Denmark's Policy towards Europe after 1945:
History, Theory and Options

Denmark's Policy towards Europe after 1945: History, Theory and Options

Editors:

Hans Branner

and Morten Kelstrup

University Press of Southern Denmark

This publication was supported by a grant from CORE

© The contributors and University Press of Southern Denmark 2000, 2003
2. rev. ed.
Set and printed by Narayana Press, Gylling
Cover design by Unisats
ISBN 87-7838-541-5

Language revision by Steven Sampson

Proof reading by Torben Huus Larsen

University Press of Southern Denmark
Campusvej 55
DK-5230 Odense M
Phone +45 66 15 79 99
Fax   +45 66 15 81 26
E-mail: press@forlag.sdu.dk
www.universitypress.dk

Distribution in the United States and Canada:
International Specialized Book Services
5804 NE Hassalo Street
Portland, OR 97213-3644 USA
Phone: +1-800-944-6190
www.isbs.com

Contents

1. Hans Branner and Morten Kelstrup: Denmark's Policy towards Europe in a Historical and Theoretical Perspective 9

Part I: Theoretical Perspectives

2. Hans Branner: The Study of Danish European Policy – Perspectives for a Comparative Approach 41
3. Nikolaj Petersen: National Strategies in the Integration Dilemma: The Promises of Adaptation Theory 72
4. Morten Kelstrup: Integration Policy: Between Foreign Policy and Diffusion 100

Part II: Historical and Cultural Preconditions

5. Uffe Østergaard: Danish National Identity: Between Multinational Heritage and Small State Nationalism 139
6. Hans Branner: The Danish Foreign Policy Tradition and the European Context 185

Part III: External and Internal Determinants

7. Johnny N. Laursen and Thorsten Borring Olesen: A Nordic Alternative to Europe? The Interdependence of Denmark's Nordic and European Policies 223
8. Karl Christian Lammers: Denmark's Relations with Germany since 1945   260
9. Ulf Hedetoft: The Interplay Between Mass and Elite Attitudes to European Integration in Denmark 282
10. Jens Henrik Haahr: Between Scylla and Charybdis: Danish Party Policies on European Integration 305

Part IV: Options and Decision-Making

11. Hans Branner: Options and Goals in Danish European Policy Since 1945: Explaining Small State Behavior and Foreign Policy Change 333
12. Søren Z. von Dosenrode: Danish EU-Policy Making 381
13. Kurt Klaudi Klausen: Integration from Below: Local Government in the Process of Europeanization 403
14. Morten Kelstrup: Danish Integration Policies: Dilemmas and Options 414

Preface

Denmark's policy towards Europe – and in particular Denmark's policy towards and within the EU – has become one of the most important issues, if not *the* most important issue in Danish politics after 1945. Why is this so? In what ways is Denmark a special case in regard to European policy? What are the fundamental conditions for the formation of the Danish European policy? What are the determinants? What are Denmark's options? And how may the study of the Danish European policy contribute to the field of foreign policy analysis? These are some of the questions which this book attempts to answer. Thus, it is our hope that the book provides the reader with a better understanding of the Danish policy towards Europe in both a historical and a theoretical perspective.

We want, in particular, to thank our co-authors for their contributions to this volume. The book is produced as a part of the Copenhagen Research Project on European Integration (CORE) which has been supported by the Danish Social Science Research Council. In addition, we want to thank Steven Sampson and Torben Huus Larsen for linguistic help with the book and our student assistants Pernille Vejby Nielsen and Nikolaj Egerod for their practical assistance.

Hans Branner and Morten Kelstrup
Copenhagen, April 2000

CHAPTER 1

Denmark's Policy towards Europe in a Historical and Theoretical Perspective

Hans Branner and Morten Kelstrup

This book is about Denmark's policy towards Europe after 1945. The book is an attempt to analyse the Danish policy in a historical as well as a theoretical perspective. Thus, the book is not an ordinary historical description of Danish policy. Rather, it is an attempt to analyse the main determinants of the Danish policy towards Europe *and* to contribute to the development of an analytical, theoretical framework which is suitable for such analysis. The theoretical framework draws on existing theories on foreign policy analysis but supplements such analysis with concepts fit for analysing integration policies. In addition, it has been an ambition to combine historical and theoretical analysis in order to make the Danish case comparable to other cases and to use the framework to contribute to a discussion of the main options in Denmark's policy towards Europe.

Simultaneously, the book is an anthology with chapters on a range of different topics. Our ambition has been that the book should be a 'rich' empirical analysis which describes and analyses many aspects of Danish policy towards Europe in general, and European integration in particular. We have included chapters on Danish foreign policy traditions and Danish national identity and culture in a historical perspective, and we have specific chapters on external aspects of Denmark's policy towards Europe and chapters on particular domestic sources of influence on this policy. By this we hope to contribute to a differentiated understanding and discussion of Denmark's European policy. This also implies that, while it has been our ambition to integrate the different contributions into some kind of common conceptual and theoretical framework, we realise that in the end we have only partly been successful in this. Each contributor has to a certain extent developed his own conceptualisations and perspectives. Yet, in spite of this the book at least *attempts* to establish a common perspective and is also intended as a contribution to such endeavours within the social science disciplines more generally.

1. Former research on Denmark's European policy

Until 1989-90, Denmark's policy towards Europe and towards European integration was only to a very limited extent a topic of research. Indeed, research conducted on Denmark's foreign policy had to a large extent concentrated on questions of security. More specifically, the main focus was on the general conditions confronting Denmark in the international system and on the changes in Danish policy after 1949, when Denmark by entering NATO decided to depart from a long held policy of neutrality vis-a-vis great power conflicts. Danish foreign policy was mainly seen in an Atlantic and – to a lesser degree – in a global or a Nordic context. The so-called 'European pillar' was mainly regarded as an aspect of Denmark's foreign *economic* policy rather than as an element in Denmark's general orientation towards the outside world. Even after 1973, when Denmark had become a member of the EC, this remained the most influential perspective. The narrow, economic approach to European questions on part of the Danish policymakers did not elicit great interest among researchers. Thus, in the 1960s and 1970s there were only very few analyses made of Denmark's European policy, and the analyses that were made were mainly preoccupied with economic perspectives on Denmark's relations to the rest of Europe.

However, this state of affairs has changed in the 1990s. Today scholars in a wide range of fields are engaged in research with the purpose of understanding Danish attitudes and Danish policy towards Europe. The literature on this topic is expanding – part of it in English. In the appendix to this introduction we have included a list on the most important literature in English on Denmark's policy towards Europe after 1945. Much of the literature is of a rather general character and a relatively high number of titles deal with the Nordic aspect of Denmark's position and policy. But during the last decade we have had a growing number of analyses which specifically deal with Danish relations to the EU, and rather many of the studies have theoretical ambitions. In many ways this book builds on these studies and continues a trend in the existing literature. A more thorough comment on the existing literature in English concerning Danish European policy is included in the appendix.

Both external and internal factors account for the growing interest in Denmark's policy towards Europe. Externally, the end of the Cold War, the changes in Europe after 1989-90 and the development of the European Community have in a rather fundamental way altered the political situation for Europe as a whole and for each of the European states. Like the governments of other members of the European Community the Danish Government cannot evade taking a stand on the many intricate issues concerning the overall European development and the role of the European Union in this process. It has become important for the Danish Government, as it has for other European governments, to deal with a number of new questions, for example questions related to: the new security situation after the end of the cold war and the new conflicts in Europe; enlargement of NATO and the EU; reform of the treaties and of the institutional structure of the EU; the initiation of the Economic and Monetary Union; sector policies of the EU; and the EU's relations to Russia, the United States and to other parts of the world outside Europe.

The growing importance of the European Union in European politics has had the effect that the hitherto upheld *distinction between European policy and se-*

curity policy, no longer is sustainable. And it has opened a whole series of issues related to the policy of integration, both generally, regarding the degree and form of integration between the European states and peoples, and more specifically, regarding the various policies pursued within the European Union. Thus, the growing integration of Denmark into the European Union has created a special policy-agenda, an agenda which is not entirely new but which on the other hand poses new questions and demands new kinds of analysis. And Denmark is not the only European state which is confronted with these new practical and theoretical challenges that follow from integration.

Internally, the 'European issue' has become increasingly politicised in Denmark since the first Danish referendum on EC membership in 1972. There has been a growing awareness of European questions in the Danish population, and the European issue has contributed to new cleavages in the Danish social and political system. The European Community, now the European Union, has developed into a new policy-making unit which pursues substantial policies in most issue areas, which directly affects the citizens of the member countries. This has had the effect that the traditional *distinction between foreign and domestic policy* is disappearing as well. Also this opens a series of issues related to policies of integration, not only questions related to policy formulation but also questions about the relationship between the way in which Danish politics has functioned until now and the way the Danish political system is changing as a consequence of the process of Europeanisation.

Furthermore, the continued deepening of European integration means that it is no longer possible to evade discussions of the consequences of this process on core values of the Danish society, e.g. questions related to national identity, the welfare system, the conception of democracy and the institutionalisation of democratic processes. The practice which hitherto has been upheld, that every new integration step should be decided by a referendum, makes such discussions even more unavoidable. Perhaps, Denmark is – because of the intensity of the political debate in Denmark on European issues and because of this evolving tradition of referenda in regard to this policy area – a special test case on the legitimacy problems for the European Union. The fact that, with a slight majority, the Danish population in June 1992 rejected the Maastricht Treaty has contributed to the status of Denmark as such a test case, and this has further added to the interest in studies concerning Denmark's European policy.

These are some of the reasons that, as a research field, Danish European policy has become a very interesting area. It is a field which involves not only international relations and comparative politics but many other research areas, also outside political science. A range of researchers within the disciplines of history, sociology, law, economics and the humanities are today engaged in studying the various aspects of the Danish approach to Europe and the resulting policies.

2. The need for a combination of historical analysis and theoretical perspectives

As indicated already, the present book is a reflection of this new interest and focus in research on Denmark's policy towards Europe. In particular it is the ambition of the book to contribute to a combination of historical and theoretical approaches to the study of Denmark's European policy.

It is our contention that traditions and different forms of institutionalisation within the different states have immense influence on the way in which the policies of those states are formed and implemented, and that concrete analysis and policy-making for an individual concrete state must be understood in a historical perspective and include the specific historical and institutional background for the state in question. But it is also our contention that in spite of the uniqueness of each individual state, its traditions and institutions, we are witnessing the development of a new 'field' of policy-formation, 'integration policy', defined as the policy which states, and possibly other actors, pursue in regard to integration processes. In this new policy area we see a new kind of interplay between external and domestic factors and between different policy areas, and we find that the European integration process itself is influencing the political processes within the participating states in a profound way. Thus, integration policy – and policies of what we might call semi-integrated states – is different from foreign policy and from domestic policy. These contentions imply that we should on the one hand pursue a historical-institutional analysis which identifies the specific conditions for the Danish European policy, but on the other hand also pursue a theoretical and comparative analysis in order to open for a better general understanding of the Danish case.

In spite of historical differences there are actually great similarities between states engaged in stronger forms of regional integration, in particular within the EU. Our view is that it is fruitful to attempt to compare the policies of different states in regard to European integration. It is a major challenge to systematic policy analysis to study integration policies, and to discuss to which degree it is possible to make this policy area an object for comparative analysis and some kind of generalisation. The comparative perspective will not only give a possible basis for generalisations. It will also contribute to our understanding of the peculiarities of specific states. This kind of analysis may thus contribute to the self-understanding – and possibly even to the political identity – of the states in question.

Two key concepts in this book are: 'determinants' and 'options'. They are both considered crucial in understanding Danish European policy. We understand *determinants* as factors, institutions or sets of problems that have decisive influence on policy formation, in this case on Denmark's policy towards Europe. And we understand *options* as the different possible policies or strategies that an actor, here Denmark, has and/or perceive at a given time. The basic understanding is that there is an interplay between determinants and options. The contention is *not* that the foreign or European policy of Denmark – or of any other independent unit in the international system – is totally 'determined' by either internal or external factors or by a combination of the two. But neither is it the contention that policy makers have a completely 'free choice' in deciding their course of action. Rather, the premise is that in the policy processes – also in a small state – there is a combination of determinants and room for policy choice. In regard to policy choice, the political and ideological preferences of policy-makers are assumed to play an independent role. Thus, although decisions are conditioned and sometimes rather heavily influenced by 'determinants', there are also different options for decisions makers at any point in time.

A consequence of this view is that in the analysis of political processes we regard it as important to identify the different social conditions, social relations and specific actions which have had an impact on the formation of the policies, in casu on the Danish policy towards Europe. One aspect of this is to identify *internal 'determinants'* which have influenced the policies of successive Danish governments. Thus, we regard it as important to identify historical preconditions that may have had an impact upon Danish preferences regarding Europe, and to identify the nature of Danish foreign policy 'traditions' in general. Further, it is important to identify interests as well as norms and discourses in Denmark that at different times have been of important influence. In this volume we, in particular, take a closer look on cultural preconditions, Danish foreign policy traditions and the influence of Danish political parties. We would have liked to include more on Denmark's economic relations to the EU and the economic interests of different groups within the Danish society in the European integration process but we had to renounce on covering this aspect as it deserves. Another aspect of the determinants behind the Danish policy towards Europe relates to the external conditions that can be interpreted as *external 'determinants'* for Danish policies, i.a. Denmark's position in the international system and in relation to closer neighbours, the policies of other states, the character of the European integration etc.

In regard to *'options'* we have been particularly interested in two perspectives. One has been to identify the options which Danish decision makers at different times have perceived as the main possible policies which Denmark could follow. How has for instance the perspective of a closer Nordic integration been regarded relative to the European 'option'? And how have the views been in regard to reservations concerning Denmark's participation in European integration? The focus of this part of the analysis is directed towards the various integration strategies that have been available for Danish decision-makers and the choices that have been made between these strategies. Of special interest in this regard is: decision-making in crucial situations; perceptions of political actors (i.e. political parties) regarding the available options; and changes over time as to the number and character of the options. The other perspective on options that we have been trying to develop in this volume has been aimed at identifying and discussing the options available to Denmark in regard to the European integration process – especially as it unfolds by the beginning of the 21st century. We do not pretend to give an exhaustive analysis of Danish options. But we want in all modesty to relate our historical and theoretical analysis to the discussion on options and perspectives for Denmark in regard to Europe's future.

3. On the uniqueness of the Danish case

While we see common features in the kind of problems which European states face in regard to the development of the European Union, our view is as mentioned that the policy of every state is also marked by unique features, formed as it is by the particular traditions and institutions of the state. This is also true of the European policy of each European state. Thus, theory-building and theory-testing has to take into account the wide variety of specific problems and conditions confronting each state and at the same time try to formulate and use general concepts and propositions. The present study attempts to illuminate this dialectic between the general and the specific. We take as a point of departure that many of the apparently unique features of the Danish situation are – on closer investigation – apt to contribute to generations of general propositions on policy formulation. Yet, without going into detail at this point, we would like to explain in what way we regard the Danish 'case' as important and interesting when dealing with the general field of policy formulation, not least pertaining to the question of integration and integration strategies. In this connection, Denmark can indeed be characterised as unique, and therefore interesting, in a comparative perspective. The following five characteristics should illustrate this point:

- *Denmark is an almost pure 'nation-state'*. Seen in a European context – and probably even more so in a world wide context – Denmark is characterised by having an unusually homogeneous population with – so far – only negligible national and ethnic minorities within its borders. This fact is almost bound to have an influence on the direction of Danish policy towards Europe, especially in light of the progressing integration process in the EU. However, in an analytical perspective, it is not possible beforehand to stipulate in what direction this 'nation state factor' influences a country's integration policy. Two opposite hypothesis may be put forward: A 'pure' nation state will be reluctant to give up sovereignty since the existing political system enjoys broad popular support. On the other hand the 'strength' of the state makes it easier to do so because the threat to 'national' survival may be regarded as negligible.
- *Denmark's economic and geographic position has provided latent alternatives to continental European integration.* The 'nation state factor' and ideological conceptions related to this factor may account for some of the problems Denmark has experienced in finding her place in 'the new Europe'. But these problems may also be seen in light of the fact, that Denmark to a greater degree than most other EU countries historically has had other – at least perceived – options than EU membership. The alternatives are derived from Denmark's position on

the fringe of the European continent with close cultural, economic and political ties to the other Nordic countries, and in some respects also to the UK and the US. The existence of these alternative options raises some interesting general questions: Are they real or only perceived? Which factors account for their viability or non-viability over time? In what way are the alternative options – if available – used in the internal political debate?

- *Denmark pursues an 'atypical' strategy compared to other small states in the EU.* At least until recently it has been rather unique that a small member state has shown as reluctant an attitude towards European integration as Denmark, a fact which is especially noteworthy when comparing Denmark to the other economically advanced and older member states (i.e. the Benelux countries). The sceptical Danish attitudes may in part be explained by the two above mentioned characteristics, but also the 'small state factor' may be of importance. A traditional problem in foreign policy theory of defining a specific small state behaviour is hereby accentuated. But even without pretending that such generalisation about small states is possible, small state theory may still be useful at another level. Even when small states behave differently, it may be worthwhile to try to identify different small state strategies in regard to integration, and to discuss the specific dilemma confronting small states, for instance the problems related to the so-called 'integration dilemma'.

- *The institution of referenda and the intensity of the public EU debate in Denmark poses special challenges to Danish policy-makers.* Hardly any other country in the EU has experienced such a high degree of popular involvement in questions related to EU membership as Denmark. Again, this unique feature may be of a more general interest – especially when one considers future perspectives. As mentioned, the integration process is increasingly blurring the traditional distinction between foreign and domestic policy. This development will undoubtedly involve more and more groups in the decision-making process in all member countries and add to its politizisation. The analysis of Danish experiences with the consequences of greater popular involvement may thus also be useful for others. One consequence observable in Denmark is the split between mass and elite opinion on integration issues. It remains an open question, whether it will be a general trend that mass and elite opinion differ, or whether this divide in Denmark is conditioned on the specific Danish circumstances.

- *Denmark has a unique decision-making system regarding day-to-day politics in the EU.* One of the unique characteristics of the Danish decision-making system in regard to EU-participation is that it tends to involve the Danish parliament to a greater degree than elsewhere. Although the way that parliamentary control over Danish European policy functions has often been the subject of criticism within the country, it is just as often regarded as a model for other member states to follow. The ever growing focus on the 'democratic deficit' in European decision-making and the prevailing scepticism towards federalism in Europe are likely to add further intensity to the existing interest in understanding the Danish experiences with national, parliamentary control. In this connection it will be vital to discuss the contingent effects of increased parliamentary control, e.g. on the integration strategies of individual countries. These effects may differ substantially among different countries, due to differences in institutional and political contexts.

4. Denmark and Europe: a short historical sketch 1945-2000

Since most of the following chapters presuppose some historical background information, we include in this section a short sketch of major events and developments of importance for Danish policies and attitudes towards Europe since 1945.

In 1945 all European countries had to shape their relations with the rest of Europe anew; but although external changes, with the fall of the German great power, were as profound for Denmark as for any other state, the European question in Danish foreign policy was from the very beginning conceived of in a predominantly economic and pragmatic way. No strong internal pressure for Danish participation in the construction of a new Europe developed. Security questions, visionary conceptions and value promoting policies were reserved for other pillars in the foreign policy edifice. Denmark was in 1947-48 eager to join the Marshall plan and its institutional extension in the form of OEEC, but officially it was stressed that Danish participation should be seen in a purely economic context with no implications for security policy. In 1949, Denmark was among the ten founding members of the Council of Europe, but in the ensuing discussions of extending the powers of the Council, Danish representatives, who were among the most 'European' oriented of Danish politicians, were firmly placed in the functionalist camp which did not wish to extend federal powers to the Council.

In the 1950s Danish Governments found it increasingly difficult to accommodate the emergence of the European Communities with its foreign economic policy and its general foreign policy orientation. Danish functionalist inclinations had never been of the dogmatic art; the surrendering of sovereignty could be a means towards obtaining practical goals or securing concrete national interests. The possibility of joining the club of six first in the ECSC and later the EEC was not ruled out beforehand, but economic considerations as well as close political affinity with the Nordic countries and Great Britain kept Denmark outside the formative phases of the continental integration process. However, the issue of Denmark's European orientation was not an easy one at the end of the 1950s. The country was caught in a serious dilemma when negotiations on the wider free trade area broke down and its two most important export markets, Germany and the UK, subsequently were placed in separate camps. The politically still very influential Danish farmers were at the same time confronted with the unpleasant prospect of being excluded from the common agricultural policy of the EEC. The Liberal Party, advocating the interests of farmers, had as early as 1957 pledged to work for Danish entry into the EEC.

Denmark eventually opted for the less ambitious European Free Trade Area, but the issue of EC membership was only temporarily put aside. During the 1960s a consensus grew that Denmark might later join the EC, should the international conditions change to favour such a cause of action. Indeed, as the UK overcame its reservations towards the EC and applied for membership in 1961 and 1967, applications for membership were simultaneously forwarded by the Danish government. In both cases, however, the enlargement foundered on French opposition to British entry. Upon the second failure of enlargement Denmark initiated negotiations with Norway, Sweden and Finland on the creation of a Nordic economic Union (NORDEK). A treaty was ready to be signed, when 'the Six' at the Haag Summit of 1969 pledged to reconsider the applications. It soon turned out that this development represented a deadly blow to the Nordic plan, and in 1973 Denmark finally joined the Communities together with the UK and Ireland.

Before the accession membership had been approved in a public referendum, with 63.3% of the votes in favour and 36.7% against, see table 1. This result was rather less decisive than one would have expected, considering the generally sympathetic public sentiments towards the EC during the preceding years – less than 10 percent of the electorate seemed to be against Danish EC membership during most of the 1960s. However, as the negotiations picked up speed in 1970/71, there was a massive increase in voter dissatisfaction over the prospect of joining the EC, an increase which held in the years after membership had become a reality. In fact, as illustrated in figure 1, until 1985 opinion polls almost consistently showed a majority for Denmark to leave the Communities.

The sudden rise of negative sentiments among the voters was partly prompted by a strong anti-EC movement, the People's Movement Against the EC, as well as internal opposition to the EC from within the dominant Social Democratic Party and the Social Liberal Party. In Denmark, the Euro-sceptic feelings have traditionally been most prevalent on the left, where both the Socialist People's Party and various groupings on the far left have been ardent critics of the European Com-

Table 1: Danish referenda on EC/EU questions

Date	Topic	Participation in %	Yes in %	No in %
2.10.1972	Danish membership	90.1	63.3	36.7
27.2.1986	Single European Act	75.8	56.2	43.8
2.6.1992	The Maastricht Treaty	83.1	49.3	50.7
18.5.1993	The Maastricht Treaty and the Edinburgh Agreement	86.5	56.7	43.3
28.5.1998	The Amsterdam Treaty	74.8	55.1	44.9
28.9.2000	Adherence to the euro	?	?	?

Figure 1: Danish attitudes towards the EC/EU (numbers = %)

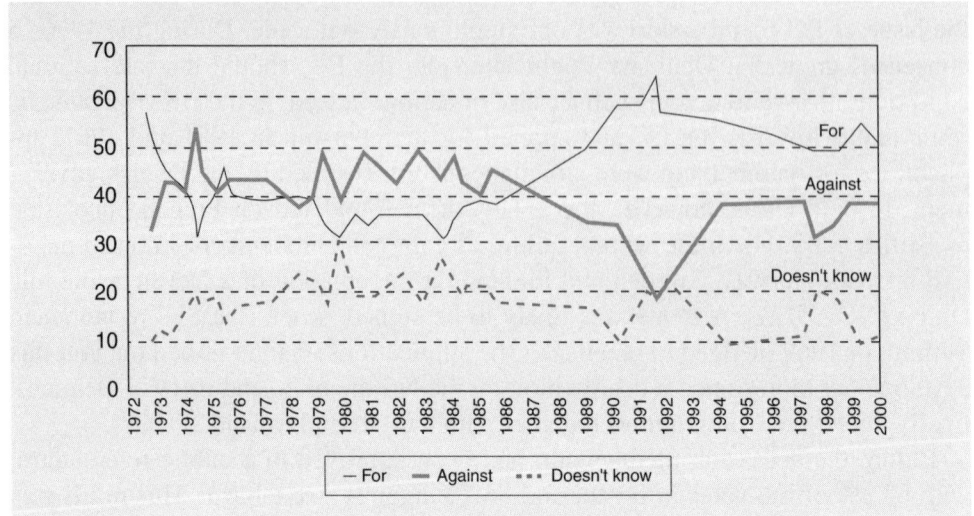

Answer to the question: If you today should vote about Danish adherence to the European Union (before 1993: The European Community), would you vote for or against Danish membership?

Source: Gallup

munity. The Social Democratic Party marks the dividing line between the core of the EC sceptic left and the more pragmatic centre – having been split on the issue in every one of the referenda concerning European integration from 1972 onwards. Right wing parties have until the 1990s been strong supporters of Danish membership – with the Liberal Party in the lead. Until recently, federalist inclinations have only been found in the small centre party, the Centre Democrats.

Domestic political conditions led Danish Governments in the 1970s and 1980s to pursue a rather reserved policy towards the strengthening of integration, especially concerning institutional questions. Denmark was reluctant to support the introduction of direct elections to the European Parliament, and also had strong reservations in regard to various other plans for further integration. At the first election to the European Parliament in 1979, four out of 15 members represented the People's Movement Against the EC. Also the later elections to the European Parliament have given a rather strong representation of movements against the EU (see table 2). In 1986, a majority in the Danish Parliament voted down the SEA on account of its federalist implications. However, on a number of occasions – when concrete interests were involved – Denmark played an active and constructive role in the further development of EC policies, e.g. the creation of the EMS in 1979.

The SEA was eventually passed in the Danish Parliament following a referendum in which 56.2% of the voters were in favour and 43.8% against. In the wake of this outcome internal conditions for Danish EU policy-making changed dramatically. During the late 1980s the polls showed increasing majorities in favour of continued Danish participation in the Communities, the proportion of the electo-

Table 2: Elections in Denmark to the European Parliament (numbers = %)

	1979	1984	1989	1994	1999
Social Democrats		19.5 (3)	23.3 (4)	(3)	16.5 (3)
Social Liberals	3.3 (0)	3.1 (0)	2.8 (0)	8.5 (1)	9.1 (1)
Conservative People's Party	14.0 (2)	20.8 (4)	13.3 (2)	17.7 (3)	8.5 (1)
Centrum Democrats	6.2 (1)	6.6 (1)	8.0 (2)	0.9 (0)	3.5 (0)
Socialist People's Party	4.7 (1)	9.2 (2)	9.1 (1)	8.6 (1)	7.1 (1)
The June Movement			(3)[1]	15.2 (2)	16.1 (3)
The People's Movement Against the EC/EU	21.0 (4)	20.8 (4)	18.9 (4/1)	10.3 (2)	7.3 (1)
Danish People's Party					5.8 (1)
Christian People's Party	1.8 (0)	2.8 (0)	2.7 (0)	1.1 (0)	2.0 (0)
Liberals	14.4 (3)	12.4 (2)	16.6 (3)	18.9 (4)	23.4 (5)
The Progress Party	5.8 (1)	3.5 (0)	5.3 (0)	2.9 (0)	0.7 (0)
Participation in %	47.8	52.4	46.2	52.5	50.5

Source: Official Danish statistics

rate which supported membership reaching around 60-70% by the beginning of the 1990s. Parallel with this change in public attitudes was a reorientation of policy among parties that traditionally had been sceptical or negative towards the EC. The Socialist People's party, more than other parties representing the no-voters, stopped advocating Danish withdrawal. And the Social Democratic Party and the Social Liberals (which have been in government since 1993, in the beginning together with the Centre Democrats) have gradually become supporters of the European Union, although the issue remains contested among the grass-roots of the two parties. In 1990 all major parties were able to agree on a common EU memorandum stating the Danish positions in regard to the conferences to be held on what was to become the Maastricht Treaty. The membership question was no longer relevant politically, what mattered was instead how far Denmark was willing to go in regard to the Union's development.

---

1 Three representatives from the People's Movement Against the EU changed during the election period to becoming representatives of the June Movement, founded in 1992.

Since the 1980s, the public debate on European integration had also shifted somewhat, so that the matter of Danish membership of the EC had been toned down, whereas the development of positive political authority within the EU came to the fore. This change of focus mirrors the general development of the European integration process at large, and is undoubtedly the most important reason why – despite a growing acceptance of Danish EC-membership among the voters – the European issue is still one of the most contentious issues on the political agenda.

The referendum on 2 June 1992 turned out with a majority of 50.7% against Danish ratification of the Maastricht Treaty and 49.3% for. This result largely caught the political establishment 'off guard'. The result forced through a considerable change in Danish policy towards the EC. A new movement against the Maastricht Treaty was formed, the June Movement. The politicians were under heavy pressure to define a policy in regard to Denmark's future relation to the EC. The result of intense negotiations was a 'national compromise' fashioned between seven of the all together eight parties in Parliament, including the Socialist People's Party which had been one of only two anti-Maastricht parties. This compromise set out four Danish reservations to the Maastricht Treaty, which were afterwards accepted by the 11 other governments in the EC at the Edinburgh Summit in December 1992. The combination of the Maastricht Treaty and the Edinburgh Agreement was approved by the Danish electorate in a referendum on 18 May 1993 with 56.8% for and 43.2% against. The political compromise binds the Government in future to avoid far reaching Danish participation in four areas of EU policy: the single currency, defence cooperation, the common citizenship, and supranational cooperation in justice and home affairs. Any Danish involvement in these four areas needs prior approval in a public referendum.

As can be understood from the above, recurrent referendums now form an integral feature of Danish politics regarding the European issue. This may partly reflect the need of Danish minority governments to assure a broad political basis for their actions, or it may bear testimony to the salience of the issues in Danish politics. Furthermore, the use of the referendum is specifically sanctioned by the Danish Constitution, as a result of a revision made in 1953. At this time it was decided to include a special section (section 20) in the Constitution, a section which obliges the Government to hold a referendum whenever a transfer of sovereign powers from Parliament to an international organ is not supported by a ⅚ majority in Parliament. In the intergovernmental treaty conferences, the Danish Government is thus tightly constrained in its ability to relinquish national sovereignty, knowing that the final result of the negotiations will have to stand the test of public referendum.

The above mentioned section 20 of the Constitution has also been the object of a much debated court case which was taken to the Danish Supreme Court. The plaintiffs – a number of Danish citizens – claimed that the Maastricht Treaty is in breach with the Danish Constitution, which only allows sovereignty to be transferred 'to a limited extent'. The argument was that the Treaty opens for wide reaching political changes affecting all areas of domestic politics, and that the Danish ratification should thus be deemed to be unconstitutional. The Supreme Court issued its ruling on 6 April 1998. The ruling stated i.a. that the Maastricht Treaty was not in breach with the Danish Constitution and that the provision in section 20 of the Constitution – in accordance to which authority can only be transferred to other, intergovernmental bodies "i nærmere bestemt omfang" (more specified extent) – had not been violated. Very importantly, the Supreme Court provided through this case its interpretation of the relationship between the EU-treaties and the Danish constitution, giving primacy to the Danish constitution, but accepting the constitutionality of the transferred authority.

The ruling of the Danish Supreme Court came during the debate on the treaty amendments which followed the 1996 intergovernmental conference and the agreement negotiated at the Amsterdam Summit of June 1997. The Amsterdam Treaty was put to a referendum on 28 May 1998. Danish ratification of the treaty was supported by a broad majority around the political centre, while there was an opposition at the right as well as the left – represented in Parliament by the Danish People's Party and the Progress Party on the far right, and by the Socialist People's Party and the Red/Green Alliance on the left. The Government had in spite of the Danish reservations participated fully in the negotiations of the Amsterdam Treaty, and the four Danish exemptions, which had formerly only been politically accepted, were at least partially inserted in various provisions of the Amsterdam Treaty. At the referendum 55.1% of the electorate voted for and 44.9% against the ratification of the Amsterdam treaty.

The immediate result of the acceptance of the Amsterdam Treaty was a relative comfortable situation for the coalition Government between the Social Democrats and the Social Liberals in regard to their EU-policy. But after the coming into force of the Amsterdam Treaty in May 1999 difficulties became gradually more severe in regard to the Danish "reservations". New steps were taken in regard to co-operation in the fields of justice and home affairs. The crises in Kosovo led to new steps towards a common European defence dimension, making it more difficult for the Danish Government to live up to the reservation from 1993 about the Danish "exemptions" in regard to European defence. And the realisation of the third phase of the EMU and the introduction of the EURO in the beginning of 1999 made it more pressing to define Denmark's future relation to the EMU. In addition, it seemed likely that the intergovernmental conference which began in 2000, would include proposals which would be difficult to accept for the Danish Government. In the Spring 2000 the Government decided to hold a referendum on 28 September 2000 about one of the Danish reservations, the reservation regarding Danish participation in the third phase of the EMU. Obviously, the decision about this reservation seems to be extremely important for Denmark's future relation to the European Union.

5. The content of the book

Part I deals with the three theoretical perspectives – the comparative approach, adaptation theory and integration policy – that are used throughout the book. Together, the three chapters of the first part indicate the main theoretical thrust of the entire book, but they should also be seen as contributions in their own right, hopefully inspiring other studies in the field.

In *chapter two*, written by **Hans Branner**, focus is on the comparative potential of single country studies with Danish European policy after 1945 as the point of departure. The issue of comparison is approached from three different angles, including a part on conceptualisations, a part on the relevance of a historical dimension, and finally, a part on perspectives for further development of the comparative approach. Regarding conceptualisation, the usage of the term 'European policy' in Danish political discourse is described and discussed; and on this basis some observations are put forward aiming at making the concept more apt for comparisons. Special emphasis is placed on the distinction between the two levels – national and European – upon which the European policy of a particular state unfolds; but the concept is also discussed in the context of the terminology of 'foreign policy aspects' and of the increasing difficulties involved in separating domestic and foreign policy.

In the following section, Hans Branner argues for the necessity of including a historical dimension when comparing European policies of states. Again the Danish case forms the basis of the discussion; and by drawing on the conceptualisation set up he identifies four trends enforcing the impact of historical variables. An attempt is made to present an approach for systematic analysis of such variables, stressing some of the main themes taken up in part II of the book. This last part of the analysis is undertaken after having examined the field of foreign policy theory for possible contributions to the study of historical variables. It is argued that such contributions are conspicuously rare, and that the few existing ones are of limited value in the present context.

The following *chapter three* by **Nikolaj Petersen** is on *"national strategies in the integration dilemma: the promises of adaptation theory"*. Nikolaj Petersen takes his point of departure in the view that one of the lacunae of classical integration theory is its failure to produce a theory of national integration policy. The article is an attempt to contribute to such theory on integration strategies of individual states by discussing the so-called 'integration dilemma' and by using the approach of 'adaptation theory'.

After a definition of the integration dilemma the article presents a conceptualisation of modes of adaptation and strategies which the states use in their integration policies. The 'adaptation theory' is – in combination with some elements of game theory – used to sort out the external as well as domestic policies and strategies which nations adopt in the course of a cross-national integration process. Thus, the article presents conceptual categories for describing different external and domestic strategies by which decision-makers may try to cope with the integration dilemma and the integration process, mainly based on the 'influence capability' and 'stress sensitivity' each state has in regard to the integration process.

In the last part of the chapter Denmark is used as an illustrative case for analysing the integration policy of an individual state. First, Denmark's basic values and preferences in regard to European integration are described within the general understanding that Denmark's policy is in some way within the 'balanced mode'. Then follows a historical overview of Denmark's external integration strategies 1973-95, both general aspects and policies in specific issue areas, and some brief comments on Denmark's domestic integration strategies.

The article concludes that the concepts of the adaptation approach and their use of the integration dilemma is a fruitful way of understanding the fundamental conditions under which nation-states formulate their concrete integration strategies, i.a. because it provides concepts with which national policy can actually be described and understood, and because it focuses on the interaction of external and internal forces. Yet, the approach also has its weak points, and the problem of national integration strategies remains a conspicuous lacuna in the integration theory.

In *chapter four* **Morten Kelstrup** writes on *"integration policy: between foreign policy and diffusion"*. The article is an attempt to develop the concept of integration policy and to use it to analyse policies which states might follow in regard to European integration. It is concerned with different dimensions of integration policies and, in particular, with the relationship between the study of integration policy and the study of foreign policy. The article discusses different approaches to the study of integration policy. The emphasis is on integration policies towards and within integration systems with a relatively high degree of integration in which the state as a semi-integrated actor is entangled in a new political system which is not merely an intergovernmental system. It is argued that integration policy must be seen as highly dependent on the character of the integration system, and that in the EU there is an important difference between integration policies towards an intergovernmentally dominated EU and such policies towards a supranationally-transnationally dominated EU. A major contention is that if and when integration proceeds, new kinds of politicisation will arise, and integration policies will be marked by increasing diffusion.

Part II is devoted to an examination of historical and cultural preconditions for the European policy of Denmark in the post-war period. It is no easy task to pin down such conditions, and not easier to arrive at a categorisation apt for comparisons. Nevertheless, the two chapters in this part are meant as contributions to such endeavours.

In *chapter five* by **Uffe Østergaard** on national identity and political culture focus is on internally generated determinants for Danish European policy.

As a major point Uffe Østergaard emphasises that the name 'Denmark' historically denominates two different kinds of state: a multinational, composite state-nation of second rank, whose size gradually was reduced until the middle of the 19th century; and a more recent, ethnically homogeneous nation-state, whose external power in part has been based on a high degree of 'societal security', i.e. internal cohesiveness. He argues that the two pasts both have an impact on present day Danish foreign policy behaviour, and in large measure account for the apparently contradictory attitudes to international cooperation characterised by combining internationalism, parochialism, extreme self-confidence and a tradition for stressing smallness and lack of importance.

The repercussions of "Denmark's" transition from one type of state to another and the manner by which this transition has been tackled are, according to Uffe Østergaard, essential in explaining central features of Danish political culture and national identity. The small size of the country made possible the establishment of an ideological hegemony stressing egalitarianism, consensus and 'folkelighed' – a concept based on the teachings of the influential Danish priest, philosopher and poet N.F.S. Grundtvig denominating a special feeling of identity and community in the population. These values were in large measure taken over by the rising labour movement whose political strategy became much less class based than in other countries. Altogether the ideological heritage and the circumstances accounting for the development of a strong state and a strong society make the Danes apprehensive of participating in the construction of a Europe in which state, nation and society no longer refer to an identical entity.

In *chapter six* **Hans Branner** narrows the pespective by focusing on the specific Danish foreign policy tradition. While discarding the conventional reference to neutrality as the key constituting element in the tradition, he attempts instead to define its main content by basing the analysis on a dualistic conception: on the one hand a passive, adaptive behaviour characterised by a desire to stay out of great power conflicts, labelled determinism; and on the other hand, active engagement in efforts towards the establishment of a more just, peaceful and legally regulated international order, labelled internationalism. This duality, developed in response to the gradual deterioration of Denmark's European power position, also dealt with in the preceding article by Uffe Østergaard, has previously been identified by Carsten Holbraad in a study on the history of Danish foreign policy. However, Hans Branner rejects the interpretation given by Holbraad, according to whom the effect of both trends has been that Denmark in large parts of its history has 'contracted out' of international politics. Instead, he views the two trends as an integral and mutually reinforcing part of a Danish small state tradition. By introducing a broader concept of power and by distinguishing between a short and a long run perspective, he argues that the Danish tradition is characterised by involvement in rather than by withdrawal from international politics.

The analysis leads to the advancement of a cyclical rather than a linear conception of the evolution in Danish foreign policy, thereby countering a hitherto pre-dominant interpretation of the extent and character of changes in Denmark's post-war foreign policy, changes that have been especially manifest at the end of the 1940s and in the 1990s. Danish activism since the end of the Cold War is not primarily seen as a novel development but rather as a new turn in the cyclical process. Also, Danish reluctance towards full participation in the European integration process is seen in a historical context. In part, this reluctance reflects the continued influence of the determinist strand of thought stemming from negative experiences with traditional European power politics. An increase in Denmark's relative power position since 1945 has given more scope to the internationalist part of the tradition, but Danish European policy exhibits greater inertia in regard to adapting to changing external conditions than other aspects of foreign policy.

Part III of the book deals with the external and internal influences on Denmark's policy towards Europe. Four determinants are singled out for separate treatment: Danish relations with the other Nordic countries and with Germany, popular attitudes and party politics.

In the post-war period Nordic cooperation has for Denmark had a role similar to the role which Commonwealth cooperation has had for Britain: the possibility of relying on – or at least referring to – an alternative integration framework than the Continental one. In the title of their contribution in *chapter seven* **Thorsten Borring Olesen** and **Johnny Laursen** ask whether a Nordic alternative to Europe existed. The chapter demonstrates how complicated this question is; and while they are not able to give a clear-cut answer the authors are able to come up with a number of clues to the role which Nordic cooperation has played in the internal Danish debate and in the formulation of official policy.

It is shown that Nordic cooperation, besides functioning as an *alternative,* has to a certain degree been viewed also as a *supplement* to western European integration or as a *platform* for the promotion of Nordic values in a broader European context. Most important, however, Nordic cooperation has throughout functioned as a *de-legitimiser* of European integration. This function has been closely associated with the impact of what the authors name 'The Nordic Vision'; i.e. the belief that the promotion of Nordic cooperation could be a lever for a specific model of society which would in important respects deviate from the one prevailing in the original EC countries. It is stated as a main point in the article that, apart from the early post-war period, "this vision has not functioned as a real engine for intensifying Nordic cooperation or integration. Rather, from the 1950s onwards it has been used as a defensive weapon aimed at safeguarding and fending off European challenges to Danish sovereignty and independence." While the de-legitimising function of the Nordic vision in the first half of the period primarily is to be observed in Social Democratic policy and discourse, it has since Danish membership of the EC been exploited by the organised EC opposition movements. As such it plays a major role in explaining the continued Danish scepticism towards European integration.

When analysing the role of Nordic integration as a part of the overall European policy of Denmark the authors identify a recurrent pattern characterising three subsequent historical phases beginning after the peak of Nordic aspirations in the period 1945-49. The cycle starts out with Nordic disappointment, followed by new Nordic endeavours and hopes and ends with Nordic individual strategies vis-à-vis Europe. Conditions for repeating this pattern seem to be fundamentally altered after the latest EC enlargement of 1995 providing membership for Sweden and Finland. What kind of prospects these new conditions leave for Nordic cooperation in the future are discussed at the end of the chapter.

Although relations with the Nordic countries and with Germany are of a very different kind – both in regard to policy formulation and in regard to popular perception – they have had similar consequences for the direction which Danish European policy has taken in the post-war period. Both have contributed to the Danish reluctance towards full participation in the western European integration process. One could have expected that the German factor had driven Danish policy in the opposite direction. But as emphasized by **Karl Christian Lammers** in his contribution in *chapter eight*, Danish European policy has been guided by a different integration perspective than the one which has prevailed in other small states bordering on the German great power, i.e. the Benelux countries. To a certain degree the fear of entrapment has been more pronounced than the desire to participate in the 'Einbindung' of Germany.

The underlying theme in the analysis made by Lammers is not only Germany as a problem for Denmark but also the opportunities created by the multilateralisation of Danish relations to Germany. He starts out by quoting Per Hækkerup (Danish foreign minister 1962-66) who, while holding office, is reported to have told his undersecretaries that Danish foreign policy had three main problems: Germany, Germany and Germany again. And, when evaluating the situation in the 1990s at the end of the chapter he not only states that Germany "still makes up a first-rate determinant in Danish foreign policy" but also "as earlier continues to make up a problem for Denmark." This problem, according to Lammers, in part stems from a fear to end up *de facto* being a formally independent appendix to Germany, a northern Bundesland.

This emphasis on Germany as a continuing problem does not mean that the immense changes characterising Danish-German relations in the post-war period are not taken up as well. A milestone is said to have been the solution of the minority question at the common border by the Bonn-Copenhagen declarations of 1955. Great importance is also attached to the transformed security relationship created by the membership of both countries in NATO and in the EC/EU. These factors all have contributed to a 'normalisation' of relations increasingly basing them on a high degree of mutual trust and common interests. However, it is also shown that in the development of a close Danish-German partnership, the motivation on the Danish side has been based on narrow economic and military considerations. Furthermore, the developments mainly reflect changes in official attitudes, while on the informal level, changes are slower and the fear of a German domination in Europe still vivid.

In *chapter nine* **Ulf Hedetoft** writes on *"Danish Mass and Elite Attitudes towards European Integration"*. The article asks how the relationship between the Danish masses and the Danish elites has affected Danish policy towards Europe, and how this relationship has in turn been affected by Danish membership of the EU and by the process of deepening European integration. It is argued that a typically Danish political culture which ties elites to masses within a framework of consensus, homogeneity of identity, and middle-of-the-road politics has provided the interpretative prism for approaching and understanding European integration in 'minimalist' and pragmatic terms. Further, Danish political culture has supplied a number of instruments with which Danish membership of the EU has been regulated. However, this culture-based Danish approach to integration, prevailing in the 1970s and 1980s, has increasingly been perceived to have been put in jeopardy by the deepening of European integration. In the 1990s, the integration process has been seen by an increasing proportion of the Danish population to impinge on issues of national identity and on the cultural symbolics of national sovereignty. In a sense, a gap between elites and masses has been exposed and exacerbated by EU integration. In another sense, however, recent developments have also shown that such a gap has been accompanied by a new type of consensus, namely that Danish membership of the EU is by now regarded as 'given' by almost the entire Danish population.

The relationship between mass and elite attitudes also plays a crucial role in *chapter ten*. Analysing Danish party attitudes towards European integration. **Jens Henrik Haahr** starts out by identifying two stable determinants of Danish party attitudes: (1) the electorate's scepticism towards supranationalism, and (2) Danish political and economic dependence on its European surroundings. On these premises Danish political parties are confronted with a basic dilemma between pleasing the electorate and maximizing its influence. However, different solutions to this dilemma mark the political spectrum. Electoral opposition to supra-nationality is not equally strong in all parties, and party behaviour towards European integration can be divided between influence seeking behaviour and what is called 'symbolic positioning'. On the basis of an analysis of the Danish political parties, it is possible to single out three parties, to which the basic dilemma prove especially difficult: the Social Democratic Party, the Social Liberal Party and the Socialist People's Party.

In the empirical part of the chapter, Jens Henrik Haahr first deals with the various tactics employed by the three vulnerable parties in coping with the dilemma, and he ends by stating that "the dilemma cannot be escaped, it can only be confronted". It is, however, characteristic of the parties analysed that their positions on the integration issue have undergone significant changes since the middle of the 1980s. They have all moved further towards influence seeking, they are in favour of majority voting in specific areas, and they have in general reversed their predominantly negative attitude towards the Union project. On the basis of a framework for the analysis of party policy change, Haahr then shows how societal conditions have changed following the adaption of the Single European Act and the emergence of a new security situation in Europe upon the demise of the Cold War. These two changes influence the possibilities for achieving the general political goals of the three parties and can thus account for the changes in their integration policies. But since there has been no equivalent development in the electorate, the basic dilemma remains. The Socialist People's Party is seeking to edge back towards a symbolic anti-integration position, whereas the dilemma looms larger for the two other parties. Since they all hold the key to the formulation of Danish European policy, Haahr predicts new and intensified political battles as more referenda are coming up.

Part IV concerns some of the options and dilemmas that have confronted Danish policy-makers, as well as the process by which Denmark's policies towards Europe have been formulated.

In *chapter eleven*, **Hans Branner** examines Danish foreign policy options in both a historical and a theoretical perspective. The scope of options confronting Denmark since the end of World War II is first illuminated by contrasting this period with the one preceding it, characterised by a one-sided Danish dependency on Germany. He then goes on to discuss some of the general factors which can account for this increase in options, i.a. evaluating the importance of the European integration process in this regard. In the main part of the chapter, Danish responses to the post-war options are analysed – not by investigating concrete decisions, but by attempting to identify some general features. On this basis he is led to the conclusion that 'the European option' all along has had a remarkably low priority among Danish decision-makers. Part of the reason for this can be found in the historical context dealt with in the beginning of the article: starting from scratch in 1945, policy-makers have tended to give high priority to options which had not been feasible before the war but which might prove more realistic in the new, post-war environment – i.e. the Nordic and universalistic orientations of the Danish foreign policy tradition came to the fore. Hereby Branner is drawing on his contribution in part II, showing that a dualistic foreign policy tradition continues in the post-war period.

Two further theoretical perspectives are included: Throughout the chapter Danish policy is analysed in the context of the 'small state' concept; and at the end, theories of foreign policy change are evaluated by focusing on the relative weight of external and internal factors determining the evolution of Danish foreign policy since 1945.

It is a widely held conception that the Danish decision-making system on EU matters has a very strong democratic basis, and – not least for this reason – stands out as rather ideal and suitable for imitation by other member states. However, both contentions are opposed in the next contribution, *chapter twelve,* by **Søren Z. v.**

Dosenrode analysing the Danish national policy formulation process. The article applies the analytical framework of the policy analysis approach, especially the concepts of the policy cycle and that of policy network. A short discussion of five phases in the making of Danish EU policy is followed by a detailed analysis of the two primary networks involved in Danish EU policy formulation: the administrative-corporative network and the parliamentary network. Distinguishing between actors, functions and power-relations Dosenrode emphasises the strength of the first network and the weakness of the second one, thereby supporting the thesis that an important part of legislation directly influencing Danish citizens is not made by parliamentarians, but in networks dominated by civil servants and interest organisations.

Although acknowledging that this 'democratic deficit' is more pronounced in regard to daily low-key decisions than in regard to major, politicised questions, Dosenrode concludes the article by stating that "in spite of its formal powers, the Danish Parliament is on its way to get disconnected from the decision-making procedure", the main reasons being a "paralysing fear for unpopular decisions and a tremendous workload in the European Affairs Committee." Part of the problem thus stems from the gap between mass and elite opinion, which entails that the initiative in EU matters drifts from parliamentarians to the civil servants, who are backed up by interest organisations. A further implication is a very reactive Danish approach to the decision-making in the EU, aggravated by the weak interplay between the Danish and the EU decision-making system in the first phases of the policy cycle.

When we ask about the determinants of Denmark's policies towards Europe – or more specifically about Denmark's policies towards the European Union – we tend to ignore the involvement which substate actors have with the world outside Denmark. In *chapter thirteen*, **Kurt Klaudi Klausen** discusses *"Integration from below – Local Government in Denmark in the Process of Europeanisation."* The article rests on research into the role of local governments in processes of internationalisation and Europeanisation, and deals with the impact of the EU on local government. More specifically, it asks how Danish local authorities have reacted upon the challenges presented by Europeanisation, and it is described in which ways and through which institutions local governments have actively engaged in the process of Europeanisation. While local governments are not directly involved in the formulation of Danish foreign policy nor of Denmark's EU-policy, local governments have engaged in inter-regional integration and in the institutional system of the EU, since the ratification of the Maastricht Treaty also within the Committee of the Regions. The involvement of the local authorities in the integration process has been steadily growing, in particular during the last decade. Thus, local governments have also had a growing indirect influence on the integration process and on the Danish EU-policy. It is concluded that although local governments have not until recently been important in the integration process and in relation to the formulation of the Danish EU-policy, this might change in the future. Thus, one might even talk of a 'silent revolution' in the process of integration challenging deep-rooted conceptions of which actors are the relevant ones in the formulation of Danish integration policy.

Chapter fourteen by **Morten Kelstrup** focuses on *"Danish Integration Policies: Dilemmas and Options"*. This article characterizes different integration policies which Denmark has followed historically in regard to the process of European integration. It attempts to characterize main features of the external conditions for the Denmark's policies towards the EU at the beginning of the new century, and to analyse the internal conditions which through the historical and institutional development in Denmark places different constraints on the Danish Government in regard to Denmark's participation in European integration. On this basis major dilemmas of the Danish Government are identified and it is discussed which major strategies and policies Denmark might follow in regard to the future European integration. The article is touching a highly politicised topic and is in many ways tentative. The aim of the article is not to reach any specific, normative view on 'recommendable strategies', but rather to recommend better 'strategic analysis' in regard to integration policies, regardless of political preferences.

Appendix on literature in English on Denmark's policy towards Europe

A separate biography listing the main contributions is attached at the end of this chapter. On the basis of this list we may, more specifically, characterize the existing literature by emphasizing the following four general features:

- **In regard to comprehensive studies covering the entire spectrum of Denmark's European relations in the post-war period there is a serious gap.** Five items on the list have pretensions of this kind, but all have obvious shortcomings. The dissertation by *Gunnar P. Nielsson* ("Denmark and European Integration", 1966) is a detailed investigation into both political and economic aspects of Danish European policy since the beginning of West European integration, also including a long historical perspective. However, this study was undertaken before Denmark became a member of the EC, is almost entirely based on secondary sources, and has never been published (it is available on microfilm). The book edited by *Lise Lyck* ("Denmark and EC membership evaluated") contains valuable contributions, some of them listed separately, but it consists mainly of rather short and narrowly based articles on specific aspects of Danish EU policy. The volume edited by *Carsten Due-Nielsen and Nikolaj Petersen* ("Adaptation and Activism") contains two articles which, taken together, examines Danish EC policy in the period 1967-1992. Again, the time scope is limited, and the two contributions stand alone in a book devoted to a more general treatment of Danish foreign policy during the 25 years mentioned. Also, in the book edited by *Morten Kelstrup* ("European Integration and Denmark's Participation") the main focus is not on Danish European policy. The greater part consists of studies on theoretical aspects of European integration, and those dealing specifically with Denmark (listed separately) analyses rather circumscribed issues and themes – without pretending to establish an over-all coherence. Finally, an overview of the entire period may be obtained in the book which has been edited by *Birgit Nüchel Thomsen* ("The Odd Man Out? Denmark and European Integration 1948-1992"). However, this publication is a severely abbreviated English version of the corresponding Danish one, on the whole leaving out contributions based on primary sources. The result is a rather sketchy presentation of main lines in the Danish policy.

- Another general conclusion to be drawn when studying the list is the relatively **high number of works dealing with Danish policy in a Scandinavian context**. No doubt, the proportion of such works is higher than it would have been on a list of titles in the Danish language. When accounting for this feature we may start out by pointing to different perspectives underlying the interest in Danish policy. From a domestic perspective this policy is, quite understandably, to a large extent studied in its own right, whereas the outside perspective – Denmark being a small country with limited international influence – tends to be broader, not least geographically. Thus, attention is easily directed at the Scandinavian context when the audience is international, not least because the attitude of the Scandinavian countries – in spite of differences in concrete policies vis-à-vis European integration, both past and present – exhibit a number of similar traits. These similarities are the points of departure for the classical work by *Toivo Miljan* ("The Reluctant Europeans"). Two anthologies on the list are indicative of the same tendency to focus on Scandinavia, i.e. the volumes edited by *Thorsten Borring Olesen* ("Interdependence versus integration. Denmark, Scandinavia and Western Europe 1945-1960") and by *Tiilikainen and Petersen* ("The Nordic Countries and the EC"). Drawing in some of the other titles it is possible to identify two additional factors accounting for the interest in the Scandinavian context. The first has to do with the process of integration which – parallel to the Continental one – has taken place among the Scandinavian countries themselves in the post-war period. Characteristic features of this process – both historically and theoretically – has been dealt with in quite a number of studies, but since we are here dealing with a separate field of research only a few are included in the list (*Laursen*, *Nielsson* and *Straath*). But this factor spills into another one, which more directly pertains to the formulation of Danish European policy: The dilemma derived from being placed in both a Nordic and a Continental foreign policy circle. Some of the works included are inspired by, or take up, this dilemma: *Gunnar P. Nielsson* (1966 and 1971), *Martin Sæter* (1993) and *Vibeke Sørensen* (1995).

- Thirdly, when looking at the year of publication, a conspicuously **large part of the literature has been produced within the last decade**. For a number of titles which are the result of historically oriented research this may easily be explained by recent release of archival material[2]: the studies by *Hans Branner, Just and Olesen, Johnny Laursen* and *Vibeke Sørensen*. By these contributions various aspects, not least in the economic field, of Danish policies during the formative period of European integration have been investigated, although a comprehensive historical analysis based on primary sources is still lacking. The deepening of European integration since the middle of the 1980s has internationally given a new upsurge in European studies, and this general trend is also reflected in the vast number of new titles in the 1990s. As mentioned earlier recent research includes a wider spectrum of fields, taking in questions like national identity and political culture, see the works by *Hans Mouritzen et al., Tim Knudsen, Uffe Østergaard, Lene Hansen* and *Ole Wæver*. Furthermore, developments in the 1990s have drawn special attention to the role of Denmark in European integration, thus giving further impetus to internationally oriented research. This factor is not yet highly visible on the list, although it forms part of the background for studies already referred to (*Nüchel Thomsen, Sørensen* and *Mouritzen et al.*) and more explicitly dealt with in *Mouritzen* (1993), *Petersen* (1993 and 1995) and *Wæver*. Public opinion and voting behaviour at the two referenda held in 1992 and 1993 has been analysed in *Nielsen, Sauerberg, Svensson* and *Worre*. Finally, it should be added that the 1990s has seen the first comprehensive presentation in English of the history of Danish foreign policy, i.e. *Holbraad*. A substantial part of the book deals with the post-war period, but the main focus is on security policy rather than European policy.

- As a last point it is worth emphasizing that the biography contains a **number of studies with theoretical pretensions**. Most characteristic is the implementation and elaboration of the adaptation approach, sometimes referred to as the Scandinavian school in foreign policy analysis. The article by *Peter Hansen* (1974) is the first attempt to revise the original scheme of this research tradition set up by James Rosenau. And in the studies by *Nikolaj Petersen (1995)* and *Hans Mouritzen* (1993 and 1996) the adaptation approach is applied to Danish European policy on the basis of further revisions undertaken by both authors in their previous works. Conceptualisations aiming at connecting adaptation theory with the study of integration policy is also to be found in *Kelstrup* (1993). In this study, and in the ones by Mouritzen, an additional theoretical perspective is included by discussing the position and options of small states in the integration

---

2 Compared to other Western European countries Danish legislation has traditionally been more restrictive in giving permission to access to historical material, upholding until 1992 a 50 year rule.

process, hereby taking up another traditional interest of Danish scholars in the international relations field (Søren Z. von Dosenrode, *Westeuropäische Kleinstaaten in der EU und EPZ*, Chur & Zürich: Verlag Rüegger, 1993). At least three other theoretical approaches are represented on the list: *Jens Henrik Haahr* has studied party strategies applying and revising neo-functionalist integration theory; *Thomas Pedersen*, in the article included, discusses Danish European policy in light of theories on foreign policy change; and *Heurlin* and *Schou* (1980) have viewed Danish attitudes and policies in the context of the main postwar approaches to integration, a theme also taken up in all three titles by *Hans Branner*.

Literature

Arter, David (1993): "The 'Six' becomes the 'Nine'. The Accesion of Britain, Denmark and Ireland to the European Community in 1973", ch. 6, pp. 145-88 in David Arter, *The Politics of European Integration in the Twentieth Century*, Aldershot: Dartmouth Publishing.

Auken, Svend, Jacob Buksti and Carsten Lehmann Sørensen (1975): "Denmark Joins Europe: Patterns of Adaption in the Danish Political and Administrative Process as a Result of Membership of the European Communities", *Journal of Common Market Studies*, Vol. 14, No.1, pp. 1-36.

Branner, Hans (1993): "Danish European Policy since 1945: The Question of Sovereignty" in *Kelstrup (ed.)* (1993a).

Branner, Hans (1995): "Denmark and the European Coal and Steel Community, 1950-1953" in Borring Olesen (ed.), *Interdependence Versus Integration. Denmark, Scandinavia and Western Europe, 1945-1960*, Odense: Odense University Press.

Branner, Hans (1997): "Small state on the sidelines: Denmark and the question of European political integration" in George Wilkes (ed.), *Britain's Failure to Enter the European Community 1961-63*, London: Frank Cass.

Buksti, Jakob A. (1980): "Corporate Structures in Danish EC Policy: Patterns of Organizational Participation and Adaption", *Journal of Common Market Studies*, Vol. 19, No. 2, pp. 140-159.

Carlsen, Hanne Norup, J.T. Ross Jackson, Niels I. Meyer (eds.) (1993): *When no means yes: Danish visions of a different Europe*, London: Adamantine Press.

Dahl, Aghnete (1995): *National freedom of action in EU environmental policy: Denmark and the Netherlands*, EED-report 1/1995, Lysaker: The Fridtjof Nansen Institute.

Dosenrode, Søren von (1998): "Denmark: The Testing of a Hesitant Membership", ch. 4, pp. 52-68 in Kenneth Hanf and Ben Soetendorp (eds.), *Adapting to European integration: small states and the European Union*, London: Longman.

Due-Nielsen, Carsten and Nikolaj Petersen (eds.) (1995): *Adaptation and Activism. The Foreign Policy of Denmark 1967-1993*, Copenhagen: DJØF Publishing.

Due, Ole (1999): *Denmark and the Court of Justice of the European Communities*, DUPI working paper 1/1999.

Friis, Lykke (1998): *Denmark's Fifth EU-Referendum: In Denmark nichts Neues?*, DUPI working paper 13/1998.

Friis, Lykke (1999): "EU and Legitimacy – The Challenge of Compatibility: A Danish Case Study", *Cooperation and Conflict*, Vol. 34, No. 3, pp. 243-271.

Featherstone, K. (1988): "Denmark", ch. 4, pp. 76-106 in *Socialist parties and European integration: a comparative history*, Manchester: Manchester University Press.

Fitzmaurice, John (1976): "National Parliament and European Policy-Making: The Case of Denmark", *Parliamentary Affairs*, 29(3), pp. 281-292.

Gulmann, C. (1987): "The single European Act: Some Remarks from a Danish perspective", *Common Market Law Review*, Vol. 24:1.

Haahr, Jens Henrik (1992): "European Integration and the Left in Britain and Denmark", *Journal of Common Market Studies*, Vol. 30, pp. 77-100.

Haahr, Jens Henrik (1993): *Looking to Europe. The EC Policies of the British Labour Party and the Danish SDP*, Aarhus: Aarhus University Press.

Hansen, Lene and Ole Wæver (eds.) (2000): *Between Nations and Europe: Regionalism, Nationalism and the Politics of Union.* Routledge.

Hansen, Peter (1969): "Denmark and European Integration", *Cooperation and Conflict*, 1969/1, pp. 13-46.

Hansen, Peter (1974): "Adaptive Behaviour of Small States: The Case of Denmark and the European Community" in McGowan (ed.), *Sage International Yearbook of Foreign Policy Studies,* Beverly Hills/London: SAGE Publishers.

Hansen, Peter, Melvin Small and Karen Sinne (1977): "The Structure of the Debate in the Danish EC Campaign: A study of an opinion-policy Relationship", *Journal of Common Market Studies*, Vol. 15, No. 2, pp. 93-129.

Heurlin, Bertel (1998): "Federal Conceptions in Denmark: Traditions and Perspectives", manuscript, forthcoming 2000 in a revised German edition.

Heurlin, Bertel (1996): "Denmark: a new activism in foreign and security policy" Ch. 8, pp. 166-185 in Christopher Hill (ed.), *The actors in Europe's foreign policy*, London: Routledge.

Holbraad, Carsten (1991): *Danish Neutrality. A Study in the Foreign Policy of a Small State*, Oxford: Clarendon Press.

Ingebritsen, Christine (1998): *The Nordic states and European unity*, Ithaca, New York: Cornell University Press.

Jensen, Frede P. (1998): "The National Interests of Denmark", pp. 36-46 in Wolfgang Wessels (ed.): *National vs. EU foreign policy interests: mapping "important" national interests final report of a collective project by TEPSA and member institutes*, Cologne/Brussels: TEPSA.

Just, Flemming and Thorsten B. Olesen (1995): "Danish Agriculture and the European Market Schism, 1945-1960" in *Borring Olesen (ed.).*

Jørgensen, Birte Holst (1999): *Building European cross-border co-operation structures: Ph.D. thesis*, Copenhagen: Institute of Political Science University of Copenhagen.

Jørgensen, Knud Erik, Johnny Laursen and Henrik D. Høyer (1995): *Made in Denamrk: essays on Danish legal, historical, and political science research on the European Community and the European Community*, Aarhus: Department of Political Science, Aarhus University.

Jørgensen, Knud Erik (1998): *Denmark: The Royal Danish Ministry of Foreign Affairs*, Aarhus: Department of Political Science, Aarhus University.

Kelstrup, Morten (ed.) (1993a): *European Integration and Denmark's Participation,* Copenhagen: Copenhagen Political Studies Press.

Kelstrup, Morten (1993b): "Small States and European Political Integration. Reflections on Theories and Strategies" in *Tiilikainen and Petersen (eds.).*

Knudsen, Tim (1993): "A Portrait of Danish State-Culture: Why Denmark Needs Two National Anthems" in *Kelstrup (ed.).*

Larsen, Henrik (1999a): *Denmark and the CFSP in the 1990s. Active Internationalism and the Edingburgh Decision*, DUPI working paper 4/1999.

Larsen, Henrik (1999b): British and Danish Policies towards Europe in the 1990s: A Discource Approach", *European Journal of International relations,* 5(4).

Laursen, Finn (1988): "The Discussion on European Union in Denmark" in Walter Lipgens and Wilfried Loth (eds.): *Documents on the History of European Integration,* Vol. 3, pp. 566-627, Berlin/New York: Walter de Gruyter.

Laursen, Finn (1992): "Denmark and European Political Union" in Laursen and Vanhoonacker (1992), *The Intergovernmental Conference on Political Union, Institutional Reforms, New Policies and International Identity of the European Community*. Maastricht: European Institute of Public Administration.

Laursen, Finn (1993): "The Maastricht Treaty: Implications for the Nordic Countries", *Cooperation and Conflict*, Vol. 28, No. 2, pp. 115-142.

Laursen, Johnny (1994): "Blueprints of Nordic Integration. Dynamics and Institutions in Nordic Cooperation, 1945-72", *EUI Working Paper*, RSC No. 94/20.

Laursen, Johnny (1996): "Next in Line: Denmark and the EEC Challenge" in S. Ward and R.T. Griffiths (eds.), *Courting the Common Market. The First Attempt to Enlarge the European Community 1961-1963*, London, pp. 211-227.

Lawler, Peter (1997): "Scandinavian Exceptionalism and European Union", *Journal of Common Market Studies*, Vol. 35, No. 4, pp. 565-594.

Lyck, Lise (ed.) (1992): *Denmark and EC Membership Evaluated,* London: Pinter.

Miljan, Toivo (1977): *The Reluctant Europeans. The Attitudes of the Nordic Countries towards European Integration*, London: C. Hurst.

Mouritzen, Hans (1993): "The Two Musterknaben and the Naughty Boy: Sweden, Finland and Denmark in the Process of European Integration", *Cooperation and Conflict*, Vol. 28/4, pp. 373-402.

Mouritzen, Hans, Ole Wæver and Håkan Wiberg (1996): *European Integration and National Adaptations. A Theoretical Inquiry,* Commack: Nova Science Publishers, Inc.

Møller, J. Ørstrøm (1983): "Danish EC Decision-Making: An insiders view", *Journal of Common Market Studies*, Vol. 21, No. 3, pp. 245-260.

Møller, J.Ø. (1988): "The Nordic Angle III: The single European Act – A Danish view", *The World Today*, Vol. 11, pp. 195-199.

Nehring, Niels-Jørgen (1998): *The Illusory Quest for Legitimacy. Danish Procedures for Policy Making on the EU and the Impact of a Critical Public*, DUPI report/reprint 3/1998.

Nielsen, Hans Jørgen (1993): "The Danish Voters and the Referendum in June 1992 on the Maastricht Agreement" in *Kelstrup (ed.)*.

Nielsson, Gunnar P. (1966): *Denmark and European Integration. A Small Country at the Crossroads*, unpubl. Ph.D diss., University of California, Los Angeles (microfilm at Royal Library, Copenhagen).

Nielsson, Gunnar P. (1971): "The Nordic and the Continental European Dimension in Scandinavian Integration: Nordek as a Case Study", *Cooperation and Conflict*, no. 3-4, pp. 173-81.

Olesen, Thorsten Borring (1995) (ed.): *Interdependence Versus Integration. Denmark, Scandinavia and Western Europe 1945-1960,* Odense: Odense University Press.

Pedersen, Ove K. and Dorthe Pedersen (1995): *The Europeanization of National Corporatism: when the State and Organizations in Denmark went to Europe together*, COS-report no. 4/1995, Copenhagen: Copenhagen Business School.

Pedersen, Thomas (1994): "Denmark and the European Integration" in Georgi Karasimeonov and Mette Skak (eds.), *Bulgaria and Denmark and the new Europe*, Sofia: St. Kliment Ohridsky University Press.

Pedersen, Thomas (1995): *Changing course Denmark, Sweden and the EU*, Aarhus: Departement of Political Science, Aarhus University.

Petersen, Nikolaj and Jørgen Elklit (1973): "Denmark Enters the European Community", *Scandinavian Political Studies*, 8, 204.

Petersen, Nikolaj (1993): "Game, Set and Match. Denmark and European Union from Maastricht to Edinburgh" in *Tiilikainen and Petersen (eds.)*.
Petersen, Nikolaj (1995a): "Adapting to change: Danish security after the cold war", pp. 99-116 in Birthe Hansen (ed.), *European security – 2000*, Copenhagen: Copenhagen Political Studies Press.
Petersen, Nikolaj (1995b): "Denmark and the European Community 1985-93" in *Due-Nielsen and Petersen (eds.)*.
Petersen, Nikolaj (1996): "Denmark and the European Union 1985-96. A Two-level Analysis", *Cooperation and Conflict,* Vol. 31/2, pp. 185-210.
Petersen, Nikolaj (1998): "National Strategies in the Integration Dilemma: An Adaption Approach", *Journal of Common Market Studies*, Vol. 36, No. 1, pp. 33-54.
Royal Danish Ministry of Foreign Affairs (1993): *The Danish referendum, May 18, 1993: views of the political parties and political groups on the referendum issues*, Copenhagen: Royal Danish Ministry of Foreign Affairs. Secretariate for Cultural and Press Relations.
Royal Danish Ministry of Foreign Affairs (1998): *The referendum in Denmark on 28 May 1998 on the ratification of the Amsterdam Treaty: the views of political parties and groups – in their own words*, Copenhagen: Royal Danish Ministry of Foreign Affairs.
Rüdiger, Mogens (1995): "Denmark and the European Community 1967-85" in *Due-Nielsen and Petersen (eds.)*.
Sauerberg, Steen (1992): "Parties, voters and the EC" in *Lyck (ed.)*.
Schou, Tove Lise (1980): "Denmark: The Functionalists" in Valentine Herman and Mark Hagger (eds.), *The Legislation of Direct Elections to the European Parliament*, Gower.
Schou, Tove Lise (1993): "The Debate in Denmark 1986-91 on European Integration and Denmark's Participation" in *Kelstrup (ed.)*.
Stillman, Edmund (Director of Study) (1977): "Denmark and the EEC", Ch. 4, pp. 120-160 in Hudson Report: *Denmark in Europe*, Paris: A/S Forlaget Børsen.
Straath, Bo (1978): *Nordic Industry and Nordic Economic Cooperation*, Stockholm: Almqvist and Wiksell International.
Straath, Bo (1980): "The Illusory Nordic Alternative to Europe", *Cooperation and Conflict,* Vol. 15, pp. 103-14.
Svensson, Palle (1994): "The Danish Yes to Maastricht and Edinburgh. The Referendum of May 1993", *Scandinavian Political Studies* 1994, Vol. 17, No. 1, pp. 69-90.
Sæter, Martin (1993): "The Nordic Countries and European Integration. The Nordic, the West European and the All-European Stages" in *Tiilikainen and Petersen (eds.)*.
Sørensen, Henning and Ole Wæver (1992): "State, society and democracy and the effect of the EC" in *Lyck (ed.)*.
Sørensen, Vibeke (1986): *Danish Economic Policy and European Cooperation on Trade and Currencies (1948-59)*, EUI Working Paper 86/251, Florence.
Sørensen, Vibeke (1991/92): "The Politics of Closed Markets: Denmark, The Marshall Plan and European Integration, 1948-1963", *International History Review*, Vol. 14/1.
Sørensen, Vibeke (1992a): "National Welfare Strategies and International Linkages in a Small Open Economy: The Danish Social Democratic Party and European Integration, 1947-1963" in Richard T. Griffith (ed.), *Socialist Parties and the Question of Europe in the 1950s*, Leiden: E.J. Brill.
Sørensen, Vibeke (1992b): "How to Become a Member of a Club without Joining. Danish Policy with respect to European Sector Integration Schemes, 1950-1957", *Scandinavian Journal of History,* Vol. 16, pp. 105-25.

Sørensen, Vibeke (1993): "Between interdependence and integration: Denmark's shifting strategies" in Alan Milward and Vibeke Sørensen (eds.), *The Frontier of National Sovereignty,* London and New York: Routledge.

Sørensen, Vibeke (1995a): ""Free trade" versus regulated markets: Danish agricultural organisations and the Green Pool, 1950-54" in Brian Girvin (ed.), *The Green Pool and the Origins of the Common Agricultural Policy.*

Sørensen, Vibeke (1995b): "Nordic Cooperation – A Social Democratic Alternative to Europe?" in *Borring Olesen (ed.).*

Thomas, Alastair, H. (1975): "Danish Social Democracy and the European Community", *Journal of Common Market Studies,* Vol. 13, No. 4, pp. 454-468.

Thomas, Alastair H. (1995): "Danish Policy-Making, Regionalism, and the European Community", ch.13, pp. 281-288 in Barry Jones and Michael Keating (eds.), *The European Union and the regions*, Oxford: Clarendon Press.

Thomsen, Birgit Nüchel (ed.) (1993): *The Odd Man Out? Denmark and European Integration 1948-1992*, Odense: Odense University Press.

Tiilikainen, Teija and Ib Damgaard Petersen (eds.) (1992): *The Nordic Countries and the EC,* Copenhagen: Copenhagen Political Studies Press.

Worre, T. (1988): "Denmark at the Crossroads: The Danish Referendum 28 February 1986 on the EC Reform Package", *Journal of Common Market Studies* vol. 4, pp. 361-88.

Worre, Torben (1995): "Danish Public Opinion and the European Community", *Scandinavian Journal of History*, Vol. 20/2.

Wæver, Ole (1995): "Danish Dilemmas – Foreign Policy Choices for the 21st Century" in *Due-Nielsen and Petersen (eds.).*

Østergaard, Uffe (1992): "Danish identity: European, Nordic or peasant?" in *Lyck (ed.).*

Part I

Theoretical Perspectives

CHAPTER 2

The Study of Danish European Policy – Perspectives for a Comparative Approach[1]

Hans Branner

1. Introduction

When analyzing the foreign policy of a single state covering a certain span of time, one is normally tempted to emphasize the peculiarities of behavior, the specific internal and external circumstances which have determined the policies pursued and the uniqueness of the major decisions involved in policy formulation. Notwithstanding the ambitions and endeavours by foreign policy analysts since the end of the 1960s to develop a common framework or relevant theories, the "historical trap" is still all too evident in most studies pretending to have a generalizing aim. This aim remains only superficially attached to the concrete investigations, and the results rarely inspire those scholars who deal with the foreign policy of other states. The problem of accumulative research in the field of international relations seems difficult to overcome.

We need both the well-documented historical inquiry revealing the distinctive character of the foreign policy of an individual state and how this policy has evolved over time, as well as the construction of concepts, models, and theories able to show how the behavior of a specific state fits into a larger pattern enabling the analyst to draw more general conclusions valid for other states. This book contains both, and hopefully, each article is valuable on its own merits. Yet the book should also be seen as an integrated whole, so we are confronted with the above-mentioned problems of combining empirical findings and theoretical endeavours – and of accumulation.

Without pretending to solve these problems and with Danish experiences as a point of departure – I shall attempt here to place the study of European policies of single states into comparative perspective. The article takes up the thread from the introduction, which dealt with comparisons on the basis of the Danish case; but the scope in regard to concrete comparisons is more restricted. At the same time, I focus more on the comparative approach per se.

---

1 This contribution as well as my two other chapters in this book are also offsprings of my previous attachment to the research project "Danish Policy in Transition 1945-1985", sponsored by the Danish Social Science Research Council. I am grateful for the opportunity I hereby was given for investigating into Danish European policy in a historical perspective.

Three aspects of the problematique will be taken up.[2] *First,* I shall elaborate on the above mentioned gap between empirical and theoretical studies in the field of foreign policy. It will be argued that a closing of the gap is not in sight, but that the lack of such a closing should not prevent us from advancing comparative research. In other words: we should learn to live with it and get the best out of it, in part by refining single country studies. *Secondly,* on the basis of the Danish experience I attempt to pin down the concept of "European policy" and relate it to other relevant concepts. This is done in order to make it more useful for comparative purposes. A few indications of how the conceptualization presented may be applied in further research are given. In the *third* part, divided up into two sections, focus is on the historical dimension as an element which increasingly enters into the analyses of European policies. A number of post-war developments which account for the importance of historical determinants are identified, with special emphasis on the Danish case. This discussion is then further elaborated by scrutinizing the position of these determinants in existing foreign policy theory. It is shown that existing theory only insufficiently provides a basis for including the past, when analyzing and comparing European policies. Altogether, this third part vindicates the position of history in foreign policy research and casts new light on the discussion of a "historical trap" in foreign policy analysis.

2. On integrating empirical and theoretical ambitions in foreign policy studies

This is not the place for an overview of the history of foreign policy theorizing or the present state of research in this field.[3] Suffice it to say at this point that not least Danish – and Scandinavian – scholars have been attracted by the field and have in various ways contributed to it or have attempted to employ models set up by others.[4] Lately the focus of these studies have almost exclusively been directed towards the understanding of integration policies, e.g., Kelstrup (1993), Jerneck (1993), N. Petersen (1995), Mouritzen (1996), Th. Pedersen (1996).

The point of departure for the discussion to be taken up in this section is not the concrete theories but the "meta issue" just raised as to how to deal with the existing gap between empirical and theoretical ambitions.

For clarification one may start by specifying what exactly is meant by this gap. In its most extreme form, the gap exists when separate studies are carried out

---

2 The two articles which follow also attempt to contribute to the comparative approach: the first refines adaptation theory in light of developments in Danish European policy, the second develops and applies the concept of integration policy.
3 For an introduction to foreign policy theory in regard to integration policies see chapter 3. This issue is also discussed below, sections 4 and 5.
4 This is particularly true with respect to adaptation theory, doctrine studies and frameworks for studying foreign policy change.

covering the same area of research without linking empirical and theoretical insights. On the one hand we have empirical studies focusing on a detailed chronology of events or on the various forces at work in a specific situation by accumulating and analyzing a large amount of data. On the other hand are theoretical studies primarily concerned with conceptualizations and broad generalizations with only scant regard to the intricacies of the historical development or the historical situation.

This kind of gap relates to *different disciplines and aims* and – although important – is not our main concern here. As already stated, foreign policy research needs both, and a further advancement of the field cannot be achieved without input from both the empirical and the theoretical side. Furthermore, it should be noted that in the area of international relations a certain tendency to fill the gap between the two disciplines of history and political science can be observed, especially on the part of historians who increasingly show a willingness to relate their work to research belonging to the theoretical discipline.

Instead, I would like to focus on the gap that for long has existed *inside the field of foreign policy studies itself*. The dissolution of the "comparative foreign policy movement" of the 1960s and 1970s may to a large extent be accounted for by the apparent impossibility of overcoming the gap between theoretical and empirical aims. By lowering ambitions to middle range theories the field has in the 1980s again gained some momentum, and a number of remarkable studies which indicate a continued drive to move the field ahead have appeared.[5] Nevertheless, a closing of the gap is still only in the making.

I would like to point to two interrelated ways in which this gap still manifests itself. The *first* one relates to the tendency in certain studies to cover up a predominantly empirical investigation by introducing a few theoretical concepts whose relevance are demonstrated throughout the analysis and which the conclusions are hinged upon. The problem is that concepts or frameworks applied in this way seldom add to empirical understanding nor to the development of theory.

The *second* – and probably most fundamental way in which the gap is revealed – pertains to more sophisticated analyses where the empirical and theoretical parts are more fully integrated. Although such studies may seem fruitful from a purely theoretical point of view, on closer inspection they may not lead to the kind of understanding to which they pretend. The problem is usually that theories either become too crude or too refined – in both cases their value for comparative purposes is restricted.[6] However, even studies which have seemingly struck a fruitful middle course in this respect often fall short of creating a basis for relevant comparisons.[7]

---

5 Cf. the article by Ole Wæver in Carlsnaes and Smith (1994).
6 This problem is to some degree inherent in the field of IR studies and, thus, of a very general nature; cf. the difficulties encountered by neo-functionalist integration theory in the 1960s and 1970s.
7 This point is further elaborated in my discussion (in section 4) of a recent work comparing the European policy of six European states in the frame of adaptation theory.

How then to get on? And is it at all possible to close the gap between empirical and theoretical ambitions in the field of foreign policy studies? I shall argue that instead of continuing to deplore the situation it should be accepted as a necessary and a desirable pre-condition for further studies.

Although existing research conditions always reflect former institutionalization and the way priorities have been set in the past, they are also indicative of scholars' deep-rooted inclinations in respect to their own research objectives.

Some scholars are attracted to a more empiricist approach and others by a more theoretical one. This appears evident when comparing historians with international relations specialists, but also holds within IR itself. This observation, while trivial, nevertheless is often forgotten or suppressed. Moreover, the plea for more tolerance among scholars from different fields of research is particularly relevant considering the contributions made to the present book.

Quite apart from the "fundamentals" cited above, it can be argued that understanding the "real" world and the problems confronting states is best advanced by sticking to two- og multifold objectives without necessarily integrating the findings into a coherent whole. Reality itself cannot be confined to those phenomena which are immediately observable. Understanding the "real" world also requires the identification of long-term trends and other variables of a general kind; variables which have an impact even if they are not perceived by decision-makers. These dimensions of reality might best be understood by keeping empirical and theoretical studies separate – at least to a certain extent. Thus, we may look at the gap we are discussing not only from the point of view of a necessary but also of a desirable pre-condition for advancing research.[8]

On this – in regard to theoretical ambitions – rather modest basis a few indications as to how the study of Danish European policy may contribute to an understanding of the European policy of other countries, and how it may inspire studies towards this aim. First, however, we must define what we are talking about, hereby admitting that conceptualization is a necessary step in every comparative endeavour.

3. The "European policy" concept in Danish and comparative perspective

Comparing the European policies of several states is no easy task. Because of the encompassing character of the term the problems inherent in this task are not necessarily easier to grasp than the ones confronting the researcher dealing with general foreign policy comparisons. One may even argue that in the context of present

---

8 It should be added that this observation does not imply that efforts aimed at combining empirical and theoretical studies should be abandoned; rather that "understanding" and "theorizing" should be regarded as separate aims.

day political conditions "European policy" is even more difficult to pin down for comparative purposes than the more familiar but very elusive "foreign policy". Furthermore, in spite of all the difficulties of the foreign policy approach, a certain consensus has always existed in regard to the main object of research and on the main issues. Since the same kind of research tradition does not exist with regard to "European policy", a similar consensus is not at hand. Consequently, one finds a variety of meanings attached to the term by scholars; e.g. by some it is taken to be synonymous with "integration policy", by others the concept has a wider content.

In order to make "European Policy" apt for comparative purposes we shall first deal with its meaning and its usage in a Danish political context and then attempt to define its main elements. I will introduce two analytical levels on which the term "European policy" should be conceptualized, although in a concrete analysis these levels may be hard to distinguish. On this basis some further distinctions will be elaborated, not least the one between "European policy" and "integration policy".

It is remarkable that the term "European policy" (Europapolitik) as an aspect of Danish foreign policy has only in recent years acquired a more widespread usage in official declarations, in statements by the political parties and in public debate.[9] In contrast, the European great powers have always had a "European policy" also in Danish political discourse, the most illustrative example being the century-old balance-of-power policy by Great Britain in regard to the European continent. In the post-war period the course of European integration has been closely linked to the fluctuations of French European Policy. Similarly, a new European policy was the major element when after the war the United States chose to abandon its long-held isolationist stand and instead embarked upon an internationalist foreign policy.

If a systematic analysis was undertaken of how the term "European policy" has been articulated in the foreign policies of *small states* and *great powers*, respectively, a common pattern would probably emerge. No doubt, political discourse in this respect reflects differences in the scope and character of foreign policy interests by states of varying size, and consequently, of the state's self-perception concerning its role and position which prevails among decision-makers and in the general public. A closer look at the Danish case supports an interpretation of this kind.

Since the latter part of the 19th century and until the end of World War II, when the external conditions of Denmark were almost exclusively determined by the behavior of a single European great power (i.e. Germany) there was no talk of a Danish European policy. For Denmark, the question of what kind of relations the country should have towards the rest of Europe was more or less limited to a discussion of what kind of a policy Denmark should pursue towards Germany. In the Danish discourse, Denmark had a "Tysklandspolitik" = *German policy* (i.e. policy towards Germany), but no *European policy*.

---

9 In this preliminary and historically based discussion of the term, European policy is seen as an aspect of foreign policy. This premise will be challenged at the end of the section.

After the war external conditions changed dramatically. Relieved of the German problem, Denmark was confronted with a range of new foreign policy options. However, small state thinking and small state terminology survived, which meant that more narrow terms continued to be applied when dealing with those issues today covered by the term "European policy". The major questions now centered around Danish policy towards European integration, which was persistently referred to as Danish *market policy* reflecting an official interpretation defining this aspect of Denmark's foreign relations as belonging to an exclusively economic sphere. The terminology applied, however, was also indicative of a continued perception of closely circumscribed Danish interests in regard to European affairs.

No change of terminology occurred when Danish policy, after joining the European Community in 1973, was no longer primarily occupied with the question of choosing between different "market" blocs. The parliamentary committee set up to control government policy in this field, now endowed with new functions, continued to be called the "Market Committee". This was still the case by the middle of the 1980s, when European integration again moved ahead; questions concerning Danish positions on the Union plans leading to the Maastricht Treaty of 1991 were all referred to the Market Committee; and so was the subsequent discussion of how the Danish "No" vote of June 1992 should be handled. Not before October 1994 was the committee renamed the "*European* Committee". At this point the term "market policy" was finally regarded as obsolete, and was gradually replaced by the term "European policy".[10]

This short terminological overview shows that use and non-use of the term "European policy" in the Danish political context has been closely associated with changes in Denmark's role as a small state and how this role has been perceived by those occupied with the formulation of foreign policy. A certain inertia with regard to terminological change was characteristic of the post-war period. When a change finally materialized in the 1990s it had become evident that – although still a typical small state – Denmark not only needed to define its relations to the rest of Europe on a wider basis and in a more explicit and coherent way, but was now also able to independently influence European developments.

Although Danish use of the term "European Policy" has been limited to the present, it is possible to apply "European policy" to earlier historical periods as well. Furthermore, the evolution of the Danish discourse can provide a suitable basis for comparing the "European policy" concept with others applied in earlier periods of Danish relations with Europe.

The distinction between market policy and "European policy" – as already indicated – has to do with the division between different aspects of foreign policy, i.e. security policy, foreign economic relations and normative policy.[11] Obviously,

---

10 This change of terminology was foreshadowed at the reorganization of the Danish Foreign Ministry in 1991, when the newly created N1 department was explicitly charged with handling "European policy".

11 For these distinctions see chapter 11.

market policy relates solely to the foreign economic aspect, and does not even cover all of this. In order to speak of "European policy", we need to identify some consistent perceptions within the foreign policy community concerning the role of the state in relation to the rest of the region – or parts of it at least. These perceptions are not exclusively conceived in terms of international economic relations. When we speak of British, French and US "European policy" we assume that this policy, besides its economic aspects, also contains some distinct elements of security policy. To use an expression from integration theory, one could say that without some element of *high politics* present one cannot speak of a European policy. In this perspective the term "market policy" has been used not to denote Danish European policy, but, rather, that Denmark pursued a "market policy" because a perceived need for a true European policy had not yet materialized in the Danish foreign policy debate (whether this is historically correct is another matter).

Pursuing foreign economic interests, while an important aspect of a European policy, can never be the sole purpose of such a policy.[12] If foreign economic policy (or trade policy) is a foreign policy category for itself, then market policy is just one distinct element of this policy (albeit probably the most important), defined by its concern with trade issues in Europe. If Danish trade relations were directed exclusively towards Europe, foreign economic policy and market policy would overlap with each other. Due to the character of the distinction between foreign economic policy and security policy, a similar translation of market policy into European policy is not possible.

The distinction between these different aspects of the European policy concept will be taken up again below, but first the meaning of the concept will be illustrated through a comparison with another foreign policy concept, namely that of *German policy*. Just as it is possible to imagine a market policy without a European policy, one should be able to have a "German policy" without a European policy. However, the relation between the policy types is different in the two cases.

In the Danish discourse not all relations to other countries are expressed in the form of a *policy*; this is especially true for small powers such as Denmark, which has relatively limited foreign policy interests. Of course, it is possible for a small country to develop quite elaborate policies towards even rather distant – and in security terms relatively insignificant – states, e.g. Denmark's policy toward Vietnam or South Africa. Such policies have been pursued where these states have been involved in political conflicts in which Denmark took an active interest. On the other hand, there has been no specific labelling of Danish policy towards a nearby great power such as France, despite the close economic and cultural ties between Denmark and France. As is the case with the European policy concept, the deciding factor in defining a "country policy" seems to be whether the relations

---

12 I am aware of the fact, that the distinction between economic policy and security policy can in some cases be difficult to maintain. However, this criticism can be directed towards any such analytical distinction between different aspects of a policy, and in the analysis here, it should not cause us to totally abandon such analytical distinctions.

between Denmark and the respective country or region encompass elements of security policy – or at least political elements not related exclusively to foreign economic policy. Danish "German policy" is a case in point.

During the years just preceding both World Wars, Danish foreign policy sought to develop a coherent stance towards the security threat posed by the expansive German state. Relations between the two countries were further complicated by the problems surrounding their common border. Under these circumstances, the Danish Government followed a policy of accommodating German interests. After World War II "the German problem" became a general feature of European politics through the military occupation and the subsequent political division of the German state. Denmark had to relate to this overall security issue as did other European states. Moreover, a "German policy" was needed in light of the size and economic importance of the new West German state, although this need had been lessened by the "multilateralization" of the issue within West European fora such as the EC (EU). German re-unification in 1990 has not lessened the significance of economic issues.

From the above we can conclude that, in principle, there is no difference between Danish European policy and Danish "German policy" regarding the foreign policy aspects involved in the two policies. Neither is it possible to claim that one policy (German policy) should be subordinate to the other (European policy). In so far as Denmark had a European policy in the 1930s, it largely reflected Danish policy towards Germany. The same can be said of French policy in the post-World War II era. Conversely, a policy towards Germany can also be viewed as part of an overall European policy.

When trying to distinguish between the two kinds of policy the most useful criterion is geographic. Use of "European policy" would be appropriate insofar as "German policy" were conceptualized within a wider European context. However quite apart from its spatial demarcation, the term "European" needs some further elaboration in order to fully grasp the content of European policy concept.[13] Thus, we propose a distinction between two analytical levels, *European* and *national*, which are not applicable to the "German policy" concept. This distinction has roots in the above mentioned Danish policy of adaptation pursued in the 1930s.

Altogether this policy – at least theoretically – may be understood on three separate levels. The first level is strictly *bilateral*, signifying a Danish "German

---

13 If a policy is directed only towards a group of European countries, e.g. Western Europe or the EU, it may still be covered by the "European policy" concept. In the Danish case a problem exists in regard to the distinction between "European" and "Nordic" policy. Due to unique cultural and historical bonds between the Nordic countries, relations to these states have a different character than relations to other states. On this basis, and since it is possible to conceive of a Danish "Nordic policy" without relating this policy to Denmark's position in Europe (like Danish "German policy"), Nordic policy should be seen as a separate category and not only as an element in European policy.

policy" perceived in a narrow geographical context. Focus is on Germany as a potential military threat, and adaptation is seen as a means of averting the threat – without regard to its wider international implications. In a concrete analysis these wider implications cannot be ignored. Thus, it becomes relevant to ask: is the policy pursued by the Danish Government really a manifestation of indirect support for specific alliances of European powers, so that Denmark – despite of its official neutrality – is taking sides in the power game by positioning itself in a certain way within the overall picture? One could also ask, whether the policy signifies a general unwillingness to deal with the larger questions of European politics? Are defensive national interests being given priority over broader, more long term goals?

These questions pertain to the second analytical level, i.e. the *national level of Danish European policy*, which concerns Denmark's position and role in Europe. Like "German policy" the focus of attention here is still on the traditional nation-state as actor. It is possible, however, to perceive of a third level where focus is moved above the nation state towards some kind of European entity. This third *European level* concerns the identification, institutionalizing and pursuit of goals, common to European states, or a group of them, e.g., promotion of security, economic growth, human rights protection, and the relations of these states with the outside world (European foreign policy). If regarded as a case of "anti balance-of-power policy", the Danish adaptation policy of the 1930s can be said to include an element of European policy at this level, in this case by in fact counteracting the common security goal.[14] According to the predominant interpretation, Denmark – by adapting to Germany – contributed towards tipping the balance between the great powers in a way detrimental to the maintenance of peace. If Danish policy could be interpreted as reflecting a preference for a German model of a new European order, it might also have been an illustration of what kind of policies can be included on the European level.

Figure 1 attempts to illustrate main concepts brought up in the discussion so far. An additional distinction, between internal and external level, is added when dealing with the European level of European policy. The internal level is placed in the middle of the figure, indicating that the policies involved here belong to the low politics category (see also fig. 2 and the overlap between European and integration policy).

Focusing specifically on developments since 1945, not least the process of European integration, the scheme may be taken as a point of departure for some further observations relevant to the identification and application of the European policy concept.

We may start by elaborating on the previously made observation concerning the

---

14 "Anti-balance-of-power" policy is a term applied by Anette Baker Fox when characterizing typical small state behavior in the latter part of the 1930s; see Baker Fox (1959).

Figure 1: The concept of "European policy" in the frame of various analytic distinctions

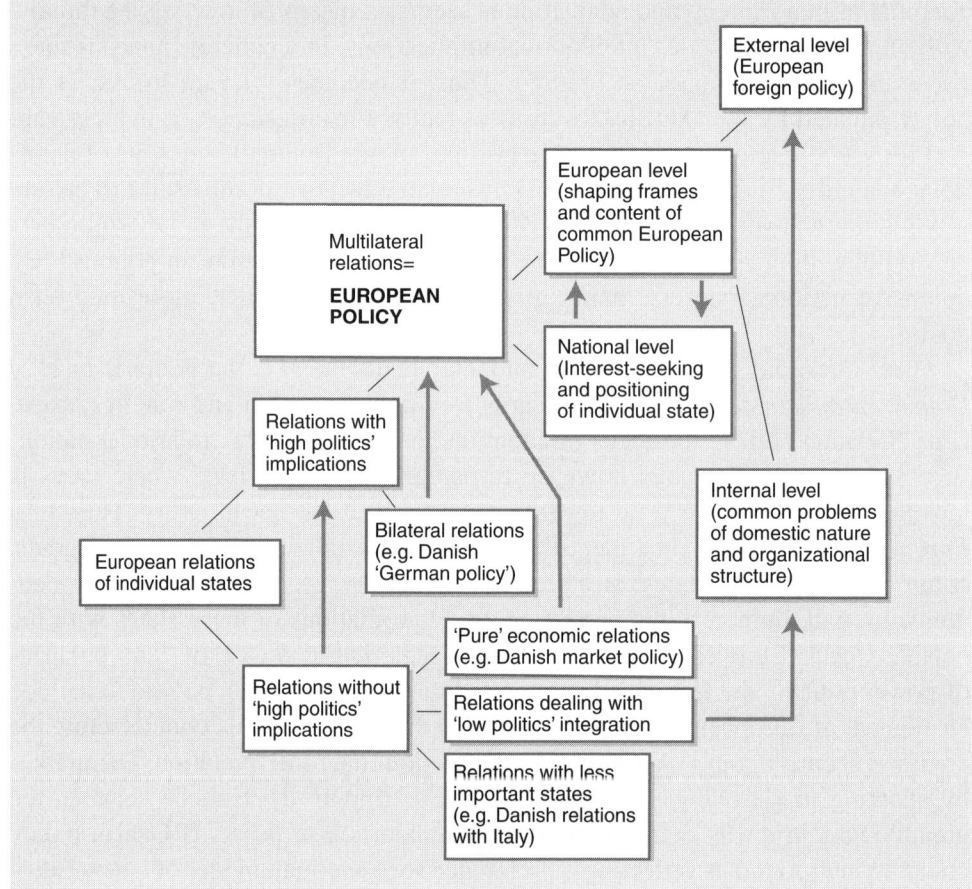

different use of the concept in regard to small states and great powers, respectively. Due to greatly increased interdependence between states and a parallel development towards linking of various policy areas in the post-war period, relations and levels placed in the upper part of the scheme in fig. 1 tend to gain importance. To a certain degree the arrows pointing upwards reflect these general trends, which are common to all European states: bilateral relations become multilaterilized, "low politics" becomes intertwined with "high politics", the nation-state as a frame of reference for policy formulation becomes undermined. As a consequence, focus is increasingly placed on "European policy" which then no longer remains an exclusive domain of Great Power politics.

With regard to the connection between the *national* and *European* levels of European policy, an upward as well as a downward arrow is included, in general signifying the difficulties involved in separating the two levels. Most often it is only with a post hoc interpretation and evaluation that we can determine the level at which a specific European policy is conceived. Sticking to a realist view, one could even maintain that only a national level exists, references to "international community" and "common interests" being regarded as mere rhetoric.

Notwithstanding these considerations, we shall argue that the distinction is a helpful analytic device for investigating European policies of individual states and for comparing such policies.

Thus, regardless of motives, the increased institutionalization of European politics since 1945 makes it necessary for most states to at least formulate a policy on both levels. Using a parallel but not synonymous distinction, decision-makers have to play a two-level game: one with their internal, another with their external environment (Putnam 1988). In the internal game, a European policy of a specific state will typically be dominated by considerations belonging to the national level. However, in the external game the European level will necessarily play an important role. Institutions – no matter how they are conceived as actors – are a forum for solving common problems and, thus, also for formulating positions which do not stick solely to a narrow national point of view. This tendency to focus on the European level is enhanced by the way national interests are legitimized in the external game, i.e. by reference to overall goals such as peace, stability and economic growth. Compared to previous periods, what we have termed the European level has now become much more manifest in the policy formulation process of individual states.

When applying the distinction between national and European levels, this development opens up for some interesting comparative perspectives from a discursive point of view. Thus, we may undertake a diachronic analysis measuring the relative weight of the two levels in the European policy formulation of single states. Typical questions to be asked would be, "To what degree are the solutions to important political problems perceived to exist at the European level? Which integration scenarios and visions of Europe as an international system are the most salient? Which European goals are given priority, and what means are deemed to be most appropriate for the task?" Comparing the policies of the various European states along these lines for a period just after World War II would certainly bring out some rather significant differences. Furthermore, these differences need not correspond to the existing descriptions, which have for the most part relied too heavily on analyses of "integration policies", thus neglecting the more general European policy concept (see below for the distinction between integration policy and European policy). Theoretically, it is possible to imagine policy formulation which emphasizes the European level without at the same time endorsing a supranational development. This seems to be occurring in present-day Danish political discourse.[15]

Keeping the two levels analytically distinct also seems helpful when analyzing

---

15 Other possible differences between states in such discursive analyses could be the degree to which the European level also enters into the internal game. In some states, European policy steps might very well also internally be legitimized by reference to common rather than national goals.

the *integration policy* of a specific state. The concept of integration policy is dealt with at length in chapter 3 of this volume. In the present context, two points are relevant with respect to conceptualization.

To start with, integration policy includes one key aspect of European policy, i.e. the one dealing with European integration. A range of issues in the military and economic spheres as well as questions related to "cooperation" and not the "integration" of states are thus exclusively reserved for the European policy concept. Prior to World War II, European policy hardly included any elements of integration policy.[16] However, a dominant trend in the post-war development for most states has been, that the space covered by European policy is "filled" by integration policy. This is reflected in every day usage, where the two terms often are made synonymous.

Sticking to our conceptualization as illustrated in fig. 1, however, it should also be pointed out that the content of the European integration process not only implies a substantial diminishing of the domain exclusively reserved for the European policy concept but also in some respects makes the integration policy concept the wider term. European integration is not mainly concerned with matters of "high politics" but is increasingly directed towards questions belonging to the "low politics" category. Consequently, a strict application of our definitions entails that for member countries of the European Union and applicant states, "integration policy" tends to become a more encompassing term than "European policy" (see fig. 2).

Figure 2: Conceptual relationship between "European policy" and "integration policy"

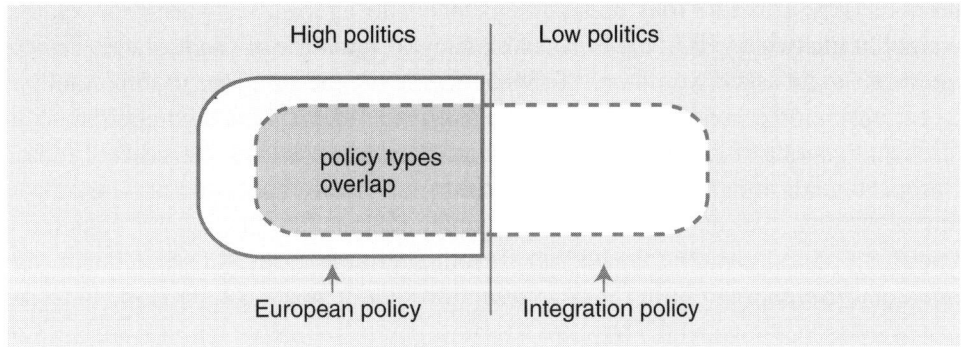

For most European states, intensified European integration now represents the major external condition to which their policies, be it domestic or foreign, must relate. On this account, the interplay between the two analytic levels, the national and the European, becomes relevant when trying to understand the integration policies of individual states. The Danish case seems apt to illustrate this point.

During the 1990s reservations towards the Maastricht Treaty have dominated

---

16 The well known proposal of 1930 by French foreign minister Aristide Briand on the creation of a European Union clearly belonged to the category of "cooperation" and not "integration".

Danish political discussions on European affairs. These reservations are typical examples of integration policy on the national level – having to do with the safeguarding of Danish sovereignty and with the position of Denmark in the European political architecture. This emphasis on the national level came about as a result of a preceding large step forward in European integration, which for Denmark involved a pre-occupation with the European level. Such a feedback process, amounting to what could be termed a reverse spill-over effect (or spill-back), is symptomatic of how Danish integration policy has been shaped during the past, and with the deepening of integration, might increasingly be observable in other countries too.[17] Again, studies aiming at diachronic and synchronic comparisons would be of interest, in this case based on the interplay between the two levels of integration policy.

Finally, the distinction between two levels of European policy is useful when exploring the relation between the concepts of *European policy* and *foreign policy*. At first glance, it seems most helpful to regard the foreign policy concept as the most general of the two, so that European policy is merely one part of a country's foreign policy. However, by drawing in the two levels, the discussion becomes somewhat more complicated.

Where the national level is in focus, it is indeed appropriate to speak of European policy as an aspect of a country's foreign policy in general. Here we are concerned with Denmark's foreign policy interests vis-à-vis a specific part of the world, including the priorities given to its relations with specific states within this area. This is absolutely within the limits of the traditional foreign policy concept. On the European level, however, though normally considered also to be foreign policy, it becomes more difficult to separate European policy from domestic policy.

The difficulties connected to the separation of domestic and foreign policy have generally been increasing, but they have nevertheless been especially salient in connection with the processes discussed here.[18] On the European level, the starting point is that Europe should be regarded as a unity of some kind. In so far as this level becomes an integrated part of normal political practice, the domestic political sphere becomes connected to a new political unit, and the domestic political issues pulled along to this new unit. Naturally, the degree to which a fusion of domestic and foreign policy is completed depends ultimately on the level of integration within the new and larger polity. Nevertheless, by distinguishing between the two analytical levels, it becomes more evident that European policy cannot be understood exclusively as foreign policy – at least not in the conventional meaning of this concept.

---

17 Developments in Danish integration policy following the signing of the SEA and the Amsterdam treaty may be seen as exceptions to the prevailing trend. It would be interesting to take up the question of whether the trend is about to be reversed.
18 This point is further elaborated in chapter 4, where the separation is regarded as impossible.

4. Comparing European policies – the need for a historical dimension

The attempt made to conceptualize has already drawn attention to a number of comparative perspectives, especially concerning the status, content and interrelationship of the two levels on which a European policy unfolds. In the present section the comparative aim shall be made more explicit by focusing on a group of factors, which present-day European policies, exemplified by the Danish case, seem to have accorded increased weight, i.e. historical determinants. The need to include a historical dimension when analyzing the present direction of European policies of individual states may be derived from various perspectives.

In an analysis of Norwegian attitudes and policies towards Europe, Jane Matlery observes:

> "… the past may shape the present to a far greater degree than the present itself. Often one assumes that man's political preferences are instrumental in the sense that choices are made according to the "rational" pursuit of interests, and that therefore the choice *pro* et *contra* the EC is the result of such a calculation. The more I do political analysis, however, the less evidence I find for this kind of "cost-benefit"-analysis, at least when the actors are constituted by the general populace."
>
> (Matlery 1993: 44)

When trying to understand Norway's European policy such a "historical" approach seem highly relevant. Almost four hundred years of "union" experience – first as part of the Danish realm, and since the Napoleonic wars, under Swedish sovereignty – and the consequent late attainment of independence (1905), in combination with a traditional sentiment of detachment in regard to the Continent, must necessarily be seen as key determinants for the direction which Norway's policies have taken towards Europe since 1945. For most other countries – at least at first glance – it is not so easy to trace the impact of historical factors. Building primarily on the Danish case, however, we shall try to identify a number of developments which support the general view expressed in the above quotation.

As a point of departure, we may first refer to the discussion of "European policy" terminology from the preceding section. As mentioned, Danish relations with the rest of Europe were for many years stubbornly termed "market policy", indicating that this part of foreign policy had mainly to do with Denmark's current economic interests and how to position the country in order to further these interests in the most optimal way. In theory, a major part of policy formulation could thus be reduced to a rational cost-benefit calculus. Consequently, not much room was left for the impact of historical factors. The introduction of the term "European policy" signifies an important change in this regard.

Today, it is generally understood that Danish relations with Europe covers a much broader spectrum than just foreign economic interests. The dual impact of intensified integration and the end of the Cold War has necessitated – even for a small state like Denmark – the formulation of a European policy on two levels, i.e. European and national. At *the European level,* a range of questions – democratic governance, identification of internal and external threats, ability to act in common, the speed of EU enlargement – have entered into everyday political life. Dealing with such questions and the very fact that Denmark today forms part of a larger political entity represents a challenge to Denmark's traditional small state identity.

No doubt, recent developments on the world scene as well as on the regional one cause many small European states to profoundly alter the very idea of what politics is all about, not least how foreign policy and the relations between national and international issues are conceived. Existential challenges provoke existential responses, like the case is for human beings. Under these circumstances, it is not surprising that the focus of policy formulation tends to move from narrow cost-benefit calculations to broader value-related issues. In the course of this process, determinants related to national identity and national political culture, often stemming from historical experience or the way this experience has been interpreted, will acquire a greater role in decision-making.

One particular issue, which also involves the national level of European policy, strengthens the role of historical factors, i.e. *the issue of surrendering sovereignty.* In this case, the impact is felt in small as well as in large states. Whereas the saliency of this issue varies among states, it is everywhere tied up with fundamental values characterizing political life and ultimately with the very existence of independent political entities. With European policy increasingly involving the surrender of sovereignty in various fields of great symbolic value, such as army, police and currency, the tendency towards "historical" thinking will become more prevalent. Questions requiring a historical approach will loom larger in the political debate. For example, "Why do we cherish our own institutions? Why are we behaving in the way we are in foreign affairs?"

In the Danish debate, the fear of losing sovereignty has played a great role in recent decades; thus a perceived loss of sovereignty has been the single most important motivation for the great number of "no"-voters during the five Danish referenda so far held on EC/EU questions. While the sovereignty issue opens up for historical arguments, its prominence during referenda campaigns also draws attention to another factor accounting for the increased importance of historical variables: *the trend towards democratization of foreign policy,* beginning after World War I but especially conspicuous since 1945.

As long as the conduct of foreign policy was almost exclusively a matter for diplomats and the executive branch of government, the adaptation to the international environment and the definition of the "national interest" tended to take place in a rather narrow universe. With no need to legitimize behavior before the general public or the parliament, neither was there a need to include a broader, ideological appeal in decision-making. Instead, decisions could be taken solely on basis of a cost-benefit calculation. Today, however, the democratization of foreign policy has reactivated the importance of historical factors.

In the Danish case democratization of European policy acquired a specific framework with the provision in the Danish constitution requiring a referendum if a ⅚ majority in Parliament is not obtained in favor of acts entailing partial surrender of sovereignty, and by the tacit, or at least unwritten, agreement to hold a referendum at any case. Whereas the inclusion of this clause in the 1953 constitution was originally intended to ease Danish participation in European integration, it has in fact had the opposite effect. The chasm between elite and mass opinion on the issue of Danish EC membership and its implications has deepened with the continuing prospect of a new referendum.

At each referendum the presence of a fixed "yes" or "no" alternative has tended to polarize the debate even more than the saliency of the decision to be taken in itself would have merited. Polarization has been a necessary prerequisite for mobilizing voters, but the effect has been to bring the issue of sovereignty to the forefront of political debate. In this way, democratization may have had a more profound impact in Denmark than elsewhere in bringing the historical factor into the decision-making process.[19]

A final development, closely intervowen with those already discussed, is the *increased spillover of European policy into the domestic field* and the resulting blurring of the distinction between foreign and domestic policies. This tendency has led to a greater ideological coherence between policy formulation in the external and internal fields. European questions are increasingly seen in the light of traditional political preferences and thus become part of the ideological pattern by which political parties – at least to a certain extent – define themselves. Since ideologies have emerged largely out of the past and refer to deep-rooted value orientations, this feature of today's European policy may also contribute to the importance of the historical factor. On the other hand, the transformation of European issues to an ordinary part of the political game, i.e. the Europeanization of domestic politics, also open up for a more traditional cost-benefit calculus when decisions on such issues are taken. Although undoubtedly relevant, the impact of this process on the importance of historical determinants has to be evaluated on a concrete basis. We may note here that in this respect the value of the Danish case for comparative purposes is questionable.[20]

---

19 In the early phase of European integration the issue of sovereignty did not receive much attention among Danish decision-makers and did not in itself constitute a major argument for or against Danish participation in the Continental supranational integration process. In the 1960s leading members of the Government continued to perceive a possible surrender of sovereignty from a predominantly pragmatic point of view, even arguing that strong, supranational institutions would be to the advantage of small states like Denmark. For more detailed accounts see Branner (1992, 1997). Cf. chapter 11, section 3.2. For a discussion of the connection between the institution of referendum and the saliency of the sovereignty issue see Branner (1991).

20 Until recently, left-wing political parties have been either sceptical or outright negative towards further European integration, making Denmark a deviant case in terms of the

Theoretical Perspectives 57

This section has stressed that four interrelated developments in the post-war period have tended to give historical determinants a greater impact on the direction and on the concrete content of the European policies of individual states: (1) the new focus on the "European" level of European policy; (2) the deepening of the integration process involving a threat to the pillars on which nation-states are built; (3) democratization of foreign policy-making including the direct participation of voters in crucial decisions; and (4) the spill-over of European policy into domestic policy. As we have indicated the effects of these developments may vary according to specific circumstances in each state. The first development pertains especially to small states, and the implications of the second and third have probably been more significant for Denmark than for other states. Analysis of policy formulation in other states would undoubtedly reveal other characteristics modifying the impact of the four developments one way or the other.[21] What we have been trying to substantiate is, on the one hand, the over-all tendency towards greater influence of historical determinants and therefore the need to include a historical dimension when comparing European policies; and on the other hand that specific circumstances – e.g., the issue of sovereignty for Denmark – may be related to the four developments identified. When embarking on comparisons these circumstances can function as a point of departure.[22]

The need for a historical dimension is supported by the few comparative endeavours hitherto undertaken. Illustrative in this respect is a recent work by Hans Mouritzen et al. who accord the historical determinants a greater role in explaining policies than the theoretical framework presented and applied opens up for. Mouritzen and his colleagues present a carefully structured analysis of how six "non-essential" European states (Denmark, the Netherlands, Sweden, Poland, Lithuania and Ukraine) have responded to a number of major developments on the European scene in the period 1989-1994 (Mouritzen et al. 1995). Their goal is to identify the prevailing mode of adaptation, which – according to the definitions set up – is determined by establishing a "value account" for each country. The book distinguishes between five types of values which all "regimes" are supposed to

---

development towards greater ideological coherence referred to above. In the 1990s the Danish political pattern has increasingly come to reflect that prevailing in other EU member countries: European issues are being decided upon according to the conventional left-right dimension. An illustrative example is the Danish 1997-98 debate on the Amsterdam Treaty, which was characterized as a Social Democratic project.

21 It may very well be that specific circumstances reduce the effects of these four processes. Democratizing may thus have an effect quite the opposite of that shown in the Danish case. In the original EU member states, the ideological motivation for European integration was strong in the decision-making elite. Increased public participation may result in greater focus on economic considerations and cost-benefit calculations, thereby diminishing the impact of "historical thinking".

22 The institutionalization of this historical dimension in the form of foreign policy traditions will be taken up below and in chapter 6.

safeguard in their foreign policy; the specific content of these "regime values" are then analyzed in six separate country studies.

The emphasis on analyzing values would suggest that the authors take a rather liberal approach attaching great importance to domestic and subjective determinants in foreign policy, thus allowing for the considerable impact of "historical" factors.[23] This is not the case, however.[24] The values are not regarded as determinants, but rather are included in the framework because their identification is a necessary prerequisite for specifying the *dependent* variable, i.e the mode of adaptation. The *independent* variables, i.e. the main factors explaining policy behavior, all belong to the structural category. The central variable of this kind is the regional polarity structure, which in the period studied is identified as a European unipolarity with the EU functioning as the sole pole. This implies that the major preoccupation of the foreign policy of all European countries is how to relate to the EU pole. The specific policies, including the mode of adaptation, are then primarily accounted for by the objective position of the individual country in the unipolar structure, i.e. the "constellation". Three possible positions are distinguished, and states may accordingly be labelled: *insiders* (part of the pole), *would-be insiders* and *outsiders*. The book argues for the existence of a correlation between the form of constellation and the mode of adaptation. Insiders tend to pursue a policy of balance (i.e., a balanced value account), would-be insiders a policy of adaptive acquiescence (i.e., a negative value account) and outsiders either a policy of adaptive acquiescence or a quiescent mode (i.e., a negligible value account).

Notwithstanding its theoretical sophistication and the comparative insights achieved, Mouritzen et al.'s study is not, on its own premises, able to answer the central question of what kind of determinants are crucial for understanding and differentiating European policies of individual states. In reality – and contrary to the assertions of the introduction – the book ends up attributing a major influence to domestic factors, especially the historical ones.[25] This becomes most evident when the authors compare the European policies of the two insiders, Denmark and the Netherlands, both of which are said to pursue a policy of balance.

Denmark and the Netherlands have a number of structural preconditions in common: Besides long-time EU membership, they are both typical small states located next to the same great power with whom relations in the past rather have

---

23 One may quote the first sentence of the preface: "In this book, we shall paint a value picture of Europe."
24 This is stated by the authors themselves on pp. 14-15, where they find it necessary to "pre-empt the misunderstanding that we are naive believers in values as the driving forces behind regime behavior." See also p. 274.
25 Hence "our primary assumption is that the unipolar structure and its three constellations are the main determinants of non-essential nation-states' behavior." (Mouritzen et al. 1996, p. 3) Later on, when discussing the importance of the size variable, this point is re-emphasized: "The view held here is that for the non-essential powers, size – or even pure actor attributes, for that matter – mean little to their external behavior, compared to which constellation they are located in" (p. 23).

been characterized by enmity rather than by friendship. However, even a superficial perusal of the historical record reveals that they have pursued very divergent European policies. Whereas Denmark is commonly regarded as one of the most reluctant member states concerning the deepening of integration, the Netherlands have consistently advocated steps which could bring a European federal structure closer to reality. Accordingly, observers and analysts tend to apply opposing categories when characterizing the integration strategies of the two countries.[26] Applying the concept of balance policy to the behavior of both countries may be useful at a high level of abstraction, but it is not apt to convey much insight relevant to the comparative study of concrete policy behavior.

The fundamental difference in integration strategy between the two insider countries does not go unobserved by Mouritzen et al. The concluding chapter contains not only a cross-constellation but also an intra-constellation comparison, and here the authors explicitly state: "Within the broad category of a balanced mode of adaptation ... we may find integration enthusiasts as well as integration sceptics." In direct continuation, they emphasize that "when accounting for integration attitude, *historical experience* will play a decisive role" (Mouritzen et al. 1996: 270, emphasis added). This last point is further elaborated when the concrete reasons for the Danish-Dutch differences are analyzed. Elements in the foreign policy traditions of the two countries are identified, and it is concluded that "two *factors with deep historical roots* are probably essential for an explanation" (p. 271, emphasis added).

This is not the place to take up the adaptation approach as such.[27] And concerning the above citations it should be noted that the authors do not regard the great importance attached to historical factors as a theoretical problem. On the contrary, it is an integral part of the model to show that the behavior of insiders is characterized by heterogenity, whereas for the would-be insiders the leeway for independent actions, and thus also for the impact of domestic factors, is much more restricted. Furthermore, the specific explanations that can account for the Danish/Dutch difference are considered exogenous to the model (p. 272). Notwithstanding the stipulations and theoretical aims of the adaptation approach, it is precisely such differences that should be the focus of comparative endeavours. Despite its structural basis – or maybe even because of this basis – Mouritzen et al.'s study ends up to explain key differences in behavior by using the historical dimension.[28]

---

26 See for example Thomas Pedersen (1996). This is also the case in v. Dosenrode's (1993) important comparative work dealing with both Denmark and the Netherlands.
27 The approach is dealt with in detail in chapter 3, although not in the version developed by Hans Mouritzen.
28 It may be added that their concluding chapter points to a number of policy differences and behavioral changes which the model is not able to account for, and which further reveals the elusive character of the various modes of adaptation; for example, the possibility of a dominant mode by Germany and France; a continuous Danish balancing mode in spite of remarkable policy changes in the end of the 1980s; the change from acquiescence towards a more balancing mode in Swedish behavior in light of the referendum campaign, etc.

5. Historical determinants, foreign policy traditions and the search for a comparative framework

Having argued for the important role of history in understanding the direction of present-day European policies, especially when analyzing the Danish case, we shall now ask how the historical determinant is treated in existing foreign policy theory. To what extent can this theory contribute to a comparative endeavour focusing on historical factors. In a wider context, the discussion concerns the question of institutionalization of foreign policy behavior and whether the search for such "institutions" is apt to narrow the gap between empirical and theoretical endeavours discussed in section 2.

Special – but not exclusive – attention will be devoted to the concept of *foreign policy traditions*, which often function as a central explanatory variable in both scholarly and journalistic analyses of state behaviour. By foreign policy tradition we refer to fundamental conceptions regarding the goals, role and/or options of a given country in international politics viewed as a part of the political heritage of this country (cf. chapter 6).

The first place to look for a theoretical contribution is the field of comparative foreign policy, initiated at the end of the 1960s with the ambition of developing an analytical scheme encompassing all variables relevant for comparisons.[29] In an attempt to categorize existing foreign policy research of the time, Patrick J. McGowan and Howard B. Shapiro have elaborated one of the more well-known schemes with 11 independent variables explaining the foreign policy behavior of individual states (McGowan and Shapiro 1973).

Among the nine sets of internal variables in the McGowan-Shapiro scheme it is only the "linkage variables" that are relevant for our purpose. In the authors' presentation, linkage variables are said to "represent the historical traces of the actor's past foreign policy behavior"; and it is supposed that "traditions of past foreign economic and political involvement are likely to influence current and future behavior"(p. 45). When discussing the more precise stipulation of these traditions, however, the focus is confined to "all the past official actions of decision-makers and their agents as manifested in treaty ties, diplomatic representation, international organization memberships, and foreign aid"(p. 45).[30]

For McGowan and Shapiro the historical determinant primarily refers to past commitments undertaken by an actor (p. 133) and not to the broader category of variables which analyses of the past may reveal, i.e. national and state identities, foreign policy traditions, etc.. Considering the fact that quite a large number of studies have tried to establish the content of such factors in individual countries

---

29 The initiator and chief representative of this approach has been James N. Rosenau (1966).
30 Compare the overview given in East et al. (1978: 23). The interpretation is somewhat broader here.

Theoretical Perspectives 61

(and that these also existed 25 years ago), the omission of these variables in a major work on comparative foreign policy is remarkable. Are foreign policy tradition and similar categories too diffuse for an analytical scheme? Is past behavior in the broad sense implicitly rejected as a variable that could account for later policies? Or has the omission to do with methodological problems regarding the possibility of measuring the influence of these factors?

We shall return to some of these questions below. At this point, it should be added that despite omissions such as these the comparative foreign policy approach is not completely void of theorizing on the broader historical determinant. In a model set up by David Wilkinson to be used for comparative purposes in a number of single country studies, the author comes closer to identifying historical factors (Wilkinson 1969).

According to Wilkinson, two main factors account for the foreign policy of a country: capabilities and "will". Although the first factor ranks higher than the second, the "degree of will" has a great impact on the behaviour of a given country and on its role in international politics. In characterizing this impact "will" is contrasted to another central concept in the model: prescription. The more the "will factor" is absent the more important is "prescription". Prescription is "the living presence of the past in current policy-making; it is that sanctification of tradition, that bureaucratic inertia, that permits us to explain a decision of today by referring to the policy of yesterday and saying "nothing has changed"; it is the persistence of memory"(p. 73).[31] Later on, Wilkinson explains that all the determinants regarded as belonging to the prescription concept should be understood as residuals (p. 87). Whereas McGowan and Shapiro interpret the historical determinant in a very narrow way making it virtually non-existent in the sense used here, Wilkinson, by introducing the concept of prescription, endows it with a very broad meaning. Nevertheless, a major point in the model is the inferior role attributed to the historical determinant. This determinant is viewed in contrast to will, implying that history is a very passive factor which influences behavior only when a country lacks leadership "characterized by conscious, original and decisive action" (p. 74). While this logic sustains the argument for the inferior role of history, the contrast between the two factors seems dubious from an analytical point of view. The presence of a historical tradition in the minds of decision-makers may very well lead to decisive action and an active foreign policy.[32]

The various empirically-based research projects, spawned by the comparative foreign policy approach in the late 1960s and in the 1970s died without achieving their ambitious goal of establishing an authoritative general theory of foreign po-

---

31 The will factor is a characteristic of the political leadership and not of the nation, see East et. al. (1978: 128).
32 British and French foreign policy since 1945 undoubtedly provide ample evidence hereof.

licy.³³ From this brief overview, it seems fair to conclude that this approach in its original version fails to offer the kind of contribution we are searching for. The historical determinant as understood here is relatively absent. Instead, the impact of the past is analyzed in terms of either previous commitments or as routine behavior more characteristic of bureaucrats than politicians. In the only instance of theorizing, the historical determinant is treated in a problematical fashion and the postulated relationships not empirically substantiated.

Instead taking theoretical inspiration from comparative foreign policy, we should look to other approaches. We should search for approaches in which the historical determinant plays a greater role; and which also may provide clues as to what part of the past is deemed relevant. In focusing more specifically on contributions to the study of foreign policy traditions, we shall deal here with only two approaches: decision-making analysis and doctrine studies.

Decision-making analysis may be regarded as both a predecessor to the comparative foreign policy approach and as an integral part of it. Since the object of study (concrete decisions, not foreign policies in general) – and hence the comparative aim – is narrower in decision-making analysis, this approach may be deemed less relevant. However, it is precisely the historical determinant that so often occupies a prominent position in decision-making analysis. This is due primarily to the focus on the *perception* of decision-makers characterizing this approach.³⁴

Studying perceptions – or to use a central concept in one of the better known models "the psychological environment" – means that attention is focused on subjective rather than objective factors, something the comparative foreign policy approach otherwise tends to do.³⁵ Among the subjective factors, research has pointed to the use of historical arguments as one of the most important, especially when national values of high priority are at stake (Paige 1968 and Branner 1972). Models of decision-making analysis reflect these findings, e.g. that of Michael Brecher referred to above. In this model, "traditions, which derive from the cumulative historical legacy" (p.11) are one of the main societal factors that make up the so-called "attitudinal prism" crucial to the perception of decision-makers.

As a kind of offspring from decision-making analysis, historically oriented research has placed special emphasis on studying the influence of the past on crucial foreign policy decisions. Best known is Ernest May's effort to explain a number of post-war decisions made by the U.S. Government as a reflection of perceived historical insight drawn from previous U.S. policy.³⁶ May demonstrates that

---

33 The fate of the Wilkinson project is illustrative in this respect. Only part of the envisiged 10 case studies were actually carried out, and those "are not sufficiently uniform in approach and data base to serve as a basis for comparisons" (Faurby 1976: 150).
34 The classical work is *Foreign Policy Decision-Making*, Snyder et al. (1962).
35 On psychological environment see Brecher (1972).
36 *"Lessons" of the Past. The Use and Misuse of History in American Foreign Policy,* (New York: Oxford University Press, 1973).

the past must be regarded as one of the main determinants behind the direction taken by American foreign policy during the first half of the Cold War period.

For present purposes, however, a two-fold problem exists regarding the use of analyses inspired by the decision-making approach. First, in continuation of what has already been stated, focus has been on studying foreign policy decisions per se and not as part of a general foreign policy orientation. This is certainly true for the research done on a theoretical basis. In this respect, the historically based literature, like the study by Ernest May, seems more relevant in the present context.[37]

A more serious problem, pertaining especially to this article, has to do with the way history is used as a determinant in existing decision-making analysis. Focus is directed not towards the broader concept of foreign policy traditions but instead towards inferences based on analogies with past events – either in a negative or a positive form.[38] According to the decision-making approach, the use of history is also revealed when inferences are based on a conception of inertia in regard to the past. This is the case when it is argued that a certain political or economic development / trend is likely to continue (i.e., extrapolation) or that existing conditions will not change.

The impact of history in this rather specific sense is not the main concern in the present analytical context. A foreign policy tradition is not equivalent to concrete decisions made in the past, not even when such decisions have had a long lasting effect on foreign policy thinking. Obviously, however, the two research objects overlap. A tradition as conceived here is not a completely static phenomenon. It tends to evolve over time and in this process the interpretation of major decisions of the past – in combination with the effect of important outside events – plays a central role. Hence, insights from decision-making analysis may bring us a step forward, although we still lack investigations into the specific role of foreign policy traditions.

In our second approach, the less well-known *doctrine studies*, the object of research seems more closely related to this purpose.[39] Like the comparative foreign policy approach, the analysis of foreign policy doctrines may be considered a legacy of research efforts undertaken in the late 1960s and the 1970s, efforts which have expired. In both cases, initial ambitions have not been fulfilled, but in the case of doctrine studies there at least exists a basis.

---

37 It may be noted, however, that in an article based on Michael Brecher's framework, Nikolaj Petersen has demonstrated the importance of historical determinants when trying to explain differences between Danish and Norwegian alliance policies in the late 1940s (Petersen 1979).
38 The "Munich 1938" analogy being a negative one, while the 1962 Cuban Missile Crisis is often invoked as a positive example.
39 Research belonging to this approach has mainly been restricted to Sweden and Finland, with K. Brodin as the leading figure. The concept of foreign policy doctrines also refers to more or less binding statements made by individual statesman, e.g. the Monroe and Truman doctrines. Such "personal doctrines" should be viewed as elements of the doctrine concept discussed here.

In the works undertaken by the most prominent representative of this approach, the Swedish scholar Katarina Brodin, the objects of study are official foreign policy doctrines, defined in the following way: "one of the official power holders' openly articulated system of generalized views and ideas, including normative ones, with impact on the international system and one's own state's role in this system" (Brodin 1977: 26, my translation from Swedish). Although not part of the definition, it is presupposed that such doctrines are more or less constant during a certain time-span, which enables the researcher studying the doctrine of a specific country to gather material covering a longer period.

It seems evident that on the basis presented above, doctrine studies may contribute to the kind of understanding we are trying to achieve in this article: they concern fundamental conceptions regarding the foreign policy of a given country. A basic premise is the very existence of such conceptions. Moreover, they take a diachronic perspective. In the original Swedish version doctrine analysis also has a predictive aim. The identification of a doctrine is regarded as a tool to help decision-makers in other countries foresee the doctrine-holder's future behaviour. Finally, by setting up a framework of analysis to be used when studying the individual cases, this approach aims explicitly at comparisons.[40]

Unfortunately, doctrine analysis has generated only a very limited number of research projects, and the results obtained are not impressive. The shortcomings of doctrine studies have to do with inherent weaknesses in the original research scheme. In combination with other characteristics of the approach, these weaknesses make doctrine studies less valuable for our endeavour than indicated above.

Methodological considerations and predictive aspirations have led doctrine researchers to focus on "official" doctrines as these are formulated by political leaders occupying formal positions. This research design assumes that the identification of doctrines is simplified in this way, which is undoubtedly true; at the same time, however, it narrows the scope of the studies making them less relevant when trying to identify the broader concept of a foreign policy "tradition" (see below).

Doctrine analysis research also assumes that declarations by official leaders have a restrictive influence on the future behavior of leaders. Since a deviation from the officially proclaimed doctrine will presumably be met by negative reactions at home and abroad, leaders will tend to avoid such deviations, which means that official doctrines may result in a self-fulfilling prophesy. Quite apart from the doubtful validity of this hypothesis, focusing on the predictive aspects represents another narrowing of the scope of the studies.[41] Our interest in the historical determinant is not restricted to such self-fulfilling mechanisms. Rather, we seek to elucidate the continued presence and importance of long held fundamental foreign

---

40 A foreign policy doctrine is considered to be based on two main elements: strategy and argumentation. Strategy is subdivided into instrumental goals and means; argumentation into basic goals and world outlook (further classified into universal and regional outlook); see Brodin (1977).
41 See the review by Hans Mouritzen in *Statsvetenskabeligt Tidsskrift* (1980).

policy conceptions not necessarily formulated in a way, which make a deviation from them part of the conscious deliberations of decision-makers.[42]

It follows that on closer inspection, the object of study when dealing with official doctrines differs considerably from the object to be taken up in this article and its continuation in chapter 6. As understood here official doctrines and foreign policy traditions are far from identical. As clarification we may cite three major differences:

First, the content of a tradition may not, like official doctrines, be solely derived from proclamations made by decision-makers; instead, traditions are identified by the historical record and include both verbal statements and actual behaviour. This means that the data to be used for analyses of traditions are rather dispersed, requiring more subjective interpretation as compared to doctrine analysis.

Second, the sources of foreign policy traditions tend to make them less logically coherent than is the case with foreign policy doctrines. Elements of a tradition may have different origins in terms of historical period, personalities and ideologies. This does not preclude logical coherence, but neither does it preclude the possibility that a tradition comprises competing strands of thought alternately dominating official policy (e.g. isolationism and internationalism in the US foreign policy tradition).

The preceding differences point to a third: studies of traditions are concerned with a much longer time-span than doctrine studies. Whereas doctrines tend to be replaced when basic changes take place in internal or external political conditions, traditions are almost by definition not exposed to sudden changes. While traditions certainly evolve according to altered circumstances, what is more striking is precisely their relative immunity to change.

The framework for analyses set up by the doctrine study approach certainly enables us to identify important elements, which may be regarded as ingredients in a foreign policy tradition. It may be the empirically safest way to arrive at such an identification. However, the approach does not fully grasp all the relevant elements and cannot be considered a satisfactory basis for understanding the kind of variables we are looking for here.

Comparative foreign policy, decision-making analysis and doctrine studies were all developed during a period when "European policies" had not taken the shape which they have today. This may explain some of the shortcomings cited here, especially the failure to broaden the scope when analyzing historical determinants. However, the new directions in the theoretical study of foreign policy observable in the last 15 years hardly bring us much further.

One of the latest versions of *adaptation theory* has already been dealt with. The discussion has shown that undertaking a comparative study of European policies in

---

42 A related field are studies specifically aiming at predictions; cf. Stenelo (1981) who identifies a number of "hereditary mechanisms" as a basis for foreign policy predictions using American Vietnam policy as an illustrative case.

the 1990s requires the inclusion of a historical dimension, and even that this dimension should be accorded a decisive explanatory role. In the version presented in the preceding section this inclusion does not follow from the theoretical groundwork itself.

Another approach, still very much in its beginning, i.e. *discourse analysis*, holds the promise of casting new light on the importance of historical factors. The existence of relevant foreign policy discourses cannot be understood without viewing them as part of a long-term development. In this sense, discourses may very well be regarded as part of – or more correctly as reflecting – a foreign policy tradition. Yet it remains to be seen to what degree discourse analysis can contribute to systematic research on the tradition variable.

At this stage, it does not seem possible to set up a fruitful framework for studying foreign policy traditions, not to say historical determinants at large. We might even be overstretching the potential for integrating historical and theoretical research endeavours by insisting on developing such a framework (cf. the remarks made in section 2). Nevertheless, the two articles included in part two of this volume, dealing with historical determinants influencing the direction of present-day Danish European policy, comprise attempts to systematize the historical variables.

For one thing, the specific features of the European policy concept analyzed in section 3 have been taken into consideration when selecting the objects of study, defining the focus of attention and interpreting the material presented. The first article is thus based on the premise that European policy not only relates to the field of foreign policy but also includes aspects of what is normally regarded as belonging to the domestic sphere. The article by Uffe Østergaard focuses on developments accounting for traits characterizing the over-all political culture in Denmark and the various paradoxes of Danish national identity, variables which are usually more essential to analyses of internal than of external policies. The second article takes up the foreign policy tradition as a part of Denmark's European experiences in the past. By focussing on the dualism of the tradition, it illustrates the two levels on which European policies unfold.

Secondly, the attempt to identify national values and identities with an impact on Danish European policy is made by basing the analysis on three types of historical developments which in the Danish case are closely interrelated. The first – and probably most fundamental (discussed in both articles) – concerns self-images and role perceptions derived from the kind of state/nation constructions prevailing in the past, the degree to which these constructions have altered over time, and the conditions bringing about alterations. All existing states have experiences in this regard, but obviously their significance as part of the historical development and the extent to which they are stored in the "collective memory" of a nation varies considerably.[43] In the case of Denmark, the almost complete identity of state and nation is often referred to as a major factor influencing the Danish position on

---

43 The concept of "collective memory" is dealt with in chapter 5.

European integration. Østergaard's treatment of the history of "Denmark" also contains a very different tradition on this point – with possible repercussions on present foreign policy attitudes.[44]

State/nation constructions and the way they have been modified or transformed quite often spill over into other essential historical developments and have long-ranging implications. The analysis of Danish history allows for the identification of two such developments. One has to do with the evolution of specific rules, norms and structures characterizing the state apparatus and its functioning; the other with the emergence of specific ideological patterns establishing some of the pillars of political discourse and political conflict/cooperation. Both developments, especially the latter, will be analyzed in chapter 5.[45]

Thirdly, we should mention the stipulations guiding the analysis of the Danish foreign policy tradition in chapter 6. In itself it is an indication of the broadness of scope, already dealt with, when the historical determinants are treated in separate chapters, signifying that foreign policy traditions only cover one aspect. While the concrete analysis is based on the premise that foreign policy traditions do exist and also have an impact on the formulation of policies, it is at the same time acknowledged that both their identification and an assessment of their influence are not easy tasks. Chapter 6 focuses on identification; two sets of stipulations have been important for this endeavour.

Foreign policy traditions are often invoked in political debate and in various historical accounts which attempt to present an overview of a longer time-span. For the present purpose, the identification which may be obtained from this kind of analysis is regarded as unsatisfactory – or at worst, misleading. A major effort must be made towards a critical evaluation of existing perceptions concerning the content of a tradition. An alternative interpretation should be relieved of the fallacies inherent in identifications based on political premises and/or the need for reductionist simplicity.

In acknowledging the complexity of foreign policy traditions, it is furthermore stipulated that their content may be of a two-fold or even multi-fold nature, without any necessary logical coherence between the elements. In contrast to doctrines, traditions develop only partly as the result of conscious deliberations of decision-makers, hence they should be analyzed accordingly. This does not preclude the observer from being able to detect a common pattern among seemingly divergent elements, perhaps in the form of a common basis for their emergence. In fact, the search for such patterns should be an essential part of the analysis of traditions, not least because they may provide a clue to understanding their influence.

---

44 Many observations could be made regarding a comparative analysis of the impact of past state/nation constructions on present European policies. The importance of this factor may be illustrated by the very divergent experiences of the four great powers (or former great powers) of the European Union: France, Germany, Italy and Great Britain, especially in regard to national unity and colonial past.
45 It was originally envisaged to include a separate chapter on this development; for a previous treatment see Knudsen (1992).

6. Summary and conclusions

This article has covered a broad field of study. Focus has been on conceptualization and historical determinants in comparative perspectives, but in neither respect has the analysis been able to draw up an elaborate or easily applicable framework for further research. The shortcomings may in large measure be due to the limited number of studies, which hitherto have attempted to answer the central question raised in the article: how do we compare present-day European policies of states? Notwithstanding the theoretical lacunae still existing and still too apparent, it is hoped that the observations made, not least the presentation of the Danish experience, have moved research in the field a few steps ahead and may inspire other studies with similar objectives. Summarizing the article with these hopes in mind, three points should be stressed:

- At the level of methodology and research strategies, the article started out with a few reflections on the relationship between theoretical and empirical efforts in the field of foreign policy studies. The arguments for less ambitious theoretical research designs and for acceptance of "natural" inclinations on the part of scholars in different fields of study (primarily historians and political scientists), should be linked with the main thesis advocated in the last part of the article: the need to accord greater attention to historical determinants. The crucial role of history in contemporary European policies not only points to the intimate connection between history and theory in any comparative endeavour but also to the necessity of including both disciplines on their own terms.

- Concerning the thesis of historical determinants as explanatory variables, we have sought to identify a number of factors significant to present day European policies and presented, albeit in a rudimentary form, a skeleton for systematic analysis. The key elements have to do with the way former and present state/nation constructions have become part of the historical legacy – be it in the form of paradoxical (as in the Danish case) national identities, specific and deep-rooted ideological trends permanently influencing the political culture, or characteristic features of the state apparatus and its relations to society at large. Foreign policy traditions form part of this legacy, but they may also be studied as a separate category. This means that historical determinants of European policies have both an internal and an external aspect. The complexities which so often characterize the content of foreign policy traditions and the challenges involved in identifying them have been emphasized.

- Finally, as concerns conceptualization, let us recapitulate the four observations from section 3, in which an attempt was made to sketch the content of the European policy concept. First, it was argued that in order to speak of a European policy elements of high politics, security policy considerations must be involved. Second, we identified two levels at which European policies unfold, and cited the possible comparative insights to be derived from this distinction. Third, on the basis of the distinctions made, the relationship and differences between the two concepts of European policy and integration policy were identified and discussed. We saw that the term "integration policy", while not including all elements of "European policy", covers additional policy areas which now tend to make it the more widely used term. The final and fourth observation has to do with the intermediary position of European policy between foreign and domestic policies. This intermediate position was further highlighted in the subsequent analysis of historical determinants.

In all fields of study, research efforts will always remain incremental. As we have indicated, some of the above points are given more substance in the empirical part of the book. Others do not form an integral part of the efforts undertaken here. Hopefully, however, this does not make them any less relevant for future research.

Literature

Branner, Hans (1972): *Småstat mellem stormagter. Beslutningen om mineudlægning august 1914*, Copenhagen: Munksgaard.
Branner, Hans (1991): "Da suværæniteten blev en hellig ko", *Information* (Danish daily), 3-4 August.
Branner, Hans (1992): "Danish European Policy Since 1945: The Question of Sovereignty" in M. Kelstrup (ed.): *European Integration and Denmark's Participation*, Copenhagen: Copenhagen Political Studies Press, pp. 297-327.
Branner, Hans (1997): "Small State on the Sidelines: Denmark and the Question of European Political Integration" in G. Wilkes (ed.): *Britain's Failure to Enter the European Community 1961-63*, London: Frank Cass.
Brecher, Michael (1972): *The Foreign Policy System of Israel*, Oxford: Oxford University Press.
Brodin, Katarina (1977): *Studiet av utrikespolitiska doktriner*, Stockholm: Utrikespolitiska Institut.
v. Dosenrode, Søren Z. (1993): *Westeuropäische Kleinstaaten in der EG und EPZ*, Chur/Zürich: Verlag Rüegger.
East, Maurice et al. (eds.) (1978): *Why Nations Act: Theoretical Perspectives for Comparative Foreign Policy Studies*, Beverly Hills: Sage Publications.
Faurby, Ib (1976): "Premises, Promises, and Problems of Comparative Foreign Policy", *Cooperation and Conflict*, vol. 11, pp. 139-162.
Fox, Annette Baker (1959): *The Power of Small States. Diplomacy in World War II*, Chicago: The University of Chigago Press.
Jerneck, Magnus (1993): "Sweden – the Reluctant European?" in Tiilikainen and Damgaard Petersen (eds.), *The Nordic Countries and the EC*, Copenhagen: Copenhagen Political Studies Press.
Kelstrup, Morten (1993): "Small States and European Political Integration" in Tiilikainen and Damgaard Petersen (eds.): *The Nordic Countries and the EC*, Copenhagen: Copenhagen Political Studies Press.
Knudsen, Tim (1992): "A Portrait of Danish State-Culture: Why Denmark needs two National Anthems" in Kelstrup (ed.): *European Integration and Denmark's Participation*, Copenhagen: Copenhagen Political Studies Press, pp. 262-293.
Matlery, Janne Haaland (1993): "And Never the Twain Shall Meet? Reflections on Norway, Europe and Integration" in Tiilikainen and Damgaard Petersen (eds.): *The Nordic Countries and the EC*, Copenhagen: Copenhagen Political Studies Press.
May, Ernest (1973): *"Lessons" of the Past. The Use and Misuse of History in American Foreign Policy*, New York: Oxford University Press.
McGowan, Patrick J. and Howard B. Shapiro (1973): *The Comparative Study of Foreign Policy. A Survey of Scientific Findings*, Beverley Hills: Sage Publications.
Mouritzen, Hans (1980), Review of K. Brodin (1977): *Statsvetenskapligt Tidskrift*, vol. 1980/2.
Mouritzen, Hans (1993): "The Two Musterknaben and the Naughty Boy: Sweden, Finland and Denmark in the Process of European Integration", *Cooperation and Conflict*, vol. 28/4, pp. 373-402.

Mouritzen, Hans, Ole Wæver and Håkan Wiberg (eds.) (1996): *European Integration and National Adaptation. A Theoretical Inquiry*, Commack: Nova Science Publishers, Inc.
Paige, Glenn D. (1968): *The Korean Decision*, New York: The Free Press.
Pedersen, Thomas (1996): "Denmark and the European Union" in Lee Miles (ed.), *The European Union and the Nordic Countries*, London and New York: Routledge, pp. 81-100.
Petersen, Nikolaj (1979): "Danish and Norwegian Alliance Policies: A Comparative Analysis", *Cooperation and Conflict*, vol. XIV, pp. 193-210.
Petersen, Nikolaj (1995): "Denmark and the European Community 1985-93" in Carsten Due-Nielsen and Nikolaj Petersen (eds.) (1995): *Adaptation and Activism. The Foreign Policy of Denmark 1967-1993,* Copenhagen: DJØF Publishing.
Putnam, Robert D. (1988): "Diplomacy and Domestic Politics: The Logic of Two-level Games", *International Organization*, vol. 43/3, pp. 427-59.
Rosenau, James N. (1966): "Pre-theories and Theories of Foreign Policy" in Farell (ed.): *Approaches to Comparative and International Politics*, Evanston: North Western University Press, pp. 27-92.
Snyder, Richard et al. (1962): *Foreign Policy Decision-Making*, New York: The Free Press.
Stenelo, L.-G. (1981): "Prediction and Foreign Policy Heritage", *Cooperation and Conflict,* vol. XVI, pp. 3-17.
Wilkinson, David (1969): *Comparative Foreign Relations: Framework and Methods*, Belmont: Dickenson.
Wæver, Ole (1994): "Resisting the Temptation of Post Foreign Policy Analysis" in Carlsnaes and Smith (eds.), *European Foreign Policy. The EC and Changing Perspectives in Europe*, London: Sage Publications, pp. 238-273.

CHAPTER 3

National Strategies in the Integration Dilemma: The Promises of Adaptation Theory

Nikolaj Petersen

1. Introduction

One of the lacunae of classical integration theory is its failure to produce a theory of national integration policy. This is somewhat surprising, considering the role of national policies as input to the European integration process, and in view of the fact that national interests and sensitivities have repeatedly served to boost a lagging integration process or – just as often – as a brake for it (for other statements regarding this point, see Kelstrup 1993, Friis 1995 and Petersen 1998).

This article attempts to sort out the external as well as domestic policies and strategies which nations adopt in the course of a cross-national integration process. The analysis is predicated on the notion that integration offers important benefits as well as poses serious problems to nation-states. There will be costs as well as benefits to every integration process, but these costs and benefits will not necessarily be distributed evenly among the participants or be judged in the same way by them. Each national government's integration policy operates under different constraints, each is rooted in its international position, its domestic structures, its dominant ideologies, etc. Yet however different in background and interest, all participants in an integration process are likely to experience what Morten Kelstrup terms the "integration dilemma", i.e. difficult choices between the costs and benefits of international integration (Kelstrup 1993: 154). This "integration dilemma" concept thus has parallels to the "security dilemma" concept.

This article will take its departure in a short elaboration of the integration dilemma and the insights which can be gained through a comparison with the security dilemma. It then focuses on the prospects of an adaptation theory approach to the integration dilemma, with a special view to the definition of concrete external and domestic strategies by which decision-makers may try to cope with it. Finally, the integration dilemma and its strategies will be illustrated through an empirical example, namely Danish integration strategies over the last twenty years.

2. The Integration Dilemma: What Is It?

2.1. The Security and Integration Dilemmas Compared

In his article on "The Security Dilemma in Alliance Politics" Glenn Snyder (1984) discusses national strategies for coping with the security dilemma from a game-theoretical point of view. The security dilemma operates in two games, the alliance game and the adversary game, respectively. The alliance game, which is most relevant here, encompasses the dilemmas associated with politics within an alliance, dilemmas which can be coped with by applying either a C strategy (C for cooperation) or a D strategy (D for defection). A C strategy stands for strong political support for the alliance, a credible commitment to the common defence and for firm adherence to the alliance mainstream in political and strategic questions. A D strategy implies only conditional support for the alliance and a tendency to take up independent policy postures.

The choice between C and D strategies hinges on the government's ranking of respective benefits and drawbacks or its "goods" and "bads". A C strategy in the alliance game is linked with the "good" of enhanced security on the one hand and the risk of entrapment "bad" on the other, while a D strategy may be associated – on the good side – with relative independence and freedom of manoeuvre and – on the bad side – with the risk of abandonment, i.e. of being deserted by one's allies in a crisis situation. This is the well-known "entrapment vs. abandonment" dilemma (cf. Petersen 1993).

The integration dilemma highlights the difficult choices states encounter in integration projects like the European Union. The integration dilemma has many similarities with Snyder's version of the security dilemma, but there are also important differences: the integration dilemma is simpler but also often starker than the security dilemma. Briefly stated, the differences are the following:

- For obvious reasons the adversary game, i.e. relations with the "enemy", is less pronounced in integration politics than in alliance politics; the internal game between member states, henceforth the union game, is paramount.
- Compared to the alliance game, the union game places heavier demands and stresses upon its participants. Union politics go deeper than alliance politics, because it touches the neuralgic points, i.e. sovereignty, of its members, and also in the sense that it is more intrusive. Union politics penetrates deeper into the domestic systems of its member states and – in some respects at least – deals directly with the citizens.
- The impact of integration is broader than that of alliance-building. The European Union, for example, is nearly all-encompassing and covers most of the issue areas which are of concern to national governments.[1] In this respect, too, the integration process is much more of a challenge to national governments than the alliance.

---

1 In Denmark the Minister of Church Affairs is the only minister not involved in Union politics.

- Finally, the integration process is progressive by having a developmental aspect to it, while alliances are normally status quo-oriented. Hence, the integration dilemma is likely to grow or at least remain constant over time, while the alliance dilemma will either remain constant or decline.

2.2. The Goods and Bads of the Union Game

The dilemmas of the Union game thus appear to be stronger and starker than those of the alliance game. But what exactly are the dilemmas and the trade-offs associated with taking part in an integration process as seen from the perspective of its member states?

The goods of the Union game touch upon the basic motives for international integration. The most universal motivation, in the sense that it is subscribed to by all participants, is to increase welfare by removing transaction costs and exploiting the potentials of an economy of scale.

Another universal motivation for integration is to reduce or eliminate conflicts between member-states and overcome regional anarchy. This motivation was prominent in the first integration initiatives after World War II and has recently come to the forefront as an important argument for enlarging the Union to the east.

Other goods associated with integration are more controversial. Thus, integration may be sought in order to build up a great power and increase the clout and status of the participating states in international politics. This good is one of the central motivations of the European integration process but is less universally accepted, especially among the smaller nations.

A final highly ambitious goal of community-building is that of creating a joint identity and, ultimately, a new state. Again, this has historically been an important motivation behind the European integration process, but it is a goal which is not shared by all. In the present Union, it is held more or less by the original members (with the exception of France), but (apart from Spain) not by the later arrivals to the process. During the Maastricht process, the "federal goal" of the Union became a hotly contested symbol which had to be eventually abandoned.[2]

Seen from a nation-state point of view there are also general drawbacks (bads) associated with integration, the most important being the equivalent to entrapment in the alliance game. This is the diminution of sovereignty and independence, which is hardly separable from the integration process, and which, in its weaker form, implies the compromise of national priorities. As an example, welfare may be bought at the expense of the possibility for national regulation and suppression of particular national preferences.

---

2 The goods sought from integration can also be given a more inter-governmentalist twist by pointing to the need for strengthening the ailing European nation-state after World War II (Milward 1992) or governments' goal of strengthening their domestic position by controlling integration policy (Moravcsik 1994).

Other bads are associated with the goal of external security and power. Some participants, like Britain, may see it as a threat to other objectives such as trans-Atlantic cooperation, while others, such as Denmark, may find it difficult to see themselves as part of a regional power and prefer to view the Union as a pure civilian power.

Finally, there are significant bads associated with the good of community-building. The bad is not only potential loss of formal sovereignty, but also the compromise of national identity and the potential withering away of the nation-state. As demonstrated by the reaction to the Maastricht Treaty, this bad is much feared, especially at the public opinion level.

2.3. Strategic Choices in the Union Game

As rational actors, member-states in the Union game must be presumed to seek the goods and avoid the bads of integration. However, hard choices often have to be made, as goods and bads are closely intertwined and, in many cases, two sides of the same coin. Whatever strategy is chosen, it will have at least some bads associated with it. Game theory posits two potential strategies to solve this dilemma. One is a C strategy, i.e. a cooperative "core" strategy, the other a D strategy, based on limited support of the goals of integration. A cooperative strategy entails a fairly close identification of national priorities with the goals of integration, most notably the community-building goal. In concrete terms a C strategy involves a willingness to suppress or compromise on national interests so as to reach the goals of integration, active consideration for other participants' interests, and a constructive attitude in bargaining processes. This is the kind of foreign policy behaviour predicted by the liberal theory of international relations. In the European Union, Germany and the Benelux countries probably come closest to this ideal-type.

The goods of a C strategy are primarily the enjoyment of the collective goods produced by integration: i.e., welfare, security, and community. Besides, a C strategy may increase influence on the integration process by generating respect and reputation for loyalty and team spirit among the partners. The bads of a C strategy, on the other hand, are connected with the willingness to accept compromises of national priorities and – in a wider sense – of national sovereignty. In the last instance, a C strategy may lead to the loss of sovereignty and national identity. While a C strategy can be presumed to increase influence over the integration process as such, it may also lead to others taking advantage of its practitioners in specific conflicts of interest.

The D strategy, in contrast, is characterized by a high priority of national values and interests over those of the community and only weak identification with the long-term goals of integration. Common solutions to problems are subordinated to acceptable national solutions, and other members are treated as rivals rather than as partners. Finally, the political style can be uncooperative, "selfish" and intransigent. This is the foreign policy behaviour predicted by the realist school in international relations. Prominent examples are France under de Gaulle and Britain under Margaret Thatcher and John Major.

The goods of a D strategy consists mainly in avoiding or reducing the bads of the C strategy. The protection of national interests and the avoidance of sovereignty loss are among the prominent goods of this orientation, as is the increased bargaining power which may follow from a reputation for intransigence. As a matter of fact, in most cases the uncooperative partner cannot be prevented from enjoying the collective goods produced by the integration process. Hence, there is an important "free-rider" aspect to a D strategy.

The bads of the D strategy lie primarily in the risk of exclusion or (less strongly) marginalization. Formally member states in the Union cannot be expelled, but the fear of political isolation and de facto exclusion has often been a strong motive for modifying D strategies. A related bad is the lack of allies if needed; a country with a reputation for selfishness may find it more difficult to mobilize assistance from other participants if it runs into difficulties than C strategists.

Figure 1 sums up the goods and bads associated with the two strategies in the union game:

Figure 1: C and D Strategies in the Union Game

C Strategy	D Strategy
Goods:	**Goods:**
• Enjoy collective goods (welfare, security, community)	• Reduce loss of sovereignty
• Increase influence	• Protect national priorities
• Enjoy respect	• Increase bargaining power
• Enhance reputation for loyalty	• Enjoy collective goods by non-exclusion (free-riding)
Bads:	**Bads:**
• Compromise national priorities	• Risk marginalization
• Risk progressive loss of sovereignty	• Risk exclusion
• Risk loss of identity	• Risk loss of respect and reputation
• Risk exploitation by others	• Risk loss of allies

2.4. The Limitations of Game Theory

The game-theoretical approach to solving the integration dilemma, while providing useful insights into the strategic choices open to national players, also has certain weaknesses. First, being without a theory of national preferences, it cannot predict which strategies governments actually choose. Second, the predicted strategies, C and D, are not distinct enough, as they seem to cover several modes of behaviour. The ideal-type D strategy, as described above, refers to a policy which is dominant and slightly "bullying". However, an uncooperative D strategy may also have a more passive side, whose main characteristics are withdrawal, isolation or

Theoretical Perspectives

non-commitment. Likewise, the ideal-type C strategy is one of active participation in the give and take of integration politics. However, a cooperative attitude may also have a more passive flavour and be characterized by unwilling concessions to the integration process rather than full-blown participation in it.

Finally and most important, game theory does not take into account the Janus-faced aspect of the integration dilemma, i.e., the fact that the Union game is played not only on the international level, but also at the domestic one. This problematique may be illustrated by the so-called "strategic triangle", in which decision-makers must select policies which are not only acceptable to themselves and compatible with the policies of other integration partners, but which also satisfy the demands and fears of their own publics, cf. fig. 2. With the growing scepticism of European publics towards the integration process, this aspect must be taken fully into account. This is where adaptation theory enters the picture.

Figure 2: The Strategic Triangle of the Union Game

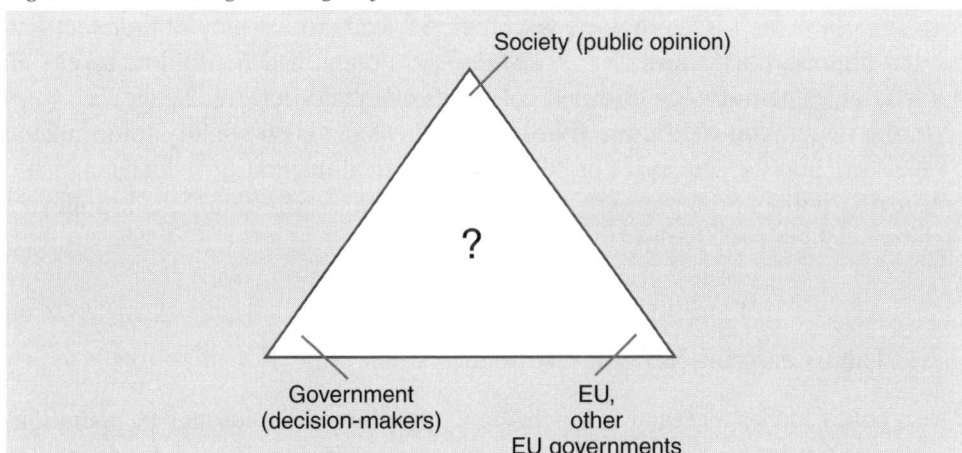

3. Adaptation Theory Revisited

3.1. Adaptive Modes and their Strategies

Mouritzen (1993; cf. Kelstrup 1993, Petersen 1995) suggests that adaptation theory may provide a useful framework for analyzing national integration strategies. Adaptation theory assumes that foreign policy consists of policy-makers' actions to manipulate the balance between their society (i.e. the internal environment) and their external environment in order to secure adequate functioning of societal structures in a situation of growing interdependence (Rosenau 1970). This is a conception somewhat similar to Robert Putnam's conceptualization of foreign policy as a two-level game, where policy-makers try to balance their external and internal constituents against each other (Putnam 1988). In fact, however, adaptation theory is a three-level type of analysis, as decision-makers and their values are also ascribed an active role in the balancing process.

3.2. The Union Game and Its External Strategies

Adaptation to the *external* environment can take four basic forms (modes), depending on the underlying balance between internal and external forces. Put differently, the foreign policy mode of a country depends on its degree of control over its external environment, i.e. its influence capability (IC), as well as its degree of sensitivity to the outer world, i.e. its stress sensitivity (SS) (cf. Hansen 1974; Petersen 1977). The essence of adaptation theory, then, is its focus on the interface between the external and internal environments of the state and the relative balance between them.

A combination of high IC and low SS permits the nation to conduct a *dominant* foreign policy; high IC combined with high SS leads to a policy of *balance*; low IC, but high SS only allows for an *acquiescent* policy; and finally low scores on both variables permit a low-profiled policy of *quiescence*, cf. fig. 2 page 77.

In the integration field these four orientations have been slightly reformulated by Kelstrup into the categories of "dominant political integration", "balancing and optimizing political integration", "reluctant political integration" and a policy of "relative isolation"(Kelstrup 1993: 153).

3.2.1. The Underlying Variables: Influence Capability (IC)

These policy modes and their independent explanatory variables may be operationalized in different ways. Theoretically, *influence capability (IC)* can be defined as a function of those positive and negative measures (sanctions) which a nation-state can use to influence its external environment. In the case of integration, this is meant to be the other participants individually or as a group.

IC hinges on both tangible and intangible elements. Evidently, economic power is an important tangible factor of IC, especially in an integration context; it is expressed in measures such as overall GDP, GDP per capita, foreign trade, economic and monetary stability, etc. However, military power is also of increasing importance, as integration spills over into the fields of foreign and security policy. This means that factors such as the capability to protect other partners (e.g. through an independent deterrent) or to provide military means for common political-military operations (e.g. expeditionary or peace-keeping forces) will exert increasing influence in the European Union.

Throughout the history of European integration, Germany has based her influence on her economic pre-eminence in the Union. After the end of the Cold War the general expectation was that Germany – as the European civilian power *par ex-*

cellence – would grow even more powerful and influential in the Union. This has not turned out to be the case partly because her lack of military prowess (including the self-imposed limitations on its use) has severely handicapped Germany vis-à-vis her sister great powers France and Britain.

IC, however, also depends on such intangible characteristics as prestige and reputation, willpower, diplomatic skill, etc. In the EU, Germany's reputation for loyalty, France's willpower and British diplomatic skill are all relevant aspects of their influence capability. An especially important variable is "coalitional power", i.e. the ability to form or operate as an influential party in winning coalitions. France and Germany have both benefitted considerably from their bilateral coalition, which usually forms the core around which winning coalitions form.

Besides depending on actor characteristics, IC also depends on structural and situational factors. Thus, the expansion of the European Union from an early main focus on economic integration to a much more broadly based political and military integration naturally leads to shifts in the balance between economic, political and military influence factors.

Finally, IC depends on the policy type in question and the relevant decision structures and rules. The politics of the Union may be roughly divided into three broad policy areas: 1) pragmatic regulatory and (re)distributory policy, the EU's domestic policy so to speak; 2) foreign and security policy; and 3) constitutional-institutional policy. In the first area, economic power and coalitional power count for more than in the CFSP area, with its emphasis on political and military power elements and its demand for consensus. In the constitutional field, where every member has a veto and where supreme interests are often felt to be at stake, influence is even more diffuse than in the former two areas. The joke about Chancellor Kohl driving to Maastricht in a Mercedes and returning on a bike captures some of the problems of influence in the constitutional-institutional field.

3.2.2. The Underlying Variables: Stress Sensitivity (SS)

Stress sensitivity (SS) is mainly, but not exclusively a structural variable. In terms of actor characteristics, its main feature is modernization, which implies high sensitivity of societal structures to international events. Dependence on foreign markets, i.e. a high foreign trade/GDP ratio, in general leads to high SS, as does a concentration of trade in the EU market in particular. Small, rich countries like Denmark or the Benelux countries typically belong in this category, but so does Germany. Another factor of dependence is dependence on redistribution schemes within the Union, which places the Southern European members and Ireland in the stress-sensitive group. In contrast, France and Britain score relatively (though not absolutely) low on this variable, because of their relatively low trade ratio (France) or relatively low proportion of trade in the European market (Britain).

An integration system like the European Union tends to be biased in favour of balanced policy modes, i.e. policy behaviours rooted in high influence capability and high stress-sensitivity. This is because taking part in the integration process in itself provides important influence capabilities, such as access to all formal policy bodies and a formal veto in many questions, including the important constitutional-institutional field. In theory, and in many cases in practice as well, even the weakest member of the Union can veto or sabotage policies which other members have agreed upon; that is, if it is prepared to bear the political costs involved. In questions where qualified majority voting applies, votes are skewed in favour of the minor countries, and about 30 per cent of the votes are enough to block a decision. No member, however weak in material terms, is therefore without substantial influence in an integration project.

Likewise, the very fact of integration presupposes mutual sensitivity among partners and increasing interdependence among them. In the earliest presentation of adaptation theory, Rosenau (1970) predicted that the balanced (or preservative as he termed it) mode would increasingly prevail in international politics because of growing interdependence among nation-states. As integration represents the most developed form of interdependence, it follows that balancing policy modes tend to prevail. However, as there are still important differences between member states with respect to their position on the two variables, balancing policies will often be coloured by characteristics and strategies belonging to the dominant, acquiescent or quiescent policy modes.

3.2.3. Adaptive External Strategies

In his dissertation, Mouritzen (1988: 75 ff.) concentrates on discussing strategies associated with the acquiescent mode, such as the strategy of concessions, the strategy of non-commitment, the bastion strategy, and the so-called counterweight strategy. A strategy of concessions involves conceding domestic values and interests to external pressures, e.g. those of the integration process. Non-commitment aims at avoiding or limiting external commitments that may limit national autonomy; an example would be to evade or seek exemptions from new EU obligations. The bastion strategy aims at protecting especially sensitive and vital interests through rhetorical or other forms of self-commitment, e.g. public statements which make concessions harder to give and constitute a "barrier" on the slippery slope of concessions to the integration process. Finally the counterweight strategy aims at engaging "allies", external or internal, in support of a specific policy; an example would be using public opinion as a bargaining chip in EU negotiations.

Mouritzen's list of strategies is incomplete because he is solely interested in the strategies of acquiescent actors. Nor do all his strategies belong convincingly to this mode. Non-commitment is basically a quiescent strategy, in that it aims at reducing links of dependence to the environment, while counterweight rightly belongs to the balancing mode because of its bargaining aspect. Concessions may be part of a balancing mode of give and take as well as being the core strategy of acquiescence (cf. Petersen 1989).

Mouritzen's typology can be expanded by including the assertive or active counterparts of some of his strategies. Thus, we may postulate a strategy of demands (the inverse of a strategy of concessions), a strategy of "sine qua non" (the opposite of the bastion strategy), and a strategy of commitment (non-commitment in reverse). A strategy of demands involves formulating active demands on the external environment, e.g., the European Union, and is closely associated with the strategy of commitment, which is used to increase influence over outcomes. Both typically belong in the balancing mode, even though a strategy of demands can also be part of a policy of dominance, of course. Obviously, the "sine qua non" strategy, which entails raising ultimate demands in negotiations, is the hallmark of the dominant mode. Britain's strategy in the "mad-cow" controversy seems an almost quintessential version of this posture. Finally, as the strategy of demands is the corollary of commitment, non-commitment is closely associated with a strategy of exemptions, i.e. a strategy which aims at an outsider status in certain areas so as to reduce the negative impact on societal values of the integration process.

Recently, Mouritzen (1993) has added another pair of concepts to the typology of integration strategies. Taking his point of departure in Denmark's integration strategy, he argues that prior to the 1992 referendum, Danish politicians gave priority to offensive power, i.e. influence on EC developments, over defensive power (autonomy), but that subsequently autonomy concerns have won out over wishes for more offensive power.

These various strategies as well as hypotheses concerning participation level, are summarized in fig. 3, which shows the main characteristics of the four foreign policy modes of dominance, balance, acquiescence and quiescence.

Figure 3: Adaptive Modes and Strategies in the Union Game

	Influence capability (IC)	
Stress sensitivity (SS)	Policy Dominance Medium degree of participation Strategies: • Demands • "Sine qua non" Offensive power priority	Policy of Balance High degree of participation Strategies: • Demands • Commitment • Counterweight • Concessions Offensive power priority
	Low degree of participation Strategies: • Non-commitment • Exemptions Autonomy priority **Policy of Quiescence**	Medium degree of participation Strategies: • Concessions • Bastions Autonomy priority **Policy of Acquiescence**

3.3. The Four Adaptive Modes and their Background

The four modes of behaviour described in fig. 3 are classical ideal-types, of course, i.e., they cannot be expected to be found in pure form, but only in approximations. All kinds of intermediate positions can be imagined, depending on the degree of influence capability and stress sensitivity of the nation in question, and modified by the relevant perceptions of decision-makers. Over the short- to medium-term strategies are likely to evolve on the basis of decision-makers' (possibly erroneous) perception of their country's position in the IC-SS space, but in the longer run the "objective" position is likely to set itself through (cf. Petersen 1977).

3.3.1. Dominance

As a point of departure, it may be hypothesized that *ceteris paribus* governments prefer to conduct a dominant integration policy. Dominance is characterized by the ability to make demands on integration partners, even ultimate "sine qua non" demands, without having to make significant concessions in return. The balance between externally and internally generated forces is thus skewed in favour of domestic interests. A clear offensive power priority prevails. In game-theoretical terms, dominance equals a D strategy in the union game.

Several conditions must be met so as to make possible such a policy. The country in question must have a high score on the influence variable. In concrete terms, this means *inter alia* a strong material base, e.g. great economic (and military) power, a strategic position in the Union (considerable coalitional power), diplomatic skill and not least a willingness to accept the costs of a dominant strategy. At the same time, dependence on partners and on the integration process must not be too heavy, and there must be some leeway for independent action outside the Union as well as inside it. Therefore, participation in the integration process will typically lie in the middle range. In various phases of European integration, France (under de Gaulle) and Britain (under Mrs. Thatcher and Mr. Major) have attempted to pursue dominant policy modes, but their examples also demonstrate the limitations of such a policy in an integration context. In most cases, SS (stress sensitivity) will be too high for such a policy to succeed, especially in the long run.

3.3.2. Acquiescence

The acquiescent policy mode is obviously at the other end of the preference scale from dominance. If governments can avoid it, they would prefer any alternative to a policy mode whose defining strategy is to give concessions, i.e., to subordinate domestic priorities to externally defined ones. In its pure form, acquiescence is hardly compatible with participation in integration because integration processes are by definition based on shared interests and cooperation rather than on unbridled economic and political competition. Besides, the formal voting procedures and veto rights inherent in membership limit the degree of acquiescence a government can be forced to endure. Therefore, applicants to the European Union are more likely to exhibit this kind of adaptation than countries already inside (Mouritzen 1993).

Even though a country's integration strategy is based on conceding to the integration process (without necessarily sharing its goal), such concessions will normally be given piecemeal and reluctantly so as to avoid stepping onto "the slippery slope of concessions" (Mouritzen 1988). In the Danish debate the Union process is very often referred to as such a "slippery slope" entry which will inevitably take a country into the full union. To counter this risk, a bastion strategy may be chosen in which a country seeks to limit concessions by putting up a spirited defence of certain central principles or interests outside the realm of acceptable concession. This is often done through self-binding commitments. Of course, the formal rights of membership favour such a strategy, even though it can best be used in extraordinary circumstances, when high interests are at stake.

Acquiescence presupposes a limited degree of influence capability and a great dose of stress sensitivity. The purest example of acquiescence, therefore, can be found among applicants who desire to enter the Union and must adapt their policies to membership by a wholesale acceptance of the *acquis communitaire*. Acquiescent insiders will typically be small and comparatively poor member states without political or economic clout, and, furthermore, countries essentially dependent on the Union, either for access to the Internal Market or for transfers from the Union's redistributive funds. Countries like Ireland, Portugal and Greece may be the closest approximations to an acquiescent policy in the Union, even though Greece has felt free to demonstrate her nuisance value on several occasions. In game theoretical terms, this strategy mode has elements of the more passive version of a C strategy.

3.3.3. Quiescence

For countries with limited influence capability, quiescence may be a preferred alternative to acquiescence. Quiescence is basically a low-key policy aimed at limiting concessions to the integration process; it is more intent on avoiding its bads than enjoying its goods. Participation is low, and autonomy is preferred to offensive power, i.e. influence over the Union process. The prevailing strategy is non-commitment, i.e. a loose tie to the process, perhaps with a concentration on a few goals or aspects, such as the trade arrangement. In some cases, non-commitment may be expressed in a policy of exemptions, that is, limiting participation to preferred policy areas and being exempted from unrewarding ones. Quiescence is related to the passive version of a D strategy referred to above. It is clearly a policy for low-influence countries, but it also presupposes a limited stress sensitivity, which may be difficult to maintain when participating, even though at a low level, in an integration project. Therefore, a full-blown quiescent policy does not seem possible in the European Union; on the other hand, the temptations of non-commitment or exemption strategies will very likely be felt when national interests are threatened by the integration process.

3.3.4. Balance

A balanced policy mode is the archetypal integration mode. As already mentioned, James Rosenau (1970) postulated that, with the growth of international interdependence a balanced policy mode would become increasingly prevalent, and, in fact, this mode is the only posture which is theoretically compatible with full participation in international integration.

The balanced mode is characterized by a multitude of strategies and a high degree of participation. Basically, it is a policy of give and take, of accepting the conditions of interdependence and trying to exploit it to further national interests. Concessions are given in the expectation that they will be more than balanced by the benefits of integration. Such benefits are actively sought through a strategy of demands, i.e. putting concrete and specific proposals in all arenas. Demands are often combined with a counterweight strategy to give further weight to arguments. Fundamentally, the balanced mode is characterised by a commitment strategy and an offensive power orientation. In game theory it corresponds to the active side of a C strategy.

The balanced mode is determined by high scores on both underlying variables, i.e. high influence capability and high stress sensitivity. These are, as already mentioned, closely related to interdependence and integration. However, not all states are equally influential and stress-sensitive. In the European Union, Germany comes closest to the ideal-type, but the other major powers as well as the medium powers, e.g. the Netherlands and Belgium, also belong in this category.

3.4. The Union Game and its Internal (Domestic) Strategies

Compared to the external aspect of the Union game, its domestic aspects, including overall policy modes and concrete strategies, remain virtually unexplored. The following is but an initial attempt to come to grips with some of the intricacies of the domestic game; it will be neither a full-blown parallel to the operationalization of the external aspects above, nor an attempt to integrate the external and internal games into some kind of a integration "super-game". However, the analysis will try to demonstrate the enormity of the challenges of this "super-game", at least in cases where the corners of the strategic triangle (see fig. 2), especially the societal and international corners, are incompatible or near-incompatible.

As in the external game, it is reasonable to surmise that the domestic game is defined by two underlying factors, one denoting policy-makers' control over society, the other their susceptibility to societal influences. These concepts seem roughly parallel to "influence capability" and "stress sensitivity" in the external game and to avoid confusion the terms "control capability" (CC) and "influence susceptibility" (IS) will be adopted.

3.4.1. Underlying Variables: Control Capability (CC)

Control capability (CC) is a function of all those positive and negative measures by which decision-makers may influence their societies on a given issue. In democratic societies like those engaged in European integration, control capability is generally low, but it may vary across political systems and across issues. An important aspect of CC is political control, by which is meant governments' influence on public opinion via political parties, public organizations, the mass media, etc.

At least until recently, modern mass society often gave governments important control powers over public opinion. Such important channels of influence have included strong, hierarchically organized party organizations with firm control over the party's rank and file, economic interest organizations (labour unions, farmers' unions, etc.) and loyal party presses. These structures still play a role in some countries, as in southern Europe, but in northern Europe such control mechanisms have weakened considerably over the last generation. In Denmark, for instance, the political parties are rapidly losing members, ties between the political parties and economic interest organisations are becoming attenuated, and the party-controlled press is a thing of the past.

Another potential control mechanism is the power of the purse. With respect to European integration, a potentially important lever is the concrete welfare benefits of integration, whether these accrue to society as a whole, or are being distributed to key segments of society. Presently, economic benefits are a potent control mechanism in the hands of Southern European governments; to a lesser degree this also used to be the case with respect to Danish integration policy (benefits from the Common Agricultural Policy).

In the relative absense of organizational and economic controls, governments must rely on what could be termed "agenda control". Even though it has been eroded by modern mass media, as well, governments are still in possession of important privileged information for influencing public opinion, especially concerning strategic questions; i.e., what can and what cannot be done. Furthermore, governments still have some remaining analytical advantages, even though it is eroding fastly. The precondition for influencing the political agenda-setting seems to be a high degree of internal cohesion in the decision-maker group (no discordant voices), reasonable powers of persuasion and the like.

Because of their relative loss of traditional forms of public opinion control governments can no longer take it for granted that the public will follow its advice. At the same time, publics are less prepared than before to accept political admonitions from above. This is a function of the general democratization which has triumphed over the last generation in advanced societies. Basic to this development is the decline of authority, i.e. of people's willingness to accept government or expert recipes uncritically, which again is rooted in increased feelings of personal competence on the part of individuals.

3.4.2. Underlying Variables: Influence Susceptibility (IS)

The other side of the government-public relationship, susceptibility, also flows from the democratization of Western society and its overflow into the foreign policy area. Traditionally, foreign policy, including economic and political integration, was considered part of high politics and almost entirely within the purview of the government; the only relevant segment of society with some influence was elite and organizational opinion, which, however, was usually co-opted into the political establishment. Thus, the domestic game existed only in a very weak form. In some countries, especially in southern Europe, this is still the overall picture, which means that government normally has the freedom to formulate its integration policies without much public interference. However, if concrete economic interests become affected, societal influence on politics may become direct and dramatic; French policy shows numerous examples of this mechanism.

Generally, though, governmental integration policies tend to grow increasingly susceptible to public opinion. An important precondition for this are individuals' growing analytical capabilities (information and insight) and the political competence at the individual level. People are simply better informed and better capable of forming relevant opinions about issues of international integration. This tendency is strengthened by the fact that integration policy increasingly spans the foreign policy/domestic policy divide. What in the early days was seen as an aspect of foreign policy pure and simple now crosses into domestic politics in a myriad of ways. Integration policy is thus fast becoming an aspect of domestic policy with an everyday impact on people's lives. People's motivation for holding opinions is therefore increasing.

The impact of public opinion on the government is aided by the proliferation of potential channels of influence, such as grassroots organizations and the like, outside the control of the political establishment. Furthermore, structural changes have facilitated formal organizations' access to the policy-making field. Corporate structures channel inputs from organized, mostly economic interest groups, into the decision-making process, and political reform has increased the influence of Parliament and the political parties over government policy. The ultimate democratization of integration policy occurs when significant integration issues are decided by referendum.

In conclusion, the trend in the government/society relationship is towards decreasing government control and increasing government susceptibility to societal influences. Governments therefore operate under considerable constraints in their integration policy. There are degrees, though. Southern European governments are generally less constrained than northern ones, societal influence is weaker in France than in Germany, etc. It is probably fair to say that nowhere are domestic constraints stronger than in Denmark.

For the sake of simplicity, the analysis will now concentrate on the domestic integration game as it is played out in political systems characterized by low government control and high government susceptibility. In such situations, the domestic aspect of integration policy may become as important or even more important than its external aspect. Another assumption, basic to the following argument, is that there will tend to be important divergences between the values and interests of the decision-makers' external and internal environments, or – phrased differently – there will be great distance between the societal and EU corners of the strategic triangle. If not, the integration dilemma does not arise in any marked form, and adaptation theory becomes less useful.

3.4.3. Adaptive Domestic Strategies

Given the constraints governing integration policy in countries like Denmark, what strategies are available to decision-makers to cope with these constraints? The basic overall policy mode in this case is likely to be one in which "acquiescence" to public opinion combines in an uneasy way with a balance policy towards the external environment. This combination is uneasy, because "acquiescence" to a critical public opinion as its ideal counterpart has an external policy of dominance, one which is entirely governed by domestic concerns. However, given the facts of external constraints, governments normally cannot just follow a strong-willed public and pursue such a policy.

The main government strategy for coping with public opinion could be termed a "strategy of representation". That is, the government sees it as its primary task to represent societal demands to its international partners. This is, of course, what governments are normally supposed to do in the integration process, and in most cases this results in a give and take, which leaves public opinion with a mixture of satisfaction and frustration depending on where the necessary compromises are struck.

The strategy of representation works best in cases where the distances between the three corners of the strategic triangle are rather small. If so, government has no qualms about representing societal demands abroad, and their reception among other governments is likely to be positive. Problems arise, however, if the strategic triangle expands. This may happen in two important cases.

In the first case, the distance grows between public opinion and decision-makers in the country and the external environment. Domestic consensus is preserved, but there is increasing tension surrounding the external aspects of integration policy.

In the second case, the distance grows between society and establishment, but not between government and the external environment. Domestic consensus ruptures, while relations around the external aspects of integration policy remain stable, at least as long as the opinion factor is kept neutralized.

In both cases, decision-makers are in a difficult position. In the first-mentioned case the problem is mainly one of handling the external environment, which lies outside the present discussion. However, decision-makers may also see a major problem with the public, despite the fact that they basically agree with it. This stems from the different perspectives of government and public. The public can afford to be and tends to be more absolutistic than the government in its demands to the other world. Even though the government may share the sentiments of the public, it will not ruin its long-term relationship with its partners by appearing immoderate and intransigent. Therefore, it may mix its basic representation strategy with a mild form of persuasion strategy vis-a-vis the public, aiming at reducing the public's demands and preparing it for the necessary compromises. This strategy could also be termed a "dialogue strategy".

The second case is much more critical, however. The government cannot choose a representation strategy in good faith, because it does not sympathise with the sentiments of the public. Several strategies can then be followed, even though none are entirely satisfactory. One would be a strong version of the persuasion strategy, in which the government makes a determined effort to sway public opinion and to explain its own position to it. The normally weak CC of the government works against this strategy, which may have limited effect.

In this situation, the government may choose to strengthen its power of persuasion through a domestic variant of the counterweight strategy (inverse counterweight so to speak), e.g. by "allying" with other governments in order to explain to the public the seriousness of the situation, in which the public has placed the country. This strategy may backfire, though, if a significant part of the public smells collusion. A more radical version of the persuasion strategy could be termed a strategy of threats, in which the public is threatened by pointing out the negative consequences of its positions.

If the strategies of persuasion and counterweight are not feasible, an alternative strategy might be one of concessions, which is characterized by the government accepting that its policy must be based on the views of the public – at least to the extent they are known. Concessions will be limited, though, to the extent necessary to persuade the public.

This version of representation strategy is likely to be less credible to a suspicious public and may therefore be strengthened with a more explicit concession strategy on certain issues whereby the government openly commits itself to representing certain policies or views in the integration process. The external form of the explicit concession strategy is the bastion strategy discussed above.

Finally, the government may want to increase its freedom of movement in coping with the integration dilemma through a de-coupling strategy vis-à-vis the public. A decoupling strategy may consist of reluctantly entering into a dialogue with the public or in attempts to reduce public debate to the elite level.

3.4.4. Domestic Policy Modes

We have now tentatively isolated a number of possible strategies for coping with public opinion in a situation where the government's control capability is limited and its influence susceptibility is pronounced. Intuitively, these strategies fall into two major patterns, a defensive one and an offensive one. The defensive pattern includes strategies of de-coupling, concessions and explicit concessions, while the offensive pattern encompasses strategies of dialogue, persuasion, threats and counterweight. The strategy of representation falls somewhere in between.

4. Denmark: An Illustrative Case

As mentioned, we predict a balanced policy mode with its associated strategies (within a large range of variation, of course) for policy in an integration context, usually coupled with a domestic strategy of representation. This policy is predicated on high scores on both influence capability and stress sensitivity, combined with low scores on control capability and high scores on influence susceptibility. However, it is also typically associated with a high degree of identification with the immediate and ultimate goals of integration; it is a characteristically centrist, insider position.

But what about participants who do not share (all) the goals of integration, who do not have much influence capability to pressure their own agenda, but who nevertheless share a high degree of sensitivity to the integration process? That is, countries for whom the bads of the integration dilemma come close to overshadowing its goods, and who, because of the lack of influence capabilities, are unable to change the balance in a more favourable direction.

4.1. Basic Values and Preferences

The Danish case illustrates important aspects of this *problematique* (cf. Rüdiger 1995; Petersen 1995). Denmark joined the European Community in 1973 on a highly selective identification with EC goals. The primary motivation was economic, and politicians focused almost entirely on the economic benefits of joining in the referendum campaign prior to membership.[3] Since then, the promotion of pragmatic cooperation in the economic sphere has been the main priority of

---

3 This understanding was shared by the population. Among those who voted for membership an overwhelming majority did so for economic or other pragmatic reasons. On the other hand, political and ideological arguments, most notably the loss of sovereignty and the dangers of European Union, predominated among nay-sayers (Petersen 1978).

Denmark's EC/EU policy, i.e. promotion of free trade and the internal market, support for monetary cooperation in the EMS, the struggle against unemployment, promotion of joint environmental policies, and the like. Thus, there has been a fairly high degree of goal identification in the field of pragmatic, economic-social policy, including a willingness to accept majority voting in high-priority fields.

On the other hand, goal identification has been low in the areas of foreign and security policy and especially in constitutional-institutional policy. In the foreign and security area the Danish preferences have been ambivalent: a high measure of support for foreign policy coordination, both in the former EPC (European Political Cooperation) and the present CFSP (Common Foreign and Security Policy), combined with stubborn resistance to extending cooperation into the fields of security and defence policy. In the dominant view, determined primarily by the Social Democratic Party, defence cooperation should be a matter for NATO and NATO alone, and the EC/EU is in no need for a defence policy of its own, let alone a European Army. As a consequence, the WEU, Western European Union, has usually been viewed by Danes with great scepticism.

On the other hand, there has been some fluctuation over the years, as the political right-of-center forces (Conservatives and Liberals) have been more willing to accept a European security policy. When a conservative coalition was in power during 1982-93 (though lacking a firm majority in European affairs), the official posture became less negative, but after 1993, when a Social Democratic coalition took over, it hardened once again.

In the constitutional field, Denmark has been a persistent adherent of inter-governmentalism; only one political party, the Liberals, has (or rather had) some federalist sympathies. In the dominant view, most clearly represented by or rather had the Social Democrats, the EU is and should remain a voluntary association of states which have decided to solve certain problems in common. Hence, any talk of federalism is more or less taboo, and the defence of national sovereignty figures high on the political agenda. Consequently, the Council of Ministers is seen as the absolute center of power in the Union, while the Commission and the Parliament are given subsidiary roles. This preference is usually expressed in terms of support for the existing institutional balance in the Union. Again, during the 1982-93 period, there was a certain relaxation of this basic attitude, but since 1993 inter-governmentalism has been quite firmly in the saddle.

The prevailing official attitudes have their background in an even more sceptical public. For many years, from 1973 to about 1988, the public was uncertain about the pros and cons of membership itself and, in fact, those regretting 1973 were in a majority most of the time. Even when this issue faded away in the late 1980s, sceptical attitudes towards integration and unionism remained. The first Maastricht referendum in 1992 ended in a disaster for the political establishment, which had underestimated the public's fear of the slippery slope towards the Union. Such aspects of the Union as common foreign and security policy, common defence, common currency, and Union citizenship were all rejected by majorities or pluralities of the respondents in polls at the time. Policy-makers thus operate under difficult domestic constraints, which are increased by the fact that constitutional requirements and political convention give referenda a crucial role in the making of Danish European policy (Siune et al. 1994; Worre 1995).

Under these circumstances, the dominant priorities in Denmark's European policy have been under pressure from the integration process during most of the period since 1973, though mainly in the periods between 1973 and 1982 and after 1993, when the more sceptical views have held sway. Nevertheless, even in the 1982-93 period, when governmental priorities were more in tune with the European mainstream, the integration process was perceived as stressful by conjuring up domestic conflicts which were difficult to handle for the government. Thus, in a sense, the integration process itself has been an important element of Denmark's stress sensitivity vis-à-vis Europe.

Other more fundamental aspects of Denmark's high stress sensitivity are its high foreign trade/GDP ratio and a high concentration of trade on the European market. This dependency, which has been most prevalent in the agricultural sector, has further increased with the recent accession of Sweden and Finland to the Union. Besides, Denmark is also dependent on the EC/EU as a major receiver of funds from the CAP, the Union's Common Agricultural Policy. In fact, over the years, Denmark has been an overall net receiver of funds from the EC/EU.

On the influence side, the limited identification with Union goals and the associated "foot-dragging" image has limited Denmark's influence on Union affairs, although it is difficult to prove how much. On the other hand, in the more active period before 1992, Denmark was able to exert some influence on the process, e.g. during IGC 1991, and Denmark has also been able to use the prerogatives of membership, including her veto in constitutional affairs. This veto, however, has been most effective in small and special policy cases or in cooperation with other reluctant integrationists, such as Britain.[4] A special case of influence was the adroit exploitation of the "nuisance value" which Denmark gained as a consequence of the first Maastricht referendum in 1992.

4.2. Denmark's External Integration Strategies 1973-95

4.2.1. Pragmatic Politics

In the area of pragmatic Community/Union politics, Denmark's policy posture has mainly been balancing. In order to secure vital economic interests deriving from high dependence on external markets, successive Danish governments have shown a high degree of participation and followed a policy of commitment in most policy areas, most notably relating to the Internal Market and the CAP. The same has been

---

[4] One example is the Danish ban against foreigners' (including EU citizens') purchase of summer homes in Denmark.

the case in the field of fishery policy despite very strong internal pressures opposing a common fishery policy with its strong regulatory impact on Danish fisheries. In this case, however, counterweight arguments (opposition from strong and militant fishermen) were also used. The most characteristic feature of this issue-area, therefore, has been a mixture of demands and concessions, i.e. a policy of give and take with an offensive power priority. During the last decade, offensive power priority has been especially pronounced in issues like the environment, worker protection (the EU's social dimension) and consumer protection. Here Denmark has pursued a fairly aggressive policy of demands, e.g., at the Inter-Governmental Conference of 1996.

In a few areas, however, an autonomy priority has prevailed. Before the Single European Act (1986), this applied to environmental policy, because of fears that high national standards would be eroded by EC harmonization measures. After the introduction of minimum directives, this fear was assuaged and Denmark shifted to an offensive posture. Another sensitive area is taxation, where Denmark has consistently opposed harmonization, both of direct and indirect taxes.[5] A further case is the third stage of the Economic Monetary Union (EMU). Successive governments have been highly favourable to economic and monetary cooperation in the Union, but both in the political establishment and (particularly) in public opinion there has been strong resistance to the idea of a common currency. As a concession strategy was impossible for domestic reasons, and a demand strategy futile for external ones, policy-makers instead opted for an exemption strategy. In the Maastricht Treaty itself, Denmark was allowed to postpone her decision to join the third stage until after a referendum at that time. After the first referendum, this exemption was strengthened by the December 1992 Edinburgh Decision, where Denmark was permanently exempted from the third stage. Subsequently, in connection with the 1993 referendum, this exemption was turned into a bastion, as policy-makers promised the public that it would not be changed unless approved in another referendum.

With the above-mentioned exceptions, Danish strategies in the EU's "domestic policy" have been characterized mostly by a cautious balancing. It is possible to identify a more active posture after the mid-1980s, reflecting a more pro-integrationist policy leadership and gradually also a more permissive public, but the basic balancing posture has not changed significantly.

4.2.2. Foreign and Security Policy

In the field of foreign and security policy, Danish strategies have been more mixed. In foreign policy proper, a straightforward balancing strategy has been pursued.

---

5 As a consequence of uncontrolled border trade, Denmark has had to lower taxes on goods like tobacco, beer, alcohol and gasoline.

Denmark has participated actively in the give and take of both the EPC and CFSP, making a number of demands, but it has also been willing to adapt national policy to the common policy.[6] In the security field, however, strategies have been different, being characterized by a continuous rearguard action of small, harshly resisted concessions against the expansion of EPC. For many years (until the SEA) the "political aspects" of security were the limit of the acceptable, then "the political and economic aspects". Prior to the 1991 Inter-Governmental Conference, the Government set up a small bastion in a memorandum agreed with and inspired by the Opposition, which rejected "the idea that the (EPC) should come to include co-operation in defence policies, i.a. the setting-up of common military forces" (Memo 1990).

In Maastricht, however, the Government accepted – against some criticism from the Social Democratic opposition – that the CFSP would cover all aspects of foreign and security policy, including in time a common defence (TEU, Art. J. 4.1). Following the negative referendum of June 1992, however, the old bastion strategy was reinstated and supplemented by an exemption strategy. First, a National Compromise was negotiated between seven out of eight parties in Parliament, according to which "Denmark does not participate in the so-called defence policy dimension, which involves membership of the Western European Union and a common foreign policy or a common defence" (Denmark in Europe 1992). Subsequently, the Edinburgh European Council meeting turned this bastion into an exemption and the Danish position was generally accepted. Finally, prior to the 1993 referendum the bastion was further reinforced when the parties behind the National Compromise promised that it could only be repealed if approved by another referendum. Thus, while balance strategies characterise Denmark's participation in the common foreign policy, the defence area abounds with bastion and exemption strategies, i.e., with strategies related to the acquiescent and, especially, the quiescent policy mode and reflecting a desire not to be associated closely with the development of a European defence policy. As a consequence, Denmark has chosen not to join the Western European Union (WEU), but to remain an observer.

4.2.3. Institutional Politics

Institutional politics has created most difficulties for Danish policy-makers over the years. Because of Denmark's basic orientation towards the status quo and intergovernmentalism, the Union process has repeatedly produced strains and conflicts domestically and in relation to the European partners. Under the circumstances, Danish policy has been characterized by rearguard fighting in defence of bastions, large and small, such as the principles of unchanged institutional balance and the

---

6 A primary area for Danish demands has been the opening of the EC/EU to Central and Eastern Europe. Concessions have been most prominent in Denmark's Middle East policy.

primacy of the Council. The growing strength of the European Parliament has created particular difficulties. Denmark fought in vain against direct elections to the EP, the expansion of the EP's powers in the SEA, and expressed important reservations prior to the 1991 IGC. The strengthening of the Parliament (the co-decision procedure) in the Maastricht Treaty caused little domestic opposition, however, and since then the Danish policy towards the Parliament has mellowed somewhat with the realization that it could be an effective ally for Denmark on issues of environmental policy, consumer protection, etc. Despite this, the core of Danish institutional policy remains the defence of the Council of Ministers as the absolute core of decision-making in the Union.

In recent years, institutional policy has acquired a less foot-dragging aspect, as Denmark has taken the lead in promoting openness and democracy in Union affairs. Such demands were voiced for the first time in 1990 (Memo 1990), only to be strongly reinforced after the failed 1992 referendum. Denmark subsequently pressed successfully for including increased openness in the Edinburgh Decision, and since then openness, subsidiarity (what the Danes call "nearness") and democracy have been catch-words in Denmark's EU policy, including her policies at IGC 1996.[7]

Some elements of balance, therefore, have come to colour the Danish strategy on constitutional development. Nevertheless, certain bastions are still vigorously defended, for instance, the rejection of federalism. During the final Maastricht negotiations the Danish government had to dig in its heels after heavy criticism from the Social Democratic opposition and it's demand that the "federal goal" be removed from the Treaty text.[8] In the same vein, Denmark opposes the "communitarization" of the inter-governmental parts of the Union, i.e. Pillars Two and Three; one of the Edinburgh bastions (not a proper exemption) was that Denmark would not accept the transfer of parts of Pillar Three to Pillar One. When this happened in the Amsterdam Treaty, Denmark demanded – and received – an exemption concerning the transferred parts.

4.2.4. General Patterns in External Strategies

Denmark's European strategy has varied both across issue areas and over time. Balancing strategies have become more prevalent, even though bastion and exemption strategies have been taken up as a consequence of the public opinion backlash in the first referendum in 1992. This tilt against balancing strategies is probably

---

7 In the Danish reading, "subsidiarity" is exclusively a decentralizing concept, hence the translation into "nearness". It is not realized that subsidiarity may also entail centralization, if that is called for.
8 British opposition obviously meant more to the final result than that of Denmark.

due to a slowly growing, but still far from perfect identification with the goals of integration, as well as an increasing familiarity with the Union. As demonstrated by the 1992-93 debacle, however, there is no linearity; strategy shifts, *in casu* to bastion and exemption strategies, may be occasioned by public opinion backlashes, government shifts (the France of Chirac), and other domestic changes.[9]

Strategies have also varied across issue areas. In low politics, balance strategies have prevailed, while other strategies have been more common in high politics, especially in the areas constitution and defence policy. The overall image is one of a bifurcated policy mode, somewhat at variance with the popular, general characteristic of Danish "foot-dragging" across the entire field of European integration.

4.3. Denmark's Domestic Integration Strategies

Like external strategies, domestic integration strategies vary over issue areas and to some extent over time.

4.3.1. Pragmatic Politics

The basic domestic strategy in the realm of pragmatic EC/EU politics, has been the representation strategy. Successive governments have usually had no difficulties in identifying themselves with those economic and other interests which emanate from society. A pertinent case is the way Danish governments have represented agricultural interests throughout the entire membership period. Other economic sectors have been supported as well, such as shipbuilding and (to a lesser degree) the fishing industry. In the latter case, Danish governments have sometimes had to resort to complementary strategies of dialogue and persuasion in order to ward off excessive demands on the part of the industry. Other segments whose interests have been regularly represented by Danish governments is labour; Denmark has been an ardent proponent of employment policies in the EC/EU. In recent years representative strategies have been expanded to include environmental protection and consumer interests.

As mentioned above, the waters have divided between government and the public over the third stage of the EMU. While EMU is (or at least was) rejected by the public, most decision-makers want Denmark to join. In this particular case, decision-makers had to resort to an explicit concession strategy by accepting a binding ban on Danish participation until the public gives its acceptance in a popular referendum. This strategy is followed, however, by various alternative strategies.

---

9 Denmark was not the only country which modified its European strategies as a consequence of the public reaction to the Maastricht Treaty.

The present government of Social Democrats and Social Liberals prefer a mild dialogue-cum-persuasion strategy, while opposition is more tempted by threat strategies in order to change public opinion.

4.3.2. Foreign and Security Policy

In this policy area domestic strategies have been more mixed. Over a broad number of issues a de facto de-coupling strategy has prevailed, which has limited public debate to the political and elite level. This is the area mainly covered by the old EPC and the foreign policy part of the present Common Foreign and Security Policy. Here the government has had considerable freedom of maneuver to pursue what has mostly been a balanced external policy mode.

In security and defence policy a similar situation has arisen as with the EMU, Third Stage. Strong public doubts concerning the wisdom of including security and defence policy in the Maastricht Treaty contributed to its defeat in the 1992 referendum. Subsequently the government had to accept an explicit concession strategy vis-à-vis the public and have Denmark exempted from the relevant aspects of the Treaty. In this case, decision-makers are split as to secondary strategies. While the government parties – at least until recently – seemed content to stick to the explicit concession strategy, the opposition loudly demands decisive attempts to turn public opinion around, using a blend of persuasion and threats.

4.3.3. Institutional Politics

Finally, because distances are rather small government-society relations are comparatively calm in the field of institutional-constitutional politics. Both the public and the political elite basically agree that the constitutional development of the EU should not be forced ahead, and that the Union should keep its present inter-governmentalist character. This field is therefore characterized by representative strategies.

5. Conclusion

The aim of this article has been to conceptualize national integration strategies. The point of departure is an identification of the manifold problems and benefits associated with integration. The concept of the integration dilemma (with heavy borrowing from the alliance dilemma concept) seems a fruitful way to understand the fundamental conditions under which nation-states formulate their concrete integration strategies, a crucial notion being that integration processes involve both costs and benefits (goods and bads) for the participants.

In attempting to conceptualize the concrete integration strategies, two theories were explored, game theory and adaptation theory. The application of game theory brings important insights, but it is hampered by the fact that it cannot explain national priorities; and the two main strategies of game theory, cooperation and defection, remain crude.

Adaptation theory somehow makes up for these deficiencies. It has an underlying theory, however broad and general, and it allows for the specification of concrete strategies within the predicted broad policy modes. As the empirical example demonstrates, it is useful in providing concepts with which national policy can actually be described and understood. Another strength is that it focuses on the interaction of external and internal factors, which is of increasing importance in European integration after Maastricht.

Adaptation theory is not without its weaknesses, however. It is universal and, hence, fairly general in its theoretical categories. This problem is exacerbated by its theoretical bias towards one particular policy mode, balancing, in the case of integration. The latter problem, while genuine, does not invalidate the theory. Balancing in itself is a broad category which encompasses many different mixes of the underlying variables and of their attendant strategies. Furthermore, balancing strategies may borrow heavily from the arsenal of adjacent policy modes, i.e. dominance, quiescence and acquiescence, thus adding nuance to the tenor of national policies.

Another relevant criticism is that adaptive policies presuppose interest differences between the nation-state and its environment. As Mouritzen (1988) points out, adaptation makes no sense if interests are identical. If, therefore, a nation does not feel any integration dilemma, if there are only goods and no bads associated with taking part in integration, then there is no need to worry about the balance between society and its external environment. However, as the discussion of the integration dilemma has brought out, this situation is highly unlikely. The integration dilemma varies in terms of severity, but it is always there calling for adaptive strategies.

The foregoing analysis has not tested out the potential of integration theory proper. This reflects the author's theoretical point of departure, but also the fact that even intergovernmentalism is of little help when it comes to theorizing state behaviour. For this reason, the problem of national integration strategies remains a conspicuous lacuna in integration theory.

Literature

Denmark in Europe, October 1992.

Friis, Lykke (1995): *Challenging a Theoretical Paradox: The Lacuna of Integration Policy Theory.* Copenhagen: CORE working paper 2/1995.

Hansen, Peter (1974): "Adaptive Behaviour of Small States: The Case of Denmark and the European Community", *Sage International Yearbook of Foreign Policy Studies*, vol. 2, pp. 143-174.

Kelstrup, Morten (1993): "Small States and European Political Integration", in Teija Tiilikainen & Ib Damgaard Petersen (eds.), *The Nordic Countries and the EC*, Copenhagen: Copenhagen Political Studies Press, pp. 136-162.

Matlàry, Janne Haaland (1993): "Beyond Intergovernmentalism: The Quest for a Comprehensive Framework for the Study of Integration", *Cooperation and Conflict*, vol. 28, pp. 181-208.

Memo (1990): *Memorandum from the Danish Government*, 4 October 1990.

Milward, Alan S. (1992): *The European Rescue of the Nation-State*, London: Routledge.

Moravcsik, Andrew (1994): *Why the European Community Strengthens the State: Domestic Politics and International Cooperation*, Cambridge, MA: Harvard University Press.

Mouritzen, Hans (1988): *Finlandization: Toward a General Theory of Adaptive Politics*, Aldershot: Avebury.

Mouritzen, Hans (1993): "The Two Musterknaben and the Naughty Boy: Sweden, Finland and Denmark in the Process of European Integration", *Cooperation and Conflict*, vol. 28/4, pp. 373-402.

Petersen, Nikolaj (1977): "Adaptation as a Framework for the Analysis of Foreign Policy Behaviour", *Cooperation and Conflict*, vol. 12, pp. 221-250.

Petersen, Nikolaj (1978): "Attitudes towards European Integration and the Danish Common Market Referendum", *Scandinavian Political Studies*, vol. 1 (new series), pp. 23-42.

Petersen, Nikolaj (1989): "Mod en generel teori om adaptiv politik", *Politica*, vol. 21, pp. 174-188.

Petersen, Nikolaj (1993): "Abandonment vs. Entrapment: Denmark and Military Integration in Europe", in Norbert Wiggershaus & Roland G. Foerster (eds.), *The Western Security Community, 1948-1959*, Oxford & Providence, N.J.: Berg Publishers, pp. 199-226.

Petersen, Nikolaj (1995): "Denmark and the European Community 1985-1993" in Carsten Due-Nielsen & Nikolaj Petersen (eds.): *Adaptation and Activism. The Foreign Policy of Denmark 1967-1993*, Copenhagen: Danish Institute of International Studies & DJØF Publishing, pp. 189-224.

Petersen, Nikolaj (1998): "National Strategies in the Integration Dilemma: An Adaptation Approach", *Journal of Common Market Studies*, vol. 36, pp. 33-45.

Putnam, Robert D. (1988): "Diplomacy and domestic politics: the logic of two-level games", *International Organization*, vol. 43, pp. 427-459.

Rosenau, James (1970): *The Adaptation of National Societies: A Theory of Political Systems Behaviour and Transformation*, New York: McCaleb-Seiler.

Rüdiger, Mogens (1995): "Denmark and the European Community 1967-1985" in Carsten Due-Nielsen & Nikolaj Petersen (eds.): *Adaptation and Activism. The Foreign Policy of Denmark 1967-1993*, Copenhagen: Danish Institute of International Studies & DJØF Publishing, pp. 163-188.

Siune, Karen, Palle Svensson & Ole Tonsgaard (1994): *– fra et nej til et ja,* Aarhus: Politica.

Snyder, Glenn (1984): "The Security Dilemma in Alliance Politics", *World Politics*, vol. 36,4, pp. 461-95.

Worre, Torben (1995): "First No, Then Yes: The Danish Referendums on the Maastricht Treaty 1992 and 1993", *Journal of Common Market Studies*, vol. 33, pp. 235-257.

CHAPTER 4

Integration Policy: Between Foreign Policy and Diffusion

Morten Kelstrup

1. Introduction

This chapter is a discussion of 'integration policy'. Tentatively, we can understand integration policy as the policy of an individual state or actor towards and within the formation of a new international political centre with some kind of supranationality. The chapter discusses what we mean by integration policy, how it can be exemplified as policies which states might follow in regard to European integration, how we might define different dimensions of integration policies, and what the relationship is between integration policy and foreign policy. In addition, the chapter discusses how some of the major dynamic developments in relation to integration policies seem to create diffusion and new kinds of politicisation.

A point of departure in the understanding of integration policy can be taken in the view that, although we in general find that the most important actors in the international system are the states, there are many features of the international political system which are at odds with its state-based character. One of the developments which does not "fit" with the so-called Westphalian international political system, is the emergence of regional political integration with supranational features since the end of the Second World War. In particular, we have in Europe – with the formation of the European Communities, now the European Union – experienced a very strong form of regional political integration which goes far beyond the formation of intergovernmental regional, international organisation. The European Union has emerged as an important new kind of political entity which mixes a supranational character with intergovernmental and transnational aspects. It has developed in a dynamic way, yet it has also shown rather stable features. The 'European project' has grown so as to have a major impact on nearly all aspects of European politics and a deep influence on the societies of the participating states, even on states outside the Union, for instance the many states applying for membership in the European Union and the states in EU's vicinity, e.g. Norway, the Maghreb countries and Albania.

The impressive development of the European Union means that practically all European states are confronted with the problems of formulating their policies towards – and for the members also within – this new entity. Thus, the challenge for research which arises from regional political integration is not only to understand the major lines of development of the regional system, the European Union, but

Theoretical Perspectives 101

also to analyse the strategies and policies of individual states in relation to the new regional political system and the effects of European integration on the individual states and societies. This also implies that studies of the policies of individual states should be seen in such broader context. With the gradual steps towards further European integration, lately the steps taken with the Maastricht Treaty of 1993, the Amsterdam Treaties of 1998, and the many important issues on the EU's present and somewhat overloaded agenda (described in chapter 14), it has become even more important for governments to formulate their strategies and policies related to the EU.

The contention of the following analysis is that with the confrontation of individual states with developed forms of regional political integration, a special kind of policy is of increased relevance: *integration policy*. The aim of the following chapter is to consider how we can use the concept of 'integration policy' as an analytical concept which might help us understand the problems of policy formation for actors which participate in integration processes. One aspect of this problem is to analyse which types of policy, towards regional political integration, states have been pursuing historically. Another aspects is to consider how we might use the concept of 'integration policy' constructively. Can it, for instance, be used in specifying which alternative types of policy states might choose when they are confronted with specific forms of integration, or when they have taken the first steps within a specific integration process? In this perspective, the aim is to develop a concept fit for analysis of political options of what we might call semi-integrated actors. The empirical basis for the following discussion is, in particular, Denmark's policies towards the EC/EU, but the aim of the chapter is conceptual and theoretical in order to develop a more general perspective for a kind of analysis which also applies to other states that participate in the process of European integration. The specific interest is to discuss how the study of integration policy somehow transgresses the study of foreign policy and to discuss how one should understand integration policy in relation to and within very integrated regional and political systems.

The perspective of the following analysis is not only that regional political integration – from a certain stage of the integration – provokes a new kind of policy of participating actors, *integration policy,* but also that states participating in integration experiences an *integration dilemma*. Further, it is the contention that – from a certain stage of integration – regional integration provokes *a "societialisation" of political issues related to integration*, and possibly also *a new politicisation of integration issues*. Said differently, political questions related to integration will move from being predominantly a question of foreign policy and questions of governmental policy to becoming issues that involve more societal actors and are marked by a diffusion of involved actors and issues. The integration issues might be linked to domestic or crossboundary cleavages in societies and lead to new political disagreements.

Section two of the chapter discusses the definition of integration policy and differentiates between different dimensions of this kind of policy. *Section three* discusses how integration policy can be studied, and it tries in particular to clarify the relationship between integration policy and foreign policy. The discussion takes its point of departure in two approaches to analysis of foreign policy: the decision-making approach and the adaptation approach. These are illustrated by two different models. The perspective is not only how we are to analyse the structures and actors which might influence a concrete state's integration policy. The perspective is also how we are to analyse the opposite chain of influence: the wider consequences which the external development of a regional system might have for national policy-making. Special attention is given to the problems related to the so-called *'by-pass'* and the *'integration dilemma'*.

Section four discusses in which way the regional political integration in the European Union might be understood. The basic view is that integration policies depend on the character of the system in which the actor in question is being (semi-) integrated. The EU is here seen as a political system with a mixture of different structural features, primarily as a combination of intergovernmental, supranational and transnational structures.

Finally, in *section five* it is discussed how the character of alternative regional systems might influence the contexts of integration policy and, thus, also the policies themselves and their dynamic development. The section presents two different kinds of regional political integration, i.e. integration as a) being dominated by an intergovernmental structure, and as b) being dominated by supranational and transnational decision-making. In a somewhat simplified discussion on the basis of two models it is attempted to specify what the effects of each kind of integration are on the integration policy and the dynamics of integration. Special attention is paid to the effects that different forms of integration have on the participating societies. One might also say that the topic is how participation in the European Union implies processes of *socialisation* and *Europeanisation* in the participating societies. Some of these perspectives are illustrated by reference to problems in Denmark's policy towards the EC/EU. The chapter is concluded by a brief summary and a discussion of perspectives which link the chapter to other parts of this anthology.

2. On concepts and problems in the study of integration policy

2.1. Integration policy and its different dimensions

In a *broad* understanding of 'integration policy' we might define it as *the strategies and policies which an actor pursues in relation to a – more or less – 'integrated system'*.[1] A more narrow definition corresponds roughly to the one mentioned

---

1 More generally, we might claim that a social system is integrated when it has a high degree of coherence, either by constituting a community, by a high degree of interaction or by a binding common decision making process. Thus, one might regard a social system as an integration system when it contains processes which show the existence of a common community/common identity, a strong interdependence or a common decision making centre.

above: *the strategies and policies of individual states towards and/or within the formation of new international political centres with some kind of supranationality.*[2] If we talk about international political integration, integration policy is the policy which actors pursue in relation to the new regional political entity. Applied to the EU, integration policy is the policy of actors in relation to and/or within the EU. Often we will talk of the integration policies of states or governments, and for the sake of simplification, I will mainly do so in the following discussion. But integration policy is also relevant for other actors, and – from a certain stage in the integration process – the primacy of focus on states has to be abandoned. Thus, we might also speak of integration policies of other actors (for instance the integration policy of a political party, a social movement and possibly a governmental agency).

It should be noted that by integration policy we do *not* mean a policy which needs to support integration or contribute to further integration. A policy which for instance aims at *de*creasing the degree of supranationality in a given integration system, is also an integration policy.[3] Neither do we, by using the word, intend to apply any value judgement in regard to whether integration is a good or bad thing.

We might distinguish between *different dimensions of integration policies.* One aspect of a state's integration policy towards a more or less integrated unit relates to its participation or non-participation in the new unit, for instance by *becoming a member* or not. Other aspects relates to the problems which a state has – when it has become a member – in defining and pursuing more concrete integration policies. Thus, a second aspect of integration policy relates to the state's (or actor's) *position* in the integration system. For instance whether it is a powerful or weak member, what rights it can claim for itself, whether it places itself in the centre of the decision-making structure or at its margin etc.[4] A third aspect refers to the views that the state/actor in question might have in regard to *changes* in the institutionalisation of the new integration system. Actors might have very different views on the preferable future of the integration system, and an important part of an integration policy has to do with the ways in which the state/actor in question attempts to influence the future institutionalisation of the integration system. A fourth aspect has to do with the wishes which a state/actor might have about the integration

---

2 I include the word strategies in the definition in order to underline the analytical aspect of the term. Integration policy has not only to do with concrete policies but is also related to the definition of strategies and strategic options.

3 One could talk of such a policy as a "disintegration policy", but I prefer to use the concept integration policy in a broad sense, leaving it open whether the policies do lead to more or less integration. Sometimes we might experience that policies which aim at integration, lead to disintegration and vice versa, and in order to leave it as an open question whether an integration policy actually leads to more or less integration, one should avoid making prejudgements on this in the term itself.

4 It is somewhat unclear what exactly we mean by "position". It is assumed, though, that the integration system has some kind of structure, and that an actor has at least some choice in "positioning" itself within this structure. But it should be discussed further how one can reach a clearer view of this aspect.

system's *internal policy output,* i.e. its political output in relation to the participating societies. We might here distinguish between the economic, socio-cultural, legal, political, military and possibly other aspects of the policy output and relate these distinctions to sector policies. Thus, also the policy which a state/actor might wish pursued in regard to a specific sector – for instance in regard to participation in further economic integration, in regard to the character of the environmental policy of the new entity, or in regard to its security policy – is part of its integration policy. Finally, an aspect of integration policy has to do with strategies and policies in regard to the new unit's *external policy output,* i.e. its policies as an entity towards different subsystems in its external environment, towards other states, towards international organisations, or for instance towards external negotiations or crises.

If we, for instance, focus on the relation between Denmark and the EU, the integration policy of the Danish government comprises 1) the policy which the Danish government has pursued in relation to becoming a member of the EC/EU and also the policy – if it should become a policy – of possible withdrawal; 2) the policies which the Danish government pursues concerning Denmark's position in the EU (for instance in regard to the Danish reservations from the Edinburgh Agreement); and 3) the policies of Denmark towards the future character of the EU and it institutional development (for instance in regard to institutional changes at future intergovernmental conferences, in relation to enlargement or in relation to "openness"). The integration policy of the Danish government includes, in addition, 4) the policies which Denmark pursues within the EU in specific areas (for instance in regard to agricultural policy, environmental policy or competition policy); and 5) the Danish policy in regard to the action that EU should or should not undertake in relation to other states (for instance EU's policy towards the United States, EU's policy in Kosovo, – in general, the Common Foreign and Security Policy, the CFSP).

We might add that there are some kinds of policies that indirectly are part of an integration policy. It could for instance be 6) the policies concerning the way in which a state organises its decision-making in regard to the EU (for instance the policy which in Denmark regulates the interaction between the interests organisations, the administration and the parliament, "Folketinget", in the Danish EU-decision-making); or 7) the policies which the Danish government might pursue internally in Denmark in order to adapt (or not to adapt) to the policies of the EU.[5] In another terminology we might claim that the integration in the EU involves important processes of 'Europeanisation of national policy-making', and that this aspect also is involved in the states' integration policies.

---

5 Thus, in a broad understanding of 'Denmark's' integration policy, we might also include these policy areas. We could also include policies which other Danish actors (for instance Danish local governments, Danish interest groups or Danish members of the European Parliament) follow towards or in the European Union. If we include this, it is important to distinguish between the integration policy of the Danish government and Denmark's integration policy.

It is possible to differentiate further between different integration policies. In particular, it might be relevant to include a time-dimension which takes into account that an integration system might develop from one degree and kind of integration into another, and that – partly as a consequence – the political challenges from participating in the integration process might include changes in integration policy.[6]

We do not in the academic literature find much theory concerning the study of integration policies. Most studies treat integration policy as part of the foreign policy of the state in question. We might – with Lykke Friis – talk of 'the lacuna of integration policy theory' (Friis 1995). Theories of political integration – the 'classical integration theories' – have mainly examined integration processes 'as seen from the centre'. When, for instance, Ernest Haas discussed different ways in which states could negotiate with each other and became fascinated by the possibility that in proper institutional settings, states could be moved from reaching the 'lowest common denominator' to 'splitting the differences' and even – if power was given to a common, independent actor – to the 'upgrading of the common interests', then this was seen in the perspective that the whole regional political system could be integrated through gradual processes (Haas 1961). The classical integration theories, functionalism, neofunctionalism, federalism, transactionalism or intergovernmentalism, have also focussed on the development of the integration system as such, typically the EC/EU, from the viewpoint of the new institutional centre, typically the Commission. They have, in general, not analysed the process and problems as seen from the position of those who are (or are not) to be integrated.[7]

Sometimes a parallel is drawn between the problems of integration policy, and the problems related to the foreign policies of small states, and we might ask how the relationship is between theories of integration policy and the so-called 'small states theory'.[8] Some of the literature on small states has been concerned with international cooperation and for instance with the interests of small states in the formation of regimes.[9] But little attention has, at least until recently, been paid to the policies

---

6 Thus, we might also differentiate between integration policies in regard to different phases within an integration process. We might also differentiate between strategies in regard to different levels of – or parts of – the integration system.
7 For recent discussions of integration theories, see Kelstrup (1998), and Rosamond (2000).
8 It is frequently discussed, what we mean by a small state and whether we need special theories for small states. Without going into an elaborate discussion, I'll just state that I prefer to talk about a small state not as defined by its size nor – a priori – as a state with a certain behaviour, but as *a state which has relatively few resources as compared to other states*. This also implies that small states might be strong states in the sense that they have a high degree of internal coherence, but they might also be weak states, i.e. being characterised by internal cleavages. A special category of small states are 'mini-states' which in a comparative perspective hardly have any resources at all.
9 For early 'small state theory' see for instance Amstrup (1976). For 'adaptation theory' see i.a. Rosenau (1981), Petersen (1977, 1989, 1995, 1998 and contribution to this volume) and Mouritzen (1988 and 1993). See also Kelstrup (1993b) and Mouritzen, Wæver and Wiberg (eds.) (1996).

of small states in regard to stronger forms of integration. When 'integration' has been in focus, it has mainly been treated as international cooperation, and the specific problems that follow from the stronger forms of integration which affect the authority and character of the states, have in general been neglected. In addition, within the so-called 'small-state theory' the highest priority has been given to the study of the dependencies which small states experience in relation to power politics and the different ways in which small states might survive through different ways of balancing and adaptation. But small states are not only greatly affected by stronger forms of integration, they might also get special opportunities within such new political systems. There seems – also from the point of view of small states – to be a special need for attention to integration policies.[10] But, obviously, integration policy is relevant for all states confronted with or participating in international political integration.[11]

2.2 On approaches to integration policy

The study of 'integration policy' can be approached from different perspectives. The most obvious perspective is to link the study of integration policy to policy analysis in general. In this perspective, which is the predominant approach in this volume, integration policy is regarded as a special kind of state policy which may be studied in parallel with studies of other kinds of state policies, domestic and foreign. Thus, we may analyse how collective decisions are made in the concrete state in question. We should ask about the importance of rules, formal organisation, different domestic actors and their strategies, common views, common traditions and historically specific circumstances etc. This implies interest in and focus upon the historical settings, traditions, institutions, public opinion, interest organisations, social movements, parties, constellations in the parliament, government views and perceptions. Many of the analyses in the following chapters of this volume aim at analysing such aspects of the Danish policy towards Europe after 1945.

Another approach takes its point of departure in the study of foreign policy and discusses ways in which 'integration policy' is linked to foreign policy, but also differs from this, the presumption being that the two are not identical but closely connected. In this perspective the study of 'Denmark's policies towards Europe' can be seen as closely associated to the special part of Denmark's foreign policy which relates to European affairs, but which includes aspects of this policy which "transcends" foreign policy and relates more directly to policies and strategies pursued towards and within the new political entity, now the European Union.[12] The

---

10 For analyses which include this perspective, see Sundelius (1995) and Hansen (1997).
11 Some large states might depend very much on integration. For instance, it has been of crucial importance for Germany to pursue an integration policy.
12 See the discussion in chapter 2 of Denmark's policy towards Europe and the discussion in chapter 3 on adaptation theory.

following discussion in this chapter takes its point of departure in the study of foreign policy, in particular in the so called adaptation theory, and discusses how the study of integration policy transgresses the study of foreign policy.

A third approach to the study of integration policy relates the concept to the so called integration theories, but develop the special aspect of these which relates to the position of individual states.[13] Thus, instead of asking – as it is most frequently done in the integration theories – about the dynamics which form the processes of regional political integration as such, the approach here is to ask in which way we shall interpret the policies of individual states in relation to different kinds of regional political integration, in casu different basic structures within European integration. A major perspective in this approach is that the policy of the state towards an integration system must take into account which kind of integration system it relates to and incorporate an understanding of the dynamic features of this. For instance, there are important differences between a situation when a state is integrated in a rather loose intergovernmental structure, for instance an international regime, and a situation in which a state is integrated in a more comprehensive and tight political system which comprises a high degree of supranationality and a comprehensive negotiation system. The last part of this chapter elaborates on this approach. It is done, first, through a description of major features of the EU, and then – in section five – through a discussion of the dynamics that are at play in relation to different "paradigmatic structures" of the integration system of the EU.

3. On the study of foreign policy and integration policy

Foreign policy can be regarded as the policy of a state (or, if we distinguish between state and government, the policy of a government) towards other states and/or international organisations and other actors outside the state itself. Thus, foreign policy has a decision-making aspect and can be regarded as a special kind of policy analysis. There is no generally accepted 'theory' of foreign policy, but considerably much controversy about approaches to the study thereof.[14] Here, I shall distinguish between two different approaches which might not be mutually exclusive and each have different variants, the traditional decision-making approach and the adaptation approach.

---

13 As mentioned, recent overviews of integration theories can be found in Kelstrup, 1998, or Rosamond (2000).
14 See i.a. Snyder et al. (1954), Rosenau (1966), Allison (1971), Smith (1986), Hermann et al. (1995), Carlsnæs and Smith (1994), Wæver (1994). A small overview is in Gustavsson (1998).

3.1 The traditional decision-making approach

The approach, which we call the 'traditional' approach to the study of foreign policy, or the *foreign policy decision-making approach,* focuses particularly on the decision-making process which leads to the foreign policy of a particular state. The decision-making approach to analysis of foreign policy can in some ways be seen as an alternative to another approach which mainly sees the foreign policy of an individual state as dependent on the position of the state within the international system, i.e. the realist or neorealist approach.[15] The decision-making approach is in particular concerned with the domestic structures, institutions, rules, actors and perceptions which – as they are institutionalised historically – form the policy decisions of the state in question. Thus, there is a close link from this kind of analysis to the study of national policy-making in other issue areas. Important questions are: which domestic *actors* (for instance parties, interest groups, voters), which specific historical *'circumstances'* and/or which *perceptions* (traditions or doctrines) *and goals* have influenced the policy process and the outcome of the foreign policy decision-making process?

In general, the traditional decision-making approach put much emphasis on domestic variables, but we find different variations of the approach which give different weight to different aspects. One variation, in particular based on the early studies of Snyder, Bruck and Sapin (1954/1962), sees the foreign policy decision making as dependent not as much on 'objective factors' as on the decision-makers 'subjective definition of the situation'. In another variation the focus is mainly on structural conditions, formal institutions and the influence of actors and their interests on the central decision-makers in the state. Partly, this was formulated as a "pre-theory" by James Rosenau (1966) and in the early 1970s developed into quantitatively based research programs on comparative foreign policy. The results of this endeavour was relatively meagre. The quantitative comparative foreign policy approach was heavily criticised (Smith 1986), and there has been very few attempts to continue it in the quantitatively oriented comparative foreign policy approach.

Foreign policy analysis has since then operated with "middle-range theories" which often operate with alternative approaches, but let the individual studies focus on the influence of one particular explanatory factor (see also Gustavsson 1998). A classical example of a study which contrasts different models which all

---

15 We find such a view in the realist or neorealist perspective which see the international political system as having its own (anarchic and polar) structure and see this as determining the overall development of the international system as well as the position of each individual state. We do not find a neorealist theory of foreign policy, understood as a theory which explains or predicts a certain behaviour of individual states. But we find a theory about the external conditions of each state, and these conditions are seen as having fundamental importance for the 'room' of action of the state (e.g. Walt 1987).

relate to the decision-making approach, is Graham Allison's study of the American decision-making process concerning the Cuban missile crisis in 1962 (Allison 1971). Allison contrasts a model of rational decision making with an organizational-process model and a bureaucratic-politics model and uses them all in the interpretation of the decision-making in relation to the crisis. In some variations psychological and cognitive aspects get special emphasis (i.e. Jervis 1976). A permanent problem in the decision-making approach is how to treat the link between "objective factors" and "perceptions". One might say that it is very hard to find solutions to this problem, although different attempts have been made. In recent years the use of discourse analysis in relation to foreign policy analysis has contributed to a new perspective on this problem.[16]

With the danger of oversimplification we can illustrate the decision-making approach to foreign policy in the following model, also using it as one approach to the understanding of integration policy. In model 1 it is shown how the foreign policy of a state can be seen as formed mainly through the internal decision making processes of the state in question. The foreign policy appears as a result of the domestic policy-processes which lead to the decisions of the government. The foreign policy is influenced by the institutions, rules, norms and perceptions which characterise the historical institutionalisation of the policy system of the state. The public opinion and sub-actors in the society in question, for instance interest groups, parties, the parliament and the administration, will have influence. But also traditions and other internal constraints have importance. Major influence is usually attributed to the government itself, possibly also to people in charge, i.e. the prime minister and the foreign minister.

In such a somewhat simplified view of the foreign policy decision-making, the policy towards the EU is regarded as part of the state's foreign policy. The addition, by introducing the EU as an "integration system" or an international organisation, is that the state in question also, *within* its foreign policy, has to formulate a policy towards this body, for instance towards the EC/EU. In this interpretation 'integration policy' is seen mainly as an aspect of cooperation between states, i.e. as part of a state's intergovernmental relations within international regimes or institutions.

---

16 Discourse analysis puts special emphasis on the discourses which dominate communication in the system that leads to the formulation of foreign policy (and integration policy), e.g. Weldes (1996), Larsen (1999). In my view this kind of analysis can be seen as a special variant of the decision-making model. It offers a positive contribution to overcoming the difficulties created by the distinction between "objective" and "subjective" factors. Yet, it might be subject to the criticism of putting too little emphasis on the environment of the state.

Model 1

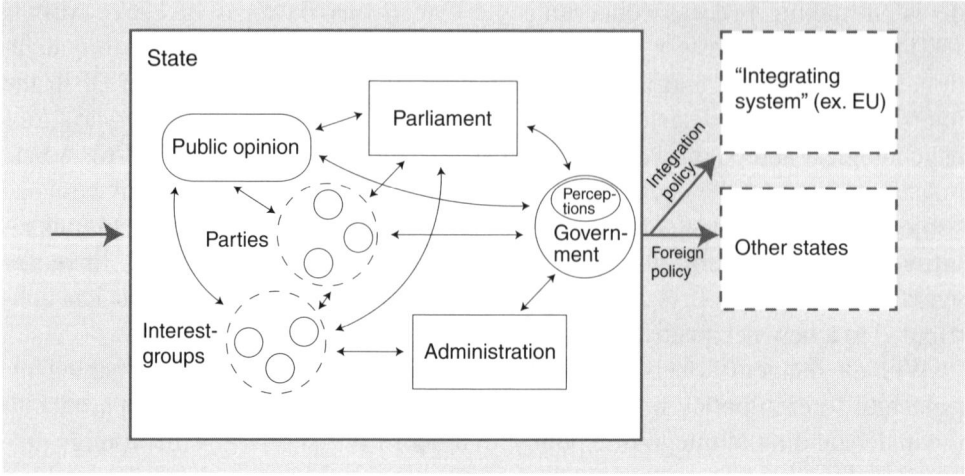

As the model indicates, the government is considered responsible for the foreign policy of the state, and the integration policy is seen as a part of the foreign policy. The decision making process which leads to the governmental policy is influenced partly by the actors at the domestic political scene and partly by the perceptions of the decision makers. Public opinion, parties, interest groups, parliament and administration – and possibly other institutions – might have influence, but also perceptions, based i.a. on tradition and cognitive structures are important. The model illustrates that the institutions interact in conjuncture with perceptions, but there is not a clear picture of this interaction. If this model is taken as a 'paradigm', the purpose of a concrete analysis is to describe the foreign policy and the integration policy of the state and to find out, how the final outcome is determined by the internal policy processes in the state.

In general, the decision-making approach can be useful in organising an analysis of the foreign policy of a state and possibly also in an analysis of a state's integration policy, for instance in an analysis of the integration policy of Denmark. But the approach seems to be misleading in two important aspects. The first is that the approach tends to place an insufficient weight – and a too undifferentiated view – on the external environment of the state in question. The second is that it seems to be insufficient in regard to more developed forms of integration. As it shall be illustrated later in this article, when integration proceeds beyond a certain degree of integration, integration policy changes character and "proliferates" away from being a special kind of foreign policy.

These reservations are particularly important in relation to the situations in which small states become semi-integrated actors. Since small states have relatively scarce resources as compared to other states, they are in general very vulnerable and sensitive to their international environment. And when small states become deeply involved in integration processes, it is quite insufficient to analyse

Theoretical Perspectives *111*

their problems and options as if they were dealing with other states in an intergovernmental framework and not in much more binding and complex integration systems.

In spite of these reservations, the traditional decision-making approach does constitute a usable framework for more elaborate analysis of special aspects of a state's European policy. The application of the approach implies an elaboration of historical-contextual descriptions, in casu of the importance which different actors, circumstances, perceptions and goals have had for the Danish policy towards Europe after 1945.

3.3 The adaptation approach to foreign policy

Another approach to the study of foreign policy is as mentioned the so called *adaptation approach*.[17] The main perspective in this is that the foreign policy of any state, also a small state, is seen as determined by internal *and* external forces. The essence of this thinking is that different balances between internal and external forces (related to 'stress sensitivity' and 'influence capability') leads to different 'modes of adaptation' and, thus to different types of foreign policy. Thus, the theory of adaptation has developed a typology of foreign policy modes. Each mode corresponds to a special 'balance' between internal and external determinants. Briefly summarised, major alternatives for a government exposed to external and internal influences are:

a) The actor might attempt to change or shape its environment in accordance with its domestic interests, following a *'dominant' mode of adaptation*. This is typically the foreign policy mode of great powers.
b) The actor might attempt to find a balance between internal interests and external demands, following a *'balanced' mode of adaptation*. This is typically the foreign policy mode of powers which have important influence on their environments but not the capacity to dominate.
c) The actor might be weak but attempt to avoid the external demands by seeking isolation (*'quiescent adaptation'*). This is a typical small state option.
d) The actor might be weak but attempt to solve the problems of conflicting internal and external demands by – partly – giving in to demands from the outside, yet maximizing the realization of internal interests (*'acquiescent adaptation'*). This too is a typical small state option.

Without going deeply into the discussion of the theory of adaptation, we might ask how this approach deals with the special problems of integration policy. Seen in the

---

17 See i.a. Mouritzen (1988 and 1993), Mouritzen et al. (1996), Petersen (1977, 1989, 1995 and 1998), see also Nikolaj Petersen's discussion in chapter 3.

perspective of adaptation theory, integration policy is still regarded as a part of the foreign policy of a state. A small state still has to evaluate its policy towards other states, and also in regard to integration, on the basis of its (relatively weak) position among great powers. It is an important perspective, though, that integration might give states – and not least small states – better possibilities of influencing the external environment and thereby greater possibilities for pursuing a balanced foreign policy than they would otherwise have. In addition, if integration involves a change in the international environment from power politics to other forms of politics, for instance consensual politics, the relative influence capability of a small state can be seen as greater than in a system dominated by power politics. If integration evolves from being a rather unimportant aspect of the environment to becoming an important part of the environment of a state, then the character of the integration system itself might become one of the 'determinants' of the integration policy of the individual state.

The perspective on the study of integration policy which rest on 'theories of adaptation', but includes the adaptation to an "integration system", here the EU, might be illustrated in the following model:

Model 2

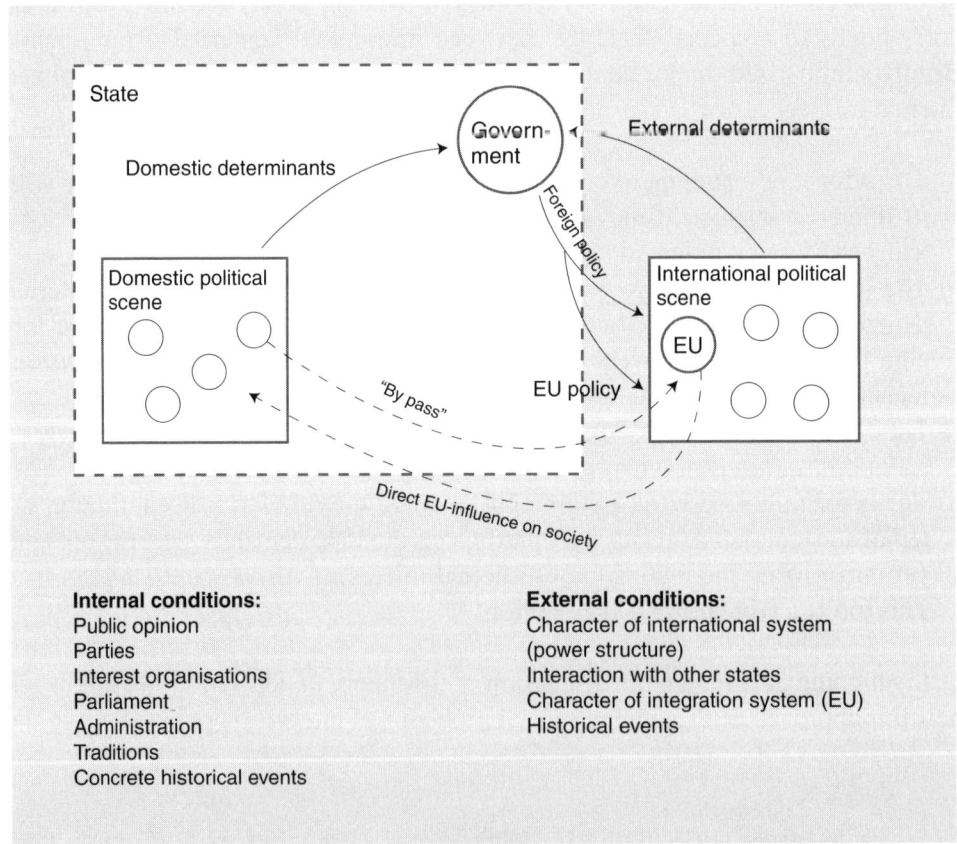

The model illustrates how the government of an individual state simultaneously is exposed to internal and external pressures. It might be assumed that sometimes these pressures are externally dominated, sometimes internally dominated. Further, it is likely that some government might experience severe cross pressures between internal and external demands, and maybe the government will be in a practically impossible situation, for instance in a situation in which it either has to follow "double standards" or take serious conflicts either internally or externally.[18] At other times there might be a great "room of manoeuvre" for the government within the external and internal constraints. I have in the model illustrated how the EU policy of the government in question is part of its foreign policy, and how the EU can be seen as an important part of the state's international environment. The two dotted arrows should be seen as indications of links which the model does not cover sufficiently. They illustrate that the integration might go further by 1) direct influence of the EU directly in the national society, and 2) by direct influence from the national society on the EU which "bypasses" the state and goes directly into the integration system.

According to this approach the study of a state's integration policy, in this case the EU-policy, can be seen as being in a cross pressure between internal and external demands. An investigation requires *both* an understanding of the domestic scene of the individual state in question *and* an understanding of the external scene, in casu the phenomenon of European political integration. Only on the basis of an analysis of both of these 'complexes' and the ways in which they have influenced the decision-makers historically can we reach an understanding of the determinants of the concrete integration policy. It is important to include the historical dimension, also because of changes on the domestic as well as on the external scene.

The model does at a general level generate important questions. It is an interpretation which places itself between a traditional decision-making analysis and a (neorealist inspired) interpretation which holds that the external environment *determines* or dominates the foreign policy of some states (in particular small states). In relation to the traditional decision-making approach it turns the focus on the balance and interplay between domestic and external developments. In relation to the neorealist-inspired interpretation it points to limitations of such a view.

We might argue that it is a question for empirical investigation to find out how the balance and interplay has been between domestic and international developments. Using the model on integration politics also implies that we ask whether we shall interpret the external pressures on a specific state mainly on the basis of its position in relation to other states/powers/poles or give weight to the integration

---

18 One might find many instances in which a government has had an inconsistent policy of which one part is directed towards parts of its international environment, and other parts are more for domestic use. An example is the "double" Danish policy in regard to acceptance of nuclear weapons on the Thule air base. One of the advantages of the adaptation approach is in my view that it exposes the double pressure on governments.

system as such, and if so – what kind of weight? Another important question is, whether we see the influence of the integration system as one of the factors which influence a state's integration policy, what importance we attribute to the *character* of the integration system? In the following section I shall return to these questions.

A major problem in the 'adaptation-approach' to the study of foreign policy is the rather broad categories in relation to strategies or 'modes of adaptation'. In particular, it is necessary to be more specific in regard to the analysis of 'balanced' adaptation, because this category becomes too broad and might have several subcategories. For instance, it is not very concrete to say that Denmark, because of its participation in integration, has the possibility of a balanced mode of foreign policy. Another problem is that the adaptation approach has the same difficulties concerning the relationship between "objective" and "subjective" factors as the decision-making approach. One might argue that the two approaches do not differ fundamentally, and that some of the thoughts from the one could be used on the other. A third problem which is of special relevance in regard to the study of integration politics, is that the adaptation approach does not effectively capture the situation in which the integration has proceeded so that a state has become a semi-integrated actor within a new integration system. Said differently, the adaptation approach has important limitations in relation to analysis of deeper forms of integration.

3.4 How the study of integration policy transcends the study of foreign policy

I shall argue that integration politics can only be regarded as part of the foreign policy of an individual state when the integration in question has not proceeded long and is still on an intergovernmental stage. In relation to more integrated systems, i.e. systems in which there is a significant amount of supranationality and in which there are important direct links between institutions and bodies outside a state and citizens within the state, integration policy cannot be subsumed as a part of foreign policy. And this is problematic, in theory as well as in practice.

The problem, though, is how we find a framework for analysing integration policy in constellations in which states are not in possession of an immutable authority where regional political systems have gained (limited, but substantial) supranational powers, and states are being involved as semi-integrated actors in a new political decision-making system. Obviously, the way of posing the problem implies that we regard authority as a quality that can be transferred partially to new entities and new organizations within functionally specific areas.[19] The study of integration policy should include this perspective, i.e. we should include the study of policies which relate to transfer of authority to the EC/EU, and we should see these policies as bound not only by external, but also by internal concerns. Typically the

---

19 I prefer to speak of transfer of authority rather than to talk of division of or partial transfer of sovereignty, see also discussion later in this article.

new decision-making centre makes collective decisions which implies that parts of the state authority is transferred to the new decision centre, and the new multi-level decision making systems might evolve in a way which affects the authority of the individual government vis à vis its own society. Thus, we are discussing the way in which individual states are affected by relatively 'deep' and yet functionally 'uneven' integration.[20]

One way ahead is to link the conceptualisations of integration policies closer to an understanding of regional integration and of different kinds of regional integration, also of different forms of regional political integration. Since there is a close relationship between integration theories and policies of integration, it is quite natural that the way in which we understand regional integration has a major influence on the way in which we view the possible policies towards regional integration.[21]

4. On different types and degrees of regional political integration: The character of the European Union

This section is particularly concerned with different types and degrees of international political integration. The basic understanding behind the somewhat sketchy analysis which follows is the view which introduced the article: The international political system is, particularly in some areas, moving away from being primarily state-based. In the European Union we find a rather integrated regional political system, and we cannot discuss integration policies in regard to such a system without considering more explicitly what the character of this integration system is. Furthermore the contentions are that the basic structures of the EU can be seen as a mixture of different patterns, that the relative weight between these patterns, respectively intergovernmental, supranational and transnational substructures, has been shifting over time, and that this influences integration policies in important ways. The EU is neither a pure intergovernmental, supranational nor transnational system, but rather an intermediate mixture which contains different structural elements and dissolves the "hard shells" (borders) of the individual states.

4.1 On the concept of regional political integration

Obviously, it is important how we view – and define – integration and how we specify different forms of integration.[22] In a very abstract terminology *integration*

---

20 The integration might also be geographically uneven.
21 This seems to be true not only in theory, but also in practice. Thus, the difficulties in understanding the complexities of the EU seems to increase the difficulties of finding concepts to define practical integration policies.
22 For discussions on this, see i.a. the classical integration theories. See also Kelstrup (1992b and 1998), and Rosamond (2000).

might be said to refer either to a process or a state of affairs. As process, integration can be defined as *the process through which units are becoming parts of a greater unit*, and as a state of affairs, integration can be defined as the degree of *internal coherence* in the system in question. We might talk of different *degrees of integration,* and of integration in relation to different kinds of social systems, i.a. in relation to political systems, economic systems or legal systems, and in parallel we may talk of *political, economic, legal and socio-cultural integration.*

In the international system we can define regional international integration as the formation of regional units within the international system and regional political integration as the formation in the international political system of new, regional political systems with decision-making centres and a basic political community, possibly a common political identity, yet, most likely without developing into a new state. Regional political integration implies that the states involved somehow become parts of a greater unit in the international political system. It is much discussed in the academic literature how such 'new' political units are to be characterized, and a basic – if not *the* basic problem in integration theory – is how they emerge and develop. Without going into discussions on details here, I shall indicate that I prefer the terminology which describes international political integration as the *formation of new political systems.* This can combine the institutional and community-/identity-aspect of integration.[23] A strong form of international political integration is in this perspective equal to the formation of a strong political system with common institutions, a common decision making centre with an ability to produce collective decisions which are binding for a new and greater political constituency, combined with a strong legitimacy based on a strong sense of political community.[24]

Our main concern in this context is with integration which is more than cooperation between states. We might see cooperation between states – for instance formation of international regimes and intergovernmental institutions – as 'weak' forms of integration. But crucial problems in the understanding of integration and integrations policies are related to stronger forms of integration, i.e. to processes which lead to the formation of new entities which affect the states in their decision making, affect their position as unitary centres of authority and involve their societies in new supranational and transnational processes.[25] Thus, the core of integration theory has to do with the historical and institutional formation of new units

---

23 The term 'political system' has the advantage of combining the perspective of on the one hand formal institutions and decision-making and on the other hand identity aspects related to political community. I have discussed this in other articles, see for instance Kelstrup (1992b and 1993a).
24 Legitimacy is here seen as a dimension which combines community and authority. It is important that strong integration is not necessarily equal to supranationality. It refers to coherence of a political system – in many different dimensions.
25 See later for a brief discussion of sovereignty, a concept which I, on purpose, do not use here.

which are new political systems and more than a set of international regimes or institutional frameworks for cooperation between states.

It is clear that the formation of the EC/EU is a very important case of regional political integration, probably at present the most important one. In the international systems we find much cooperation between states, many international regimes and international institutions. But in no other cases do we find new regional entities which have the same degree of institutionalisation, such a scale of common decision making and such a degree of legal integration as the EU. Thus, the questions related to 'strong' forms of regional integration are of particular relevance in relation to the processes which in Europe have lead to the formation of the European Community, now the European Union. Some will argue that the EU is a system 'sui generis'. This is true in some sense, since we do not find similar systems. Yet, the EU can, in spite of its uniqueness, be regarded as an example of regional political integration, and the problems which we meet in studying integration policies in regard to the EU, have a more general nature. We do see other examples of regional political integration (for instance in NAFTA, MERCOSUR and ASEAN), and the comparative perspective on regional political integration is important.

Although I characterise the European Union as a (relatively) new political system with new formal institutions, a common decision making system and at least some degree of political community, we experience – in the literature and in different interpretations among politicians and others – great uncertainties concerning the character of the European Union. There are still analysts who regard the EU as mainly an *intergovernmental political system* in which the states still are 'sovereign', although they might have 'pooled' some of their powers. Others view the EU as 'nearly' a federation, i.e. as a *semi-federation* characterised by a substantial amount of common, supranational decision-making and by a Treaty of the European Union which functions as a kind of constitution. Others, again, view the EU as essentially a *transnational system* – or as a political framework for comprehensive multi-level negotiations – which involve new interactions, communication and decision-making across traditional states borders and which does not stop at the borders of the EU but involves actors outside the community as well. I shall return to these different perspectives, which we find among practitioners as well as in the theoretical literature.

4.2. On different types of integration

As mentioned already, we might distinguish between different types of political integration. This discussion might be elaborated in many ways and in relation to many dimensions. For the sake of simplicity, I want only in this context to distinguish between three major forms of political integration: 1) Political integration as *cooperation* between states, 2) political integration as *the making of common, binding decisions,* either in functionally specific areas or with a broader scope, encompassing many decision areas, and 3) political integration as *transnationalisation.*[26] Each of these types or forms of integration places the government of an individual state in a different position facing different choices. Thus, the problems which a government has in formulating its integration policy are very different in relation to the tree forms of political integration.

It can be added that the different forms of political integration might be linked to major phases in integration processes. Thus, integration in the EU was first characterised by the formation of a common decision-making system in rather narrow functional areas (coal- and steal, market cooperation, atomic energy). It expanded gradually to include broader, intergovernmental cooperation, still in combination with common decisions within narrow functional areas.[27] From this European integration has entered a new phase in which we find a still broader common decision-making system – in an expanded community – in combination with elements of intergovernmental cooperation and of transnationalisation. The point here is not to engage in an interpretation of EU's history, but to stress that the character of integration is changing historically, not necessarily in any predetermined way, but with the consequence that the individual state cannot once and for all fix its integration policy. The integration policy of a state must depend on the perceived character of the integration system and predicted changes. For instance, policy formulations in the earlier stages of the integration process should foresee the problems which might arise from the later phases.

One form of political integration is, as mentioned, characterised as still being essentially *cooperation between states.* This is the well-known intergovernmental interpretation of political integration. The characteristic feature is that each government is responsible for – and has the ultimate authority over – its own society, that a government in its foreign concerns is mainly oriented towards other states, and that the agreements in the integration system (the international organisation, the regime, here EU's political system) are directed towards governments, binding the governments, but not directly binding the citizens (the traditional view in international law). Common decisions are essentially subject to the veto of the individual government, and implementation is made through governmental action, not in a direct link between the international institutions and the citizens.

Another form of political integration can be characterised as *common decision making,* i.e. encompassing common decisions, which are binding directly for the citizens. We might characterise this as supranational decision making.[28] The supranational element can either, as mentioned, be functionally specific or have a

---

26 It will be clear from the definition above that I here omit considerations concerning different degrees and kinds of community and focus mostly on the decision-making aspect of the integration system.
27 Many will here refer to the concept "spill over" which in particular has been heralded by the neofunctionalist integration theory.
28 If there is a veto-power for the individual state in the system, it should be considered as a mix between an intergovernmental and a common decision-making system, depending on the extend and conditionality of the veto power.

broader and more general scope. The decision making process might be institutionalised in many different ways, possibly with formal as well as real powers to common institutions. Thus, there are very many variations of common decision making, and they might give greater or lesser influence to the individual states, maybe in a rather asymmetrical way. The integration policy of the individual state is in this form of political integration very dependent on the concrete institutionalisation of the decision-making system in the integration system (in this context, the EU), its position within the system, not only it position as compared to other states, but also its position in the institutionalised structure of the system. The integration system might give possibilities for influence for the state in question, but it might also have formal or informal structures and rules which prevent much influence or limits state influence to specific policy areas.[29] At the same time, the common decisions might seriously affect the domestic authority of the individual government.

It is in particular in relation to this form of integration that a state in the integration process might be confronted with an *'integration dilemma'*: the dilemma of an 'either/or' choice: *either* the state gives up a substantial part of its political authority with the danger of being *'entrapped'* in the integration system, i.e. being so constrained that it loses its freedom of action and thereby its ability to pursue its own interests, **or** the state insists on its independence with the danger of being *'abandoned'*, i.e. not included in the integration process with the disadvantages which might ensue.[30] This dilemma might be posed both to non-members when they consider joining an already strongly integrated system, or to members in a system when integration intensifies. The members might, at one and the same time, be afraid of being 'entrapped' in further integration and afraid of being 'abandoned' and marginalised.

It is relevant to conduct case studies to see when integration dilemmas occur. We might assume that states which – like the states in Central and Eastern Europe – have regained their national sovereignty recently, might especially be exposed to the integration dilemma. Also Denmark seems in practically all basic choices in regard to the EC/EU to have experienced an integration dilemma, and this dilemma has been articulated in all of the untill now five referenda on EU questions.[31] Clearly, the character of the integration dilemma depends on the character of the integration process. Furthermore the dilemma within an irreversible integration process is much greater that in a reversible process, thus it seems to become stronger within a stronger form of integration. The integration dilemma is of particular importance

---

29 Formal thinking on this must link to theories of federations.
30 I have developed the idea of the 'integration dilemma' in Kelstrup (1991, 1992a and 1993b). The basic idea is to draw a parallel to Glenn Snyders analysis of the 'alliance dilemma', Snyder (1984). The thought has been developed further by Nikolaj Petersen (see Petersen, 1998, and his contribution to this volume).
31 See also the introduction to this volume. Further analysis of the integration dilemma could include a distinction between "objective" and "subjective" factors therein. Thus, it might not be all perceived or articulated dilemmas which – in fact – are such dilemmas.

when the integration process moves very fast, since the learning processes which should make the actors accustomed to the new levels of integration, will have difficulties in keeping up with the integration process. We might add that economic circumstances might exacerbate the integration dilemma. The danger of 'being left out' becomes greater when economic interests are also at stake. Here, I shall only point to the existence of these problems. It is a matter of more detailed analysis to find out when, in a concrete integration process, an integration dilemma exists, when it is perceived as existing, and when its articulation serves specific purposes.[32] Furthermore, the question as to whether there are ways of avoiding the dilemma or of circumventing it, deserves special discussion.

A third form of political integration sees political integration as closely related to *transnationalisation,* i.e. as processes through which the borders between societies loose importance and in which collective decision-making is developing across state borders within different areas of transnationalisation. Transnationalisation can take place at many levels at the same time, economic, socio-cultural, legal and political. It is closely linked to processes of globalization and to the emergence of "governance without government".[33] Typically, the individual government will be *'by-passed'* in a transnational environment, i.e. political demands and support will be channelled to other authorities than states, often authorities with an unclear legitimacy and a very temporal institutional basis, and these other authorities will take decisions concerning the authoritative allocations of values in societies, thus perform basic political tasks in a non-governmental institutional form.

4.3. The EU as an integrated system which combines intergovernmental, supranational, and transnational patterns

The European Union might be regarded as a combination of the three kinds of integration which we have just described. Others might use other concepts to characterise the EU, for instance the EU can be seen as a system of multilevel governance (Jachtenfuchs 1997) or characterised as a "negotiated order" (Smith 1996). Using the term multilevel governance points to the existence within the EU of negotiations at different levels with participation of different supranational, state and sub-state actors. And the term "negotiated order" points to the fact that the EU is a system in which negotiations are going on permanently at different levels with the

---

32 As indicated, the articulation of one side of the integration dilemma: the danger of being left out or the danger of being entrapped, might serve concrete and often different political purposes.

33 Globalization and the emergence of new and stronger form of "governance without government" represent major trends in the understanding of international relations and in IR-literature. See i.a. Rosenau and Czempiel (1992), Väyrynen (1999), and Hewson and Sinclair (1999). The governance perspective is very relevant in the study of the EU, see i.a. Jachtenfuchs (1997).

consequence that a single negotiation is linked to earlier negotiations, simultaneous negotiations in other decision areas and prospects in regard to future negotiations.[34] While each of these perspectives are important, I prefer in this context to regard the EU as a combination of the three different patterns mentioned, a combination in which the internal balance might shift over time.[35]

When a state or government takes part in an integration process, possibly as a semi-integrated actor, we might assume that it wants to pursue its interests in relation to all the aspects of its integration policy which was mentioned earlier. Thus, a differentiated integration policy has to be developed with regard to the states' *position* in the integration system, it attitudes towards institutional *change*, its wishes regarding the *internal output* of the integration system, and in regard to its *external output*. But analyses of these dimension require understanding of the basic structures of the integration system and an assessment of their dynamic features. The implication is that in order to analyse the integration policy of a particular state in regard to the EU (and, for a government or other actors, to make an analysis which leads to a differentiated integration policy) more detailed analysis is needed on the one hand of the positions and interests of the individual state/actor, and on the other hand the many different aspects of the EU. It lies beyond the scope of this article to go further in such an attempt. Instead I shall – in a somewhat simplified and paradigmatic way – continue this thinking and discuss how integration policies depend on the very different institutional dynamics which we find in relation to different substructures of the integration system. The purpose is, in particular, to illustrate that further analysis of integration policies have to include reflections on the interaction between the state and the system in which it integrates itself and to show how the character of integration policy itself changes when integration proceeds.

5. Integration policies and institutional dynamics in relation to the EC/EU

5.1. Further categories of integration policies

A major point in the discussion above has been that from a certain stage of integration, the integration policy of a state transcends beyond foreign policy. One might say that it becomes a mix between foreign and domestic policy, but this is an

---

34 For the negotiation approach, see i.a. Friis (1996 and 1999).

35 By doing so, I take the stand that the EU should not "solely" be seen as an intergovernmental system, nor as only a common decision-making system nor as only a transnational system. It might easily be argued that EU's decision making system is far more complex than the one presented here, for instance by pointing to the more concrete provisions of the treaties and to the practices in different parts of the system. Some will, for example, argue that the "system of comitology" (the many committees engaged in concretizing EU-decisions) comprise a special "infra-national" kind of decision making (Weiler 1999: 283ff.).

imprecise expression. Thus, it is very unclear what we mean by "domestic" when borders are transgressed.[36] Instead, it has been suggested above that we might distinguish between different dimensions of integration politics. Further, it has been argued that the integration policy of a state in regard to the different dimensions must depend on the character of the integration system, in casu on the more concrete institutionalised patterns within the European Union. It has been suggested that the basic pattern of the European Union might be understood as a dynamic mixture between intergovernmental, supranational and transnational structures.

The differentiation between dimensions of integration policy lead to the understanding that a state must follow policies in regard to its *position* in the integration system, in regard to institutional *changes* in the system, and in regard to the *internal* as well as the *external policy output* which it might want of the integration system. The thoughts on this might be elaborated.

In regard to *the position* in the system, a state might choose between "pro-active" and "reluctant" (or reactive) participation. In both cases the state might – or might not – have special reservations, i.e. areas or sectors in which it wants in some specific way to keep outside the integration process.[37] This gives us the following spectre of strategies in regard to position in the integration system:

	Pro-active participation	Reluctant participation
Without reservations	1	2
With reservations	3	4

The integration strategies of individual states in regard to the European Union might be characterised according to this rather simple picture. Typically, Germany has together with the Benelux countries and Italy pursued a policy of pro-active participation, only with minor reservations, being "front runners" in European integration (policy option 1). The picture is somewhat more mixed for France, and in characterising the French strategy one should distinguish between different historical periods. Great Britain and Denmark are examples of states which mostly have pursued a policy of reluctant participation, yet for Great Britain there has been an important shift with the "New Labour" in Government. Thus, the Great Britain can at one and the same time be pro-active in regard to the security dimension of EU and keep its reservation in regard to the EMU (policy option 3). The major Danish policy has been reluctant participation, though shifting in the late 1980s to a more active policy (a move from policy option 2 to policy option 3). Yet, in 1992-93 the Danish "no" in the refer-

---

36 One might talk of "EU-domestic" politics, but also this is unclear – for instance seen in its relation to the "normal" domestic politics of the individual states.
37 The reservations might be more or less formal. The Danish reservations which were formalised in the Edinburgh Agreement have an unusual formal status.

endum on Danish ratification of the Maastricht Treaty and the later acceptance in 1993 of the combination of the Maastricht Treaty and the Edinburgh Agreement ended in a Danish position which might be characterised as "reluctant participation with reservations" (policy option 4). The Danish reservations were made manifest in the so-called "National Compromise", and they have formed an important part of Danish EU-policy since. We shall not elaborate this perspective on pro- and reactive integration policies, but leave it to other analyses eventually to expand this further.

Integration policies concerning *institutional change* in the EU might be differentiated according to major institutional issues. There might, in particular, be different policies in regard to 1) the possible enlargement of the EU, 2) the efficiency of EU's decision making, and 3) the measures for greater democratic legitimacy of the EU. Other aspects might also be relevant. Some of the participating EU-states, including Denmark, are very much for the enlargement of the EU, other states are more reluctant in regard to this kind of institutional change of the EU. Some are very much for strengthening the efficiency of EU's institutions, i.e. by increased use of Qualified Majority Voting and fewer commissioners. Others, among them Denmark, are less inclined to accept further authority transfer to the EU. In parallel, there are different policies in regard to the democratic aspects of the EU. There are different views on giving further power to the European Parliament, different views on practices in regard to control, openness etc.

Another dimension of the integration policy is concerned with the *internal policy output* of the EU. Two important dimensions of the concern with policy output are 1) the political wish for greater economic markets, i.a. the realisation of the so-called "negative" integration within the EU and in relation to associated members, and 2) the political wish for regulation on the scale of EU (and, thus, for "positive integration") which might give possibilities that do not exist for the individual state. The relative weight on "marketisation" versus "regulation" can be seen as a major dimension in the fight within the EU between different political projects (linked, respectively, to liberal vs. social-liberal or social-democratic ideologies).

Some will argue that in the analyses of European integration too much attention has been paid to debates about "the nature of the beast", i.e. what kind of system the EU is and debates on what kind of political system it should be (Risse-Kappen, 1996), but that too little attention has been paid to debates on "the colour of the beast", i.e. debates on the kind of regulatory policy output which one should wish from the EU (Johansen 1998). Interestingly enough, we have in recent years seen growing concerns and debates – in theory and in practice – about the kind of regulatory and distributive policy the EU should follow. For instance, in the development of the Economic and Monetary Union, important debates have been about the kind of economic policy the European Central Bank should follow, especially on whether the economic policy should be linked to anti-inflation as the prime goal or also give high, or even higher, priority to employment measures. In parallel, we have a serious debate on the balance between market forces and environmental concerns. These are some of the dimensions which should be included in a differentiation of integration policy in regard to policy outcome.

Finally, it is an important dimension of integration policy what kind of *external policy output* the EU should provide. Also here we have the argument that the development of a capacity at the regional level, i.e. an external capacity of the EU, makes it possible to do things in the international setting – in trade as well as security – which the individual states cannot do. The debate is closely related to the debate about the questions whether the EU shall be an important actor in the international system, how active it should be etc. From the beginning of the EEC-cooperation it was important that the EEC should have a common external trade policy. Later dimensions in external affairs have been related to EU's tasks in relation to developing countries. After the end of the Cold War we have a debate – linked to institutional change and enlargement on EU's role in Europe, not least the recent debate and the recent measures to expand EU's foreign and security policy by adding a military dimension. The most controversial part of this dimension of integration policy is probably EU's future military dimension and the disagreements which exist concerning EU's role in this area.

This differentiation of integration policies is included to indicate areas in which the perspective of integration policy can be expanded. In the following I shall discuss features of integration policies in relation to two different kinds of integration system, respectively an intergovernmentally dominated integration system and a supranationally-transnationally dominated integration system. The main purpose is to illustrate how the major dynamics of the integration process are different in the two instances, and how this influences the problems in regard to the formulation of integration policies. It should be kept in mind, though, that the major interpretation here is that the EU contains both of these structures in combination. Thus, the interpretation that the EU either corresponds to one or the other model, should be avoided.

5.2 On integration policy towards an intergovernmentally dominated integration system

Let us first assume that a state is taking part in an intergovernmentally dominated integration system, here illustrated with an "ideal type" of this view on the EU.[38] The integration policy of the state is assumed to be formulated by its government as part of the state's foreign policy. The government takes part in the negotiations in the EU. These negotiations are mainly negotiations between states, they lead to major results, and these results are assumed to be fed back into the societies of the states. The feedback from the integration system will not only influence the society in question, but might also have influence on internal dynamics within the societies and within the political systems of the participating states. Over time, the effects of integration might also have effects on the integration policy and, thus on the future integration. These dynamic relations might be illustrated in the following model 3.

---

38 I use the "ideal type"-approach only for illustration, it is not intended to pass any judgement as to which structure the EU should have.

Model 3

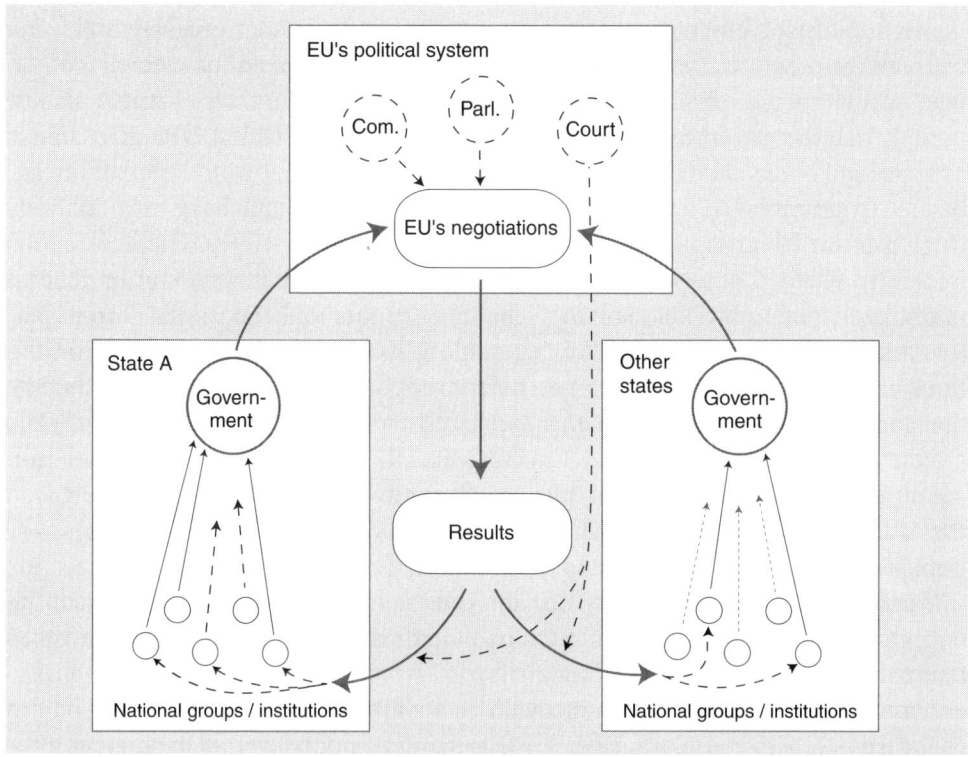

The model illustrates these relations, taking two states, A and B, as "paradigm". Negotiations are assumed mainly to take place in or in relation to the Council or at intergovernmental conferences. The Commission and the Parliament are assumed to have some, but limited influence on the negotiations which (according to the paradigm) are mainly the result of intergovernmental bargaining. It is illustrated how the Court has influence on the way on which the legal results of the negotiations are interpreted and applied.

This model might give rise to interesting reflections. Fundamentally, each government is seen as being involved in two different negotiation systems, one in relation to domestic politics, the national political system, another in relation to the EU-process.[39] The government might sometimes be so locked by internal constraints – for instance by internal positions or agreements – that it has "tied hands" in the EU negotiations. There are plenty of examples of this. For instance, the "National Compromise" which was formulated as an internal Danish agreement on the Danish policy towards the EU in 1992-93 is an example of giving the Danish government such "tied hands" in regard to the EU.[40]

---

39 There is a certain parallel to the understanding of foreign policy as "two level games" (Putnam, 1988), only here we are separating the EU as one level. We might also include the international level and use a three level perspective.
40 For a more extensive discussion of negotiations in the EU and negotiation strategies, see Moravcsik, (1994 and 1998), and Friis, (1996 and 1999).

The model also illustrates another dynamic relationship: the government might, through the involvement in the EU-negotiations, come under pressure and – because of the pressure from the other states – accept certain solutions which it otherwise would not accept. Such a participation in the EU negotiations might also be used to free the government of domestic restraints ("cut slack"). The government can use (and misuse) this in getting policies through which it would not, otherwise, be able to get accepted on the domestic political scene.[41] Some have used this view to give an explanation of why states integrate (Moravcsik 1994). The explanation is, briefly stated, that governments through participation in the integration process might be helped in problem solving. The more or less real "necessities" from participating in the intergovernmental negotiations in the EU, give legitimacy to solutions which otherwise would lack sufficient support.[42] It should be added, though, that an extensive use of this dynamic mechanism might create its own limits. When governments follow the strategy of making the EU responsible for unpopular decisions, while they themselves take the credit for popular decisions, the effect is in the long run that the EU, and, thus, the integration project as such, becomes very unpopular.[43]

Further, the model illustrates that the effects of the integration process influences the different social groups in the participating societies. It is in many ways an interesting question, how the EU decisions – directly and indirectly – affect different groupings, and how existing inequalities are affected. One picture could be that active groups, which already have resources and positions, get an even greater advantage through the integration project, while other less privileged groups tend to loose relatively by the integration project. Another picture could be that the gains of integration are spread out very broad, while the losses are more concentrated. Obviously, it should not be assumed that the gains and losses from integration represent a zero sum. Empirical investigations of the topics related to winners and loosers in the integration process are important, yet beyond the scope of this article. It is important that the effects of integration are seen in relation to the already

---

[41] Another variation in this interplay could be that a government which within a specific problem-area is "getting captured" by a certain interest group (for instance the French government being heavily influenced by French farmers), might be strengthened through its participation in EU's decision-making.

[42] Moravcsik has in an analysis, which in important aspects run parallel to the one in model 3, argued that the integration strengthens the state (Moravcsik, 1994). It is important, though, in this context to distinguish between state and government. The argument here is that integration might strengthen governments by giving legitimacy to solutions which otherwise would be difficult, thus, mainly that integration – notably in this model of or phase of integration – strengthens governments.

[43] Also in this respect there might be other dynamic relations at play: If it is recognised that the EU helps *other* governments in taking unpopular decisions, for instance decisions which do *not* solve the problems on the expense of other states, this might *increase* the popularity of the EU.

existing social and historical context. In some countries, not least in the Southern European states, the EU project has an image of being "a project of modernisation", giving advantages to new, active groups in society. In other states, notably the Nordic, it is much more problematic whether the EU's regulatory policies represent "progress" as compared to the already existing social and environmental regulation.[44]

An interesting aspect is to ask how the traditional cleavages in a society are affected by the society's participation in the integration process. Probably, it is hard to generalise about this topic since traditions, institutions and cleavages are very different among the participating countries. There are signs that the cleavages linked to integration develops across existing borders and barriers. In parallel, we might ask how integration affects the pattern of politicisation in the society in question, and to which degree questions in regard to integration policy are politicised.[45] The politicisation – and division between the pro's and con's of integration – might very well cross traditional patterns of politicisation.

In general, the intergovernmental model of EU negotiations illustrates that although we are dealing with an intergovernmental model, a more profound consideration of the dynamics involved show that integration politics involves problems which go far beyond interstate relations and traditional foreign policy. Even when we assume that states are unitary actors, the dynamics from integration affect internal processes in the societies of the participating states. In the consideration of cleavages and politicisation it seems relevant to point to one specifically problematic "mechanism": If the general pattern is that the results of the negotiations within the integration system are to the advantage of those being already active and engaged in integration, but not for others, the overall effect of integration will be the creation and growth of a cleavage between those getting advantages of and those becoming disadvantaged by the integration. Thus, further integration is, through this mechanism, also provoking a pattern of we/they identity which causes greater resistence against integration. It should be added that it is, at least partially, beyond the reach of the individual governments to decide on the distribution of the advantages of integration. These relationships represent, however, only one aspect of integration.

---

44 The Danish government's declaration of Denmark as being "a benchmark country" corresponds to such a self-image. One of the issues in the Danish debate is whether such an image is true or not.

45 Some might go even further and claim that questions in regard to integration might be "securitised" (Wæver et al. 1994). We lack in this respect more concrete analyses of the relationship between politicisation and securitisation in relation to integration.

5.3 On integration policy towards a supranationally-transnationally dominated integration system

Now, as claimed above, the integration system might develop beyond being intergovernmentally dominated. The integration system might get supranational features which – in different forms – give the institutions of the system great and relatively autonomous importance. It might also acquire transnational features, giving influence to substate and transnational actors and opening for dynamic relations across state borders.[46] As argued above, the EU has important supranational and transnational traits, although it can be considered as an open questions to which degree it is the intergovernmental or the supranational-transnational structures that at present are dominating.

In model 4 I have in a rough sketch illustrated some of the basic features of a supranationally-transnationally dominated integration system. They are here exemplified as "ideal types" of this aspect of EU's negotiation system, an image which, notably, is not taken to be a true picture, but to represent one important aspect of the EU. The basic features are:

- that the main EU institutions (in particular the European Commission and the European Parliament) are strong participants in the decision-making and negotiations in the EU,
- that the negotiations in the EU (in particular in the Council) are regulated, i.a. by rules allowing for qualified majority voting
- that the Parliament has its own basic democratic legitimacy through direct elections
- that the Commission has a direct link to some actors (in particular to governments, but also to sub-state actors, regional and transnational organisations, interest groups and individual experts),
- that there are possibilities that governmental agencies develop their own sub-policies within their policy area with the effect that governments are not always or by necessity unitary actors, and that the foreign ministries are overloaded and in practice unable to secure the unity in state policies.

---

46 In this context I treat supranational and transnational perspectives as part of one model in order not to create too many models. It is obvious, though, that the supranational and transnational aspects could be separated further than it is done in this analysis.

Theoretical Perspectives

Model 4

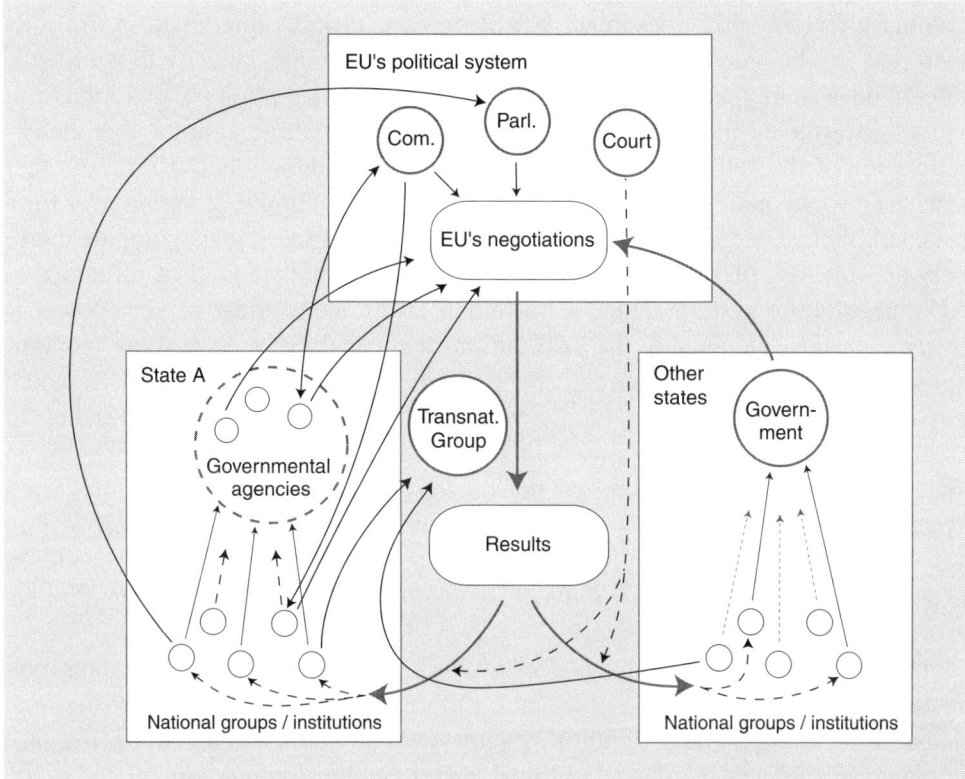

What are the dynamic features of such an integration system? One tendency is that the integration policies of the individual states are undermined. The direct links between independent actors in the society and the institutions and processes in the integration system/EU mean that there is an extensive "by pass" of the state. Such direct links can be the inclusion of interest representation in EU's negotiation system (for instance private enterprises participating in negotiations on standardisation), national courts accepting the preliminary rulings of the European Court of Justice, local and regional political bodies' participating in the Committee of the Regions etc. Even more important, the direct election to the European Parliament has established a link which fundamentally is at odds with the privileged position of the state. In addition, there might be internal competition within the states between different agencies and (as assumed) tendencies for governmental agencies to pursue their own policies within their field of competence. The counter move from the state might be to establish procedures for formulating as unitary a state policy as possible. The Danish procedure for such coordination is certainly such an attempt. But this seems to be a move against the current. The major perspective is that *in a more integrated, supranationally-transnationally dominated system there is a tendency towards a diffusion of the integration policy of the state.*

Another tendency is that the processes within the EU are transcending the control of the individual government. This is most obvious in relation to the extended use of qualified majority voting in the Council. Obviously, to the degree this is becoming effective and widespread, it will prevent an individual state in using its veto power. The gain from this will probably be a stronger capacity to act for the integrated system, the EU, but it also implies that the integration policy of the individual government might be circumvented. One might argue, though, that the deterioration of the veto power for some states will strengthen the position of other states. Thus, the major picture is not so simple that the demise of veto power for a state simply leads to less influence for that state. But if the state is going to "compensate" for loss of veto power, it must be through another kind of influence in EU's negotiation system. Thus, a movement away from effective veto power is likely to lead to a change in the distributions and capabilities control (or "governance"). Some might claim that the change in the decision-making practices which move towards extended use of majority voting will give greater influence to smaller states, but it is very uncertain whether this is true or not. A more certain statement is that the character of the decision-making in the more integrated system will give influence to those actors that are able go gain influence within very complex networks. Thus, *the diffusion of integration policies and the changes in governance-structures seem to be accompanied by changes in the style of interest representation and governance.*

The inclusion of more sub-state actors in the policy making of the integration system implies that it becomes relevant for more actors to develop their wishes and demands in regard to the integration system. And one might add that this is the case in regard to a greater number of political issues. Said differently and related to the EU, it becomes necessary for many more actors and institutions to define their role and practice to many very different problems related to European integration. *The questions of European integration are becoming "societal" in the sense that they involve more actors and more issues.*

It is a special problem whether such a development implies that questions concerning European integration are becoming more politicised, understood as becoming a topic for controversies between social actors. One might argue that the two tendencies are at play simultaneously, and that they draws somewhat in opposite directions. The "societalisation" of integration policy tends to further politicisation. But the tendency of diffusion pulls towards depoliticisation. Yet, these reflections are on a very general a level and should be taken with corresponding reservations. Whether politicisation will actually take place will most likely depend on the interest constellations and the possible correlation between new and old cleavages.

A major implication of these considerations is that a state will have problems in pursuing a clear integration policy within a more integrated system. It is an open question whether we in practice will see formations of differentiated "integration policies" or rather the disappearance of clear state policies towards integration.[47]

---

47 Special problems are whether there exists a set of "high politics issues" that are exemptions to this, or whether it might be possible to have such a "securitisation" of integration issues that the appeal to security concerns justifies a state in breaking with the obligations that have emerged through integration.

Theoretical Perspectives 131

One might add that a special mechanism could be at play: If the interest of the dominant political groups are to avoid politicisation, the interest in actively supporting a "diffusion" of integration policies could be great.

5.4. On the move from an intergovernmentally dominated integration system to a supranationally-transnationally dominated system

The two models sketched above have only been rough illustrations of different paradigmatic structures in an integration system. Obviously, they only represent aspects of the actual structures in such a complex decision system as for instance the EU, and only do so in a very superficial way. But the considerations do help to illuminate problems related to integration policies. These considerations should be supplemented with two important perspectives:

The first perspective is that one might assume that a state does not just meet an integration system with a given structure. Rather, the state is involved in a historical development and is taking part in a formation process in which the structure of the integration system is not stable but – partially – open for influence. The possibilities of changes in the structure (or in the balance between different structures) make the integration system contingent, depending also on the action and policy of the state itself. This implies that the dimension of integration policy which is concerned with changes in the integration system, and power structures between different "projects of change", is of particular relevance. It is important for the state to take into consideration what kind of decision making structure it wants in the integration system and to have a policy on this. One might say that this becomes *the* crucial part of a state's integration policy.

The second perspective is that developments within a state and in its environment takes place in social settings with institutional and conceptual inertia. Sometimes we will see new practices develop without being able to describe them.[48] Often we will see old descriptions upheld, supported by interests in upholding these old and insufficient images. It is my understanding that the EU is a system which – very far – has developed practices which we have not described yet. In this perspective there are many reasons for, in practice, to uphold and confirm descriptions of the EU which do not correspond to reality.

Applied to the two paradigmatic models described above, one might claim that the reality of the EU already is rather close to the complex model of supranational-translation negotiation. But the most likely picture is that politicians and many others will have an interest in keeping and reproducing the picture of the EU as still being an intergovernmentally dominated system. Obviously, this might also serve as an explanation of the relative neglect in regard to the problems that arise when integration policy transcends foreign policy.

---

48 Joseph H. Weiler has a beautiful description of this phenomenon in regard to the EU in his article: "We will do, and hearken" in Weiler (1999).

6. Conclusions

A major contention of this article has been that we need to develop studies of integration policy. I have tried to show that integration policy is different from foreign policy, and that integration policy has many dimensions which in some ways transcend foreign policy. I have also tried to show that integration policy might be studied on the basis of decision making analysis and might be linked to the adaptation theories.

The difference between foreign policy and integration policy is not obvious when we are dealing with weak forms of integration. But when integration reaches stronger forms, important differences emerge. And when integration is so strong that we might speak of semi-integrated actors, the political decision-making in the original actor have changed. We might say that the decision-making proliferates: First, it becomes necessary for the governments in question to find out which policy it will pursue in regard to a) membership, b) position in the system, c) future changes in the system, d) policies within the system and e) policies outside the system. Later, the process goes even further in the direction of diffusion. Integration policy is by then no longer a monopoly for the government. Sub-state actors, also individual governmental agencies, might pursue different policies. Most likely, in a transition phase, a government might attempt to secure a "unitary" policy. But as it is the case already now in the EU, the institutional structure of the integration system might make it very difficult.

This implies that from a certain stage in the integration process it becomes important to link the understanding of integration policy with the understanding of the character of integration systems. I have – for simplicity reasons – only sketched two basic structures, and have attempted to show that the dynamic relationship around integration policy is very dependent on the dominant structure in the integration system. The reflections on the basis of the models have led to the conclusion that the dynamics of integration – if it moves from an intergovernmental to a supranational-transnational structure – lead to a phase in which integration policy will simultaneously become societal and diffuse, and – possibly – also to politicisasion. There seems to be a tendency that further integration will lead to a "proliferation" of integration policies which in itself is part of the process of policy diffusion. It is on this basis that I conclude that integration policy should be understood as being "between foreign policy and diffusion". But it should be stressed that there is quite a bit to be done concerning analysis of integration policies between these two extremes.

Literature

Allison, Graham T. (1971): *Essense of Decision*, Boston: Little Brown.
Amstrup, Niels (1976): "The Perennial Problem of Small States: A Survey of Research Efforts", *Cooperation and Conflict*, 1976/3, pp. 163-182.
Carlsnæs and Smith (ed.) (1994): *European Foreign Policy. The EC and Changing Perspectives in Europe*, London: Sage.
Friis, Lykke (1995): *Challenging a Theoretical Paradox: The Lacuna of Integration Theory*. Copenhagen: CORE working paper 2/1995, also published in *Global Society*, vol. 11, no. 3, 1997, pp. 359-381.
Friis, Lykke (1996): *When Europe Negotiates. From Europe Agreements to Eastern Enlargement*, Copenhagen: Copenhagen Political Studies Press.
Friis, Lykke (1999): *An Ever Larter Union? EU Enlargement and European Integration*, Copenhagen: Danish Institute of International Affairs.
Gustavsson, Jakob (1998): *The Politics of Foreign Policy Change: Explaining the Swedish Reorientation on EC Membership*, Lund: Lund University Press.
Haas, Ernst B. (1961): "International Integration. The European and the Universal Process", *International Organization*, vol. XV, no. 4.
Hansen, Lise Bøgh (1997): "Småstaters indflydelse i Den Europæiske Union", CORE arbejdspapir 3/1997.
Hermann, C.F, C.W. Kegley jr, and J.N. Rosenau (eds.) (1995): *New Directions in the Study of Foreign Policy*, London: Harper-Collins.
Hewson, Martin and Timothy J. Sinclair (eds.) (1999): *Approaches to Global Governance Theory*, New York: State University of New York Press.
Jachtenfuchs, Markus (1997): "Conceptualizing European Governance" in Knud Erik Jørgensen (ed.): *Reflective Approaches to European Governance*, London: Macmillan Press.
Jervis, Robert (1976): *Perceptions and Misperceptions in International Politics*, Princeton, NJ: Princeton University Press.
Johansen, Helle (1998): "Exploring the Colour of the Beast: Hegemony and Political Projects in the European Union" in *Wivel (ed.)* (1998): pp. 297-320.
Kelstrup, Morten (1991): "Danmarks deltagelse i det internationale samarbejde – fra pragmatisk funktionalisme til aktiv internationalisme?", in Henning Gottlieb et al. (eds.) (1991), *Fred og Konflikt*. SNU, Copenhagen, pp. 289-311.
Kelstrup, Morten, (ed.) (1992a): *European Integration and Denmark's Participation*, Copenhagen Political Studies Press.
Kelstrup, Morten (1992b): "European Integration and Political Theory" in *Kelstrup (ed.)* (1992a): pp. 13-58.
Kelstrup, Morten (1993a): "EF's politiske system", *Politica*, 1993/3, pp. 253-268.
Kelstrup, Morten (1993b): "Small States and European Political Integration", in Tiilikainen and Damgaard Petersen (eds.), *The Nordic Countries and the EC*, Copenhagen: Copenhagen Political Studies Press.
Kelstrup, Morten (1994): "Dansk EU-politik: Politikfastsættelse i et dilemma mellem diffusitet og fastlåsning" in Bertel Heurlin (red.): *Danmark og den Europæiske Union*, Forlaget Politiske Studier, pp. 20-53.

Kelstrup, Morten (1998): "Integration Theories: History, Competing Approaches and New Perspectives" in *Anders Wivel (ed.)* (1998): pp. 15-55.

Larsen, Henrik (1999): "British and Danish Policies towards Europe in the 1990s: A Discource Approach", *European Journal of International relations*, 5(4).

Moravcsik, A. (1994): "Why the European Community Strengthens the State: Domestic Politics and International Cooperation", *Center for European Studies Working Paper* 52. Cambridge: Harvard University.

Moravcsik, A. (1998): *The Choice for Europe: Social Purpose and State Power from Messina to Maastricht*, New York: Cornell University Press.

Mouritzen, Hans (1988): *Finlandization: Towards a General Theory of Adaptive Politics*, Aldershot, Avebury.

Mouritzen, Hans (1993): "The two Musterknaben and the Naughty Boy; Sweden, Finland and Denmark in the Process of EU integration", *Cooperation and Conflict*, vol. 28/4, pp. 373-402.

Mouritzen, Hans, Ole Wæver and Håkan Wiberg (eds.) (1996): *European Integration and National Adaptation. A Theoretical Inquiry*, Commack: Nova Science Publishers, Inc.

Matlery, Janne Haaland (1993): "And Never the Twain Shall Meet? Reflections on Norway, Europe and Integration" in Tiilikainen and Damgaard Petersen (eds.), *The Nordic Countries and the EC*, Copenhagen: Copenhagen Political Studies Press.

Pedersen, Thomas (1996): "Denmark and the European Union" in *Lee Miles (ed.)*, *The European Union and the Nordic Countries*, London and New York: Routledge, pp. 81-100.

Petersen, Nikolaj (1977): "Adaptation as a Framework for the Analysis of Foreign Policy Behavior", *Cooperation and Conflict*, Vol. XII, pp. 221-250.

Petersen, Nikolaj (1989): "Mod en generel teori om adaptiv politik", *Politica*, 1989/2, p. 174-188.

Petersen, Nikolaj (1995): "Denmark and the European Community 1985-1993" in Carsten Due-Nielsen & Nikolaj Petersen (eds.): *Adaptation and Activism. The Foreign Policy of Denmark 1967-1993*, Copenhagen: Danish Institute of International Studies & DJØF Publishing, pp. 189-224.

Petersen, Nikolaj (1998): "National Strategies in the Integration Dilemma: An Adaption Approach", *Journal of Common Market Studies*, vol. 36, pp. 33-45.

Putnam, Robert D. (1988): "Diplomacy and Domestic Politics: The Logic of Two-level Games", *International Organization*, vol. 43/3, pp. 427-59.

Risse-Kappen, T. (1996): "Exploring the Nature of the Beast: International Relations Theory and Comparative Policy Ananlysis Meet the European Union", *Journal of Common Market Studies*, vol. 34, pp. 53-80.

Rosamond, Ben (2000): *Theories of European Integration*, London: Macmillan.

Rosenau, James N. (1966): "Pre-theories and Theories of Foreign Policy" in Farell (ed.), *Approaches to Comparative and International Politics*, Evanston: North Western University Press, pp. 27-92.

Rosenau, James N. (1981): *The Study of Political Adaption*. Pinter, London.

Rosenau, James N. and Ernst-Otto Czempiel (eds.) (1992): *Governance without government: order and change in world politics*, Cambridge: Cambridge University Press.

Smith, Michael (1996): "The EU as an International Actor" in *Jeremy Richardsson (ed.)*, *European Union. Power and Policy Making*, London: Routledge, pp. 247-262.

Smith, Steve (1981): *Foreign Policy Adaptation*. Aldershot: Gower.

Smith. Steve (1986): "Theories of Foreign Policy: An Historical Overview", *Review of International Studies,* 12.1, pp. 13-29.

Smith, Steve (1994): "Foreign Policy Theory and the New Europe" in *Carlsnæs and Smith (eds.)* (1994), pp. 1-20.

Snyder, Glenn (1984): "The Security Dilemma in Alliance Politics". *World Politics,* vol. 86, no. 4.

Snyder, Richard et al. (1954): "Decision-Making as an Approach to the Study of International Politics", *Foreign Policy Analysis Project Series,* No. 3, Princeton University.

Snyder, Richard et al. (1962): *Foreign Policy Decision-Making,* New York: The Free Press.

Sundelius, Bengt (1995): "Sverige bortom småstatsbindingen: Litet men smart i ett internationaliserat Europa", SOU 1995, pp. 61-85.

Väyrynen, Raimo (1989): "Constraints and Opportunities in the Foreign Policies of Small States". In Bertel Heurlin and Christian Thune (1989): *Danmark og det internationale system* Copenhagen Political Studies Press, Copenhagen, pp. 52-64.

Väyrynen, Raimo (ed.) (1999): *Globalization and Global Governance,* New York: Rowman and Littlefield Publishers.

Watson, Adam (1992): *The Evolution of International Society,* London: Routledge.

Weiler, J.H. (1999): *The Constitution of Europe,* Cambridge: Cambridge University Press.

Weldes, Jutta (1996): "Constructiong National interests", *European Journal of International Relations,* vol. 2(3), pp. 275-318.

Walt, Stephen (1987): *The Origins of Alliances,* New York: Cornell University Press.

Wivel, Anders (1998) (ed.): *Explaining European Integration,* Copenhagen: Copenhagen Political Studies Press.

Wæver, Ole (1994): "Resisting the Temptation of Post Foreign Policy Analysis" in *Carlsnaes and Smith (eds.),* pp. 238-273.

Part II

Historical and Cultural Preconditions

CHAPTER 5

Danish National Identity: Between Multinational Heritage and Small State Nationalism

Uffe Østergaard

"The Dane who never refrains from underlining the smallness of his country, at the same time feels strongly that his country is surpassed by no one."

(SNU 1995: 20)

Self perceptions, Nation-building and State-building

Denmark in particular and the Nordic countries in general represent variations over general European patterns of state- and nation-building and political culture. Sweden and Denmark rank among the oldest, most typical nation-states. Accordingly, together with France, Britain and Spain they should be studied as variations over the early modern European state-nation rather than as typical 'small states'. In heavy competition, the two states together exercised a supremacy over most of Northern Europe from the late Middle Ages onwards. Mainly as a result of mutual exhaustion, Russia, Prussia and to a degree the United Kingdom gradually replaced Denmark and Sweden, who were subsequently reduced to the status of smaller powers.

As a result of simultaneous changes in great power politics in the eighteenth and nineteenth centuries, the major conflicts in Europe were relocated away from Northern Europe and produced a virtual 'neutralization' of the Scandinavian countries north of the Baltic Sea. This relatively peaceful situation has struck a deep chord among Danes. Regardless of many years' membership in NATO and the European Union, neutralist ideology still has a strong resonance in the population. A side effect of the experience as a privileged periphery in Northern Europe was the rise of a trans-national common Nordic identity on top of the independent national identifications. Even today, Nordic unity is regarded as a viable alternative to European culture and integration by large numbers of the population. This supranational identity is of a particular kind, as strong national identifications were the very precondition for successful Nordic cooperation at a practical level since the early twentieth century, not a competing identification as seems to be the case at a European level (Østergaard 1997b).

Such paradoxes are deeply ingrained in the Nordic political cultures in general and Danish political culture in particular. As a result of history, Danish self-perceptions oscillate between that of a small state with a moral right to exercise influence because of its strong and coherent society and that of a small state with no influence in the world. Often both understandings are invoked, albeit in different contexts. The self-perception of the country as weak often translates into the saying: 'Denmark is a little land'. On the other hand, Denmark's disproportionately high influence in some aspects of world affairs is justified by reference to the country's homogeneous character and high moral standards. The latter comes to the fore primarily when Danish democracy is – favourably – compared with that other European countries.

The concepts of small state and strong society, does not exhaust the list of possible characterizations, yet they indicate some of the ways Danes and foreign observers have understood Denmark's situation in the world. The distinction between weak power and strong state was originally introduced by Barry Buzan (1983) and has been elaborated among others by Ole Wæver (1995) and Bertel Heurlin (1996). By juxtaposing military and economic power with social or societal strength, Buzan seeks to draw attention to the fact that influence in the international community is exercised on the basis of more factors than sheer size and military might. Internal cohesiveness and economic strength combined with national as well international trading power, are alternative sources of strength, not to speak of morality. Buzan has since elaborated this line of thinking under the heading of 'societal security' (Buzan 1993). Obviously, it is no coincidence that such alternative sources of influence in international politics are stressed by the socalled 'Copenhagen School' of international studies.

A 'strong society' is an older concept which has resurfaced, recently provoked by observations of so diverse societies as the former Soviet Union and Italy. Among others, the American political theorist Francis Fukuyama has pointed to the importance of the social and cultural mechanisms which precondition the rule of law (in German, *Rechtsgesellschaft*). These cultural factors he calls 'trust' (Fukuyama 1995). Arguing in a similar vein, the American political scientist Robert D. Putnam, investigating the long-term factors influencing the working of civic culture and local democracy in Italy, has pointed to the influence of age old traditions of civic behaviour in Central and Northern Italy (Putnam 1993). Putnam finds that democracy, and with it market capitalism and the rule of law, flourish where the civil society is strong and cohesive. These recent observations are strikingly similar to early explanations of the Nordic welfare states such as Marquis Childs' now classical study of Sweden as a representative of a 'middle way' between capitalism and communism (Childs 1936). Childs wanted to impress on his fellow Americans the need for a social order in the vein of Roosevelt's New Deal. However, his book at the same time heavily influenced Scandinavian reflection on our own so-called 'Nordic' model of society.

This belief in a Nordic model of the welfare state in particular, and social democracy in general, has led many Scandinavians to assume a major difference between their small, coherent and peaceful societies and the larger, conflict-ridden and aggressive European (and American) states. Among the Nordic countries, these beliefs are most widespread in Denmark and Sweden. At the same time, however, these two countries dominated all of Northern Europe and were locked in mortal competition over the Baltic Sea, the *Dominium Maris Baltici*, in the centuries between 1500 and 1800. This conflict arose from the geopolitical realities of two multinational state-nations both trying to exercise hegemony over the Baltic region. This warlike past, though, has largely been forgotten by the populations of both the major protagonists.

Compared with most other states in the European Union, present-day Denmark appears as the very archetype of a 'small state'.[1] Accordingly, its foreign and European policy is often interpreted exclusively as a consequence of an age old tradition of determinism and neutralism. In an influential book, a Danish scholar working in Canada, Carsten Holbraad, has traced this tradition back to the peace settlements after the Great Northern War in 1720 (Holbraad 1991). As Hans Branner points out in his contribution to this volume, this analysis does not grasp the internal paradoxes and ambiguities in Danish foreign policy positions, among the elites as well as in the broader public. Holbraad identifies a so-called 'Danish' policy of neutrality extending from 1720 well into the twentieth century. He distinguishes between different versions of this neutralism in different periods: aligned neutrality 1720-1807; isolated neutrality 1814-1920; defenceless neutrality 1920-1945; non-aligned neutrality 1945-1949 and latent neutrality 1949-1989. Basically, however he sees the foreign policy of Denmark as variations over the fundamental attitudes of a typical 'small state' with interests only in her own survival. This approach does not allow for the present policy of 'active internationalism' (cf. Holm 1997). It also misunderstands the very meanings of 'Denmark' and 'Danish', being based on the misleading assumption that the 'Denmark' of the different periods was one and the same entity. Since Denmark no longer refers to herself as a 'small state', having instead embarked upon an unprecented active multilateralist – some would even say interventionist – policy in her Baltic 'Near Abroad' (the area Mouritzen [1997: 47] refers to as her 'salient action sphere') and in the Balkans. This interventionism has been backed by armed force on a hitherto unknown scale, from naval vessels in the Persian Gulf and heavy tanks in Bosnia to military cooperation with Poland, the Baltic countries (Heurlin 1994 and 1996) and from 1999 with France (in Kosovo).

Other oberservers have at times preferred to refer to the country as a 'small nation'. At other times, Denmark has been referred to as a 'small people' on a pair with the Catalans, the Scots, the Bretons, the Corsicans or many other of Europe's

---

1 The concepts of 'small state' and 'small power' are investigated in more detail in other contributions to this volume. A classic description of the behavior and self-imposed limitations of a small power was put forward by Robert L. Rothstein in 1968. According to him, 'a Small Power is a state which recognizes that it cannot obtain security primarily by use of its own capabilities, and that it must rely fundamentally on the aid of other states, institutions, processes, or developments to do so' (quoted from Hans Branner 1972: 24). Branner's book is the fundamental work on Danish small state politics; it also gives an introduction to the international literature on the concept.

so-called 'stateless' peoples. This is obviously wrong. Denmark is a small state yes, but hardly a small people, as Denmark is a nation with its own state, uncontested membership in the United Nations and a long historical legitimacy. Countries like Denmark belong to a restricted, privileged group of small states ranging from Luxembourg to the Netherlands, who by historical accident exercised national independence in the crucial years in the middle of the twentieth century when European cooperation was launched on the basis of sovereign nation-states – cf. the telling title of Alan Milward's seminal work on the early phases of European integration, 'The European Rescue of the Nation State' (Milward 1992).

It is hard to determine any precise logic behind the different statuses of Catalonia, Scotland and Bavaria, on the one hand, and Luxembourg, Denmark and Ireland on the other. However, regardless of their 'accidental' background,[2] the sovereignty of the latter states is now a fact which has allowed these particular entities a disproportionately large say in European – and for that sake global – political and economic affairs. In the era of nation states, independent statehood plays a major role, regardless of how formal it might be. Therefore, it is not completely ridiculous when the Danish electorate clings to the sovereignty of their country, however imprecise the term may seem, while Germans and Italians seem fairly keen on handing over their national sovereignty to European institutions. The problem for Denmark as a player in international politics is that many Danes mistake formal sovereignty for real power to decide the outcome of European politics. Thus they feel frustrated or cheated when realizing the limits of the influence of small state, regardless of the strengths and cohesiveness of its society.

Indeed, if we investigate the political debate in Denmark on European integration and on related elements in the political culture, we find a number of features normally taken to be characteristic of recently independent or even not yet independent countries. Slovenia offers an interesting case for comparison, as there are a number of similarities between the national mentalities of the two peoples as expressed in political discourse and world view. The geographical and geopolitical differences, however, are equally striking. The Slovenian lands have as long a history as Denmark, but only as separate provinces in what eventually became the multinational Habsburg Empire. They were never the legitimate basis of a recognized 'national' Monarchy of their own with an unbroken history. The Slovenes are a small people held together as a cultural nation and only in 1991 rose to the rank of state. Thus, it personifies the small, ethno-national nation-state of the theoretical literature (cf. Connor 1994).

---

2 Social scientifically biased readers should note that for historians 'accidence' and 'coincidence' are not to be confused with pure chance. On the contrary, these *termini technici* refer to outcomes that can be explained afterwards, once they have happened, but could hardly have been predicted before, as the combination of the necessary structural factors only coincided because of a particular historical *conjuncture*. The sudden demise of the Soviet Union between 1989 and 1991 is a major example of a development which historians would label accidental in this sense (cf. Østergaard 1997d on the use of counterfactual analysis in historical explanations).

Denmark, on the other hand, has been around for more than a thousand years. Not exactly the present entity, but an entity carrying the name Denmark, can be identified as far back as the formative years of Europe in the early Middle Ages. Originally Denmark was a rather typical state-nation consisting of several entities.[3] In contrast to other old state-nations such as France, Spain and the United Kingdom, Denmark was defeated in its wars with Sweden and Prussia and, consequently, lost most of her territories. Contrary to Poland, however, Denmark was not swallowed by stronger neighbours as the great powers of the day had an interest in preserving a small sovereign state at the entrance to the Baltic Sea. In the nineteenth century, the core provinces of this multicultural and multilingual composite state gradually evolved into a homogeneous nation-state with a political culture based on identity between language, people (*folk*), nation and state.[4]

In the following contribution I analyze the confluence of the long legitimacy of the state, the small nation-state of the nineteenth century, the nationalistic rejection of an ever closer European Union since 1972 and the policies of active internationalism in the 1990s. At first sight, the relation between the strong Danish, civic or civil society, national identity and the different strategies and perceptions in the foreign policy of this small country appear paradoxical. A small state with only 5.3 million inhabitants and limited military might at times behave as if it were a big state. On other occasions the state might emphasize her smallness, particularly when confronted with issues of handing over national sovereignty to the European Union.

---

3   State-nations are the territorial states which originated in early modern Europe between 1500 and 1800, mainly in the West. Some of these states later developed into nation-states with a national identity created in a top down process. The distinction between state-nation and nation-state dates back to Hans Kohn's classic account (1944), *The Idea of Nationalism*. It is developed in E.J. Hobsbawm (1990), *Nations and Nationalism*. To add to the terminogical confusion a nation-state is called *état-nation* in French. Many state-nations were organized as monarchical unions or composite states (see following note).

4   'Composite state' has become a *terminus technicus* for the territorial states of early modern Europe. For a definition and elaboration of the British concept of sovereignty, see J.C.D. Clark, 'Britain as a composite state – Sovereignty and European Integration' in Østergaard (1991: 55-84). The nature of the British composite state is further elaborated in Clark, 'English History's Forgotten Context: Scotland, Ireland, Wales', *Historical Journal* 32 (1989: 211-28); for an elaboration of the phenomenon in European context see H.G. Koenigsberger, 'Composite States, Representative Institutions and the American Revolution, *Historical Research* (62, 1989: 135-53) and J.H. Elliot, 'A Europe of Composite Monarchies', *Past and Present* (137, 1992: 48-71). Competing denominations are 'conglomerate state' and 'multiple kingdom'. The first attempt to apply these concepts on Danish and Nordic history are O. Feldbæk, 'Clash of Culture in a Conglomerate State: Danes and Germans in 18th century Denmark', C.V. Johansen et al. (eds.), *Clashes of Culture,* Odense University Press (1992: 80-93) and Jens Rahbek Rasmussen, 'The Danish Monarchy as a Composite State', in N.A. Sørensen (ed.), *European Identities, Cultural Diversity and Integration in Europe since 1700,* Odense University Press (1995: 23-36).

Integral nationalism in a rump territorial state-nation: a 'Danish' Paradox?

In a comparative context, Danish national identity and political culture combine features of what is often referred to as East European *integral nationalism* typical of smaller, recently independent nation-states and the *patriotic concept of citizenship* in the older West European state nations (Brubaker 1992). The explanation of this apparent paradox is that Denmark belongs to both families. A former multinational, composite state was cut down to a size that enabled peasant-farmers to establish an ideological hegemony in the diminished and nationalized state.

Only few foreign observers have correctly identified the historical and geographical reasons behind the simultaneous existence of negative feelings towards European integration and a concerned and well-informed internationalism. One of these is the former British ambassador to Denmark in the late 1980s, Peter Unwin,[5] who, in the context of a broader reportage and political analysis of the reemerging Baltic region, observes: 'Denmark seemed at first sight the most transparent of national societies. But closer examination revealed paradoxes as inexplicable as any I had encountered as a diplomat in Hungary, Germany, the United States and Japan' (Unwin 1996: 9). Unwin formulates these paradoxes as follows:

> "I found the Danes an intriguing people, straightforward and perverse by turns. ... [Who] think of themselves as relaxed and humour-loving, but the astonished stare with which they so often greet everyday statements spoke to me rather of well-controlled insecurity.
> Long before their 1992 vote on Maastricht, the Danes were manifestly ambivalent about their place in Europe and about the impact of the European Community on their country. They seemed to me quite as reserved, as confused even, as my own countrymen, and more introverted by far than the British. And yet the Danes were polyglot citizens of Europe and the world, much travelled, cultivated, good judges of red wine, and a people with global conscience, pouring their money into relief of distant hardship."

(Unwin 1996: 208)

The explanation Unwin finds in Denmark's geopolitical situation:

> "If geography is the clue to history, history is the key to to national psychology. The Danes, I found, were no exception to this rule. They cherish 1,000 years of continuity. They remember that their king's writ used to run to the gates of Hamburg, as far as the North Cape and across the Sound deep into southern Sweden. Gradually they lost their empire, and its loss, along with wars with Sweden and Prussia and high-handed British arrogance has left its mark on the national psyche. Similarly, the Danes' passionate

---

5 Peter Unwin, *Baltic Approaches* (1996). It seems to have become a virtual tradition for British ambassadors to write perceptive accounts of Danish identity, from Robert Molesworth's *An Account of Denmark as it was in the Year 1692* (1694) to James Mellon's *Og gamle Danmark* (1992, not published in English).

egalitarianism is a peasant nation's response to memories of royal absolutism and a harsh, German aristocracy. [...] The Danish psyche seems to have come to terms with this long history of loss with admirable equanimity. Animosity towards Sweden, for example, runs no deeper than the Oxford versus Cambridge variety. But with Denmark's readiness to face reality came passivity, a sense that she lies exposed to the mercy of her neighbours and of superior force."

(Unwin 1996: 209-210)

This even holds true in the face of recent Danish activism in international affairs:

"[R]ecent Danish self-assertion reminds one that their emphasis on the littleness of Denmark has always had something self-consciously whimsical about it, almost Yiddish in its self-depreciation. For the Danes are rightly a proud people, with a proud history. [...] Many Danes find that their self-depreciating whimsicality sits uneasy with their proud past. Yet the modern history of little Denmark is a triumphant success story. When the Danish crown ceded its richest provinces to Germany in 1864, the Danes set themselves to develop the bleak heathland of Jutland and to create wealth there to replace the lost riches of Sleswig-Holstein. At the same time they began to lay the educational and socially egalitarian foundations of today's Denmark. [...] To Danes, and to many foreign observers, Denmark is an ideal society. No one is very poor; few are very rich. [...] The state and its police are surprisingly intrusive, but their intrusions are accepted as necessary to that fairness and order which the Danes prize so highly."

(Unwin 1996: 211-212)

These are the words of a highly perceptive and intelligent outsider. They point to the dilemma between a long and relatively uncontested past as a composite European state-nation of second rank and the more recent ethnically homogeneous 'little Denmark' sharing many characteristics with the smaller and younger nations on the peripheries of core Europe. As the collective memory of the Danes tends to neglect the multinational past, and the majority of outside observers share this mistake, it seems relevant to begin the analysis of the present national identity and its repercussions on European integration policy with a recapitulation of the historical evolution of this state-nation. A major reason for confusion is that the older composite monarchy bears the same name as today's ethnic nation-state. More precise than 'Denmark' would be to talk of the Oldenburg Monarchy from 1448 to 1863.

From Composite State to Peasant-Farmers' Democracy

Until the loss of the Norwegian half in 1814, the name 'Denmark' referred to a rather typical European composite state. The official title of this middle ranging, absolutist power in Northern Europe was 'Kron zu Dennemarck', 'The Danish Monarchy' or 'House of Oldenborg'. Today, if rembered at all in its entirety, this state is referred to as the 'Double Monarchy' or 'Denmark-Norway'. This name, however, is so imprecise that it must be considered wrong. Geographically, the state consisted of the two kingdoms, Denmark and Norway, the two duchies Sleswig and Holstein, of which the latter belonged to the Holy Roman Empire of the German Nation. Furthermore, the composite state comprised the Atlantic dependencies of Iceland, the Faroe Islands and Greenland, which from a position originally under Norwegian suzerainity, gradually came to be ruled directly from Copenhagen.

Furthermore, the Danish Monarchy in the seventeenth and eighteenth centuries acquired a full set of colonies in the West Indies, West Africa (Christiansborg in present-day Ghana) and India (Serampore and Tranquebar). This colonial empire enabled the state to have a stake, albeit a minor one, in the triangular Atlantic trade between a European centre, the slave-producing West Africa and the sugar-cane growing West Indian islands of St. Croix, St. John and St. Thomas (Degn 1974) supplemented with a stake in the East Asian trade (Feldbæk and Justesen 1980). In the late eighteenth century the main cities in the European part of the conglomerate state were Copenhagen, Altona and Kiel in Holstein, Flensborg in Sleswig and Bergen in Norway; except Copenhagen, all lay outside the frontiers of present Denmark. The port of Charlotte Amalie on St. Thomas in the West Indies and Serampore (formerly Frederiksnagore) in India up the Hoogh river from Calcutta ranked second and sixth, respectively, in terms of trade volume and number of inhabitants in the whole Danish empire.[6]

The main financial basis of the Danish state stemmed from duties levied on ship traffic through the Øresund channel to and from the Baltic Sea. For a long time, the

---

6   An indication of the composite nature of the Danish state is the founding years of the universities of the multinational state before its final dissolution in 1864: Copenhagen 1479; Kiel 1665. (Strictly speaking the University was founded as a German speaking university by the Duke Christian Albrect from the House of Gottorp, that is, by a vassal of the Danish king who at the same time acted as his competitor in alliance with his Swedish enemies. After the incorporation of Sleswig and Holstein in the monarchy in 1720/73 the university continued as German, but its graduates were fully qualified as civil servants in the whole of the monarchy also after the introduction of the so-called act of Indigenous Rights in 1776; cf. Lange 1996: 224), Kristiania (Oslo) 1811, Frederiksnagore (Serampore) 1821/27. Even after the demise of the composite state universities were founded in various parts of the surviving realm (in Danish *Rigsfællesskab*). They include the University of Iceland in Reykjavik (Háskolí Íslands 1911), Frodskapasetur Føroya in Tórshavn in the Faroe Islands 1952/65 and the University of Greenland in Nuuk (formerly Godthaab) in 1983. A further important example of the national significance of these seats of scholarship is the founding of the university in neighboring Lund in 1668. In the Middle Ages Lund had been the ideological center of the Danish state as the seat of the archbishop. When the Danish king was forced to cede the provinces of Skaane (Scania), Halland and Blekinge to Sweden in 1658, the Swedish state founded a new university in the area in order to present an alternative to the University of Copenhagen. Only in the 1820s were Swedish subjects allowed to cross the frontier to visit Denmark (and vice versa). The political logic of the university in Lund was to educate a new generation of priests who would help swedisize the Danish speaking peasant population. As we shall see later, Sweden was surprisingly successful in this rather unique undertaking of renationalizing a province this early (cf. Fabricius 1906-58; Åberg 1994).

Danish Monarchy owed its strong financial situation to this position at the entrance to the Baltic sea as demonstrated in the impressive castle at Elsinore (Helsingør) which was built just in time for Shakespeare to use as location for that most famous of plays, *Hamlet*. Because of a favourable geopolitical position, the Danish Monarchy from the late Middle Ages was able to exercise hegemony over Northern Europe; *de facto* for approximately 400 years, *de jure* in the form of the Kalmar-Union from 1397 to 1523. Because of its possession of the main islands in the Baltic, Rügen, Bornholm, Gotland, Dagö and Ösel, the state even secured a dominating position in the Baltic for another hundred years, the so-called *Dominium Maris Baltici* (Ahnlund 1956).

Being a composite state stretching from the North Cape to Hamburg, equivalent to the distance from Hamburg to Sicily, and possessing various islands in the North Atlantic, the military, technological and political backbone of the empire was the navy. This navy had to be big enough to fight simultaneous wars in the Baltic against the emerging Swedish rival and protect the far reaching Atlantic possessions. The Danish state succeeded in doing this for more than 150 years until the middle of the seventeenth century. Then, having overstretched its resources, it suffered a series of humiliating defeats at the hands of the rising competitor Sweden. Between 1645 and 1660, the Monarchy lost its hegemony over Northern Europe to a newly established Swedish empire around the Baltic (Roberts 1979). Yet, the Danish navy was still in a position to deal crushing blows to the Swedes in the Scanian war 1675-79. Only Swedish military success on land enabled Sweden to retain the newly won territories of what today constitutes western and southern Sweden. Even in the eighteenth century, however, the might of its navy kept the composite state of Denmark-Norway-Sleswig-Holstein ranked second in Europe only to great powers such as France, Great Britain, Spain, Austria (*Casa d'Austria*), Russia and the rising Prussia.

From a comparative point of view, we may note that this geographically somewhat overstretched and financially overburdened state nevertheless succeeded in modernizing itself from the top down by the end of the seventeenth century and again in the late eighteenth century (Horstbøll and Østergaard 1990), an endeavour at which most other contemporaries failed. In many ways, this Northern European Monarchy embodied the ideals of the philosophers of the Enlightenment. That is why its political system was eagerly debated among political observers from Venice to London. Not always favourably as we know from Montesquieu's *De l'esprit des lois* (1748); but debated it was (cf. Østergaard 1995a).

In theory, the political system was unconditionally Absolutist since the revolution in 1660 and the subsequent drafting of a sort of Absolutist 'constitution' (*Lex Regia* or King's Law) of 1665. Yet the political reality was far less despotic. So different was the reality that the Norwegian historian Jens Arup Seip has somewhat paradoxically characterized the system from the 1770s onwards as 'Absolutism guided by opinion' (Seip 1958). Less clumsily, this political culture could be termed 'Absolutism by consent' (Østergaard 1995a; Horstbøll and Østergaard 1990). This tradition for consulting public opinion explains why Denmark-Norway succeeded where the very epitome of Absolutism, France, failed. Where France came to unleash the uncontrollable forces of democratic revolution, the Danish kingdom revolutionized itself from above in a series of relatively coherent reforms of the agrarian system, civil liberties, customs and trade regulations in the years from 1784 to 1814 (cf. Løfting, Horstbøll, Østergaard 1989; Østergaard 1995a).

Subsequent international political catastrophes in the nineteenth century reduced this multinational composite state to a tiny nation-state. So small was its size after the loss of the duchies of Sleswig and Holstein in 1864 that many in the dominant elite wondered whether it would be able to survive as an independent state and neighbour to the recently united, aggressively dominant, self-confident Germany. Competing new elites devised different programs for the survival of the mini-state. Parts of the national-liberal intelligentsia advocated a union with Sweden and Norway, the Scandinavianism (which de facto would have meant Swedish hegemony cf. Østergaard 1996b and 1997b).[7] A small minority advocated alignment with the new Germany, a much larger group neutrality vis-a-vis Germany combined with an economic orientation towards the British empire. Gradually, the latter program was chosen and led to a small, successful democracy, truly one of Barrington Moore's 'small states.'[8]

What is important, however, is not to mistake this second, extremely homogeneous nation-state, for the composite state, even though they are normally referred to by the same name, "Denmark". That would be even more wrong than confusing present day's Russia or Serbia with the Soviet Union or Yugoslavia. There is some continuity, obviously, but in many areas the discontinuities are more important. First of all, many areas outside the core lands are completely left out of most analyses of European history, while at the same time the role of the larger composite states in international politics is completely misunderstood when concieved only in terms of Europe after 1919. Today, both the multinational middle ranking power as well the amputated social-democratic Danish nation-state of the twentieth century are referred to as 'Denmark' in the multi-volume histories of Denmark. In fact, however, apart from a certain geographical continuity of the two provinces Jylland (Jutland) and the islands of Sjælland and Fyn they do not have much in common.[9]

---

7   Cf. Bo Stråth, 'Scandinavian Identity: A Mythical Reality', in (Sørensen 1995: 37-57) and the 'Illusory Nordic Alternative to Europe', *Cooperation and Conflict* 15, (1980: 103-114).
8   In Moore's opinion small states can be disregarded in comparative studies because of their lack of originality and importance (Moore 1966, x). The lack of importance Moore attributes to small states in history is certainly debatable, but there is no reason to debate the subject matter at great length here, as I have done so elsewhere. Barrington Moore uses 'small state' as a historical sociological characterization rather than as a term for small military and economic capabilities of international politics (Østergaard 1991b).
9   A logical corollary to this neglect of the other parts of the monarchy is the denial of differences within the resulting nation-state. Denmark turned out an extremely centralized state but in the nineteenth century attempts to turning the multinational monarchy into a federal state as well as later federalist projects for the 'rigsfællesskab' cannot be ignored, as demonstrated by Steen Bo Frandsen in a major analysis of the Jutland question (Frandsen 1993 and 1996, Østergaard 2000).

Danish observers tend to take the continuity of Danish history so much for granted that they never reflect on the name of the state. Yet it is crucially important to bear in mind that the nationally homogeneous 'Denmark' of the last 150 years was very different from the political entity we encounter in international politics of the early modern period. The result of the reduction in size was an extremely homogeneous population which enabled the rising class of peasant farmers to establish ideological hegemony over the political culture in the remaining Danish state. Such ideological hegemony over a legitimate and fully recognized old territorial state was (and still is) relatively unique.[10]

Contrary to other states with strong peasant movements, the Danish peasants actually managed to take power in this small monarchy and turn it into a homogenous national democracy. Popular values permeated all sectors of the society, in contrast to other modernizing societies where they had to compete with stronger forces. The peasant farmers were not the only social force. However, as will be demonstrated below, after the turn of century, the values of the peasant farmers came to set the conditions for the ideological, party political and economic struggles within the new, smaller Denmark and made their fundamental imprint upon the other forces such as the commercial bourgeoisie and the rising working class (cf. Østergaard 1992a).

A few years ago, my colleague Helge Paludan, argued that the structural conditions for these peasant values in the core lands of the Monarchy date back to the High Middle Ages (but not back to the Viking Age) when the Christian *familia* was established by law in 1305. According to Paludan, this family structure enabled the peasants to emerge as a separate class following the enormous restructuring of land holding in the wake of the agrarian crisis of the Late Middle Ages (Paludan 1995). Although the overwhelming majority of the peasants were tenants, they held their farms on relatively secure terms. Because of protection from the Crown, it was difficult for aristocratic estate-owners to incorporate individual farms into their directly run estates.

If Paludan's interpretation holds true, the long-term structural explanation of the peculiar agrarian development of the Danish core lands, that is Northern and Southern Jutland (Sleswig/Sønderjylland), Zealand and Southern Sweden (Scania), date back this far. These values then helped the peasant farmers successfully survive the agrarian reforms of the late eighteenth century and resurface as a hegemonic class in the nineteenth and twentieth centuries. They even made it into the industrial era, as

---

10 In this particular context, hegemony is used in a relatively precise way as *terminus technicus* for those forces who have the ability to set the terms of the discourse in a given society. The Italian Marxist thinker Antonio Gramsci used this term to understand how a minority group was able to exercise power over a society with different and even conflicting interests (Gramsci 1930-36). The three Baltic states, with all their internal differences, could serve as a point of reference for comparative studies of popular political attitudes. However, the parallels should not be overemphasised as the historical background of the apparently similar attitudes are different (Kirby 1990 and 1994).

will later be described. This social continuity, however, does not imply any direct continuity in the political nation. National sentiments were primarily reserved for the politcal class, i.e., the aristocracy. And the aristocracy was oriented towards manorial possessions in the broader multinational realm in Scandinavia and the Duchies.

These liberal peasant values also help explain some of the paradoxes of national identity and political culture of today. Why is it that a relatively open minded political culture has gone back on its own professed internationalism and rejected the European project as a grand idea and a challenge? Minor tactical disagreements aside, most of the Danish political spectrum agrees on a fundamental mistrust of everything 'big' i.e., transnational and 'European'. The disagreements between Left and Right are based on differing perceptions of the economic benefits they see coming from the European Union and different evaluations of the necessary adjustments of economic distribution policies. In European matters, however, both sides basically agree to do as little as possible, as late as possible, as cheap as possible, and with as little enthusiasm as possible reflecting a century and a half of Danish foreign policy.

On the one hand Danish, national identity reflects the parochial mental horizon of the class of middle-sized landowners. On the other hand, these peasant farmers themselves produced in an agrarian-industrial way for the global market. They had inherited a complete, legitimate state which enabled them to deal at an international level as the equals of other powers, albeit somewhat smaller. Internationalism *and* parochialism were combined: an extreme self-confidence and a tradition for stressing smallness and lack of importance are characteristic of the Danish worldview, a view which helps explain the apparently contradictory attitudes to international cooperation. Economic cooperation is considered fine and military alliances necessary, but political cooperation is predominantly perceived as a loss of sovereignty. In order to understand how this particular combination of factors came about, we need to examine the Danish historical experience in more detail.

Composite States at War – the Swedish and Danish Empires

The present boundary between Denmark and Germany dates back to only 1920, which means that strictly speaking modern Denmark is a result of the peace settlements after World War I. Yet Denmark also has a much older history which sets it apart from most other European countries. Even the Nordic countries have had different experiences. The past of Finland, Norway and Iceland is closer to that of small nations in Eastern Europe or even that of decolonized peoples in the Third World.[11] Denmark and Sweden, on the other hand, belong to a different group of classic Western state-nations, i.e., France, United Kingdom and Spain. The United

---

11 Norway, of course has a long history as an independent state. In many ways the medieval monarchy of Norway can be considered the most centralized and unitary state in medieval Northern Europe. Because of a combined ecological and social disaster in the 14th century, however, its native elites were extinguished and the state fell under Danish-Holsteinian hegemony for almost 400 years.

Kingdom began as a personal union between England (including Wales) and Scotland in 1604, later developing into a parliamentary union in 1707. Spain came into being in 1492 with the unification of Castille and Aragon, albeit Catalonia was only formally incorporated in 1714. France gradually acquired its present borders (*l'Hexagone*) in a steady process of expansion from 1500 to 1700. The end result is a curious mixture of extreme centralization and jealously guarded localism. As suggested by the British historian Hugh Kearney, it is instructive to compare developments in Northern Europe with those of Spain, Britian and France, not only in order to gain a better grasp of the history of the North, but also in order to better understand the major polities which are most often accorded prominence as classic examples of the nation-state (cf. Kearney 1991).

One might wonder why the unification of the North did not take place in the Middle Ages or early modern period, as was the case in Spain, Britain and France. The answer is Sweden. The Late Middle Ages saw a Danish Monarchy striving to achieve mastery of the entire Baltic region, *Dominium Maris Baltici* as the strategy was called (Ahnlund 1956). Ultimately, Sweden broke away and transformed herself into a competing composite state with a huge Baltic empire. The competition between these two northern European states explains the present situation. In order to compensate for their humble population figures, the relatively poor states of Denmark-Norway and Sweden established themselves, each in its own particular way, with a state apparatus that was 'heavier' than was the norm elsewhere in Europe (Anderson 1974: 173-91). The degree of centralization and extent of taxation are still evident in the magnificence of the monumental buildings in the two capitals of Copenhagen and Stockholm. This exploitation of the population in its entirety was later depicted by 'anti-colonialist' Norwegian, Finnish, Icelandic and Faeroese historians as Danish and Swedish national oppression, respectively. Yet this description is not accurate. Broadly speaking, Danish and Swedish peasants were exploited on an equal footing with the Norwegians, Sleswigers, Holsteiners, Icelanders, Faeorese, Finns, Samis and others.

Denmark had long been the most populous of the three Scandinavian monarchies, and its efforts to achieve sole supremacy failed only because the Danish nobility, prior to its defeat in the seventeenth century, refused to be tamed by a strong monarchy. Furthermore, the transnational nobility, with landed estates in both Sweden and Denmark, also failed in its attempts to create an aristocratic republic under elected kings, as occured at the same time in the Polish-Lithuanian *rzeczpospolita* or *res publica* (cf. Davies 1984: 296). Instead, Sweden acquitted itself so well that between 1645 and 1709 it was able to assume the hegemony over Denmark-Norway in the Baltic and Northern Europe and establish a much more successful empire. Denmark avoided being annexed by Sweden between 1658 and 1660 only because the great power of the day, the Netherlands, was interested in a weak state controlling the approaches to the Baltic.

The Netherlands came to the aid of Denmark in 1658, just as Britain and Russia were subsequently to lend Denmark their support for fear of finding themselves faced with a single great power at the entrance to the Baltic (the Sound). This narrow escape has left deep traces in the collective memory of Danes, something approaching genuine trauma.[12] Only after a series of attempts to undo the Swedish conquests and challenge her newly won hegemony did Denmark accept the losses. Denmark's acquiescence, on the other hand, eventually caught on to such a degree, that the history of Danish-Swedish conflict has been virtually obliterated from the institutionalized historical memory. The conflict lives on, but as Peter Unwin remarked, it remains at a level comparable to the competition between Oxford and Cambridge (Unwin 1996: 210).

As a result of this national amnesia, the overwhelming majority of Danes today consider the inhabitants of Skaane not as 'lost Danes', but as Swedes. This renunciation is rather perplexing to outsiders, as the landscape of Skaane to this day positively exudes 'Danishness', if one only abstracts from the application of a thin coat of Stockholmian state-Swedishness. After the Swedish annexations in 1658-60, and especially after the check-mate situation of the War of Skaane in 1675-79, radical measures were taken to reorient the Scanian population towards Sweden. What is remarkable seen in European perspective is not these efforts in themselves so much as the fact that they were successful. As the Danish historian Knud Fabricius has demonstrated, Skaane constitutes just about the only known example of such a massive policy of indoctrination having succeeded (Fabricius 1906: 3-16). Whether this may be attributed to the skill of the Swedish state or to the realism (or weak national identification) of the Danish peasantry remains an open question (cf. Åberg 1994 for an open minded Swedish analysis). What is worth noting today is that Swedish-Danish antagonism in Skaane has since been effectively buried. Of course, there are still wide clefts between Danes and Swedes, but this is not due to the wars of the past, but to the fact that until quite recently the Swedes succeeded in presenting themselves as the epitome of modernity.

The demand to bring Skaane 'home to Denmark' is stone dead and has been so now for almost 300 years. This massive repression of history can be traced to the realignment of the Danish state following defeats at the hands of Sweden in the mid-1600s. The relinquishing of Skaane, Halland, Blekinge, Gotland, Ösel, Bohuslen, Herjedalen and Jämtland between 1645 and 1660 led to the introduction of the Absolutist monarchy in 1660. This implied an administrative reorganization or 'modernization' of the state, but also a geopolitical reorientation towards Sleswig and Holstein, which were now gradually incorporated into the core of the kingdom as the competing state-nation project in northern Europe, that of the Gottorp fam-

---

12 By 'collective memory' I refer to the authoritative interpretation of history handed down in history books as well by other more popular means of recollection. The concept was originally developed by the French sociologist of the Durkheimian school, Maurice Halbwachs, who died in Buchenwald in 1945. In two pathbreaking studies, 1925 and 1950, now translated into English, Halbwachs analyzed several of its implications. The French historian Pierre Nora took the 'collective memory' concept as a point of departure for his masive investigation of the 'places of (French) memory' (les 'lieux de mémoire') in 7 massive volumes (Nora 1984-92). Recently an entire industry analyzing the differences between history and memory has sprung up. A valuable Danish introduction to various aspects of remembrance and forgetting in the lives of nations, groups and individuals in B.E. Jensen et al. (1996).

ily (1490-1773) gradually lost out to the Oldenborg family. This realignment was almost of the same magnitude as the simultaneous transformation of Sweden from an East-West to a North-South axis. The Danish Monarchy was to prove unsuccessful in its attempts to regain the provinces lost to Sweden in the two wars of revenge of 1675-79 and 1709-20, but the increase in the power of the Crown, was to be otherwise achieved with the annexation of the Gottorp regions of Sleswig and Holstein in 1720.

During the war of 1675-79, the Duchy of Sleswig was occupied by Danish troops, though no lasting result was achieved, and in 1689 the king was forced to accept the reinstatement of the Duke of Gottorp. In 1700 Denmark again fought Sweden, each in union with separate European great powers. As a result of the Swedish defeat by the Russians at Poltava in present day Ukraine in 1709, Denmark achieved its revenge but gained no lands. As compensation, Sweden, France and Britain in 1720 finally accepted the incorporation of Gottorp by the Danish king, enshrined in the Act of Incorporation of 1721. The Law of Succession of 1665 (*Lex Regia*) was now extended to the whole of Sleswig. Administratively, however, Sleswig was to remain together with the royal portions of Holstein, both of which were to be administered by the German Chancellery (in Copenhagen since 1523, which resembled a kind of 'Ministry of Foreign Affairs' under Absolutism).

The Monarchy thus lived up to its official name, the Low German 'Kron zu Dennemarck'. This designation referred not merely to Denmark proper, north of Kongeåen, but to the Crown's possessions in their entirety, Norway and the Norwegian dependencies Greenland, the Faeroes and Iceland, as well as the duchies of Holstein and Sleswig. All in all, this multi-national state comprised a medium-sized European power on the level of Prussia and, thanks to Norway, possessed the third largest navy in Europe at the end of the eighteenth century. In 1767, after a major military crisis, an exchange was agreed with the Gottorp heirs, whereby the Danish king gained unchallenged possession of all Holstein. The move was effected in 1773, making the united monarchy a tangible reality within the framework of the Danish-Norwegian Dual or Double Monarchy. Thus, the foundations were laid for the great reform process of 1784-1814. These reforms were initiated primarily by representatives of the German-speaking aristocratic elite within the composite state. This elite, however, saw no reason to make any adjustments to the administrative division of the realm, so that the Danish-speaking regions in Sleswig were to continue to be administered together with Holstein, as was stipulated in the 'Treaty of Ribe' of 1460, by which the Danish king had promised to keep the two duchies 'unde dat se bliven ewich tosamende ungedelt' (forever undivided, Gregersen 1981: 178).

The foundation for this tightly organized state was laid in the 1670s and 1680s, when the Absolutist monarchy reformed itself on the pattern of the France of Louis XIV.[13] The all-encompassing bodies of laws, *Danske Lov* of 1683 and *Norske Lov*

---

13 According to the recent and highly original research by Gunner Lind and others, the structural foundations for these legal innovations date back to the wars between 1614 and 1662, the Danish version of the European wide military-political revolution of the seventeenth century (Cf. Lind 1994, 1996).

of 1687, modernized, systematized and made uniform the many varying medieval provincial laws, introducing a chancellery in the European mould (Horstbøll and Østergaard 1990). A completly new survey of the productivity of the arable land and other natural resources enabled the state to collect taxes on a fairer basis than before. The central administration was rebuilt on the Swedish-European model of specialized colleges somewhat similar to today's ministries. The administration of the army and navy was the first to be modernized. Then followed the administration of finance, whose college was made up of four nobles and four burghers. That the path to a government career in this way was opened to persons of non-noble birth was something quite new. The old regional administration of state territories in the Danish and German Chancelleries, respectively, was incorporated into the college system as 'domestic' and 'external' administration, and by the end of the seventeenth century the territorial state had gradually been replaced by a tax-based 'Machtstaat' (power-state, cf. Ladewig Petersen 1984).

In a brief episode from 1770 to 1772, Johann Friedrich Struensee, physician to the Absolutist King Christian VII', tried to revolutionize the entire state by introducing radical reforms from the top down of the type recommended by Enlightenment philosophers. Though born in Altona, i.e. within the borders of the multinational Monarchy, most of Struensee's career had been spent outside Denmark, and he was thus perceived by the majority of population as a foreigner. His reforms quickly ran into disrepute when he was exposed as an adulterer and the queen's secret lover. His arrest and subsequent execution provoked some anti-German sentiments among Danish-speaking middle classes who hoped to profit from the expulsion of the so-called 'Germans' (Feldbæk 1991-92: I).

In an attempt to forestall further criticism, the government, in 1776, passed a law reserving government jobs for those born inside the realm, the 'Indfødsret'. This law was backed by a whole series of well meant – but futile as it turned out – attempts to build a common patriotic feeling in the whole of the realm in general and for the king in particular (Feldbæk 1991: I-II and Rasmussen 1995: 28-29). Examples of this ideological enterprise was the publication in 1776 of a history of the Monarchy (Suhm 1776) and Ove Malling's 'Lives of Eminent Danes, Norwegians and Holsteinians' in the tradition of Plutarch in 1771 (1992).

In 1800, the Danish king still ruled over a vast, though thinly populated realm, stretching from Greenland, Iceland and Norway to the suburbs of Hamburg, in distance half the total European coast-line. According to the reliable census of 1801, the total population of the kingdom was 2.5 million. Denmark-Norway had 1.8 million, 51% of which lived in Denmark proper; Sleswig-Holstein had 600,000 inhabitants, of which 54% were in Holstein; other German possessions counted for some 90,000 people and the North Atlantic islands some 50,000. No reliable census for the colonies exists, as their status was different (Rasmussen 1995: 25).

The Enlightment reforms of the late eighteenth century were based upon reform of the civil laws, which ended the personal dependency of peasants upon landowners, a reform of the system of cultivation comprising abolition of the common field system and enclosure of the individual holdings, establishment of a comprehensive school system (1814), and liberalization of the customs as the most important changes. In 1805, serfdom in Holstein was abolished, a move which alienated the German landed aristocracy of this province and made them the embittered opponents of the Monarchy they had been supporting, or at least accepted as legitimate. In 1806, following the abolishment of the Holy Roman Empire by Napoleon, Holstein was incorporated into the Danish monarchy. From 1720 to 1807, the Danish Monarchy enjoyed a hitherto unparalleled prosperity, based on better prices for its agrarian products and on huge profits in neutral trading during the repeated European and colonial wars. In the early nineteenth century, however, Denmark-Norway overplayed its hand and ended up an adversary of Britain in the Napoleonic wars. The battle of Copenhagen in 1801, the British bombardment of the capital in 1807, the subsequent loss of the navy and final defeat at the hands of the anti-Napoleon coalition led to bankrupcy of the state in 1813 and the loss of Norway to Sweden in 1814.[14]

These events completely altered the balance between the German and Nordic elements in the composite state. The number of German speakers rose from less than 20% to 35% and nationalist sentiments began to tear the state apart (Rasmussen 1995: 26). As mentioned, in 1806, the Duchy of Holstein was annexed to Denmark as a consequence of the disintegration of the Holy Roman Empire. However, with the establishment of the German Confederation in 1815, Holstein was reestablished as an independent duchy, which implied that the Danish king participated in the Federal Assembly in his capacity as Duke of Holstein. As punishment for the alliance with France, the Danish king was compelled to cede the kingdom of Norway to Sweden, 'in return' for which he received the tiny Duchy of Lauenburg (Nørregaard 1954). With that, the Dual Monarchy gave way to the so-called *Gesamtstaat* ('Helstat' or United Monarchy).[15] Though reduced, this state was still a composite state in legal terms, and it retained its multinational character. It consisted of the Kingdom of Denmark proper (North Jutland to the Kongeåen plus the islands) and the duchies of Sleswig, Holstein and Lauenburg. The latter, no larger in size than the minor Danish island of Lolland, retained its independent status and its particular institutions. Furthermore, the realm comprised the dependencies of Iceland and the Faroe Islands, and the colonies of Greenland, the Danish West Indies, Tranquebar and Guinea. In short, still a multi-nation polity in the mould of the Austro-Hungarian Monarchy, only smaller. As was the case with the Habsburg Empire, however, the multi-national state was soon to be torn apart by two antagonistic, national programmes, a Danish-(Scandinavianist, i.e. Danish-Swedish), and a German-(Sleswig-Holsteinian).

---

14 The British Bombardment of Copenhagen gave rise to the expression 'Copenhagen a city' i.e. exposing a civilian population to a terror bombardment.
15 On the *Gesamtstaat* and the historical development of the Danish-German state see K. Bohnen, S. Aa. Jørgensen (Hrsg.), *Der dänische Gesamstaat: Kiel – Kopenhagen – Altona* (Wolfenbütteler Studien zur Aufklärung 18, Tübingen 1992). On Denmark-Norway as a Gesamtstaat, see Feldbæk 1998-99.

Civil War, Break-up of the Composite State and the Nationalization of the Peasant Masses

Nationalization is the most convenient and relevant term denoting the processes of national identification and democratization in Europe in the nineteenth century. It denotes processes of deliberate nationalization from above (cf. Mosse 1975), that is indoctrination as well as broader, more democratic processes from below combined with deliberate national indoctrination by the school system and the media (Weber 1976).[16]

The demand for the creation of a national state with a written constitution was first formulated in liberal minority circles in the first half of the nineteenth century, primarily among students and younger civil servants. In Denmark and Holstein, the move from international or supranational liberalism to national liberalism happened between 1836 and 1842. Until then the liberal movements in Copenhagen and Kiel had been allied in their resistance to the almost unlimited power of the Absolute Monarchy, which continued to prevail even after the introduction of the consultative assemblies in 1830/34. Being so few in number, the bourgeoisie alone was in no position to shake the despotic regime. Had this not been apparent before, it certainly became so following the accession of Christian VIII to the throne in 1839. The liberals had believed that Christian VIII would transfer the free Norwegian constitution, over which he had presided in 1814, to Denmark. Astute as he was, however, Christian VIII nourished no desire to curtail his own powers and deliver himself into the hands of the increasingly nationalistic liberals. Under these circumstances, the two liberal reform groups in the capitals of Copenhagen and Kiel each established their own strategic alliances. In Denmark, the liberals allied themselves with the peasant farmers, an alliance which in 1846 was capped by the establishment of a political party, *Bondevennerne* (Friends of the Peasant). In Holstein, a more informal alliance was established with the landed aristocracy that later developed into the Sleswig-Holsteinian "movement". The confrontation of 1848 was not the result of the situation in Sleswig, however, but the fact that neither of the two liberal groups were able to gain power without polarization over the abstract ideology of nationalism (Waahlin & Østergaard 1975).

The nationalistic radicalization of the language employed eventually led to war and ended with the dismemberment of the united Danish Monarchy after the self-inflicted defeat of 1864. Denmark survived as a sovereign nation-state only by the skin of its teeth, and not without help from the outside. Again it was the interests of the great powers, first and foremost Russia and Britain this time, in maintaining a neutral power at the entrance to the Baltic, that saved Denmark as a sovereign state. Had this not been the case, the country would have become either German or Swedish (the latter eventuality being termed Scandinavianism). Today we have

---

16 A combination of the two understandings of the term is applied by Østergaard in several analyses of the Danish process (1992a and 1993a). A general presentation of the theoretical literature on national identity in Østergaard (1992c), Hettne, Sörlin and Østergaard (1998).

grown used to considering this development as both inevitable and positive. This view reflects the swift exploitation by popular movements of the exceptional situation of a whole sovereign state having been rendered so weak that it allowed the peasant movement, and subsequently the workers movement, to gain control over the state. Such popular movements were not altogether uncommon in an international context, but it was quite unique for such movements to gain cultural, economic and eventually political hegemony within a sovereign state (Østergaard 1992a). This is what the slogan 'Outward losses must be made up by inward gains' came to mean for the Danes in the period following 1864.

The programme for a romantically, ethnically and historically motivated definition of the nation was, as previously noted, formulated by the National Liberal 'party' – party here being placed in inverted commas because the liberals in principle did not recognize political parties at all, only representatives of the whole nation, motivated only by their own convictions (Lehmann 1861). This conception, however, was out of tune with the political and social realities. The years 1830-1848 saw the rise of modern political ideas in Denmark. As a result, the lower classes began to organize themselves from the bottom up. According to the liberals, members of society ought to organize on the basis of their own ideas and compete for political power through free elections – although the liberals meant that only those who understood how to govern should vote, the socalled 'best and brightest' (Lehmann 1861). But this was all theory.

In practice, it was to become apparent already prior to the political upheaval of 1848 and the subsequent civil war between 'Danes' and 'Germans' (the Danish version of a bourgeois revolution cf. Østergaard 1998) that the dividing lines ran parallel with social or class-based affiliations. Liberal academics, officials and other pillars of the liberal community sought to conceal these class cleavages by shrewdly elaborating appeals in the name of 'the people'. The means for creating this alliance across class divisions was the so-called 'national revival' (or more aptly, nationalistic incitement) concerning the status of the Duchy of Sleswig within the national framework. The strategy worked well for a number of years, but ended in the abortive attempt to annex Sleswig in November 1863 and the National Liberals' subsequent collapse. Stubborn and intransigent quibbling by Danish National Liberal politicians and their misjudgement of the international situation enabled Bismarck to establish a united Germany, without Austria, and under Prussian dominance (Nielsen 1987). The international political climate and international agreements notwithstanding, the National Liberals demanded a Danish nation-state within the 'historical' framework, meaning all of Sleswig to the river Ejder, regardless of the opinion of the inhabitants. This move would have resulted in a large German-speaking minority within Denmark. Instead Prussia and Austria took all of Sleswig and Holstein, with a large Danish population in Northern Sleswig (Østergaard 1996a).

This led to the proclamation of a new German Empire in 1871. The presence in the middle of Europe of this unstable and all too domineering new major power provoked in its turn a national unification in Denmark, as well as in other neighbouring countries. In Denmark, this was achieved in a quite exceptional manner by means of a combination of outside pressures and initiatives from below, primarily from the class of peasant farmers. On the basis of this conscious demarcation towards Germany and all things German, the modern, popular and democratic Denmark emerged, i.e. everything Danes today celebrate as being particularly Danish about Denmark and the Danes (Østergaard 1984).

During the 1870s, the opposition successfully engaged in a virtual *Kulturkampf* with the conservatives and the urban liberals over control of the schools and the congregations. The struggle over the schools was to have far greater importance for the establishment of cultural hegemony than the better-described conflict of literary cultures in the 1880s (Østergaard 1984). The latter has always been the subject of attention from social-liberal intellectuals owing to the quality of the contributions from the critic and politician Edvard Brandes (1847-1931), the literary historian Georg Brandes (1842-1927), the journalist and politician Viggo Hørup (1841-1902) and other so-called 'European intellectuals'. Despite their intellectual brilliance and apparent victory with the founding of the newspaper *Politiken* in 1884, the cultural hegemony they sought, did not materialize. The religious and social movements of the Grundtvigians and their opponents in the Pietist 'Inner Mission', however, were more successful. From their efforts ensued a hegemony that in the twentieth century subsequently was to be appropriated by the Social Democratic workers movement, in alliance with the successors to the European left.

With social unification, however, came a high degree of national mobilization among the rural masses and in the rest of the nation. This nationalism, in its turn, made it extremely difficult for the responsible government to strike the necessary compromises with the rising German power next door. Only the defeat of the German Reich in World War I provided an opportunity for Denmark to retrieve the Danish speakers in North Sleswig. Because of clumsy attempts to Germanize them, the Danish-speaking Sleswigers had become ardent Danish nationalists, organizing a sort of parallel society (Japsen 1983). Yet it took almost superhuman efforts on the part of courageous and far-sighted representatives of the Danish minority in Sleswig, such as H.P. Hansen Nørremølle (1862-1936) to bring about the necessary change in the Danish political line and arrive at a vital national compromise with its great neighbour (Østergaard 1996a).

One of the prerequisites was the building of new self-confidence within the population. An important element in this process was a reorientation away from Europe and towards the North (Østergaard 1996b). Whether the shift from a European to a Nordic orientation has been worth the cultural price is a matter for debate. However, it is incontestable that in the short run, the reorientation involved major political advantages in terms of a homogenous and self-important nation-state that was able to hold together, even after having surrendered to German forces almost without firing a shot on 9 April, 1940.

The Peasant-Farmer Roots of Danish National Identity

Contrary to the situation in most other nineteenth century nation-states, the small size of the amputated Danish state allowed a numerous class of relatively well-to-do peasants who had turned independent farmers via the reforms of the late eighteenth century, to assume economical and political hegemony. This did not occur without opposition, but through the latter part of the nineteenth century, the middle peasants gradually took over from the despairing ruling elites. The latter were recruited from the tiny urban bourgeoisie, the civil servants of the state trained at German-style universities inside the Monarchy as well as outside, and the manorial class. After the debacle of 1864, and the subsequent establishment of a strong united Germany next door they had lost faith in the survival of the state. Some even played with the thought of joining this neighbouring state which already dominated the culture of the upper classes.

In this situation, however, an outburst of so-called 'popular' energy proclaimed a strategy of 'winning inwards what had been lost to the outside'. This slogan was turned into a literal strategy of retrieving the lost agrarian lands of Western Jutland, now deserted because of the deforestation of the sixteenth and seventeenth centuries. It also took the form of an opening up of 'Dark Jutland' in an attempt to turn the economy of the peninsula away from Hamburg and redirect it towards Copenhagen. This movement, provocatively called 'the Discovery of Jutland' (Frandsen 1995 and 1996), entailed the exploitation of Jutland by the capital Copenhagen, situated on the far eastern rim of the country as remnant of the former empire, much like Vienna in present day Austria. This battle between metropolis and province is not yet over, as demonstrated in the heated controversies whether or not to build a bridge between the islands of Fyn and Sjælland or to connect Sweden and Copenhagen directly with Germany over the gulf of Fehmern (Østergaard 2000). The attempt to hold the Danish nation-state together and keep Jutland away from Hamburg won out, as the former bridge has now been completed. However, the decision was achieved only by a very narrow margin.

More important, however, is the cultural, economic and political awakening of the middle peasants who became farmers producing for the world market precisely during this period of time. The basis of their success was the relative weakness of the Danish bourgeoisie and the country's late industrialization. The take-off happened only in the 1890s and the final break-through as late as the 1950s (Hansen 1970). The middle peasants developed a consciousness of themselves as a class and understood themselves to be the real backbone of society. Their ideology supported free trade, not surprising as they were beginning to rely heavily on the export of food to the rapidly developing British market. Trade links to Britain were so important that Denmark, economically speaking, was de facto a part of the British empire from the mid-nineteenth to the mid-twentieth century. More surprising is the fact that their ideology also contained strong libertarian elements because of their struggle with the existing urban and academic elites. The peasant-farmers' movement achieved hegomony because it succeeded in establishing an independent culture with its own educational institutions. This was in turn possible because of the unique organization of the agrarian industries: the cooperative.

Basic agrarian production had remained individual production on independent farms, albeit of an average size somewhat larger than usual in a European context. However, the processing of the dairy and meat produce into exportable products took place in local farm industries run on a cooperative basis. The cooperative associations were run democratically on the basis of equality, regardless of the initial investment. The cooperative movement formulated this in a slogan of votes being cast 'by heads instead of heads of cattle' (i.e., one man, one vote regardless of the initial investment). This pun (in Danish *hoveder* and *høveder*) is less true when one starts investigating the realities of the cooperatives. Yet the myth remained, producing a sense of community which by means of various political traditions has been transformed into a long-lasting hegemony that laid the ground for a national consensus. This consensus, while hard to define, until very recently, made it possible for members of the Danish community to communicate through means of words, symbols, and actions. Humour and understatement thrived on a common understanding that precedes the spoken word.

The libertarian values, though, were not originally meant to include other segments of the population. The agrarian system was based on a crass exploitation of the agricultural labourers by the farmers. The latter, along with the urban elites, were often not even considered part of 'the people' by the peasant-farmers. However, in an interesting and surprisingly original ideological manoeuvre, the rising Social Democracy adapted its ideology to the unique agrarian-industrial conditions in Denmark and developed a strategy very different from the Marxist orthodoxy of the German mother party. The Danish Social Democracy even agreed to the establishment of a class of very small farmers called *husmænd* (cottagers). Thus, the Social Democrats fulfilled the expectations of their landless members among the agricultural workers but at the same time undermined the possibility of ever obtaining an absolute majority in the Parliament, as did their sister parties in Sweden and Norway.

This apparently suicidal strategy, as well as subsequent compromises in housing policy, ruled out any position of a virtual Social Democratic monopoly of power, as took place in Norway and Sweden (Esping-Andersen 1985). Yet as far as we can judge, they did so knowingly and on purpose. During World War I, it became clear to the Social Democratic leadership that the party would never be able to achieve an absolute political majority. Under Thorvald Stauning's thirty-two years of charismatic leadership (1910-1942), the party restructured its line from a class-based to a more 'popular' one. The near concensus line was first openly formulated in 1923, and later on adopted in slogans such as 'the people's cooperating rule' and, somewhat less clumsily, 'Denmark for the people' (1934). The platform resulted in a stable governing coalition, from 1929 to 1943, of the Social Liberals (*Det Radikale Venstre*) and the Social Democratic Party. The Social Democratic leaders apparently accepted the ultimate check on the influence of their own movement in the interests of the society at large. Perhaps they did not distinguish between the two. Developments might have turned out differently in Germany had the Social Democracy in that country in the 1920s adapted a policy directed towards the people as a whole and not just the working class in the Marxist sense.

The eminent German socialist theoretician Karl Kautsky (1854-1938) never really understood the role of agriculture in modern societies. He saw it as something of the pre-capitalist past which would be better run according to the principles of mass-industrialization as happened in the Soviet Union after the collectivizations of the 1930s. The Danish Social Democrats, in their practical policies had a better understanding of agriculture. But proved unable to turn this understanding into coherent theory. At the level of doctrine, the party stuck to the formulations in the 1913 program. These formulations reflected the international debates in the Second International rather than the Danish reality and the practical policy of the party. The very fact that the program of 1913 remained unchanged until 1961 testifies to the lack of importance attributed to theory in this most pragmatic of all reformist Socialist parties. Danish Social Democracy was never strong on theory, but the labour movement, on the other hand, has produced an impressive number of capable administrators and politicians.

This lack of explicit strategy enabled remnants of the libertarian peasant ideology to take root early on within the party and in the labour movement as such. The Social Democrats embarked upon a policy for the people as such, and not just for the working class. This testifies to the importance of the liberal-popular ideological hegemony dating back to the peasants-farmers' ideological hegemony in the last third of the nineteenth century. The leaders realized that they would never gain power on their own. The farmers proper constituted only a fragment of the population as a whole, but small scale production permeated the whole society then as it still does today. Ironically, the Marxist who understood Denmark best was Lenin. In a discussion of the Agrarian Program of the Social Democracy (Lenin 1907) he discussed at length the Danish cooperatives, which he had studied on the spot (in the Royal Library in Copenhagen). Lenin turned out rather positively disposed towards such a self-reliant strategy but refused to endorse it for Russia for a number of reasons. Maybe he should have done so. That a strategy directed towards the majority of the people would turn out more rewarding seems pretty obvious from today's point of view. Yet a sophisticated socialist party such as the German Social Democrats embarked only on this strategy as late as 1959 in Bad Godesberg; the British Labour and the French Socialist Party took even longer to make up their minds; and what happens in former Eastern Europe still remains to be seen.

The main reason why a libertarian ideology of solidarity ended up dominating a whole nation-state was the small size of this particular state. Danish historians and sociologists have eagerly discussed whether the peasant ideological hegemony resulted from a particular class structure dating back to the 1780s or even further back to the early sixteenth century, when the number of farms were frozen by law, or whether it was this ideology that created the particular class-structure of the Danish nineteenth century society (Paludan 1995). Constructed in such terms, the discussion is almost impossible to solve, as both positions reveal some truth. My own view is that the outcome can best be explained in terms of the existence of a particular form of populism or 'popular' ideology (*folkelighed*) stressing the importance of consensus among people. This status was first and most coherently formulated by the important Danish thinker, virtually untranslated and untranslatable philosopher, Nikolaj Frederik Grundtvig (1783-1872) who was a historian, priest, and poet. That is I stress the importance of what historians label 'chance' or 'accidence' (cf. note 2). This does not imply that I refrain from explaining the course of history, but I accept that a different outcome would have been possible (Østergaard 1997d, cf. note 2).

The Grundtvigian Synthesis – National and Social Consensus

Depressed by the defeat of Denmark by Great Britain in the war 1807-1814, the young priest N.F.S. Grundtvig took it upon himself to reestablish what he took to be the original 'Nordic' or 'Danish' mind. He translated the Icelandic Sagas, the twelfth century historian Saxo Grammaticus, the Anglo Saxon poem *Beowulf* and many other sources of what he considered to be the true but lost core of 'Danishness'. His sermons attracted large crowds of enthusiastic students. His address on *The Light of the Holy Trinity*, delivered in 1814 to a band of student volunteers willing to fight the British, inspired a whole generation of young followers, including the priest Jacob Christian Lindberg (1791-1857), who later organized the first Grundtvigian movement. When Grundtvig embarked upon a sharp polemic with his superiors in the church on matters of theology, he was banned from all public appearances and publishing. This drove him into what he called his 'inner exile' in the 1830s. This inner exile, however, gave him time for reflection where he formulated a program for the revival of the stagnant official religion. When the ban was lifted in 1839, he burst out in a massive production of sermons, psalms, and songs, a literary legacy which until at least a few years ago formed the core of the socialization of most Danes.

Grundtvig then formulated an all-embracing view of nature, language, and history. In 1848, after the outbreak of the civil war over Sleswig, he produced a refined definition of national identity which helped set the tone for a nationalism less chauvinistic than most in the nineteenth century. As is sometimes the case with prolific writers, his most precise theoretical expressions were to be found in the restricted form of the verse:

> People! What is a people? What does popular mean?
> Is it the nose or the mouth that gives it away?
> Is there a people hidden from the average eye
> in burial hills and behind bushes, in every body, big and boney?
> They belong to a people who think they do,
> those who can hear the Mother tongue,

those who love the Fatherland.
The rest are separated from the people, expel themselves, do not belong.
(from the poem *Folkelighed* 1848 by N.F.S. Grundtvig, my translation)

This definition, though produced in the heat of battle with the German-speaking rebels in the duchies of Sleswig and Holstein, resembles most of all the definition of national identity produced by the French thinker Ernest Renan in what has since become one of the standard texts on nationalism, *Qu'est-ce qu'une nation?* (1882). Originally Renan's intention was to 'scientifically' demonstrate the right of the French population in Alsace-Lorraine to its French nationality after the provinces had been signed over to Germany by the peace treaty in 1871. After their defeat in the Franco-German war, the French changed their minds as to whether a nation should be defined in cultural or political terms. The same happened in Denmark after the defeat in 1864, which in 1867 was followed by the incorporation into Prussia of all of Sleswig. But Grundtvig anticipated this change of thinking – at least in some of his writings.

Renan's statement has since become the standard formulation of an anti-essentialist definition of national identity. This could be labelled a voluntaristic-subjective definition, stressing as it does the importance of the expressed will of people. The rival definition in modern European thinking could be called the objective-culturalist definition. It dates back to the German thinker J.G.H. Herder and has permeated all thinking in the nineteenth and twentieth centuries up until Fascism and Nazism (Østergaard 1991a). It is surprising that the Danish thinker Grundtvig should present a democratic definition of nationality as early as 1848. No military defeat had preceded it, as was the case in France. Until 1870, French thinkers had defined nationality in terms no less essentialist than any German would after that date. Moreover it should be recalled that Grundtvig wrote these lines in a highly explosive political situation when a majority in the two predominantly German-speaking provinces of Sleswig and Holstein had seceded. Grundtvig left those who opted for the German language to their own choice as non-Danes, which in his opinion was a most deplorable fate. Yet he left them the choice and would never dream of interfering with it.

Through a long and complicated history, this understanding of national identity later became official Danish policy and has successfully been applied in the border region between Denmark and Germany after 1920, and particularly after 1955. There is much more to say about the thinking of Grundtvig and his influence on Danish political culture. The core of his thinking was the assumption that culture and identity are embedded in the unity of life and language. Although this kind of thinking invites one to label it as chauvinism, Grundtvig himself, like his opposite number Herder, did not assume a hierarchy of nationalities. Cultural diversity yes, cultural dominance no. Whether these assumptions are really viable need not concern us here. What is important is that Grundtvig's thinking caught on among a class of people in the small Nothern European state left over from the wars of the middle of the century.

It began immediately after 1814, with the students. The breakthrough occured around 1839, when various religious and political movements decided to transform his thinking into practice. First, it influenced the revivalist religious movements, later on the more explicitly political movements and eventually his thinking came to serve as the foundation for independent economic and educational institutions. Grundtvig himself did not seek such popular support. He delivered his message either in writing or orally, and then stood aloof when others decided what to make out of it. This is why some of today's guardians of Grundtvig's thoughts speak of him as having been 'taken prisoner by the Grundtvigian movement' when his message was transformed into an ideology known as 'Grundtvigism' (Thodberg and Thyssen 1983).

No doubt there is some truth to this, as is always the case when an individual's thought is transformed into social practice, for example with Marx and Marxism. The only ones who have not suffered such fate are the likes of the existentialist philosopher Søren Kierkegaard (1813-55), i.e. those who formulate their ideas without reference to their relevance for society. Grundtvig's thinking, however, certainly struck a chord with many groups in society, but he did not care whether it did or not. He normally refused to meet people and, if he did, he talked incessantly and never listened. Consequently, the reasons behind the influence of his thinking are not to be found in his personal behaviour, but in the thought itself and its relevance for the surrounding society.

The revivalists came to Grundtvig of their own accord. This religious movement of the first half of the nineteenth century resembled many other Pietist movements throughout Europe. Because of the negative attitude of the official Lutheran state church, they chose to meet outside the churches, and were thus called *Forsamlingsbevægelsen* ('the Meeting Movement'). They were attracted by Grundtvig's independent interpretation of the Lutheran heritage. Grundtvig, however, succeeded in giving an optimistic tone to the normally somewhat gloomy Pietism of German origins. In their struggles with the officials of the Absolutist state, these revivalists learned an organizational lesson which they would soon put to political use. The leaders of the peasant movement of the 1840s were recruited from their ranks. Initially working under the tutelage of the liberal intellectuals, the peasant party gradually broke away from the National Liberals, as they called themselves.

The various political factions of the peasant party would soon establish their own independent institutions, beginning with the church. With the transformation of the monarchy from an Absolutist to a constitutional regime in 1849, the organization of the church had to be changed accordingly. However the result of these endeavours differed in important ways from the otherwise comparable situation in the Lutheran monarchies of Sweden and Norway. A state church with a proper constitution never came into existence, though it had been envisaged in the constitution of 1849. This was a result of the influence of Grundtvig and the revivalist movement. They wanted guarantees of religious freedom, so the church should be the creature of the state, or its agent of socialization, as it had been under Absolutism. They found these guarantees best preserved in an anarchic state of affairs (Lindhardt 1951).

In this way, Denmark acquired a most peculiar mixture of freedom and state control in religious matters. The minister of religious affairs is called Minister of the 'People's Church' – a contradiction in terms that does not seem to bother Danes. The minister presides over church administration and the upkeep of church buildings, most of which is financed by a separate tax whereas 60% of the pay for the pastors is provided by the state. However, it is left to individual priests and their congregations to interpret the actual teachings of the church. Councils of the local parishes (Menighedsråd), elected every four years, run these congregations. Nowadays the most influential groups in these counties are the fundamentalist Inner Mission and the Social Democrats! In spite of their differences, they often collaborate in order to control the elected priests. The latter are normally academically trained at the universities and represent an intellectually refined Lutheran theology which often does not appeal to ordinary believers.

Most of the apparently non-religious Danish population belongs to this church in the sense that 86% pay the taxes even if relatively few attend services except for Christmas, baptisms, burials, and weddings. Still, I think, the Lutheranism of the People's Church plays an enormous and insufficiently recognised role in defining the political culture. In fact, we should probably talk of Lutheran or Protestant Democracy rather than Social Democracy when analyzing the social and political model advocated by Denmark in particular and the Nordic countries in general.[17]

In the 1870s, the ideological battle was carried into the field of education. The National Liberals who now sided whole-heartedly with the conservative estate owners in a party called *Højre* ('the Right') wanted a comprehensive school system under the supervision of the state. This, was vehemently opposed by the majority of the farmers' party *Venstre* ('the Left'), who believed in the absolute freedom of education and attacked the socalled 'black' schools of learning where Latin was still taught. This they could do because the peasant movement, from 1844, had established a network of 'folk high schools' throughout the country. Over the years, Grundtvig had produced a series of programs for a new and more democratic educational system. Like many of his other ideas they did not constitute a coherent system. Rather, they can be seen as an appeal for a more practical schooling in democracy. What these schools lacked in coherent programs, however, they made up for in flexibility. Today, most of them are institutions of adult education, supplementing the formal educational system.

On top of this, the anti-institutional thinking of Grundtvig ultimately permeated the Danish educational system to such a degree, that even today there is no compulsory schooling, only compulsory learning. How one is educated is a personal choice. Again, this might not sound terribly surprising for an American audience,

---

17 Mouritzen uses these terms in a recent analysis of Danish foreign policy (Mouritzen 1997). Another perspective is to underline the origins of the particular Nordic version of Enlightenment thinking among the local priesthood as does Nina Witoszek and others in the forthcoming *The Cultural Construction of the Nordic Countries* ed. by Bo Stråth and Øystein Sørensen (1997). Lately I have analyzed the relationship between the universalist welfare state and Lutheranism (Østergaard 1998).

but in the context of highly centralized European states with a Lutheran heritage, it is most surprising. Furthermore, these schools helped produce an alternative elite. Until very recently there were two or maybe three different ways of recruiting Denmark's political, cultural, and business elites. The university system was one, the workers movement another, at least until the democratization of the official educational system in the 1960s. Both are well-known in other countries.

The third line of recruitment, through the folk high schools however, is a uniquely Danish phenomenon. Grundtvig and his followers accomplished what amounts to a genuine cultural revolution. He hated the formal teachings of the official school system and favoured free learning with an emphasis on story telling – 'the living word' – and discussion among peers. This program gave rise to a system of autonomous 'free schools' for children, plus folk high schools and agrarian schools for the farmer sons and daughters in their late teens and early twenties.

It is difficult to estimate the importance of the Grundtvigian schools in precise quantitative terms, as their influence has been almost as great outside the schools as in them. There is no doubt, however, that the very fact of the existence of two or three competing elites has helped agrarian and libertarian values to make inroads into the mainstream of Danish political culture, thus contributing heavily to defining 'Danishness'. The informal and antisystematic character of the teachings of Grundtvig suited the peasant movement extremely well. They could provide inspiration without restricting innovation. It also helps explain why Grundtvig has never been a favourite of academics; his thinking does not amount to a coherent theoretical system. His enmity toward all systems let him even to deny that he himself was a 'Grundtvigian' (much as Marx denied that he was a 'Marxist'). 'Grundtvigians' never used this term themselves. They talked of 'Friends' and organized 'meetings of Friends'. This organizational informality, too, turned out to be a major advantage, at least in the early stages of the movement. Furthermore, it explains why the influence of this farmers' ideology was able to cross the boundaries of the class it originally served so well.

Grundtvig's teachings were permeated by a fundamental optimism with regard to people's capacities. He demanded economic and ideological freedom and the right of citizens to education. This program corresponded precisely to the needs of the large class of highly self-conscious and class-conscious farmers, men and women alike. In Danish literature and history, it has become commonplace to interpret Grundtvigism narrowly as the ideology of the well-to-do farmers. This identification of class and ideology dates back to the communist author Hans Kirk (1888-1962). He contrasted the farmer religion of Grundvigism with the more traditionally revivalist Inner Mission (*Indre Mission*) founded in 1853. According to Kirk, this competing religious movement better suited the poorer farm hands and fishermen. While the Grundtvigian farmers could reap their rewards in this life, the lowly farm workers and fishermen would have to wait until the next.

This convincing description presents three different social environments, each with a specific religion. It is a most satisfying materialist explanation which has dominated Danish social history; a good example is the overview by the leading church historian P.G. Lindhardt (1953). The problem with Kirk's explanation is that it is simply wrong. Later research has called into question the simplistic association between class position and religious belief (Thyssen 1960-75 and Waahlin 1987). Examinations of membership lists of Grundtvigian parishes, for example, show that they included more than just well-off farmers. The general pattern turns out to be that entire parishes were either Grundtvigian, or Inner Mission, or nothing at all. The determining factor seems to be the choice made by the elites of the parishes. In most parts of Denmark, in spite of openings toward other social classes, the well-off farmers constituted the core of both Inner Mission and the Free Grundtvigian churches. But they also dominated the great number of parishes that did not undergo any sort of revival, be it Grundtvigian or Inner Mission. These so-called 'dead' parishes – religiously committed to neither movement – actually accounted for 50% of all votes the first parish church council elections in 1909.

These findings do not completely refute class-based explanations of religious beliefs, but they do force us to refine them. It turns out that Grundtvigism was not the only relevant ideological medium for the rising class of petty bourgeois entrepreneurs. What is important, however, is the function of both ideologies as a means of obtaining self-reliance. Both revivalist movements had their roots in, and helped to express, the needs of this class vis-a-vis government officials and influential businessmen. Whereas the function of these doctrines was similar, the difference lies in the content. Apparently, it did not matter what was said; what was important was that it was said independent of the authorities. Most countries witnessed the spread of revivalist movements such as Inner Mission during the transition to industrialized modernity. The United States is full of them. In this sense Grundtvigism is a revitalist movement, regardless of professed antagonism between the Grundtvigians and Inner Mission.

What is particular for the Danish Grundtvigism is its emphasis on the unity of land, country, God, and people (*folk*). It has turned out to be virtually impossible to export this particular synthesis. Grundtvigism even has played a negligible role among Danish immigrants to the American midwest. Today it has almost vanished in those communities, mainly in Iowa and South Dakota, where it was transported in the nineteenth century; Inner Mission, however, is still thriving (Simonsen 1990). 'Grundtvigism' is thus to be understood as a shorthand for all the revivalist ideologies of self-reliance thriving in Denmark at the time regardless of their precise teachings.

In a now classic account of Danishness, Robert Molesworth (1656-1725) British ambassador to the king of Denmark from 1689 to 1692, denounced what he called Danish 'mediocrity and pettiness'. Molesworth hated everything Danish, the petty peasant slyness and shortsighted scheming. He apparently loathed every minute he had spent in the country. The conclusion of the account runs as follows:

> "To conclude; I never knew any Country where the Minds of the People were more of one calibre and pitch than here; you shall meet with none of extraordinary Parts or Qualifications, or excellent in particular Studies and Trades; you see no Enthusiasts, Mad-men, Natural Fools, or fanciful Folks; but a certain equality of Understanding reigns among them: every one keeps the ordinary beaten road of Sence, which in this Country is neither the fairest nor the foulest, without deviating to the

right or left: yet I will add this one Remark to their praise. That the Common People do generally write and read."

(Molesworth 1694: 257)

Molesworth's book was presented to the British audience as a travel account, but the actual intention was to warn the aristocracy, who in 1688 had expelled James II, of the dangers of Absolutism. Denmark had been proclaimed an Absolutist regime in 1660 after the disastrous defeat in its wars with Sweden. One might say that on principle it was the most Absolutist regime in all of Europe, as its Absolutism was actually written down in 1665 (se p. 147), albeit made public only in the early 18th century (partly published in *Danske Lov* of 1683). This was never done in the France of Louis XIV, the very country where Absolutism was invented. Warning against this ominous fate was Molesworth's intention, so one should probably pay no more attention to his descriptions than to those of his friend, and contemporary, Jonathan Swift when describing the country of the Lilliputians or Brobdingnagian. Yet Moleworth's characterizations remind us of any number of subsequent descriptions by Danes as well as foreigners. What varies is the valuation put on mediocrity and mundaneness in a society; some see it as the utmost boredom, others as the egalitarian heaven on earth.

Another way to look at this ideology of mediocrity is to accept it as the prerequisite of popular consensus. If laws and reforms are to work, they must be based on general acceptance among people. And acceptance has more often than not been the case in Denmark. At a time when the overwhelming majority of intellectuals in a Europe of rising nation-states talked of the necessary 'nationalization of the masses' or the necessity of transforming peasants into citizens through policies from the top down, Grundtvig developed an ideology centered on the concept of *folkelighed* ('popular spirit') denoting a common feeling of consensus in the population. According to Grundtvig, the feeling can take root only in a historically developed national community and is manifested in actions of solidarity. At the level of ideological discourse, at least, Grundtvig succeeded in transforming the traditional amorphous peasant feelings of community and solidarity into symbols and words relevant to constructing a modern industrialized imagined community.

It remains to be seen whether the resulting mentality can survive the transplantation to entities larger than the Danish nation-state. Maybe it cannot. For a time, however, it was capable of influencing the majority of an industrial working class and establishing a welfare state distributing universal benefits. By means of easily remembered lyrics and slogans such as 'Freedom for Loke as well as for Thor'[18], Grundtvig succeeded in influencing the mentality of a whole nation. The original Herderian concept of nation, on the other hand, was independent of state unity in Germany; one might even say that it compensated for the lack of a unified German state. As a result of this experience, the 'Germanic' tradition of national identity is based on a notion of a people (*Volk, Folk*) which does not necessarily coincide with the inhabitants of the territory. The Danes who lost the wars with Prussia and Aus-

---

18 Grundtvig, *Preface to 'Nordens Mythologi'*, 1832, *Udvalgte Værker* I.

tria, in real terms shared ideological positions with their German enemies. Yet contrary to the German experience, Danes have been indoctrinated at school and at home that they are different from and more democratic than the suppressed, authoritarian Germans. Whether people actually live by these values, of course, is another question. At the level of discourse, however, that is in the conscious and preconscious (not subconscious) political culture, the concepts of liberty and egality have had great impact on determining what can be expressed and what can not, what does not have to be expressed at all, and which values are considered worthy of persuit.

These are the 'peasant roots of Danish modernity' or the 'peculiarity of the Danes'. They help explain many of the apparently paradoxical features of Danish political and social life, including its anarchistic party political system. Real national values are at stake in the present process of European integration, and many Danes fear that they will disappear when society, nation, and state are not longer coterminous, as has been the case the last hundred years and so. This is why Danes have been so reluctant to fully participate in 'the construction of Europe'. What they have failed to realize is how recent this identification of the society-nation-state is and how dangerous the geopolitically exposed situation in the center of Europe at the entrance to the Baltic Sea is. When the Baltic region opened up to the rest of Europe with the fall of the Iron Curtain, old tensions dating from before the rise of the nation-states reemerged and put back on the table the necessity to choose between different international options. Denmark cannot any longer have it both ways, as she had during the Cold War.

Foreign Policy and National Identity in a Small State

In many ways, Denmark seems to provide the perfect illustration of Barry Buzan's and Ole Wæver's concept of 'societal security'; i.e. a militarily weak power which, however, is strong in the sense that it is difficult to control by military means because of its internal cohesiveness (Wæver et al. 1993). This is no mere coincidence; social and national integration as an alternative to military armament actually formed the basis of the policies of the Social Democrats and Social Liberals who governed Denmark from 1929 to 1940.

The minister of foreign affairs at that time was the social liberal P. Munch (1870-1948). Munch started out in the 1920s as a convinced internationalist and stalwart believer in handing over power and possibly sovereignty to the League of Nations. He was never a doctrinaire pacifist, even though the official policy of the Social Democrats and the Social Liberals (*Radikale Venstre*) was anti-militaristic. On the contrary, Munch seems to have supported the idea of enabling the League of Nations to use military force when acting with a mandate from the involved parties in international conflicts (Pedersen 1970). Only when he realized the diffidence of the major powers and lack of determination in the international community to implement the initial ideals of the international organisation did Munch and his coalition government, under the Social Democrat Thorvald Stauning (1873-1942), endorse a policy of unarmed neutralism towards Germany (Pedersen 1970).

P. Munch defined the fundamentals of his international policy in three lectures delivered at L'Institut Universitaire des Hates Etudes Internationales in Genèva in 1931.[19] The main topic was the 'moral authority' of the small nations, mainly the neutrals of World War I: Denmark, Norway, Sweden, the Netherlands and Switzerland. In Munch's thinking, these five states were particularly able to 'réaliser l'impartialité que est l'idéal de la Société des Nations' (Munch 1931: 17). Of course these smaller powers did not have the same influence as the great powers. In Munch's own words. 'Certes nous ne prétendons pas a une influence correspondante à celle des Grandes Puissances' (Munch 1931: 18). Munch argued that another kind of influence was possible, one based on economic and moral factors.

A precondition for display of such a strength of the weak was a high degree of cohesion within the national community. In the eyes of the Social Democrats and Social Liberals, military disarmament could be possible if society was 'strong', that is, insulated against totalitarian temptations from the Right as well as from the Left through social integration. The strategy was to hold the totalitarian ideologies at bay by means of a 'Nordic' welfare state. This alternative to the sterile radicalism of the German Social Democrats and Communists, respectively, was explicitly formulated by the respected classical scholar and Marxist theoretician, Hartvig Frisch (1893-1950) in the 'Nordic Preface' to his book, *Pest over Europa* ('Plague over Europe'), published shortly after Hitler came to power, in 1933.

In this perceptive political analysis of, and warning against, all totalitarian movements, Fascism and Nazism as well as Communism, Frisch endorsed the move from liberalism to social democracy. Only a socially just society, in his opinion, would be able to resist the dangerous temptations and easy promises put forward by the various enemies of liberal democracy. Frisch was never a pacifist, although he bravely defended the appeasement policy and cooperation with the German occupation forces during and after the war. This defence reflected intellectual honesty and personal conviction, it was definitely not unconditioned doctrinal pacifism (Christiansen 1993). Although not a member of the inner circles of power in the Social Democratic party of the 1930s, Frisch was the first to explicitly formulate the Scandinavian strategy of political compromise between the Agrarians and organized labour in order to prevent Nazism and fascism.

The Scandinavian Social Democrats developed this strategy in order to avoid the mistakes of their fellow social democrats in Germany and elsewhere in Central Europe. In January 1933, on the eve of Hitler's takeover in Germany, the Danish Social Democrats and the Social Liberals pushed a major crisis agreement with the Conservatives and the Liberals through parliament, the *Kanslergadeforlig* – named after the street on which prime minister Thorvald Stauning lived. With this package of laws, the Social Democrats offered the agrarians in *Venstre* subsidies for the farmers and devaluation of the currency in exchange for public works programs

---

19 Published later the same year under the title *La politique du Danemark dans la Société des Nations*.

and a social security bill which primarily included higher unemployment compensation – the very policy the strong Social Democracy in Germany had failed to carry through in 1928.

The purpose of the agreement was primarily to save the parliamentary system; not for its own sake, but as a means of defending and extending the societal processes upon which the labour movement relied. The price included some political sacrifices, but the Social Democrats and Social Liberals accepted these because they had a higher political goal in sight, to preserve the social order and thereby national coherence (Lindström 1985: 156 ff.). Thus began the building of the strong society of the post-war period. In the public debate that followed the *Kanslergade* compromise, its advocates repeatedly returned to the crisis agreement as a superior alternative to the events in Continental Europe. This parliamentary policy was explicitly promoted in the new working-program in 1934, 'Denmark for the People'. The closing paragraph of the party congress the same year read:

"We want a Parliament fit for work and thus an active cabinet. We want to work on the basis of the legal, parliamentary foundations and preserve democracy and popular government for the protection of the right to work and of the working-class, and for the protection of the free prosperity and preservation of the Danish nation and the Danish people."

(Lindström 1985: 171)

Munch's policy of *de facto* pacifism regarding military means fell into disrepute in the Second World War during the German occupation ending with the Danish resistance movement and Denmark's entry in NATO in 1948. Seen with the advantage of historical hindsight, however, one must admit that the policy 'worked', in the sense that Denmark escaped the trials of war and occupation almost intact as a democratic society and polity, though her moral reputation had suffered. In a way she even fared better than Norway, as the extreme cohesiveness of Danish society discouraged the Germans from attempting to install any kind of Quisling regime. Norway kept a high moral profile during the war as an occupied nation formally at war. This situation, however, left room for the Germans to install a regime of their own under Vidkun Quisling and this brought to the surface the divisions within the Norwegian polity. The effect of these divisions made itself felt long after the war and can still be observed in the difficulties of dealing with the legacy of Quisling.[20] In contrast to the Netherlands, the Danish political system also succeeded in keeping the administration free from Nazi infiltration. The main factor in this survival as a nation was the other element of Munch's non-offensive foreign policy, the strategy of immunizing the society against divisions coming from the outside.

In a long-term perspectives, the strategy of 'societal security' thus worked and

---

20 See, for instance, the reception of H.F. Dahl's pathbreaking biography of Quisling (Dahl 1991-92) and Øystein Sørensen's original analysis of the striking similarities between the social programs of the Norwegian (and German) National Socialists and the Social Democrats in Norway and Great Britain (Sørensen 1991 and 1993). A short presentation of the political debate over the findings of the historians can be found in Figueireido (1995).

has left deep marks on Danish society and collective psychology. This is less true for the 1930s, when the foundations of the welfare state were laid, but very much for the 1950s and 1960s, when the social democratic welfare state came into existence as an alternative to the two dominating ideologies of the Cold War, totalitarian Communism and unmitigated Capitalism. As argued by Poul Villaume, this so-called 'Third Way' between unmitigated capitalism and Communist central planning was probably more important as an ideological alternative to the cleavages of the Cold War than remembered today (Villaume 1995).

In Denmark in particular and in the Nordic countries in general, the program stuck and has survived the disappearance of Communism. Instead, a stereotype of a supposedly 'Catholic', 'Southern' or 'Latin' Europe without universal welfare values has taken its place as the predominat 'enemy' image. After 28 years of membership of the European Community, this image still plays a role in the public debate. The problem with these stereotypes, which may have been relevant in the 1930s, is that they are outdated, as the remaining countries in the European Union have long ago embarked upon the road towards various versions of the welfare state (Ploug and Kvist 1994). This new situation, however, has not really dawned upon the majority of Danes, who still guard the sovereignty of their small state as if she were still a great power with real sovereignty. Such is the power of collective memory at the preconscious level that the members of this strong and successful society still deep down tend to think that they are citizens of a strong power, though no sane Dane would be caught saying it aloud.

'Folk' and 'Folkishness' as Positive Concepts – Society, People, Nation, State and Sovereignty in Danish Political Thinking

When analysed in this historical context, the reluctant Danish attitudes towards Europe and European integration become less of a paradox. Ambivalence has characterized the Danish attitude towards European integration from the very beginning. Reluctantly, the majority of the population has let itself be dragged into European cooperation by the arguments of dire economic necessity coming from political and economic elites. But there has never been any enthusiasm, not even among the intellectuals and others who stand to profit from the greater opportunities of intellectual exchange on a larger scale. The socialist Left mistrusts Europe for trying to undermine the supposedly unique Danish welfare state, while the Right doubts Denmark's ability to compete on equal terms. This defensive attitude may change, but it has not yet been translated into significantly different political opinions.

Why has mistrust of Europe and everything European been the dominant theme in Danish politics and permeated the political culture? Another way to summarize 'Danishness' of today is to say *Denmark is a little land*. Danes say this all the time when they want to impress foreigners with how amazingly well we have done. The saying dates back to that philosopher of Danishness, N.F.S. Grundtvig, who in a poem from 1820 struck a core with the Danish attitudes of social levelling and the search for the middle ground:

> Far higher mountains shine splendidly forth
> than the hills of our native islands.
> But we Danes rejoice in the quiet North
> for our lowlands and rolling hills.
> No towering peaks thundered over our birth.
> It suits us best to remain on earth.
>
> (N.F.S. Grundtvig, *Langt højere Bjerge,* 1820, my translation)

The song ends on a note of flat hill self-satisfaction: 'Even more of the ore, so white and so red (the colours of the flag, u.ø.). Others may have got mountains in exchange. For the Dane, however, the daily bread is found no less in the hut of the poor man; when few have too much and fewer too little then truly we have become wealthy.'[21] This is not a program for social or economic equality – Grundtvig at this time was a conservative – yet it is a clear proclamation of political anti-elitism and egalitarianism which later came to embody the ideology of Danishness.

There is a certain unpretentious, self-ironic note in this version of Danish national discourse. It is hard to detect for foreigners because it is considered bad form to be a nationalist in Denmark, as in most other European countries after 1945. Nevertheless, this subtle form of nationalism surfaces immediately when foreigners start criticizing anything Danish. Danes love to criticize everything themselves, but put up the defences as soon as somebody else points out a fault with Danish behaviour or something Danish. Luckily Danes are not very often confronted with such criticism, as Denmark has had a surprisingly good press in the international community – that is, when she is not mistaken for Sweden. This, of course, is mainly a reflection of the relative lack of importance attributed to this small country in world affairs. This attitude has nevertheless helped foster a feeling of what could be termed 'humble assertiveness' if not Lilliputian chauvinism: We know we are the best, therefore we don't have to brag about it. One must never mistake the apparent Danish or Scandinavian humility for genuine humility. It often conceals a feeling of superiority.

Over the last ten to fifteen years, this security has been challenged by the arrival of a small number of immigrants, some 250,000 foreigners out of a net total population of 5,3 million, i.e. little more than 4%. Many of these immigrants have felt uncomfortable with the unspoken Danish way of life and have challenged it in ways never experienced before. That has produced a certain uneasiness among Danes in the public. May the reason why there was no racism earlier on be that there was nobody to discriminate against? An American colleague, the cultural sociologist Jonathan Schwartz, who has been living in Denmark for more than thirty years, has characterized Danish culture as follows:

---

21 N.F.S. Grundtvig, *Langt højere Bjerge* 1820 (my translation u.ø.).

"Danish Academic culture, like agriculture, tends to be enclosed, fenced in and hedged. The *gård* (farm) likewise, is self-contained, and even the house is surrounded by protective trees and bushes. What is Danish in Denmark is so obvious to the foreigner here. *Hygge* (cosiness), *Tryghed* (security) and *Trivsel* (well-being) are the three Graces of Danish culture and socialization. Faces look towards a common *gård* (yard), or a table with candles and bottles on it. Hygge always has its backs turned on the others. *Hygge* is for the members, not the strangers. If you want to know what is Danish about Denmark, ask first a Greenlander and then a guestworker ... An American asked me the difference between Denmark and America. I ventured an answer. In America there's one politics and fifteen ways to celebrate Christmas. In Denmark there are fifteen political parties and one way to celebrate Christmas ... 'Denmark is a little country'. That's canon number one. A close second is: 'Danish is a difficult language'. How many times have I been chastised for my foreign accent?"

(Schwartz, 1985: 123-124).

Ultimately, this is a rather different way to express what most Danes do when they brag about their friendly, small, and democratic culture. Of course, Danes tend to regard as positive those features that irritate the American Schwartz. This only demonstrates how difficult it is to be accepted in such a closely knit national culture. Yet both positions highlight the importance of the size of the country as an explanation of the specifics of the political culture. For some, small is beautiful, for others small means petty, mediocre, and tedious. From a cultural and historical sociological perspective, the Danish nation-state of today represents a rare situation of virtual identity between state, nation and society. As we have argued, however, this unity is a much more recent phenomenon than normally assumed by Danes as well as foreign observes.

Ideologically, Danish identity unequivocally belongs to the family of Germanic, Celtic, and Slavic identity discourses, where, in the tradition of the German thinker Johann Gotfried Herder national identity is conceived primarily in terms of language and culture. This differs from French thinking, where state-nation is a core concept and state and nation mutually help in defining the Other (Renan 1882). The ethno-cultural notions of *Volksgemeinschaft* (Danish: *Folkefællesskab*) as an organic, linguistic or racial community were first formulated by German intellectuals in the early nineteenth century. They sought to distance themselves from what they saw as shallow rationalism and cosmopolitanism in the Enlightenment and the French Revolution. This rejection led them to celebrate cultural particularism. In the social and political thought of Romanticism, nations were conceived as historically rooted, organically developed individualities, united by a distinctive *Volksgeist* and by the infinitely ramifying expression (*Geist*) in language, custom, law and culture.

It was this interpretation that came to dominate the German understanding of nationhood. This is a somewhat surprising development as the unified Germany of Bismarck was not originally inspired by nationalism, still less by ethno-cultural nationalism (Østergaard 1995b and 1997c). The original Herderian concept of nation did not envisage the political unification of all Germans; on the contrary, one could claim that its cultural unity compensates the lack of a unified German state. As a result of this experience, national identity in the 'Germanic' tradition came to rely on the existence of a people (*Volk, Folk*) which did not necessarily overlap with the inhabitants of the territory. In Contrast with the German experience, the Danes, after having lost the wars with Prussia and Austria, were dependent on having a sovereign state if they should preserve their identity. This nation-state, however, was difficult to define theoretically, as the Danes shared ideological positions with their German adversaries. Here lies the theoretical basis behind the intellectual paradoxes of Danish attitudes towards sovereignty and integration. These paradoxes can still be identified in surveys of Danish values (cf. Gundelach 1993).

The German *Reich* of 1871 contained no unified citizenship; the Germans were citizens of the individual principalities of Bavaria, Hannover, Württemberg, Prussia, etc. Prussia, of course, dominated the others, comprising as it did two-thirds of the territory and its king simultaneously emperor of the whole empire (the second). In principle, both the German Empire and the Weimar Republic were organized as federal states. The federal system was cancelled only after 1934 as a result of Nazi *Gleichschaltung*. German citizenship came to be defined in linguistic, cultural (and therefore eventually biological) terms only in 1913, in the *Bürgerliches Gesetzbuch*, the legal code of Prussia; this definition has survived into the present German constitution of 1949 (Brubaker 1992), only modified by the Social Democratic and Green coalition government in 2000. Nonetheless, Germany was understood as a nation-state, and gradually came to understand itself as such. This change was due to the paradoxical combination of inclusion and exclusion. As *kleindeutsch* it excluded millions of German speakers in the Austrian-Hungarian Empire and elsewhere in Eastern Europe. At the same time, the state included millions of French-oriented German speakers in Alsace-Lorraine, Poles in eastern Prussia and Danes in North Sleswig. The intensifying conflict between Germans and Poles in eastern Prussia reinforced the ethno-cultural and differentialist strand always existent in the intellectual German understanding of nationhood helping to translate it into practical politics (Wehler 1962).

How this notion was carried into the twentieth century by defeat in the First World War, perverted by Nazi *völkisch* propaganda and translated into official doctrine in the Federal Republic because of the massive migrations of Germans from Eastern and Central Europe after 1944-45 need not occupy us here. Suffice it to say that there is a striking similarity between the Danish and German understanding of nationhood at the level of ideology. On the other hand, the Danish version of this common ideology of national identity took root precisely because of the fatal clash with Germans in and over Sleswig. The clash was inevitable because both sides demanded a sovereign state based on parallel ethnonational principles. This parallelism, has left a profound duality in Danish political thinking, which helps explain some of the Danish ambiguities concerning sovereignty, European cooperation and national identity.

Danish identity is firmly rooted in ancestry, language and a whole way of being.

In reality, Danish nationality is based on blood, not soil (*jus sanguinis* not *jus soli*) although it used to be easier for a foreign immigrant to acquire citizenship in Denmark than in Germany. In other words, Denmark firmly belongs to the group of ethno-national European nations where culture has priority to state in defining the political nation (cf. Brubaker 1992). On the other hand, as we have seen, Danishness has always been intimately linked with the existence of a sovereign state. For long periods, this state was multi-national in character. However, because of the continuity of the name, Denmark, the Danish national variant of the ethno-political program succeeded in monopolizing the multi-national prehistory, appropriating the label 'Denmark' for use in constructing its collective memory.[22] This continuity is demonstrated at the symbolic level in a number of ways, from the myth of the origins of the Danish flag, which supposedly fell from heaven in present day Estonia in 1219, to pride in the impressive cultural heritage of the Absolutist capital of Copenhagen, to the contradictory nature of today's uneasy co-existence of three nations within the so-called *Rigsfællesskab* which in reality is a subtle mixture of a commonwealth and an empire (cf. Østergaard 1996a).

The present day national identity born out of the 1864 defeat, depended even more on a nominally sovereign state than did the French and even British identity project. This dependence on the state explains the apparent contradictions in Danish collective mentality and political behaviour when confronted with the prospect of European integration. In an even closer collaborating Europe with state characteristics dispersed at more levels, the etno-cultural concept of nation seems to exhibit a series of relative advantages over the exclusively state-based concept we find in the traditional British identification of national sovereignty with the sovereignty of Parliament and unlimited parliamentarianism (Clark 1991). The French notion of republican, state-based national identity, on the other hand, might eventually come to grips with the new European-wide dispersal of sovereignty, provided the definitions are clear cut. The great loser, eventually, will be the peculiar Danish conflagration of the two, nation and state. It is therefore not surprising to see a majority of the Danish populace, for different reasons, rejecting the loss of national sovereignty, although this sovereignty, in real terms, is hard for hard headed outside observers to detect.

Small State, Strong Society and Active Internationalism

Denmark represents a series of apparent and genuine paradoxes. On one hand, Danish policy since World War II has been supremely active in advocating international norms, also in areas where power politics predominate, i.e. security. Though

---

22 This interpretation has formed the ideological back-bone of Danish historiography, professional as well as otherwise. See the critiques in Østergaard (1992b), Engman (1991), Kjærgaard (1989) and Rasmussen (1995: 32).

the UN has been the primary arena for Danish active internationalism, in recent years, by undertaking its own independent initiatives, Denmark has not relied solely upon UN actions (Holm 1997: 65). Moreover, in the course of the last ten years, Denmark has embarked upon a policy of building a sphere of influence in the Baltic area and, thus, no longer acts as a small state. Now it must be called a 'non-small state', whatever that is (Mouritzen 1997: 47). On the other hand, the reluctant Danish EU policy has severely undercut her possibilities for effectively using these international norms because of the difficulties in building strong alliances with other members of the EU and the EU itself. The basis of this apparent paradox is a massive satisfaction in being Danish among her citizens and a negative feeling towards European citizenship.[23] 'Danish' values thus help explain Danish behaviour in foreign politics (cf. Gundelach 1993).

The major problem, however, is that the 'Denmark' referred to is far from unequivocal. On one hand the name refers to a typical multinational state-nation with a long standing role in European politics; on the other hand, this very same name refers to an atypical homogeneous small nation-state. This duality is nicely reflected in the use of two national anthems (cf. Knudsen 1992). The first is *Kong Christian* written by Johannes Ewald in 1779; this martial song praises the warrior king who defeats the enemies of the country – and politely forgets how he lost everything in the end. The other song is *Der er et yndigt land* ('There is a lovely land') written in 1819 by the romanticist poet Adam Oehlenschläger, praising the beauty of the friendly and peaceful country and its national inhabitants. This latter is the one song, at national football-games, regardless of the result. Denmark, the Danes and the 'Danish' national consensus are caught between these competing and at times even antagonistic notions of Danishness.

---

23 A comparative survey of these feelings in the various EU memberstates can be found in 'Citizens Attitudes towards Europe', *Eurobarometer* 45, 1996, 86-10.

Literature

Adriansen, Inge (1987): "Mor Danmark, Valkyrie, Skjoldmø og fædrelandssymbol", *Folk og Kultur*, pp. 105-163.
Ahnlund, Nils (1956): "Dominium maris Baltici" in Ahnlund, *Tradition och historia*, Stockholm, pp. 114-130.
Anderson, Perry (1974): *Lineages of the Absolutist State*, London: NLB.
Bagge, Sverre og Knut Mykland (1987): *Norge i dansketiden*, Copenhagen: Politikens Forlag.
Baldwin, Peter (1990): *The Politics of Social Solidarity. Class Bases of the European Welfare State* 1875-1975, Cambridge University Press.
Barrington Moore, Jr. (1966): *The Social Origins of Dictatorship and Democracy*, N.Y.: Basic Books.
Berggren, Brit (1992): "Det baltiske og det atlantiske Norden" in Hastrup (ed.), *Den nordiske verden* 2 Copenhagen: Gyldendal, pp. 11-18.
Bjøl, Erling (1966): "Foreign Policy-making in Denmark", *Cooperation and Conflict* 2, pp. 1-17.
Bjøl, Erling (1970): "P. Munch, sociologisk og historisk set", *Historie* nyrk. IX,1, pp. 123-141.
Bohnen, K. und S.Aa. Jørgensen, (1992) (Hrsg.): *Der dänische Gesamtstaat: Kiel – Kopenhagen – Altona*, Wolfenbütteler Studien zur Aufklärung 18, Tübingen.
Branner, Hans (1972): *Småstat mellem stormagter. Beslutningen om mineudlægning august 1914*, Copenhagen: Munksgaard.
Branner, Hans (1992): "Danish European Policy Since 1945: The Question of Sovereignty", in *M. Kelstrup* (1992), pp. 297-327.
Brubaker, Rogers (1992): *Citizenship and Nationhood in France and Germany*, Cambridge MA: Harvard University Press.
Brubaker, Rogers (1996): *Nationalism Reframed. Nationhood and the National Question in the New Europe*, Cambridge: Cambridge University Press.
Buzan, Barry (1983): *People, States and Fear. The National Security Problem in International Relations*, 2. ed. Brighton: Wheatsheaf.
Buzan, Barry (1993): "Societal Security, State Security and Internationalization" in O. Wæver et al. (eds), *Identity, Migration and the New Security Agenda in Europe*, London: Pinter Publishers, pp. 41-58.
Childs, Marquis (1936): *Sweden: The Middle Way*, New Haven: Yale University Press.
Christiansen, Niels Finn (1993): *Hartvig Frisch. Mennesket og politikeren: En biografi*, Copenhagen: Chr. Ejlers' Forlag.
Christiansen, Palle Ove and Uffe Østergaard, (1993), "Folket, landet og nationen" in Østergaard, pp. 13-56.
Christmas-Møller, Wilhelm (1970): "De små stater: Sokraterne i international politik", *Økonomi og Politik*, 1970/4, pp. 380-93
Clark, J.C.D. (1989): "English History's Forgotten Context: Scotland, Ireland and Wales", *Historical Journal* 32, 1989: 211-28.
Clark, J.C.D. (1991): "Britain as a composite state" in *Østergaard (1991b)*, pp. 55-84.
Connor, Walker (1994): *Ethnonationalism: The Quest for Understanding*, Princeton: Princeton University Press.
Dahl, Hans Fredrik (1991-92): *Vidkun Quisling* I-II, Oslo: Cappelen.
Davies, Norman (1984): *The Heart of Europe. A Short History of Poland*, London: Oxford University Press.

Degn, Christian (1974): *Die Schimmelmanns im atlantischen Dreieckshandel. Gewinn und Gewissen,* Neumünster: Karl Wachholtz Verlag.
Due-Nielsen, C. and N. Petersen, (eds.) (1995): *Adaptation and Activism. The Foreign Policy of Denmark 1967-1993,* Copenhagen: DUPI.
Due-Nielsen, C. (1996): "Vindskibelighed eller vankelmod. Nogle spørgsmål til dansk neutralitetspolitik", H. Jeppesen et al. (eds.), *Søfart – Politik – Identitet tilegnet Ole Feldbæk,* Kronborg: Handels og Søfartsmuseets søhistoriske Skrifter XIX, pp. 315-24.
Elliot, J.H. (1992): "A Europe of Composite Monarchies", *Past and Present,* vol. 137, 1992: 48-71.
Engman, Max (1991): "Historikerna och nationalstaten", *Historien og historikerne i Norden efter 1965,* Studier i historisk metode 21, Aarhus: Aarhus Universitetsforlag.
Esping-Andersen, Gösta (1985): *Politics against Market: The Social Democratic Road to Power,* Princeton: Princeton University Press.
Esping-Andersen, Gösta (1990): *The Three Worlds of of Welfare Capitalism,* Princeton: Princeton University Press.
Eurobarometer 45, Europakommissionen, Bruxelles, 1996.
Fabricius, Knud (1906-58): *Skaanes Overgang fra Danmark til Sverige* I-IV, Copenhagen: Kildeskriftselskabet (reprint 1972).
Feldbæk, Ole (ed.) (1991-92): *Dansk identitetshistorie* I-IV, Copenhagen: C.A. Reitzels Forlag.
Feldbæk, Ole (1992): "Clash of Culture in a Conglomerate State: Danes and Germans in 18th century Denmark" in C.V. Johansen et al. (eds.), *Clashes of Culture,* Odense: Odense University Press, pp. 80-93.
Feldbæk, Ole (ed.) (1998-99): *Danmark-Norge 1380-1814 I-IV,* Oslo: Universitetsforlaget
Feldbæk, Ole og Justesen, Ole (1980): *Kolonierne i Asien og Afrika,* Copenhagen: Politikens Forlag.
Figueireido, Ivo de (1995): "Historikerne og okkupasjonen", *Dagbladet* (Oslo). December 31, p. 32.
Fink, Troels (1955): *Sønderjylland siden genforeningen i 1920,* Copenhagen: Schultz Forlag.
Fink, Troels (1958): *Geschichte des Sleswigschen Grenzlandes,* Copenhagen: Munksgaard.
Fink, Troels (1959): *Spillet om dansk neutralitet 1905-1909,* Aarhus: Aarhus Universitetsforlag, 2nd. ed.
Fink, Troels (1961): *Ustabil balance. Dansk udenrigs- og forsvarspolitik 1894-1905,* Aarhus: Aarhus Universitetsforlag 2nd. ed.
Frandsen, Steen Bo (1993): "Jylland og Danmark – kolonisering, opdagelse eller ligeberettiget sameksistens?" in *Østergaard (1993a),* pp. 103-129.
Frandsen, Steen Bo (1995): "The Discovery of Jutland: The Existence of a Regional Dimension in Denmark" in *Sørensen (1995),* pp. 111-126.
Frandsen, Steen Bo (1996): *Opdagelsen af Jylland. Den regionale dimension i danmarkshistorien 1814-64,* Aarhus: Aarhus Universitetsforlag.
Frisch, Hartvig (1933): *Pest over Europa. Bolschevisme – Fascisme – Nazisme,* Henrik Koppels Forlag Copenhagen (new ed. with an introduction by Uffe Østergaard, Copenhagen: Fremads forlag 1993), V-XIV.
Frisch, Hartvig (1933): "Nordisk Forord" in *Pest over Europa,* Copenhagen, pp. 10-14.
Fukuyama, Francis (1995): *Trust: The Social Vitues and the Creation of Prosperity,* London: Hamish Hamilton.
Gad, Finn (1984): *Grønland,* Copenhagen: Politikens Forlag.
Gramsci, Antonio (1930-36): *Fængselsoptegnelser (Quaderni del Carcere)* I-II, translated and ed. by Gert Sørensen, Copenhagen: Museum Tusculanum.
Gregersen, H.V. (1981): *Slesvig og Holsten før 1830,* Copenhagen: Politikens Forlag.

Grundtvig, N.F.S.: *Udvalgte Værker* 1-10 ed. by P.A. Rosenberg, Copenhagen: Forlaget Danmark.
Gundelach, Peter (1993): "Danskernes særpræg", *Dansk Udenrigspolitisk Årbog*, pp. 133-47.
Halbwachs, Maurice (1925): *Les cadres sociaux de la mémoire* (Engl. transl. by L. Coser [ed.] 1992), *On Collective Memory*, University of Chicago Press.
Halbwachs, Maurice (1950): *La mémoire collective*, Paris: PUF 1950 (Engl transl. with introduction by Mary Douglas 1980), *The Collective Memory*, N.Y.
Hansen, S. Aa. (1970): *Early Industrialization in Denmark*, Copenhagen: Academic Press.
Henningsen, Bernd (1980): *Politik eller kaos*, Copenhagen: Berlingske Forlag.
Hettne, Bjørn, Svesker Sörlin and Uffe Østergaard (1998): *Den globale nationalisme*, Stockholm: SNS Förlag.
Heurlin, Bertel (1994): "Aktivismen og europæiseringen af dansk sikkerhedspolitik" in B. Heurlin (ed.): *Danmark og den Europæiske Union*, Copenhagen: Forlaget Politiske Studier, pp. 129-137.
Heurlin, Bertel (1996): "Denmark: a new activism in foreign and security policy" in C. Hill (ed.), *The Actors in Europe's Foreign Policy*, London: Routledge, pp. 166-185.
Holbraad, Carsten (1991): *Danish Neutrality. A Study in the Foreign Policy of a Small State*, Oxford: Clarendon Press.
Hobsbawm, E.J. (1990): *Nations and Nationalism since 1780: Programme, Myth, Reality*, Cambridge: Cambridge University Press.
Holm, H.-H. (1997): "Denmark's Active Internationalism: Advocating Intenational Norms with Domestic Constraints", *Danish Foreign Policy Yearbook*, pp. 52-80.
Horstbøll, H. and Uffe Østergaard (1990): "Reform and Revolution. The French Revolution and the Case of Denmark", *Scandinavian Journal of History* 15, pp. 155-179.
Hroch, Miroslav (1985): *Social Preconditions of National Revival in Europe: A Comparative Analysis of the Social Composition of Patriotic Groups among Smaller European Nations*, Cambridge: Cambridge University Press.
Hroch, Miroslav (2000): *In the National Interest. Demands and Goals of European National Movements of the Nineteenth Century: A Comparative Perspective*, Prague: Chates University.
Japsen, Gottlieb (1979): "Statspatriotisme og nationalfølelse", *Historie* 1979:2, pp. 107-122.
Japsen, Gottlieb (1983): *Den fejlslagne germanisering*, Åbenrå: Historisk Samling for Sønderjylland.
Jensen, Bernard E. et al. (eds.) (1996): *Erindringens og glemslens politik*, Roskilde: Roskilde Universitetsforlag.
Jespersen, K. (1994): "Rivalry without Victory. Denmark Sweden and the Struggle for the Baltic, 1500-1720" in Rystad et al. (eds), pp. 137-176.
Kautsky, Karl (1899): *Die Agrarfrage. Eine Übersicht über die Tendenzen Landwirtschaft und die Agrarpolitik der Sozialdemokratie*, Stuttgart.
Kearney, Hugh (1991): "Nation Building – British Style" in *Østergaard (1991b)*, pp. 43-54.
Kelstrup, Morten (1991): "Danmarks deltagelse i det internationale samarbejde – fra pragmatisk funktionalisme til aktiv internationalisme" in H. Gottlieb, B. Heurlin, and J. Teglers, (eds.), *Fred og konflikt*, Copenhagen: SNU, pp. 289-311.
Kelstrup, Morten (ed.) (1992): *Europen Integration and Denmark's Participation*, Copenhagen: Copenhagen Political Studies Press.
Kirby, David (1994): *The Baltic World, 1772-1993*, London: Longman.
Kirk, Hans (1928): *Fiskerne*, Copenhagen: Gyldendal.
Kirk, Hans (1953): *Skyggespil*, Copenhagen: Gyldendal.
Kirby, David (1990): *Northern Europe in the Early Modern Period, 1492-1772*, London: Longman.

Kjærgaard, Thorkild (1989): "The farmer interpretation of Danish history" in *Scandinavian Journal of History* 10, pp. 97-118.
Koch, Hal (1944): *N.F.S. Grundtvig,* Ohio, 1952 (Danish 1944).
Koenigsberger, H.G. (1989): "Composite States, Representative Institutions and the American Revolution", *Historical Research,* vol. 62, 1989: 135-53.
Kohn, Hans (1944): *The Idea of Nationalism,* New York.
Knudsen, Tim (1992): "A Portrait of Danish State-Culture: Why Denmark Needs Two National Anthems" in *Kelstrup (1992),* pp. 262-97.
Knudsen, Tim (1995): *Dansk statsbygning,* Copenhagen: Jurist og Økonomforbundets Forlag.
Ladewig Petersen, Erling (ed.) (1984): *Magtstaten i Norden i 1600-tallet og dens sociale konsekvenser,* Odense: Odense Universitetsforlag.
Lahme, Hans Norbert (1982): Sozialdemokratie und Landarbeiter (1871-1901) Odense: Odense University Press.
Lange, Ulrich (1996) (ed.): *Geschichte Sleswig-Holsteins,* Neumünster: Wachholtz Verlag.
Lehmann, Orla (1861): "For Grundloven. Tale ved en politisk Fest i Vejle 1861" in *Efterladte Skrifter* IV, Copenhagen 1874.
Lenin, V.I. (1907): "The Agrarian Program of the Social Democracy", *Works,* Vol. 13, Moscow.
Lind, Gunner (1994): *Hæren og magten i Danmark 1614-1662,* Odense: Odense University Press.
Lind, Gunner (1996): "Gamle patrioter. Om kærlighed til fædrelandet i 1600-tallets Danmark" in H. Jeppesen et al. (ed.), *Søfart – Politik – Identitet tilegnet Ole Feldbæk,* Kronborg: Handels og Søfartsmuseets søhistoriske Skrifter XIX, pp. 91-114.
Lindhardt, P.G. (1951): *Grundtvig: An Introduction,* Oxford: Cowley.
Lindhardt, P.G. (1953): *Vækkelse og kirkelige retninger,* Copenhagen.
Lindström, Ulf (1985): *Fascism in Scandinavia 1920-1940,* Stockholm: Almquist & Wicksell.
Linvald, Axel (1965): *Christian VIII før Eidsvoldgrundloven,* Copenhagen: Gad.
Løfting, C., H. Horstbøll, U. Østergaard, (1989): "Les effets de la révolution française au Danemark" in M. Vovelle (ed.), *L"image de la révolution française* I, Oxford: Pergamon Press, pp. 621-42.
Malling, Ove (1777): *Store og gode Handlinger af Danske, Norske og Holstenere,* ed. by E. Hansen Copenhagen, Gyldendal 1992.
Mellon, James (1992): *Og gamle Danmark,* Aarhus: Centrum.
Milward, Alan (1992): *The European Rescue of the Nation State,* London: Routledge.
Molesworth, Robert (1694): *An Account of Denmark as it was in the Year 1692,* London.
Moore Jr., Barrington (1966): *The Social Origins of Dictatorship and Democracy,* Boston: Beacon Press.
Mouritzen, Hans (1997): "Denmark in the Post-Cold War Era: The Salient Action Spheres", *Danish Foreign Policy Yearbook,* pp. 33-51.
Mosse, George L. (1975): *The Nationalization of the Masses,* New York: Howard Fertig.
Munch, Peter, Ministre des Affaires étrangères du Danemark (1931): *La politique du Danemark dans la Société des Nations,* Genève.
Møller, Erik (1948): *Skandinavisk Stræben og svensk Politik omkring 1860,* Copenhagen: Gad.
Møller, Erik (1958): *Helstatens Fald* I-II, Copenhagen.
Neumann, Iver B. (ed.) (1992): *Hva skjedde med Norden?* Fra selvbevissthet til Rådvillhet, Europaprogrammet, Oslo: Cappelen.
Nielsen, Johannes (1988): *1864 – Da Europa gik af lave,* Odense: Odense University Press.
Nora, Pierre (ed.) (1984-92): *Les lieux de mémoire* I, La République, II La Nation (1-3), Les Frances (1-3), Paris: Gallimard.

Nørregaard, Georg (1954): *Freden i Kiel,* Copenhagen Rosenkilde og Bagger.
Paludan, Helge (1995): *Familia og familie. To europæiske kulturelementers møde i højmiddelalderens Danmark,* Aarhus: Aarhus Universitetsforlag.
Pedersen, Ole Karup (1970): *Udenrigsminister P. Munchs opfattelse af Danmarks stilling i international politik,* Copenhagen: G.E.C. Gad.
Pedersen, Ole Karup (1975): "Den hidtidige forskning af dansk udenrigspolitik", *Synsmåder i studiet af dansk udenrigspolitik,* Copenhagen: Samfundsvidenskabeligt forlag, pp. 59-66.
Petersen, Nikolaj (1996): "Denmark and the European Union 1985-1996: A two-level analysis", *Cooperation and Conflict* 31:2, pp. 184-210.
Ploug, Niels and Kvist, Jon (1994): *Overførselsindkomster i Europa. Systemerne i grundtræk* I-IV, Copenhagen: Socialforskningsinstituttet 1994-98.
Putnam, Robert D. (1993): *Making Democracy Work. Civic Traditions in Modern Italy,* Princeton: Princeton University Press.
Rasch, Aage (1966): *Dansk Ostindien 1777-1845,* Copenhagen: Fremad.
Rasmussen, Jens Rahbek (1995): "The Danish Monarchy as a Composite State" in Sørensen (1995), pp. 23-36.
Renan, Ernest (1882): "Qu'est-ce qu'une nation?", *Oeuvres Complètes* I, Paris: Calman Lévy: 1948 pp. 887-906.
Rerup, Lorez (1981): *Slesvig og Holsten efter 1830,* Copenhagen: Politikens Forlag.
Roberts, Michael (1979): *The Swedish Imperial Experience 1560-1718,* Cambridge: Cambridge University Press.
Roberts, Michael (1993): *Gustavus Adolphus,* London: Longman.
Rokkan, Stein (1987): *Stat, nasjon, klasse.* Essays i politisk sosiologi (red. Bernt Hagtvet), Oslo: Universitetsforlaget.
Rothstein, Robert L. (1968): *Alliances and Small Powers,* New York.
Rystad, G., K.R. Böhme, W.M. Carlgren, (eds.) (1994): *In Quest for Trade and Security.: The Baltic in Power Politics, 1500-1990* vol. I-II, Lund: Lund University Press 1994-66.
Schwartz, J. (1985): "Letter to a Danish Historian", *Den Jyske Historiker* 33, pp. 123-24.
Seip, J.A. (1958): "Teorien om det opinionsstyrte enevelde", (norsk) *Historisk Tidsskrift* 38, pp. 397-463 (reprint in *Politisk ideologi.* Tre lærestykker, Oslo: Universitetsforlaget 1988, 13-66).
Simon, Erica (1960): *Réveil national et culture populaire en Scandinavie. La genèse de la Højskole nordique 1844-1878,* Copenhagen: Munksgaard.
Simonsen, Henrik Bredmose (1990): *Kampen om danskheden. Tro og nationalitet i de danske kirkesamfund i Amerika,* Aarhus: Aarhus Universitetsforlag.
Sjøqvist, Viggo (1966): *Danmarks udenrigspolitik 1933-1940,* Copenhagen: Gyldendal.
Sjøqvist, Viggo (1973): *Erik Scavenius. Danmarks udenrigsminister under to verdenskrige,* Copenhagen: Gyldendal.
Sjøqvist, Viggo (1976): *Peter Munch. Manden. Politikeren. Historikeren,* Copenhagen: Gyldendal.
Sjøqvist, Viggo (1995): *Nils Svenningsen. Embedsmanden og politikeren. En biografi,* Copenhagen: Gyldendal.
SNU (Det Sikkerheds- og Nedrustningspolitiske Udvalg) (1995): *Dansk og Europæisk sikkerhed,* Copenhagen: SNU.
Steensgaard, Niels (1996): "Slotsholmen og verdenshavet. Kan adelsvældens og enevældens Danmark placeres i det kapitalistiske verdenssystem" in H. Jeppesen, et al. (ed.), *Søfart – Politik – Identitet tilegnet Ole Feldbæk,* Kronborg: Handels og Søfartsmuseets søhistoriske Skrifter XIX, pp. 81-89.
Stråth, Bo (1980): "Illusory Nordic Alternative to Europe", *Cooperation and Conflict* 15, pp. 103-114.

Stråth, Bo (1995): "Scandinavian Identity. A Mythical Reality", in Sørensen (1995), pp. 37-57.
Stråth, Bo and Ø. Sørensen, (eds.) (1997): *The Cultural Construction of the Nordic Countries*, Oslo: Universitetsforlaget.
Suhm, Peter Frederik (1776): *Historie af Danmark, Norge og Holstein udi i tvende Udtog til den studerende Ungdoms Bedste*, Copenhagen.
Swienty, Tom (ed.) (1994): *Danmark i Europa*, Copenhagen: Munksgaard.
Sørensen, Gert (1993): *Gramsci og den moderne verden*, Copenhagen: Museum Tusculanums Forlag.
Sørensen, N.A. (ed.) (1995): *European Identities, Cultural Diversity and Integration in Europe since 1700*, Odense: Odense University Press.
Sørensen, Ø. (1991): *Solkors og solidaritet. Høyreautoritær samfunnstenkning i Norge ca. 1930-1945*, Oslo: Cappelen.
Sørensen, Ø. (1993): *Verdenskrig og velferd. Britiske, tyske og norske sosialpolitiske planer under annen verdenskrig*, Oslo: Cappelen.
Thodberg, C. and A. Pontoppidan Thyssen, (eds.) (1983): *N.F.S.Grundtvig. Tradition and Renewal*, Copenhagen: Det danske Samfund.
Thyssen, Anders Pontoppidan (ed.) (1960-75): *Vækkelsernes frembrud i Danmark i første halvdel af det 19. århundrede*, I-VII, Copenhagen: Gads Forlag.
Thorsteinsson, Björn (1985): *Island*, Copenhagen: Politikens Forlag.
Unwin, Peter (1996): *Baltic Approaches*, Norwich: Michael Russel.
Villaume, Poul (1995): *Allieret med forbehold. Danmark, NATO og den kolde krig. En studie i dansk sikkerhedspolitik 1949-1961*, Copenhagen: Eirene.
Weber, Eugen (1976): *Peasants into Frenchmen. The Modernization of Rural France, 1870-1914*, Stanford University Press.
Wehler, Hans-Ulrich (1962): *Sozialdemokratie und Nationalstaat, Nationalitätenfragen in Deutschland 1840-1914*, Göttingen: Vandenhoek 1971.
Winge, Vibeke (1991): "Dansk og tysk 1790-1848", in O. Feldbæk (1991), pp. 110-149.
Wæver, Ole (1992): "Nordic Nostalgia", *International Affairs* 68:1, pp. 77-102.
Wæver, Ole, Barry Buzan, Morten Kelstrup, and Pierre Lemaitre, (1993): *Identity, Migration and the New Security Agenda in Europe*, London: Pinter Publishers.
Wæver, Ole (1995): "Danish Dilemmas. Foreign Policy Choices for the 21st Century" in C. Due-Nielsen and N. Petersen (eds.), *Adaptation and Activism. The Foreign Policy of Denmark 1967-1993*, Copenhagen: DJØF Publishing.
Waahlin, Vagn (1987): "Popular Revivalism in Denmark", *Scandinavian Journal of History* 12, pp. 363-87.
Waahlin, Vagn og Uffe Østergaard (1975): *Klasse, demokrati og organisation. Politiserings- og moderniseringsprocssen i Danmark 1830-48 I-VI*, Aarhus Universitet.
Østergaard, Uffe (1984): "Hvad er det danske ved danskerne?", *Den Jyske Historiker*, pp. 29-30, 85-134.
Østergaard, Uffe (1991a): "Definitions of Nation in European Political Thought", *North Atlantic Studies* 1:2, pp. 51-56.
Østergaard, Uffe (ed.) (1991b): *Britain – Nation, State, Decline*, Special issue of *Culture and History* 9/10.
Østergaard, Uffe (1991c): ""Denationalizing" National History – The Comparative Study of Nation-States", *Culture & History* 9/10, 1991, 9-42
Østergaard, Uffe (1992a): "Peasants and Danes", *Comparative Studies in Society and History*, pp. 5-31, reprinted in G. Eley and G. Suny (eds.), *Becoming National. A Reader*, Oxford: Oxford University Press 1996, 179-222.
Østergaard, Uffe (1992b): "Danmarkshistorie mellem statshistorie og nationshistorie", *Historie*, pp. 265-89.

Østergaard, Uffe (1992c): *Europas ansigter,* Politisk kultur i et nyt, gammelt Europa, (ph: Rosinante 1998.)
Østergaard, Uffe (ed.) (1993a): *Dansk identitet?,* Aarhus: Aarhus Universitetsforlag.
Østergaard, Uffe (1993b): "Politisk kultur og landskabsopfattelse i Danmark" in L. Bek o.a. (eds.), *Syn for rum. Om byers og landskabers æstetik,* Aarhus: Aarhus Universitetsforlag, 21-32.
Østergaard, Uffe (1995a): "Republican Revolution or Absolutist Reform?" in G.M. Schwab and J.R. Jeanneney (eds.), *The French Revolution of 1789 and Its Impact,* Westport Connecticut: Greenwood Press, pp. 227-56.
Østergaard, Uffe (1995b): "Norden, det tyske och det moderna" in Anders Björnsson and Peter Luthersson (eds.), *Vändpunkter. Europa och dess omvärld efter 1989,* Stockholm: Svenska Dagbladet, pp. 179-210.
Østergaard, Uffe (1995c): "Der Aufbau einer färöischen Identität – Nordisch, norwegisch, dänisch – oder färöisch?" in C. Dipper and R. Hiestand (eds.), *Siedleridentität,* Frankfurt a.M.: Peter Lang Verlag, pp. 113-140.
Østergaard, Uffe (1996a): "Danmark og mindretallene i teori og praksis" in J. Kühl (ed.), *Mindretalspolitik,* Copenhagen: DUPI, pp. 44-105.
Østergaard, Uffe (1996b): "The Nordic Countries: Roots of Cooperation and Early Attempts" in Péter Bajtay (ed.), *Regional Cooperation and the European Integration Process. Nordic and Central European Experiences,* Budapest: Hungarian Institute of International Affairs, pp. 13-50.
Østergaard, Uffe (1996d): "Stat, nation og national identitet" in H. Andersen og L.B. Kaspersen (eds.), *Klassisk og moderne samfundsteori,* Copenhagen: Hans Reitzels Forlag, pp. 474-93 (English transl. forthcoming Basil Blackwell).
Østergaard, Uffe (1997a): "The Nordic Countries in the Baltic Region" in P. Joenniemi (ed.), *Neo-Nationalism or Regionality. The Restructuring of Political Space around the Baltic Rim,* Stockholm.: Nord Refo 1997:5, pp. 26-54.
Østergaard, Uffe (1997b): "The Geopolitics of "Norden" – States, Nations and Regions" in Stråth and Sørensen (1997), pp. 25-71.
Østergaard, Uffe (1997c): "Skandinavien und Deutschland – Vergleiche und Unterschiede", Katalog zur Ausstellung Skandinavien und Deutschland. Eine Wahlverwandschaft, Berlin: Deutsches Historisches Museum.
Østergaard, Uffe (1997d): "Kontrafaktiske hypoteser", *Kritik:* 128, pp. 1-17. Swedish transl. "Vad hade hänt ... Kontrafaktiske hypoteser och "öppna" situationer i historien och historieforskningen", L.M. Andersson and U. Zander (eds.): *Tänk om ... Nio kontrafaktiska essäer,* Lund: Historiska Media 1999.
Østergaard, Uffe (1998): *Europa. Identitet og identitetspolitik,* Copenhagen: Rosinante 1998/2000.
Østergaard, Uffe (1999): "Danmark i Europa"/ Poul Erik Tøjner (ed.): "1749" in *Weekendavisen* 8/1/1999 no 2.
Østergaard, Uffe (2000): "Regions and Regionalism in Denmark", *Newsletter of the Jean Monnet Center Aarhus* 2, 2000, 4-13
Østerud, Øyvind (1987): *Det moderne statssystem og andre politisk-historiske studier,* Oslo: Gyldendal Norsk Forlag.
Åberg, Alf (1994): *Kampen om Skåne under försvenskningstiden,* Stockholm.: Natur och Kultur.

CHAPTER 6

The Danish Foreign Policy Tradition and the European Context

Hans Branner

1. Introduction

In political, economic, and cultural terms Denmark has been closely tied to the rest of Europe and – as a small country – been strongly dependent on and influenced by developments on the European scene. Less evident, however, is the degree and manner in which Denmark's European experiences have had an impact on its post-war foreign policy, and particularly the European aspect of this policy.

This chapter will try to present and discuss part of the necessary background for taking up these questions. In doing so, it rests on two important, closely interrelated, assumptions. *First*, it assumes that history is a major variable in explaining present policies; *second*, it operates with the existence of a specific Danish foreign policy tradition. These two assumptions are interrelated insofar as the relevance of identifying a tradition is due to the importance of history. Apart from this, however, the two assumptions have a different status.

The question of whether the first and more general assumption holds true is dealt with in chapter 2 (esp. section 4); the concrete influence of history on post-war Danish policies is taken up in other chapters of this book, in particular chapter 5. Below, the focus will be on the second and more controversial assumption of a specific Danish foreign policy tradition. It is the purpose of this chapter to define the content of this tradition, as part of an endeavour to stipulate main determinants of Denmark's post-war European policy. By "foreign policy tradition" is meant fundamental conceptions regarding the goals, role and/or the options of a given country in international politics viewed as part of the country's political heritage.[1]

Throughout the post-war period the content and not least the impact of a Danish foreign policy tradition has received much attention in public debate and political analysis. It is not surprising that major policy changes spark off reflections about the main elements constituting past policies and the historical premises on which these elements have emerged. Furthermore, a preoccupation with traditions is aroused if changes are controversial or if their implementation seems to be ham-

---

1 In chapter 2, section 4 the differences between the concept of a tradition as defined here and the concept of foreign policy doctrines are discussed.

pered by "old thinking". The history of Danish foreign policy since 1945 is characterized by a conspicuous presence of such conditions, in particular those related to the crucial decisions of joining the Atlantic alliance (1949) and the European Community (1972). In both cases the full-blown consequences of membership were not drawn, which in large measure can be explained by inertia in foreign policy thinking and by the existence of deep-rooted conceptions concerning the role and position of Denmark in European and in world politics – what is often referred to as "neutrality thinking".

A new direction of Danish foreign policy in the 1990s, turning a predominantly cautious and passive policy mode into a more engaged and active one is apt to cast new light on the content and impact of "traditional" elements in Danish behavior.[2] On the one hand, ongoing changes may be interpreted as the culmination of a fundamental reorientation which began at the end of World War II, but which has its roots in the 19th century.[3] On the other hand, Danish activism in the 1990s may be seen as demonstrating the continued presence of a tradition exhibiting dualistic traits and whose origin can be traced even further back than the 19th century. It is the identification of such a dualism which is the focal point of the following analysis. In the end we will show how this second interpretation is validated by present Danish policies, also – and not least – when including the European part hereof.

Our first task, however, is a critical assessment of a still widely held conception regarding the foundation of a Danish foreign policy tradition, i.e. the policy of neutrality.

2. A Danish Tradition of Neutrality?

2.1. The Perception of a Neutrality Tradition in Historical Literature and in Political Discourse

In surveying the literature on the history of Danish foreign policy, the concept of *neutrality* occupies a central position, if not *the* central position. Almost unanimously, we are told, since at least the end of the Napoleonic Wars and up until 1945 – or more often until 1949 – that the maintenance of neutrality was the paramount goal of Danish foreign policy.[4] Consequently, both in historical research and in political discourse, it is generally accepted that when searching for a Danish foreign policy tradition with implications for present behavior the closest one gets is the policy of neutrality pursued during the largest part of modern Danish history.

It is worth noting, that this observation holds true although more than 50 years

---

2 For details see chapter 14, section 5.
3 In section 5 we shall discuss the attempt made in a recent and very thorough biography of the Danish diplomat Henrik Kauffmann to identify two main lines in Danish foreign policy thinking, a national and a cosmopolitan. Implicitly, this identification supports the interpretation just made of a tradition that has been overcome (Lidegaard 1996).
4 See e.g. the attempt to trace the "long lines" in Danish foreign policy in Fink (1958).

have now passed since the policy of neutrality was officially given up. This may be accounted for by the conditions prevailing for discussing foreign policy in Denmark. For the adherents of the new post-war direction in Danish policy – both at the time of the change and later on – it has been important to emphasize the negative effects of postures hitherto upheld and the continued urgency of the fight against them. The content of post-war Danish foreign policy, often characterized as semi-neutrality or semi-alignment, has provided plenty of reasons for maintaining this struggle (Ørvik 1986). In this way, the former Danish policy of neutrality rightly seems to deserve the label of a foreign policy tradition. The existence of a tradition is revealed by the tenacity of positions and basic disagreements which seem to override official policy changes.

The next section presents Carsten Holbraad's book *Danish Neutrality. A Study in the Foreign Policy of a Small State* (1991). While this book is the only in-depth analysis of the history of Danish foreign policy in modern times, it also attempts to identify characteristic features of Danish behavior over a long time-span, i.e. a Danish foreign policy tradition. In accordance with the usual interpretation, Holbraad gives – at least at first glance – the policy of neutrality a central position in the Danish tradition. "Neutrality" is not only used in the title as a general characterization of Danish policy throughout the entire period; it is also the ordering concept for structuring the book. Thus the five chronologically arranged chapters are entitled: "Aligned Neutrality (1720-1814)", "Isolated Neutrality (1814-1922)", Defenseless Neutrality (1922-1945)", "Non-aligned Neutrality (1945-1949)" and "Latent Neutrality (1949-)"; the sixth and last chapter follows this line with the title "Future Neutrality"?

Sticking with the "neutrality" concept throughout all the chapters is an integral part of the author's goal with the entire book (cf. below). So is the characterization of Danish policy after 1949 as latent neutrality. Holbraad's major thesis is that important features of pre-war policy persisted not only in the immediate post-war period but also after Denmark became a member of the *North Atlantic Alliance*. In so doing Holbraad's work accords with a recent trend in Danish historical research emphasizing the reluctance of the Danish government in 1948-49 towards membership in the Atlantic Pact and the subsequent hesitant and low profile policy as an alliance member (cf. Heisler 1985; Branner 1990; Villaume 1994; Borring Olesen 1994).

Major aspects of Danish policy towards the EC/EU might also be interpreted as influenced by a Danish neutrality tradition, not least the four exemptions from the *Maastricht Treaty* obtained in the *Edinburgh Agreement* of December 1992. It has been a widespread conception in the interpretations made by political commentators and analysts that Danish EU positions reflect the continued presence of a neutrality stance in Danish foreign policy. Although the main focus is on security policy and the account ends in 1990, a parallel interpretation is to be found in the analysis by Holbraad. For him the "qualified commitment and limited participation [in the EC], which ... may be explained with reference to traditional attitudes and ideas" (p. 152) is another sign of the latent neutrality prevailing in Danish foreign policy since 1949 (p. 154).

Thus, a widely held conception of a neutrality tradition with continuous impact on policy formulation has not only survived the international and domestic upheavals following World War II and the resulting changes in Danish foreign policy, but has been reinforced by historical research and concrete Danish behavior. Nevertheless, it may argued that neutrality is both an inadequate and in some respects misleading term when trying to identify the Danish foreign policy tradition. The following analysis will try to substantiate this position by providing five reasons for attaching less importance to the neutrality tradition, and subsequently – in the next sections – by discussing an alternative way of determining a Danish tradition.

2.2. Five Arguments against Neutrality as the Central Concept in the Danish Tradition

The reasons for rejecting neutrality as the central concept in the Danish tradition may be summarized as follows:

- The practice of neutrality in foreign relations is *far from being an exclusively Danish phenomenon*. Indeed, throughout the history of modern Europe up until the Second World War, neutrality seems to have been an accepted foreign policy goal of most small states, several of whom have traditions of neutrality that go just as far back if not further than the Danish tradition. Obvious cases are Sweden, Switzerland, and the Netherlands.[5]
- In the Danish case, neutrality is *far from being a consistent practice*. On the contrary, as noted in Holbraad's five chapters, this policy can take different forms over time, various Danish politicians having pursued it in different ways. Moreover, further nuances can be added to Holbraad's typology. Starting from 1720, when the Danish neutrality tradition is normally considered to have been formed, the following different types of neutrality policy can be identified: neutrality with/without alliances; neutrality with a strong/weak military basis; neutrality in isolation/not in isolation; neutrality oriented equally towards all great powers/oriented primarily towards Germany; guaranteed/non-guaranteed neutrality; classical/neo-neutrality; overt/latent neutrality.[6]

---

5 The relation between a neutrality-oriented foreign policy and the relative size of the state in question is a common subject in the existing literature on small states. See Baker Fox, Rothstein and Frei, or my own comparative discussion of foreign policies of Denmark and other small states in Europe during the 1930s, in Branner (1987: 261-75).

6 I shall not attempt to offer a final definition of the concept of neutrality. See Ørvik (1953) for a discussion of the concept and its evolution. The aim here is merely to point out the fact that the concept of neutrality has been used to characterize Danish foreign policy practice since 1720, while at the same time the many different shapes that the policy takes within this period make it very difficult to identify the existence of a tradition within this Danish policy practice.

This abundance of different forms of neutrality, which to some extent have all characterized the history of Danish foreign policy, makes it difficult to use the concept of neutrality for identifying a distinct Danish foreign policy tradition. The only fitting solution would be to define neutrality simply as "a tendency to stay out of war", but such a definition would be susceptible to the above argument that the concept of neutrality can not be said to describe anything peculiar to Danish historical experience, i.e., something not found in the foreign policy traditions of other countries.[7] It seems more convincing to regard the goal of neutrality, insofar as such a goal can be said to have been part of Danish policy, as a concrete manifestation of more deep-rooted – or more fundamental – views and perceptions held by decision-makers.

- It can further be argued that neutrality has been *far less deeply rooted in early Danish foreign policy* than is often maintained, or far less than seems to be implied by most summary overviews of Danish history. This is especially the case if a distinction is drawn between clear cut neutrality on the one hand and a policy of alliances on the other – a distinction quite commonly made, at least since 1949.

During the first period of Danish neutrality, ostensibly lasting from 1720 to 1814, this policy did not prevent the making of peace-time alliances.[8] On this background, the tradition of neutrality could indeed be just as appropriately said to have started at the end of the Napoleonic wars. However, even within this more limited time span the motivations for alliance-making have been shown to be lurking right under the surface of neutrality. A closer analysis of the Danish policy during this period would thus lead to the conclusion that in several particular instances the Danish government was actually inclined to abandon its policy of neutrality – and indeed, it went this far in some cases, e.g. in 1815, 1864, 1870, 1906-07 and 1937.[9]

---

7 In August 1914, when Danish politicians were to respond to the German demand for laying mines in Danish waters, it was exactly the hope of avoiding direct participation in the impending First World War that led to consensus around neutrality as the proper choice of policy under the existing circumstances. Behind this consensus, however, quite varied perceptions existed as to how to react to the German demand, how to relate to the great powers, as well as how the policy should be pursued in more concrete terms. General consensus on the course of neutrality could thus be consistent with quite contradictory foreign policy views. See Branner (1972: 219).

8 Denmark made alliances with Britain, France and Russia at different times during this period.

9 In pursuance of the peace settlement of 1815, Denmark made an attempt, though not very successful, to enter into an alliance with England. Likewise, during the war of 1864, Denmark hoped for military agreements with England as well as with Sweden and Norway, a hope which turned out to be just as futile as in 1815. Later on, at the beginning of the Franco-Prussian war in 1870, Denmark made a rather half-hearted declaration of neutrality while actually being on its way to signing an agreement with France; the early military successes of the Germans, however, quickly forced the Danish government to reconsider its course of action. In the 20th century, during 1906-07, negotiations were conducted with Germany on

- From a more contemporary point of view, there are inherent advantages of not stressing the tradition of neutrality too hard. One avoids the rather pointless *terminological discussion*, which would otherwise ensue in relation to the seeming break with tradition in 1949. There are many good reasons to regard the Danish NATO decision as important in relation to the question of break/continuity in the Danish foreign policy tradition (see chapter 11). However, it seems less fruitful to connect this question exclusively to the neutrality aspect of this tradition. In 1949, the alliance is chosen, although half-heartedly, over the alternative of continued neutrality, and at no point since then has there been any question of altering this fundamental choice. To talk of semi-neutrality or latent neutrality when characterizing the period since 1949, therefore, constitutes a rather inappropriate way of stressing the continuity in Danish foreign policy during this period. This continuity should be seen in a different and broader context than that of neutrality.
- With this we touch upon a final point, which is that the whole question of neutrality versus alliance-making and the choosing among many different kinds of neutrality – notwithstanding the many implications of these choices – *constitute only one element of foreign policy practice*. Foreign policy has many aspects, and it would be exceptional if all these aspects could be understood in light of the choice for or against neutrality.[10] When trying to describe the Danish foreign policy tradition, therefore, it will be an unavoidable task to seek out other possible starting points for this description.

---

the creation of some form of military convention between Denmark and Germany (the so-called 'Lütken discussions', thoroughly studied by Fink 1959). In the 1930s, the Danish Prime Minister Stauning, in spite of the cautious and basically Germany-oriented policy of neutrality practiced at the time, actively investigated the possibilities of an alliance with England. He did this during a visit to London, and without any prior agreement with Foreign Minister P. Munch, who would undoubtedly have strongly resisted the idea at the time. It can be shown that even P. Munch, who for many stand as the incarnation of the Danish neutrality policy, was in principle not opposed to the making of alliances. For an account of Stauning's visit to London, see Sjøqvist (1966) and Seymour (1982). For Munch's position on the question of alliances, see Bjøl (1970; 1983: 25).

10 It is a question of degrees or shades rather than of black and white. In the case of Sweden it is possible to show that the policy of neutrality has had a determining impact on a range of other aspects of that country's foreign policy during most of the post-World War II era, e.g. in its overall European policy (see Malmborg 1994). A similar point can be made about the special Finnish version of neutrality. However, these examples must be said to constitute exceptions to the general picture.

3. A Dualistic Interpretation: Determinism, Internationalism and Their Interaction

3.1. Carsten Holbraad's Analysis

In continuation of the previous arguments we shall again discuss the analysis by Carsten Holbraad. This may seem paradoxical, since neutrality is such a central concept in his book – at least when looking at the title and the headings of the chapters. On closer inspection, however, we see, that Holbraad's ambition is not limited to tracing different forms of Danish neutrality policy in their historical context.[11] Holbraad's main concern is to explain the evolution of Danish foreign policy by demonstrating the impact of two contradictory ideological tendencies, i.e., *determinism* and *internationalism*. Although at times he seems to assume that the two tendencies constitute the specific content of Danish neutrality, they are also studied in their own right. And the examination of their origin and their importance may be considered the main contribution by Holbraad in identifying a Danish foreign policy tradition. In addition, by relating the Danish tradition to these tendencies, he makes Denmark's European experiences more explicit, thus facilitating the discussion of the relevance of the tradition variable in the post-1949 context – and for the present purpose.

Determinism represents a widely held perception among Danish decision-makers and is most distinctly expressed by the Danish foreign minister during the two world wars, Erik Scavenius (1913-20 and 1940-43). In an often quoted passage Scavenius wrote that Danish foreign policy was only apparently determined by Danish authorities; in reality, decisions reflected the power balance in Denmark's surroundings. The main task for Danish decision-makers, therefore, was to adapt to external demands, especially those emanating from the most important great powers.[12] This kind of deterministic thinking, of course, is not atypical of Small Powers, but according to Holbraad and also other observers, historical experience has given it a firmer grasp on the minds in Denmark than elsewhere.

---

11 It is probably indicative of his main research interest that he omits a discussion of the concept of neutrality; cf. the review by Niels Amstrup (1992).

12 In full the passage reads as follows: "It is a widely held view in this country that the foreign policy of Denmark is determined by the Danish Government and Parliament. This, however, is correct only insofar as the formal decisions through which this policy is given expression appear as a decision of these organs. In reality, Danish foreign policy is determined by factors on which the Danish Government has little influence. The main task of Danish foreign policy, therefore is to keep the government informed about these factors and their interaction and in this connection to form an opinion on the right moment in which to exploit the prevailing situation to further Denmark's interests. Decisive among the factors whose interplay determines Danish foreign policy are the actual power relations in the world around us, especially the power balance between the great powers near to us" Scavenius (1948: 9). (The translation from Due-Nielsen and Petersen 1995). Surprisingly, the quotation is not to be found in Holbraad's book.

At the same time the Danish version of determinism is peculiar because of its interaction with the opposite tendency, i.e. internationalism. Whereas determinism leads to a more passive policy, internationalism leads to an active one. The basis for this second ideological tendency is the conception that in the long run possibilities exist for changing conditions in the international system to the advantage of small states; and, furthermore, that these states themselves may contribute to the realization hereof, primarily by working for the substitution of power by law in relations among states. According to Holbraad, the internationalist tendency has even longer historical roots than determinism, and he is able to trace its significance back to the 18th century. The unique feature in the Danish tradition, however, is its dualistic character: both tendencies are conspicuously manifest in Danish history, and through their interplay they have shaped the main characteristics of Danish foreign policy behavior. Although key conditions have changed, Holbraad tries to demonstrate the continued importance of this dualism.

This short account of the central thesis of Holbraad's book will now be followed by a more elaborated presentation and discussion of its main elements. Our intention is to demonstrate both the advantages and some of the shortcomings of his analysis and clear the ground for an alternative means of identifying a Danish foreign policy tradition (section 4).

3.2. The Independent Variable: The Reduction of Danish Power

The concept of power – rather than the concept of neutrality – is central to an understanding of the way Holbraad depicts the evolution of Danish foreign policy. It is on the background of the decline in the relative power position of Denmark and the interpretation hereof by decision-makers that his main thesis is formulated.

Although departing from a "realistic" approach to international politics, Holbraad is pre-occupied with the internal conditions for foreign policy-making. Without explicitly discussing the relationship between the impact of external and internal factors on the development of Danish foreign policy, he operates with the idea that there exists some intricate form of interaction between the two. Holbraad's main objective is to identify the ideologies that are effective in forming Danish foreign policy. Thus, domestic factors has been given some weight in the analysis. For Holbraad, however, the ideologies are at the same time primarily a reflection of external conditions at the time when they were developed and embedded in Danish policy. First among these external conditions is the marked reduction over time in the relative size and power of the Danish state within the European system of states.

This aspect of Danish history is well known in the literature and is dealt with at greater length in chapter 5 of this volume. For the sake of later argument, however, I shall give a short overview.[13]

---

13 For a fuller account see also Fink (1958).

Historians normally cite the year 1720 as a turning point in Danish history. This was the year when a peace settlement was reached between the Nordic powers, Denmark and Sweden, after several years of war. The settlement embodied an implicit acknowledgment by Denmark of the significant losses of territory that Denmark had experienced during the 17th century in its wars with Sweden. Although Sweden was the immediate loser of the war, the war had thus finally shown that Denmark would not be able to recover these territories. Denmark no longer had the capacity to make its own way in European power politics. From being at least a kind of great power, Denmark was from now on reduced to a medium-sized power.

The next major turning point came a century later, when Denmark in 1801 chose the wrong side in the Napoleonic wars, a mistake that cost Denmark its relatively strong fleet as well as control of the Norwegian territory, which then came under Swedish authority. Loss of Norway occurred without compensation in the form of territories in Northern Germany, which the Danish government fought for at the Vienna Peace Conference in 1815. On the contrary, by the establishment of a German confederation, Denmark was destined to become ever more dependent on developments in the German territories, because German speaking Holstein was still under Danish rule. Later in the century, this would lead to yet another reduction in the size of the Danish state.

The two wars that were fought over territories in southern Jutland (Sleswig-Holstein) in 1848-50 and 1864 were indirectly caused by the difficult constitutional questions surrounding the demarcation of the Danish state in relation to the German confederation. The immediate catalyst was the emergence on both sides of the border of strong nationalist movements, Danish as well as German. At the same time, the wars illustrate the fact that by 1914 Denmark was effectively reduced to the status of a "pawn in the game", totally dependent on the European great powers for its survival.

The first of these wars resulted in a Danish victory on the battlefield. However, Denmark was not allowed by the great powers to carry out the political changes that had been the aim of the war effort, – known as the Eider-policy, which would have strengthened Danish control in these territories. Later on, in 1864, as a result of some risky foreign political manoeuvrings on the side of the Danish government, Denmark was finally defeated in another war against the then much stronger Prussia. In spite of several declarations from other European states, which seemed to support Denmark's position, it eventually appeared that Denmark stood isolated within the international community – no others were willing to confront the armies of Bismarck for the sake of Denmark.

The result was yet another reduction in the size of the Danish state, this time by about a fifth of its territories and the loss of a third of its population. Yet, that was not all. The war of 1864 constituted but one among a number of events that were eventually to unite the German states under the supremacy of Prussia in 1871. Over the following decades, this new German state developed into the most powerful single actor on the European continent. For Denmark, these events therefore led to a reduction in relative as well as absolute power resources. The decimated Danish state was now placed in the shadow of a dominant and expansionist European great power.

In broad terms, this state of affairs did not change significantly until 1945. The German defeat in World War I and the resulting return to Danish rule of parts of southern Jutland in 1920 cannot be said to have constituted any fundamental change in the balance of power that had been established after 1871. Rather, these developments were instrumental in making the Danish position in international politics even more precarious over the subsequent years. The tough conditions imposed on the German state in 1919 by the Treaty of Versailles created fertile ground for the reemergence of strongly nationalist tendencies within Germany, which under Hitler in the 1930s took on a character of unprecedented aggressiveness. Under these circumstances, it was an extra disadvantage for Denmark to have within its borders a minority of German speaking people, of which a majority actually supported Hitler's revisionist policies.

In sum, the period from 1720 until World War II was characterized by a gradual but significant reduction in the international power position of the Danish state – as evaluated against the most commonly used standards. This took place across a number of dimensions: the territory that was controlled by Denmark, the importance with which it was regarded by other European states, and the relative dependence of Denmark on its relations to neighboring states. The German occupation of 1940-45 was the absolute low-point in this development. This extreme situation, which was brought about by the international war conditions, can thus be regarded, perhaps somewhat cynically, as no more than the mere effectuation of underlying realities in the Danish power position, conditions that were present already in the 1930s and even earlier.

3.3. "Contracting Out" and the Evolution of a Dualistic Tradition

According to Holbraad's analysis, the "external" events, which have been recounted above, constitute only one element in the Danish deroute from being an important power to becoming an insignificant state, dependent on its German neighbor. Developments in the international power structure occurred along with developments in behavior and self-perception, which reinforced the trend towards retraction of Danish state power until Danish politics was almost decoupled from European international power politics. At the beginning of his book, Holbraad sums up the characteristics of the policies pursued by the Danish state after 1720:

> "Over the centuries, [Denmark] took leave of one means after another of conducting foreign policy and, apart from two wars by its southern border in the mid-nineteenth century, adopted an increasingly passive role in European politics. While becoming ever more preoccupied with international trade, international law, international morality, and international society, it nearly turned its back on international politics"
>
> (Holbraad 1991: 1)

Through the three stages of its exit from the international power game, Denmark relinquishes, one by one, three important instruments of security policy: active involvement in war after 1720, alliances with other states after 1814, and, finally after 1870, an effective military defense capability. Even if this last surrender of military capability takes place only gradually and is accompanied by some internal political conflict, it nevertheless seems to have been more or less implemented by the 1920s. According to Holbraad, the gradual dismantling of Danish military power also influences the various forms that the Danish neutrality policy assumes over the centuries.

In Holbraad's view this self-imposed decoupling from the game of international power politics is connected with two ideological strands in Danish foreign policy thinking: internationalism and determinism. The apparent conflict that would appear to exist between the two is in fact quite superficial, as both happen to work in favor of the prevailing policy of neutrality. Both tendencies illustrate the way Danish politicians have interpreted the loss of power experienced by Denmark over the centuries.

Elements of the first strand, *internationalism*, can be found as far back as the very first years after 1720, where Holbraad finds a tendency to "sentimentalize" the nature of international politics (p. 19). The international position of Denmark was relatively benign throughout the 18th century, partly due to a successful policy of neutrality as well as the renunciation of its earlier revisionist goals. While other states were preoccupied by issues of survival and security, Danish leaders could concentrate on domestic economic welfare. Consequently, an idea developed that matters of economy and welfare could be separated from the more crude issues of international security. Issues of foreign relations were therefore constrained within a rather limited scope, and what was to endure of Danish policy within this field was henceforth based on a conviction among its practitioners that it was somehow morally superior to the policies of other states. For example, the elder Bernstorff, who was the main architect of this new Danish foreign policy, regarded "with dismay" the practices of "war politics" among other European states.[14]

The same ingredients can be identified in foreign policy identities from later parts of Danish history. Especially after 1864, the process of sentimentalization intensifies. With the addition of some new elements, it transforms itself into the major strand in the Danish foreign policy tradition that Holbraad calls internationalism. More specifically, this intensification takes the form of a series of attempts to integrate legal procedures into relations between Denmark and other states. It is evident that the earlier tendencies of casting foreign relations in a moral light still affects the Danish policies during this period. Especially the political opposition parties are concerned about this aspect – something which can also be seen in the fact that after the liberal farmers party, *Venstre*, comes to power, Denmark becomes

---

14 In a confidential letter from 1757, Bernstorff wrote to one of his friends that "a war started without just reason – I will go even further: without necessity, seems to me to be the most dreadful of all decisions that human beings could take" (Holbraad 1991: 3).

one of the leading countries regarding the conclusion of treaties concerning arbitration.[15] In the same period, steps are taken by the Danish government to make the neutral status of Danish territory permanent, backed by treaties with the interested great powers. Another element of internationalism in Danish foreign policy of this period is the effort to bind together more strongly the Nordic countries in an area of peace and international harmony between states.

Together, these efforts represent a desire to avoid entanglements in international conflicts. Thus, one could say that in Holbraad's interpretation, internationalism becomes a means by which Denmark seeks to decouple itself from international politics.[16] As such though, it constitutes only one of two ideologies behind the Danish neutrality policy. As we shall see, the other one, determinism, has a number of further implications, although in practice they give rise to almost similar results.

The presence of a *deterministic* ideology in Danish foreign policy can hardly be traced as far back as that of internationalism. Of course, the separation of international economics from international security policy, which constituted the hallmark of the new foreign policy of the 18th century, has some affinity with deterministic ideology. However, it was not really until the defeat to Prussia in 1864 – and even more clearly after German unification in 1871 – that determinism became an integrated part of the Danish foreign policy tradition. A new concept is introduced in this period: *the European necessity* – expressing a widespread belief that the small size and the geostrategic position of Denmark made any notion of an independent foreign policy illusory.

The new ideology had substantial effect on policy behavior, of which two are taken up by Holbraad. The first is the emergence of a tendency towards "introversion of national efforts". Holbraad does not mention the famous slogan of E.M. Dalgas: "What is outwardly lost, must be inwardly regained."[17] Yet it would make a very suitable title for this aspect of deterministic thinking. A basic notion in the reevaluation of Danish foreign policy was that the future survival of the Danish state would be much better served through internal political measures rather than through political initiatives on the international scene. Relative passivity in the field of foreign policy was thus compensated by activism in matters of domestic policy. The broad mobilization of the rural population, including institutional innovations like the folk high schools and the farmer-cooperatives, and the gradual development of an egalitarian and prosperous society, should – at least in part – be interpreted in this context.[18]

---

15 In this connection, it might be worth mentioning that in 1908 a Dane, Frederik Bajer, was awarded the Nobel peace prize for his work for a more legally regulated international society. See Henning Nielsen (1977: 75).
16 On this background it can be argued that the label 'internationalism' is really not very appropriate. Holbraad's usage of the term has to be seen in connection with his general approach to international politics (Holbraad 1991: 7), as will become clear in the discussion below.
17 Dalgas (1828-1894) organized the cultivation of the moors in western Jutland into arable land during the latter part of the 19th century.
18 For details on folk high schools and cooperatives see chapter 5. Using concepts from mod-

The second – and internationally most conspicuous – element in Danish policy change was the adaptation to German interests. In one way this adaptation was closely connected to the "introversion of national efforts." If Denmark was to expend its energies on domestic political and economic development, it needed to maintain a good relationship with its dominant neighbour, which after all was the most potent threat to the desired tranquility in foreign relations. However, this policy did also have its own fundamental reasons, as was flatly stated by the right-wing prime minister and strong proponent of military defense J.B.S. Estrup: "the next time Denmark comes to stand as the enemy of Germany in a military conflict will be the last one for Denmark."[19] It was Denmark's very survival that was at stake. One had to recognize the fact that Denmark was situated within an area that was increasingly dominated by Germany.[20] As long as this situation persisted, i.e. until 1943/45, it was to become a guiding principle in Danish foreign policy always to accommodate German interests.

Also a third element in Danish determinism, though treated by Holbraad in a later context, should be included at this stage: the sort of nihilism developing around Danish defense policy towards the end of the 19th century. German dominance and the new emphasis on welfare policies formed the basis of the still stronger criticism directed against Danish defense expenditures. "What is the good of it?", a famous slogan coined by one of the liberal opposition leaders, Viggo Hørup, obtained high standing in the political debate of the time. Taken literally, the quotation can be interpreted as signaling a deep political disillusionment regarding the prospects of foreign policy and defense. As such it contributed to laying the ground work for the sharp decline in Danish defense spending after World War I. However, Hørup's campaign against the Danish military was primarily a cultural-political struggle to ignite a new spiritual awareness in the Danish population, and, thus, formed part of the development which would eventually strengthen the Danish state.

As said, the two ideological strands in Danish foreign policy – according to Holbraad's interpretation – both worked towards the same overall result: namely the gradual decoupling by Denmark from the game of international power politics in Europe. This development reached its climax during the inter-war years, when Denmark in effect relinquished its capability for independent military defense of its own territory. This occurred with the defense laws of 1922, and no changes were subsequently made in this regard, even when in the 1930s the threat of German militarism was again clearly felt in Denmark. On the contrary, under the lea-

---

ern political theory, one could say that Denmark after becoming a "weak power" was turned into a "strong state" and a "strong society"; cf. Buzan (1991) and the contribution by Uffe Østergaard. This line of thought will be further pursued in the discussion of power below in section 4.

19 See chapter 11.

20 There was some disagreement, however, as to how Denmark was to ensure its neutrality while at the same time avoiding a direct confrontation with Germany. For a discussion of this within the tradition of adaption theory, see Nikolaj Petersen (1979).

dership of foreign minister Peter Munch, Denmark pursued a consistent policy of adaptation towards Nazi Germany. While following this pragmatic, determinist course in his policy towards the immediate threat, Munch took an active interest in the work that went on within the League of Nations to create a tighter legal framework for the international community.[21] Hence, internationalism still had a prominent place in the Danish foreign policy universe, but neither internationalism nor determinism – and the manner in which they became politically manifest during this period – were of much benefit, when Hitler's quest for European domination was directed against Scandinavia in early 1940.[22]

The course of events leading to the April 1940 German invasion thus seem to substantiate the contracting-out thesis put forth by Holbraad. Looking at the 1930s, one could almost say that the two tendencies of Danish dualism mutually supported and reinforced each other. At the same time, this example shows that the combination of internationalism and determinism led to unrealistic perceptions of international politics among Danish decision-makers: on the one hand an exaggerated pessimism, on the other hand an exaggerated optimism. Moreover, the decoupling from international politics in this period takes on an especially extreme form in the so-called 'neo-neutral' doctrine, which is formulated by the Danish expert of international law Georg Cohn, a close adviser to foreign minister Munch.[23] This doctrine does not stop with the recommendation that neutral countries stay out of war, but takes the argument further in a total renunciation of war as a means of international politics. As for the older Bernstorff, neutrality policy is thereby invested with an ideal and moral quality which sets it apart from all other forms of foreign policy.

According to Holbraad, internationalism and determinism become the two main variables of the Danish foreign policy tradition; and it becomes one of the objectives of his book to show how they are still present in the making of Danish foreign policy in the post-World War II period. He argues that the most important change in Danish policy after 1945 is the appearance of a new form of internationalism very different from the earlier one, and which is illustrated by Denmark's participation in the Western cooperation fora of NATO and the EC. As a further tendency, however, Holbraad points to the fact that in participating in these fora, Denmark has generally taken on the role of "foot-dragger" rather than enthusiastic member.[24] Since the two

---

21 The policies of Munch are elaborated below in section 4.3.
22 It should be added – even if it is not spelled out by Holbraad – that the "Scandinavian option" also plays a role in the 1930s. Prime minister Stauning, in this respect, is more active than Munch, although he qualifies his position somewhat after his famous speech of 1937 (Lænkehundstalen); see Sjøqvist (1966). However, when Munch, in May 1939, takes steps to gather the Scandinavian countries behind a joint response to the German offer of a non-aggression pact, this is in part also motivated by a hope that the Scandinavian territory could be kept out of the impending confrontation between the great powers.
23 It seems plausible that the neo-neutral doctrine had some influence over Munch's thinking as well as his behaviour. For a discussion of this possibility, see Pedersen (1970: 477-78).
24 This is by no means a controversial evaluation of the Danish policy within these fora. Unfortunately, however, Holbraad fails to relate this practice to his variables of the Danish foreign policy tradition. In chapter 11, such a detailed analysis will be at the center of the discussion.

Historical and Cultural Preconditions 199

Figure 1: The Danish Foreign Policy Tradition: Background conditions and Main Features (based on C. Holbraad's analysis)

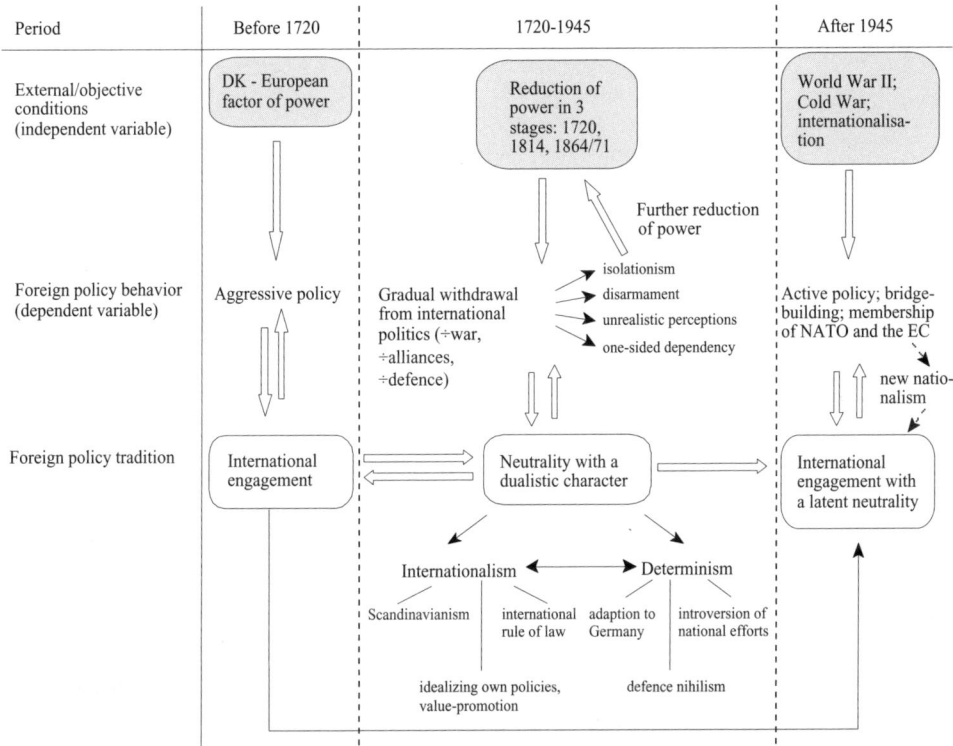

ideological strands are regarded as constituent parts of the Danish neutrality tradition, and since they are both – although in altered forms manifest in the post-war period, Danish foreign policy after 1949 as a whole is labeled "latent neutrality".[25] A strong impetus for the development of this "latent neutrality" is said to have been the emergence of a Danish nationalism. Thus, at the end of the book Holbraad identifies a third ideological strand not included in his analysis of the previous periods.

An overview of the entire set of variables and elements included in Holbraad's analysis is attempted in figure 1.[26] Some factors only partly referred to in the book are also included in order to give the scheme a maximum degree of analytical coherence. Consequently, the figure represents an interpretation and extension of the main lines of Holbraad's argument. Nevertheless, the figure may act as a useful

---

25 The years 1945-49 constitute a transition period in which the new forms of internationalism take root, in the early years as a result of the occupation experience, but later also influenced by the first impressions of Cold War in Europe.
26 It should be mentioned that it has not been the intention to introduce all of Holbraad's categories and determinants. In his analysis, economic interests, the development of industry and party politics are also influential factors. However, such factors are bound to play a role in the historical development of any country. Hence, they are not included here, since our aim has been to develop variables specific to the Danish case.

frame of reference for the following discussion, which draws on the scheme set up by Holbraad, but – on the basis of a critical assessment of central concepts and implied assertions – seeks to develop an alternative way of identifying a Danish foreign policy tradition.

4. The Content of a Danish Small State Tradition

4.1. The Need for a Broader Definition of Power

Before turning to criticism and further elaboration, we may emphasize three main elements in Holbraad's analysis which will be used as a basis for the discussion in this section.

First, we shall assume that it is actually possible to induce from the varied history of Danish foreign policy a number of general variables that characterize the special Danish tradition within this field – and that any such variables will also have made an imprint on Danish policy during the post-World War II period.[27]

Second, it will be assumed that external factors, including "objective" conditions such as the territorial size and location of Denmark in the international system, influence the development of a Danish foreign policy tradition. More specifically, we accept Holbraad's contention that the gradual reduction in the external power of the Danish state, which took place during the 18th and 19th centuries, has had a marked impact on this tradition. Indeed, the foreign policy tradition has in large part evolved through a continuing process of interpretation and reinterpretation connected with this decline in external power.[28]

A *third* starting point for the analysis will be Holbraad's definition of the Danish tradition as being constituted by a basic duality between two ideological strands. We thereby accept one of the main conclusions of his book, that the Danish foreign policy tradition is indeed characterized by some kind of dualism.

Our main line of criticism, however, departs from the way this dualism is conceived by Holbraad and the implications he attaches to it. Basically, Holbraad has a negatively biased view of the tradition he is studying. According to his inter-

---

27 For an oposite view see the review of Holbraad's book by Armstrup (1992).
28 In figure 1, the influence of the external/objective factors are pictured with the use of arrows pointing downwards from these. In the first instance, the result is a specific political behavior, but out of this behavior a tradition is developed, the content of which is included in the lower part of the model. It seems obvious that also a number of other factors will be influential in the development of foreign policy behavior as well as the foreign policy tradition. Thus, the figure does not pretend to be an exhaustive model for the explanation of foreign policy. The model is specifically designed to cover the issues related to the present discussion. Furthermore, the interesting dynamics that develop between tradition and behavior is not covered by the model.

pretation, both parts in Danish foreign policy dualism, and consequently also the Danish policy of neutrality, are connected with a strategy of decoupling from international politics, which has been highly disadvantageous to Danish national interests. Through its membership of NATO and the EC Denmark has only to a limited extent transcended the historically defined constraints on its ability to engage in international politics.[29] These constraints have been potentially present ever since 1945, such that a constant danger exists of Denmark sliding back into the old habits. The introduction of the concept "nationalism" to describe recent trends in Danish foreign policy ideology is indicative of his pessimistic view in this regard.

The sharp distinction between, on the one hand, the neutrality tradition as it existed prior to World War II, and, on the other hand, the internationally oriented policies of the period after the war is of little use in clarifying the neutrality concept, since neutrality has by no means been a hindrance for effective participation in international affairs. The policies of Sweden during the post-World War II period are a case in point. The basic problem inherent in Holbraads understanding and evaluation of permanent traits in Danish foreign policy thinking has to do with his narrow use of the concept of *power*. It is exactly this narrowness, which induces him to link the former Danish policy of neutrality to a strategy of decoupling from international politics – and thereby to a negative evaluation of past as well as present consequences of the Danish foreign policy tradition.

In many traditional accounts of diplomatic history – and Holbraad's analysis is not different in this respect – the concept of power is regarded from the view of the *realist* school of international politics. According to this view, international politics are conducted through relations between formally sovereign states, and the most fundamental determinant of these political relations is the relative distribution of power resources among the participating states. When Holbraad talks about decoupling from international politics it is exactly this kind of politics that comes to mind. This is especially the case when he points to Denmark's efforts to stay out of military conflicts as the primary illustration of his argument. However, power relations, both between states and in the international system more generally, can also be seen from other perspectives.

Without going into too much detail about the definition of power I shall here introduce three points.[30] First, the concept of power has both an *offensive* and a *defensive* aspect. Power tends mostly to be associated with the offensive aspect, i.e., the power of a particular state to induce other states to act in a preferred way. Conversely, the defensive aspect involves the ability to avoid being subjected to the power of other states. In this connection the internal cohesion and institutional structures of the state can be just as important as traditional power resources such as the size of territory and population.

---

29 As the analysis ends by 1990, only the term "EC" is used.
30 A discussion of power concepts introducing the distinctions employed here can be found in Goldmann and Sjøstedt (1979). For a brief overview of the various power dimensions, see Branner (1996: 52-55).

This brings us to the second aspect, which is that power can be obtained through both *material* and *immaterial* resources, tangible and non-tangible power base elements.[31] The immaterial resources, as they are inherently difficult to quantify, are often neglected. Moreover immaterial resources are mainly defensive in character, and, thus, do not cause the same dramatic and visible effects in diplomatic history as do the more material and offensive powers of the state. Finally, it seems appropriate to include *time* as a distinct variable in the discussion of power. Different forms of power do not have the same effects at different points in time but are closely related to general developments and conditions in *the international system*. Thus, it is not irrelevant to take into account whether the international climate is marked by tension or lack of tension, war or peace, separation or interdependence between the units, and whether the degree of anarchy in the international system more generally is increasing or decreasing. These factors are important for assessing the effects of power resources both positive and negative, material and immaterial.

By noting these distinctions, we should be able to develop a fuller and more qualified understanding of the content and persistence of the Danish foreign policy tradition, in the post-World War II period.

The starting point for this reformulation remains the relative reduction in physical power resources of the Danish state that has taken place since the beginning of the 18th century.[32] However, by using a more refined concept of power, we may offer an alternative interpretation of the ensuing duality in the Danish tradition. Instead of viewing the political effects of the two separate but still complementary tendencies of determinism and internationalism amplifying the consecutive losses of Danish state power, we shall argue that the duality can just as well be understood as an attempt to compensate for the reductions in physical power resources by the development of other type of resources. Furthermore, it will be argued that the two roles in this duality are logically related to developments in the external environment as well as to each other, and that they have thus constituted a coherent and appropriate basis for the formulation of Danish foreign policy.

4.2. Internationalism and Determinism as Part of a Power Strategy

As defined here *internationalism* is composed of the three elements shown in figure 1: (1) active pursuit of a more legally regulated international order including the promotion of general principles of conduct and of common values; (2) a ten-

---

31 So-called PBE's. Petersen (1977) makes use of this distinction in his analysis of Danish power and its development during the course of the 20th century. See also Goldmann and Sjøstedt (1979).
32 As described earlier, there was in fact no physical reduction of the size of the Danish state in 1720. That this year continues to be identified as a turning point in Danish history is because it was during this period that it was finally recognized that Denmark would never regain its former, dominant position in the northern part of Europe.

dency towards idealizing own policies, hereby stressing the avoidance of war and the priority of economic interests; (3) cooperation with like-minded states, especially the other Scandinavian countries, with the purpose of enlarging the "peace-zone". It would be worthwhile to discuss how deeply rooted these elements are as part of a Danish tradition and whether it is appropriate to classify all three of them under the label "internationalism". However, these questions are not our focus here. In the present context the important point is that all three elements may be said to represent an alternative conception of power-policy – when applying the more elaborated power-concept from the previous section.

As regards the first element, which in short may be labeled "value promoting policies", it is not difficult to see this as part of a power strategy in the meaning of "power" described above.[33] The less anarchy in the international system, the greater the chance that sheer physical power occupies a reduced role in relations among states, provided the regulation of the system does not take the form of a hegemony by one or a few great powers. It follows that value promoting policies may be seen as an important ingredient of the security policies especially of small states.

Viewed in this perspective, the first element in the Danish "internationalist" tradition should not be interpreted as a way of "contracting out" of international politics. On the contrary, it represents an active endeavor on the part of Danish decision-makers not only to change the frame in which international politics are carried out, but also to enhance the possibilities for a small state like Denmark to pursue its own interests vis-à-vis other states. This effect will be obtained when non-tangible power-base elements such as diplomatic skill, good arguments and reputation acquire greater weight, what tends to be the case in a non-anarchical international system.[34]

Neither should the other two aspects of Danish internationalism in fig. 1 be regarded as a way of "sentimentalizing the nature of international politics". Both are – like the first one – apt to enhance alternative power base elements, especially elements which small states may profit by. Avoiding war, stressing economic interests and enlarging the peace-zone are strategies for reducing the importance of military power. This does not necessarily mean that these strategies entail a withdrawal from international politics; rather, they are means by which small states can participate in international politics despite their size – and despite of their military weakness.

---

33 In the analysis of Danish foreign policy other terms have also been applied, e.g. "normative policies" in Karup Pedersen (1970) and "policies of ideas" in Hækkerup (1965).

34 The term "non-tangible power-base elements" is used in Goldman and Sjøstedt (1979). Obviously, not all parts of the Danish tradition of value-promoting policies reflect these long-term endeavors aiming at system change. It would require a more thorough investigation than intended here to demonstrate the kind of motives that have dominated this aspect of Danish foreign policy. However, it seems appropriate to make three points: first, the interpretation by Holbraad is not based on such a documentation but seems to be deduced from his overall, only implicitly stated paradigm concerning international relations; second, the interpretation given above corresponds with findings in the literature on small states; finally, in the next section we shall demonstrate how closely tied together were the long- and short-term goals of Danish foreign policy in the 1930s.

So much for the internationalist part of the Danish tradition. Apart from a few possible exceptions when investigating the historical record, this part may without great difficulty be interpreted as an alternative power-strategy.[35] Such a direct link between the other part of the tradition, i.e. *determinism*, and a power-strategy is less easily established. By definition and as employed in the Danish context the term relates to a conception according to which a country has to accept its subordination to outside forces and consequently its inability to take care of its foreign policy interests by its own means. The three elements in the Danish determinist tradition as analyzed by Holbraad – adaptation to Germany, defense nihilism and introversion of national efforts (see fig. 1) – are all ways to cope with a lack of physical power, but in this case there is apparently no inherent strategy of power compensation aimed at creating possibilities for independent international action. On the contrary, determinism may rightly be interpreted as a way of "contracting out" of international politics.

Nevertheless, it is misleading *only* to interpret Danish determinism in this way. The broader power definition opens for an alternative interpretation. When applying the distinction between offensive and defensive power, it is evident that all three elements in the determinist tradition create a basis for strengthening Danish *defensive* power.

The introversion of national efforts exemplified by the establishment of peasant ideological hegemony in the latter part of the 19th century, followed by the subsequent incorporation of the labor movement into a broad national consensus (see chapter 5), has contributed to making Denmark a stronger state, i.e. increasing its defensive power. Obviously, defense nihilism may have the opposite effect, since a strong military posture may reinforce both offensive and defensive power. In the Danish case, however, defense nihilism has not been advocated primarily on pacifistic premises, but rather as a way of strengthening the nation, thereby building up what has been labeled a "cultural defense". Finally, the adaptation to Germany should not only be viewed in a deterministic light. While this policy on the one hand has reflected the conception of a high degree of impotence vis-à-vis Germany, it has at the same time been motivated by a desire to minimize external influence and consequently enhance the country's defensive power.[36]

By building up its defensive power, the Danish tradition of determinism in foreign policy has thus been part of a power strategy. However, this does not necessarily mean that determinism has been part of an *international* power strategy. Increasing one's defensive power may be motivated by a desire to "contract out" of international politics.[37] When Holbraad interprets Danish determinism in this way,

---

35 The strategy of neutralization attempted at the beginning of the 20th century may be seen as such an exception.
36 This line of thought is reflected in the distinction made by foreign minister Munch (see section 4.3) between security for the state and security for the people as analyzed in Karup Pedersen (1970); cf. Wæver (1997: 33-34).
37 That is, in an attempt to move from an acquiescent to a quiescent mode of foreign policy behavior according to adaptation theory (see chapter 3).

he is surely in agreement with the conventional wisdom held by analysts of the Danish "tradition". According to this view, the foreign policy of Danish governments until the German invasion in April 1940 rested on the illusory assumption that Denmark was able to pursue its own domestic goals without much concern for what was happening on the international scene.[38] After the war the official policy has been purged of such illusions, to which Danish membership of NATO and EU bear witness.

Without going into any empirical proof, a number of critical points against this conventional interpretation of Danish determinism should be raised.

First of all, this interpretation fits well into a very simplistic view of the past inspired by political conditions in post-war Denmark. A highly negative evaluation of past policies has led to a dominant political discourse which has seen the Danish foreign policy tradition confined to the determinist past associated with an outdated neutrality and a humiliating dependence on an aggressive great power. It is a logical extension of this concept that the former policy has been regarded as being inward looking, whereas the present one, by contrast, is outward looking. Previously Denmark opted out of international politics, which led to disaster; now Denmark is opting in with much more rewarding consequences.

In pursuing this critique further, two more points have to be added, both parallel to the ones made regarding the internationalist part of the tradition (p. 202-03). For a small state like Denmark, the motives for increasing defensive power at the expense of offensive tend to differ from the motives of the great powers. For great powers, self-reliance and isolationism may be deliberate and feasible policy goals; increased defensive power becomes part of a strategy aiming at these goals. But neither in this regard do small states have the same freedom of choice as great powers. They may outwardly pursue similar objectives, as Danish governments actually did before World War II, but such objectives are less easily obtainable and consequently they often tend to be intermingled with other objectives. At least this is what seems characteristic of Danish foreign policy – in the past as well as in the present.

Hereby we touch on the second point: the connection between the two parts of the tradition. If it is possible to demonstrate that determinism has been a means towards internationalism, it becomes less evident to interpret the determinist strand in Danish foreign policy thinking as part of a "contracting out" strategy. This kind of interrelation between the two parts is hard to construct on the basis of historical documentation, whereas it is easier on the level of theoretical speculation.

In principle, the security policy of some states, especially small ones, may essentially be motivated by a desire to establish a legally based world order allowing all states to pursue their interests on more equal terms than has hitherto been the case. As the achievement of this goal, at any rate, belongs to a distant future, the same states may – under prevailing international conditions – find it expedient to

---

38 During World War I this view was expressed in literary form, in a passage written by the well-known Danish poet, Jeppe Aakjær: "Little baby land smug in its coziness while the earth burns around its cradle" (my translation).

play a passive and reserved role in regard to immediate concerns, i.e. threats from and conflicts between great powers. The rationale for such behavior would thus be to enable the state to play a constructive role in regard to the long-term goals, implying a transformation of the entire international system. Prospects for a transformation may – even in the long run – seem meager, and instruments for achieving it difficult to find or invent. The passive (determinist) elements of a foreign policy of this kind will thus be more conspicuous than the active (internationalist) ones.

It would undoubtedly be stretching the historical evidence too far to attempt to empirically substantiate the relationship between determinism and internationalism developed here. The aim of the next section is less ambitious. However, by presenting and interpreting a number of key elements in the Danish foreign policy of the 1930s, I attempt to illuminate some of the propositions advanced above in a more concrete way.

4.3. The Foreign Policy Conception of Peter Munch and the Logic of Danish Dualism

Is the Danish foreign policy tradition characterized by a "contracting in" rather than a "contracting out" strategy? Is it possible to conceive the two elements of the tradition as mutually dependent rather than partly contradictory? These questions will now be taken up in light of Danish policy in the 1930s.

The reason for choosing this period is three-fold. *First*, Danish foreign policy in the period leading up to World War II is generally regarded as the most extreme expression of the Danish tendency to contract out of international politics – as understood by Holbraad. We thus have a clear case for the formulation of an alternative interpretation. *Second*, the policy of the 1930s has been used in the post-war period as a highly negative point of reference when arguing for a 'new' foreign policy, not least because the catastrophe and humiliation experienced by Denmark on 9 April 9, 1940 has been accounted for by this policy. The tendency – in large measure politically inspired – to emphasize discontinuity rather than continuity has thus distorted the perception of the former policy and prevented a correct unveiling of main elements in the Danish tradition. *Third*, in the entire period from 1929 to 1940 the post of foreign minister was occupied by *Peter Munch,* leader of the Social-Liberal Party, who since the beginning of the century had played a prominent role in the formulation of Danish foreign and defense policies, and who in a very pronounced way had developed a conception of Denmark's position in international relations.[39] Munch's views contain a number of elements normally considered central to traditional thinking. Although narrowing the scope of the analysis somewhat, the focus on Munch is deemed a relevant basis for the coming discussion.[40]

---

39 Cf. the detailed, theoretically based, analysis by Ole Karup Pedersen (1970) as well as Sjøqvist's historical biography (1976).
40 It should be stressed that by focusing on a foreign minister we are dealing with foreign policy *doctrines* rather than with foreign policy *traditions.*The purpose of the present section,

The picture most often conveyed of Danish foreign policy in the 1930s – and thus also of the policy associated with the name Peter Munch – is, to put it briefly, one of exaggerated adaptation to German security interests, including minimal defense efforts, and almost over fulfillment of the demands made by the great power neighbor, i.e. a "stay-put policy".[41] As a consequence Denmark became increasingly isolated in the international community and in effect contributed to German expansionism and the outbreak of war. Subsequent criticism has not only been directed toward Danish foreign policy proper but also to the repercussions of the policy pursued into the domestic field: quasi-censorship of the press, restrictive refugee policy, etc. While post-war assessment has paid little attention to the idealistic elements which also formed part of Munch's foreign policy (see below), the idealism was at the time often ridiculed as being out of line with the realities prevailing in the international system. Altogether the picture drawn up in political discussions and historical accounts is quite similar to the interpretation presented by Holbraad: Denmark almost completely contracted out of international politics.

As a point of departure for an alternative interpretation of Danish foreign policy in the 1930s we may quote from an article written by Munch three years after taking office and a few months before the advent to power of Adolf Hitler in Germany:

"... the passive foreign policy pursued until 1914 is now a thing of the past which is not going to return. ... In the world an interdependence, mutual relations between the states, had now been created calling for an active foreign policy in small as well as in large states. As a member of the League of Nations, Denmark must do its part of the work. Also our destiny depends on the development in international politics. If it leads to new fierce battles, this will mean disaster for us as well as for others. If it leads to the safeguarding of peace, this will mean safety and progress for our people and for all of mankind. Together with other states which have no part in the kind of interests pursued by large states, Denmark must contribute its share in carrying out the tasks that the League of Nations was established to solve."

(*Fyens Venstreblad*, 1 October, 1932, here quoted from Sjøqvist 1976: 167, my translation)

Although such statements may seem rather trivial from a contemporary perspective, they contain a number of key elements characterizing Munch's conception of the role and position Denmark held in international relations in the interwar period. It is thus worth noting that – as an over-all foreign policy orientation – Munch himself does not advocate "stay-put" behavior, which in many later analyses has been seen as the essential feature of his policy. On the contrary, he acknowledges that the

---

however, is not to analyze the conception of Munch for its own sake, but to show how elements in this conception may be interpreted as part of a Danish foreign policy tradition.

41 In Danish: "ligge død" = "lie dead" This term has been applied by Nikolaj Petersen when operationalizing the quiescent policy mode of adaptation theory, see Petersen (1977: 244); cf. Bjøl (1983: 24-25).

world has undergone fundamental changes since the beginning of the century, changes which entail that all states, irrespective of their size, have to play an *active role in international politics*. This conclusion on his part is also remarkable in light of his own former views on Denmark's role, and considering the fact that Denmark succeeded in remaining out of World War I by sticking to a predominantly passive foreign policy stance.[42]

The above quotation is furthermore indicative of the explicit *differentiation between the role of small and large states* essential to Munch's thinking. According to his conception, the two types of states engage in international politics on very different premises. Large states, being used to playing an active role on the international scene, continue to involve themselves on traditional premises, i.e., attempting to further their own nationally defined interests. In comparison, the small states, handicapped with regard to the power game of the great powers, have – besides the traditional role – a new and different one, necessitated by the increased interdependence among states: the framing of international norms, the promulgation of common interests and the exertion of moral authority.[43] All these functions are apt to contribute to the overriding goal of avoiding the catastrophe of another world war. In pursuing this goal, the policies of small states may have an impact if they collaborate closely.

Finally, as a third and basic point, in contrast to previous periods a framework existed within which it was meaningful for states to act with the hope of achieving the international goals deemed essential by Munch. The effectiveness of Danish activism as well as of small state solidarity, in spite of all its deficiencies, was dependent upon the institutional innovation represented by the *League of Nations*. It was quite in conformity with prevalent stipulations in the new scientific field of international relations when Munch adhered to the idea that the creation of the League heralded the beginning of a new world order in which the possibility of war among states would gradually diminish and in the end become obsolete. However, it is also in conformity with Munch's thinking at the time, when actual developments showed that none of the persons responsible for great power foreign policy were in line with the theoretical stipulations.[44] Munch had no illusions as to the motives, which had induced the European great powers, i.e., Great Britain and France, to support the creation of the League of Nations, nor to the opportunities

---

42 In 1905 Munch had expressed the view that "the first and last thing we should demand from Danish diplomacy is that it keeps quiet and does its utmost so that we may live as unnoticed as possible." Quoted in Karup Pedersen (1970: 417); cf. Petersen (1979: 258) and Due-Nielsen and Petersen (eds.) (1995: 25).

43 This enumeration, not to be found in the above quotation, draws on the study by Karup Pedersen (1970).

44 Cf. the observation in a recent British textbook dealing with the first great debate of the discipline between realism and liberal internationalism: "The unfortunate truth was that liberal internationalist ideas were not dominant in the minds of any statesmen other than Wilson", (Brown 1997: 25).

the new organization had given them for sticking to old-time diplomacy. Nevertheless, the League had opened up for practicing an alternative form of diplomacy, and hard work by small states held out the prospect of turning this form into an effective instrument for keeping peace.

It is not difficult to demonstrate how these basic elements in the view held by Munch regarding the role and position of Denmark with respect to ongoing external developments, here mainly derived from a few passages in a newspaper article, by and large correspond to the content of the internationalist strand in Danish foreign policy thinking as stipulated above. Studying the conception of a single individual will always reveal specific traits, but there is no doubt that Munch, on the basis of the above analysis, must be seen as a very distinct – if not extreme – representative of this part of the Danish tradition. It is important to keep this characterization in mind, since his policies – as already stated – in post-war perception most often have been associated with the other part, determinism. Both parts, however, are essential to his thinking.

The turn of events, especially the outbreak of a second world war despite or – as sometimes asserted – because of all endeavors by liberal internationalists and the subsequent humiliating occupation of Denmark by German troops, has brought the entire foreign policy conception on which pre-war policy was based into disrepute. Accordingly, later assesments have focussed on the determinist, passive elements of Munch's policy; and furthermore, other elements – to the extent that they have elicited attention at all – have been seen largely as an appendix to this passivist thinking or merely as a reflection of a utopian world view without any connection to the exigencies of practical politics.

At this point, two important premises for the present analysis should be reiterated.

First, one of the challenges involved in the identification of foreign policy traditions has to do with the relative permanency of such traditions, i.e. their apparent recurrence in actual behavior in spite of historical upheavals pointing to their disappearance. By stressing the dual character of Danish foreign policy in the 1930s – instead of a one-sided focus on the determinist side – it seems possible to identify a line in Danish behavior which not only cuts across the immediate reactions of the first post-war period but stretches into the 1990s (cf. below).

The *second* premise pertains to the need to look beyond specific subjective interpretations like the ones to which the policies of Munch have been subjected. No doubt all interpretations are more or less subjective, but this only points to the need to keep alternative interpretations in mind. The disaster of the Second World War and the failure of Danish neutrality policy of the 1930s surely represent a historical evidence apt to support a negative interpretation of the foreign policy conception held by Munch. However, historical evidence is always manifold and often contradictory. Viewed in a long term perspective, taking other events into consideration, the "historical verdict" and the scientific deductions to be drawn might very well take on a new shape. What we are postulating is the impossibility of reaching a final conclusion as to the validity of either a realist or an idealist interpretation of international politics on the basis of historical evidence.

Basing our analysis on these premises and on the account hitherto presented of major elements in Danish pre-war policy, we may thus subscribe to Munch's own characterization of its activist inclinations, and furthermore interpret this activism as part of a "contracting in" strategy. What still remains to be discussed is the more precise character of the relationship between the internationalist and determinist part of the policy. Our contention here is that this relationship is logically more coherent than often assumed, entailing that the internationalist part should not be interpreted as totally subordinated to the determinist one. It may even be maintained that the contrary is the case. This kind of conclusion may be arrived at by drawing in further elements of Munch's thinking and specifying the ones already mentioned.

The view expressed in his article on changing conditions in the international system from 1932 formed part of a generally held and often formulated belief in historical progress.[45] According to Munch, ever higher forms of civilization would continue to replace each other. Although this fundamental optimism with regard to the international development had been seriously shaken with the advent of two world wars during his own lifetime, it never seemed to have completely left him. Actually, the setbacks encountered – although undoubtedly more radical than he had envisaged – also formed part of the ideological construction on which his policies were based. And it is exactly this duality in his thinking which explains the intimate connection between the internationalist and determinist aspects of his policy. It led to the already mentioned distinction between the role of large and small states, but also to a very explicitly formulated distinction between *short and long run objectives* in Danish foreign policy.

By introducing this distinction we are able to resolve the apparent contradiction in Danish pre-war policy. In the short run, a small state like Denmark in order to secure its own survival, had to act on the basis of an international order dominated by big powers. Personal preferences for one or the other of these powers and their policies had to be disregarded. What mattered in the case of Denmark was its position as a neighboring country to Germany and the meager or non-existent prospects of seeking protection from other big powers against possible German threats. The determinist or 'realistic' aspect of Danish policy belonged to this short-term perspective, whereas the internationalist or "idealistic" aspect belonged to the long-term perspective. Both policies, even when pursued simultaneously, supplemented rather than contradicted each other.

In case of conflict between the two aspects 'realism' had the upper hand; there was a "German primacy" in Danish foreign policy in the 1930s. On this account, it may be maintained that internationalism was subordinated to determinism. Yet Danish subordination to Germany was a matter of necessity and survival, dictated by prevailing power relations. It did not reflect the priorities of Danish foreign po-

---

45 This view is found in his extensive production of textbooks and during debates with political opponents in parliament; cf. Karup Pedersen (1970: 89-90).

licy. Priorities can not be deduced without taking the two time perspectives into consideration.

We may summarize by stating that the "idealistic" objective in the Danish policy had a "realistic" basis. This conclusion can be further substantiated by investigating closer the motives behind Munch's internationalism and the concrete steps taken. Two kinds of considerations – both applicable in the short-run perspective and both derived from a small state way of thinking – were essential to him.

The *first* and most fundamental consideration pertains to the use of military means in relations between states. Munch was no pacifist and would even have considered an alliance option if it had been available to Denmark.[46] Prevailing circumstances in the international system, however, led him to reject the idea of a Danish security policy based on military means. This negative attitude towards defense in the traditional sense was also part of his internationalist strategy. In the envisaged new world order, the monopolization and reduction of armaments was essential for achieving a higher degree of equality among states. In the short run, possibilities existed for working for this goal, primarily as a consequence of the creation of the League of Nations. Fulfillment of the disarmament objective laid down in the treaty was regarded by Munch as crucial for the failure or success of the organization, and from the start he became strongly involved in these endeavors.

In continuation, one should mention Munch's attitude towards art. 16 of the treaty providing for economic and military sanctions. All Danish political parties, including Munch's own Social Liberals, had agreed upon the exemptions obtained by a number of small states in regard to this clause, but Munch was a staunch supporter of the principle of collective security. Again, the different time perspectives are a clue to understanding his attitude. Exemptions were essential because of the still existing great power dominance and because small states ran a risk of getting entangled in their conflicts. However, if the application of the clause turned out to be a step towards the ultimate goal of a true collective security system, the same caution was no longer needed. When in 1935 the Council enacted sanctions against Italy upon this country's aggression against Abyssinia, it was strongly endorsed by the Danish government and proclaimed by Munch as a milestone in the history of the League.[47]

The *second* consideration also relates to the way Denmark with Munch as foreign minister, attempted to make concrete use of the new opportunities for international action which the creation of the League of Nations had opened up. It is commonplace for small state theory that increased regulation of the international system tends to work to the advantage of the lesser powers. Basically this has to do with the fact that regulation normally strengthens the rule of law at the expense of the rule of force. More specifically one may emphasize that in a regulated system decisions, at least in principle, are taken on the basis of common procedures, argu-

---

46 See note 9.
47 When it later turned out that the sanctions enacted would not be enforced by the great powers, i.e. Great Britain and France, the disappointment was equally pronounced. It led to a partial withdrawal from League obligations by Denmark and a number of other small states.

ments advanced and in consideration of the interests of a larger group of states than is the case in an anarchical system. These are some of the main reasons why Denmark and many other small states in general have been more eager supporters of international regulation than have large states. The opportunities hereby given to small states, however, may be exploited in various ways, and more or less consciously deliberated.

In regard to the day-to-day workings of the negotiating system of the League, Danish behavior was characterized by a high measure of activism. To a certain degree one may even speak of innovative thinking. In his study, Karup Pedersen identifies a "policy of demonstration", initiated by Munch.[48] The rationale behind this policy was the conception that a group of small states, by sticking together on matters of principle, could make the legal and normative stipulations on which the League was based more visible and pronounced and endow them with a higher degree of authority, thereby creating an effective instrument for the pursuance of the interests of small states. The policy of demonstration as practiced by Munch in the League of Nations is strikingly similar with the neutralist activism developed by Third World countries after World War II (cf. Christmas-Møller 1983: 46).

Any account of Danish foreign policy behavior in the 1930s runs the risk of being characterized either as a legitimization or a condemnation. The one given above tends to be of the first kind. At this point, before going on to the conclusions, it should be kept in mind that the purpose of including this section transcends usual political discourse. Elements of Danish policy have been stressed and interpretations presented not for the sake of legitimization, but because these elements and interpretations allow us to identify a line in the history of Danish foreign policy not easily discernable and not in accordance with the one usually established, but nevertheless a line which is deemed the most correct and most fruitful when attempting to understand present dilemmas, peculiarities and apparent contradictions in Danish behavior. The concluding section will be a further attempt to illuminate the long line, i.e. the foreign policy tradition.

5. Conclusions: Three Alternative Interpretations and a Contemporary Perspective

We all construct images of the past and of how the past is related to the present. Some of these images are based on myths or serve specific political purposes. Hence, they may often be invalidated as correct historical accounts by way of empirical analysis. Other images, albeit often the same ones, can be shown to have had a considerable impact on actual behavior, and as such, irrespective of their historical correctness, are worth examining when explaining past and present events.

In this article we have also been concerned with constructing images. Any attempt to detect a foreign policy tradition of a specific country, besides historical documentation, must rely on a high degree of subjective interpretation. As a result, image-

---

48 See note 36.

building is more conspicuous in the present analysis than is normal in historical studies. Hopefully, the image set up is not of the first kind mentioned above. And although the possibility of a foreign policy tradition becoming self-sustaining by its function as an independent motivating factor in decision-making is an interesting object of study, this aspect has not been the focus of attention here. Rather we have attempted to identify central components in past foreign policy behavior and thinking of Denmark and Danish decision-makers in order to understand long-term trends in Danish policy, including the possible recurring traits characterizing this policy.

More or less explicitly, such endeavors at establishing a Danish foreign policy tradition have also been undertaken in previous historical studies. When comparing existing analyses, including the one presented here, we may distinguish between the following three approaches or interpretations.[49]

The *first*, and undoubtedly most established, focuses on a long, unbroken policy of neutrality, which officially came to an end in 1949, but whose after-effects have influenced foreign policy thinking up to the present and also to some degree has manifested itself in the actual behavior exhibited by Denmark in the post-war period.[50] An essential part of this "construction of the past" is the conception that the Danish neutrality tradition increasingly assumed the shape of a passive foreign policy stance characterized by attempts to keep Denmark away from the international scene as much as possible; and that a reaction against this passivity began to be felt after the occupation by Germany in April 1940. Slowly, a new foreign policy thinking gained foothold gradually replacing the old one. Milestones in this development have been Denmark's active engagement in the UN from its founding, Danish membership of the Atlantic alliance in 1949, followed by admission to the EC in 1973. The present very active Danish involvement in international politics, according to this interpretation, is seen as the final relinquishment of an old and outdated tradition.

Basic elements in the established version have been discussed and criticized in this chapter, especially its emphasis on neutrality and passivity – and its intimate relation with a politically felt need for dissociation from past policies deemed as a failure. The evaluation made may be supplemented by a few further observations in order to bring our own interpretation in the right perspective.

A few years ago a voluminous biography was published on the Danish diplomat Henrik Kauffmann, ambassador to the United States during the entire period from 1939 to 1958 (Lidegaard 1996). On a number of occasions and in a remarkable way, Kauffmann acted on his own[51] and his views on Denmark's position in the

---

49 A more elaborated version of the three approaches with greater focus on the Euopean aspects of Danish foreign policy is presented in Branner (2000).
50 In regard to the period until 1949, the work of Fink (1958) is representative of this interpretation. The accounts by Haagerup (1956) and Nielsson (1966) belong to the same category.
51 After Denmark was occupied by German troops, Kauffmann declared himself representative of the Danish king, not subject to instructions from the still existing puppet government in Copenhagen. In this capacity he negotiated and signed a treaty in 1941 giving the US the right to set up bases on Greenland, owned by Denmark. After the war, Kauffmann displayed on a number of occasions an independence not normally characteristic of the ambassadorial role.

world were different from the ones prevailing in the foreign ministry. In a concluding chapter *Bo Lidegaard*, discusses the content of main trends in Danish foreign policy thinking. Two basic strands of thought are defined, a national and a cosmopolitan; the national being synonymous with the traditional one, the cosmopolitan with the thinking which slowly emerged after 1940 and in the early phase most forcefully represented by Kauffmann. The existence and importance of a clash between the two lines within the foreign ministry is convincingly documented in the study, and it is also shown that the decision to join NATO was but only one step towards the final victory of the second line.

Returning to our three-ways division of interpreting Danish foreign policy, Lidegaard's account is not totally in conformity with the first one, presented as the established one. Neutrality is not seen as the fundamental element in traditional thinking. Instead, he distinguishes between an earlier national and a subsequent cosmopolitan position. By attaching only limited importance to the alliance decision of 1949, he allows the continuity factor to play a greater role than is normally the case in the established version. In spite of such modifications, Lidegaard's attempt to define the main lines of thought on Danish foreign policy and their evolution reflects the fundamental premises behind interpretation no. 1.

Lidegaard's one-sided characterization of the former policy is indicative in this respect. More important is that he argues on the implicit premise that the evolution of the foreign policy of a country is characterized by *linear* progression and not by *cyclical* movements; during a given period of time, one foreign policy mode prevails and is then gradually replaced by a new one, leaving the first as a remnant of the past.[52] This perspective is relevant when the object of study is a relatively short span of time as is the case in a biography. On the basis of his material, Lidegaard has produced a very stimulating analysis of competing world views held by Danish decision-makers, and he has provided useful insight into the historical process leading to the replacement of one view by another. However, the understanding obtained is restricted to a few, albeit crucial, decades in the history of Danish foreign policy. Thus, this kind of analysis closes its eyes to the recurring behavior, which only a longer time perspective can detect. In his last chapter, Lidegaard has contributed to the identification of a foreign policy tradition by providing building blocks, but his attempt does not in itself amount to such an identification.

The *second* interpretation, dealt with at length in this article, is represented by the thorough investigation of the history of Danish foreign policy undertaken by Carsten Holbraad. Compared to the established interpretation, Holbraad does not

---

52 The distinction between linear and cyclical historical developments deserves an elaboration which space does not allow here. It should be noted, however, that the concept of circular development points to greater influence of internal factors on the formulation of foreign policy than is the case with the concept of linear development. Cycles are more likely if long-term patterns of thought (traditions) have an impact on policies, whereas linearity tends to be prevalent if one assumes that foreign policy must be understood predominantly as adaptation to changing external conditions.

view the historical development as a linear progression. The great advantage of his approach, from the point of view of tradition analysis, is his focus on recurrent patterns of thought, observable over a long period of time stretching back into the 18th century. According to Holbraad, the external changes during this period, transforming Denmark from a composite, middle-range power to a small nation-state, has been an underlying, independent variable in the process establishing a Danish foreign policy tradition. However, its main constitutive parts, internationalism and determinism, are also analyzed as reflections of domestic political conditions. A central thesis of the book is that the two parts and their interaction have resulted in a Danish withdrawal from international power politics, an effect still observable in post-war policies in spite of Denmark's adherence to NATO and to the EU.

Only a few points of the detailed criticism of Holbraad's interpretation need to be emphasized here. While the emphasis on dualistic traits represents an original contribution to the study of the Danish foreign policy tradition, Holbraad, by linking this dualism to the policy of neutrality, is caught in a conventional and less convincing conception of what constitutes the tradition. His discussion of post-war policies characterized by half-hearted Danish support of Western institutions is thereby hampered by terminological inconsistencies. Another criticism is that by basing the analysis on a narrow, not explicitly stated, definition of the concept of power, the impact of the two strands of thought in Danish foreign policy thinking is exclusively interpreted as leading to a "contracting out" strategy. By over stressing both determinism and internationalism, during long periods of its history, Denmark has disengaged itself from the realities of European power politics – to the detriment of its own interests.

It is the contention here that the analysis by Holbraad, although clearing the way for a more rewarding approach to the study of a Danish tradition, has failed to comprehend the nature of this tradition. Holbraad's failure lies in his misinterpretation of some of the main objectives guiding Danish foreign policy in the past, and his failure to adequately consider the framework on which his analysis is constructed. These flaws are manifest with respect to his treatment of post-war Danish foreign policy. "Internationalism" is now being linked to Danish participation in NATO and the EU and, thus, suddenly viewed in opposition to the 'old' neutrality thinking of which it previously formed an integral part. And in order to satisfactorily explain Danish hesitancy towards full integration into the two novel institutions, Holbraad is led to introduce a third strand of thought, i.e. nationalism. Altogether, one is left with a confusing picture of the relationship between the elements of the tradition, carefully elaborated in the first part of the book dealing with the period up till 1945, and subsequent Danish policies – notwithstanding his ambition to draw such a line. In reality, Holbraad comes close to contradicting basic tenants of his analysis, almost conveying a linear conception of historical development.

The presentation and critical discussion of the first two interpretations above has established the main pillars on which the *third* interpretation, developed in detail in section 4, has been constructed. In short, this interpretation maintains that the evolution of Danish foreign policy should be studied as a series of cyclical movements. As understood here, this implies that external shocks, exemplified by the German invasion of Denmark on 9 April, 1940, while undoubtedly entailing rethinking of important premises, do not necessarily lead to an adaptation of the foreign policy mode matching the degree of external change. Alteration of the policy line may take place, but such changes will be rivaled and sometimes even repudiated by the cropping up of "old thinking". Second, and more important for comprehending the content of a tradition, it is presumed that the recurrence of patterns of thinking is not only observable when dealing with a relatively short span of time, i.e. a few decades, but also when analyzing longer epochs.

The patterns identified as being characteristic of Danish foreign policy behavior during modern history are essentially of a dualistic nature: precaution against involvement in great power politics is balanced by active pursuance of policies apt to overcome the restrictions, which existing conditions have set up for safeguarding Danish external interests. This dualism has in large measure developed as a corollary to the gradual reduction of Denmark's physical power and has therefore over time – until 1945 – become increasingly conspicuous. In this sense it may rightly be characterized as representing a small state tradition. The first component should be seen as the attempt by the small state to enhance its defensive power, the other to enhance its offensive power; the strategies relate to two different time perspectives.

On these premises and on the basis of this identification, one can interpret contemporary Danish foreign policy in a much longer time perspective than is usually done, including the detection of a pattern enabling us to fit the Danish activism of the 1990s into a cyclical historical development. The discussion which follows, however, should be seen as a very preliminary attempt to interpret present policies in light of the Danish tradition.

Starting out with the thesis that foreign policy thinking in Denmark in large measure has reflected the gradual reduction of Danish power over the centuries, we may postulate that this trend has been reversed since the end of World War II; the main reason being that increased multilateralization and Danish participation in relevant organizations has reduced Denmark's vulnerability with regard to great power security threats and at the same time has greatly enhanced Denmark's ability to take part in decisions affecting its international position (cf. chapter 11). Internal factors have contributed to this trend. Ethnic homogeneity and comprehensive welfare legislation entailing a high degree of social equality compared to other European states have turned Denmark into a strong state and enhanced its defensive power.

Sticking to our own premises, the above development is bound to have had an influence on Danish foreign policy thinking. With dualism still present, the increased power of Denmark tends to diminish the tension between its two parts, making determinism less necessary and internationalism less unrealistic. Nevertheless, the impact of the power variable is mainly manifest in the long run. The existence of an imminent security threat during the entire post-war period combined with inertia in foreign policy thinking have counteracted the increased power position. As a consequence, changes in the basic foreign policy posture of Denmark remained marginal. A great part of the population and leading members of the dominant Social Democratic party have also looked upon Danish membership of NATO and the EC with great hesitancy, and the two organizations have almost exclusively been used to promote narrowly defined national interests in the security and in the economic fields. In spite of vastly altered conditions for foreign policy-making, Denmark continued to steer out of great power politics inside the organizations most directly affecting Danish interests and reserved its internationalism for two other fora: the familiar small state community of Nordic countries and the global and equally less binding community of UN members.

The post-war period, brought to an end by the dramatic events of 1989-91, represents an intermediate phase in the evolution of the Danish foreign policy tradition. Turning to the present, the end of the Cold War has – in the context of our tradition analysis – had two important effects: (1) the altered conditions on the world and on the European scene have once again enhanced the Danish power position in both its defensive and offensive aspects; (2) these conditions, characterized by a hitherto unprecedented similarity in regard to societal structures (democracy and market economy) and value outlook among leading actors in the international system, have been particularly conducive for the promotion of key elements in traditional Danish internationalism. On this account, we are able to explain the apparent dramatic shift in Danish foreign policy towards a genuinely active role in international politics (officially labeled "active internationalism"), while at the same time being able to interpret the Danish policy orientation of the 1990s in accordance with long held views characterizing the Danish foreign policy tradition.

It remains to be explained how and to what degree the dualistic element in this tradition still manifests itself. If present external conditions continue to prevail, it seems likely that Danish foreign policy dualism will tend to fade away, opening up for an unequivocal emphasis on the internationalist part of the tradition. However, as we have stressed traditions are by definition long lasting, and since international developments seldom stick to a straight and foreseeable course, the determinist aspect of the Danish tradition is apt to reemerge time and again.

We may take note of to two current features in the Danish policy which demonstrate the continued relevance of our dualistic interpretation. The first has to do with the remarkable intensity, vigor and unanimity by which internationalism is being practiced. In several respects, the Danish foreign policy line of the 1990s can best be understood as an attempt to overcome the frustrations resulting from the need (more exactly: the felt need) to give priority to determinism over internationalism for many decades in the past. Key elements of today's policy represents a reversal of determinism, now in internationalist guise, e.g. the emphasis put on military means as part of collective peace-keeping in Europe and the abandonment of a non-provocative behavior by actively supporting Baltic integration into Western institutions despite Russian opposition. At least officially, Danish Baltic policy is based on the principle of formal equality among states, entitling all states – whatever their size and past history – to the same opportunities with regard to choosing external affiliations. Whereas the policy of "active internationalism" only indirectly testifies to the continued impact of dualistic thinking, contemporary Danish policy also directly demonstrates its significance. Dualism in the 1990s only manifests itself in moderated form. Despite the priority given to "active internationalism", remnants of determinism remain visible in Danish European policy, primarily as this policy is pursued within the framework of the EU.

Determinist thinking has evolved as a response to Danish experiences with the European power game, more specifically as a reflection of Denmark's neighborhood to the German great power. Although Denmark has been a member of the EU since 1973, it has never felt quite at ease belonging to a narrow and exclusive club of Western European states, encompassing most of the former great powers of Europe. It is not surprising that this uneasiness continues, observable mainly in the way Denmark has stubbornly rejected all attempts to equip the EU with a military dimension. As the only member country also belonging to NATO, Denmark has so far chosen to stay outside the WEU, not even opting for associate status, as has non-member Norway. One of the nightmares of almost all Danish political parties is the prospect of the EU turning into a new superpower acting independently on the world power scene. In this sense, Danish small state determinist thinking has not yet been overcome. EU enlargement with former members of the east European bloc will undoubtedly diminish Danish apprehension towards strengthening the EU in the security field.

As an overall conclusion about the direction of Danish foreign policy, our attempt to identify a Danish foreign policy tradition has revealed three main propositions: *First*, the "new" Danish policy is not as new as often maintained, but should be seen as a manifestation of a new turn in the evolution of the Danish tradition, highligtning the cyclical movement of history. *Second*, since "active internationalism" is based on deep historical roots, it is not apt to disappear even when encountering major external obstacles, although overall developments in the international system will determine the balance between the internationalist and determinist strands in the tradition. *Third*, a spill-over effect from the general foreign policy orientation is increasingly likely to become evident in Danish European policy.[53] However, the tenacity characteristic of foreign policy traditions will undoubtedly manifest itself more in this policy area than in others.

---

53 Prime Minister Nyrup Rasmussen's behavior at the Amsterdam summit in June 1997 is indicative in this respect. See *Politiken*, 15 June, 1997.

Literature

Amstrup, Niels (1992): Review of Carsten Holbraad: Danish Neutrality, *Politica*, no. 2.
Bjøl, Erling (1970): "P. Munch, sociologisk og historisk set", *Historie: Jyske samlinger*, Ny rk. IX, 1.
Bjøl, Erling (1983): *Hvem bestemmer? Studier i den udenrigspolitiske beslutningsproces*, Copenhagen: DJØF Publishing.
Borring Olesen, Thorsten (1994): "Jagten på et sikkerhedspolitisk ståsted. Socialdemokratiet og holdningerne til sikkerhedspolitikken 1945-1948" in Nüchel Thomsen *Temaer og brændpunkter i dansk politik efter 1945*, Odense: Odense University Press.
Branner, Hans (1972): *Småstat mellem stormagter. Beslutningen om mineudlægning august 1914*, Copenhagen: Munksgaard.
Branner, Hans (1987): *9. april 1940. Et politisk lærestykke?*, Copenhagen: DJØF Publishing.
Branner, Hans (1990): "Vi vil fred her til lands ... En udenrigspolitisk linie 1940-1949-1989?", *Vandkunsten,* no.3, pp. 47-90.
Branner, Hans (1996): *Det ny Europa. International politik i forandring*, Copenhagen: Columbus.
Branner, Hans (2000): "Traditioner og optioner i dansk udenrigspolitik" in v. Dosenrode (ed.): *Dansk udenrigspolitik. Muligheder og udfordringer ved det 21. århundredes begyndelse*, Copenhagen: Rådet for Europæisk Politik.
Brown, Chris (1997): *Understanding International Relations*, London: Macmillan.
Buzan, Barry (1991): *People, States and Fear. An Agenda for International Security Studies in the Post-Cold War Period*, London: Harvester Wheatsheaf.
Christmas-Møller, Wilhelm (1983): "Some Thoughts on the Scientific Applicability of the Small State Concept: A Research History and a Discussion" in Otmar Höll (eds.), *Small States in Europe and Dependence*, Vienna.
Due-Nielsen C. and N. Petersen (eds.) (1995): *Adaptation and Activism. The Foreign Policy of Denmark 1967-1993,* Copenhagen: DJØF Publishing.
Fink, Troels (1958): *Fem foredrag om dansk udenrigspolitik efter 1864*, Aarhus: Aarhus University Press.
Fink, Troels (1959): *Spillet om dansk neutralitet. 1905-1909. L.C.F. Lütken og dansk udenrigs- og forsvarspolitik*, Aarhus: Aarhus University Press.
Fox, Annette Baker (1959): *The Power of Small States. Diplomacy in World War II.* Chicago.
Frei, Daniel (1969): *Dimensionen neutraler Politik. Ein Beitrag zur Theorie der internationalen Beziehungen*, Genève.
Goldmann, Kjell (1979): "The International Power Structure: Traditional Theory and New Reality" in Goldmann og Sjöstedt (eds.): *Power, Capabilities, Interdependence*, London: Sage Publications, pp. 7-36.
Haagerup, Niels Jørgen (1956): *De Forenede Nationer og Danmarks sikkerhed*, Aarhus: Aarhus University Press.
Heisler, Martin O. (1985): "Denmark's Quest for Security: Constraints and Opportunities Within the Alliance" in Gregory Flynn (ed.), *NATO's Northern Allies*, New Jersey: Croom Helm.
Holbraad, Carsten (1991): *Danish Neutrality. A Study in the Foreign Policy of a Small State*, Oxford: Oxford University Press.

Hækkerup, Per (1965): *Danmarks udenrigspolitik*, Copenhagen: Fremad.

Lidegaard, Bo (1996): *I Kongens Navn. Henrik Kauffmann i dansk diplomati 1919-1958*, Copenhagen: Samleren.

Malmborg, Michael (1994): *Den ståndaktiga nationalstaten. Sverige och den västeuropeiska integrationen 1945-1959*, Lund: Lund University Press.

Nielsen, Henning (1977): *Dansk udenrigspolitik 1875-1894 med særligt henblik på beslutningsprocessen*, Odense: Odense University Press.

Nielsson, Gunnar P. (1966): *Denmark and European Integration. A Small Country at the Crossroads* (unpubl. Ph.D dissertation), Los Angeles: University of California (available on microfilm at the Royal Library, Copenhagen).

Pedersen, Ole Karup (1970): *Udenrigsminister P. Munchs opfattelse af Danmarks stilling i international politik*, Copenhagen: G.E.C. Gad.

Petersen, Nikolaj (1977): "Adaptation as a Framework for the Analysis of Foreign Policy Behavior", *Cooperation and Conflict*, no. 4, pp. 221-250.

Petersen, Nikolaj (1979): "International Power and Foreign Policy Behavior: The Formulation of Danish Security Policy in the 1870-1914 Period" in Goldmann og Sjöstedt (eds.), *Power, Capabilities, Interdependece,* London: Sage Publications, s. 235-69.

Politiken, Danish Daily, 15 June, 1997.

Rothstein, Robert (1968): *Alliances and Small Powers*, New York.

Scavenius, Erik (1948): *Forhandlingspolitikken under besættelsen*, Copenhagen: Steen Hasselbalch.

Seymour, Susan (1982): *Anglo-Danish Relations and Germany 1933-1945*, Odense: Odense University Press.

Sjøqvist, Viggo (1962): *Peter Vedel. Udenrigsministeriets direktør*, vol. II, Aarhus: Aarhus University Press.

Sjøqvist, Viggo (1966). *Danmarks udenrigspolitik 1933-1940*, Copenhagen: Gyldendal.

Sjøqvist, Viggo (1976): *Peter Munch. Manden. Politikeren. Historikeren*. Copenhagen: Gyldendal.

Villaume, Poul (1994): *Allieret med forbehold. Danmark, NATO og den kolde krig. En studie i dansk sikkerhedspolitik 1949-1961,* Copenhagen: Eirene.

Wæver, Ole (1997): *Concepts of Security*, Copenhagen: Copenhagen Political Studies Press.

Ørvik, Nils (1953): *The Decline of Neutrality 1914-1941*, London: Frank Cass & Co.

Ørvik, Nils (ed.) (1986): *Semialignment and Western Security*, London and Sidney: Croom Helm.

Part III

External and Internal Determinants

CHAPTER 7

A Nordic Alternative to Europe? The Interdependence of Denmark's Nordic and European Policies

Johnny N. Laursen and Thorsten Borring Olesen

1. Introduction

The basis for Danish NATO membership in the post-war period has rested upon a broad consensus among decision-makers and voters that there existed no convincing alternative to membership in the Atlantic security framework. With respect to cooperation with the Six, the EEC and the EU, however, many Danes have seen an alternative in Nordic cooperation. The continental cooperation project of the Six during the 1950s and 1960s was thus met with only guarded enthusiasm in Denmark. Norwegian and Swedish governments were even less inclined than the Danish to consider membership, though Norway followed the path of Britain and Denmark and presented three applications for EEC membership from 1962 to 1970, the last of which the Norwegian electorate blocked in the referendum of 1972.

On the other hand, Denmark's entry into the Common Market in 1973, without the other Nordic countries, testifies to the limits of Nordic cooperation as "marketable" alternative to European cooperation.

This article focuses upon the significance of a Nordic alternative to Danish European attitudes and policies. At the outset, it is important to stress that in the post-war period Nordic cooperation has held great attraction to most of the Danish political spectrum. Yet this attraction has been particular prevalent in social democratic circles, and later within the organized anti-EEC movements. Nordic cooperation has been hailed as a vital foundation and guarantee for the Nordic (social democratic) welfare model. Within this context, Nordic cooperation and integration have acquired a semi-ideological quality with the potential to function as a de-legitimizer of European integration. These aspects will be dealt with in Part II of this article.

Part III will focus on the form and character of Nordic cooperation as it has evolved during the last fifty years. Like European cooperation, Nordic cooperation has acquired its own dynamics and character, having been shaped by a variety of national and international forces. Although cooperation on major policy issues has tended to end inconclusively or in outright failure, Nordic cooperation has also achieved tangible results in low policy areas where the EU's achievements are still patchy and incomplete. Nordic cooperation has never succeeded in developing strong institutions with the power to regulate national rules and legislation. Moreover, it has always had a popular participatory dimension. Both these features probably help explain why Nordic cooperation has never been met with the kind of scepticism shown towards European integration.

Nevertheless, it is important to emphasize that the Nordic alternative has not always been considered an "alternative" in the fundamental sense of the word. In certain periods, rather, Danish decision-makers have considered Nordic cooperation a supplement to or maybe even a training ground for Danish EEC membership. Today the idea is often propounded that the Nordic countries should aim at forming a regional pressure group within the EU in order to promote "Nordic values" in a broader European context. In other words, it should be recognized that, when measured against the Nordic backdrop, European attitudes have changed radically over time, and that with time one can observe a growing disparity between elite and more popular views as to the importance of Nordic concerns in shaping Denmark's European policies.[1] Part IV and Part V of the article will be dedicated to discussing the swings and turns of these processes up to the present.

We will approach the problem by way of historical analysis. Only within an historical context is it possible to understand how Nordism and Nordic cooperation evolved as response to and even as an alternative to European events. Only a historical analysis can capture the full paradox of this process: that the vision of intensified Nordic cooperation was created and propagated by elite groups, not least by social democrats, who later abandoned it again when they gradually came to realize its limitations with respect to guaranteeing, i.e financing, the welfare state, that the original vision, however, continued to live on in broader circles of the social democratic labour movement and on the Left; and that these groups have, at least until lately, employed the Nordic vision to counter Danish participation in the European integration process.

2. The Nordic Vision

Within traditional geographic and political definitions, the Nordic Countries (Danish: *Norden*) are a part of Europe; a subsection within Europe.[2] History lends ample justifi-

---

1 Nikolaj Petersen has analyzed the growing disparity in the 1990s between elite and popular attitudes towards Danish participation in the European integration process using the concept of "the Danish strategic triangle". According to Petersen Danish policy towards Europe has increasingly been decided within a triangle consisting of Danish public opinion, the political establishment and the Danish EU-partners, with the Danish political establishment acting as broker between the mainstream positions of the EU partners and the Euro-scepticism of large segments of public opinion (N. Petersen 1993: 87f.) Thus, it is important to note that within the present article the concept of "elites" relates to decision-making political and administrative elites, not the cultural elites which have always been strongly represented within the Danish Euro-sceptic wing.

2 The term *Norden* has no precise English parallel (though some Anglo-Saxon authors frequently expand the term "Scandinavia" to cover the entire Nordic area). Nevertheless, when we talk about "Nordic cooperation", the terms can be used with some precision. Thus, Nor-

cation to this classification, as Nordic and European history have been closely interrelated. Still, the concept of a united *"Norden"* based on common and shared values and traditions of religious, linguistic, social and/or political nature has often been evoked to mobilize the Nordic populations against perceived European threats to the Nordic area and/or the individual Nordic nation states. During the 19th century, such endeavours were carried out under the banner of "Scandinavianism", in a thrust inspired by and directed against the nationalist ambitions of pan-Slavism and pan-Germanism. Due to the contentious rivalry between German and Danish national ambitions over the Duchies of Schleswig-Holstein, the staunchest supporters of Scandinavianism were generally found in Denmark (Østergaard 1994; Rerup 1994; Stråth 1995).

However, due to the lack of real commitment to the idea the Scandinavian unification process never achieved tangible results. The individual processes of nation-state formation in Scandinavia were driven forward not only by a process of demarcation against third parties, but also against each other. Unlike their German and Italian counterparts the Scandinavists never succeeded in their ambitions to transform the Nordic area into one compact nation state.

Nevertheless, Scandinavianism or Nordism as an idea survived, but generally within settings and associations with more limited ambitions for Nordic cooperation. It was very difficult to achieve Norwegian consent to more than the most basic expressions of Nordic cooperation as Norway only obtained full independence as late as 1905. During the 1930s the instability of the European security structure and not least the Nazi seizure of power in Germany gave a new incentive to considering perspectives for closer Nordic cooperation, particularly within the field of defense. Nothing resulted from these half-hearted attempts and on the eve of war, the Nordic countries found themselves confronting the German threat on an individual basis. As a consequence, the Nordic countries would experience the war very differently with Sweden defending her neutrality position, Finland tied to the German war effort, and Denmark and Norway being occupied by the Wehrmacht (Holtsmark and Kristiansen 1991; S.O. Hansen 1994a and 1994b; Blidberg 1994).

---

dic cooperation covers cooperation among the five states (Denmark, Finland, Iceland, Norway and Sweden) and the three home-rule territories of the Aaland Islands, the Faeroe Islands and Greenland. However, this has not always been the case. In the 19th and first half of the 20th century, Scandinavia and *Norden* were often employed indiscriminately to designate Denmark, Norway and Sweden (of which the present home-rule areas were part), but not Finland. Thus, at that time, Nordic state cooperation in fact meant cooperation carried out by the governments in Copenhagen, Oslo and Stockholm. Following Finland's independence in 1917, and especially in the period after 1945 when Finland has increasingly participated in the cooperative frameworks of the three Scandinavian countries, Nordic cooperation has been adopted as the precise term for this undertaking. For a long time, however, no uniformity has characterized the use of the terms "Scandinavian" and "Nordic". The discussions on establishing a Scandinavian Defence Union in 1948/49 very often were/are described as the Nordic Defence Union negotiations, though Finland did not take part. Today it is rather politically incorrect to talk about Scandinavian cooperation because it leaves out the Finns and the home-rule territories, whereas the Finns are eager to "prove" that they are "genuine" Nordics despite language and historical differences (for these last efforts, see Engman, 1994).

Denmark's experience with the German occupation led to a revival of Nordism, which gave strong impetus to inter-Nordic exchange and cooperation both at the interstate level and among private organisations and institutions. This trend embraced most of the political environment and must be termed a cross party trend as all political parties (except the Communists) shared in this new Nordic effort. From the point of view of national psychology, this re-orientation towards the North can be seen as a reaction against the domination from the South, which had been forced upon Denmark in the wartime period. The immediate lesson gathered from the German occupation raid – what many contemporaries branded, the "9 April experience", referring to the date and the way it occurred (only a few armed skirmishes before the Danish army was ordered to surrender) – was that Denmark could not once again be left to face European threats on her own. "Stronger Nordic ties" and "intensified Nordic cooperation" became popular catchwords to create an effective psychological, political and military bulwark against such dangers in the future (Olesen 1994a and 1994b; L.H. Sørensen 1996: 100ff.).

Evidence of the non-partisan character as well as the widespread backing behind these Nordic sentiments is shown by the impressive growth of the Danish section of the Norden Association. Sharing the European Movement's cross-political character the Norden Association (which was founded with individual branches in the different Nordic countries just after World War I) worked to diffuse and promote Nordic contact and cooperation. The Danish section sought to take cooperation the furthest (in the deepening sense), and was also the largest, with a paid membership rising from approximately 30,000 members in 1945 to 65,000 around 1960, a membership which the Danish European Movement has never approached (Andersson 1991: 111; L.H. Sørensen 1996: 85f.).[3]

Although Nordism was close to a catch-all phenomenon in Denmark in the first two decades after World War II, its weight and character varied considerably among different political parties and pressure groups. In agriculture, which until the beginning of the 1960s still accounted for the highest share of Danish exports, the Nordic market could never replace British and German markets. The Liberal Party (*Venstre*), the main representative of farmer interests in Denmark, was in 1957 the first Danish party to openly call for Danish membership in the EEC even if this meant leaving the rest of *Norden* behind (Just and Olesen, 1995; Laursen, 1993). Of course the Liberals supported Nordic cooperation. However, this support took the form of obvious and pragmatic exchange between neighbours intent on solving mutual problems, not on operating together in common.

The opposite was true of the Social Democratic Party. The Social Democrats entered the post-war period with an ambitious programme inspired by Keynesian demand management and American productivist ideas with the aim of securing economic growth, a sustained process of industrialization and full employment. These ideas overlapped nicely with similar ideas in Norway and Sweden, where so-

---

3 For the sake of comparison, the Swedish section of the Nordic Association, with the second largest membership basis among the Nordic countries counted around 15,000 individual members in 1945, rising to about 30,000 in 1960.

cial democratic parties not only formed majority governments, but also possessed much more structural power within society in general. After 1945 the Danish Social Democrats did not return to government until 1947, and then only as a fragile minority government. Worse still was the fact that as the prime foreign currency earner in an era characterized by a shortage of export earnings, agriculture constituted the most vital link in the Danish economy. It is hardly surprising that agricultural interests did not pursue cooperation in policies aimed at investment, trade and consumer controls as part of a planned exercise to boost industrialization (V. Sørensen 1987, chapter 5; Just and Olesen 1995; Molin and Olesen 1995).

Nordic cooperation appealed to Danish Social Democrats as a lever to achieve political ends. However, it is important to note that Social Democrats would also evoke the desirability in a vein similar to most other Nordists: Just after the war, party chairman Hans Hedtoft praised Nordic cooperation using the following cultural terms:

"Such a striving towards greater unity in *Norden* finds its natural justification in the solidarity which is rooted in the Nordic peoples' mutual descent, common linguistic heritage and the rest of the cultural affinity binding the area together for more than a thousand years; an affinity which has found its special expression in the Nordic peoples' common ideals concerning democracy and the conception of law".

(Speech by Hans Hedtoft, Stockholm, July 1945, Social Democratic Party Archive, box 322, file 2, our translation)

Such "folkloristic" appeals to Nordic cultural heritage were commonplace in most quarters advocating closer Nordic cooperation, inspired as they were by the predominant cultural-political current in Denmark, known as Grundtvigianism.[4]

But Hedtoft would also sound another note with a specific social democratic tone:

"I have not said too much when I say that Scandinavian Socialism after World War II has become quite *an institution*. The unshakeable democratic and reform-socialist tradition that we represent has set an example for the international labour movement. Everyone can see that after this war private capitalism as a system has come to an irrevocable end and will now be replaced by other forms of society"

(Manuscript for speech, Copenhagen, 24 February 1947, Hans Hedtoft's Archive, box 2, file 1, our translation)

---

4 N.F.S. Grundtvig (1783-1872) was a priest, philosopher and educator who inspired large sections of the Danish society with his ideas on Danish identity as being rooted in old Nordic mythology, based on the egalitarian concept of popular participation (*folkelighed*). Grundtvig's ideas laid the foundation for the Danish folk high school movement, which in the late 19th century and well into the 20th century functioned as a political and cultural vehicle for the ambitions of the Danish farmers. It has also been claimed that Grundtviganism was so fundamental for the creation of Danish national identity through this period that even Danish Social Democracy was to a large degree "Grundtviganized" (Østergaard, 1992: 51-83, see also Østergaard's contribution to the present volume).

Hedtoft presents a vision of a society representing an alternative or "third way" between American capitalism and Russian communism. Hedtoft would be specific on this point in a speech in 1948:

> "The consequence of political democracy is economic democracy. That is what we are fighting for today. ... It is a bit general, but in this respect I think one can be allowed to say that the world of today is characterized by the struggle between two systems: American capitalism and Soviet coerced collectivization. The Scandinavian Social Democratic Labour Movement desires neither."
>
> (Manuscript for speech, Malmö, 27 May 1948, Hans Hedtoft's Archive, box 3, file 14, our translation)

Inserting Nordic cooperation within a solid social democratic framework not only promised to relieve the party of the "squeeze of domestic politics", but also to bolster social democracy and the social democratic model of society as a third way between capitalism and socialism. In Denmark, Norway and Sweden the idea was nourished that Scandinavian Social Democracy represented a unique synthesis, combining high levels of social consciousness and responsibility with impeccable democratic credentials. Scandinavian Social Democracy not only embodied a vision of society which differed profoundly from both the American and the Soviet way of society. In fact, it was already administering such a society, the Scandinavian model having been under construction at least since the 1930s. It was in order to secure and develop this model in Denmark that Nordic unity and cooperation appeared so essential to Danish Social Democrats (Villumsen 1991: 48 ff.; Olesen 1994a: 30ff.; Molin and Olesen 1995: 73ff.; V. Sørensen 1995: 41ff.).

As we shall see below, this strong belief in Nordic cooperation as a vehicle for a specific model of society experienced severe setbacks; all the major attempts to consolidate Nordic cooperation into a binding and highly institutionalized cooperative framework failed, from the collapse of the Nordic defence union plans in 1948/49 to the failure of the Nordic common market project, NORDEK, in 1970. However, the political disillusionment and frustration generated by this experience made themselves felt only at the political elite level. Among the Social Democratic rank-and-file, among trade unionists and even among parliamentarians the Nordic orientation lived on untainted. In their eyes, the functional cooperation that developed among the Nordic states, underpinned by a plethora of private exchange and collaboration schemes, testified to the success and viability of Nordic solidarity and cooperation.

The appeal of Nordic cooperation can be linked to three basic perspectives. First, Nordic cooperation was perceived as a cooperation among equals. It was cooperation among states of a fairly similar (small) size, and among states and populations that cherished the same values. Social Democrats tended to stress the similarity of the Nordic welfare state projects, whereas various liberal and conservative groups hailed the participatory dimension of Nordic democracy (*Folke-*

styret) or the common religious, linguistic and historic bonds. Second, the Nordic vision evolved and gained strength to demarcate what was non-Nordic in the classical sociological context of "we-and-they", the "they" being American capitalism, Soviet bolschevism or – of special relevance within the present context – European integration. Third, Nordic cooperation was seen as a remedy to relieve Denmark of her historical trauma of having to face external challenges on her own. Nordic cooperation could thus be promoted as an alternative to the dilemma of either being left alone or joining a club of which you did not want to be a member.

These three perspectives account for why the Nordic appeal has played such a prominent role in the Danish debate on European integration. This debate has taken place since 1957, when the European question was first raised with some weight, until the present, although the Nordic appeal seems to have lost some of its credibility once Finland and Sweden became members of the EU in 1995. Already in 1957 the chairman of the Economic Council of the Labour Movement, Frederik Dalgaard, had played the "equal size" – and "we-and-they"-cards in rejecting the idea of Danish membership of the Six. With reference to Nordic cooperation, he maintained:

"Also within the context of international cooperation, the old saying, birds of a feather flock together ('lige børn leger bedst'), seems relevant. At least it provides certain advantages if the cooperating parties share more or less the same cultural and social traditions and at the same time match each other in power and influence".

(Dalgaard quoted in Engberg 1986: 67, our translation)

Dalgaard proceeded by warning against Danish membership of, as he put it, "a German-Latin union". A similar view was presented by Niels Matthiasen, internal secretary of the Social Democratic Party in a "standard lecture" on the party's line on EEC membership. Promising that Denmark would never join a market arrangement in which the other Nordic countries did not take part, Niels Matthiasen made it clear:

"As a member of the Common Market we would become the seventh country in a union dominated by the Catholic church and Right-Wing political movements. It serves no purpose to claim that the Danish concept of democracy is the same as the German, the French or the Italian. It is evident that Danish democracy and political life is based on a different foundation equalling to some extent what you find in Britain, and in certain respects in Canada and the USA, but first and foremost in the other Nordic countries".

(Engberg 1986: 68, our translation)

Such rhetoric directed against a Europe dominated by of the three C's Catholicism, Christian Democracy and Capitalism (or Cartels) – became mainstream thinking within the EEC-opposition groups during the 1960s and 1970s. Within the labour movement it faded somewhat when Denmark's Social Democratic government, in 1961, followed in the wake of the UK and submitted an application to join the EEC. That it did not disappear completely is evidenced by the campaign against Danish membership in the Common Market prior to the 1972 referendum. Both within the Social Democratic Party and within the trade union movement, substantial groups came out against membership. The Danish trade union confederation, LO, endorsed membership with a slim majority, but the two trade union heavyweights, the Unskilled Labourers Union (DASF) and the Metalworkers' Union called for a "No" on a platform in which the "three C's threat" played a prominent role (Engberg 1986: 100-109; Martens 1979: 140ff.; Kaarsted 1992: 479ff.).

Groups outside the Social Democratic labour movement also employed this kind of rhetoric. A very strong nucleus within the early organized opposition against Danish membership of the EEC was composed of former resistance movement veterans. Politically they ran the gamut from Communists on the one extreme to right-wing nationalists on the other. However, in their opposition to the EEC, they were able to join ranks, and there was a remarkable correspondence in their argumentation against a Europe of the three C's and especially against the threat of German domination in Europe generally and in Denmark in particular. In the September 1972 issue of "*Frit Danmark*" ("Free Denmark"), a resistance movement paper continued into the post-war period, one reads that "In the Catholic dominated EEC, the position of women is limping half a century behind what we have achieved in the Nordic countries – equal pay is a 'will of the wisp' (*lygtemand*)." The influential shipping magnate A.P. Møller generously supported anti-EEC activities out of fear that Denmark should become "a German satellite" ("*et tysk biland*") (quoted in Rasmussen 1997: 69). And in 1962 the communist writer Carl Scharnberg caricatured – in the form of a speech by a German general to his comrades – what the EEC would do to Europe. His speech ended this way:

> "Europeans! In the year to come we enter (the era of) unbreakable super-European cooperation, everyone under the Treaty of Rome's all-decisive paragraph 240: 'The present treaty is of indefinite duration', during which we as stated in the preamble 'will build the foundation for an ever closer union of the European people', and this will occur for the benefit of our common race and culture. May this be accomplished within the year 1962. Im namen Gross-Europas. Prost, meine Zuhörer, Volksgenossen".
>
> (quoted in Rasmussen 1997: 70, our translation)

Within the labour movement context as within the organised EEC opposition, the alternative to German-European domination was Nordic cooperation. All the groups mobilized under this banner. Two opposition groups established in the early 1960s even used the word "Nordic" to their names, the "Information Fund on Denmark and the Union of Rome – Nordic Action" (Oplysningsfonden om Danmark og Rom-Unionen. Nordisk Aktion), and the group "Free Norden" (Frit Norden). During the electoral campaign prior to the October 1972 referendum on membership, references to *Norden* were skilfully used to signal that an alternative to the

Common Market existed and that Denmark would not face the world alone if she decided to reject membership (Engberg 1986: 65ff., 100ff.; Rasmussen 1997: 63-81; Laursen & Olesen 1994: 127-160).

One of the most famous examples of such Nordic brotherhood is represented by a newspaper advertisement inserted by the dominant opposition movement, "The People's Movement against the EEC" (*Folkebevægelsen mod EF*) picturing the Danish Prime Minister, J.O. Krag, shoulder-to-shoulder with his Swedish Social Democratic counterpart, Olof Palme. The text below the picture stated: "The Prime Minister will be able to bring congratulations from the Danish people, when the Nordic Ministers soon meet again. Our "No" to Danish membership in the EEC represents a "Yes" to a strengthened *Norden* able to cooperate with the rest of the world. We need each other, all of us" (reprinted in Skovmand 1979: 45). Again, the other side of this dichotomy, cooperation with a *Norden* demarcating itself from Europe, was displayed in another *Folkebevægelsen* campaign advertisement entitled "Poor Holland" (*Stakkels Holland*). In an attempt to dismantle the fairy tale image of "idyllic Holland" the advert asserted:

> "It is possible that this image was once correct. But we know it is no longer true. We know the economic situation of Holland is more serious than anybody envisaged. That unemployment is on the rise. That inflation is ravaging and undermining salaries. That the Dutch population are fighting with guest workers in the streets of Rotterdam. We know that the Dutch workers have started occupying their factories in order to secure their living. That taxes are rising and rising. That administration is growing. That the Dutch farmers demonstrate against the encroachments from Brussels".
>
> (reprinted in Skovmand, 1979: 43, our translation)

Moderation was a rare guest in both the "Yes" and "No" camps during the electoral campaign of 1972. The "No"-movement's effort to distance itself from Europe was counterbalanced by employing *Norden*, Nordic values and Nordic cooperation as an alternative with positive connotations or at least as a common denominator for cultural or political-economic traditions alien to the ways and traditions of Continental Europe. The vital message was that Denmark did not face the European challenge alone. She had friends and allies of her own calibre.[5]

There is every reason to believe that the Nordic vision in all its looseness and heterogeneity, was effective with voters. The "No"-movement appealed to these

---

5 On the other hand, the Nordic argument faced a severe handicap during the referendum campaign of 1971-1972 on the heels of yet another failure in Nordic cooperation. This occurred in 1970, with the collapse of the NORDEK negotiations to establish a joint Nordic common market (see part IV of the present article). The collapse seemed to lend credibility to those arguing that Nordic cooperation could never be an alternative to the EEC but has also stimulated the interpretation that the Danish government's main interest in the project was to secure its back before being presented to the decisive European round of negotiations (Engberg 1986: 90-109).

ideas during its campaigns in the 1960s and 1970s. Even the Danish Communist Party (DKP), which had never even paid lip-service to Nordic fraternity, unfurled the Nordic colours during the referendum period of 1972. As demonstrated by the election result, however, Nordism had its limits. The Norwegian "No" pronounced just ten days before the similar referendum in Denmark, did not suffice to convince the Danish electorate to give the same verdict. With a comfortable majority of 63.3% to 36.7%, EC membership became a reality. The prospect of joining a market arrangement which would comprise Denmark's two major trading partners and the success of pro-EEC forces in watering down the political implications of membership, and instead highlighting its economic benefits helped convince the electorate even to put Nordic solidarity on the back seat (Hansen, Small & Siune 1973: 93-129; Martens 1979: 180-182).

However, as later events were to prove, Denmark's entry into the EC did not once and for all settle the dilemma of choosing between Europe and *Norden*. During the referenda campaigns linked to the Danish decision on the Single European Act (1986), the Maastricht Treaty (1992) and Edinburgh Agreement (1993) the Nordic alternative was again actively promoted by the various opposition movements. The Nordic card was not the strongest or the one most often played during these campaigns (Petersen 1994: 213 ff., 254ff.; 1995: 195 ff., 208 ff.). The most prominent "No"-arguments, rather, were attached, as in the Single Act campaign, to fears of losing the veto right accorded by the Luxembourg compromise, to the strengthening of the legislative power of the EC Parliament and to the prospect of having to accept less stringent environmental and social standards. In addition to these issues, the vote "No" campaign during the Maastricht process was also strongly focused on (1) the dangers of Denmark becoming subordinated to EC Common Security and Foreign Policy and to the Economic and Monetary Union (CSFP and EMU), (2) threats to the Danish collective bargaining system and (3) the alleged incompatibility between the Treaty and the Danish Constitution. In the wake of the 1992 "No" the new referendum held in 1993 was fought very strongly on the grounds of the legally binding character and sustainability of the four Danish "opt-outs" (i.e. non-participation in the third phase of the EMU, in common defence policy, in common policy in justice and home affairs, and in the EU citizenship). During all three referenda campaigns, however, the Nordic alternative functioned as a positive backdrop for the criticism and scepticism directed against the European Community.

In contrast to the 1992-93 debacle, the 1986 referendum derived a special flavour from the fact that the main political parties split on the issue. The Social Democratic party and the small but influential "Social Liberals" (*Radikale Venstre*) rejected the Single European Act (not EC-membership as such). This was precisely the reason why the four-party conservative-liberal minority government called a referendum as it faced a majority in the Danish Parliament rejecting the Act. Most leading Social Democrats and Social Liberals did not argue that Nordic cooperation was an alternative to European cooperation, but pointed to the fact that the SEA might endanger Nordic foreign policy cooperation and Nordic agreements, such as the passport union and free mobility of the Nordic labour market. Within broader sections of the Social Democratic labour movement, however, the idea of a Nordic alternative to Europe was still nourished, as within the Union of Semi-skilled Workers (SID), whose chairman, Hardy Hansen, cooperated with the vote "No" group called "Nordic Alternative Campaign" ("Vi prioriterer Norden højest", "Pakken vil flytte nordiske grænser" and "En verden uden for unionen", all in *Notat* 18, 22 and 27 February 1986).

In the anti-EC movement's weekly (during the campaign period daily), *Notat,* the Nordic alternative was periodically embraced, but this perspective culminated in the period just after the referendum on the 27 February had produced its verdict of 56,2% in favour of the SEA. In the period 28 February-14 March *Notat* boomed with headlines such as "Nordic Politics Must Take the Offensive" and "Denmark Slipped Away From *Norden*" (5 March), "We Must Keep the Danes Attached to the Nordic Path" (6 March), "Let's Establish a Nordic Environmental Eureka" (8 March), "Denmark is Lagging Behind *Norden* Socially" (11 March) "A Wedge Between Denmark and *Norden*" (12 March) and "*Norden* is the Future" (14 March).

During the 1992-93 campaign the Nordic banner seems to have been raised higher and with more insistence than in 1986. One reason for this is probably the fact that the Maastricht referendum was interpreted as a decision with implications much more far-reaching than the SEA and as a more clear-cut issue "for-or-against" European integration as such, even though a prominent part of the No-movement maintained that their opposition was directed against the EU and not the EEC. More importantly, a radical new development obviously also contributed to the stronger Nordic focus: the prospect of the Nordic countries joining the EU. In 1991 Sweden officially applied for membership, and the following year both Finland and Norway followed suit. This immediately played the Nordic card into the hands of the Yes side which now saw a chance to present European integration as a precondition for Nordic cooperation. From now on, European integration could be presented as a vehicle for instead of a impediment to Nordic aspirations.

Inside the major umbrella organisations, *Folkebevægelsen mod EF* and *Danmark 92/Junibevægelsen* ("The June Movement" – a name acquired after the "No"-victory in the June 1992 referendum) which contained most of the parties, organisations and groups opposing the EC and/or the EU, groups such as Free Norden and Nordic Alternative based opposition on an explicitly Nordic platform. However, these groups were rather marginal, but also the more important representatives of the "No"-front engaged in Nordic rearmament in order not to lose the Nordic card to the "Yes"-side. A closer look at *Notat*, Folkebevægelsen's former weekly, testifies to this rearmament.[6] Compared to 1986, the number of articles

---

6 Due to fractioning and crisis within the movement, *Notat* had established itself as an independent paper defending a broader "No" platform. This position was increasingly in harmony with the platform defended by the *Danmark 92/Junibevægelsen* umbrella organization. *Folkebevægelsen* also continued, but as an umbrella organisation with a predominantly socialist/left-wing profile which in effect was overshadowed by the campaign of the *Danmark 1992/Junibevægelsen*.

dealing with Nordic issues manifestly increased. These articles fell into three main categories: 1) articles informing on EU attitudes and the position of the anti-EU movements within the other Nordic countries, 2) articles trying to eliminate the probability of Nordic unity within the EU, and 3) articles delineating the Nordic alternative to Europe.

It is obvious that the second category was a direct response to the fear that the "Yes"-side would benefit greatly if it could persuade the electorate that the Nordic countries stood a fair chance of remaining united within the EU. In a series of articles and editorials, *Notat,* therefore, tried to present this perspective as a mere chimera, as politically wishful thinking based on the fallacious assumption that the Nordic populations would endorse membership. In continuation of this logic *Notat* proposed that Denmark postpone any decision on whether or not to join the Union until it was clear what the verdict of the other Nordic countries would be. In other words an additional reason for voting "No" was constructed ("Wait until *Norden* has voted on Union Membership", "*Norden* will never be united in the EC", "Danmark should wait for *Norden*" and "A Divided Denmark", in *Notat* 6, 13, 20 and 29 March 1992).

At the same time – concerning the last category – the "real Nordic alternative", a united *Norden* untied by the paragraphs of the Maastricht Treaty was hailed and highlighted elsewhere in the pages of *Notat*. No single or well-developed Nordic vision was propagated and defended. Rather, arguments varied between how a Danish "Yes" would jeopardize existing Nordic institutions and ambitious visions on how the Nordic countries might develop into a fully integrated unit, a "European Canada" as one reader envisaged it. Hence, we read articles such as "Denmark must choose between *Norden* and EC", "Nordic agreements hanging by a thin tread" and "*Norden* as Europe's Canada", (*Notat* 17 and 31 January and 8 May 1992).[7]

The marginal anti-Maastricht majority (50.7%) delivered in the Danish Maastricht referendum of 1992 was turned into a more convincing "Yes" (56.7%) in the

---

7 The Norwegian peace researcher Johan Galtung, a frequent guest in the columns of *Notat,* delivered a double message, that Denmark on the one hand took on a heavy responsibility if it voted "Yes" because this would sabotage Nordic cooperation, and, on the other hand, that Nordic cooperation held the potential to be a genuine ("democratic", "environmentally conscious", "less militaristic") alternative to the EU with an equally strong institutional build-up as the latter. Galtung's vision, however, was not exclusive, but envisaged Nordic cooperation as a force in a broader European and world cooperative framework (See *Notat,* 29 May 1992, 22 January 1993 and 8 May 1993).The problem for Galtung's vision, as indicated by an interview survey carried out jointly by the Norwegian newspaper *Dagbladet* and the Danish *Information* during this period was that Galtung's own countrymen were very reluctant to consider any union at all, be it Nordic or European. Responding to the question "Do you prefer a Nordic or a EC union?", 40% of the Danes interviewed pointed to the Nordic alternative with 35% preferring the European counterpart. Among Norwegians, only 56% supported the idea of a union, with equal percentages (28%) divided among the alternatives (See *Notat,* 5 May 1993).

subsequent Edinburgh referendum of 1993. As in the 1972 referendum, it was economically motivated arguments which motivated voters for the "Yes" in 1993, and the same type of argument which persuaded voters to shift from "No" in 1992 to "Yes" in 1993 (whereas political arguments played a prominent role on the "No"-side – Siune, Svensson & Tonsgaard 1994: 112ff.). Hence, throughout the 1972 to 1993 period, pragmatic economic considerations go a long way toward explaining why Denmark has opted for Europe over *Norden*.

Until the 1992-1993 elections, it was clear that a Danish "Yes" would mean a break with Nordic solidarity. Thus, on the front page of its first issue following the Edinburgh referendum, *Notat* commented upon the defeat with the headline "Lonely Swan" (an allusion to the Nordic symbol of five swans 21 May 1993). However, it is paramount to stress that the Nordic vision has never been able to rival the national vision. On the contrary, as the Swedish historian Bo Stråth has maintained:

> "Supported by history, we can say that Scandinavian popular movements have been prominent as identity producers, not of a Scandinavian or Nordic identity, but of national identities. An important element of these national identities in the Scandinavian countries is the belief in Nordic values given by a common past, whereby the mythification of the belief in Nordic values makes them take on real proportions. However, this Scandinavism has not replaced the national values, but strengthened them. Scandinavism has served as a sounding board, a dialogue, a mirror of the national".
>
> (Stråth, 1995: 54)

Within the Nordic context, despite the high sounding ideals, common institutions have seldom existed through which the Nordic vision could translate into tangible political results. Had the Danish Social Democrats in the immediate post-war period been more successful, such institutions might have emerged. Yet, one should not forget that their ultimate purpose was also national: to strengthen, through Nordic integration, Social Democracy within Denmark. This "national" link was much less pronounced when Social Democrats in Norway and Sweden considered the benefits of Nordic cooperation. To a large extent, they actually felt that national interests might be jeopardized by entering into too binding forms of cooperation, demonstrating that even among Nordic Social Democrats political-ideological affinity and solidarity counted less than national imperatives when these could not be seen to reinforce each other.

The fundamental perspective to be highlighted in relation to the impact of the Nordic vision on Danish European attitudes is that apart from the early post-war period, this vision has not served to intensify Nordic cooperation or integration. Rather, from the late 1950s onwards, it has been used as a defensive weapon aimed at safeguarding and fending off European challenges to Danish sovereignty and independence. The Nordic references have served to bolster the sustainability and credibility of Danish anti-EC politics. In the end, these endeavours proved unsuccessful, as the Danish electorate came to believe that national interests were better served within the European framework. At least until 1992-93, however, references to Nordic solidarity and to the existence of an alternative to European integration have been invoked by Euro-sceptic groups with insistence and have probably contributed effectively in securing continuing high levels of "Euro-reluctance".

3. The Institutions of Nordic Cooperation

If Nordic visions at times reached a high-sounding and ambitious note, Nordic political and state cooperation generally followed more down-to-earth tunes, albeit with occasional outbursts of hectic pursuit of ambitious cooperation projects. Although these endeavours generally collapsed, leaving disillusionment in their wake, the Nordic cement was nevertheless strong enough to keep pragmatic and functional inter-Nordic cooperation on track.

When, after the war, the Nordic governments resumed cooperation, they were quick to return to their tradition of informal, mutual consultations concerning matters of common interest. The tradition of periodic meetings between the Scandinavian foreign ministers was re-established immediately after the war. Since then foreign ministers have met regularly for informal, ad hoc consultations (Lindström & Wiklund 1967: 171-187; Kalela 1967: 158-170). Very often, these talks have aimed at finding a coordinated Nordic platform within international bodies such as the UN, OEEC, CSCE, etc.. This strategy has proved to be particularly successful in UN peace-keeping operations and in aid programmes for the developing world. One recent example of this pragmatic, functional approach is the Nordic-Polish UN brigade operating in ex-Yugoslavia today. In a certain backdoor way this ad hoc cooperation in peace-keeping operations has smuggled a security dimension into Nordic cooperation, which has otherwise been absent since the failure of the Nordic defense negotiations in 1948/49. The informal character of these cooperative initiatives is demonstrated by the fact that it has taken place within a very loose institutional framework.

While cabinet ministers and civil servants have tended to avoid Nordic initiatives which one way or another might limit the pursuit of national interests, the efforts by Nordic parliamentarians have had a more dynamic character. Until the creation of the Nordic Council in 1952, the Nordic Interparliamentarian Union was particularly effective as an engine of closer cooperation in minor policy areas such as traffic, civil legislation, social rights, etc. A number of inter-Nordic committees of parliamentarians have prepared parallel legislation and facilitated cooperation agreements. In 1951 the Nordic national aviation companies created the Scandinavian Airline System better known as SAS. A Nordic passport union was established in 1952, a common labour market in 1954 and a social convention signed in 1955 (Wendt 1979: 12-13, 113-114, 144-146, 149-151; Larsen 1984: 198-200).

In 1952, Nordic cooperation took a leap forward with the creation of the Nordic

Council by Denmark, Norway, Iceland and Sweden (Finland joined in 1956). The institutions and procedures of the Council were carefully designed not to cede significant powers to the new body. It was not established by a treaty, but by individual endorsement by the national parliaments. Delegations from the national parliaments (still) simply meet on an annual basis to discuss matters of common interest. The Council is headed by a presidium, with one member from each member state. Until the 1970s, national secretariats attached to the national delegations combined to form the full Secretariat during sessions. The Council has precious few formal powers. It can issue recommendations and discuss proposals. The national governments, for their part, are obliged only to report on progress. They are not bound by recommendations. Relying on the work of its committees, the Council has nevertheless been able to pave the way for common initiatives, either by influencing national governments or through the preparation of parallel legislation.

Even though parliamentarians occupy the central role in the Nordic Council, government representatives are present as well. By having cabinet ministers join the national parliamentary delegations, take part in plenary debates and discuss proposals with the Council's committees, a direct link is established between this body and the national executives, thus facilitating a harmonisation of the political agendas at the Nordic and national levels. The rules of the Council, however, do not allow cabinet ministers to vote (thus forestalling political embarrassment). Furthermore, the Presidium has often met with the prime ministers outside session in order to agree on a productive agenda for imminent meetings (Anderson 1967: 26ff.; Wendt 1959: 106ff.).

These informal procedures have ensured that national governments generally have been closely informed and consulted about the progress of Council proposals. Especially when dealing with low policy issues, this system has been a dynamic factor in promoting Nordic cooperation in a manner described by the Swedish political scientist Nils Andrén as "cobweb-integration". In contrast to the binding institutional obligations known from supranational integration schemes, the Nordic cooperative framework has been much more informal. According to Andrén the success of the pragmatic, functionalist approach lies in a slowly growing ethos of cooperation from which a cobweb of practical cooperation results. This procedure has proven very effective as a means of overcoming the dilemma between the Nordic versus national orientation, and between the determination to seek solutions through cooperation and the desire to retain the option of individual policy formulation (Andrén 1966: 377-78, 384).

While Andrén's "cobweb-ethos" delivers a convincing functional explanation to how Nordic cooperation developed, it does not enlighten us on why this approach has worked only at the minor policy level and has never been sufficient to promote joint Nordic responses in areas of high-level politics. The fact remains that the cobweb ethos has not been strong enough to solve the dilemma between a Nordic and a national approach in the latter areas, or to build a foundation from which

Nordic cooperation could develop into more binding integration EEC/EU style (Ørvik 1974: 62ff., 83ff.).

To explain this characteristic feature, we must broaden the spectrum from focusing only on the internal dynamics of Nordic cooperation to consider also the effects and challenges posed by the international environment. Nordic institution-building and the choice of fields of cooperation have been closely linked to changes in the relations between the Nordic countries and the rest of Europe as well as with the international community in general. However, the pressure generated by external developments has exerted a double-edged impact on Nordic cooperation (Stråth 1980: 104ff.).

On the one hand, external challenges have tended to invigorate and reinforce Nordic initiatives. During the late 1940s the escalation of the Cold War and rumours of plans to incorporate Scandinavia into a Western defence arrangement and the efforts to create a European customs union within the ambit of the Marshall Plan were decisive for initiating a process with the aim of producing a Nordic alternative to these broader international plans. On the other hand, such international developments also impeded efforts to obtain lasting and concrete results from these Nordic initiatives. In the NATO case, the firm American preference for Danish-Norwegian membership in NATO, in contrast to the establishment of an independent Scandinavian Defence Union also encompassing Sweden, complicated the Scandinavian negotiations (Lundestad 1980: 338ff.; DUPI 1997: 92 ff.; Malmborg 1994: 88 ff.). The Soviet Union also frowned upon ambitious Nordic cooperation schemes, believing them to be a cover for Western domination in the area. Finland's withdrawal from the Nordic common market plan, NORDEK, in 1970 was a product of uncertainty as to whether NORDEK was meant to be a stepping-stone to the EC, which would be an open challenge to Finland's delicate foreign policy balance vis-a-vis the Soviet Union (Wiklund 1970: 334-335; Archer 1971: 115).

Nevertheless, it would be wrong to convey the impression that external pressure is the decisive factor in explaining why Nordic ambitions always failed in the major policy areas of defence or economic cooperation. Responsibility must also be located in and among the Nordic states themselves, as a real choice has often existed between individual national strategies and a coordinated Nordic approach *vis-à-vis* the international challenges. In high policy areas, however, the first approach has been the preferred or at least the dominant one because it proved impossible to harmonise the various national interests into a mutual Nordic strategy (Laursen 1994a: 5-6; Olesen 1994b: 165ff.; Schiller 1984: 226ff.; V. Sørensen 1993 & 1995; cf. quotation in section 4).

Explanations for this fact must be sought in varying geo-political and socio-economic conditions, in differing political preferences as well as in dissimilar historical experiences. At the structural level, differing geo-political and economic conditions have tended to complicate Nordic solutions. Denmark's exposed strategic position at the outlet of the Baltic Sea and its border with Germany have sometimes demanded other security arrangements than those preferred by Swedes or Norwegians, or vice versa determined by other, but equally compelling, geo-strategic considerations. The same kind of explanation can be applied in considering the limitations of the diversity of economic structures. Denmark has searched for market outlets for her large and efficient agricultural sector while the other Nordic countries wanted to protect their farmers. Sweden had a similar objective for her competitive industry while Norway and Finland especially have wanted to protect their domestic industry (Ørvik 1974: 83 ff.).

In addition to these nationally rooted, structural problems, Nordic cooperation itself also faced a structural problem: that of size and efficiency. During Nordic negotiations on vital policy areas a lingering doubt existed as to whether a Nordic solution could constitute a genuine alternative to the greater Atlantic or European frameworks. Could Nordic cooperation generate sufficient security on its own? Would the benefits be large enough to offset the political costs involved in creating a Nordic common market (Pharo 1994: 216 ff.; Stråth 1980: 111 ff.)?

There has probably never been any simple yes or no answer to such questions. However, had the political determination been strong enough, solutions to these problems might have been found. This was the case with the Danish Social Democratic Government, which was willing to endorse the creation of an independent Nordic Defence Union in 1949 (and was extremely disappointed when it proved to be futile) precisely because a synergy was perceived to exist between the country's security interests and the party's domestic political interests, both of which could be promoted via Nordic cooperation. Such synergies have seldom existed. Rather the tendency has been that internal rivalry or competition have functioned as barriers towards more committed forms of cooperation involving real and/or formal transfer of sovereignty to Nordic institutions. Fear of Swedish power ambitions or Danish unaccountability (or European orientation) were underlying causes behind the inter-Nordic reservations. And so were the dissimilar historical experiences described above. Norway's history of being part of Danish or Swedish dominated states seems to have worked as a psychological barrier to participation in more binding Nordic cooperation schemes, just as the very different second world war experiences of the Nordic countries have complicated efforts to achieve common security policy frameworks (Olesen 1994b: 165ff.).

Nordic cooperation has thus tended to circumvent the "hard" or demanding areas of cooperation because of the domestic political costs linked to it, because of the incompatibility of perceived national interests or because of external restraints. If Nordic cooperation in low priority policy areas can accurately be described as "cobweb cooperation", the overall Nordic approach to cooperation may be termed cooperation based on the principle of the lowest common denominator. This does not mean that Nordic cooperation has been irrelevant or without ambition. Rather, "lowest common denominator cooperation" points to the fact that the great visions of Nordic cooperation have been abandoned and that concrete cooperation initiatives have been determined by what is obtainable when five or more members have to agree. Because of the Nordic ethos, this minimalist approach has produced results which in some respects – such as social harmonisation, labour mobility or border openness – compare positively with what has been achieved by the EEC/EU (Andrén 1984: 259ff.; Stråth 1995: 208ff.).

The Nordic ethos may also be seen at work in what has been called a "Phoenix effect": each time a great political initiative has foundered, a new, but less ambitious initiative has been launched in compensation so as to secure the cooperative framework and safeguard previous achievements. In this way, Nordic cooperation has to a large extent developed as a parallel, supplementar cooperative framework alongside the more binding commitments demanded of those Nordic countries who were members of Western organizations such as NATO and EEC (Stråth 1980: 111; Laursen 1994b: 183). The "Phoenix effect" may be seen to be at work in the creation of the Nordic Council in 1952 a few years following the disillusion generated by the collapse of the Nordic defence plans; by the signing of the Helsinki Treaty in 1962 (for the first time anchoring Nordic cooperation in an official treaty), itself a response to the miscarried Nordic common market discussions which instead resulted in Danish-Norwegian-Swedish membership of EFTA; or by the surge of reform and expansion that characterized Nordic cooperation of the 1970s in the wake of the NORDEK failure and the Danish decision to join the EC. In this last instance idealist and tactical pressures from practical nordism combined with new functional tasks to breathe new life into the would-be alliance after the NORDEK debâcle.[8]

Evidently, Danish membership in the EC did not deliver the kiss of death to Nordic cooperation. On the contrary – and in contrast to the stalemate of the EC – the 1970s gave new impetus to Nordic cooperation. In 1971 the Helsinki Treaty was amended to include the statutes of the Nordic Council. The mandate of the Council and its Presidium were strengthened by the creation of a permanent secretariat in Stockholm. The same year a cultural agreement was signed and a secretariat for cultural affairs established in Copenhagen. Finally, the intergovernmental character of Nordic cooperation was reinforced by the decision to appoint ministers for Nordic cooperation and to establish a Nordic Council of Ministers with a secretariat in Oslo. Although operating on the basis of unanimity, the Council of Ministers came to function as an important liaison body for the many new Nordic initiatives taken during the 1970s. However, the most far-reaching reform may well have been the decision by the Danish Foreign Ministry to insert a Nordic liaison officer within its EC Secretariat. Correspondingly, Sweden and Norway expanded their activities and their embassies in Copenhagen. This way Copenhagen became the Nordic conduit to the EC, a position retained until the Swedish-Finnish entry into the EU in 1995 (Wendt 1979: 13-14, 42-43, 109, 260; Amstrup & Sørensen 1975: 29 ff.; Seip 1975: 15-23).

---

8 The Phoenix concept was formulated by Anderson (1967: 118ff.). See also Laursen 1994b: 183, 193-196).

The above analysis reveals that the traditional picture of the Nordic Council and of Nordic cooperation as reflecting a preference among Nordic decision-makers for a particular kind of cooperative spirit and framework is an over-simplification. The institutions of the Council and the parallel legislation procedure were products of the clash between strong Nordic ambitions and national resistance to too-binding Nordic commitments. Furthermore, external pressure also worked to give Nordic cooperation its special institutional form.

4. The Role of Nordic Cooperation in Denmark's European Policy

Any analysis of the impact of Nordic cooperation on Denmark's European policy must begin by considering Denmark's Nordic policies and the extent to which these policies were formulated in terms of European issues. It is evident that Nordic cooperation in the post-war period took place in competition or interaction with the European integration process. Therefore, since 1945 an important aim of Danish foreign policy has been to deal with both Nordic and European priorities.

However, it has not always been possible to conciliate the two. In Copenhagen as well as in the other Nordic capitals, the attraction of European cooperation schemes has often prevailed over Nordic plans and ambitions. Such a realization was voiced early. In a 1950 speech by the young Minister of Commerce, Jens Otto Krag, one reads:

> "In my office in the Ministry of Commerce in Copenhagen I have a cabinet where I file important documents. In this I also have a drawer marked: 'Reports and Minutes Regarding Nordic Cooperation'. It is already filled up. It is piled with paper. However, there exists no drawer marked: 'Results from Nordic cooperation'. But had it been there, it would unfortunately have been, if not completely empty, very close to. ...
>
> It is no wonder that the Nordic goodwill has not produced great practical results. We cannot deny that compared with international trends, a certain disillusionment with the results of Nordic cooperation standout clearly. The explanation for why international, or European or European-American cooperation seem to be much more successful is not hard to find. We have to look within ourselves, among our own economic problems.
>
> The matter simply is: the main economic problem of the Nordic countries today are such that it can only be solved on an international basis. Nordic cooperation may contribute positively to solving the difficulties, but compared to the character and size of the problems, this contribution can only be supplementary, indeed only secondary".
>
> ("Skandinavisk og international økonomisk samarbejde", handwritten manuscript for speech in Oslo, 18 February 1950 in J.O. Krag's archives, box 17, our translation)

This critical and ironic evaluation of Nordic cooperation was without doubt coloured by the disappointment linked to the failure of the Nordic Defence Union a year earlier, but it was also a view increasingly shared by the Danish elite. In this respect a gap emerged between the Nordic perceptions by the majority of the elite and the Nordic visions as they prevailed in the Danish public.

As we have seen, this gap between the guarded realism of the elite and the strong Nordic dedication prevailing in broader circles did not fully come to the fore in the public political debate until the debate on Denmark's entry into the EC in 1971-72. One explanation for this delay is that European realism did not generate much electoral support. Another is that it was not until 1972 that a binding European decision acquired a really urgent quality. Finally, a great number of the internationally oriented decision-makers were not immune to Nordic appeals and were themselves actively involved in Nordic cooperation. In the speech quoted above, Krag also went out of his way to stress the need to defend and expand Nordic cooperation within the existing international frameworks.

Thus, to many Danish policy-makers such as Krag, it was not a question of whether Denmark should pursue either a Nordic or a European orientation. The question was how to establish a nexus between Denmark's European and Nordic policies, how to define priorities and how to develop a political strategy to match these priorities. This rather technocratic approach, however, was difficult to sustain because no Danish government was able to control the external setting; therefore, one priority tended to exclude the other. This might have been a minor problem if choosing between *Norden* and Europe had not been symptomatic of more profound cleavages within the Danish society – agriculture versus industry, social democracy versus liberalism – and, thus, also tended to divide the elites internally. Denmark's Nordic strategies have thus vacillated due to deep seated political struggles within the Danish polity and to developments in the external environment (V. Sørensen 1995: 40ff.; Molin & Olesen 1995: 65, 75ff.; Laursen 1994b: 5 ff., 36).

Nevertheless, the variations of Nordic and/or European strategies seem to suggest a certain pattern over time. The European-Nordic nexus of Danish foreign policy-making can be grouped into three overall constellations, defined by how Nordic strategies have been perceived or related to Denmark's European policies.

The clearest and most distinct of these constellations is Nordic cooperation as an *alternative* to Europe. Four main currents of inspiration have nourished this more or less utopian vision: 1) the ideological, social and cultural similarities among the Nordic countries; 2) a preference for cooperation among countries of equal size; 3) the perception of *Norden* as a bulwark against European threats and challenges; and 4) personal contacts among Nordic decision-makers due to existing traditions of Nordic cooperation. As suggested by Krag's remarks about *Norden*'s need for broader international frameworks, the belief in *Norden* as an alternative has not been very influential in the decision-making elite since the failure of the Nordic Defence Union negotiations. As demonstrated above (see section II) this fact has not prevented the vision from staying alive among broad segments of the population and the anti-European movements, either as a true objective or a handy propaganda tool.

A position that has appealed more to the Danish foreign policy decision-makers is that of Nordic cooperation as a *platform* for formulating joint Nordic policies towards Europe and the West. The primary raison d'être for this strategy must be located in the assumption that closer Nordic alignment would strengthen the bargaining position of *Norden vis-à-vis* Europe. Included in this strategy one also finds the ambition to defend and/or develop the Nordic countries' position within the international division of labour, their welfare model, and their tradition of foreign policy cooperation and coordination. It could be argued that this strategy in some respects represents the offensive version of the more defensive, insular strategy of Nordic cooperation as an alternative to Europe. Two more aspects are connected to this position. First, a Nordic line to Europe has generally been considered much more effective in providing legitimacy and in rallying political support for cooperation with the Continent than accomplishing this on a strictly national basis. Thus, the *Norden*-first approach to European cooperation has been developed with an eye toward mending the internal schism within the labour movement between the longings of the heart and those of the purse. Second, the strategy has obviously also been motivated by party political preferences. In the eyes of many top-ranking Social Democrats, the Nordic link would bolster the domestic defense of national welfare provisions and market regulations *vis-à-vis* liberal claims for free market policies.

Seen in a longer historical perspective, the third position, Nordic cooperation as a *supplement* or *parallel* integration strategy to a European strategy has predominated in actual Danish policy-making. The supplementary, pragmatic strategy has typically been the Danish response to the failure of more ambitious Nordic projects or to the establishment of closer links with Continental Europe. In fact, it is hardly correct to speak about a strategy. To a large degree the choice of the supplementary option has been caused by the miscarriage of previous efforts within the "platform" strategy. Furthermore, the supplementary approach is ambiguous. On the one hand it can be interpreted as the victory of a "Europe first" policy which has driven Nordic priorities into a supplementary or perhaps even compensatory role. Thus, this policy reflects a "realist" strategy to give European or extra-Nordic affairs first priority in Danish foreign policy. The long historic tradition of formulating Danish foreign policy with an eye to developments in Germany has worked as a powerful obstacle for ceding first priority to a common Nordic policy; particularly since Norway and Sweden have historically been reluctant to intensify relations with continental Europe. On the other hand, it would be misleading to explain the prominence of the supplementary approach only in terms of realpolitik. The supplementary strategy has also been the product of a genuine determination to uphold Nordic aspirations and translate them into new fields and new forms. A combination of Nordic idealism, political tactics and practical problems has infused Nordic cooperation with new dynamics every time it encountered internal or external obstacles.

Even though it would be a simplification to view the three strategies outlined above as clear-cut alternatives chronologically succeeding each other in good order, it is tempting to describe Denmark's Nordic policies from 1945 until 1994 in terms of four cycles. The first cycle, between 1945 and 1949, was the peak of Nordic aspirations and is marked by the rise and fall of the Nordic Defence Union. This phase was followed by three phases: the 1950's and 1960's until 1972 and, finally, the period from 1973 to 1994. These phases seemed to go through a cycle beginning with Nordic disappointment (e.g. 1950-51 in the wake of the Nordic Defence Union failure), followed by new Nordic endeavours and hopes (a Nordic platform attempt) and ending with country strategies *vis-à-vis* Europe (in Denmark a "Europe first" choice plus Nordic supplement) (Laursen 1994b).

4.1. The Period 1945-1949/52

In the period 1945-49 the Danish Social Democratic elite regarded Nordic cooperation as a window of opportunity. Within these circles it was believed that intensified Nordic cooperation possessed a fair chance of materialising, using the UN framework as a platform for advancing mutual ambitions about welfare, social compromise and political détente in Europe. Reservations about this prospect among the Swedish and especially the Norwegian Social Democrats, however, prevented real progress before the escalation of the Cold War and the failure of the Nordic Defence Community in 1949 dealt the final blow to these aspirations. The collapse of the NDC had severe repercussions on Danish European policy, and was a first serluos warning of the difficulties in steering a middle course between Europe and *Norden* (Olesen 1994b: 160 ff.).

The dilemma was not confined to security. Of the three Nordic countries, Denmark was the one most willing and interested in binding and committed cooperation linking *Norden* to Western Europe. The different Nordic approaches became apparent from 1947/48 onwards in the policies of Denmark, Norway and Sweden towards the Marshall Plan and OEEC cooperation (Malmborg 1994: 79ff.; Sevón 1995: 203 ff.). The divergent attitudes in areas such as security, trade and international payments, however, did not always come out into the open. The fact that Danish, Norwegian and Swedish foreign policies reflected rather different views on closer European commitments was played down by leading politicians and governments (cf. Milward 1984: 251ff.). Instead, the governments sought to repair and relaunch Nordic cooperation in a less formal set-up and in less conspicuous areas. This praxis resembled the logic of the slogan: "Nordic unity is dead, long live Nordic unity", and one of the effects of this silent neglect of Nordic divergencies was to create room for the emergence of the gap between elite and popular attitudes regarding to the future role of Nordic cooperation in Danish foreign relations.

Following the breakdown of the Nordic Defence Community the 1950s marked the beginning of a new and more sober-minded phase. From a position where the Nordic course, for a brief period in 1950-51, was only a supplement to Danish ties with Western Europe, the Common Market issue gave *Norden* a chance to return to centre-stage. Giving up treaty-bound cooperation in "high politics", the Nordic countries moved into a strengthened cooperation in "low policy" areas mediated through inter-parliamentary connections. The creation of the Nordic Council in 1952 was such an effort to raise the Nordic Phoenix from the ashes (Wendt 1987: 460ff.; Anderson 1963: 23ff.; Laursen 1994a: 181ff.).

4.2. The Period 1949/52-1959

Despite the achievements of the Nordic Council and other cooperation schemes, "cob-web cooperation" did not spread into the world of economic diplomacy. Even though the Scandinavians, in 1950, had established UNISCAN together with the UK and also functioned as a loosely knit club in the OEEC, their divergent positions *vis-à-vis* European cooperation remained. Studies of the possibilities of forming a Nordic common market had been taking place since 1948, but made little progress because of what was conceived as incompatible economic interests (Amstrup 1980: 166ff.; Milward 1984: 251ff., 316ff.; Nordisk økonomisk samarbejde 1950: 15ff., 25ff., 42ff.). A new round of inquiries regarding a Nordic customs union (1954-59) marked a serious attempt to bind the Nordic countries together in an economic union. The Danish strategy was clearly to pull *Norden* together as a platform for Denmark's economic diplomacy and integration strategies. Once again it was the Social Democrats who were particularly eager to see Denmark's European relations channelled through a Nordic club.

The same combination of external pressure and internal division that had stopped the Nordic Defence Union contributed to the failure of the Nordic common market. The Treaty of Rome negotiations of 1956-57 produced a first challenge to Nordic cohesion, and the OEEC free trade discussions initiated by the UK during the same period produced a second (V. Sørensen 1995: 55ff.; Laursen 1994a: 188ff.).

The will to protect and carry through the Nordic common market project to a positive conclusion was a powerful influence on Denmark's European policies in the late 1950's. Already in 1955 Denmark had been invited to establish an association agreement with the European Coal and Steel Community, but – despite strong commercial interests – had declined in order to give the Nordic common market first priority. The creation of the EEC was of even more importance to Denmark's national economy in general and to her farming community in particular. Still, the Social Democrat-led government did not act to join the EEC despite the clamour of the farming lobby (and despite invitations). In 1957 the Danish government insisted that the Nordic investigations should be carried through, while continuing the work to establish closer connections with the EEC and keep the membership option open. Thus, on the domestic scene a "*Norden*-first" and an "EEC-first" strategy competed with each other (Laursen 1993: 65ff.; Laursen 1994a: 188ff.; V. Sørensen 1991: 116ff.; Branner 1992: 307f.).

4.3. The Period 1960-1972

In 1959 the precarious Nordic unity collapsed and the Nordic governments scurried to develop national strategies to meet the European challenge. One of the consequences of this was the creation of EFTA in 1960. As support for EFTA entailed abandoning the Nordic "platform" strategy, many leading decision-makers tended to view this as if the Nordic constraints on Denmark's integration strategies had also been lifted. The opinion was slowly forming that the best solution to Denmark's economic problems would be for Denmark to follow the UK in obtaining EEC membership. This realization was limited, however, to the political elite level and had to deal with a heavy legacy of the first public EEC discussion in 1957-59; a legacy containing a high degree of scepticism toward the EEC as a result of the long debate over "EEC-first" or "*Norden*-first"; or – as some would put it – the farmers against the rest (Laursen & Malmborg 1995: 201ff.; Laursen 1996: 214ff.).

Therefore, like the 1950s, the 1960s also opened with Nordic disappointment. The British application for EEC membership in 1961 brought Nordic aspirations from disappointment to the danger of a real division. Denmark took part in the efforts to reform and strengthen the Nordic Council and Nordic intergovernmental liaison, but the Danish application for EEC membership relegated Nordic co-operation to a clear second priority. The split was patched over by the EFTA council with the so-called London declaration of EFTA solidarity. Nevertheless, the "musketeers oath" from London could not conceal the fact that the Danish and Swedish Social Democratic governments stood deeply divided over the EEC issue. The attempt during the Danish negotiations with the Six in 1962 to launch a treaty on Nordic co-operation (1962) to consolidate the Nordic achievements failed to improve the situation. Even though the Helsinki Treaty consolidated the Nordic achievements, it contained only few commitments. It was at this point that Denmark and Sweden parted ways in their policies towards the EEC (Norway's position was less clear-cut). Nordic cooperation was relegated to a second priority in Denmark's actual foreign policy formulation (Laursen 1996).

France's veto of Britain's EEC application, in 1963, brought a moratorium to the inter-Nordic struggle over choosing between Europe and *Norden*. The Danish EEC application remained open, but had lost its sense of urgency. At the same time Nordic cooperation picked up momentum once again. A number of small incremental steps moved cooperation ahead, mainly within the economic area. The Nordic Council pushed this process forward, and intergovernmental cooperation on development aid and UN-peacekeeping troops bolstered the political alignment of the Nordic foreign policies.

In 1968, as a consequence of this gradual growth in the supplement strategy and as a rebuttal to the second 1967 British application to join the EEC, Danish foreign policy-making made its last turn to the "*Norden*-first" strategy. Or so it seemed. However, the attempt in the years between 1968 and 1970 to construct a NORDEK, a Nordic economic union, had – from a Danish elite point of view – a double purpose. The explicit one was to foster binding Nordic economic integration. Nevertheless, as the negotiations were to demonstrate, NORDEK was also meant to function as a common platform for approaching the EEC question either through Danish membership of both groups or through an association between the two market groups. While this was particularly appealing to many Social Democrats and Centre-left Liberals, the farmers and the Liberal Party worried that closer Nordic alignment would harm the relationship to the EEC. This became particularly evident, when the Six in 1969 reopened the enlargement issue (Christensen 1993: 140ff.; Wendt 1979: 71ff.).

When it proved impossible to reach a compromise between Danish insistence that NORDEK should keep the door open for EEC membership and the equally manifest Finnish opposition to this claim, the brief harmony between elites and masses in Danish European policy came to an abrupt end. The NORDEK experience contributed significantly to Denmark's subsequent entry into the EEC by demonstrating that the Nordic alternative had been attempted but also exhausted. Norway's application for EEC membership was also helpful to that end. Nevertheless, as demonstrated above, the referendum campaign on Denmark's entry was marked by recurrent references to the EEC as a break with Nordic solidarity and Nordic values; an argumentation which had a strong impact on large parts of the labour movement and within the Social Democratic Party and within the Radical Liberal Party (see above section II; C.L. Sørensen 1978: 62f., 77ff.).

4.4. The Period 1973-1994

Prime Minister Jens Otto Krag's signature on Denmark's accession treaty opened a new phase in Denmark's European and Nordic relations, a phase stretching from 1973 to 1994. Denmark's EC membership meant the demise of the Nordic alternative as well as of the "*Norden*-first" strategy. Yet for the next ten years Danish foreign policy went to great lengths to salvage and revitalize Nordic cooperation. EC membership was accompanied by administrative reforms in the Danish foreign service designed to allow Denmark to function as a bridge-builder between the EC and the Nordic partners. Furthermore, the Nordic institutions were strengthened by measures such as the Nordic Council of Ministers. The new council seemed as a signpost to the Nordic commitment, but was also intended to serve as a political and bureaucratic liason to facilitate practical co-operation in new policy areas. The 1970s and 1980s witnessed a continuation in the expansion of Nordic cooperation into new areas (Wendt 1979: 23ff., 42ff., 110f.; Laursen 1994b: 32ff.; Wiklund & Sundelius 1979: 104f., 110 ff.).

Such initiatives naturally played an important role in assuaging the impact of EC membership on domestic public opinion. However, this hardly suffices as an explanation for the continued Nordic emphasis. Nordic aspirations remained strong within the Social Democratic Party and the Social Liberals, and Nordic cooperation in areas such as industrial policy had an important function in a period when EC cooperation was stagnating. Thus during the 1970s one can distinguish a two-sphere integration strategy within which the Nordic supplement grew and prospered (Turner & Nordqvist 1982: 229ff.; Sundelius & Wiklund 1979: 104f., 110ff.).

This picture changed in the 1980s. At the official level the ten years of coalition governments between 1982 and 1992 dominated by the Liberal (Venstre) and Conservative Parties strengthened the official EC commitment, not least through the efforts of the Liberal Foreign Minister Uffe Ellemann-Jensen. The reorientation went hand in hand with a less committed *Norden* policy. This shift was also facilitated by a reorientation of the European policy of the Social Democrats. While the moderate EC sceptics had as their spokesman the dedicated Nordist and chairman of the powerful parliamentary market committee Ivar Nørgaard, the chairwoman of the parliamentary group, Ritt Bjerregaard, built a working understanding with the Foreign Minister (Olsen 1994: 317ff.; Haahr 1993: 199ff., 218 ff.).

Finally, the attempts to balance the Continental orientation with Nordic ties came under pressure when the EC, under Jacques Delors, threw itself into a period of institutional innovation with the Single European Act and the renewed efforts to create a forum for European Political Cooperation (EPC). This expansion of the fields of EC competence had important repercussions for Nordic cooperation. Most important was the ascendancy of the EPC and the challenge it posed to the tradition of Nordic foreign policy consultations in the UN and elsewhere. The pragmatic intergovernmental Nordic consultations, together with the Nordic Council and the rest of Nordic cooperation outlets, were still accorded prominence, but these traditions and institutions no longer functioned, as they had done in the 1960s, as a platform for designing Danish European policies. This was considered a by-gone phenomenon as long as the Nordic partners remained outside the EC. Nordic cooperation could and still did function as an important and appreciated supplement. However, as the variety of strategic choices was by now down to two, the only alternative path pointed in the direction of choosing *Norden* as a clear-cut alternative to Europe, a path desired by the anti-EC opposition.

As the Maastricht and Edinburgh referenda of 1992 and 1993 demonstrated, a strong proportion of the Danish electorate was ready to defy the Danish decision-makers' European policies and strategies and accept the Nordic strategy as an alternative. However, even this option came under growing strain as it became clear that Denmark would no longer be the only state defending the Nordic colours within the EU.

5. Denmark, *Norden* and Europe towards the Millennium: A Balance Sheet

With Finland's and Sweden's entry into the EU in 1995 the conditions for Nordic cooperation changed radically. The change could have been even more pronounced had the Norwegian electorate not rejected membership the second time in 22 years.

The Norwegian decision revitalized hope among Euro-sceptic groups that Europe was not a destiny, but a choice, and it kept the vision of Nordic cooperation alive as a platform for anti-European mobilization.

Following the referendum, the Norwegian "No" movement has been very active in rallying support behind a policy of both strengthening Nordic cooperation and ensuring that the existing Nordic institutions, not least the Nordic Council, would act as forums of Nordic cooperation in their own right and not just bodies working to coordinate Nordic policies vis-a-vis issues on the European agenda. This view has obtained wholehearted support from Euro-sceptic groups in Denmark and Sweden. In fact, already during the referenda campaigns of 1992-93 various Danish opposition groups organized to foster this goal. An organization called "Alternative Nordic Council" was created on a platform demanding a Nordic customs union and an enlarged Nordic Council elected directly by the Nordic populations. The two major Danish umbrella organisations, *Folkebevægelsen mod EF* and *Junibevægelsen*, still clung to the independent Nordic alternative as late as 1994, when during the elections for the European Parliament they both ranked the demand for "ever closer Nordic cooperation" among their top political priorities. ("Nordisk union mere spiselig", in *Notat* 5 March 1993; "Folkebevægelsen mod EF", 1993; "JuniBevægelsen", 1994; *Weekendavisen* 13-17 May 1997).

Despite the "No" movements' continued embrace of the Nordic cause in recent years, there is no doubt that the Nordic vision suffered a severe blow when it became a fact that more than 4/5 of the total Nordic population would come to live within the borders of the EU. At the political elite level, there was an instant realization/determination that Nordic cooperation would come to receive lower priority or would at least have to be organized along new lines and principles. The change in the international environment due to the demise of the Cold War and the ensuing democratization process in Eastern Europe had already begun to challenge the way Nordic cooperation functioned. During the session of the Nordic Council of 1995 it was therefore decided to reorganize Nordic cooperation technically as well as substantively, partly in line with the recommendations by a lengthy joint report on *Norden* and Europe elaborated by the Danish, Finnish, Norwegian and Swedish foreign policy institutes and the University of Reykjavik, and published in 1991 (*Norden* i Europa, chap. 7, 1991; Nordiskt samarbete i en ny tid, 1995).

Technically it was decided to centralize Nordic institutions by merging the secretariats of the Nordic Council and the Council of Ministers into one office located in Copenhagen. The hope was to improve coordination among the Nordic institutions, but financial considerations also played their part. When it became clear that Sweden would join the EU, the Swedish government announced that it could no longer find the resources to finance the activities of the Nordic Council and the Nordic Council of Ministers at existing levels. Although there is no doubt that Swedish funds were severely strained, it is difficult not to read into the Swedish intentions the signal that Nordic cooperation did not possess the same attraction as it used to. While Sweden reduced her transfers to *Norden*, she accepted the role of net-contributor to the EU. However, the cut-back in Nordic funds was not disastrous, the diminished Swedish contribution to a large degree being offset by increased contributions by Denmark and Norway (contributions are regulated on a GNI-basis). Measured in DKK (fixed 1997 prices) the budget for the Council of Ministers has dropped from 747.9 million Danish Kroner to 702.6 million Kroner from 1995 to 1997. Compared to 1993, however, the drop equals only 6.6 million (Planerne för det nordiske samarbetet (C2) samt Nordiska Ministerrådets budget för 1997: 1f., 40 ff.).

Concerning actual policy formulation, it was agreed to change procedures within the Nordic Council to the effect that political initiative would rest more firmly with the four dominating party political groups (Social Democrats, Conservatives, Liberal Centre Group and Left Socialist Group) to which the 87 Nordic parliamentarians belong. At the same time, these political activities were reorganized to function within three main committees: The Nordic Committee dealing with inter-Nordic matters, The European Committee preoccupied with EU and EES matters, and The Committee for Adjacent Areas, treating issues related to the Baltic, North Russian and Arctic areas. As previously mentioned, in the statutes of the Nordic Council it had originally been stipulated that the Council was not a forum for foreign and security policy discussions. Although this rule had never been enforced on a strict basis, such discussions had been the exception until the 1990s. The 1995 reorganization changed this pattern dramatically. Now two of three pillars on which Nordic cooperation explicitly would be based dealt with *Norden*'s external environment (Nordiskt samarbete i en ny tid, 1995; see also http://www.Norden.org)

The aim of the European pillar was to promote "cooperation on important EU/EES issues where the Nordic countries share a common ground of value and interest. Nordic cooperation must constitute a platform of initiative from which to influence the European agenda" (Nordiskt samarbete i en ny tid, 1995: 4). This description should also be seen against the backdrop of a new guiding principle for Nordic cooperation, termed "Nordic usefulness" (nordisk nytte). This new principle amounted to a redefinition by which it was sought to pinpoint the goals of Nordic cooperation on a more concrete basis than the often rather lofty and idealistic invocations of the past:

> "All activities conducted under the aegis of official Nordic co-operation are evaluated according to a set of principles known as Nordic Usefulness. To qualify for consideration all Nordic activities must meet basic criteria. They must: 1) be related to activities which would otherwise be conducted on a national level, but where tangible, positive effects can be achieved by joint Nordic action; 2) demonstrate and further Nordic solidarity; 3) raise the levels of Nordic knowledge, skills and competitiveness".
> (http://www.Norden.org/NordicCo-operation/NordicUsefulness)

To the dismay of the Norwegian "No"movement the Norwegian Social Democratic government, not least during the "reign" of former Prime Minister Gro Harlem

Brundtland, has been very active in fostering this redefinition and turning the Nordic Council into a kind of European liaison office (Siune 1996). As the outsider among the Nordic states, excluded from the decision-making processes in Brussels, the Norwegian government hopes that the Nordic institutional framework will function as a reserve-platform from which Norway can present and project her views into the EU. This way the Nordic institutions may become a political remedy for enhancing – in the eyes of the government – the Norwegian national interest vis-a-vis Europe.

It would be wrong, however, to interpret Gro Harlem Brundtland's motives simply as national "Realpolitik". There is also a 'touch of Nordic idealism in the way she conceptualizes the link between Nordic cooperation and European integration. In her view – stated at the Nordic Council's Europe conference i Copenhagen in 1996 – the Nordic countries must take on the task of imposing Nordic values onto the rest of Europe: it is on the ideological battleground of the EU that the Nordic and the European welfare state model must be defended:

"Within this field Europe recognizes the Nordic priorities given to job creation, environmental issues, transparency, equal rights. Therefore, when it is possible this mutual Nordic approach should translate into specific proposals and initiatives. When possible *Norden* – and here I willingly include EFTA countries like Norway and Iceland – should forward their views jointly".

(Siune 1996: 21, our translation)

During the same conference, Gro Harlem Brundtland was supported by the other Nordic (also Social Democratic) Prime Ministers. They agreed that *Norden* had a major role to play in the European discussion on how to meet the combined challenges of globalization and the restructuring of Eastern Europe. As Danish Prime Minister Poul Nyrup Rasmussen put it: "The strong Nordic solidarity is our guarantee that the welfare society which we cherish and have worked so hard to achieve may also be the trend-setting agenda for Europe in the future. … We must take the lead" (Siune 1996: 22).

The praise of these alleged Nordic values was occasioned by the start of the EU inter-governmental conference, and the specific address for the many appeals to Nordic policy coordination were aimed at Denmark's, Finland's and Sweden's draft proposals for that conference. However, despite the many appeals to present a joint Nordic draft, the three countries have in reality presented and defended individual platforms. Hardly any effort has been made to coordinate activities or discuss a mutual approach to the items on the IGC agenda (Petersen 1996: 13f.; Babic-Odlander 1997: 6ff., 25f.; *Politiken* ("EU-konference uden fodslag i de nordiske lande") 3 March 1996; *Weekendavisen* (Anna Libak: "Nordisk Uråd") 13-17 February 1997)

This is all the more remarkable, since the general preferences of the three governments, as evidenced by their individual draft proposals, were in fact very similar. Especially within the areas where the offensive interests of the Nordic countries manifested themselves, one finds a nearly complete congruence in outlook. According to Nikolaj Petersen, these offensive interests cover welfare objectives (employment and labour market relations), democratic control (transparency, subsidiarity, democracy) and post-material interests (environment, consumer protection, equal opportunity). In contrast, a certain degree of incongruence characterized the formulation of the defensive interests, i.e., positions on the common foreign and security policy, cooperation on juridical and police matters and institutional change – issues which dominated the IGC (Petersen 1996: 4ff.). The disparity in outlook within these areas was not radical. It was a question of nuances and different accentuation, caused partly by the four Danish rejections of elements of the Maastricht Treaty. This prevents a more flexible approach by the Danish government. However, because the Swedish and Finnish governments also possessed restricted manoeuvrability due to increased Euro-scepticism among their electorates, policies tended to converge even within the defensive interests (*Eurobarometer* no. 46, "Support for European Union membership", p. 9).

Thus, the behaviour of the Nordic governments towards the EU inter-governmental conference may be seen as emblematic of the way Nordic state cooperation has functioned throughout most of the post-war period. The individual draft proposals revealed that Nordic (Social Democratic) political thinking is animated by a mutual set of political and cultural values. This is a continuation of a long-observed trend. At the same time, continuity is equally evidenced by the fact that the Nordic countries, despite all the rhetoric, were unable to meet the IGC-negotiations on a joint and coordinated platform.

One may argue that good, pragmatic reasons exist for this lack of cooperation such as a desire not to present the Nordic countries as a compact bloc vis-á-vis the other EU-members and the realization that not much additional negotiational clout would be gained by coordination, as preferences would be quite similar all the same. Nevertheless, such explanations hardly convey all the truth. There is every reason to suspect that the three governments have also sought – as usual – to pursue national interests by maximizing operational independence and exploiting individual bargaining assets and flexibilities (Babic-Odlander 1997: 25f.). This is wholly analogous to the way the Nordic countries have been conducting relations with the Baltic region. On the one hand, joint Nordic programmes and political initiatives are being launched to boost cooperation with the newly independent Baltic states; at the same time they scramble to position themselves as the most important friend of the Balts by overbitting the joint Nordic programmes. The prime victim of this policy is probably Nordic cooperation, not the Balts (*Politiken*, 13 April and 26 August 1997).

Throughout this chapter we have discussed Danish attitudes to Nordic cooperation with an eye to how attitudes have varied over time and how elite and popular approaches have often differed due to antagonistic perceptions of the European challenges. Analyzing the future scenario Karen Siune has pointed to four distinct situations in which Nordic agreement is present: 1) The Nordic governments are in agreement about their European priorities and are backed by their populations on this; 2) the Nordic governments are in agreement but are not supported by their electorates; 3) the Nordic countries have differing opinions on European development, but within each country there is concurrence between government and electorate; 4) the Nordic populations share common attitudes towards Europe, but these attitudes are not shared at the governmental level (Siune 1996: 4f.).

Apart from the observation that 2 and 4 appear to be inverted versions of the same situation, all four versions are relevant when discussing scenarios for the future. The first one, the ideal one, is the one that Gro Harlem Brundtland and likeminded Social Democrats praise from the rostrum of the Nordic Council. Nevertheless, a mix between versions (2) and (3) most resembles today's situation, with the Nordic countries kept in an uneasy balance between pursuing a policy which the governments find necessary and one they can make their electorates accept. Keeping this balance entails sacrificing considerations for obtaining a joint Nordic approach as well as presenting a coherent European policy. Finally, it is scenario (4) which the Nordic EU-opposition movements refer to when they demand a new Nordic Council dedicated to *Norden* and not to Europe.

These scenarios notwithstanding, Nordic cooperation seems to have entered a new phase with Sweden's and Finland's entry into the Union. Nordic institutions, despite protests from the anti-EU lobby, have been modified to become a meeting ground for discussing Europe. But even these groups may find it very difficult in the future to rally under the Nordic flag to keep the EU at bay. In the late 1990s there exists no convincing Nordic alternative to Europe. The irony is that the only coherent albeit still idealistic vision remaining – at least in the short run – is Gro Harlem Brundtland's idea of making Nordic cooperation into a greenhouse for cultivating joint Nordic initiatives towards Europe. This may also explain the new approach to the Nordic alternative now discernible within the ranks of the opposition movements. Comparing the June Movement's 1996 IGC platform paper with its 1994 election manifesto mentioned above, Nordic aspirations are much attenuated. The strategy now appears to consist of ensuring that existing Nordic cooperation practices can continue, despite three of the countries' EU member status, rather than working to enlarge Nordic cooperation (JuniBevægelsen, 1996)

In the long run perspectives may change. As a permanent ad-hoc organization, the EU is a shaky construction, maybe even more so than the less pretentious Nordic one. However, the EU will most likely be the more adequate body to counter the challenges of globalization/transnationalization and the general restructuring of Europe after the Cold War. Still, history is open-ended and it is premature to rule out a development where European or global developments may not once again foster a Nordic "grand design". However, this is difficult to envisage unless seen as a consequence of as yet unforeseeable external challenges or, maybe less unforeseeable, within the context of a broader EU flexibility scheme. Hence, it has been argued that a multi-speed EU might reintroduce Nordic regionalism within a less demanding EU context (Wæver 1995: 289ff.). The point is that this perspective may arise through a new alliance between Brussels and the Nordic body politic. If until now the relationship between Brussels and the Nordic countries has primarily been regulated on an elite-to-elite basis, the flexibility scenario may reveal a shift to an alliance which on the Nordic side is connected to those broader sections of the population preferring Nordic cooperation.

This would be a new dawn for Nordic aspirations, but for the moment, it must be a speculative one.

Literature

Archives

Social Democratic Party Archives, Arbejderbevægelsens Bibliotek og Arkiv (The Labour Movement's Library and Archive), Copenhagen.
Hans Hedtoft's Archives, Arbejderbevægelsens Bibliotek og Arkiv (The Labour Movement's Library and Archives), Copenhagen.
Jens Otto Krag's Archives, Arbejderbevægelsens Bibliotek og Arkiv (The Labour Movement's Library and Archives), Copenhagen.

Newspapers and Web Sites

Notat: 1986, 1992 & 1993.
Politiken: 1996-1997.
Weekendavisen: 1997.
http://www.Norden.org: various entries.

Books and Articles and Other Published Sources

Amstrup, Niels (1980): "Nordisk samarbejde – Myte eller realitet? Planerne om økonomisk samarbejde fra 1945 til 1950" in *Nær og Fjern. Samspillet mellem indre og ydre politik*, Copenhagen, pp. 155-180.
Amstrup, Niels & Carsten L. Sørensen (1975): "Denmark – Bridge between the Nordic Countries and the European Communities" in *Cooperation and Conflict*, vol. 10, pp. 21-32.
Andersson, Jan A. (1991): *Idé och verklighet. Föreningarne Norden genom 70 år*, Stockholm.
Anderson, Stanley V. (1963): "Negotiations for the Nordic Council", *Nordisk Tidskrift for International Ret*, vol. 33, pp. 22-33.
Anderson, Stanley V. (1964): "The Nordic Council and the 1962 Helsinki Agreement", *Nordisk Tidskrift for International Ret*, vol. 34, pp. 278-300.
Anderson, Stanley V. (1967): *The Nordic Council. A Study of Scandinavian Regionalism*, New York.
Andrén, Nils (1966): "Nordisk Integration – synspunkter och problemstälningar", *Internasjonal Politikk*, pp. 370-387.
Andrén, Niels (1984): "Nordic Integration and Cooperation – Illusion and Reality", *Cooperation and Conflict*, vol. 19, pp. 250-262.
Archer, T.C.: Nordek (1971): "Shadow or Substance?", *Integration*, 1971(2), pp. 108-116.
Babic-Odlander, Lidija (1997): *Norden i EU:s regeringskonferens 1996-97*, the Nordic Council.
Blidberg, Kersti (1994): "Ideologi och pragmatism – samarbetet inom nordisk socialdemokratisk arbetarrörelse 1930-1955", *Den jyske Historiker*, vol 69-70, pp. 132-150.

Branner, Hans (1992): "Danish European Policy since 1945. The Question of Sovereignty", in M. Kelstrup (ed.): *European Integration and Denmark's Participation*, Århus, pp. 297-327.

Branner, Hans (1993): "På vagt eller på spring? Danmark og europæisk integration" in B. Nüchel Thomsen (ed.), *The Odd Man Out? Danmark og den europæiske integration, 1945-1992*, Odense: Odense Universitetsforlag, pp. 29-64.

Brückner, Peter (1990): "The European Community and the United Nations", *European Journal of International Law*, vol. 1, pp. 174-192.

Christensen, Jens (1993): "Danmark, Norden og EF 1963-1972", in: B. Nüchel Thomsen, (ed.), *The Odd Man Out? Danmark og den europæiske integration 1948-1992*, Odense: Odense Universitetsforlag pp. 135-152.

Due-Nielsen, C. & N. Petersen (eds.) (1995): *Adaptation and Activism. The Foreign Policy of Denmark 1967-1993*, Copenhagen.

Danish Institute of International Affairs (DUPI) (ed.) (1997): *Grønland under den kolde krig. Dansk og amerikansk sikkerhedspolitik 1945-1968*, Copenhagen: DUPI.

Engberg, Jens (1986): *I minefeltet. Træk af arbejderbevægelsens historie siden 1936*, Copenhagen.

Engmann, Max (1994): "Är Finland ett nordisk land" in *Den jyske Historiker*, no. 69/70 (1994), pp. 62-79.

Etzioni, Amitai (1965): *Political Unification*, New York.

Eurobarometer, no. 46, May 1997.

Folkebevægelsen mod EF: "Valggrundlag for liste N", manifesto for European Parliament elections 1994, 1993.

Hansen, Peter (1973): "Die Formulierung der dänischen Europapolitik", *Öster-reichische Zeitschrift für Aussenpolitik*, vol. 13, pp. 1-31.

Hansen, P., M. Small & K. Siune (1973): "The Structure of the Debate in the Danish EC Campaign: A Study of an Opinion-Policy Relationship", *Journal of Common Market Studies*, vol. 15(2), pp. 93-129.

Hansen, Svein Olav (1994a): *Drømmen om Norden. Den norske Foreningen Norden og det nordiske samarbeidet 1919-1994*, Oslo.

Hansen, Svein Olav (1994b): "Foreningen Norden 1919-1994 – ambisjoner og virkelighet", *Den jyske Historiker*, no. 69-70, pp. 114-131.

Haskel, B.G. (1976): *The Scandinavian Option. Opportunities and Opportunity Costs in Postwar Scandinavian Foreign Policies*, Oslo.

Holtsmark, Sven G. & Tom Kristiansen (1991): "En nordisk illusjon? Norge og militært samarbeid i Nord 1918-1940", *Forsvarsstudier* Oslo, 6/1991.

Haahr, Jens Henrik (1993): *Looking to Europe. The EC Policies of the British Labour Party and the Danish Social Democrats*, Aarhus.

Johnsson, Per-Olaf (1964): *The Projected Scandinavian Customs Union, 1945-59*, Ph.D. Thesis, Florida State University.

JuniBevægelsen: "Stem mod Union", manifesto for European Parliament elections 1994, 1994.

JuniBevægelsen: "Demokratisk samarbejde i Europa", political platform for the 1996 Intergovernmental Conference, 1996.

Just, Flemming & Thorsten B. Olesen (1995): "Danish Agriculture and the European Market Schism, 1945-1960", Thorsten B. Olesen (ed.): *Interdependence Versus Integration. Denmark, Scandinavia and Western Europe 1945-1960*, Odense: Odense Unversity Press, pp. 129-146.

Kalela, J. (1967): "The Nordic Group in the General Assembly", *Cooperation & Conflict*, pp. 158-170.
Kaarsted, Tage (1992): *De danske ministerier 1953-1972*, Odense: Odense Universitsforlag.
Kelstrup, Morten (ed.) (1992): *European Integration and Denmark's Participation*, Aarhus.
Larsen, Knud (1984): "Scandinavian Grass Roots: From Peace Movement to Nordic Council", *Scandinavian Journal of History*, vol. 9, pp. 183-200.
Laursen, Johnny (1993): "Mellem fællesmarkedet og frihandelszonen. Dansk markedspolitik 1956-1958" in B. Nüchel Thomsen, *The Odd Man Out? Danmark og den europæiske integration 1948-1992*, Odense: Odense Universitetsforlag, pp. 65-87.
Laursen, Johnny (1994a): "Fra Nordisk Fællesmarked til Helsingfors Konvention – nordisk økonomisk samarbejde, 1945-62", *Den jyske Historiker*, no. 69-70, pp. 179-200.
Laursen, J. (1994b): "Blueprints of Nordic Integration. Dynamics and Institutions in Nordic Cooperation, 1945-72", *EUI Working Paper*, RSC no. 94/20.
Laursen, J (1996): "Next in Line: Denmark and the EEC Challenge" in S. Ward & R.T. Griffiths (ed.) (1996), *Courting the Common Market. The First Attempt to Enlarge the European Community 1961-1963*, London, pp. 211-227.
Laursen, J. & Mikael af Malmborg (1995): "The Creation of EFTA" in Thorsten B. Olesen (ed.): *Interdependence versus Integration. Denmark, Scandinavia and Western Europe 1945-1960*, Odense: Odense University Press, pp. 197-212.
Laursen, Johnny & Thorsten B. Olesen (1994): "Det europæiske markedsskisma 1960-1972", in T. Swienty (ed.): *Danmark i Europa 1945-1993*, Copenhagen, pp. 93-160.
Lindgren, Raymond E. (1959): "International Co-operation in Scandinavia", *The Yearbook of World Affairs*, vol. 12, pp. 95-114.
Lindström, J. E. & C. Wiklund (1967): "The Nordic Countries in the General Assembly and its Two Political Committees", *Cooperation and Conflict*, vol. 3, pp. 171-187.
Lundestad, Geir (1980): *America, Scandinavia and the Cold War, 1945-1949*, Oslo.
Malmborg, Mikael (1994): *Den ståndaktiga nationalstaten. Sverige och den vesteuropeiska integrationen 1945-1959*, Lund.
Martens, Hans (1979): *Danmarks ja, Norges nej*, Copenhagen.
Miljan, Toivo (1977): *The Reluctant Europeans. The Attitudes of the Nordic Countries towards European Integration*, London.
Milward, Alan S. (1984): *The Reconstruction of Western Europe, 1945-1951*, London.
Molin, Karl & Thorsten B. Olesen, (1995): "Security Policy and and Domestic Politics in Scandinavia 1948/49", in T. B. Olesen (ed.): *Interdependence Versus Integration. Denmark, Scandinavia and Western Europe, 1945-1960*, Odense: Odense University Press, pp. 62-81.
Nielsson, Gunnar P. (1971): "The Nordic and the Continental European Dimension in Scandinavian Integration: NORDEK as a case study", *Cooperation and Conflict*, no. 3-4, pp. 173-181.
Norden i det nye Europa (1991), report by the four Nordic Institutes of Foreign Affairs and the University of Reykjavik, Helsinki.
Nordiskt samarbete i en ny tid. Det nordiska samarbetet i ljuset av folkomröstningarna om EU-medlemskap för Finland, Norge och Sverige (1995), report by the Nordic Council and the Nordic Council of Ministers.
Nordisk økonomisk samarbejde. Foreløbig rapport til Regeringerne i Danmark, Island, Norge, og Sverige fra Det fælles nordiske udvalg for økonomisk samarbejde, Copenhagen 1950.

Olesen, Thorsten B. (1994a): "Jagten på et sikkerhedspolitisk ståsted. Socialdemokratiet og og holdningerne til sikkerhedspolitikken 1945-1948", in B. Nüchel Thomsen (ed.): *Temaer og brændpunkter i dansk politik*, Odense, pp. 15-54.

Olesen, Thorsten B. (1994b): "Brødrefolk, men ikke våbenbrødre – diskussionerne om et skandinavisk forsvarsforbund 1948/49, *Den jyske Historiker*, no. 69-70, pp. 151-178.

Olesen, Thorsten B. (ed.) (1995): *Interdependence Versus Integration. Denmark, Scandinavia and Western Europe, 1945-1960*, Odense: Odense Universitetsforlag.

Olsen, Lars (1994): "Den stenede vej til Europa. Ivar Nørgaard, Ritt Bjerregaard og Socialdemokratiets EF-politik 1986-1993", *Vandkunsten*, no. 9/10, pp. 315-339.

Petersen, I. D. & T. Tiilikainen (eds.) (1993): *The Nordic Countries and the EC*, Copenhagen.

Petersen, Nikolaj (1993): "Game, Set and Match" in Ib Damgaard Petersen & T. Tiilikainen (eds.) *The Nordic Countries and the EC*, Copenhagen, pp. 79-106.

Petersen, Nikolaj (1994): "Vejen til den europæiske Union 1980-1993" in T. Swienty (ed.), *Danmark i Europa 1945-1993*, Copenhagen: Munksgaard pp. 195-271.

Petersen, Nikolaj (1995): "Denmark and the European Community 1985-1993" in C. Due-Nielsen & N. Petersen (eds.), *Adaptation & Activism. The Foreign Policy of Denamrk 1967-1993*, Copenhagen, pp. 189-224.

Petersen, Nikolaj (1996): *Norden og EU's regeringskonference 1996*, the Nordic Council.

Petrén, Gustaf & Claes Wiklund (1987): "Norden och EG inför 1990-tallet", *Nordisk tidskrift för vetenskap, konst och industri*, vol. 63, pp. 379-384.

Pharo, Helge (1994): "Scandinavia and the Cold War. An Overview" in D. Reynolds (ed.), *Origins of the Cold War in Europe*, Yale, pp. 194-223.

Planerne för det nordiska samarbetet (C2) samt Nordiska Ministerrådets budget för 1997, Nordic Council of Ministers, 12.11.1996.

Rasmussen, Søren H. (1997). *Sære alliancer. Politiske bevægelser i efterkrigstidens Danmark*, Odense: Odense Universitetsforlag.

Rerup, Lorenz (1994): "Nationalisme og skandinavisme indtil første verdenskrigs udbrud", *Den jyske Historiker*, no. 69-70, pp. 79-87.

Reynolds, D. (ed.) (1994): *Origins of the Cold War in Europe*, Yale.

Saeter, Martin (1993): "The Nordic Countries and European Integration. The Nordic, the West European and the All-European Stages" in Ib Damgaard Petersen & T. Tiilikainen (eds.), *The Nordic Countries and the EC*, Copenhagen, pp. 8-22.

Schiller, Bernt (1984): "At Gun Point: A Critical Perspective on the Attempts of the Nordic Governments to Achive Unity After the Second World War", *Scandinavian Journal of History*, vol. 9, pp. 221-238.

Seip, H. (1975): "Den reviderte helsingforsavtalen og följgene for det nordiske samarbetet" in *Nordisk Kontaktmandsseminar*, Aarhus 13-14th of May, pp. 15-21.

Sevón, Cay (1995): *Visionen om Europa. Svensk neutralitet och europeisk återuppbyggnad 1945-1948*, Helsinki.

Siune, Karen (1996): *Hvad kan Norden give EU?*, the Nordic Council.

Siune, Karen, P. Svensson & O. Tonsgaard (1994): *– fra et nej til et ja*, Aarhus.

Skovmand, Sven (ed.) (1979): *Der var engang en folkeafstemning*, Allingåbro.

Solem, Erik (1977): *The Nordic Council and Scandinavian Integration*, New York.

Stråth, Bo (1978): *Nordic Industry and Nordic Economic Cooperation. The Nordic Industrial federations and the Nordic Customs Union Negotiations 1947-1959*, Stockholm.

Stråth, Bo (1980): "The Illusory Nordic Alternative to Europe", *Cooperation and Conflict*, vol. 15, pp. 103-114.

Stråth, Bo (1995): "Scandinavian Identity: A Mythical Reality", in N.A. Sørensen (ed.): *European Identities. Cultural Diversity and Integration in Europe since 1700*, Odense, pp. 37-57.
Sundelius, Bengt (1977): "Trans-Governmental Interactions in the Nordic region", *Cooperation and Conflict*, vol. 12, pp. 63-86.
Sundelius, Bengt (1978): *Managing Transnationalism in Northern Europe*, Boulder, Col.
Sundelius, Bengt & Claes Wiklund (1979): "The Nordic Community: The Ugly Duckling of Regional Cooperation", *Journal of Common Market Studies*, vol. 18, pp. 59-75.
Sørensen, Carsten L. (1978): *Danmark og EF i 1970'erne*, Copenhagen.
Sørensen, Lars H.(1996): "Norden som idé og praksis. Den Danske Foreningen Nordens rolle som politisk ideologisk pressionsgruppe 1945-1960", *Historie*, vol. 1, p. 84-113.
Sørensen, Vibeke (1987): *Social Democratic Government in Denmark under the Marshall Plan 1947-1950*, Ph.D. Thesis, European University Institute, Firenze.
Sørensen, Vibeke (1991): "How to become a Member of a Club Without Joining. The Danish Policy with Respect to European Sector Integration Schemes, *Scandinavian Journal of History*, vol. 16, pp. 105-124.
Sørensen, Vibeke (1993): "Between Interdependence and Integration: Denmark's Shifting Strategies" in Alan S. Milward (ed.), *The Frontier of National Sovereignty. History and Theory 1945-1992*, London, pp. 88-116.
Sørensen, Vibeke (1995): "Nordic Cooperation – A Social Democratic alternative to Europe?" in Thorsten B. Olesen: *Interdependence Versus Integration. Denmark, Scandinavia and Western Europe, 1945-1960,* Odense: Odense University Press, pp. 40-61.
Thomsen, B. Nüchel (ed.) (1993): *The Odd Man Out? Danmark og den europæiske integration 1948-1992*, Odense: Odense Universitetsforlag.
Thomsen, B. Nüchel (ed.) (1994): *Temaer og brændpunkter i dansk politik*, Odense.
Turner, Barry & Gunilla Nordquist (1982): *The other European Community. Integration and Co-operation in Nordic Europe*, London.
Villumsen; Holger (1991): *Det danske Socialdemokratis Europapolitik 1945-1949*, Odense.
Wendt, Frantz (1959): *The Nordic Council and Co-operation in Scandinavia*, Copenhagen.
Wendt, Frantz (1979): *Nordisk Råd 1952-78. Struktur – arbejde – resultater*, Stockholm.
Wendt, Frantz (1981): *Cooperation in the Nordic Countries. Achievements and Obstacles*, Stockholm.
Wendt, Frantz (1987): "Hans Hedtoft og det nordiske samarbejde", *Nordisk tidskrift för vetenskap, konst och industri*, vol. 63, pp. 451-475.
Wiklund, Claes (1970): "The Zig-Zag Course of the NORDEK negotiations", *Scandinavian Political Studies*, vol. 5, pp. 307-336.
Wiklund, Claes & B. Sundelius (1979): "Nordic Cooperation in the Seventies: Trends and Patterns", *Scandinavian Political Studies*, vol. 2, pp. 99-120.
Wæver, Ole (1995): "Danish dilemmas – Foreign Policy Choices for the 21st Century" in C. Due-Nielsen & N. Petersen (eds.): *Adaptation and Activism. The Foreign Policy of Denmark 1967-1993*, Copenhagen, pp. 269-301.
Ørvik, Nils (1974): "Nordic Cooperation and High Politics", *International Organization*, vol. 28, pp. 60-88.
Østergaard, Uffe (1992): *Europas ansigter. Nationale stater og politiske kulturer i en ny, gammel verden*, Copenhagen.
Østergaard, Uffe (1994): "Norden – europæisk eller nordisk?", *Den jyske Historiker*, no. 69-70, pp. 7-37.

CHAPTER 8

Denmark's Relations with Germany Since 1945

Karl Christian Lammers

1. The Troubled Neighbourhood: Germany as Problem for Denmark

In the middle of the 19th century Danish-German relations were fundamentally transformed: Denmark was reduced to a small power, while Germany, i.e. Prussia and the unified German Reich emerged as European Great Power. Since this transformation, Denmark's relations with Germany, for political and psychological reasons have tended to be delicate and complicated, if not strained. History, of course, plays a role in this delicate relationship. And history seems an obsession, not only for the Germans, but especially for the Danes. This may explain why Danish experiences with German aggression in 1864 and again 1940 have for so long determined Danish attitudes to Germany and, ultimately, Denmark's political relations with its German neighbour. When the Danish historian Troels Fink, in 1968, published his study of Danish foreign policy towards Germany since 1864 in German, his book gave expression to these sentiments in its title *Deutschland als Problem Dänemarks* (Fink 1968; cf. also Frandsen 1994; Petersen 1994; Øhrgaard 1990; Lammers 1998a; forthcoming).[1] In doing so, he apparently wished to indicate that Germany not only had an important role in determining Danish foreign and security policy, but also that Danish foreign policy has traditionally been affected by developments in Germany, inasmuch as such developments would affect the position and even the freedom of action of the small neighbouring state. The title of Fink's book could indeed be so interpreted that the problem or the position of Denmark vis-a-vis Germany had remained unaltered despite Germany's military defeat and collapse in 1945, its demilitarization and subsequent division into two separate and independent states, and the Federal Republic's national sovereignty-limiting integration into the European Coal and Steel Cooperation (ECSC), NATO and later into the EEC. Denmark's "Germany Problem" remained even after the fundamentally improved bilateral relations since the beginning of the 1960s.

Fink's views reappear in the behaviour of other Danish personalities, both official and unofficial. In the 1960s, then Minister of Foreign Affairs Per Hækkerup is said to have told his undersecretaries that Danish foreign policy had three main

---

1 This article is based on access to the archives of the Danish Foreign Ministry, RA UM 5.G. 12a-c until 1972.

problems: "Germany, Germany and again Germany" (quoted from Øhrgaard, 1990: 111). Hækkerup underlined this view in the Danish parliament in June 1965, noting that "our policy towards Germany plays a very great role and probably will play a still greater role in the years to come. For Denmark the relationship with Germany will practically always constitute the most important problem relating to our foreign policy" (*Folketingstidende*, 1964/65: Sp. 6307). At the same time, Germany i.e. the Federal Republic (FRG), no longer constituted a formal problem at a bilateral level, when the same Per Hækkerup in the mid-1960s – still foreign minister – issued a text book on Danish foreign policy (Hækkerup 1965). However, we find the issue in the views of former spokeswoman for the Danish Social Democratic Party Ritt Bjerregaard, when in 1992, she analysed Denmark's position in post-Cold War Europe: "Throughout history, Germany constituted a problem for its neighbours – not only for the smaller ones. It will continue to be a problem." Pointing to the de facto veto-power of Germany on European matters, Bjerregaard noted that "if Germany opposes integration in the EC, then the EC will not be integrated ... Again we have a situation, which gives 'deja vu' feelings. A new Germany, a smaller Germany, but again a Germany which is too big for Europe" (Bjerregaard, 1992: 12, 14).

Perhaps unwillingly Ritt Bjerregaard pointed to the two contexts in which appears the notion of Germany as problem and as determinant in Danish foreign policy: the bilateral and the multilateral. In this chapter we shall discuss the notion of "Germany as problem for Denmark" by asking what is in fact implied, which role Germany has played and what determining influence Germany has had on Danish foreign policy. What do Danes refer to when they stigmatize Germany as a "problem" to Denmark, and what influence does such a stigma have on bilateral and multilateral relations between the two countries? The problem here is not only that of whether it is proper to maintain Germany as a practically unchanging problem for Denmark since 1864, but rather, whether Denmark's altered international position in the form of membership in NATO and the EC and, thus, its more direct involvement in European matters, has not altered its relations with Germany so as to change the problem, if not render it superfluous altogether. However, this is not as a determinant of Danish policy. Surely, Germany would and will always take up time and cause some anxiety for the Danes, but as will become clear, the problem was objectively not always identical, as Germany during the 1950s practically disappeared as a security problem, and the determinant role of Germany began to appear as an important problem for Danish politics in European affairs.

It is further necessary to take into consideration that at least the ways and means of coping with the problem of Germany has changed, especially because it should become clear that after 1945 (eventually 1948) Denmark would break with its traditional isolationist neutrality policy and instead seek new paths in its foreign and security policy by engaging itself in the new alliances and international organisations, which were emerging and which, as they involved multilateralisation of the so-called "German question", might be politically interpreted in relation to Germany. What impact did this change have on Denmark's relations with Germany? And what role has Germany subsequently played in Danish foreign policy? In short, it meant, viewed in the narrow Danish-German perspective, that Denmark would no longer have to face Germany on its own. Denmark's political and military alliance with the Western powers in NATO and its subsequent adherence to the EEC dramatically changed its relations with Germany as they became multilaterally linked and Denmark eventually became allied to Germany. Another reason for this change, of course, was that the primary security problem for Denmark was no longer Germany but the Soviet Union, which after 1945 had expanded its sphere of influence westward and which displayed expansionist intentions with the February 1948 coup in Prague.

This chapter will try to demonstrate how these developments indeed contributed to alter the framework of Danish relations with the new West German Federal Republic: Danish-German relations were no longer primarily bilateral but part of multilateral security and political-economic arrangements which involved Germany and linked Denmark to West Germany and made them equal partners and allies. In NATO, for instance, these arrangements forced them to work closely and indeed very efficiently together on defence matters, while in the EEC they cooperated in economic matters. As in the case of France, this may be seen as a way of dealing with or controlling the German problem through partnership. But was it in fact intended this way? The options for participation in NATO and the EEC were certainly motivated with an eye to Germany politically, militarily and economically. But eventually they could not avoid making Denmark dependent on Germany in new ways. The attitude of the Danes, therefore, remained sceptical, even though the new Federal Republic had demonstrated a new attitude to its smaller neighbour in the strained Danish-German minority question by accepting Danish minority principles. The minority solution of 1955 which surely facilitated Danish acceptance of West Germany's entry into NATO, gave off new signals: it was not a treaty, but mutual declarations and a gentlemen's agreement based on faith in the good will of the other part. It was the Germans who had made a gesture of good will.

The minority question and agreement can, together with the growing commercial and trade ties, be seen as one of the crucial signs of the narrow bilateral Danish-German relations. This emerged into a deep and effective – though not always cordial – patnership between Denmark and West Germany and, after 1990, the Federal Republic of Germany. It is a healthy bilateral partnership organized in multilateral frames, which made West Germany into Denmark's most important international partner, especially in the area of economics and trade, but also in politics generally. It also meant, however, some adaptation to Germany, as it placed restraints (which the Danes accepted) on how Denmark could relate to the other German state, the GDR, though the GDR, as compared to West Germany, could surely reckon on sympathies as a small power (cf. Lammers 1999b). Another effect was on the Danish attitude to the Oder-Neisse-border question. This article will ask, finally, which role Germany plays in the Danish attitude to Europe and what

External and Internal Determinants 263

impact German reunification has had on Danish European policy. Germany is still an important determinant, but does it remain as a problem for Danish European policy?

I will argue that, officially, Germany is no longer the traditional problem for Denmark, and that there exists no major bilateral problems between the two states. However, does the relaxation in Danish-German relations mean that the weight of history has altogether disappeared? No, because the notion "Germany as problem" plays a significant role in a new way. This chapter will contrast this interpretation to the fact that Germany both in the 1960s and again in the 1990s was still perceived as a problem by Denmark. Not officially, as Danish authorities viewed the multilateral arrangements including Germany as a way of coping with the problem. Unofficially, however, I would argue that the continuing reluctance of a large proportion of Danes to enter an integrated and unified Europe probably has something to do with the fear that it will become German dominated.

The article begins with the situation after 1945 and the road to renewed relations in 1951. It then discusses the minority question, the partnership with the FRG and the relations with the GDR. Finally, it deals with contemporary issues.

2. From no Relations to Normalization of Relations, 1945-1951

When the German occupying forces capitulated on 5 May, 1945, after having occupied Denmark for five years, Danish-German relations were clearly at their lowest point. And although relations were temporarily normalized to the situation prior to the German invasion, they were broken off on 23 May when the German government was captured and the state broke down; politically Germany had ceased to exist. Instead, the Allied powers took over control of Germany, occupied it and instituted military rule. This eventually gave Denmark a new role: as it became part of the Allied occupational regime, Danish troops (the Danish Brigade in Germany with some 4,000 members), after an agreement with the British government from April 1947, assisted British occupying forces in control tasks in the British Zone until 1957. Danish forces operated at first around Oldenburg in the western part and from 1951 at Itzehoe in Holstein. Other Danes were assisting the British occupying forces with postal and telephone censoring in Hamburg.[2]

For more than six years, no official Danish relations existed with Germany. The

---

2 In terms of international law, there existed, as the Danish Foreign Minister Gustav Rasmussen put it on 23 October, 1947 " a state of war between Denmark as one of the Allied powers, and Germany. There is no German central government, and we do not have diplomatic relations with any German authority. Even if the Germans are granted some self-government within limited areas, the fact remains that no German local government or authority exercises any independent state sovereignty" *(Aktstykker II*, 1947: 243, my translation from the Danish).

problems connected with the 250,000 German refugees who had entered Denmark in the winter of 1945 were negotiated with the Western occupying powers. Relations with the German territory were managed by a new Danish military mission, which in 1946 was accredited by the Allied Board of Control in Berlin to the four military governments. From December 1949, after the Federal Republic had been established, they were at the consular level. Of course there still were commercial relations at a lower level, but exchange of goods and trade with German territory had to take place at zone level and according to bilateral agreements with the military governments of the four occupation zones. These relations were indeed restricted until the first commercial treaty with West Germany, in November 1949, opened up for free trade on a limited scale. At the beginning of 1950, the second German state, the GDR, proclaimed that it would not trade with Denmark until it received diplomatic recognition by the Danish government. Consequently, there was practically no trade between Denmark and the GDR until the mid-1950s.

Although a "Germany" was formally and officially non-existent until 1949, followed by two Germanies, of which Denmark recognized only the Federal Republic, Germany existed as a problem, and at least indirectly may be said to have influenced and determined the foreign policy and security policy of Denmark. Even if it did not for the moment constitute a direct security problem, they believed that Germany would in due time reemerge and, thus, continue to constitute a decisive factor and maybe even threat to Denmark, that its political power would survive, and that it again would exert influence on the smaller neighbouring country. And as earlier that meant Danish adaptation, for the moment, to the powers in control of Germany, and also self-restraint on the Danish side; i.e. that Danish politics acted so as to avoid creating irritations or provoking bilateral problems towards the Allied powers or towards a future Germany.

This indeed explains the quick public declaration by the new national government only a few days after the liberation that "the border of Denmark [to Germany] stands firm." For the Danish government there was no border question, and it did not intend to work for an adjustment or revision of the Danish-German border, though it very soon came under heavy pressure for just such a revision from a growing Danish minority south of the border. The Danish government let its wishes be known that the position of the two national minorities at the border be reconsidered (*Aktstykker I-III*, 1947: vol. I, 1; cf. also Noack 1991). This may further explain the rather cautious attitude taken on the question of peace and the future status of Germany. The Danes wanted to be heard at the peace conference on the question of South Schleswig, and in preparation for the Allied conference on the future of Germany, the Danish government on 31 January 1947 put forward its views on the issue. As Germany until 1945 had been a military and political threat to Denmark, the Danish government presented the task as eliminating this threat by, on the one hand creating security against new German aggression and, on the other hand, securing conditions for an economic and social development in Germany such that the German people would be given opportunity and hope of being able to construct the German society on a healthy and lasting democratic basis. (Heurlin 1971: 38ff). As a victim of the most recent German aggression, Denmark had "a special interest in the total disarmament of Germany and in German militarism being permanently extirpated." In order to prevent a new dictatorial power, the government stressed its desires for a decentralised and democratised Germany with special rights for minority groups. It pleaded for an administrative separation of Schleswig from Holstein and maintained that it was up to the people of South Schleswig to decide for themselves on the region's future. However, the Danish government did not propose "any alteration in the status of national allegiance of South Schleswig." The government otherwise failed in its efforts to have the position and the rights of the Danish minority guaranteed by the occupation powers. When the attitude of the Western Powers in the German question changed with the intensified Cold War (1947/48), the minority Danes (i.e. the organisation of the Danish minority) were told to negotiate the question directly with German authorities, i.e., with the local government in the newly constituted state of Schleswig-Holstein.

Danish relations with Germany, or occupied German territory, appeared to be based on the premise that a German state would reemerge and that Germany would again become a major European power with importance for Denmark and its security. The question was, "Which Germany?" And to that end, the Danish government had put forward suggestions in accordance with the politics of the Western allies, stressing Danish desires for an end to threatening German militarism.

Did the Danes expect that the occupying forces and Allied control would succeed in shaping a really liberal and democratic Germany? They took account of the rebuilding of especially Western Germany, they took note of the changes, but the Danish side continued to have doubts (cf. Lammers 1999a). In fact, the minority question would become the clue to Danish-German relations when a Danish mission, in December 1949, was accredited to the new Western German government in Bonn, and Denmark resumed limited bilateral relations with West Germany.

At the outset the new West German government was not permitted to pursue its own foreign policy; that occurred only in March 1951, when the occupational regime was renewed. By June 1951 it was finally time for the reestablishment of diplomatic relations between Denmark and Western Germany. Two years previously Denmark had concluded a first bilateral treaty agreement with Western Germany, which in November 1949 was followed by a new treaty according to which the trade between the two states became practically fully liberalized.

3. The Minority Question and West Germany's entry into NATO

In 1947 Denmark had officially put forward its views on a future Germany, and it was the Danish desire that Germany should be transformed. Danes had profound misgivings about the Germans and their will to accomplish this change (cf. Lammers 1999a). Germany would still constitute a problem for Denmark. Hence, the Danish attitude to the new Germany, the FRG, changed very slowly in the 1950s. Of course, *Realpolitik* and state logic spoke in favour of establishing good terms with the German neighbour. It seemed, however, as if the Danish side was looking for a German gesture in order to fully accomplish this. And they got it.

In this sense, it was indeed a "remarkable fact", as influential commentator Erik Seidenfaden, editor-in-chief of the daily *Information*, put it, that preparations to bring Denmark even into an alliance with Germany, something which would be the consequence of West German participation in the NATO-Alliance, "was met with practically no objection from Danish politicians, something which might be argued to have its motivation in our traditional fear of Germany" (Seidenfaden 1952: 5). As already indicated, the reappraisal of Germany followed the solution of the two great problems in the Danish-German relationship: (1) the question of German rearmament, and (2) the bilateral problem with the Danish minority south of the border. In fact, the minority question, i.e., the question of securing equal civil rights to ethnic Danes, became crucial to the development of the Danish-German relations. It was politically linked to the question of a German defence contribution in the form of membership in NATO. German NATO membership actually became the basis of a solution to the minority problem.[3]

To the Danes, the minority question was at the forefront. Danish scepticism towards the Germans appeared above all in the problems concerning the Danish minority in South Schleswig, i.e. in the attitude of the Germans toward it. As such, the minority question was complicated, not least because the Danish side was not inclined to see it settled according to a treaty. In the view of the Danes, a treaty would give a great power, i.e. Germany, the possibility to interfere in the internal matters of the small power, Denmark. Danish faith in the good will of the Germans was very limited. This is one reason why the Danes tried to have the rights of the Danish minority written into the new occupation statute, but they were unsuccessful because the Allies were now greatly interested in good relations with the Germans. Although the Kiel declaration on the Danish minority, issued by the Schleswig-Holstein Landesregierung on 26 September 1949, was a result of British pressure, the Danish government was highly satisfied with it. Aimed at bringing about a friendly relationship with the Danish people, the Kiel Declaration guaranteed the

---

[3] Cf. the estimation put forward by Gunnar Seidenfaden from the Ministry of Foreign Affairs in his 1966 note in the German peace note: "it was Germany's admission to NATO and perhaps also the realisation on the German side that German territory was not at stake which made the Federal government put an end to the obstinacy of the regional Schlewig-Holstian authorities" (RA UM 5.G. 12a, 1966).

Danish Minority the rights of German citizens without discrimination and declared that "the confession (Bekenntnis) to Danish nationality and culture is free". The declaration was accompanied by a wish for reciprocity on the Danish side (Published in *Aktstykker III*, 1947: 530-534; also in Jäckel 1959). The Danish government, however, was not prepared for such reciprocity, nor for a mutual treaty with West Germany on this issue; however, to its German minority, the Danish government let it be known that the Germans in South Jutland enjoyed the same civil rights as other Danish citizens (cf. Lammers 1993: 137).

The Danish aim was to ensure free cultural and political conditions for fellow Danes south of the border. But, in the early 1950s, it turned out to be rather difficult, as the local government in Schleswig-Holstein did not really live up to its declared intentions and in many ways harassed the Danish minded. Hence, the concrete policies of the local German government annoyed the Danes, it was seen as deliberate harassment, and the aversion towards Germans was very sharp and outspoken. It was formulated in a surprisingly polemic way in 1954 by the Danish Minister for Education Julius Bomholt, who claimed that German democracy would never be the same as the Danish, not even in the question of minorities. "The desire of the Germans to suppress minorities still continues," he said. The difference in the basic attitudes of the Danes and Germans on minority questions was simply too great, as Danes saw it (See Frede Nielsen, chairman of the Schleswig Committee in the Danish Parliament (*Folketinget*); Bomholt also quoted after Lammers 1993: 140). The Danes even appeared to question the political changes which had taken place in the Federal Republic.

Dissatisfaction with the attitude of the regional Schleswig-Holstein government was growing in the Danish parliament, especially concerning the question of the political representation of the Danish minority as a result of the voting barrage imposed by the government, and it eventually led the Danish government into a rather unwilling offensive on the minority question when it was time to discuss the question of West Germany's entry into the NATO in the autumn of 1954 (cf. Lammers 1993: 139).

The matter evoked considerable emotion regarding Denmark's relations with Germany. For obvious reasons, there was a good deal of Danish reservations towards Germany's rearmament, Denmark having made pleas that German militarism be abolished. However, the Cold War and Danish participation in the Western defence alliance, NATO, caused these doubts to recede for other political considerations. In the words of then Foreign Minister Ole Bjørn Kraft: "The participation of Germany in the defence of Europe is one thing, German militarism something else" (quoted from Heurlin 1971: 76). When the Western powers exerted pressure for a German defence contribution, the Danish government, in 1951, made known that on the one hand it was quite natural that "in a country like Denmark, strong doubts should arise against a rearmament of Germany ... on the other hand, the opinion that these doubts have to yield for the opinion that every possibility to strengthen Western Europe and, thus, Denmark has to be used" (Minister of Defence Harald Petersen, quoted from Villaume 1991: 151; cf. Villaume 1995: 221f.). The form of

German rearmament would thus be decisive; it would follow under strict control and be bound up with the NATO defense alliance and not be seen as a signal of a renewed militarism. Federal Germany would take part in the common defence system: "The present plans entail guarantees against German wars of aggression and against German militarism", as it was later argued (Foreign minister H.C. Hansen in the Folketing 17 February 1954, quoted from Heurlin 1971: 84). And a rearmed Federal Germany was more convenient for Danes within NATO than within the EDC in which Denmark had no part.

Hence, a vast majority of the Danish Parliament voted in favour of NATO membership for the FRG. Minister of Foreign Affairs H.C. Hansen explained that Danes' emotions were against it, but reason spoke for German membership and the Germans would come under control. As a consequence of the altered power relations, small powers had to adjust to the fact that the former potential enemy to the south (Germany) had become the necessary ally against the East (the Soviet Union), as NATO would bring Denmark into a multilateral alliance with Germany (Villaume 1995: 157). This new situation was also acknowledged by Danish public opinion. The afore mentioned commentator Erik Seidenfaden, noted the uniqueness of Denmark's recommendation of German NATO membership. For Seidenfaden it indicated that "aspects of the Danish-German relations which are combined with the years 1864 (the loss of Schleswig-Holstein) and 1940 (the German Occupation), no longer have a decisive influence on our relationship with Germany" (Villaume 1995: 5). The reasons behind this historic break were justified by national defence: "The anti-German feelings and resentments are not so strongly represented in Parliament that they could overrule the other considerations which were in favour of the new alliance with Germany" (Villaume 1995: 6). Seidenfaden sounded optimistic, but did Denmark's entry into an alliance with Germany also change overall Danish opinions of Germany?

German membership in NATO could thus indeed be regarded as a form of "tying down" Germany and the German problem. On the question of German rearmament and NATO-membership the Danish attitude, with the French, was apparently determined by selfish national interests. But did Denmark actually have the choice to veto German participation in NATO? Evidently not. For the Danes, however, the decisive factor had not been what had happened in and with Germany, but purely military-strategic und security considerations, which were the result of the positively viewed "tying down" of the Federal Republic and of the German contribution to the defence of Denmark. The positive Danish attitude also opened the road toward closer cooperation with the Federal Republic. The means accomplishing this goal was a reasonable solution to the minority-question in the Danish-German border region.

At a NATO conference held in Paris in October 1954, the Danish Foreign Minister H.C. Hansen linked the problem of the rights of a minority to the ideals of human rights. Thus, the nature in which a minority was treated might easily become the character of a symbol, and in fact a symbol of the kind of future cooperation which the Danes wanted and would like to see (Fink 1968: 121).

West German Chancellor Konrad Adenauer at once grasped the political impact of the problem, showing a willingness to make concessions. He proposed new negotiations, which finally resulted in the unique Bonn-Copenhagen declarations from 29 March 1955, by which the two governments respectively committed themselves ensuring rights to their minorities. The new Federal Germany had indeed made the symbolic gesture.

4. Bilateral Danish-German Relationship seen in the Light of the Bonn-Copenhagen Declarations

The symbolic importance of the mutual declarations was that they regulated the minority question according to the Danish desires; in the way of a treaty, from the Danish point of view, the great power (Germany) would be allowed to intervene in the internal affairs of the small power (Denmark). The two almost identical statements committed the respective government to respect the cultural and political rights of their respective minority populations (cf. Fink 1968: 120; Lammers 1995: 141). For the Danes, it was of great importance that the outcome took the form of this quite informal settlement. It was interpreted as a new and decidedly positive signal from Germany. The settlement thus not only reflected good will on part of the Germans, but showed that on the minority question the Germans now followed the liberal and democratic notion that minority and nationality were a question of sentiment, i.e. a question of one's own disposition and wishes. And it was officially considered as "epoch-making for the development of the borderland, which had formed itself in harmony and had contributed essentially to the good Danish-German relationship."[4] Hence, the minorities could actually play a role as cultural and political bridges between the two nations.

The settlement has since then functioned very well, both parties having demonstrated good will in words and in practice. As desired by the Danish part, the treatment of both minorities became a symbol of the new cooperation between Denmark and the Federal Republic, which found its organizational form within the NATO alliance. A new spirit had apparently infused Danish-German relations.

5. Bilateral Relations and the Danish-German Partnership in NATO

As a direct result of the minority-agreement and the new partnership in NATO, the Federal Republic gradually became Denmark's most important international partner. This was evident in the economic and military spheres, but it also increasingly applied to politics in general.

---

4 Aide-memoire for Danish Prime Minister Jens Otto Krag for his talks with German Foreign Minister Willy Brandt 18 April 1967, (RA UM 5.G. 12a [5.D. 29.a]).

In the economic and commercial area, the Federal Republic gained in importance as trading partner, and bilateral trade grew steadily: in 1960 the Federal Republic became the major source of Danish imports (20%) for the first time exceeding imports from the UK. It was not until 1977 that Danish exports to the Federal Republic (15.2%) also exceeded those of the UK (cf. *Statistisk tiårs oversigt*, 1967 and 1978). Whereas Danish application for membership in the new European Economic Community was at first (in 1961) argued using the importance of the UK for Danish economy and foreign trade, by 1972, when Denmark had finally been accepted, West Germany had become more important to the Danish economy.

Although Denmark had been a military and political ally of West Germany since 1955, military cooperation did not follow without some difficulties (cf. Poul Villaume 1991). Above all these difficulties were grounded in political and psychological factors. For the Danish public and many politicians, it was difficult to accept close military cooperation, not to speak of German troops on Danish soil only ten years after the German occupation. But of course, cooperation on NATO's northern tier was necessary, and it was eventually carried out with the establishment of the Baltic Approaches Command (BALTAP) of NATO, in 1962, which linked together the defence of Denmark, Schleswig-Holstein and Hamburg within NATO framework. Danish and German troops were placed under the same command – by Danish request British and American officers also took part – and in spite of loud public protests from the Danes, German troops took part in manoeuvres first in Jutland and later in all of Denmark. Danish-German military cooperation is generally considered to be very efficient and harmonious, despite differences of opinion on questions such as the deployment of new NATO rockets in the 1980s and on the role of the WEU.

In politics generally, the Danish-German relationship and partnership, has expanded in a surprising harmonious way and to the satisfaction of both sides, since 1955 and especially since 1960. Where the Germans could speak of friendship, the Danes could choose to talk of partnership. The various Danish governments were cautious not to cause problems with the Federal Republic, and criticism was kept mostly subdued. It was also reassuring that the United States "substantially are the security for the small Western powers in their relations with West Germany" which also indicated mistrust in Federal Germany (30 March 1966, RA UM 5.G. 12a.). This mistrust appeared when Prime Minister Jens Otto Krag officially welcomed the German peace note from the 25 March 1966; in internal deliberations, however Krag's appreciation was combined with slight criticism of German inflexibility towards Eastern Europe which hampered the process of deténte in Europe. In a first analysis of the German note, Gunnar Seidenfaden viewed it as an indication of Germany's realization that "motion was necessary in German politics" (30 March 1966, RA UM 5.G. 12a).[5] Seidenfaden welcomed the initiative as an expression of

---

5   A year later, Foreign Minister Per Hækkerup told the Folketing that Danish commitments to NATO "do not prevent us from recognizing the Oder-Neisse-border if we found it correct", (quoted from note for the Foreign Ministers visit to Bonn (7 December 1967, RA UM 5.G. 12a). But political considerations towards the FRG prevented such recognition.

German insight that "the up till now rigid German policies had not been fruitful, but on the contrary had rendered prospects for solution to the outstanding questions difficult and thus had to be substituted by movement" (30 March 1966, RA UM 5.G. 12a). Pointing to the German attitude on the German-Polish border question, he noted that "one can see that the German government still seems to live in the delusion that German recognition of the Oder-Neisse is an object of negotiation for which it can reckon on a Polish *quid pro quo*" (30 March 1966, RA UM 5.G. 12a). Germany's "friends" ought to let it be understood that this was not a productive strategy. When in 1966 Denmark installed a new ambassador in Bonn, he was eager to reiterate to the West German government that neither Denmark nor other partners would be tempted to undermine Germany's interests by seeking an agreement with the Soviet Union, something which the German side seemed to fear. The ambassador added that the Danish government still held the opinion that "German unification was the essential condition for the stabilisation of relations in Europe, and that it had to be fulfilled on the basis of self-determination."[6]

One should bear in mind that the rather reserved Danish attitude was still determined by the situation and attitude of Denmark as a small power in comparison with the Federal Republic, the result being a certain degree of dependence and adaptation to the Federal Republic. Officially, this entailed a cautious adaptation to Germany, if possible on a multilateral level, as well as support for the position of the Federal Republic on matters such as recognition of the GDR and the Oder-Neisse line. In this respect, the political change of 1969, with the installation of the social-liberal Brandt coalition government, proved to be of major importance. The new government displayed much greater flexibility especially in its *Ostpolitik* providing Denmark and other states with greater freedom of action towards the Eastern European states. Danish-German relations relaxed and even improved.

Unofficially, however, there was a greater distance between the two countries. One might illustrate this double-bind by Danish policies towards the second German state, the GDR, and in the Danish attitude to the German national question and the German "Zweistaatlichkeit" (two-statehood) (cf. on this question Säter 1984; 1988; Lammers 1995; 1999b).

6. Denmark, the GDR and the German Question

On the German national question, the Danish attitude was firm, and Denmark seemed more papist than the pope.[7] In the early 1950s Denmark had recognized the Federal Republic in the West as Germany, thereby rejecting all efforts by the GDR

---

6 The Danish ambassador K. Knuth-Winterfeldt (15 July 1966, RA UM 5.D. 45 [5.G. 12a]). The same attitude was shown when Denmark following a German request, gave its approval to the so-called "peace note" of the Federal government (25 March 1966, RA UM 5.G. 12a).
7 Or in the words of Nils Svenningsen: "Plus royalist que le roi" (RA UM 141.D. 1b).

to achieve recognition. Through its adherence to the October 1954 NATO declaration, Denmark had committed herself to support German reunification on West German terms and to the claim of the Federal Republic as the sole representative of Germany (Alleinvertretungsrecht); Denmark thus committed itself to not recognizing the GDR.[8] Its attitude was similar to other West European states, but the Danish stand was admittedly "in a not insignificant degree influenced by the wish to preserve good relations with West Germany."[9] The Danish stand was delicate as the relation between Denmark and East Germany was a cause of tension with West Germany:

> "While we are strictly complying with our obligation to non-recognition of the German regime in East Germany, the necessity of certain relations with East German territory adjoining us from time to time gives rise to a practice in this relation, which goes further than the West German side may wish. As long as this question can be treated with caution and with substantial consideration to the interests and views of West Germany, it will not constitute a serious difficulty for Danish-German relations."
> (Memorandum 8 March 1960 *Nogle bemærkninger fra P.J.I. om vort forhold til Tyskland*, RA UM 5.D. 29.a)[10]

The Danish government eventually gave its support to the Hallstein doctrine, even though it acknowledged that its one-state-theory caused some irritation in practice.[11]

This attitude implied that there would not exist official relations with the GDR unless the Federal Republic changed its policy towards the GDR and established bilateral state-relations with it. The Danish stand on its policy of non-recognition was firm, as Willy Brandt learned in 1967, when he visited Copenhagen. However, the non-recognition policy caused some inconvenience: In his note to Krag, Gunnar Seidenfaden noted:

---

8 "Since the admittance of the Federal Republic to the NATO 1955 the Danish side has adhered to the opinion that the Federal Government is the only free and legally formed German government and, thus, the only one authorised to speak in the name of the entire German people".(Note for the visit of the Danish Prime and Foreign Minister in West Germany, 3 March 1965, RA UM 5.G. 12a).

9 Memorandum 8 March 1960 *Nogle bemærkninger fra P.J.I. om vort forhold til Tyskland*, RA UM 5.D.29.a.

10 The problem was that Denmark was one of the only NATO states maintaining practical relations with the GDR: in the form of a rail link to Berlin the Gedser-Warnemünde ferry, (cf. Lammers 1999b: note 33).

11 This is obvious from an confidential note "Orientering om Hallstein-doktrinen" (UM PJI 28 May 1965). "Though the Hallstein doctrine can not be said to cause Danish foreign policy – i.e. its relations with the Eastern countries – special difficulties nor to hamper a not inconsiderable trade connnections with the GDR, it must be remarked that the single state theory which it has to defend gives rise to considerable irritation in connection with the entry of East German citizens into Denmark", (RA UM 5.G. 12a).

"In consequence of its geographically determined close relation to East Germany, [Denmark being the only other NATO country besides West Germany to bordering GDR] and in light of the general tendency of deténte, it is increasingly difficult, however, for the Danish public to accept the narrow limits for communication with East Germany which the policy of non-recognition imposes, not least within the formulation it has obtained within the NATO alliance."

(*Notat*, 18 April 1967, RA UM 5.G. 12a).

The Danish grievance focussed especially on travel limitations (the "TTD arrangement"), which Denmark wanted eased.[12] The Danish attitude was put firmly by Per Hækkerup in 1967, when he stressed the commitment not to recognize the GDR:

"The other side of the problem is if a general recognition of East Germany would be useful to the definitive solution of the political and security problems in Europe. Personally I don't think so. Rather, such a recognition would contribute to freezing the actual division of Germany, whose termination, of course, must be the necessary and essential part of the ultimate solution."

(*Notat*, 7 December 1967, RA UM 5.G. 12a)

The Danish attitude thus seemed firm, although Denmark did not actively engage itself in the German question. According to the Norwegian political scientist Martin Sæter, for Denmark as with the other Scandinavian NATO members, the German question was defined as

"part of the alliance policy, which did not allow a solo trip. This policy included reunification. But to engage themselves actively for it was not a priority for these countries. Rather, they had to come to terms with a policy of status quo and of partitition."

(Sæter 1984: 4)

Consequently Denmark upheld normal and good neighbourly relationships with the Federal Republic, not, however, with the socialist GDR. Nevertheless, there existed and also developed certain relations in non-political areas, such as the cultural and economic fields.

Though Danish verbal support for unification, to which Denmark had committed itself, remained, there seemed to exist an unarticulated satisfaction with the division of Germany. Whether Denmark, like some other Scandinavian countries (especially Finland), actually participated in a process of reevaluating the GDR, as Sæter claims, seems unlikely at least as concerns the official Denmark. It also seems illogical because Denmark, after many years of strain and troubles, had normalized and intensified its relations with Federal Germany in a neighbourly fashion and had no interest in risking this relationship. On the contrary, Denmark followed a very cautious line on questions which might trouble the Federal Repub-

---

12 TTD means "Temporary Travel Documents."

lic, and it was keen not to arouse German anxieties around issues such as the question of recognition of the GDR and the Oder-Neisse line.[13] The Krag-Hækkerup government, to the satisfaction of the FRG, was a strong spokesman for West German views in its relations with the East European countries.[14] As part of the policy of détente, following the modification of the Hallstein doctrine in 1967 when FRG renewed its diplomatic relations with Yugoslavia, the Danish government on behalf of the FRG, which had no diplomatic relations with Finland, told the Finnish government not to draw any wrong conclusions from the new Federal German policy by, for instance, recognizing German partition or establishing diplomatic relations with the GDR (Paul Fischer, 1 February 1967, RA UM 5.G. 12a). Unofficially, there might exist an interest in that direction, i.e., as suggested by some of the trade unions who had closer connections with East German counterparts. Some leaders did in fact engage themselves in working for recognition. The question was discussed in political parties, too. The centrist Radical Liberal Part voted at its 1966 national congress for diplomatic recognition of the GDR. In the wake of the congress, one of the best informed Danish commentators on German affairs, Adolf Rastén, spoke out in favour of recognition. Having criticized the Danish discussion on Germany for having been too much influenced by the official cautiousness, he claimed that a "wrong and absurd West German policy does not become more correct and reasonable by being protected and encouraged by Danish preservation regulations." In his opinion "West Germany [had] no greater moral right to exist as a state than East Germany." It was time for Denmark to break free of the noose made up by the claimed "sole-representation", with which Danish politics had bound itself (Rasten 1966). Although this aspect has not been investigated further, it seems as if the picture of the GDR was surely more positive in Denmark than in the FRG, even though the GDR was not at all so well known. All in all, it might be argued that the picture of the GDR in Denmark was not thoroughly negative. Many unofficial contacts existed, and a great many Danes had personal experiences with and contacts to the GDR. The Danes certainly did not love the GDR, but in the matter of state logic they were somehow fond of it. The existence of the GDR could be seen as a weakening of the "great" Germany and thereby a way of dealing with the German problem.

The Danes' perspective of a small power and their view of the GDR might explain why the treaties with socialist Eastern Europe (the Ostpolitik) at the begin-

---

13 When the Danish Social Democratic party, at its conference in 1969, discussed the Oder-Neisse line and recognition of the GDR, the Federal criticism was characterized as of "greater severity" in the report from Bonn. The German side was "betrübt" over the way in which Danes intended to make demands on the FRG on questions of central and vital importance for Germany's future. It was not seen as in accordance with "normal international politeness" to put such demands to an allied country. (H. Haxthausen on a conversation with Sahm from the German Foreign Ministry 24 June 1969, RA UM 5.G. 12a; on this question generally, see also Lammers 1999b: note 33).

14 Cf. reports on Federal commentary of speeches made by Krag and Hækkerup in Warsaw and Moscow, 1965/66, RA UM 5.D. 29.a.

ning of the 1970s and hence, the "Europeanization" of the German question on the basis of status quo in Europe, was interpreted in a somehow paradoxical way. "Europeanization" was not regarded as the beginning of a process to resolve the German question, but, rather, as its final liquidation. The German question seemed solved through division, and the German "two-statehood" fitted in a divided Europe Denmark quite well though apparently not officially (cf. Sæter 1984: 4f.; see also Petersen 1992: 37f.). Thus, Denmark strongly supported the normalization of the German question on the basis of the status quo which appeared at the beginning of the 1970s, and Denmark soon followed the Federal Republic in establishing diplomatic relations with the GDR in January 1973 and in fully normalizing interstate connections with it. This was especially true in the economic sphere, as bilateral trade was steadily growing. Despite of continued official verbal support for the West German claim for unification and for the role of unification in a European security arrangement, the German question was considered solved in what seemed the best possible way under the existing circumstances. Does that mean that after 1973 no one in Denmark expected the unification of Germany and that few continued to desire it, as Nikolaj Petersen has recently claimed (Petersen 1994: 4)? Probably not.

During the Cold War, no one expected that the situation would ever change fundamentally. The Cold War might get more and more "normalized" and, thus, lead to détente in Europe, such as was formalized in the 1975 Helsinki accords, but few imagined the Cold War standoff would ever disappear. Yet this is what would happen by the end of the 1980s.

7. Denmark, Germany and Europe

Where the Danish side saw NATO as a means of controlling Germany, the situation apparently appeared differently with the organisations for European cooperation. The organisation of a new Europe, which had been proceeding, had been envisaged by its spokesmen to deal with the German problem. The organisations sought primarily to bind or integrate Germany. It is doubtful whether the Danes had a similar view. When the Danes considered joining the evolving Western European organisations, the new European structures which included the FRG were already developing politically and institutionally. Western European states sought to treat the German problem through supranational organisations aimed especially at integrating Germany as a way of controlling it. As in the case of NATO, the topic of European economic cooperation and integration evidently had a political function in regard to Germany. West Germany's participation in the supranational coal and steel organisation, the ECSC, in 1951, and later on in the EEC (the "Six"), was thus seen by Western European countries as a means controlling the German problem via control over its economy, while European integration generally was presented as a means of coping with Europe's traditional problem: a Germany which was too big, too strong and too dominating (Herbst et. al. 1990).

Initially, it looks as if the process of European integration was seen differently in Denmark. Relations with Europe seemed marked by the fear of Germany. Danes therefore opposed the idea of Europe because its realisation would mean that Germans would-be free to settle in Denmark. When Danish participation in the ECSC was considered, it seems as if one motive against it consisted of Danish fears that Germany would dominate integration and that integration would thus become a vehicle for a new German hegemony: "The possibility is obvious that a development in that direction [the building of a 'small Europe'] would constitute a short cut to a 'Viertes Reich', a by Western Germany dominated Western European 'Grossraum'"(Erling Kristiansen from the Economic-Political Department of the Danish Foreign Ministry 1952, quoted from Branner 1992: 51; cf. Branner 1995: 122f.). Some scholars have argued that Danish decision-makers – unlike those from Germany's other neighbouring states – saw the German ghost behind integration and feared that they would become absorbed by Germany instead of helping to bind it through cooperation (Branner 1992: 51).

The Danish wish for participation in the plans for an economic cooperation between "the Six" – visible at the end of the 1950s – was argued primarily in terms of economics and trade, as the participating FRG was an important market for Danish agricultural export. However, can this be understood without the above mentioned German perspective, which was a dimension of economic cooperation? It seems as if the Danes overlooked this, especially when – to the surprise of the Danes – it turned out that the economic cooperation might result in integrating the participant countries and Europe. Although economic and commercial in its primary ends, the EEC as well as the ECSC and the EURATOM entailed above all political integration of Germany and the German economy. All these means were indeed envisaged to deal with the problem of Germany, as we know from spokesmen for European integration (cf. Herbst 1989). It remains to be seen if European integration was viewed that way by the Danes. Probably not, even if Germany also constituted a problem for Denmark. Thus, it seems as if relations with Germany played a preponderant role in Danish public life when the question of membership was discussed at the beginning of the 1960s. Again, historically determined feelings seem to be at the forefront among those arguing against Danish membership (cf. Frandsen 1994: 204ff.).

The question, furthermore, is how Germany affected Danish wishes for admission and if and how it in fact influenced Danish politics towards Europe and closer European cooperation. Danish viewpoints seemed to differ on this issue. While Western Europeans generally saw economic, military and political integration as a way to control Germany and, thus, solve the German problem, Danes at first saw integration as a vehicle for German dominance and control over Europe. Integration, which in fact had its spokesmen in the FRG, was viewed as primarily a German project. This view is still held by many Danish politicians and even scholars (cf. Bjerregaard 1992; Petersen 1995: 96ff.).

However, we also find other estimates. When commenting on the new Federal

Ostpolitik, which strengthened the position of the FRG, the Danish chargé d'affaires in Bonn, Peter Michaelsen, claimed that "beside NATO, Danish membership in the EC would – apart from the economic consequences – be desirable in order better to balance our mutual relations". (*Letter to Troels Fink*, 31 August 1972, RA UM 5.G. 12a.). This standpoint is not that far away from conceptions held by European federalists in the 1950s.

Was the EEC and later the EU a multilaterilisation of the German problem or a means to German domination in Europe? In fact, the political aspects of European cooperation and supranational integration – with the Left and Danish nationalists expected – played a less obvious and less significant role when Denmark again applied for membership in 1972 and eventually joined the EC in 1973. These concerns were not of major importance in the arguments brought forward in favour of joining. There may have been tactical reasons because the membership had to be submitted to a referendum, as the politicians knew of the Danes' sceptical attitude towards deeper integration.

As it turned out, since 1973 Denmark has come politically close to the German position in most community matters and eventually cooperated closely with the FRG on most of the practical issues which occupied the EC member states. However, they differed on basic matters, above all with regard to the political and institutional perspectives on the EC. Whereas Denmark favoured enlargement of the EC, i.e. organisation in breadth, the FRG stood for depth and further integration. While Denmark viewed the EC as an interstate and market cooperation and was hesitant towards the deepening of European cooperation, the FRG looked to the EC as a first step towards a political union or integrated Europe. A framework in which European countries might join forces, conflicted politically with the fact that Germany could play a greater and even more determining role. This is already true of the FRG as with the Bundesbank. This became evident when West Germany, together with France in the mid-1980s assumed a leading role in developing the Community. The result was the Maastricht Treaty, which Germans did not feel went far enough, while it put Danish politicians into major difficulties when the Danes voted "No". As it turned out, it was actually Germany that promoted, if not dictated, the terms for the next step, the European Monetary Union (EMU).

It is highly probable that Danish fears that the European Union will be nothing more than a vehicle for renewed German dominance in Europe will cause the Danes to oppose a united Europe and intensified integration. Clearly little progress is made neither economically, institutionally nor politically if it goes against the wishes of Germany. There are many indications in this direction; however, the question is whether it remains a problem of their own or whether it reflects the actual course of development towards an integrated Europe. When German Chancellor Helmut Kohl explains that their openness towards European integration does not imply a German-dominated Europe, but on the contrary a Europeanised Germany as final goal, what many Danes fear is precisely that an integrated and unified Europe will necessarily become a German-dominated Europe.

8. Denmark, the Collapse of the GDR and the Unification of Germany

In the autumn of 1989, the German national question, came back on the international agenda, to the great surprise of most Danes (cf. Petersen 1992: 38f). After the East German revolution its solution from the beginning of 1990 was outlined with reunification and incorporation of the GDR, something which certainly did not happen without some uncertainty. Politically, it was impossible not to applaud it, as Denmark had always officially supported the Federal Republic in its demand for reunification. However Denmark, like so many other countries, had not believed that it would ever become reality. In public one might at first notice some reservations even with Danish politicians. Prime Minister Poul Schlüter who, at the beginning of 1989, was the first Danish prime minister to have visited the GDR, was reported to have said that German re-unification was fundamentally not in Denmark's interest, because the unification of Germany necessarily ignited a certain historical fear of a big and strong Germany; it was therefore decisive, Schlüter is said to have opined, that the process of reunification follows an understanding with Germany's neighbours and in a European context (Quoted after Petersen, 1991: 115). It is more likely that this was the personal opinion of the Prime Minister, which he shared with parts of Danish public opinion. Officially, it was emphasized that Denmark welcomed reunification, as it had always supported the stand of the Federal Republic (Foreign Minister Uffe Ellemann-Jensen, February 1990, quoted in Petersen 1992: 38).

The Germany which evolved with reunification was indeed a big and powerful one in regard to territory, population and economy. The decisive questions point for Danish decision-makers, of course, were whether German reunification would have repercussions on Denmark's position towards Germany, whether it would change Danish-German relations, and whether reunification would alter Germany's international position and engagements. The official attitude became more relaxed as it appeared that the reunification would lead to no changes in German domestic, foreign and European policies. The problem that arose for Denmark was again the problem of foreign policy and alliance: would the new Germany continue the course in foreign and alliance politics which the Federal Republic had followed? For Denmark, it turned out to be the case, and the foundations of foreign policy remained unchanged. Consequently, Denmark appeared reassured over the course and results of the popular revolution in the GDR: the reunification which made possible the integration of the GDR to the Federal Republic. Danish relations with the enlarged Federal Republic remained unchanged und untroubled and in the economic field became even closer, as Denmark would actually profit from reconstruction going on in the former GDR.

Unofficially, however, many Danes seemed to be much more uncertain. In public people spoke of a new "Grossdeutschland", and the opinion was heard that Germany had again become too big for Europe and for Denmark.

9. Conclusion: Denmark and its German Problem. German Problem or Danish Problem?

Since 1945 Germany's position in Danish foreign policy has changed, as relations with the German neighbour have changed. Surely, Germany, as earlier, continues to constitute a problem for Denmark, even after 1990, and is still a primary determinant of Danish foreign policy and even of Danish European policy (cf. Bjerregaard 1992: note 5). Nevertheless, in a world which has changed dramatically since the end of the Cold War, Danish-German relations are quite different from what they were in the 1950s. Germany is no longer a traditional Great Power and it constitutes no military and security threat. It remains, of course, a political and psychological problem, and it has reappeared as a problem in Danish attitudes to Europe. Hence, Germany remains an essential determinant of Danish foreign policy, even if Denmark's relations with a Europe have multilateralised the Danish-German relationship.

The explanations for Germany's continuing dominance are obvious. The German question cannot be said to have been definitive solved with reunification in 1990, because there still is a German problem in international politics: what role and how much say should Germany have in Europe? The new Germany is strong industrially, economically and financially. In direct and indirect ways, it has decisive influence on European affairs, even if politically and militarily, it seems as if the Federal Republic intentionally tries to underplay its power and weight, also in order not to rekindle the fears among its European neighbours. At its core, the German problem consists of whether *Status quo* will remain: will Germany continue to behave in a restrained way as before, will it return to traditional nationalistic German power politics, will it hegemonize European politics in the new European institutions? Or, will the project of European integration (European unification as Germans name it) fundamentally make the nation-state less problematic, or even neutralize it? For the moment, there are no indications on the part of the Germans that they want to play a role as traditional Great Power as did Germany until 1945. This view is also recognized in Denmark and in Danish politics. Yet Germany is a very powerful and influential force in European affairs. It has a determining voice on European developments, and no EU development is conceivable against the wishes of Germany.

Although there does exist no outstanding bilateral problems between Denmark and Germany, the notion "Germany as problem" continues to play a great if indirect role in Danish politics. Denmark not only has Germany as its most important international partner, it is also in many fields – economically, financially and politically, though not militarily – extremely dependent on Germany. German politics in the economic and financial field has repercussions in Denmark, and Danish fears of ending up as a province or as a northern Bundesland should not be underestimated. Such fears do not necessarily have much to do with today's Germany. It is a Danish problem and much more closely connected with Danish feelings of inferiority toward the efficient Germans.

Literature

Branner, Hans (1995): "Denmark and the European Coal and Steel Community, 1950-1953" in Thorsten B. Olesen (ed.) *Interdependence Versus Integration. Denmark, Scandinavia and Western Europe 1945-1990*, Odense.

Branner, Hans (1993): "På vagt eller på spring? Danmark og Europæisk integration 1948-1953", in Birgit Nüchel Thomsen (ed.): *The Odd Man Out? Danmark og den europæiske integration 1948-1992*, Odense.

Bjerregaard, Ritt (1992): *Danmark i forandring*, Copenhagen.

Bührer, Werner; Ludolf Herbst and Hanno Sowade (1990), *Vom Marshallplan zur EWG. Die Eingliederung der Bundesrepublik Deutschland in die westliche Welt*, München.

Fink, Troels (1968): *Deutschland als Problem Dänemarks*, Flensburg.

Frandsen, Steen Bo (1994): *Dänemark – der kleine Nachbar im Norden. Aspekte der deutsch-dänischen Beziehungen im 19. und 20. Jahrhundert*, Darmstadt.

Herbst, Ludolf et al. (1989): *Option für den Westen*, München.

Heurlin, Bertel (1971): *Danmarks udenrigspolitik efter 1945*, Copenhagen.

Hækkerup, Per (1965): *Danmarks udenrigspolitik*, Copenhagen.

Jäckel, Eberhard (ed.) (1959): *Die Schleswigfrage nach 1945*, Frankfurt/M.

Lammers, Karl Christian (forthcomming): *Deutschland als Problem Dänemarks. Die dänisch-deutschen Beziehungen vom Krieg 1864 bis zur Partnerschaft in der NATO und der EU*, Mainz.

Lammers, Karl Christian (1999a): "Das Deutschlandbild in Dänemark und die Entwicklung der politischen Beziehungen zu den beiden deutschen Staaten" in Robert Bohn (ed.), *Die Deutsch-Skandinavischen Beziehungen nach 1945*, Wiesbaden.

Lammers, Karl Christian (1999b): "Die Beziehungen der skandinavischen Staaten zur DDR bis zur Normalisierung in den siebziger Jahren" in Heiner Timmermann (ed.), *Die DDR – Politik und Ideologie als Instrument*, Berlin.

Lammers, Karl Christian (1998): "Danmark og Tysklandsspørgsmålet. Hovedlinier i dansk Tysklandspolitik fra 1945 til ca. 1973" in H. Dethlefsen and H. Lundbak (eds.), *Fra mellemkrigstid til efterkrigstid*, Copenhagen.

Lammers, Karl Christian (1995): *Die DDR aus skandinavischer Sicht, Potsdamer Bulletin für zeithistorische Studien 5*, 1995, p. 3-14.

Lammers, Karl Christian (1993): "Nationale Minderheiten im friedlichen Zusammenleben. Die Bonn-Kopenhagen-Erklärungen vom 29. März 1955" in *Revue d'Allemagne et des pays de langue allemande*, XXV, 1993.

Noack, Johan Peter (1991): *Det sydslesvigske grænsespørgsmål 1945-1947*, Åbenrå.

Pedersen, Thomas (1995): "Den europæiske intergration" in *Danmark efter den kolde krig*, Copenhagen: SNU.

Petersen, Nikolaj (1991): *Tysklands enhed*, Copenhagen.

Petersen, Nikolaj (1992): "Danmark og det nye Tyskland", *Politica*, vol. 24, 1992, pp. 33-50.

Petersen, Nikolaj (1994): *Denmark and the New Germany: Cooperation or Adaption?*, University of Aarhus: Department of Political Science.

Rastén, Adolph (1966): "Det vesttyske reb om dansk politik", *Politiken*, 30 June.

Seidenfaden, Erik (1952) "Vesttyskland, Atlantpagten og Danmark", *Fremtiden* 8,1, 1952.

Säter, Martin (1984): *Die Deutschlandfrage aus Skandinavischer Sicht*, Oslo.

Sæter, Martin (1978): "Nordeuropa" in H.-A. Jacobsen (ed.), *Drei Jahrzehnte Aussenpolitik der DDR*, München, p. 501-512.
Villaume, Poul (1991): "Mulig fjende – nødvendig allieret? Vesttysklands rolle i udformningen af dansk forsvars – og sikkerhedspolitik 1950-1961" in Carsten Due-Nielsen et al (eds.), *Danmark, Norden og NATO 1948-1962*, Copenhagen.
Villaume, Poul (1995): *Allieret med forbehold*, Copenhagen.
Øhrgaard, Per (1990): "Offizielle Anpassung und inoffizielle Distanz – das Verhältnis Dänemarks zu Deutschland in den letzten 150 Jahren" in Per Øhrgaard (ed.), *Die Bundesrepublik Deutschland in der heutigen Welt 1989*, Copenhagen.

Files from the Ministery of Foreign Affairs:

Memorandum, Nogle bemærkninger fra P.J.I. om vort forhold til Tyskland, 8 March 1960 RA UM 5.D.29.a.
Note "Orientering om Hallstein-doktrinen", UM, PJI, 28 May 1965.
Note "for the visit of the Danish Prime and Foreign Minister in West Germany", 3 June 1965, RA, UM, 5.G. 12a.
Reports on Federal commentary of speeches made by Krag and Hækkerup in Warsaw and Moscow, 1965/66, RA UM 5.D. 29.a.
German Peace note, 25 March 1966, RA UM 5.G. 12a.
Note on german peacenote, 30 March 1966, RA UM 5.G.12a.
The Danish ambassador K. Knuth-Winterfeldt, 15 July 1966, RA UM 5.D.45 (5.G. 12a).
Paul Fischer, February 1, 1967, RA UM 5.G.12a.
Note, 18 April 1967, RA UM 5.G.12a.
Note, 7 December 1967, RA UM 5.G.12a.
Note for the Foreign Ministers visit to Bonn, December 7, 1967, RA UM 5.G.12a.
H. Haxthausen on a conversation with Sahm from the German Foreign Ministry 24 June 1969, RA UM 5.G.12a.
Letter to Troels Fink, 31 August 1972, RA UM 5.G.12a.
RA UM 141.D.1b.

Other Sources:

Statistisk tiårsoversigt 1967 and *1978*, (Copenhagen, 1967, 1978).
Aktstykker vedrørende det sydslesvigske spørgsmål, I-III, vol. I, Copenhagen 1947.
Folketingstidende 1964/65, Sp. 6307.

CHAPTER 9

The Interplay Between Mass and Elite Attitudes to European Integration in Denmark

Ulf Hedetoft

1. Introduction

This article addresses the question of how the relationship between the Danish masses and the Danish elites has affected and been affected by Danish membership of the EU and by the process of deepening European integration. It will be argued that a typically Danish political culture tying elites to masses within a framework of consensuality, homogeneous identity, and middle-of-the-road politics has provided both the interpretive prism for approaching and understanding European integration in "minimalist", pragmatic terms, and has supplied a number of instruments with which to regulate Danish membership in the EU (notably the referendum). It will further be argued that this framework has increasingly been perceived to be jeopardised by the deepening of European integration, which increasing numbers of Danes now see as impinging on their national identity and on the cultural symbolics of national sovereignty. Consequently, a gap between elites and masses has been exposed and exacerbated by EU integration. However, recent developments have also shown that such a gap has been accompanied by a new type of consensus, i.e. that Danish membership of the EU is by now regarded as a "given" by almost the entire Danish population. Disagreements – which are not confined to the cleavage between elites and masses, but also follow other sociological trajectories – now hinge on the question of how the EU should develop in the future: should it be through widening or deepening? should the EU evolve towards interstate cooperation or a federal European state-like structure?

   The argument will concentrate, first, on presenting the conceptual outline of these configurations of identity, politics and culture (sections 2 and 3). It then moves on to discuss the historical factors crucial to an understanding of the Danish mass-elite nexus, focussing particularly on the period beginning in the early 1970s (section 4). It subsequently highlights the most important issues and arguments in the Danish debate (section 5). And it concludes with a summary of the key issues (section 6).

2. Setting the Stage

Initially, two basic theoretical points need to be made about the mass-elite nexus in Denmark.

The first is that both in terms of Danish national identity and Danish political culture, and both as regards discourse and social practice, the gap between masses and elites is relatively narrow.[1] In this context, this is significant as an indication of the social, ideological and political aspiration of both the masses (whether as private citizens, employees, retirees, electors, sports crowds, grass-roots movements, or the man-in-the-street interviewed by pollsters) and the elites (politicians, intellectuals, top civil servants, the industrial middle classes, and opinion-leaders). This relative unity manifests itself, inter alia, in the Danish form of popular democracy ("folkestyre"); in the Danish popular "ideology" known as the "Law of Jante", a peculiar culture of minimalist equality; and in the colloquial way in which Danes consistently choose to address political figureheads, i.e. as if they were one's next-door neighbour and not persons in possession of power and authority. Conversely, politicians regularly cast themselves as the man-in-the-street who just happen to have been elected to Parliament.

This leads to the second point. As regards the mass-elite nexus vis-a-vis European integration, this cultural-political homogeneity implies that it is not always easy to clearly separate mass and elite attitudes from each other. This is due not only to the intermeshing that generally results from the above-mentioned peculiarity, but also because elements of "typical" Danishness can be identified at both levels and because European integration policy in Denmark has been conducted largely on the basis of popular referenda (see below). One must therefore be cautious in presuming a clear-cut division between a pro-European elite and a sceptical mass, since typical features of Danish history, identity and political culture militate against it.

On the other hand, new perspectives have appeared in the 1990s, and these will be dealt with in sections 5 and 6.

Depending on perspective, the relation between mass and elite attitudes to the European integration project in Denmark could be characterised as *ambiguous*, as *anomalous*, or as *consistent* with Danish national and political-cultural peculiarities.

---

1 A definitional note on the use of these two core concepts: "Elite" is taken in a broad sense to encompass the political class, the top echelons of private business and public administration, professional academics, and mass-media opinion leaders. The basic definitional components in different combinations are "influence", "power", "class" and "education". Sometimes it is useful to introduce a bifurcation of the elites, as will be apparent later in the chapter, where the concept of a "core elite" (identical to factual decision-makers at any given time) within this broad definition is applied. In that case the differentiation between elites and masses may be easier to handle, but to exclusively use this definition runs the danger of, for example, not recognising a given parliamentary opposition, or powerful business lobbies, or nationalistically minded intellectuals, as part of the elites. Conversely, the "masses" are made up of the "remainder", the national aggregate of the man-in-the-street, or politically speaking, the electorate. The logical inference is that the elite-mass distinction in terms of concrete persons/citizens cuts across many individuals, in the sense that it refers to social/political positions and capacities rather than to people: even the prime minister is an elector, and as such, part of the masses, though in most other capacities (s)he must be categorised with the elites.

It appears *ambiguous* because, firstly, attitudes for or against integration have had a historical tendency to vary quite considerably both within the mass and elite strata separately and when (changes along) the two axes are correlated (Eriksen 1994; Nielsen 1993; Siune et al. 1992; Worre 1995). Second, because the substantive areas weighted as significant for assessments of whether or not integration is a "good thing" (e.g. economic benefits, the Scandinavian dimension, common security, or relations with Germany) have only partially overlapped on the two levels, and as will be shown below, not always in the same way.

It appears as *anomalous* in the sense that relations between the political landscape and voter behaviour/electoral attitudes reveal a general pattern of unusual, but quite consistent and wide-ranging dealignment. Normal patterns of party loyalty apply only in the case of a few parties, whereas most parties in the political centre have regularly had to face situations of unpredictability and volatility amongst their traditional supporters. This in turn is reflected in intra-party differences of unusual openness and vehemence, particularly but not exclusively within parties left-of-centre (the Social Democrats and the Socialist People's Party). It has further led to a number of tactical as well as strategic turnabouts and unorthodox alliances.

From an international perspective, Denmark appears anomalous in terms of the distribution of support and opposition: pro-European elites have failed to obtain the wholehearted support of the national capital (overall, Copenhagen has been consistently anti-EU whereas the Jutland peninsula has been "pro" (also in June of 92)); nor have the elites been able to obtain the support of state-employed functionaries – and only recently of a majority of intellectuals (Nielsen 1993: 56 ff.). Conversely, anti-EU movements and political actors have not been able to rely on clear-cut demographic or geographic pockets of opposition or scepticism, including the rural regions (which have by and large supported the integration process). In this sense, therefore, Denmark clearly distinguishes itself from Sweden or Norway.

From a processual perspective, the overall pattern is characterised by such factors losing their importance – with the notable exception of a left-right continuum: there is still a tendency for self-styled "leftists" to be "anti" – i.e. to be substantively conservative – and for "conservatives" to be "pro" – i.e. to be substantively for change (ibid. pp. 52 ff.). Most variables, however, indicate that to all intents and purposes the attitudes of Danes towards integration are in the process of becoming fairly evenly distributed across traditional sociological categories used by political sociologists.[2]

National homogeneity, however, has another side to it. Danes seem to assess the integration process on a very similar background and in their evaluations tend to

---

2 This does not mean that differences along such lines as gender, age, and urban vs rural areas cannot still be found, only that they are much less pronounced than in other countries (for instance, Norway and Sweden). See the tables and arguments in Nielsen (1993), pp. 57-62. The divisions that nevertheless are fairly obvious originate rather in different interpretations of the extent to which European integration and institutions affect Danish identity and Denmark's interests, i.e. in individually specific modulations between "symbolic" and "pragmatic" benefits or drawbacks. In a way, this is a political continuum, but not one that corresponds neatly to the party-political spectrum.

use a quite homogeneous toolkit. The background for this is a generally positive attitude toward membership, though on an intergovernmental basis, and a continuing effort to assess advantages and disadvantages on a sliding scale with questions of Danish identity at one end ("symbolic Danishness") and questions of national interest at the other ("pragmatic Danishness").[3] Hence, differences as measured by referenda or survey results manifest different modes of evaluating the strengths and benefits of Denmark and Danishness within the EU, but not a qualitative difference of values (such as, e.g., might be expressed in oppositions such as "federalist vs. intergovernmental" or "pro-membership vs anti-membership" political battles over European integration; see Hedetoft 1995: Part II).

It is partly in this sense that the elite-mass interaction in Denmark emerges as a *consistent* and politically significant factor. It is consistent because it conforms with self-perceptions (as well as theories) of national homogeneity, both horizontally (as just described) and vertically, i.e. as regards links between state/politics and nation/the electorate, as articulated in the traditional Danish adage "the state is all of us". Three aspects of this vertical linkage are significant in this context.

First, its pertinent democratic-institutional form is that of the *referendum,* which has been used on five crucial occasions of EC integration (1972, 1986, 1992, 1993, 1998), on the assumption that each significant step forwards towards deeper integration marks a partial surrender of sovereignty (pursuant to Art. 20 of the Danish Constitution).[4] It is the referenda that most clearly show the significance of the masses for the integration process, though elite-mass interaction in Denmark has also more generally been characterised by the elite keeping their ear to the ground and retaining both discourses and policies of Europe within the parameters of caution, pragmatism, and national interest.

Second, regardless of considerable differences between elite and mass attitudes between, and sometimes immediately prior to the referenda (the tendency being for elites to favour integration and for the masses to oppose it), the result – barring the 1992 referendum – has consistently been a show of support for the Government's line. In other words, in situations of critical choice, the majority of Danes have tended to line up behind the arguments and leadership of the core elite (note 1 and below). Pragmatic considerations of national interest have overridden more symbolic-historical considerations of identity and sovereignty.

This tendency points toward the third, more fundamental (causative) aspect: that the interaction between elites and masses has been consistently characterised by a Danish reflexive linkage between the *symbolic* and *pragmatic* aspects of Danish

---

3   For more elaboration on this "symbolic/pragmatics" dichotomy, see below.
4   With the exception of the 1986 referendum on the SEA, which the government chose to call in view of parliamentary resistance, but which was neither constitutionally necessary nor, being "consultative", legally binding on the executive or the legislature. It is further noteworthy that in Denmark as in other EU countries sovereignty has continuously been eroded through the application of Art. 235 of the Treaty of Rome.

nationalism in the country's relations with and integration into the surrounding international context (Hedetoft 1995; Knudsen 1992)[5]. The former, stressing the *identity* of nation-state homogeneity and embedded in 150 years of national introspection, encompasses the protection of Danishness and territorial sovereignty and the suspicion of the foreign Other. The latter embraces a need and, to some extent, a desire for international cooperation and an instrumentally couched openness and willingness to negotiate, as long as it is arguably in the *interests* of Denmark (or can be presented as such) (see fig. 2). It is this reflexivity that might help explain both the ambiguities and the anomalies pointed out so far. The next section will take a closer look at this feature and some observations attendant on it in a historical, process-oriented perspective.

3. Symbolics – Pragmatics Reflexivity and European Integration: the Case of Denmark

Danishness as a specific form of national identity is typified both by strong symbolic-affective attachment to the idea of a separate, sovereign, territorially bounded national uniqueness, and by a pronounced feature of pragmatism in dealing with the outside world (Hedetoft 1995).[6] Sometimes the two features are kept separate – in which case, at least as ideal-types, they correlate with the pursuit of "identity"/ "mass national culture" and the pursuit of "interest"/"the policies of the elites", respectively. Sometimes they intermesh and help to mutually define each other (and to keep each other in place in the name of national consensus). As far as this duality relates to European integration and the mass-elite linkage, the principal modulations can be described in terms of the following matrix:

Figure 1

	Pragmatism	Symbolics
Elites	+ Integration	+/÷ Integration (discourse of ambivalence)
Masses	+ Integration ÷ "union"	÷ Integration (popular democracy)

---

5 I use "reflexive" and "reflexivity" to denote the kind of "causal loops" described by Giddens (1984, e.g. p. 376), where the forms and processes of the interaction between pragmatic and symbolic attitudes to Danishness are typified by their mutual awareness of each other and their mutual recognition of and feedback into each other. In that sense, they both mirror each other and modify each other, each acting interchangeably as both cause and effect.

6 This is the historical result of some painful international experiences that have demonstrated the vulnerability and dependency of Denmark in great-power conflicts – exacerbated by the fact that Denmark has often chosen to affiliate with the losing side (Feldbæk et al. 1991; Hedetoft 1993; Knudsen 1992; Østergaard 1992). This resulted in attempts to remain neutral in both the First and Second World War.

This should be read as follows. From the perspective of pursuing Danish interests in the international/European context and preferably on the basis of intergovernmental cooperation, the elites have by and large been in favour of integration. This is no more than the ideal-type, however, and needs to be modified by the realisation that it does not generally indicate any enthusiasm for European integration amongst the elites, nor does this support invariably characterise all elite substrata. For instance, political parties at both ends of the political continuum have been consistently sceptical or opposed to the integration project; large parts of the intellectual stratum have been more "anti" than "pro", though this has changed in the 1990s. The mass media, until 1988-89, were at best pragmatically ambivalent, and generally uninterested in the subject of Europe and integration (between 1973 and 1988 there was very little public debate on these issues in Denmark). The majority of members of the Danish Parliament (*Folketinget*) opposed the SEA in 1986 – against the support given to SEA by the government and also, as it turned out, against the positive vote of the electorate in the consultative referendum held that year. Thus, though the elites have no doubt on balance favoured integration, internal divisions and vacillations have been rampant, as the pragmatic/utilitarian benefits for Denmark of integrating differently at different junctures have been subjected to scrutiny.

Consequently, as far as symbolic, affective relations with Europe are concerned, it is hardly surprising that this "slot" of the matrix has been typified by discourses of ambivalence. If reasons for "integrating" are primarily of a pragmatic nature, the symbolics of an overarching European identity, culture, or future mission a single political entity must be viewed with scepticism. This ambiguity of the elites can be conceptualised in three ways taking the interaction of "interest" and "identity" into account.

One conceptualisation concerns the "national affectiveness" of the Danish elites *per se*, i.e. the extent to which they themselves are representatives of national sentiments that have historically militated against supranational enthusiasm (not least where Germany is involved) and are locked into attempts to preserve Danish sovereignty by favouring "realist" modes of international cooperation.

The second conceptualisation pertains to elite interaction with the masses. Presuming the existence of the type of Danish homogeneity described above, the question for elites is whether to integrate mass symbolic scepticism towards Europe and positive attitudes towards the specificities of Danish identity and political culture into their own modes of discourse and practice, or simply to adhere to such sentiments in a pragmatic way since one's political life is dependent on electoral support.

The third conceptualisation veers more towards the positive side of the ambivalence spectrum and became more pronounced in the 1990s: to the extent that European integration issues have developed from a discussion of membership to one of union, from economics to (high) politics, and in as much as elites have shown stronger tendencies to identify with the institutional structures of the European Union and have come to realise the extent to which Danish interests have become intermeshed with the future of the European project, the more the political identity of elites has tended to disaggregate from that of the masses. This has added a more positive European "layer" to their own identity kit. Simultaneously, they have assumed a more functional attitude towards the national-cultural identity of the masses (fig. 2). The obvious result was the 1992 split and the subsequent attempts by the elites to negotiate a way out of the morass, involving a strategy reminiscent of a two-level game: placating the EU and the Danish people at the same time. As the May 1993 referendum indicated, the strategy – termed "the national compromise" – was successful, at least temporarily.

From the perspective of the masses, it is wise to start from the opposite presumption, namely one of symbolic resistance based in specific historical structures of "feeling Danish" (bottom right-hand slot), particularly as these sentiments manifest themselves in support of territorial sovereignty (Branner 1992; Hedetoft 1994a), the democratic form of "folkestyre" (popular democracy), and historical resentment against getting too deeply involved with "Europe" (read: Germany). As the matrix indicates, however, the masses are, like the elites, locked into the specific Danish interaction between the symbolic gesturing of national identification and the pragmatic attitude dictated by (inter)dependence. Historically, this interaction has had three forms of articulation at the level of the masses.

First, as indicated above, there has been a pattern whereby resistance and scepticism have flourished particularly well *between* referenda, i.e. when the electorate could air their feelings without regard to political responsibility or consequences, or, differently put, when they could allow themselves the luxury of getting immersed in their affective rather than cognitive reactions. The results of the referenda, on the other hand, demonstrate a pronounced degree of pragmatism and "responsible behaviour" – with the notable exception of 1992.

Second, all surveys indicate that the foundation on which mass perceptions are based has shifted considerably. Whereas a majority of Danes – between referenda – used to be opposed to *membership* of the EC (until app. 1986), after that time a large majority have been in favour. Membership is a non-issue these days. What sizeable portions of the Danish masses still oppose is the notion of *political union*, i.e. ways of deepening integration away from intergovernmentalism. Where membership was formerly seen to threaten Danish identity, it is now the spectre of union, CFSP, common citizenship, open borders, and a common currency that is regarded as carrying such consequences in their wake. In other words, debates are no longer about the whys and wherefores of membership, but its hows – including the contribution that Denmark might make (in its own interest, of course) to European developments. In this sense, Denmark – elites as well as masses – has lost its innocence in terms of international cooperation. A sign of this is that even the most fervent opponents of membership, few as they are, have no choice but to argue their case in terms of the EU being the wrong kind of cooperative international scheme (hegemony, new kind of imperialism, capitalist club, oppressor of Third World countries, environmental degradation, etc.). Withdrawing into national preoccupation and self-sufficiency are not considered realistic solutions (this argument is reserved for minorities on the extreme right and left). In other words, membership has become the normal state of affairs.

Finally, the third historical tendency is for the symbolic area of identity to become increasingly intermeshed with pragmatics (where elite representatives still try to argue their separateness); in other words, there is a tendency for the affective values of sovereign Danishness to be brought to bear on the interpretation of Danish interests in Europe and on the kind of limits to be placed on the process of "deepening". Thus, in the 1990s there seemed to be a growing tendency for the (political) elites to choose options and interest-formulations that are informed by the relative imperative of international cooperation (complex interdependence) and, conversely, for the masses to veer towards more cultural-affective interpretations of sovereignty, territoriality and identity, i.e. towards a symbolic reaffirmation of the orthodox nation-state context (see fig. 2 below). This has led to a potentially more serious dichotomisation of elites and masses, because the difference now more perfectly corresponds to the ideal-type binarism between pragmatic and symbolic "Danishness", i.e. between the top left-hand slot and the bottom right-hand slot of the matrix.[7] Still, however, this is no more than a tendency; divisions are extant within the elites as well as the masses, and even the most pronounced sign of a cleavage – the June 1992 "No" to Maastricht – must be modified in light of the almost exact 50-50 division of the electorate and the ensuing "national compromise".

The argument so far can be nicely illustrated by means of the following diagram viewing the problematique through one of the important determinants of integration at both the elite and mass levels: namely, sovereignty.[8]

Figure 2

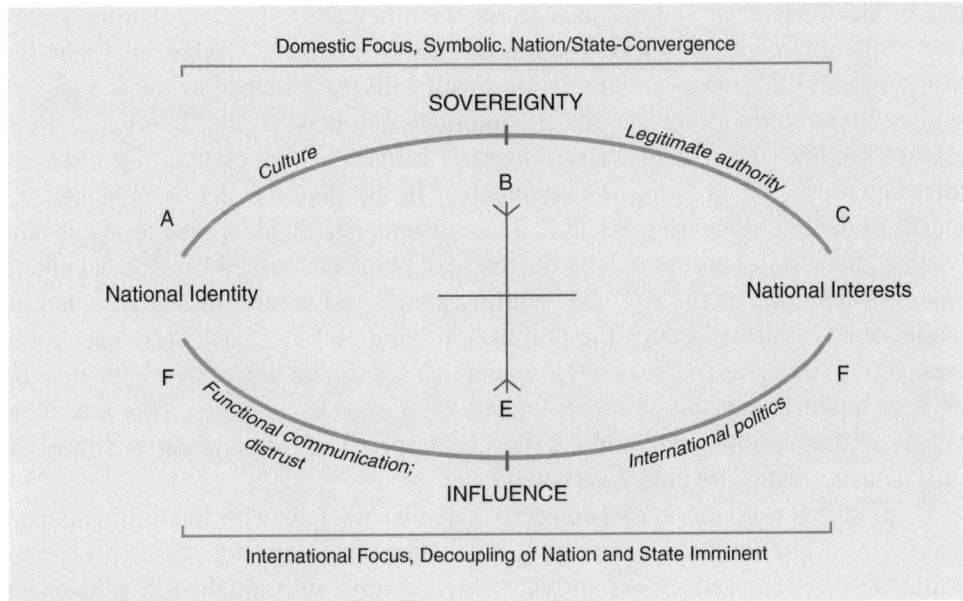

---

7 See the discussion in section 4.
8 The question of sovereignty has been shown to be the one most important factor underlying e.g. the Danish "No" in 1992. See Hedetoft (1994); Nielsen (1993); Siune et al. (1992).

The diagram tries to combine the previous elements of "symbolics" and "pragmatics" with those of (1) "identity" and "interest" and (2) "domestic" and "international". There are two different ways of linking the symbolic/affective "identity" component of nationalism with its pragmatic "interest" component, on the assumption that "identity" belongs in an ideal-type fashion with a mass perspective ("the nation"), and "interest" with an elite perspective ("the state"). At the same time the diagram tries to outline the consequences of European integration for the intertwining or, conversely, the disaggregation of national identity and national interest along the two axes (A-C and D-F), the former being informed by notions of nation-state sovereignty and nation-state cohesion, the latter more by notions of power and influence in an increasingly transnational context where different nation-state units overlap and interrelate ("complex interpenetration").

Within a classical, ideal-type conception of nationalism, the two axes are coterminous and complementary: determinants of national interest overlap with determinants of identity; sovereignty and influence as well as political power and legal authority are two sides of the same coin. The integrating elements within the domestic focus are democracy, rights and welfare. As regards the international focus, foreign policy is conducted – albeit secretively – in the national interest, using all available means to maintain and enhance national influence in the outside world. Thus, foreign influence is not simply a consequence of domestic sovereignty. It is also the prerequisite.

This is not to raise the issue of whether or not this idyllic picture has had a real-world corollary. However, I do assume that the linkages, both perception-wise and more objectively, have indeed been closer than they are today, i.e., that the structure of the international world "used to be" more "realistic". Today, interpenetration generally and European integration specifically have helped to create a partial schism between the domestic and the international axes, so that internal "sovereignty" becomes more distinct from external "influence" (which in turn is often reinterpreted as a novel form of sovereignty). In the diagram this is indicated by means of the line separating B and E. The consequence, in ideal-type terms, is that "nation" and "state" are faced with the threat of being decoupled from one another: "nation" appropriates the A-C axis within cultural and identity-based parameters, while "state" tends to occupy the D-F axis, relying on functional, "rational" communication strategies (persuasion) to maintain an intimate link between the pursuit of state interests and the political dimension of citizens' identity. This link is in danger of dissolution due to popular disenchantment with the integrative strategies of state actors (the core elite – cf. below).

Read in this way, the mass perspective ideally overlaps with the left-hand side and the A-C line (cultural sovereignty and nation/state cohesion) of the diagram, while the elite perspective overlaps with the right-hand side and the F-D movement (political influence and nation/state disaggregation). This is because for the masses "identity" subsumes "interest", while for the elites the inverse relation applies. The link between the cultural aspects of sovereignty (including its moral and legal legitimacy) and the political aspect of power/influence is threatened by the pragmatic trade-off between legal autonomy and the exercise of external influence (Hedetoft 1994a; Wæver 1995). Thus, the "rational", elite approach to integration as a means of pursuing national interests tends to have a negative impact on mass perceptions of identity and convergence between nation and state; the line connecting "national identity" with "power/influence" is increasingly typified by fragmentation or distrust and, seen from the opposite perspective, by functionalisations ("rational communication" such as persuasion strategies built on e.g. efficiency and sectoral interests).

This is generally true, but with nationally specific modifications. In Denmark, specifically, such cleavages are constantly counteracted by the intimate reflexivity between elites and masses discussed above; by a relatively low level of political distrust compared to other European countries (Goul Andersen et al. 1992; Hedetoft 1995); by the pragmatic thrust of the masses, a large part of whom are as anxious about the spectre of "being left on our own" as by deeper integration (Nielsen 1993: 73 ff.); and, finally, by a cultural confidence in the strength of "Danishness", almost regardless of what might happen to traditional legal and political sovereignty (Hedetoft 1995: Part II, Chapter III).

In other member-states, typified by another political culture and another elite-mass interaction, manifestations might differ – thus highlighting the need for specific, detailed studies which can supplement the identification of theoretical constants.

The next section proposes to look more closely at some salient historical components of elite-mass linkages in Denmark.

4. Historical factors and developments[9]

Denmark became an EU member exclusively for economic reasons.[10] Before 1973, its two main trading partners, Britain and Germany, were on either side of the EU fence. Britain's image was generally positive, Germany's less so among Danes, and in this sense the distribution of these two big nation-states between "inside" and "outside" the EU made sense from a Danish perspective. Economically, it was not a pleasant situation, but it was still tolerable. Having both countries inside the EC while remaining outside, on the other hand, was untenable; for that reason, Danish EU applications from the early 1960s onwards were tied to Britain's attempts to become accepted by the "Six" and, on the assumption that Britain would join together with Denmark, there was widespread acceptance of the prospect of membership among elites as well as the masses in the 1960s – a kind of national consensus that is superficially reminiscent of the situation in the 1990s (Worre

---

9 This section draws extensively on Hedetoft (1995), part I, chapter VII, section 3.
10 Objectively the background was the degree of dependence on Britain as an important trading partner. Whether we are facing a situation of necessity or rather of astute Danish pragmatism is a matter of dispute.

1995: 211f.). However, there was also a widespread lack of interest in the subject, particularly among the general population. Both Denmark and Britain have, partly for that reason, been described as "minimalist". However, whereas Britain's applications constituted an indisputable waving of the white flag in the face of an insurmountable political-economic reality – clearly the choice of one evil over another – Denmark's position did not contain this element of political humiliation. Where Britain's stance was guided by considerations of *political* economy (as well as sheer high politics), Denmark's was informed by political *economy* thinking: it was, in the terms often used in the '60s and '70s, a question of "pork prices" (ibid.), guided by economic pragmatism, where Britain's "minimalism" was, from its inception, both more offended and more offensive: its pragmatism was overlaid with strategic thinking; not with indifference, but with hostility to political integration and the centralisation of powers, on the popular as well as the political levels.

Thus, where a bird's eye view of European developments would naturally have identified Denmark as a very dependent variable, things looked quite different from the Danish viewpoint: the EU appeared as the dependent (and somehow dispensable) variable, a possibly necessary appendix, but an appendix none the less: the supplier of markets and trading partners, and a helpmate for an agricultural sector caught in the throes of transition – and little else. In both the 1972 and 1986 referenda, support for membership was obtained, therefore, by means of pragmatic discourses of economic expansion and maintenance of welfare standards, based on the national interest as the pivotal argumentive axis, whilst reassuring the electorate that their Danish core would not be endangered.[11]

It is therefore misleading to present Danish membership in this period as a victory of pragmatism over symbolic Danishness (though in strictly political terms it might be). Rather, the majority of Danes voted in favour of membership and for the Single European Act (characteristically referred to in Denmark as the "EU package"), because they had been convinced that their Danish culture and identity were not relevant issues, or in any case not relevant *enough* to warrant a "No" vote. The referenda were about markets, money, and – for some – welfare. And though "The People's Movement Against The EC" and other oppositional groups obtained a sympathetic hearing when trying to rally support around their affective-lyrical representations of Danishness; around the threat posed by the EU to Danish independence; and around the allegedly hegemonic German objectives; nevertheless, the majority accepted influential politicians' discursive bifurcation between the pragmatic and the symbolic, the denotative and the connotative layers of the national interest – discourses often predicated upon the allegedly limited aspirations of the EU project. It was possible to accept membership and still be affectively and cosmologically Danish.

---

11 In spite of this conflation of the two referenda under the same paradigm, it should not be overlooked that the economic pragmatism discourse had weakened somewhat by 1986. See the evidence of a higher level of pro-European "assertiveness" evident in the quotes cited in Lunde (1988: 129ff.)

EU scepticism contributed to strengthening many people's sense of their authentic identity. As EU integration proceeded in the 1980s, Danish nationalism – as mythology and as a feeling of separateness and exceptionalism – became more discursively legitimate than it had been for many decades. On the other hand, scepticism towards the EU was contained through the construction of minimalist meanings, an explicit lack of enthusiasm and involvement, and of course also through the practical demonstration that membership and Danish identity were able to go hand in hand. For the same reason, as indicated, the EU debate was very limited until 1986/87. People would rather not hear about the Community, and for those who did take an interest, therefore, relative silence and hard-headed pragmatism were seen to be the best strategies.

Hence, political jobs in the EU institutions were not coveted, and Denmark invariably elected "backbenchers" to the European Parliament. The "inner peace" could be kept, because no political-cultural symbolism was attached to the EU, no grand demonstrations of commitment beyond pragmatism made, no signs of heading for a "European identity" openly produced or embraced. Nation and state were united around the national interest and the national identity, and though strategies and political views might differ, and the pragmatic-symbolic configurations vary, all were basically committed to the same goals and the same value system as the ultimate end. Whatever the political divisions, they did not seriously impinge on the culturally homogeneous underpinning of Danish identity. EU discourse was national discourse. However, this situation began to change after the SEA referendum, spurred on by a more aggressive EU style and politics, on the one hand, and by domestic shifts in the political landscape and its EU discourse, on the other. Both cognitive and affective dissonances began to emerge, but we also observe signs of a new type of national unity more favourable towards some political aspects of integration.

There were five main signs: 1) parties and movements that had previously agitated for Danish withdrawal from the EU began to experience either failing support and/or voluntarily renounced this goal in favour of a reform-from-within strategy, some Social Democrats evolving into all-out supporters of integration; 2) pro-European intellectuals and politicians adopted a more overtly and (seen from an EU perspective) constructively integrationist line; 3) following the Single Market campaign, a public debate about the EU finally got under way in Denmark; 4) the strengthening of the Danish economy during the 1980s gave a boost of national self-confidence to opinion leaders, the business community, and public representatives; 5) finally, German Unification – though initially threatening to re-activate German enemy images in a regressive way – ultimately had the opposite effect, EU integration now becoming widely viewed as the only possible straitjacket on, and way to influence the evolving German megalith.

As previously indicated, signs of a more aggressive pro-European discourse among politicians had already been visible in the debate surrounding the 1986 referendum. In the late 1980s this tendency became clear, particularly in the wake of Prime Minister Poul Schlüter's speech in London in September of 1988 when he declared the nation-state to be dead.[12] Whatever its value, substantively speaking, the speech showed that it was now possible to put the character and future of the nation-state on the public agenda in a more provocative way, as a prelude to further integration along the road to "political union". German Unification assisted in this considerably, psychologically paving the way for the next step: the forging of the two intergovernmental conferences on economic and political integration into one document: the TEU.

As the debate pertaining to this document showed – the litmus test for this more internationally oriented line of thinking in Denmark – the immediately visible consequence of embracing European integration in this manner was a thoroughgoing divisiveness within the political debate, leading to the June 1992 rejection. This event, however, has tended to obscure that the debating agenda, discourse, and climate were quite significantly different from previous, comparable situations. Almost everyone pledged allegiance to EU membership, though interpretations of how to utilise it differed. In a sense, everyone also agreed that some measure of political integration was necessary, though perhaps not desirable; the main object of conflict was now whether or not "Maastricht" represented the right scenario for political cooperation. Since this directly impinged on national identity and sovereignty questions, the debate occasionally became vitriolic, leading to the symbolic victory of the sceptics.

Nevertheless, the debate largely took place on the premises of the "pro-Europeans". Both membership and the "1992" drive now seemed to be accepted by the electorate as a natural prerequisite, and the debate was therefore free to focus on more sensitive issues. The "state was brought back in" (Evans et al. 1985) in a new way: it was questioned, debated, relativised – in other words, became the direct object of discussion. What earlier would have been seen to be almost sacrilegious in the Danish debate, now actually happened; an axiom of Danishness, the intimate linkage between nation and state within strictly national confines, was now thematised on a predicative basis quite significantly more pro-European. In a 1990 book Professor Chresten Sørensen, a well-known Danish economist and public commentator, formerly a vigorous EU opponent, proclaimed the demise of the (Danish) nation-state and its relegation to the status of a "regional state" in Europe.[13] This development he argued, though regrettable, might not be totally bad, for "nation-states ... have caused some of the worst crimes in human history", as the author commented to a newspaper (*Jyllands-Posten*) prior to the publication of his book.[14]

---

12 Contrasting in an interesting way with a rhetorically similar but substantively very different statement in 1985 to the effect that "the Union is stone dead".
13 *Danmark, Delstat i Europa?* Sørensen (1990).
14 It is a further indication of the shifts of consensus in the Danish EU debates that a prominent champion of historical, cultural Danishness and formerly a virulent EU opponent, Ebbe Kløvedal Reich, in August 1990 announced his readiness to embrace a European Political Union if only it was constituted of "regions" all of which were approximately the size of Denmark – in other words, the larger nation-states should be broken down into their

Such statements are indicative of a radically changed "Euro-climate" vis-a-vis the role and power of the traditional nation-state. For this reason, Poul Schlüter, in the run-up to the 1992 referendum, was able to champion European integration by referring less to the pragmatic benefits of membership and more to the variant of EC idealism connected with "peace": "The EC is a safeguard for a peaceful Europe", as one headline had it.[15] In October of the same year, the writer Steen Steensen Ranum, clearly bolstered by the June "No" vote, published a "viewpoint" in *Aalborg Stiftstidende* taking the opposite, more traditionally "Danish" tack: "The nation-state is a guarantor of peace".[16] By this time, however, the Europeanists, growing in vociferousness, numbers, and general representativeness, were on the offensive. In October of 1992, *Weekendavisen* published a long interview with the Danish Foreign Minister, Uffe Ellemann-Jensen, in which he, too, predicted the inevitable erosion of the nation-state, distinguishing this from the certain survival of national (cultural) *identity* which was presented as having little immanent connection with "state".[17] In January, 1993, another ardent pro-European politician and public personality, Ritt Bjerregaard, a Social Democrat, then chairwoman of the Danish European Movement, and until recently EU Environment Commissioner, announced in *Børsen* that for reasons of international peace it was significant to make the EC work "almost at any cost"; the title of the piece was "The Limitations of the Nation-State!"[18] The article, published a month after the Edinburgh Decision and four months prior to the second referendum, addressed the open political rifts in Denmark following the June 1992 results. Rather than tactically backing off from provoking the opponents, it reasserted a commitment to Europe in its Maastricht form as a surrender of sovereignty, as a political rather than an economic question, and as a weakening of the nation-state. Bjerregaard was not alone in this view, but rather encapsulated the main spirit of pro-Maastricht agitation in a representative manner. In this new *Zeitgeist*, Thorkild Borup-Jensen, editor of an anthology entitled *The History of the Danish Identity* (Borup-Jensen 1993), contributed a lengthy piece to the daily *Information* four days before the second referendum on 18 May 1993. Though it did not in any way question the positive features of Danishness, the essay nevertheless still advocated a less inward-looking and more multiculturalist stance, a combination of (inter)national republicanism and national ethnicity. Tellingly, the essay was entitled "Nationhood – Inevitable and Dangerous".[19]

---

constituent parts (not least in order to defuse the German menace). The idealism of this notwithstanding, it is a sign of an important attitudinal change. See *Politiken*, 12 August 1990, as well as the Danish Prime Minister's response a week later (19 August).

15 *Berlingske Tidende*, 11 February 1992.
16 *Aalborg Stiftstidende*, 25 October 1992.
17 9-15 October 1992: "Don't we have to abandon the illusion of the sovereign nation-state? This state no longer exists. (...) *The territorial state* but not the nations will disappear" (original emphasis).
18 *Børsen*, 18 January 1993.
19 14 May 1993.

Clearly, the history of contemporary Danish identity was having a new chapter written for it, calling for more international commitment over and above the instrumentality of cost-benefit thinking. The discourses and platforms were undergoing noteworthy changes (across the political spectrum – this was not a partisan issue); the outcome of the second referendum practically confirmed this. Today it is not only possible to have a debate about Europe and the EU in Denmark, but the premises of the debate have been transformed, if not in kind, then at least in degree. It would seem as if the ground has shifted from Pragmatics to Symbolics, but it would be more correct to say that the national interest is undergoing a reformulation that allows it to embrace "internationalism" in novel ways. In this perspective we see a reinterpretation of Danish pragmatism, leaving the symbolic, cosmological identity terrain relatively unscathed (the peaceful transition mentioned below might have something to do with this).

It must be emphasised that this does not mean that traditional, more inward-looking Danishness has disappeared, nor that the "pro-Europeanists", to use a blanket description that conceals a number of variations, do not conceive of themselves as representatives of Danishness. Rather, the latter have been instrumental in "modernising" what I have termed the Danish Euro-discourse so that it conforms more aggressively with new conditions and politics for nation-state action in international environments. Traditional Danish fear of meddling in international affairs has been partly replaced by confidence and practical activism. The autumn 1993 decision – as a follow-up to Denmark's symbolic representation in the Gulf War and its more substantive participation in peacekeeping efforts in ex-Yugoslavia – to create a military brigade for use in NATO and UN task forces as from 1995, is a clear confirmation of this. Though *interests* are still unmistakably "Danish", the discursive and practical orchestration of them increasingly takes place within a less clear-cut and uniformly *national* mode. Politicians from both the right and left sides of the political spectrum have begun to take advantage of their new possibilities of influencing the external world through membership of both the EU and NATO. The last 7 years have witnessed a withdrawal from the small-state foreign policy of a vulnerable state, jealously guarding its hard-won sovereignty, towards the politics of influence characteristic of an international actor. The public debate is being pervaded by a Danish variant of "weltoffener Patriotismus", fighting with more traditional attitudes, discourses, and meanings for dominance and public spaces. This is a struggle that in terms of ideal-types matches the division between elites and masses (evident, for instance, within the Social Democratic Party, where there is still an obvious cleavage between a pro-European leadership and a negative, foot-dragging membership), but also one that in significant ways cuts across this bifurcation (for instance in the form of "social movements" that in Denmark often rally the support of elites as well as masses), impinging on the overall configuration of Danish national identity.

A decisive difference as compared with earlier stages is that a significant portion of the intelligentsia, who had formerly been more silent or sceptically indifferent, have become believers in a *practical* internationalisation of Danishness and Danish politics as a necessary and desirable road ahead for Denmark, and they are taking active part in public debates accordingly. This occasionally leads to accusations against academics of elitism and of having lost touch with the people.[20] Generally, however, it is more noteworthy that such apparently important changes have taken place without creating serious rifts among Danes or between different conceptions of Danishness, and without giving rise to the depth of political disenchantment and disaffection found in many other European countries (Hedetoft 1995: Part II, Chapter III). The centre of consensuality has shifted, if not imperceptibly, at least without earthquakes. No doubt the symbolic victories for EU opponents in June and December of 1992 played a significant role in this, paving the way for a new consensus on European integration – however brittle and transitional it may be.

Political divisions in Denmark belong primarily to a sphere circumscribed by pragmatics, and do not easily invade the much more symbolic-cosmological terrain of a uniform cultural identity. Between these two obviously interdependent spaces, there now seems to be a relative – and relatively important – degree of bifurcation and mutual autonomy. Previously, symbolic Danishness left hardly any space to forms of pragmatics over and above minimalist inevitability. Today, though their relationship is indeed potentially conflictual, it also appears as more balanced. However, it is a question of balancing on a knife-edge. Where the tendencies towards disaggregation between state and nation, interest and identity delineated in fig. 2 continue to push the two interpretations of Danishness away from each other, counteracting "pull" factors consist in the handed-down features of consensual political culture and the institutional mechanisms for keeping the national polity close to the "grassroots" level of prevailing attitudes amongst the people at large – especially the referendum, but on another dimension also the parliamentary "Europe Committee". This latter helps to retain in some measure the influence of parliamentarians on the free rein of the executive and top civil servants in the European Council, and to an even larger extent the public perception of such effective constraining mechanisms, and, thus, the impression that Denmark continues to ensure the pragmatic, intergovernmental nature of the EU.

---

20 See, for instance, the following outburst in a letter to *Weekendavisen,* 10 August 1990, headlined "The Professor and the Stupid Danes", responding to an article by a Danish political scientist advocating tolerance towards foreigners: "Even though [Professor] Grønnegaard Christensen is a very learned man, he is stupid in an essential way. He does not comprehend the simplest of popular emotions – that which, using an old-fashioned expression, could be termed love of one's country. He does not understand that reality is not lived on statistics and reports. He does not understand that people react to having their mother country change around them, for 'when all studies show ...' He does not understand that a bond can be so strong that it may defy his professorial reason. All he can do is sit in his ivory tower and be astonished". Although the explicit subject here is foreign immigration into Denmark, the attitude to intellectuals pontificating about the benefits of openness and internationalism is a carbon copy of the hostility occasionally found in EC matters, too – the more so since the two areas are extensively linked in the popular mind.

For this is the symbolic linchpin on which the shift diagnosed above is still primarily predicated, which also informs the interpretive prism that Danes brought to bear on the Edinburgh Decision, and which led to the reversal of majority attitudes in May, 1993: the EU must remain a cooperative scheme among sovereign nation-states, or it must at least appear as such a scheme when viewed from Denmark and in light of Danish national interests and traditional Danish sovereignty. That this to a very large extent is a question of appearances fitting the realities of European integration only in the most piecemeal and partial way – due to the continuous addition of more and more supranational and confederal qualities to the European regime – matters little when the point is to strike the right attitudinal balance in the public mind between the benefits of membership and the illusion that these can be had without yielding significant portions of traditional sovereignty. Let me deal with these points in more detail.

5. Issues and Arguments

It has already been pointed out that it would be a mistake generally to assume that the "masses" are against integration and the "elites" in favour (in that case, the different referenda outcomes would be inexplicable). There are cross-cutting cleavages at work within both domains that muddy such a neat typology. In addition, mass opinion has proved to be rather volatile, something less true for the elite; finally, mental constructions of what is at stake in terms of both issues and arguments proffered "for" or "against" have varied, and cannot be made to conform totally to one uniform blueprint set by the mass-elite cleavage.

In spite of such necessary and valid caveats, it is nevertheless true that there is both a general tendency over time for the elite *core* (and gradually also for the well-educated in general [cf. note 1]) to advocate (further) integration, and for the mass *core* to be sceptical or directly opposed.[21] By "elite core" is meant political and business decision-makers and centrally placed opinion-leaders; by "mass core" is

---

21 This could be phrased in terms of the existence of an "elite for" and an "elite against" integration (and similarly of a "mass for" and a "mass against"). This distinction has been generally true over time, in other words, sections of the elite have been consistently for (always comprising central decision-makers, notably changing governments), sections of the elites consistently against, though they have not been just as consistently for and against the same kinds of issues and developments. The major difference in historical perspective (particularly the 1990s as compared with earlier phases) is, as fig. 2 was meant to illustrate, that as "nation" and "state", "identity" and "interests", and "sovereignty" and "influence" tend to become increasingly decoupled from each other the more the integration process deepens, the more the "core elites" will also find themselves in an increasingly difficult spot, between the rock of Danish identity and its consensual political culture, and the hard place of pursuing interests and influence in the European institutions, and elsewhere too.

meant urban blue-collar workers. The point can be illustrated by looking at the party-political continuum. The staunchest opposition (formerly to membership, now to "federalism") can be found at both extremes of the spectrum, where national and democratic values are most fervently championed and traditional sovereignty discursively most in evidence (Nielsen 1993: 52 ff.). Politicians are here furthest away from executive and legislative influence; hence, this is where dealignment symptoms are weakest. This is also true for the more moderate right-wing parties (Conservatives and Liberals), since their electoral support accrues from either the urban or rural elites or from people with parallel sympathies. On the other hand, dealignment is largest among centre or left-of-centre working-class parties, particularly the Social Democrats, representing a history and ambitions of executive influence at the elite level as well as EU scepticism among traditional supporters.

For this reason the significance of the Social Democrats for rallying (enough) support to keep Denmark on the integrationist path – or for strengthening the state-nation disaggregation pattern evident in fig. 2 – can hardly be overestimated. It was the Social Democrats who carried government responsibility in 1972 and guided Denmark into the EU, primarily on a pragmatic discourse of economic necessity. When the SEA was up for debate in 1986, they were in opposition and Parliament was set to block Danish acceptance – however, the Government managed to turn the voters against this parliamentary majority. In 1992, the Social Democrats were still in opposition, and the outcome is well known. In 1993, on the other hand, they were back in government and contributed towards an acceptance of the Edinburgh Decision.

There is thus a fairly consistent pattern at work here. It does not imply that the position of the Social Democrats is all-important (the 1986 referendum shows otherwise), nor that there are not other significant factors at work (such as the mass media, the tendency for the electorate to be more change-oriented at referenda and less so between them, and perceptions of intergovernmentalism vs federalism/supranationality). However, it indicates that if the Social Democrats are not in a responsible government position, there is less incentive for the top echelons within the party to attempt to swing the marginal (but important) voters (waverers and undecideds) within their traditional ranks towards the pragmatic, structural, international interpretation of sovereignty outlined in fig. 2. In periods of opposition, emphasis shifts towards the sovereignty of Danish identity rather than the (possibly) optimal pursuit of interests and influence, in an attempt to curry favour with supporters, maintain electoral backing, and regain office (Franklin et al. 1994).

It is also important to remember, however, that over time such seemingly static political issues and arguments have played themselves out on the basis of altered conditions of integration, i.e. in different contexts. The thrust of a "yes" and a "no" has shifted considerably, as already argued. This gives rise to two different scenarios that might interlink in multiple ways: one in which elites and masses grow further apart, because the integration process, de facto, proceeds forward, gradually undermining what traditional sovereignty there might have been; and another where no matter what happens in this "real" world of political integration, the situation can still be presented as one where Danish national innocence remains intact and the EU is primarily a forum for interstate cooperation. The national compromise and the Edinburgh Decision tried to square this circle. All surveys indicate that the 1993 "Yes" should be interpreted, on the one hand, as (increased) support for both membership and gradual deepening of the integration process, but on the other as a (strengthened) wish for the retention of orthodox sovereignty (e.g. Worre 1995: 221, table 10). The Edinburgh Decision managed to combine both aspects, the pragmatics of integration with the symbolics of Danishness. Here specific opt-out issues would seem to be less important (for instance, the electoral majority has never been specifically concerned about military cooperation). What was important was that these issues were interpreted in the Danish debate as guarantees of continued sovereignty (inversely, the 1992 vote against Maastricht is widely interpreted as an apprehensive reaction to the same issue (Nielsen 1993; Siune et al. 1992; Hedetoft 1994a). The increase in "support for Europe" and in "outward orientation" among Danes that has been diagnosed as a relatively new feature in the 1990s – and which can be identified in the consistently growing support for the Danish Liberals, one of the staunchest pro-EU parties – is basically predicated on that assumption.

Here it matters little – from one perspective – that the maintenance of sovereignty is more in people's minds that in the real world – that "the separation drawn between domestic and international politics does not correspond with reality" (Erikson 1994: 75; my translation) and that "just because formal sovereignty is intact, this does not necessarily apply to real sovereignty" (ibid.). As Erikson correctly points out, it is a matter of a perception of the world that Danes want to have in spite of the fact that, in an ambiguous way, they have a clear premonition that reality is quite different. Danes want to be pragmatists and national symbolists at the same time; hence, they can only partially close their eyes to "facts".

From another perspective, however, such mental constructions of the world matter a whole lot. For they allow agents of integration to proceed with the EU project on a partly false premise, in turn permanently permitting the masses to either condone developments because they are, after all, in a legitimate Danish interest, or to withdraw their support because developments are now "seen" to have taken place within a false scenario and to have led to undesirable consequences. This last option would exacerbate the potential mass-elite cleavage that was imminent in 1992 and was papered over in 1993. It would bring the structural disaggregation between the two levels to a head.

On the other hand, both the referendum on the Amsterdam Treaty in May 1998 (Pedersen 1998) and the recent EP Elections (June 99) indicate that the pro-European political elites dominating both the Danish Parliament and the encumbent government led by Poul Nyrup Rasmussen are not (yet) ready to make a decisive move to break out of the straitjacket that the combination of exemptions, popular sentiment and a consensually bound political culture has manufactured for them.

Instead, they are holding their breath, pursuing strategies designed to win referenda and elections rather than to make decisive political headway, trying to popularise Europe by backing clean-up programs for European institutions and by keeping a high and assertive visibility on the European and world stage in domains likely to attract popular backing (environment, Kosovo, international peace-keeping, welfare standards, human rights), and all the while waiting for the most opportune moment to hold a referendum (or several) on the rescinding of the exemptions – since these currently relegate the Danish government to an uncomfortable observer position as regards monetary develoments (EMU exemption), security and foreign-policy issues (CFSP exemptions) and matters related to migration, refugees and border control (JHA exemption). Danish political culture is tying the hands of government in European affairs and the government therefore is keeping tabs on developments in popular attitudes on these crucial issues, since it has solemnly promised not to rescind the exemptions except through new referenda and cannot afford to lose once again. In that light, the EMU referendum in September 2000 entails monumental consequences for Danish participation in the EU project.

6. Conclusions

1. In an important sense – and unlike most other countries in the EU – the Danish masses have been present on the stage of European integration for the entire span of Danish membership – primarily via the institution of the popular referendum and, in terms of political culture, via the consensual tradition of Danish post-war politics. This has no doubt codetermined Denmark's more moderate, pragmatic, sometimes foot-dragging attitude toward EU. It has also, occasionally, been instrumental in keeping Danish membership and integration into Europe on track, as witnessed by the SEA issue. Finally, it has led to rocking the boat of functionalist integration, both in Denmark and across the European political landscape (1992). In this sense, the Danish masses not only thwarted the purposes of the most integration-minded elites, but also put keywords such as "sovereignty", "identity", "subsidiarity", and "cultural values" back on to the agenda. They "brought the people back in" within EU discourse and politics (Hedetoft 1994b), and reminded even the staunchest neo-functionalists of Monnet's 1979, possibly apocryphal, statement, "If I were to start all over again, I would begin with education and culture".

1992 developments ushered a new "national compromise" onto the Danish political scene, and created ripples in Europe that made both the Commission and national politicians start treading more lightly. The Treaty of the European Union (TEU) was carried, but at a price which was carried by the Intergovernmental Conference (IGC) that ended in 1997 – a price of added caution, more concessions to national interests, and more divisiveness over objectives as well as the means of achieving them. At the same time, at least in Denmark, the 1992 conundrum helped make the EU debate acceptable and diversified across the board, and it clarified beyond any doubt that arguments are now playing themselves out on a backdrop of widespread support for both membership and a certain variant of integration. It further helped overcome the traditional ostrich-like Danish attitude towards dealing with the outside world; Danes have become more outwardly oriented, more confident, and more assertive as well.

At the same time, the structural forces of antagonism between a political "push" and a cultural "pull" factor are visible and pose a threat to the traditional cohesion between nation and state in Denmark, precisely because they represent general, international forces of disaggregation and national dissolution. Such disaggragating tendencies pose a major challenge to the Danish elites: whether to pursue the structural option of following suit if e.g. the EMU and other "deep" integration mechanisms materialise for at least core parts of the EU (involving rescinding the Danish Edinburgh opt-outs); or to continue the political path of national consensus (involving the formulation of Danish integration politicies and discourses as partly hostile to the supranationality of the EU project thus far).

At present the political climate seems to favour the second option. Whether this is viable in the long term, however, is dubious in light of the objective constraints of a transnational world that to an ever greater extent is out of sync with national sovereignty and power. In that case, national interest and national identity in Denmark might collide head-on as, respectively, elites and masses.

Whatever the outcome, however, the changes and turbulence in the mass-elite relations in the context of European integration are primarily related to the fundamental fact that Danish political culture presupposes a large degree of interaction between politicians and masses and a large degree of manoeuvrability and power execution within nation-state boundaries. For the reasons already given, European integration basically questions this close linkage. It removes an increasing number of significant political decisions to a circumference not directly controllable by this type of reflexivity. The historical watershed events prefiguring the qualitative change from a broadly speaking neo-functionalist approach (applicable because of the separation between pragmatics and symbolics in Danish integration policies) were the interlinking of the disappearance of the Cold War and the deepening of political, "positive" integration in the early 1990s. Where the former removed the extraneous "necessity" for European political and security integration in depth, the latter (leading to Maastricht), as a kind of preemptive reaction, nevertheless tried to keep the process on track, introducing *inter alia* a deepening of QMV as well as movement towards a common currency, adding both the CFSP and cooperation within the third pillar comprising legal and domestic issues. All of this took place within the framework of a "Union citizenship" and a Delors-inspired discourse of European identity. It is hardly surprising that both in Denmark and elsewhere such developments were interpreted by the masses as a qualitatively new step in the history of the EU, impinging on cultural and symbolic areas that had hitherto been left relatively unscathed by the pragmatics of membership. What distinguished the Danish case was the subsequent application of political instruments originating in a political culture and a national identity now perceived to be threatened by these developments (extensive public debate and referenda).

The irony of the situation is that where the use of the referendum was initially conceived as providing a guarantee for the support of the masses to European policies, it has, since the early '90s, shown a different face: as an institution that is significantly, though not yet decisively, hampering the freedom of manoeuvre for Danish political elites as regards European integration, something which in turn has deep implications for domestic politics, too. No wonder, therefore, that political political leaders are according ever more time and energy to a kind of quiet (and sometimes not so quiet) diplomacy intended to convince the Danish population of the deleterious effects of the exemptions for the Danish possibilities of influencing European politics.

Literature

Aalborg Stiftstidende, 25 October 1992.
Berlingske Tidende, 11 February 1992.
Børsen, 18 January 1993.
Borup-Jensen, Thorkild (ed.) (1993): *Danskernes Identitetshistorie*, Copenhagen: C.A. Reitzel.
Branner, Hans (1992): "Danish European Policy Since 1945: The Question of Sovereignty" in M. Kelstrup (ed.), *European Integration and Denmark's Participation*, Copenhagen: Political Studies Press.
Erikson, Johan (1994): "Europeisk integration och dansk tvetydighet" in *Suveränitet och demokrati*, published by the Swedish Foreign Ministry, 12th Public Report 1994. Stockholm: Nordstedt.
Feldbæk, Ole et al. (1991): *Dansk Identitetshistorie*, I-IV, Copenhagen: C.A. Reitzel.
Franklin, Mark et al. (1994): "Uncorking the Bottle: Popular Opposition to European Unification in the Wake of Maastricht", *Journal of Common Market Studies*, vol. 32, no. 4 (December).
Giddens, Anthony (1984): *The Constitution of Society,* Berkeley: The University of California Press.
Goul Andersen, Jørgen et al. (1992): *Vi og vore politikere,* Copenhagen: Spektrum.
Hedetoft, Ulf (1993): "National identity and mentalities of war in three EC countries", *Journal of Peace Research*, vol. 30, no. 3 (August).
Hedetoft, Ulf (1994): "The State of Sovereignty in Europe: Political Concept or Cultural Self-Image" in S. Zetterholm (ed.), *National Cultures and European Integration,* Oxford: Berg.
Hedetoft, Ulf (1994b): "National Identities and European Integration 'From Below': Bringing People Back In", *Journal of European Integration*, 94/1.
Hedetoft, Ulf (1995): *Signs of Nations. Studies in the Political Semiotics of Self and Other in Contemporary European Nationalism*, Aldershot: Dartmouth.
Knudsen, Tim (1992): "A Portrait of Danish State-Culture: Why Denmark Needs Two National Anthems" in M. Kelstrup (ed.), *European Integration and Denmark's Participation,* Copenhagen: Political Studies Press.
Lunde, Helle (1988): *Rød-Hvid Identitet*. Unpublished MA Thesis, Aalborg University.
Nielsen, Hans-Jørgen (1993): *EF På Valg*, Copenhagen: Columbus.
Pedersen, Nikolaj (1998): "The Danish Referendum on the Treaty of Amsterdam", ZEI discussion papers, C14, Bonn: Center for European Integration Studies, Friedrich-Wilhelms-Universität.
Politiken, 12 August 1990; 19 August 1990.
Siune, Karen et al. (1992): *– det blev et nej,* Aarhus: Politica.
Sørensen, Chresten (1990): *Danmark – Delstat i Europa?,* Copenhagen: Fremad.
Østergaard, Uffe (1992): *Europas Ansigter*, Copenhagen: Rosinante.
Weekendavisen, 10 August 1990; 9 October 1992.
Worre, Torben (1995): "Danish Public Opinion and the European Community", *Scandinavian Journal of History*, vol. 20, no. 2.
Wæver, Ole (1995): "Identity, Integration and Security: Solving the Sovereignty Puzzle in EU Studies", *Journal of International Studies*, vol. 48, no. 2 (Winter).

CHAPTER 10

Between Scylla and Charybdis: Danish Party Policies on European Integration

Jens Henrik Haahr

1. Determinants for Danish Party Attitudes on European Integration

The attitudes of Danish political parties towards European integration are influenced by different types of factors. We can distinguish between those stable determinants, which have constituted the fundamental conditions on which Danish parties have had to formulate their European policies, and the dynamic determinants which have caused specific changes in party policies over time.

The most important fundamental condition on which Danish parties have had to operate, albeit to a varying degree from party to party, is the basic dilemma between the wish to please the electorate and the wish to maximise influence. This dilemma is described in more detail in the following section. Subsequently, I seek to categorise Danish political parties according to the vulnerability towards the basic dilemma, as some parties are more directly affected by it than others. In section 3 I focus on some more dynamic determinants behind changing party policies, and I attempt to explain a number of significant policy changes in three particularly important political parties: the Social Democratic Party (SDP), the Social Liberals and the Socialist People's Party (SPP). Section 4 draws together the conclusions and discusses the future perspectives for Danish party attitudes to European integration.

1.1. The Basic Dilemma:
Pleasing the Electorate or Maximising Influence

The attitudes of Danish political parties towards European integration are fundamentally shaped by a basic dilemma which can be interpreted as a dilemma between vote seeking and policy pursuit, or to put it in other words: between pleasing the electorate and maximising political influence.[1]

---

1 The ideal typical vote seeking party seeks to maximise its voting support in the electorate. The ideal typical policy pursuing party seeks to maximise its influence on public policy (cf. Axelrod 1970: 165-85 and Ström 1990).The concept of the policy pursuing party originally concerned the willingness of parties to join coalitions with other parties, implying that

This basic dilemma emerges because of two facts: First, a relatively strong scepticism towards supranationality in the electorate at large. Second, the fundamental condition of Danish political and economic dependency on its European surroundings.[2]

First the question of Danish dependency: One fundamental fact with which the political parties in Denmark have had to come to terms is the comprehensive Danish dependency on its international surroundings in a number of issue areas. These issue areas range from security policy over monetary policy and financial policy to immigration policy, international trade questions and their ramifications, and a large number of environmental issues.

In these areas, the direction of public policy is decided upon in many other settings than in the Danish parliament at Christiansborg. In isolation, legislation adopted by the Danish parliament in these areas will not have any effects. Alternatively, the effects will be contrary to the intended effects or they will be associated with disproportionate costs. Danish security is a question of the relations between and the policies of the great powers. Danish economic well-being is a question of the developments in the economies of our trading partners – not exclusively but to a very high extent. Trends in Danish interest rates are determined in Frankfurt, London and by political actions in Brussels rather than in Copenhagen. Environmental pollution flows to us from other states, just as Denmark passes on environmental damages to our neighbours.

Public policy in all these areas is decided upon outside the formal jurisdiction of the Danish political system. Consequently, any influence on these issues has to be exerted in other settings than at Christiansborg as well. Political parties have general policy goals. To the extent they wish to achieve these goals under the given circumstances of Danish dependency, they have to seek influence where influence is to be sought.

Furthermore, and closely related to this fact, the political elites of all parties have to consider the implications of the character of the international system for a small state as Denmark. This is particularly important when it comes to small state strategies for maximising political influence and avoiding direct or indirect external policy dictates. I will argue that all political forces in Denmark have an interest

---

coalitions form only between parties which are connected in policy space. Here I use the terms "policy pursuing" and "influence seeking" interchangeably. This implies a broader understanding of policy pursuit as concerning not only coalition formation but also involvement in day-to-day policy-making in bargaining with and within the national government and with other governments and supranational actors.

2 In this article, I understand the level of supranationality as defined by three variables: a) the scope of regulation adopted in international organisations and accepted as binding by participating states, b) the number of issue areas in which such regulation is adopted following majority decision making procedures, and c) the extent of authority in various issue areas conceded to international institutions. Supranationality is thus conceived as a multidimensional phenomenon, an approach which was also applied in an early classic study (Haas 1958: 32-59). Furthermore, I understand the term integration as movement towards or as a condition of a high level of supranationality.

in maximising the rule of law in international relations, in maximising the political importance of multilateral decision-making fora, and not least in supporting the principle of supranationality in those areas where public policy has transnational effects – which happens to be those areas where Denmark is dependent on its surroundings. If applied, the principle of supranationality serves to extend the rule of law in international relations and the significance of binding international cooperation, just as it makes possible flexible power balancing, enabling smaller states to influence larger states through mechanisms of flexible coalition building.[3]

The second issue concerns the importance of an electorate which is sceptical towards the principle of supranationality: It is by now a well documented fact that the Danish electorate is among the most reluctant in Western Europe when it comes to the question of European integration. The reasons for this need not concern us too much here. Suffice it to emphasise that a relatively sceptical Danish public opinion on the question of supranational cooperation in Europe is by no means a new phenomenon. Perhaps it has one of its most important roots in the "Nordic" political and cultural orientation of the Danish political elites in the wake of the two wars with Prussia and Prussia-Austria in the mid-19th century, and the development of a Nordic nationalism in Denmark as a reaction to the expansionist German nationalism of the late 19th century – a Nordic nationalism which emphasised the peculiarity of Nordic culture and that this culture should serve as a model to others (Jensen 1988: 38-60).

A second important historical feature is the significance of popular movements in the creation of the modern Danish state – the importance of the liberal peasants movement in the second half of the 19th century and the strength of the workers movement in the first half of the 20th century (For a brief overview, see Østergård 1987). In an historical view, the strength of these popular movements and their deep involvement in the modernisation of the Danish political, social and economic system has led to a sense of a deep-rooted "ownership" of the Danish state, and in particular of the Danish welfare state, in the Danish population. The welfare state is a welfare state of the Danes' own making – something to be proud of as a Dane. Correspondingly, there is a strong positive sense of identification with national symbols related to Danish state institutions.[4] All of this stands in contrast to the experience of

---

3 It should be noted that supranationalism may take different institutional forms. In the Danish debate, much attention has been focussed on the balance between the different EU institutions in this respect, and sometimes supranationalism is associated exclusively with a situation where the Commission and the European Parliament play the most prominent roles in the political process. However, I view supranationalism as a broader concept, encompassing also a situation in which the Council of Ministers acts as the key institution, namely where it may adopt binding legislation or regulation with simple or qualified majorities among the member states.

4 There are few quantitative data available about popular "ownership" of the Danish state apparatus and Danish welfare state institutions. However, one possible available indication could be the relative degree of satisfaction with the way national democracy works in Denmark. Here, the Danish electorate distinguishes itself as the most satisfied in EU12. In late 1994, 82% of the Danes were satisfied with Danish democracy, compared to an EU12-average approval rate of national democracy of 49% (*Eurobarometer* 1995: no. 42, p. 35).

several other European states, where state modernisation to a higher extent has been imposed from above, and where national state symbols often signify oppression and centralism rather than the achievements of popular movements.[5]

The more recent and focussed scepticism of the Danish electorate towards the institutions of the European Community, or the European Union, may in part be ascribed to the differences which indeed do exist between the Danish regulatory system and the Danish welfare state on the one hand and the regulatory systems which are dominant in the EC/EU on the other hand. In specific areas, for instance regarding working conditions, the working environment, consumer protection and the protection of the external environment, Danish protective standards have often been above the EC/EU average. This has led to a continuing series of incidents in which Danish standards are lowered, or are threatened to be lowered, by the introduction of common EC/EU regulation intended to improve the functioning of the common market. It seems plausible that these continuing regulatory conflicts have contributed to the scepticism of the Danish electorate, along with the fact that there are a number of differences between the universalist and comprehensive Scandinavian-type welfare state regimes and the predominant less de-commodifying Central European regimes. European integration has not affected the outlook of the Danish welfare state in any significant manner, but fears about the possible consequences of tax harmonisation have been salient at times.[6]

The effects of these and other factors for Danish public opinion are well documented. The Eurobarometer surveys repeatedly indicate that resistance to EU membership in Denmark is among the strongest in the Union, although in recent years there has been a clear majority for remaining in the club. Furthermore, until very recently there has, among other things, been strong opposition towards the Economic and Monetary Union, towards binding cooperation on internal security matters, and towards a common security and defence policy.[7] Furthermore, in the

---

5   However, there may be many similarities among the Scandinavian countries when it comes to the popular sense of "state ownership".
6   On differences between welfare state regimes in Scandinavia and continental Europe (see Esping-Andersen 1990).The main conclusion of the comprehensive public opinion survey, which was carried out in the wake of the Danish "no"-vote in the June 2nd 1992 referendum on Danish ratification of the Maastricht Treaty, can be summarised as "freedom lovers vote no, mercenary souls vote yes" (Siune et al. 1992). Voters prioritising economic benefits over political freedom of action predominately rejected the Treaty. Voters with the opposite priorities approved of it. My arguments about the significance of historical Nordic nationalism, popular ownership of the welfare state and worries about Danish regulatory standards are by no means invalidated by this. On the contrary, these features help us understand why formal national political freedom of action is valued so highly by large parts of the electorate. National political freedom of action is more valuable the more there is a perceived difference between Denmark and other nation states, and the higher specific national institutions and systems are valued.
7   The share of the Danish population judging national membership of the EU as a "bad thing" has fluctuated between 20 and 30 percent for many years. Among the electorates of the EU12 member states, this is parallelled only by the scepticism of the British and most

years following the Danish 1993 referendum on the Edinburgh agreement, which laid down certain Danish reservations concerning the Maastricht Treaty in the wake of the June 1992 no-vote, opinion polls indicated weak support for eliminating the four Danish reservations (regarding the Economic and Monetary Union, internal security co-operation, European citizenship and a common defence policy). Specifically concerning the EMU, a 1997 survey reported a majority of 60 percent of the Danes being against a common currency including Denmark with 35 percent favouring it. Among social democratic voters, a massive majority of more than 70 percent opposed the EMU (Data from Greens Analyseinstitut, quoted from *Børsen*, 1995.12.13, and *Eurobarometer* 1996: no 46, DDA3104).[8]

Under these circumstances, vote-seeking must push parties in the direction of being sceptical towards increased supranationality, towards supranationality as such, or towards Danish membership in the EU. Evidently, it should not be forgotten that there is also strong support for EU membership in some segments of the population, and that pro-integration positions are not insignificant. However, it is worth emphasising that most often, pro-integration positions in the electorate take the form of support for status quo or as an accept of reforms as the lesser evil – i.e. support for continued EU membership or accept of Treaty revisions based on fear of the consequences of a Danish rejection, EU membership being seen as a precondition for economic growth and well-being in Denmark (Siune et al. 1992: 92-93 and Haahr 1992: 25-26).

In sum, the fundamental fact of Danish dependency on its international surroundings pushes political parties in the direction of supporting multilateralism and supranationalism. Dependency implies that the EU should be used as a political battleground and that political parties should favour the adoption of common EU-policies where it works to the benefit of the realisation of general party policy goals. It also implies that parties should support strengthened supranationality where it increases de facto Danish influence, where it favours the substantial policy goals of the party in question or strengthens the rule of law in international relations. The fundamental fact of the electorate's scepticism pushes Danish political

---

recently the Spanish electorates. A larger share of the Danish electorate than in any other of the EU12-electorates prefers that countries should not have to submit to majority decisions in the future (Eurobarometer 1995). There is a massive Danish majority of 64 to 24 against a European Government responsible to the European Parliament, compared to a EU-15 average of a majority of 58 to 20 approving. And the Danish electorate is, along with the British, the one which to the highest extent defines itself as having a "national" identity rather than a "European and national" or a "European" identity (Eurobarometer 1996).

8 However, support for taking Denmark into the EMU has increased significantly after Danish ratification of the Amsterdam Treaty and after the coming into existence of the EMU in January 1999. On January 24 1999 an opinion poll for the first time indicated that a clear majority of Danes intended to vote for Danish membership of the EMU, with 49 percent being in favour of the common currency for Denmark and 30 percent rejecting it (cf. *Jyllands-Posten*, 24 January 1999).

parties in the opposite direction: In the direction of emphasising formal national sovereignty, in the direction of rejecting the principle of supranationality, and in the direction of resisting any further attempts at strengthening supranationality in the European Union. However, no matter how strongly you wish to do so, you cannot do both things at the same time.

1.2. The Vulnerable and the Not So Vulnerable

The dilemma between maximising influence and pleasing the electorate affects all Danish political parties, as in referenda the electorate holds the key to Danish approval of future EU reforms. However, the dilemma does not affect all parties in the same manner and with the same strength.

Looking at the existing Danish party system, the vulnerability of each party depends on the extent to which the party in question seeks to influence public policy and on the character of its voting support. Here it is useful to distinguish between two different categories of party behaviour and two different categories of party voting support. We can distinguish between political parties that actively, persistently and on a day-to-day basis seek to influence that public policy which affects the Danish electorate, and political parties that to a higher extent emphasise symbolic and principled policy statements – influence seeking parties and parties which to a higher extent rely on "symbolic positioning".

Influence seeking parties will typically be located close to the government. Either they will form the government or a part of it in a coalition government, they will form a part of the government's parliamentary basis, or they will participate in political compromises with the government on public policy on a regular basis. Parties adopting symbolic positioning as a dominant pattern of behaviour will similarly be located further away from government, advocating policies which diverge radically from present government policies.

Second, we can distinguish between parties of which the electoral support is predominately in favour of supranationality and parties of which the electoral support is predominately sceptical towards supranationality. The resulting four-cell matrix is displayed below.

The following points should be emphasised: First, where the voting support of the party in question is predominately in favour of the principle of supranationalism, the dilemma of pleasing the electorate and maximising influence is not valid. Whether they can be characterised as influence seekers or as parties adopting symbolic positioning, such parties will not face conflicting pressures.

Table 1: Party Behaviour and Party Voting Support in Relation to International Integration

Party Voting Support	Party Behaviour	
	Influence-Seeking	Symbolic Positioning
Voting Support in Favour of Supranationality	Harmonious pro-integration policy involvement	Symbolic pro-integration position
Voting Support Against Supranationality	"Bridging the impossible gap" – the vulnerable	Symbolic anti-integration position

Second, it could be expected that given fundamental Danish dependency on its international surroundings, the dilemma between pleasing the voters and maximising influence should become a threatening reality to all parties where voting support is predominately against supranationality. However, by moving itself away from day-to-day politics a party is also moving itself away from the practical implications of Danish dependency. By emphasising symbolic policy statements, a party may thus be able to escape the dilemma, in fact by denying or toning down the consequences of international dependency or by advocating policies which would imply a radical break with existing international economic and political relations.

As it appears, the most interesting category of parties is the category consisting of parties which are active influence seekers at the same time receiving the bulk or a large share of their electoral support from voters who are critical or sceptical towards the idea of supranationality. Given the basic fact of comprehensive Danish dependency on the outside world, these parties will have to "bridge the impossible gap". On the one hand they need to or wish to seek influence where influence is to be sought. This implies their active pursuit of policies in the European Union or other supranational bodies where this is the most efficient channel for influence. It also implies their support for increased supranationality where this would serve the accomplishment of their substantial general policy goals. On the other hand they need to accommodate their voters' resistance towards precisely this supranational framework.

How can we describe the most important Danish political parties in terms of their vulnerability towards the dilemma of influence versus electoral support? First we can identify the parties that can be characterised as influence-seekers and those which to a higher extent rely on strategies of symbolic positioning. In accordance with the definitions introduced in the above, influence-seeking parties would include parties of present or recent governments, the parties constituting the parliamentary basis of present or recent governments or parties participating in political compromises with the government on a regular basis.

Described in terms of their location on the traditional left-right scale, this would include the right-of-centre parties of the Liberals and the Conservatives, forming a part of the government from 1982 to 1993 and collaborating regularly with the governments since then. It would also include the centre parties of the Social Liberals, the Centre Democrats and the Christian People's Party (when represented in Parliament). All of these three centre parties have recently formed or are presently forming a part of the coalition governments which have ruled in Denmark since 1982 and on multiple occasions before that. Furthermore, it would include the largest party in Parliament, the Social Democrats, the main party of the coalition government since 1993 and a regular participator in large compromises with the centre-right coalition governments from 1982 to 1993.

It would exclude the right wing Progress Party and the left wing Unity Party (which was formed in 1991 on the basis of the Left Socialist Party, the Communist Party and several smaller left wing groupings). It would also exclude the left wing Socialist People's Party (SPP) until the late 1980s, but could include this party from 1989 and onwards, since the SPP has appeared increasingly to value its influence on day-to-day policy formation from this time onwards at the cost of more principled policy statements.

Looking at the voting support of the above mentioned parties, which of them should be characterised as relying on voting support predominately favouring or accepting the principle of supranationality, and which of them are to a high extent dependent on voting support from segments of the electorate which is predominately against supranationality? Two different indicators may serve to illuminate this question: The positions of the various parties' voters on the question of Danish EC/EU membership, and the positions of the various parties' voters in the four most recent Danish referenda on the development of the EC/EU in 1986, 1992, 1993 and 1998, respectively.

Table 2: EC/EU-Membership Support by Party Vote, Opinion Balances[9]

Party vote	1979	1984	1990	1996
Left Socialists*	÷78	÷94	N/A	÷76
Socialist People's Party	÷77	÷73	÷46	÷28
Social Democrats	÷1	÷13	0	+5
Social Liberals	+29	+19	N/A	+15
Christian People's Party	+29	+22	N/A	N/A
Centre Democrats	+65	+45	N/A	N/A
Liberals	+78	+74	+71	+47
Conservatives	+66	+48	+67	+54
Progress Party	+23	÷11	+30	÷22

*Succeeded by the Unity Party in 1991

---

9 "Generally speaking, do you think that Denmark's membership of the European Union / the European Community is a good thing, a bad thing, neither good nor bad?" (Data 1979 and 1984 quoted from Torben Worre 1987: 82; Data from 1990 Gallup 1990: survey DDA1640; Data from 1996 Eurobarometer 1996: no. 46.0, DDA3104).

Table 3: "No"-Vote by Party in the EC/EU-Referenda 1986, 1992, 1993, 1998[10]

Party vote	1986 (SEA)	1992 (Maastricht)	1993 (Maastricht)	1998 (Amsterdam)
Socialist People's Party	85	94	80	81
Social Democrats	77	61	41	45
Social Liberals	25	50	30	30
Centre Democrats	10	20	17	32
Liberals	2	13	12	17
Conservatives	2	15	14	20
Progress Party / DPP	N/A	82	84	88

From Tables 2 and 3, it appears that we can distinguish between three groups of parties in terms of the positions of their voters on Danish EC/EU membership and on the development of European integration.

First, there is a group consisting of the Conservatives, the Liberals and the Centre Democrats, the voting support of which is clearly in favour of Danish membership, and the voters of which display the clearly smallest share voting against Danish ratification of the Single European Act, the Maastricht Treaty and the Amsterdam Treaty respectively. According to the survey data, only up to 20% of the three parties' voters have voted "no" in the referenda since 1986, with the single exception of the 32% of the Centre Democrats' voters opposing the ratification of the Amsterdam Treaty.

Second, there is a group consisting of the Left Socialists/Unity Party and the Socialist People's Party the voting support of which is clearly opposed to membership, and the voters of which were very clearly opposed to Danish ratification of the SEA and the Maastricht Treaty. The right wing Progress Party could also be included into this group. One the one hand, the party's voters are very divided on the issue of Danish EC membership, but on the other hand there appears to be strong resistance among its voters towards any deepening of European integration, and this last question has for the past 10 to 15 years been the most relevant question of the two.

Third, there is a group consisting of the Social Democrats, the Social Liberals and the Christian People's Party, the voting support of which is highly divided on the issue of EC membership, and on whether or not to approve the deepening of European integration which was represented by the SEA and the Maastricht Treaty.

---

10 For the 1986-referendum, the figures are quoted from Tonsgaard (1987: 122). For the 1992-referendum, the figures derives from a GfK opinion poll carried out on 5-7 June 1992 (GfK 1992). The 1993-figures are quoted from Siune et al. (1994: 101). For the 1998-referendum, figures are quoted from a Gallup exit poll on 28 May 1998 (Gallup 1998). Prior to the 1998-referendum, the right wing Progress Party split into the Progress Party and the Danish People's Party (DPP). The 1998-figure concerns the voters of the DPP. Due to small n, data for the Left Socialists and the Christian People's Party have been omitted.

The leaderships of all these three parties have consistently recommended Danish EC/EU membership – at least ever since the British decision to join the Community. Furthermore, all three party leaderships recommended the Danish electorate to approve the Maastricht Treaty in 1992 and 1993 and the Amsterdam Treaty in 1998. In 1986, the Social Democrats and the Social Liberals recommended a "no" to the SEA, which presumably explains the particularly strong resistance among social democratic voters in this instance, whereas the Social Liberal leadership appears to have done a poor job in leading the party's voters in the SEA referendum.[11]

We can now combine this information on the nature of Danish parties' voting support with the previous characterisation of their behaviour as being influence seeking or predominately marked by symbolic positioning. An attempt has been made in the four-cell matrix below, where we do not distinguish between whether a party's voting support is divided on or directly against supranationality.

Table 4: The Vulnerability of Danish Political Parties Concerning European Integration

Party Voting Support	Party Behaviour	
	Influence-Seeking	Symbolic Positioning
Voting support predominantly in favour of supranationality	• Conservatives • Liberals • Centre Democrats	• None (in Denmark)
Voting support highly divided on or predominantly sceptical towards supranationality	• Social Democrats • Socialist People's Party (after 1989) • Social Liberals • Christian People's Party	• Unity Party • Socialist People's Party (before 1989) • Progress Party

In this interpretation, the Conservatives, the Liberals and the Centre Democrats have been able to follow a course of harmonious pro-integration policy involvement as regards European integration. For this group of parties, the basic dilemma between influence and electoral support has not materialised to any significant extent. Policy pursuit has not conflicted with appeals to their core voters or potential voters, as these voters basically display positive attitudes towards integration. However, this does not mean that the dilemma cannot emerge in the future, perhaps already in connection with the next IGC. This is true since support for European integration among the parties' voters appears to be instrumental and shaped by perceptions of concrete interests in and benefits flowing from integration, rather than any ideal support for a European unification process.

---

11 The Social Liberal leadership repeatedly emphasised its willingness to accept the decision of each individual voter in the SEA-referendum (Worre, 1988: 371-372). Party leadership was very "soft", perhaps suggesting that the leadership was aware of the internal divisions among the party's voters.

The course of the left wing Unity Party and the Socialist People's Party before 1989 and the right wing Progress Party can similarly be characterised as symbolic resistance to European integration. Since the risk that the policy positions of these parties will actually result in enacted policies is very small, it has been costless for them to pursue policies that are confrontational towards integration and which could possibly involve Danish withdrawal from the EU. This has enabled those parties to be in accordance with their voters and potential voters to a very high extent, and thereby to escape the dilemma of influence versus electoral support, simply by lowering the importance attached to influence, at least in the short term.

The parties which are most affected by the basic dilemma, the vulnerable parties, are characterised by a wish to exert influence over the policies that affect the Danish political system. At the same time, they are characterised by a reliance on electoral support from voters who disagree on the benefits of European integration or who are highly sceptical towards supranationality. As it appears, this group of parties comprise three important political forces located at the centre and centre-left of the political left-right divide: the Social Democrats, the Social Liberals and from the late 1980s the Socialist People's Party. When represented in Parliament, we can also include the small Christian People's Party in this vulnerable group.

2. Coping With the Dilemma: Party Tactics

How have the three largest of these parties, the Social Democrats, the SPP, and the Social Liberals, sought to "bridge the impossible gap"? Which balance has been struck between pleasing the electorate and maximising influence? And which tactics have been applied to attempt to ameliorate or escape the dilemma?

2.1. The Social Democrats

For the most important party, normally the single largest party in the Danish Parliament and the most frequent carrier of governmental responsibility, the Social Democratic Party, there was never any doubt in the party leadership that Denmark had to join the EC in the moment Great Britain did so, and that any future outside the EC under this circumstance would be bleak.

However, the deep divisions among the party's voters and internally in the parliamentary party, which were displayed both in connection with the 1972 referendum on Danish EC membership and in connection with the 1986 SEA referendum, has done much harm to the party. The leadership has therefore implicitly or explicitly adopted a range of tactics to ameliorate the most damaging effects of the basic dilemma.

One initial reaction in connection with the discussion of EC membership was to tone down the political importance of European integration and continuously to emphasise the pragmatic, economic elements in European cooperation (as the Social Democratic leadership preferred to term the EC), as well as the direct economic benefits of Danish EC membership for agriculture and the fishery industry. This emphasis of economic benefits for Denmark were closely coupled with continuous warnings to EC sceptical voters about the dire economic consequences, should Denmark choose to stay outside or leave the Community. The strategy of "economising" questions of European integration appears to have been pursued by the party leadership well into the 1980s.

A second tactic pursued by the Social Democratic leadership has traditionally been to sweep internal disagreements under the carpet, avoiding any discussion altogether of European integration. An early attempt was made by the party to put internal rifts behind it and take EC membership as the fact on which to proceed with the development of positive policies: Right from the onset of Danish membership, the party leadership decided to attempt to make use of the political system of the EC to further the obtainment of its general policy goals, acknowledging that membership provided opportunities and access to fora where a small country could not otherwise have yielded any influence (Andersen et al. 1973). But as EC opposition in the party and among its voters proved very stubborn and the discussion on Danish EC membership would not go away, an implicit tactic of reconciliation through oblivion appears to have been the party leadership's choice. This tactic worked reasonably well as long as European integration was paused in the harsh economic climate of the 1970s and early 1980s, but it turned out to backfire and reveal its harmful consequences for the party in the form of unresolved conflicts once European integration started to move forward again in the mid-1980s.

Furthermore, up, until and including, the 1986 referendum on the SEA, the party leadership openly and continuously committed itself to resist any development of the EC in the direction of a "Union". In the party's statements, "Union" was never defined in anything approaching precise terms. However, since "Union" had developed into the single most important spook-word of the popular anti-EC movement during the 1970s, being associated on any given occasion with a highly centralised, undemocratic and bureaucratic superstate, the Social Democratic party leadership sought to accommodate its EC sceptical voters by distancing itself from "Union". "Union" does not have the same negative connotations in most other Western European states as in Denmark. This subsequently caused the SDP many problems in connection with the SEA-negotiations and in particular with the Maastricht Treaty. Many observers have wondered why the Single European Act or the "Acte Unique" in French got the strange Euro-speak name it got. The explanation is to be found in Danish Social Democratic fears of "Union": In the negotiations, the French in particular pushed for some kind of reference to a Union, but the Social Democrats would not accept any name referring to this land of the condemned (Nørgaard 1985; see also Nørgaard 1989).

More generally, many of the most prominent social democratic leaders had vowed to prevent a development of the European Community in a supranational direction. This promise was made forcefully by the leading EC spokesman for many years, Ivar Nørgaard, in connection with the debate on Danish EC membership, and it was made repeatedly after membership had become a reality. The principled rejection of a strengthening of supranationality was one of the most important reasons that the party rejected Danish ratification of the SEA in 1986, pointing among other things to the limited extension of the European Parliament's powers in this reform package as a point of disagreement. That the referendum subsequently overturned the party leadership's recommendations has presumably freed many of the party's old EC advocates from an obligation to resist a further development of supranationality.

Traditionally, the Social Democratic Party has thus adopted largely defensive strategies, having sought ways of accommodating its sceptical members and voters. Alternatively, it has chosen an "easy" offensive strategy in pointing to the immediate economic consequences of resistance to EU membership or strengthened integration. Historically, very few attempts have been made to openly persuade party members and voters about the political benefits for Denmark of strong supranational institutions and Danish membership of them. Until recently, the party leadership has presumably had little faith in the power of persuasion as regards these aspects of European integration. Small-state dependency on international surroundings and the political benefits of supranationalism and multilateralism are – as it appears – abstract concepts relating to general and abstract benefits. It is not difficult to see why representatives of the Social Democratic Party have most often chosen other, more tangible arguments in direct confrontation with their voters, or have tried to avoid this divisive subject altogether.

Most lately, however, there are signs that more offensive approaches are increasingly being adopted by the party leadership. This follows the outcome of the referendum on the Amsterdam Treaty, where a majority of the Danish population opted for Danish ratification, and the coming into existence of the Economic and Monetary Union. I shall return to this fact later.

2.2. The Social Liberals

In the early phases of Danish EC membership, the Social Liberals, a small centre party, appears to have followed some of the same tactics as the social democratic party. As was the case for the Social Democratic party leadership, the leadership of the Social Liberals supported EC membership, emphasising the economic aspects of integration. At the same time, during the 1970s and most of the 1980s the party rejected any development of the EC into a political union with federal characteristics (N.H. Petersen 1984: cols. 7197-7200). As regards political rather than economic aspects of international cooperation, the party has traditionally emphasised the value of Nordic cooperation and the UN framework. The party leadership thus pointed to concerns about the future of Nordic foreign policy cooperation as an explanation for voting against Danish ratification of the SEA in 1986.

However, both in connection with the 1992- and 1993 referenda, the party adopted policies which only to a limited degree sought to accommodate its EU-sceptical voters. For instance, Social Liberal support for the EMU was clear prior to the June 2nd referendum (Minister of Economy N.H. Petersen 1990: cols.8469-8472). In the period after the May 1993 referendum, some prominent figures in the party increasingly seem willing to confront EU-sceptical voters and party members with what they see as the realities of the European situation. The party's chairwoman and Minister of Economy in the government since 1993, Marianne Jelved, has repeatedly emphasised the large costs involved if Denmark was to remain outside a future Economic and Monetary Union, and she has continuously hammered out the message that Denmark ought to join the common currency. Similarly, the party has underlined the importance of EU enlargement and the institutional reforms of the EU which this necessitates. Finally, in the party's executive board a majority in 1995 decided not to attempt to accommodate the party's EU sceptical wing in the formulation of its policies towards the 1996 IGC.

As opposed to what has been the case for the Social Democrats, the Social Liberals therefore do not to the same degree seem inclined to adopt defensive strategies towards its integration-sceptical voters. It has to remain an interpretation, but one explanation could lie in the fact that the Social Liberal Party has a peculiar profile: It is the party in Denmark which has the lowest ratio of core voters with fewer than half of its voters in each election having voted for the party in the previous election. In addition, the party has continuously placed itself precisely at the centre of the political stage, between the right and left blocks, meaning that policy changes that cost votes on the one side of the spectrum most likely capture new votes on the other side. Finally, it has been one of the party's hallmarks not to have close ties to any particular social class or organised interests. Added together, these factors suggest that the Social Liberals are more free than other parties to pursue controversial policies which they deem are important from an overall societal point of view. Indeed, the party has repeatedly argued for the necessity of revamping the expensive "something in it for everyone"-welfare state, involving proposals for changes in a range of controversial fields.

2.3. The Socialist People's Party

Looking at the left wing Socialist People's Party, the dilemma between pleasing its voters and maximising influence first became a reality after the party's change of policy style in the late 1980s. Thus, in the late 1980s the party gradually adopted a more influence-seeking attitude, seeking closer cooperation with the Social Democratic Party and the centre parties in order to affect policy outcomes. One consequence of this change of policy style, which I shall return to below, was an accept by the party leadership that Danish EC membership was a fact with which the party had to come to terms. The party leadership in effect accepted that the only alternative to the EC was an improved EC (U. Haahr, interview with Holger K. Nielsen, 27 March 1993). At the same time, as we have seen it, the party's voters remained deeply sceptical towards European integration and Danish EC/EU membership.

The party leadership was confronted with the possible effects of this dilemma quite soon after the party had adopted its new influence seeking style, i.e. in connection with the 1992 referendum on the Maastricht Treaty. The party leadership explicitly acknowledged that the Treaty contained many elements of which the party was fully supportive and that these elements were indeed quite necessary in the new European situation. But confronted with the stark alternatives between advocating a "yes" in the referendum, thereby deviating sharply from the traditional anti-EC policy of the party and most likely attracting the wrath of its voters, and recommending the "no" which voters of the party expected, the choice fell on the latter and probably easier option.

It is a noticeable but widely overlooked fact, however, that the motivation for the party's policy in connection with the referendum was not a defence of Danish sovereignty or any rejection of supranationality as such. The party had from the outset adopted a very critical attitude to the proposed economic and monetary union in the EU, but in addition Holger K. Nielsen, the party leader, and other leading members of the party's parliamentary group repeatedly emphasised that the party also advocated a rejection of the Treaty on the grounds that it did not go far enough! In particular this was the case in the fields of environmental protection and a strengthened social dimension in the EC. The party had in other words chosen the policy which the party's voters clearly preferred, but the policy in part rested on a motivation which differed very much from the SPP's traditional rejection of supranational European integration, a motivation which could pave the way for more pro-integrative future positions.

The dilemma between pleasing the electorate and maximising influence remained very salient for the Socialist People's Party in the period from the narrow no-vote in the June 2nd referendum to the second referendum on the Maastricht Treaty in May 1993. As the SPP appeared to hold the key to the outcome of the next referendum the pressure on the party leadership was immense, both from the anti-EC movements and from proponents of Danish ratification of the Treaty. Eventually, the SPP decided to join the "national compromise" – the common negotiating position of a vast majority in the Danish parliament for a solution to the situation after the June 2nd referendum.

The contents of the "national compromise" is a clear example of the balancing act the SPP leadership tried to perform between pursuing influence and pleasing its voters. Before the June referendum, the party had assured the voters that there were no risks in rejecting the Maastricht Treaty. The result would be a renegotiation of the Treaty or special escape clauses for Denmark. If the SPP were to remain a trustworthy partner for other parties with a view to future policy making, it therefore had to adopt a constructive approach to "the Danish problem". The situation after the June referendum also provided the party with a unique possibility of influencing events with wide ranging consequences. At the same time, the party had to reassure and satisfy its EC-hostile voters. The contents of the national compromise reflects this situation, as in the end its most important elements turned out to be four defensive Danish statements specifying which types of European integration Denmark would not take part in in the future. The offensive elements in the SPP's European policy therefore to a large extent disappeared in the light of the strength of anti-integration feelings among the party's grass roots among other things.

In spite of this hostility, the party leadership stuck to its commitments and chose to recommend Danish approval of the Treaty, with the escape clauses attached, when the other EC member states had agreed to the Danish requests. This was on most accounts a brave but also a very costly decision. The SPP was widely being castigated and condemned as traitors among left wing voters and by the anti-EC popular movements. The party representatives took a battering in constituency meetings, and the parliamentary election of September 1994, saw the electoral decline of the SPP and the entry into parliament of the Unity Party, the most salient policy positions of which were staunch resistance to the EU and a critical attitude to the European policy of the SPP.

Since then the Socialist People's Party has tried to edge closer to its voters without losing too much credibility in relation to previous policies. The balance has tilted towards vote pursuit, at the cost of influence seeking. The result is that the party has now moved back towards the symbolic anti-integration position it represented in the period before 1989. Moving back towards previous positions without directly having to admit failures or reverse specific policies is a difficult exercise. The strategy of the SPP has been to cling to and focus almost exclusively on the four Danish "exemptions" contained in the national compromise, which it could portray as its victory, the concrete results of the party's involvement in the national and international negotiations after June 2nd.

Thus, in the parliamentary talks on the Danish negotiating position in the 1996 IGC, it was the party's single most important priority that these exemptions should be written into the revised Treaty, even though there were few signs that the exemptions would be on the agenda – and indeed it was a Danish decision whether they would be discussed at all. The party's insistence on the codification in the Treaty itself of the exemptions caused the breakdown of negotiations. The SPP was therefore not committed to the Danish negotiation position, and thus remained comfortably free to recommend a "no" in the referendum on the Amsterdam Treaty – which unsurprisingly was the official position adopted by the party.[12] In late 1995, the party's concerns about its relation to its voters were directly confirmed by political spokesman Steen Gade, as he on 12 December held that "SPP is the party which is closest to the positions of the population, and one will have to listen

---

12 The decision to recommend a "no" in the referendum was, however, surrounded by internal controversy and disagreement, with a pro-integration faction in the party's parliamentary group openly advocating a yes-vote.

to that" (Quoted from *Information*, 13 December 1995: 3, my translation). In this instance Gade put forward precious few arguments about the actual substance of the four exemptions, whether it is a right policy or not for Denmark and Europe. In that place, he put very much emphasis on respecting the opinion of the people. This position was also reflected in the party's policy paper pertaining the 1996 IGC. This paper pointed to the marked popular resistance to supranational integration as the main rationale for suggesting a fundamentally different approach to European cooperation than the project of European Union (Socialistisk Folkeparti 1995).

In sum, there are no easy ways for the most important vulnerable parties in Denmark to escape the basic dilemma between influence seeking and the wish to please the electorate. Various tactics have been employed, but none of them have been successful for more than limited periods of time. Apparently, the dilemma cannot be escaped, it can only be confronted. This means that the party in question may choose to refrain altogether from attempting to influence the policies which affect the Danish political system directly, instead adopting symbolic policy styles. Alternatively, it may choose to confront its voters directly with the harsh message of international dependence and its consequences, however costly in terms of voting support this may turn out to be.

3. Explaining the Dynamics of Party Attitudes on Integration

Although they display a relatively high degree of stability, and although the basic dilemma is truly basic for the group of parties I have termed "the vulnerable parties" above, some Danish parties' policies on European integration have evolved over time. In particular, and as it could be expected, in the vulnerable parties the question of European integration has continuously been debated, and we have witnessed several clear policy developments during the past 15 years. Thus, in the last years of the 1980s and the first years of the 1990s all three of the most important vulnerable parties, the Social Democrats, the Social Liberals and the Socialist People's Party developed policies which were clearly more offensive in the question of European integration than the positions previously advocated by these parties.

This policy development is signified by the fact that whereas both parties had argued for a rejection of the Single European Act in 1986, the Social Democrats and the Social Liberals supported a "yes" in the first referendum on the much more wide reaching Maastricht Treaty in June 1992. Similarly, both the Social Democrats, the Social Liberals and the Socialist People's Party advocated a "yes" in the May 1993 referendum on the Maastricht Treaty with addenda, just as the Social Democrats and the Social Liberals supported the Amsterdam Treaty and favour full Danish membership in the EMU. Against the background of the analysis of the basic dilemma that these parties are confronted with, it is relevant to ask why this development occurred.

Party policy changes are most fruitfully studied as analyses of changing societal conditions for the achievement of general policy goals. As I have argued previously in this article, parties have general policy goals. Social democratic political parties for instance pursue general policy goals such as full employment and a range of universal citizen rights. But in different societal circumstances, different means or in other words different specific policies are relevant for the achievement of general policy goals. In a small, open economy, the development of a large public sector may for instance be a suitable policy for shielding the national economy against international economic fluctuations (Cf. Katzenstein 1985). In a dynamic perspective, the growing economic openness of a national economy may similarly imply that a party's policies for economic stability and full employment will increasingly focus on a large public sector as a means to this end.

Changing societal conditions may therefore translate into changing party policies in a specific area. This translation process can take place through two different channels. First, conditioned on the party's general policy goals, second through the effects of societal changes on voter preferences and conditioned on the party's electoral support concern. Thus, for political parties, some degree of support in the electorate is the *sine qua non* for survival, not to mention political influence. Whether general policy interests or electoral support concerns are most important for a given policy development depends on a range of institutional, systemic and organisational factors (For a full discussion of this model for the analysis of party policy change, see Haahr 1993: 19-40).

Figure 1: A Framework for the Analysis of Party Policy Change

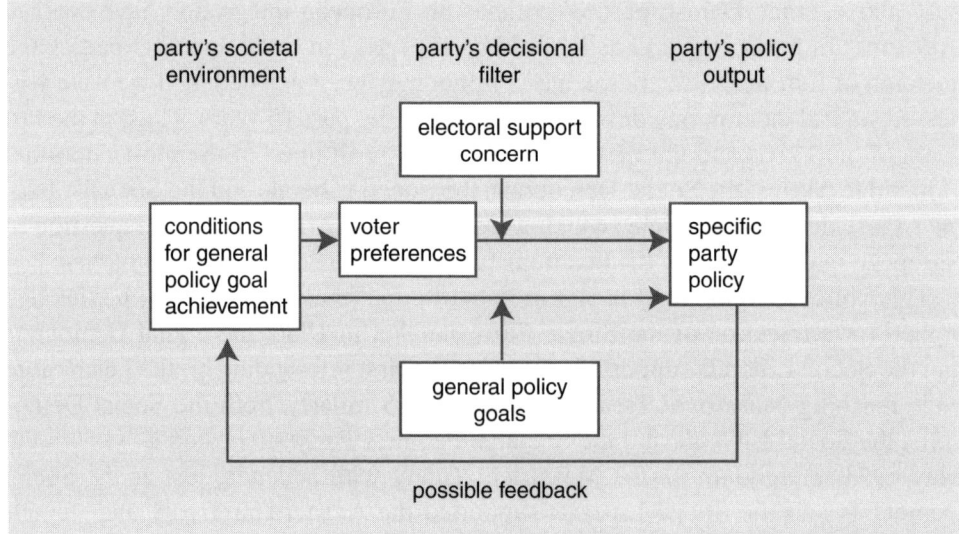

Which changing societal conditions explain the development in the European policies of the most important vulnerable parties, the Social Democratic, the SPP and the Social Liberals? Why did these parties first reject the SEA, only to endorse – eventually – the Maastricht Treaty?

Two explanations may to a certain degree account for this development. As for the first explanation, the party leaderships of the SDP, the SPP and the Social Liberals increasingly saw a need to supplement the market liberalising single market-project with regulation aimed at protecting social and for the Social Liberals in particular environmental values. However, given the realities of a revitalised EC, the SEA and the progressing single market, this supplementary regulation could only be implemented at the European level. This again required strengthened supranationality in the EC in specified areas. Second, both the SPP, the Social Democrats and the Social Liberals were as affected by the break-up of the European security political situation in 1989-90 as every other political party in Denmark. All party leaderships increasingly acknowledged that the new situation called for strengthened European institutions in certain areas, to commit Germany to multilateral cooperation and to face up to the growing challenges in Central and Eastern Europe and the Soviet Union/CIS.

The Social Democrats and the Socialist People's Party share many general policy goals: the objective of full employment, a range of universal citizens' rights enshrined in the concept of the comprehensive welfare state and protective rights aimed at ensuring a life in dignity. What more is, to a high extent they share the conviction that these general policy goals are to be achieved through state intervention in the market economy – "politics against markets" (Esping-Andersen 1985), – and indeed the realisation of these basic general policy goals inevitably involves a high degree of state intervention in the functioning of the economy and in the lives of citizens.

Against this background, it was in many ways quite understandable that the Social Democrats and the SPP decided to reject Danish ratification of the SEA in early 1986. Thus, the Single European Act must primarily be seen as a market liberalising venture aimed at strengthening the scope of market regulation of the economy on a European Community-wide scale. As such the SEA bears the unmistakable finger print of then Conservative Prime Minister Margaret Thatcher, who eventually decided to support the reform of EC decision making procedures and overwin her scepticism towards supranational institutions both on ideological grounds and with a view to the possibilities of the London City in an internal market for financial services.

For the Social Democrats and the Socialist People's Party in Denmark, there appeared to be considerable risks involved in the realisation of the single European market, primarily in relation to the SEA's majority decision making procedures. Doubts were raised in 1985-86 as to whether Danish regulatory standards in areas such as environmental protection, consumer protection and the working environment could be upheld where majority decisions would apply in the EC Council of

Ministers. Concerns were also voiced about the possible implications for the financing of the Danish welfare state of tax harmonisations in a Europe without borders. A number of other arguments against the SEA were heard from the two parties' representatives, ranging from the need to defend formal Danish sovereignty and reject any strengthening of supranational institutions, to a basic rejection of the EC as such. However, fears about the implications of the effects of market liberalisations on a Community wide scale were among the important motivations for the two parties' common decision to reject the reform package.[13]

After the February 1986 consultative referendum in Denmark, which gave endorsement to the then centre-right coalition government's approval of the SEA, the ratification process continued. During 1987-88, the single market-project even turned out to be a clear and highly unexpected political success for the European Commission. Progress on implementation of the White Book, containing 279 directives needed for the accomplishment of the single market, was faster than expected, and a range of economic and political actors mobilised in light of the emergence of a more integrated market in the EC. To the Social Democrats and the organisations and interests the Social Democratic Party represented, this was an unsought development which was by some groups – primarily trade unions – increasingly seen as a threat to working and living conditions, an understanding summarised in the concept of "social dumping". But the SEA had been adopted, with the approval of the Danish electorate, and the social democratic leadership was fully aware of the Danish dependency on EC membership.

In this situation, the most realistic solution seen from the Social Democratic Party was to try to twist the single market project in a more acceptable direction, giving more priority to social and environmental protection. In connection with the June 1989 elections to the European Parliament, this development resulted in a social democratic policy on reforms of the European Community which endorsed the introduction of majority voting procedures in the Council of Ministers as regards the establishment of minimum standards for environmental and labour market conditions (Lorenzen: 1989).

The policy of the SPP developed in parallel to this, even if with a slight delay. The party remained focussed on limiting the scope and impact of the single market project on a national basis for longer than the Social Democrats, but in the second half of 1989 the party gradually adopted a more offensive policy similar to the Social Democratic approach. Thus, in a parliamentary debate concerning the Delors-plan for Economic and Monetary Union in the EC, held in November 1989, the SPP explicitly stated its wish for an EC with stronger competencies in the fields of environmental protection and regulation on minimum social standards (SPP political spokesman Steen Gade 30 November 1989: cols. 2586-2587). For the Social Liberals, arguments against social dumping were not pre-eminent in the

---

13 For an account of social democratic positions in the debate on the SEA see Haahr (1993: 203-211).

debate about European integration. However, the party increasingly stressed the need to strengthen environmental projection in the EC-framework in the wake of the single market reforms, and in the run-up to the 1991 IGC, the party advocated the introduction of majority voting procedures in this area (N.H. Petersen 29 October 1991: cols.1125-1126).

As for the second explanation – the new security political situation in Europe after 1989 – this explanation in particular accounts for the development in the positions of the Social Democratic Party and the Social Liberals towards Economic and Monetary Union. For the SPP, it appears to have contributed more generally to the party's constructive approach to European integration in the early 1990s, whereas the party remained opposed to the EMU-plans throughout the process.[14]

Looking at the Social Democrats and the EMU, this party initially rejected all ideas about currency union in the EC, deeming it unrealistic and criticising the consequences for monetary and in the last instance finance political autonomy in the member states (the Social Democratic Party 1987: 90). However, as the EMU-plans hardened and a political consensus appeared to be emerging, social democratic scepticism was gradually replaced by an attempt to influence the coming EMU framework in a direction more acceptable to social democratic beliefs. This implied that the EMU should be based on a concern for employment as well as low inflation, not just a concern for inflation as was the view of conservative and liberal governments in Western Europe. As the intergovernmental conference commenced its work in preparation of the Maastricht Treaty, the party thus had adopted a constructive and open approach to EMU (Haahr 1993: 244-247).

A projection of social democratic values and interests to the EC-level thus partly explains this development, as was the case with social democratic policies on the introduction of more majority decisions in the EC. However, a growing realisation that there was a Danish interest in obtaining some kind of influence on German monetary policy and at the same time commit Germany irrevocably to supranational European structures was the most important motivation. This understanding was voiced particularly loudly by the then chairwoman of the SDP's parliamentary group, Ritt Bjerregaard (Olsen 1990). At the same time, social democratic support of EMU during this period should not be exaggerated. Prior to the agreement on the Maastricht Treaty, the party never explicitly endorsed the proposal on economic and monetary union, emphasising that the specific outlook of the EMU-plans were decisive. In the campaign preceding the 1992-referendum, the EMU-plans were not among the party's arguments for a "yes", and prior to the 1993-referendum the then EC-spokesman of the party, Ivar Nørgaard, emphasised that the Danish opt-out of the EMU had improved the case for ratifying the Maastricht Treaty considerably, given the contents of the EMU-plans as described in the

---

14 The Socialist People's Party's fundamentally critical attitude towards the EMU was illustrated by Steen Gade (Gade 1989a; 1989b).

Treaty. The SDP's current enthusiasm for full Danish EMU membership is thus a rather recent phenomenon, which is most likely related to the fact the EMU has come into existence and is set to be a permanent and extremely significant element of European integration. At the same time, the pro-EMU swing in public opinion in late 1998 and early 1999 has made it much easier for the party leadership to signal enthusiasm, in effect largely causing the basic dilemma between vote pursuit and influence seeking to disappear in this field – at least for the time being.[15]

In sum, the successful single market plans in the 1980s in the view of the three party leaderships constituted an important societal change. The single market success implied a change in the parties' societal conditions for the achievement of their general policy goals. This led the SDP, the SPP and the Social Liberals to support the introduction of majority voting in the EC in new areas. At the same time, the changing political landscape in Europe after 1989 also signified a change in conditions for the achievement of general policy goals which led the SPD to consider and the Social Liberals to support the single currency plans.[16] Furthermore, considering the nature of these three parties' voting support as it has been described previously, this development of specific party policies has clearly been conditioned by their general policy goals rather than by a concern for electoral support. European integration has never been a vote catcher in Denmark. This is illustrated by both the outcome of the three most recent referenda, by the outcome of the 1994 and 1999 elections to the European Parliament, where both the SPP and the Social Democrats experienced heavy losses particularly to the anti-EU movements, and by the September 1994 parliamentary election where the SPP lost heavily and saw itself confronted with a new strongly EU-critical competitor to its left.

4. Conclusions and Perspectives

Because they are operating in a small state, Danish political parties are confronted with the imperatives of Denmark's dependency on its international surroundings. At the same time they are facing an electorate which displays little enthusiasm about supranational integration. The first condition calls for strong and strengthened supranational cooperation in a number of issue areas. The second condition leads political parties to oppose or resist supranationality.

Parties, who wish to influence public policy affecting Denmark and who at the same time receive their electoral support from voters who are sceptical or critical towards supranational integration, are caught in this dilemma. They are the vulnerable parties of Danish European policy: the Social Democratic Party, the Social Li-

---

15 For a more thorough analysis of the Danish Social Democratic approach to the EMU see Haahr (2000).
16 For the Social Liberals, concerns for the then government coalition between the Conservatives, the Liberals and the Social Liberals presumably also played an important role. Both the Conservatives and the Liberals where clearly in favour of EMU.

berals and the Socialist People's Party. Danish European policy cannot be formulated without the support of at least one of these three parties, and the way in which they seek to evade or confront the basic dilemma is therefore decisive for present and future Danish policies on European integration.

As we have seen it, all three parties have reformed their policies on European integration significantly through the late 1980s and early 1990s. Both the Social Democratic Party, the Social Liberals and the SPP adopted offensive policies on the further evolution of the EC/EU from 1988 and onwards. The political success of the single market project made them attempt to pull European integration in a direction where it would have a higher social and environmental profile, implying stronger European integration in these areas. At the same time, the break-up of the European security political landscape led two of the three parties to adopt a more positive approach to the single currency plans, just as it contributed to the constructive involvement of all three parties in the Maastricht-process.

Consequently, from 1988 to 1992, the three parties have pursued a European policy which aims at maximising influence more than at pleasing the electorate. But neither for the SPP nor for the Social Democratic Party, this was a sustainable policy. The SPP's new offensive approach to European integration, both prior to the 1992-referendum and in connection with the 1993-referendum, backfired badly in the 1994-elections which also saw the emergence of an EU-hostile competitor of the party to its left side. The Social Democrats in turn fared very poorly in the September 1994 European Parliament elections.

The SPP has drawn the most far-reaching conclusions from this development, in fact seeking to edge back towards a symbolic anti-integration position – at least when it comes to issues involving European integration. This will bring the party into closer accordance with its voters, but it will also exclude the party from influence in a wide range of areas.

For the Social Democratic Party, the consequences of the 1992-1993 experience are less clear. In the months after the June 1994 elections to the European Parliament, the party leadership appeared to keep a very low profile, reverting to the familiar tactics of sweeping internal disagreements under the carpet and avoiding discussion of the subject altogether. However, in late 1995 as the IGC approached the leadership adopted a somewhat bolder and more confrontational approach. In November 1995 Prime Minister Nyrup Rasmussen thus in an interview argued forcefully for the necessity of strengthened European integration, first of all on political, not economic grounds. The Prime Minister among other things indicated his willingness to introduce majority voting in new areas and support those institutional reforms which would become necessary in light of future enlargement (Rasmussen 1995). As the IGC had concluded its work, he threw his and his party's weight behind popular approval in the referendum on the Amsterdam Treaty. Finally, and as mentioned, the party leadership has recently adopted a relatively bold approach towards full Danish EMU membership in the wake of the 1998 referendum success and the pro-EMU swing in public opinion in 1998-1999, cf. footnote 8.

What are then the future perspectives for Danish party attitudes on European integration? The three vulnerable parties are likely to continue to decide the direction of Danish European policy. This direction is in turn likely to be determined by each party's balancing of the concerns for policy influence and electoral support. In the medium term, the most likely situation to emerge will be one where the SPP remains committed to a symbolic anti-integration position, where it will be in accordance with its voters. The leaderships of the Social Democratic Party and the Social Liberals, as opposed, are more likely to accept and press for further supranational integration in a number of areas, which will lead to a further number of confrontations with its EU-sceptical voters in the future. Even if we have witnessed a significant change in public opinion as regards Danish EMU membership, more far reaching and fundamental changes in the attitudes of the Danish electorate towards the European Union are improbable.

Consequently, we are likely to experience more political battles like the ones in 1992, 1993 and 1998, where a large majority in Parliament in favour of strengthened integration (Social Democrats, Social Liberals, Centre Democrats, Liberals, Conservatives against the Unity Party, the SPP and the Progress Party/DPP) confronts a sceptical electorate where the anti-EU movements enjoy widespread support. The result is likely to be yet more narrow outcomes of future referenda and a continued strong presence of the popular anti-EU movements in European Parliament elections. Evidently, the outcome of these referenda will depend on their specific themes, but certainly also on the commitment by the main parliamentary parties and their leaderships to argue their case and risk their electoral backing.

References

Andersen, Ole et al. (1973): *EF: Hvad nu? Et debatoplæg til en Socialdemokratisk EF-politik*, Copenhagen: Forlaget SOC.
Axelrod, Robert (1970): *Confict of Interest*, Chicago: Markham.
Børsen (1995.12.13).
Eurobarometer (1996) No. 46.0, Fall.
Eurobarometer (1995) No. 42, Spring.
Esping-Andersen, Gösta (1990): *Three Worlds of Welfare Capitalism*. Cambridge: Polity Press.
Esping-Andersen, Gösta (1985): *Politics Against Markets: The Social Democratic Road to Power*, Princeton: Princeton University Press.
Gade, Steen (1989a): in *Folketingstidende*, forhandlingerne, 1988/89, 23 May 1989, cols. 10581-10583.
Gade, Steen (1989b): in *Folketingstidende*, forhandlingerne, 1989/90, 30 November 1989, cols. 2583-2587.
Gallup exit poll (1998.05.28): Gallup, Copenhagen.
Gallup survey (1990): DDA1640, Gallup, Copenhagen.
Haahr, Jens Henrik (2000): "Pleasing the Voters or Maximising Influence? The Danish SDP and European Monetary Integration" in Ton Notermans (ed.), *Social Democrats and Monetary Union*, Berghahn.
Haahr, Jens Henrik (1993): *Looking to Europe: The EC policies of the British Labour Party and the Danish Social Democrats*, Aarhus: Aarhus University Press.
Haahr, Jens Henrik (1992): "Folkeafstemningen 2. juni 1992 om dansk ratifikation af Maastricht-traktaten", Working Paper, Institute of Political Science, Århus, pp. 25-26.
Haahr, U. (1993): interview with Holger K. Nielsen, 27 March.
Haas, Ernst B. (1958): *The Uniting of Europe*, London: Stevens and Sons Ltd..
Information, (1995.12.13), p. 3.
Jyllands-Posten (1999.01.24).
Katzenstein, Peter: (1985): *Small States in World Markets: Industrial Policy in Europe*, London: Cornell University Press.
Lorenzen, Ole (1989): "S-kovending", in *Det fri Aktuelt*, 22 May.
Nørgaard, Ivar (1989): in *Folketingstidende*, forhandlingerne, 23 May, col. 10624.
Nørgaard, Ivar (1985): "Ordet Union vil vi ikke have", in *Weekendavisen*, 13 September.
Olsen, Lars (1990): "Ritt: Ellemann ødelægger EF-debat", in *Information*, 13 September.
Petersen, Niels Helveg (1991): in *Folketingstidende*, forhandlingerne, 29 October, cols.1125-1126.
Petersen, Niels Helveg (1990): in *Folketingstidende*, forhandlingerne 18 April, cols. 8469-8472.
Petersen, Niels Helveg (1984): in *Folketingstidende*, forhandlingerne, 1983/84, 28 May, cols. 7197-7200.
Rasmussen, Annegrethe (1995): "EU er et fredens projekt", in *Weekendavisen*, 3.-9. November.
Socialistisk Folkeparti (1995): *Et Europa i Flere Rum*, Copenhagen.
Siune, Karen et al. (1994): *Fra et nej til et ja*, Århus: Politica.

Siune, K, et al. (1992): *Det blev et nej*, Århus: Politica.
the Social Democratic Party (1987), *An Open Europe*, English version, Brussels.
Ström, Kaare R. (1990): "A Behavioral Theory of Competitive Political Parties", *American Journal of Political Science*, Vol. 34, No. 2, May, pp. 565-598.
Tonsgaard, Ole (1987): "Folkeafstemningen om EF-pakken", *Dansk Udenrigspolitisk Årbog 1986*, Copenhagen: DJØF and DUPI.
Worre, Torben (1988): "Denmark at the Crossroads", *Journal of Common Market Studies*, vol. 26, no. 4, June, pp. 361-388.
Worre, Torben (1987): "The Danish Euro-Party System", *Scandinavian Political Studies*, Vol. 10, No. 1, pp. 79-91.

Part IV

Options and Decision-Making

CHAPTER 11

Options and Goals in Danish European Policy Since 1945: Explaining Small State Behavior and Foreign Policy Change

Hans Branner

1. Introduction

A characteristic of international developments since 1945 is that many small states are confronted by an increase in the number of foreign policy options. In Western Europe, this tendency has been supported – and to some extent initiated – by the integration process, enabling small states to take part in international decision-making to an extent not previously experienced.

The conditions for foreign policy-making in Denmark are no exemption to this general trend. Considering Denmark's extreme dependency on Germany until 1945, the outcome of World War II represented a greater external change than in most other European states. Whereas foreign policy options since the latter part of the 19th century had been primarily a question of how much to adapt to the German great power, post-war Denmark has had to define its foreign policy orientation on a new basis. At the same time, in light of new international possibilities, this process of redefinition has been complicated by a number of factors. Among them has been Denmark's dual position as part of Scandinavia while being attached to the European continent. Another was Danish vulnerability in terms of foreign trade. And a third was the proximity of Danish territory to the Soviet Union and the new communist states of Eastern Europe. These geopolitical and economic factors have made foreign policy options more precarious for Denmark than for most other European states, not least because the post-war period in Europe has been characterized by a division between different groups of states rather than by all-European cooperation.

The multitude and the delicacy of Danish foreign policy options since 1945 have been accompanied by a deep-rooted opposition among segments of the population and by various political groups to the officially chosen course. As a consequence, on a number of occasions the choices made have been the object of intense political controversy. Both external and domestic factors have thus interacted in making foreign policy options a focal point of Danish post-war history.

It is the purpose of this chapter to discuss the totally changed situation in foreign policy options, which Denmark has experienced in the second half of the 20th century, and to subsequently explore how Danish governments have responded to these options. This will lead to an analysis of the goals and strategies pursued. Considering the importance and multiplicity of options, such a task may seem overwhelming – at least within the scope of the present article. It is therefore necessary to further, define the limits and content of the analysis of Danish foreign policy options to be presented.

First, we shall refrain from giving any detailed chronological account of external or internal developments. The external developments, establishing the main background for Danish decision-making, concern crucial events in post-war European history and may be considered more or less well-known to the reader. Discussion of internal developments will focus on identifying goals rather than on presenting a historical situation in its totality.

Second, also this chapter concentrates on the specific European aspects of Danish policy, leaving out less relevant aspects. Attention will be placed on the manner in which European options have been incorporated into Danish post-war foreign policy and on key elements of the Danish approach to European integration. In the Danish case, however, European questions cannot be considered apart from other geographical dimensions; e.g., the global and the Atlantic. Hence, it will be necessary to include observations on Danish foreign policy in this wider context.

Third, it should be stressed that this chapter has a more generalizing than historical aim. The analysis will thus concentrate on typical features regarding foreign policy options and the goals and strategies pursued. The purpose is neither to extend existing historical knowledge nor to study the concrete cases for their own sake. Instead, we shall try to identify the *kind* of options Denmark has been confronted with and the *kind* of responses given.

In pursuing these goals, we shall take our point of departure in the Danish foreign policy tradition described in Chapter 6 and in two theoretical approaches. Throughout the analysis, Denmark's status as small power will be drawn in, and in the end possible contributions to *small state theory* will be discussed. In continuation, the emerging *theories of foreign policy change* will also be taken up.[1] By covering a relatively long time-span – including two distinct historical turning points – 1945 and 1989-90 – the material presented can illuminate some of the premises behind and distinctions made in existing models and conceptualizations.

Before beginning the concrete analysis, a short remark is necessary on the concept of *option* in foreign policy.

Foreign policy options may be regarded as objective categories solely to be deduced from a correct analysis of the external environment. For certain analytical purposes such a point of departure may be worthwhile. However, if one wants to exclude politically less relevant options, the *perception* of decision-makers has to

---

1 Special focus will be on Hermann (1990). For a more comprehensive presentation of theories on foreign policy change see Rosati (1994).

Options and Decision-Making 335

be taken into consideration when delimitating the kind and number of options confronting an international actor. For large as well as for small states, an internal factor thus becomes part of the analysis of foreign policy options. This factor may be called internal acceptability, first of all involving the basic values of decision-makers and the physical and/or political costs inherent in choosing alternative policies.[2]

In the following, this delimitation of options will be applied, thereby leaving out options of a purely theoretical interest (e.g., the option of alignment with the Soviet Union after 1948). On the other hand, for the present purpose it is not considered necessary to account for decision-makers' perceptions of options in all cases. And, at an early point in the development, we shall be free to include options whose salience has only evolved over time (e.g., the option of participation in supranational integration).

Whatever the point of departure, an exact enumeration of foreign policy options confronting a given state will always be difficult to determine. The complexity may be illustrated in two additional ways.

Options may have a very *short lifetime* because their implementation soon turns out to be impossible. Normally, such cases should qualify as options (e.g., the Nordic defense pact in 1948-49), although they tend not to be regarded as such in many historical analyses in which an objective definition is applied. Nevertheless, the question remains as to what kind of time limit should be set for their qualification as options.

A further question arises because of the necessity of differentiating between the *various levels* to which options belong. In this chapter, we shall deal mainly with the higher levels relating to all-round foreign policy orientation and the fundamental decisions constituting this orientation (also labelled "strategic options", see chapter 14). However, sub-level options may be relevant to study because of their relationship to the all-round orientation, or because they – under changed external conditions – climb up the ladder and become high-level options. These considerations play a major role in the analysis to be carried out in the following section.

2. Scope and Character of Danish Foreign Policy Options – 1945 as a Turning Point

2.1. Isolated dependence on the German great power before 1945

The degree of dependence which a small power experiences when located close to a great power tends to vary according to a number of factors. Denmark's proximity to Germany in the period since the establishment of the Second Reich in 1871 and until the dissolution of the Third Reich at the end of World War II presents a case of closely circumscribed foreign policy options on the part of the small power. Concerning fundamental foreign policy orientation, i.e., the highest level of option

---

2 Cf. Petersen (1978) who presents three categories for analysing foreign policy options: internal acceptability, internal and external feasibility (pp. 200-201).

analysis, it is even questionable if – at all – one may speak of options in the objective sense of the term.³

In the period referred to – with the exception of the 1920s – Germany was an expanding and at times aggressive great power, giving rise to real and perceived threats to neighbouring countries. The resulting consequences for Denmark's international position would – of course – have been less serious, if possibilities had existed for aligning with other great powers. However, it is a striking feature of the entire period that such possibilities were either non-existent or of a highly dubious value from a Danish security policy point of view. In spite of the fact that Danish territory, covering the entrances to the Baltic Sea, was of great strategic importance in a European great power conflict the Western powers, primarily Great Britain, showed no interest in guaranteeing Danish independence in the periods leading up to the two world wars. Official declarations as well as confidential sources disclose that Britain, both militarily and diplomatically, had written off Denmark as a potential ally or even reliable neutral. In the British view Denmark was seen as part of the German sphere of interest, and there were no possibilities of changing this state of affairs. As a consequence, Danish subservience to German demands at the outbreak of World War I and the mere symbolic Danish resistance to the German invasion on 9 April, 1940 were not only accepted by Great Britain but regarded as reasonable and realistic reactions by Danish decision-makers.⁴

An evaluation of Danish foreign policy options in the period of German dominance must include an analysis of the way the German threat was perceived by leading Danish decision-makers. Such perceptions indicate how the costs involved in not adapting to Germany were measured. An early and very revealing interpretation herof was given by the long-time, conservative Danish Prime Minister in the latter part of the 19th century, J.B.S. Estrup, who in a memo argued that:

> The next battle in which Denmark came to stand (together with allies or alone) against G[ermany] would probably be Denmark's last battle, and I therefore deem it neccessary that we approach G. so much *in time*, that she cannot harbor any doubt whatever, that D[enmark] will stand at her side – in any case never against her.
> (Sjøqvist 1962: 124, trans. Petersen 1979a: 262)

---

3   A more contemporary and – in certain respects – similar case is Finland's position vis-à-vis the Soviet Union after 1945 and until the end of the Cold War.
4   Closer examination of the arguments advanced on the British side for this 'hands-off' policy towards Denmark gives further evidence of the constraints within which Danish foreign and security policy had to operate in this period. In the internal British deliberations, the small state factor was crucial for arriving at a negative conclusion in regard to military assistance to Denmark. Not only was Danish proximity to Germany a hindrance for effective military operations on Danish territory, but the sheer size of the country and the inadequacy of resources made it almost impossible for Denmark to alter the prospects of such operations by increasing its defense efforts. This means that an internally conditioned option for a more independent foreign policy line, i.e., greater spending on national defense, was non-existent or at least of a very limited value (Branner 1972: 128-30; Branner 1987: 99-109). For a contrary view regarding the situation in the 1930s see Seymour (1982).

This view was held by a person who at the same time, in the heated internal discussions, was an ardent supporter of a greater defense effort. According to Estrup, both the costs involved and her limited resources, prevented Denmark from having any 'real' option in regard to its basic policy orientation.[5]

Although Estrup's analysis was indicative of the thinking during this period, his perception of Danish foreign policy options was generally not shared by his political supporters, who saw a stronger Danish defense as a means of ensuring a more independent Danish policy. Actually, a certain degree of rearmament took place in Denmark in the years when Estrup held power, and it was exactly this rearmament which in the right-wing opinion of the 20th century, enabled Denmark to remain neutral in World War I. On the same premise, the perceived lack of options in 1939-40 was seen as a consequence of Danish disarmament during the interwar period.

As indicated above, this optimistic view of Danish options can hardly be supported by the historical sources dealing with official British attitudes towards Denmark. What matters in this analysis of perceptions is that Estrup's reasoning from the 1870s was taken over – at least in its basic form – by those responsible for Danish foreign policy in the greater part of the period since the turn of the century and until 1945. In his memoirs Erik Scavenius, foreign minister from 1913-20 and foreign and prime minister during World War II, explicitly referred to the above citation by Estrup, giving the argument his full support (Scavenius 1948: 13). Also the other central figure in Danish foreign policy during the first half of the 20th century, Peter Munch, had a similar view of the importance of Germany. Acting as foreign minister in the 1930s, Munch saw no alternative to a neutrality posture, which first of all respected German interests. Neither culturally nor ideologically did Munch have any preference for Germany among the great powers, but he saw the need to distinguish sentiments from reason when defining the Danish foreign policy line. The costs of not doing so would be catastrophic not only for the survival of the Danish state but also for the living conditions of the Danish population.[6]

Obviously, the above description gives only a very crude outline of the foreign policy options facing Denmark in this period. A full treatment would give a much more varied picture, both with regard to options in the objective and in the subjective sense of the term. This presentation of the main features, however, is a necessary prerequisite for understanding both the fundamental changes as well as the elements of continuity characterizing subsequent developments in Danish foreign policy options. A short analysis of some of the nuances, however, may also serve the same purpose.

Whereas the overall foreign policy orientation of Denmark seemed fixed, a number of options existed within this framework. In the present context, it is

---

5   The influential director of the Foreign Office in the latter part of the 19th century, P. Vedel, had a slightly more optimistic evaluation of Denmark's international situation, see Petersen (1979a), pp. 260-62.
6   Munch's foreign policy conception is analysed in Karup Pedersen (1970).

worthwhile to consider two such sub-level options: (1) *intensification of inter-nordic cooperation*; (2) *optimizing international norm regulation*.[7]

(1) Danish dependency upon Germany failed to not reduce the prevailing conception of close affiliation with the other Nordic countries. It was only natural that efforts were made to compensate for the feeling of forced adaptation to the German great power by closer contacts to those states with whom Denmark shared fundamental political values and whose general outlook on international affairs were similar. To a greater or lesser extent, the Nordic option was discussed throughout the period, and in a number of ways attempts were made to transform the Nordic option into practical politics.

During World War I, the three Scandinavian states acted in common with regard to infringements on their neutrality and intensified their trade relations irrespective of criticism on the part of the warring great powers; they coordinated their efforts during negotiations on the Versailles Treaty after the war; in the wake of renewed threats to European security in the 1930s, the institution of regular foreign minister meetings was reestablished; and by the end of the decade common neutrality rules were issued accompanied by measures facilitating communication in defense matters.

However, it is hard to avoid the conclusion that the Nordic option up to 1945 was of very limited value from a Danish foreign policy perspective. It was closely circumscribed by external as well as internal factors. Externally, Nordic cohesion was hampered by the relatively recent dissolution of the Swedish-Norwegian union and the incongruity of the respective national economies of the three Scandinavian countries being dependent on trade with outside countries. Also decisive was the fact, that Sweden, the militarily most powerful of the three, had clearly signalled its unwillingness to take part in the defense of the Danish border in Jutland. And when foreign minister Munch, on the eve of the Second World War in May 1939, appealed to Nordic solidarity in the hope of avoiding Danish isolation on the issue of signing a non-aggression pact with Nazi Germany, he was met with a cold shoulder by his Nordic colleagues. More important, nevertheless, were Denmark's own foreign policy priorities.

External limitations together with internal reservations played a role in ensuring that the intensification of inter-nordic cooperation remained a subordinate option in Danish foreign policy. It was only regarded as a feasible course insofar as it did not conflict with the over-all pattern of adaptation to Germany. For Danish policy-

---

7 Another sub-level option of a certain significance was the possibilities inherent in the trade structure between Denmark, Germany and Great Britain. Denmark's ability to maintain its neutrality during World War I may in part be explained by a successful exploitation of a German and British interest in a continuation of Danish trade relations with their main antagonist; see Sjøqvist (1973: chapter 9). At the end of the 1930s, Denmark's foreign economic position no longer gave rise to the kind of foreign policy options experienced earlier in the century; see Seymour (1982: 86-89).

makers, it was not a question of choosing between two alternative lines of action, but rather of the degree to which a main line should be supplemented by a secondary one. Internally, this way of making priorities was to a large extent conditioned on basic security policy thinking: The primary threat was of a military nature, and there was no point in Denmark, as a small power, trying to balance this threat by the same means – whether in isolation with a great power ally or with neighbouring small powers. Instead of a strategy of force, which was apt to enhance the threat, a strategy of conciliation was needed. It was on this level of diplomacy that the Nordic option could be an asset, making Denmark less vulnerable when engaged in accommodating German demands.[8]

(2) Efforts towards increased norm regulation among states received considerable international attention from around the turn of the century; and active participation in these efforts was from the outset a part of the Danish small state strategy (see chapter 6). However, considering the intensification of European great power rivalry ending in World War I the issue remained on the fringes of the international agenda until the United States was drawn into the war in 1917. With the establishment of the League of Nations in 1919, the possibility of creating a more legally based world order had suddenly become an option for which at least the member countries had to find a place in their foreign policy strategy.

The defeat of Germany in the war meant that Denmark's military-strategic position in the early part of the interwar period was more reassuring than it had been for decades. Moreover, there arose the possibility of transforming the stipulations laid down in the charter of the League of Nations into reality; this project could be seen as a continuation and expansion of endeavours which Denmark – and other small states – had already been engaged in for some time.

The historical record shows that Denmark invested as much energy as most other small states in this promising project of creating a new and more peaceful basis for relations among states – and in a number ways considerably more energy. In the 1920s, Denmark was actively engaged in negotiations striving to make treaty provisions concerning disarmament a reality. With Danish foreign minister Munch as initiator, the League Assembly in the 1930s was used as a forum for demonstrating small state solidarity, thereby attempting to give substance to the international norms, on which a new and alternative world order should be based (Karup Pedersen 1970: 234-36; cf. chapter 6, section 4.3 of this book). For his idealism, Munch was often ridiculed at home, but his efforts show how much official attention was paid in Denmark to the foreign policy option represented by the founding of the League of Nations.

Like the Nordic option, however the League of Nations option was closely circumscribed in the Danish interwar foreign policy. By the 1930s, it had become

---

8 For an extended discussion of Danish foreign policy strategies in the 1930s see Mouritzen (1988: chapter 10).

evident that the League had failed as a guardian of peace and security and therefore on external premises had receded as a major foreign policy option. Denmark declared itself an advocate of the idea of a collective security system in Europe when the treaty was signed, but it nevertheless abstained from an unconditional ratification of art. 16 providing for an effective implementation of this system. The fear that the article could be used against Germany and that Denmark ran the risk of getting involved on the 'wrong' side in a future war made the government demand exemptions from treaty obligations.

A similar foreign policy priority was disclosed concerning the principle of national self determination embodied in the charter of the League. The effectuation of this principle made it possible for Denmark to fulfill a long standing and highly valued aspiration of regaining a part of Northern Schleswig which had been lost in the war of 1864. But it was crucial to Danish negotiators at the Versailles Conference that the implementation of this principle concerning the German-Danish border issue should take place on a bilateral basis and not be subject to multilateral supervision by the League.[9]

In conclusion, it should be emphasized that intensification of international norm regulation was an integral part of Danish foreign policy behavior in the interwar years. However, a sharp distinction was drawn between the long term goal inherited in these endeavours and the short term – and more immanent – goal of establishing the best possible relations with Germany. A clear priority was given to the second goal – irrespective of the kind of regime holding power in Germany, as evidenced by Danish foreign policy behavior in the 1930s.

Summing up this section, it is evident that the question of choosing among fundamental foreign policy options hardly entered the calculations of Danish foreign policy makers in this period (cf. Petersen 1979a: 250). The over-all concern was with Germany. External developments offered no basis for changing the course outlined. Counterweight strategies were considered but not as alternatives.[10] They had to be coordinated and subordinated to the main lines of policy. And to the extent they were attempted they turned out to be rather unsuccessful.

On the morning of 9 April 1940, when German troops were crossing the border and the Danish government was confronted with an ultimatum demanding Danish acceptance of the foreign invasion, it not only became evident that the policy of accommodation had failed. The situation was also a dramatic illustration of the lack of options characterising Denmark's international situation in the preceding period.

---

9 Applying another scheme of analysis, the two sub-options dealt with here may also be considered part of the reservoir of foreign policy strategies available to Denmark when pursuing a so-called policy of adaptive acquiescence. In the terminology used by Mouritzen, both options exemplify a counterweight-strategy (Mouritzen 1988: 90-93).

10 See note 9.

2.2. Factors influencing the increase of options after 1945

2.2.1. The changing role of the German factor

The preeminence of the German factor when analyzing Danish foreign policy options before 1945 accounts for the dramatic change in the Danish position as a result of the outcome of World War II. While a similar situation arose after World War I, a closer look at external as well as internal developments after 1945, however, shows how fundamental differences were between the two situations.

From today's perspective, it is easy to point to the main elements in this difference. The post World War II period has witnessed no revival of German nationalism; the German state has increasingly been embedded in European supranational integration; and Europe as a whole has been subject to a superpower overlay which changed former patterns of relations between small and great powers in this part of the world. This development could be only partially envisaged when the war ended, and because these elements were not equally manifest from the beginning, it is not surprising that none of the European states, including Denmark, with its legacy of troubled relations with the German great power, could from one day to the other discard the possibility of a renewed German threat to their security. Like other states, the traditional perception of Germany's role and power in Europe changed only gradually – and has never been completely erased. In Denmark, suspicions about German intentions were especially pronounced up to 1955, when the minority questions at the common border were solved to the satisfaction of both countries – and when subsequently a close partnership as members of NATO developed (cf. chapter 8 in this book).

What matters with regard to the issue of options, however, is that Danish decision-makers from early on – and in great contrast to their behavior after World War I – acted on a new perception of the country's international environment, not least concerning its relations with the former great power south of the border. Although German great power resurgence was again regarded as a realistic future development and could therefore influence Danish foreign policy formulation, the exact consequences to be drawn from this insight were perceived differently from the post-Versailles era.

First, the consequences were seen as less far-reaching than earlier. The prospect of German resurgence accounted for a renewed cautious Danish attitude towards the border issue, which again popped up due to the turmoil following the German collapse. Precaution with respect to bilateral relations could only be considered natural on the part of a smaller power neighbouring a former and possible future great power. In contrast to previous behavior, this kind of precaution, however, did not inhibit Danish attempts to upgrade its global and Nordic foreign policy orientations, which had previously only represented sub-options. In general, there no longer existed serious barriers for Danish inclinations in various aspects of foreign policy to follow a line not determined by the German factor. As will be pointed out below, the Danish change of policy after World War II was of a multi-dimensional kind, amounting to what has been termed a restructuring of the entire foreign policy orientation.

Second, Denmark was – at least at the outset – actively prepared to support initiatives aimed at preventing a renewal of the German threat. From his exile in London during the war, the first Danish foreign minister after the liberation, John Christmas Møller, brought with him the conception of the necessity of a permanent, internationally supervised reduction of German power.[11] Møller's short term in office seems to have prevented him from formulating these views as minister, but they were contained in a government memorandum in 1947 outlining the official Danish stand on the future of Germany. This kind of reasoning also reflected a general internal thrust for activism and change in Danish foreign policy, a central element in the general political upheaval following five years of foreign occupation and an even longer period of humiliating subservience to its great power neighbour.

For Danish decision-makers, the German factor thus continued to play an important role in their perception of the environment, but it was more on a par with other factors. There was a possibility to control it, and there existed a pronounced will to overcome Danish foreign policy passivity, for which German dominance had been the chief cause. The immediate decline of German power was thus accompanied by a number of internal factors which opened Danish governments of the first post-war period to new international engagements.

2.2.2. Multilateralism and new foreign policy options

The changing role of the German factor is crucial to understanding the new focus on options in Danish foreign policy. Equally crucial was an external development, which during the same period offered small European powers the possibility to choose foreign policy orientations not hitherto experienced.

Besides the renewed attempt – now through the UN – to erect a world wide organization based on adherence to and strengthening of common international norms, two novel developments were the most important ones in this regard: First the emergence of the Cold War and the subsequent formation of military alliances based on the principle of collective defense; and second the beginning of the European integration process, which not only opened the possibility for various market schemes, but also held out the prospect of a united Europe constructed on a supranational basis. In large measure these developments resulted from great power initiatives and could be explained by the clash of great power interests. And although all powers in Western Europe were hereby confronted with new kinds of options in their foreign policies, the change was most remarkable for the small states.

---

11 See his articles from the summer of 1944, published in a booklet entitled *The German Problem* (1945).

In general, both developments reflected a trend towards increased multilateralisation in the international system – at the global level and later not least at the European level. This multilateralisation was more inclusive than previously seen, insofar as it was unprecedented in engaging small states in international decision-making.

More specifically, one may first mention the novelty of *collective defense* in an Atlantic framework. The quick change from the end of European hostilities in May 1945 to global confrontation between the superpowers, taking concrete form only two years later, obviously represented a highly disquieting development for all European countries. In Denmark, the magnitude of external changes described above was hardly absorbed before new dramatic changes occured, in large measure threatening the fundamentally improved security environment. However, neither the Danish situation nor that of other small (Western) European states can be characterized as 'back to the future'. From a Danish perspective, three elements constituted the difference compared to the situation before the war.

First, the elevation of the major security conflict from a European to a global level brought former great power enemies in Western Europe together into a single block. Although Denmark was again located in a frontline position – now in relation to East-West confrontation – the country on the whole enjoyed the privilege of belonging to a low tension area during the entire Cold War period. Second, and more important in terms of the character of options, Denmark was asked for the first time since the beginning of the century, to take part in a great power alliance and now with the possibility of obtaining a security guarantee from the world's leading military power. Finally, the character of this alliance was historically unique. The geographic dimension was unprecedented, and the sheer size of the Atlantic alliance made it encompass not only a superpower and most of the old European great powers but also a whole range of smaller powers. Such a construction based on the principle of collective defense was apt to be more reassuring for small states than previous security constructions between large and small states, which always contained the potential of a one-sided, highly dependent kind of relationship.

Later on we shall take up Danish reactions to external development in the immediate post-war period in more detail. At this point, we need only emphasise that in spite of the radical changes, not only in the European security situation at large but also in the means available for countering the new security threats, the Danish path into NATO-membership was not an easy one. And the decision to join did not represent an unequivocal break with the past. For this reason, subsequent decisions in the security field were not seen as straightforward steps to be logically deduced from the initial alliance decision. Internal inertia meant that the issue of fundamental security policy orientation – and thereby security options – remained alive, although not prevailingly in the shape of the alliance-neutrality dichotomy.

The second main development mentioned above, the beginning of *European integration*, was in the long run to become the most decisive factor when measuring the increase of Danish foreign policy options in the post-war period. This may be accounted for in two ways: 1) the specific economic aspects of Danish foreign policy, and 2) the general international role of Denmark.

As a small power with a high standard of living, Denmark has throughout the 20th century been strongly dependent on foreign trade, with import and export quotas amounting to 30-40% since 1950. In the same period, around three-fourths of this trade has been concentrated on Western European markets, which means that developments on these markets in a crucial way have influenced possibilities of pursuing key societal goals. Not surprisingly, from early on, Danish governments have attached great attention to the economic aspects of European integration by which it seemed possible to establish a firmer basis for trade relations, not least by abolishing existing trade barriers.

Like the alliance option, Danish participation in a greatly intensified Western European economic integration represented a new foreign policy option. However, whereas the former created great internal controversy, the latter – considering the extent of Danish dependency on European markets – could hardly *in itself* arouse political disagreement. Like most other small states, Denmark whole-heartedly welcomed the trend towards closer economic cooperation in Western Europe and was prepared to take active part in the institutionalisation of this trend. Nevertheless, for a number of reasons this aspect of the post-war European development also confronted Denmark with difficult choices, thereby accounting for the increase of basic foreign policy options.

In this regard, three characteristics of Danish foreign economic relations were of importance. First, Danish trade was not only heavily concentrated on Western Europe, but within the region trade with Great Britain and Western Germany was by far the most important. Second, in the 1950s Denmark – in contrast to other highly developed European countries – was still very dependent on the export of agricultural commodities, which made up over half of total exports. As a corollary, Danish governments had as a primary goal after the war of pursuing accelerated industrialization. And third, compared to other West European countries, Denmark had heavily relied since the 1930s on quantitative restrictions on imports, whereas it had kept a low level with regard to protecting its emerging industry by tariffs.

These specific Danish conditions combined with the external developments complicated Denmark's participation in West European economic integration in the 1950s and 1960s, as shall be illustrated in greater detail below. There was no fixed line governments could follow in their attempts to transform their initial commitment into active engagement in the integration process. Instead they found themselves confronted with a host of intricate problems to which no optimal solution was at hand. The main problem was that Denmark would have to wait until 1972 until it could choose a solution fulfilling its prime market policy, i.e. participation in an integration scheme which included both Great Britain and Germany. In regard to agricultural interests, Denmark had to balance its attraction to Continental projects with the less favourable – or rather unfavourable – conditions provided by other institutional frameworks, to which Denmark was more inclined to adhere out of broader political considerations. And from the outset, difficulties arose because plans for trade liberalization on a wider West European scale not only exempted agriculture but almost exclusively aimed at abolishing restrictions and not tariffs.

Reverting to the comparison between the fields of security and foreign economic policy, it may be useful once again to emphasize how different the question of options manifested itself in the two fields. In both cases new basic options emerged. In the first case external circumstances made it possible to make a fundamental choice at an early date by opting for membership in NATO. A similar concrete choice was not possible for Denmark in the other field. Instead various less optimal alternatives were at hand. Although alliance membership did not release Denmark from making difficult decisions, the question of options remained – until 1972 – much more alive in the field of foreign economic relations. And the reason why options in this field continued to appear as fundamental had to do with the other – political – side of the integration process in Western Europe.

The vision of a politically integrated Europe, as amply documented in historical literature, had many roots. Each of the six countries, which in the beginning of the 1950s started the concrete process towards a politically united Europe on a supranational basis, had their own individual motives for engaging in this process, below labelled the 'integration option'.[12] However, for the three smaller states, e.g. the Benelux countries, there can be no doubt that the prospect of creating an international system in Western Europe in which interstate relations were based on law rather than on power relations was a prime motive.[13] The realisation hereof was in line with traditional small state endeavours aimed at greater equality in international politics.

While we will reserve the specific Danish reactions for later treatment, two points are important when evaluating how participation in the novel development of European political integration became a Danish post-war foreign policy option. First, the prevailing interpretation of this development among leading Danish politicians and decision-makers – and, as it seems, in public opinion – parallel that which had induced the Benelux states to active participation. On a very general level, the institutionalisation of closer political ties – also of a supranational character – was seen as a historic possibility to overcome old nation-state rivalries in Europe. In other words, also in the Danish perception, there existed a choice between radically different lines of development for Europe.[14]

---

12 For this terminology, see Milward and Sørensen (1993), who distinguish between strategies of interdependence versus integration.
13 For a detailed account of the European policies of the Benelux-countries in the formative phase of European integration, see Woyke (1985).
14 Unfortunately, there is no in depth analysis of early Danish attitudes towards European integration. The perception mentioned may be deduced from the records of the parliamentary debate in May 1949 on the ratification of the Statute of the European Council, dealt with in Branner (1993: 36-37).

The other point concerns the fact that the integration option continued to be part of the political agenda in Denmark during the greater part of the post-war period. Basically this must be seen on the background of Danish hesitancy to participate in supranational political integration with the continental states – and later also with the larger group of EC/EU member countries. A consequence of this hesitancy has been, that Denmark has never – and not yet today – made a clear-cut decision for or against the integration option, thereby keeping the saliency of the integration issue alive.

When evaluating this option as a central part of the Danish foreign policy setting in the early post-war period, the complicating factor of foreign economic relations dealt with above must also be taken into consideration. From the very outset the integration option was intertwined with Denmark's difficulties in finding an optimal solution to its market problems, which at any rate made a clear-cut decision almost impossible and tended to put economic rather than political questions in the forefront of political decision-making.

Finally, the continued, externally determined, availability of the integration option should be mentioned in this connection. Not only from an objective point of view, in terms of geography and economic relations, was Denmark closely tied to continental Europe. When looking at the political perception of leading decision-makers among the Six in the 1950s and the 1960s, Denmark was regarded as an almost natural potential member country – to a larger extent than other outsiders such as the two other Scandinavian countries and Great Britain. In 1952 Denmark was offered membership, although confidentially, in the newly established Coal and Steel Community (Branner 1993: 47-49; Branner 1995: 120-21); and in 1963, upon rejection of the British application for entry into the EEC, French president de Gaulle let the Danish prime minister know, that the membership option was still open for Denmark (Nielsson 1966: 591-96; Christensen 1993: 135; Branner 1997: 146).

After 1973, Denmark's situation with regard to the integration option did not deviate from the one enjoyed by other member countries. In concluding this overview, however it should be mentioned that Denmark at the turn of the century is the only small state member country of the EU, which had retained the option of non-participation in central aspects of the integration process.[15] One more indication of how the integration option has been kept alive in the Danish political debate, and of the combination of internal and external factors which account for the continued salience of the integration issue.

A traditional way of describing Denmark's foreign policy orientations after 1945 has been to differentiate between four (or five) circles or geographic dimensions of the country's foreign policy: the global, the Atlantic, the (West) European and the Nordic (see section 3.1.). In itself, these differentiations testify to the re-

---

15 Danish reservations as are spelled out in the Edinburgh Agreement of 1992, see the introductory chapter.

markable increase of options analysed in this section. When trying to capture the entire spectre of options, however, it is not sufficient to enumerate these dimensions and the relative realism with regard to their pursuit in various periods, but also – as emphasized above – Denmark's own difficulties in prioritising among them. According to the prevailing interpretation, Denmark has been able to make use of all four dimensions by concentrating different aspects of its foreign policy on each of them. Yet this 'fragmentation' of its foreign policy may also be seen as reflecting an important internal factor, which – as shown in this section – accounts in large measure for the focus on foreign policy options in Danish post-war history. By not committing herself fully to any of the four dimensions, the question of options both high-level and sub-level options has loomed larger in Denmark's conduct of its foreign relations than has been the case in comparable countries. In the conclusion we shall argue that this characterisation of the Danish situation regarding options has remained valid in the changed European environment in the late 1990s.

The main point of this and the preceding sub-section has been to elucidate the magnitude of external changes in foreign policy options seen from a Danish small state perspective and taking the year 1945 as a turning point. The presentation given up till now forms the basis for the analysis to be made in the following sections – in at least three ways.

In the first place, the definition of a new beginning concerning options is essential for the discussion of options in the 1990s, when new fundamental external changes have taken place. To what degree has there been an increase in options in this decade? And what kind of changes have taken place in the nature of these options? In both cases, an answer must be assessed on the background of changes in the first early post-war period.

Second, when focussing on the specific European part of Danish foreign policy, the point made in this section could very well provide a valuable clue to a correct interpretation hereof. It might be that precisely the new beginning in 1945 helps to explain why the European option – to be discussed in section 4 – was accorded a relatively minor place in Danish post-war foreign policy priorities.

Finally, by taking the findings here as a point of departure, it will later on be possible to raise some interesting questions pertaining to a theoretical analysis of foreign policy change. On the basis of the Danish case, the role of internal and external factors in explaining major foreign policy changes seems more complicated than originally assumed by existing theory. This will be shown in the concluding section.

3. Characteristic Features of the Danish Approach to the Post-War Options

The myriad of foreign policy options after 1945, the continually changing external and internal conditions, and the differing perceptions and political orientations of subsequent Danish governments make it difficult to define characteristic features of the Danish approach to the new options. The present third part of this chapter is nevertheless devoted to such an attempt, being based at the same time on the presumption that characteristic features exist. Consequently, we shall refrain from embarking on any detailed empirical documentation; instead, we shall establish, by way of a three step analysis, an overview and create the basis for generalizations; the first step being a concrete comparison of available options and the way choices were perceived. On the basis of this analysis, we shall – as a next step – attempt to specify certain general features characterizing the Danish approach towards options. The third and final step – reserved for the concluding fourth section of the chapter – will be an interpretation, based on the first two steps, of the role and the priority given to the specific European part of Danish foreign policy.

3.1. The ranking of options and the choice among them

As already mentioned, Danish post-war foreign policy can be understood in terms of four main dimensions (or geographic circles, pillars): the global, the Atlantic, the West European and the Nordic. This analytical division is a product of hindsight, when the evolving pattern of Denmark's major foreign policy orientations had become clearly discernable.[16] Although all four dimensions had become manifest in the course of a rather limited time-span after the war, they did not – for obvious reasons – present themselves as options from a 1945-perspective. It is illuminating, however, to regard the dimensions as a point of departure when trying to give an overview of the direction of Danish foreign policy as well as the main deliberations behind this direction since the turning point in 1945.

Thus, an element of continuity is observable in the early Danish emphasis on the two previously analysed sub-options of the interwar period: the global and the Nordic orientation. It is remarkable how strongly the thrust for a new activism in foreign policy was channelled into these dimensions, and how stubbornly they were upheld despite counteracting developments. This tendency is especially prevalent in the security field.

---

16 The identification of the four dimensions was introduced by former foreign minister Per Hækkerup, 1962-66, in a book on Danish foreign policy published in 1965. After the end of the Cold War, a fifth is often added: the all-European; see Petersen (1990), Due-Nielsen and Petersen (1995) and Heurlin (1995).

3.1.1. Denmark and the post-war security options

After liberation, immediate attention was paid to the new possibility of creating a broader, collective basis for national security. The highest foreign policy priority of the first post-war Danish government was to be admitted to the San Francisco conference and, thus, be included among the founding members of the United Nations. The intensity of this desire must no doubt be seen in light of Denmark's dubious role during the war, but the views advocated by Danish representatives at the conference as well as subsequent Danish behavior as a member bears witness to a strong commitment towards making the UN an international organisation, which on a realistic basis could provide security for both large and small states. The Danish approach to the new global organization contained no trace of former reservations towards its predecessor concerning binding military sanctions; and in realising the necessity of continued great power cooperation for the UN's ability to fulfill its main security purpose, Denmark, at the conference, did not join the concerted attempt by almost all small powers to prevent an inclusion of the veto power in the charter.[17]

As in other areas of post-war Danish foreign policy, it soon turned out that also in regard to involvement in the UN, the new 'activism' was characterised by certain limitations. What is important to emphasize at this point, however, is that initial reliance on the UN as a main instrument of Danish security policy functioned as a barrier against other forms of security policy reorientation – or was at least used to argue against such reorientation. This was the case concerning the delicate issue of Danish defense policy, which for decades before the war had caused serious divisions between the political parties with the anti-defense forces in the front. Since the mid 1930s, a new and more positive attitude had been emerging in the leading Social Democratic Party, and in the opening statement of the liberation government, representing the entire party spectrum, the need for consensus on an effective Danish defense effort was stressed. In the years that followed, however, the Social Democrats as well as the more doctrinaire defense opponents in the Social Liberal Party continuously voted for postponement of measures meant to transform the new party consensus into reality. The reason given was that, as yet, no guidelines had been received from the UN.

Even more conspicuous was Danish behavior when, by the beginning of 1948, it had become all too obvious that the UN's collective security system did not represent any effective guarantee against foreign attack. In the course of only six months, a whole range of new security options had to be considered by Danish decision-makers: participation in the Brussels-pact, weapon deliveries and/or a one-sided security guarantee from the U.S., a Nordic defense pact and membership of the Atlantic alliance.[18] Viewing this period in retrospect and when studying the

---

17 An early but detailed account of Danish UN policy is given in Haagerup (1956).
18 A thorough analysis of Danish options in this period is to be found in Petersen (1978). See also Petersen (1991).

long lines of Danish foreign policy history, the final decision of March 1949 to bring an end to a century-old policy of neutrality and join the Atlantic alliance has naturally attracted the greatest attention. It may be argued, however, that the deliberations made in the course of this decision-making period are more revealing of characteristic features of the Danish approach to the post-war options than is the outcome itself.

In light of increasing East-West tensions, Denmark embarked already from 1946 on what was to be labelled a 'bridge-building policy'. This implied a desire not to engage the country on one side in the global confrontation and at the same time, whenever possible, work for a reduction of tensions. Although this policy thus contained the new element of activism in foreign policy, it soon turned out that a deviation from the former neutrality policy was difficult to discern. And the rapid intensification of the Cold War during 1948 made it almost impossible for a small country like Denmark to exert any influence on the course of events. What remained was an attempt to safeguard national interests in an optimal way by adapting to an emerging bipolar world (Amstrup 1978).

In this process of adaptation, Danish policy was marked by either rejection of or hesitancy towards new options, representing deviations from familiar patterns of behavior. Thus, in the first phase, in spite of the obvious dysfunctions of the Security Council, the UN continued to be considered the main basis for Danish security policy. The line was that everything should be done to overcome what were regarded as temporary difficulties among the great powers. Consequently throughout 1948 the anti-block policy remained a guiding principle of the Danish approach to the new security options.[19]

The first indication of this continuity of policy was the Danish reaction to the Bevin Plan of January 1948 proposing a West European defense union. Since Denmark – and the other Scandinavian countries – were not included in the original invitation to join such a union, this option was hardly a feasible one – at least in the short run. It is worth noting, however, that the government expressed its relief in being omitted, and upon signing of the Brussels-pact internally argued against serious consideration of this option.[20] At this point – in March 1948 – the governing Social Democratic party was prepared to abandon its reluctance towards a defense build-up not sanctioned by the UN. In internal party deliberations at the end of February, however, the minister of defense did not hesitate to stress that the object of a rearmament effort was to safeguard the Danish 'policy of neutrality' (Borring Olesen 1994a: 40).

The main indication of continuity in Danish security policy in light of still more disquieting external developments, however, lay in Danish attitudes towards plans

---

19 Cf. Branner (1990) and Villaume (1994: 100-08) whose interpretation on this point deviates somewhat from that of Petersen. See also Borring Olesen (1994b: 160-61).
20 Minutes from Udenrigspolitisk Nævn, 24 March, 1948. Danish Foreign Ministry Archieves, File no. 3.E.92.b.

for a Scandinavian defense union on which negotiations began following a Swedish initiative of April 1948. Three elements in the Danish position are important in this regard.

First, it is remarkable how resolutely the Danish government pursued a successful realisation of the Scandinavian option. This option obviously had the highest ranking with regard to desirability, and when it turned out that Swedish and Norwegian views were far from identical, Denmark undertook the role as an active mediator. It has been claimed that the Danish government had been willing to sign any agreement reached by the two other governments, irrespective of its own preferences (Petersen 1979a: 198).

Second, it seems plausible that the prospect of realizing a Scandinavian defense union was an important, if not decisive, element in convincing the government to create an effective Danish defense (Borring Olesen 1994a: 41-42). Thus, in the first instance a reorientation of the basic Danish defense posture was closely linked to the requirements of the UN collective security system, and in the second instance to the establishment of a small state alliance comprising the neighbouring Scandinavian states. While there is no question of a distinct break in the prevailing attitude towards defense, these linkages certainly indicate a continuity in foreign policy orientation.

Third, the government regarded Danish participation in the proposed defense union as a continuation of the anti-block policy. Although contested in the literature, it is hard to avoid concluding that the over-all picture disclosed by available sources on the 1948-49 Scandinavian defense negotiations shows Danish positions closer to the Swedish insistence on impartiality in the East-West conflict than to the Norwegian insistence on links to the Western powers. For Denmark, the optimal solution in this turbulent period would have been continued dissociation from the Cold War by creating a neutral Scandinavian zone sufficiently armed to deter attacks on a lower scale and providing for mutual assistance.

On this background, it is not surprising that following the collapse of the Scandinavian talks, Denmark only half-heartedly entered the Atlantic Alliance. Although this option since September 1948 had represented a fall-back position for the Danish government, the disadvantages of this option at times loomed larger than the advantages. Symptomatic in this regard is foreign minister Gustav Rasmussen's opinion, expressed in early January 1949, that membership of the Atlantic pact equalled the signing of one's own death sentence; and the characterisation in February 1949 of the Atlantic option as the 'lesser of two evils' (the other one being isolated neutrality) by Social Democratic foreign policy parliamentary spokesman and chairman of the Foreign Relations Committee of the Folketing, Julius Bomholt (Petersen 1978: 232 and Branner 1990: 69). Not surprisingly, such attitudes had an effect on subsequent Danish security policy as a member of NATO, a policy characterised as semi-neutrality (see section 3.2).

3.1.2. Foreign economic relations and integration policies

Whereas options in the security field related to all four dimensions of Danish foreign policy orientation, options in the two fields to be considered now tended to have a narrower scope by not having any important extra-European aspect. At the same time they were – as already indicated – of a more prolonged nature. Options in the fields of foreign economic relations and integration policies were not eliminated by Danish EC-membership from 1973 in the same definite way as was the case with security options after 1949. Not until the end of the 1980s did the possibility of a Danish withdrawal from the EC exit the political agenda, and at the turn of the century Denmark had not yet finally opted for a European integration scheme which opens up for full-fledged economic and political union.

Although the relevant options were narrower in scope, Danish policies in the two fields up to 1972 may be said to have evolved around two axes: a *European vs. Nordic* axis and a 'little' vs. 'great' European axis. Both are essential ingredients in post-war discussions on foreign policy orientation, with the first having a higher standing in terms of political saliency.

The European vs. Nordic solutions

When analysing the position of the Nordic dimension in Danish foreign policy since the war, it is easy to point out how often common endeavours have failed. Despite of the many concrete steps taken towards harmonisation of legislation and coordination of policies as a result of the formation of the Nordic Council in 1952, conspicuously little has been achieved on key aspects of foreign policy. The eclipse of the defense union plans in the late 1940s have already been dealt with. Plans for a customs union and of an economic union, both seriously considered, have never materialized. Even less realistic have been visions of a Scandinavian political union, held in the years before and immediately after the end of World War II (discussed by Villumsen 1991: ch. 4 and 5). These failures are usually attributed, at least in part, to the lack of basic common interests in the various fields of foreign policy, and – as a consequence – to the priority of other geographic dimensions, e.g. the Atlantic and the European.[21]

Yet, the position of the Nordic option in Danish foreign economic relations and Danish integration policy cannot be solely evaluated on the background of actual historical developments or the conventional interpretation hereof. A full assessment, treating the concept of 'option' in its subjective sense, may only be obtained by analyzing the way the Nordic option entered the political scene and how it remained there. A number of features, more fully examined in chapter 7 of this book,

---

21 For explanations of the failure of Nordic integration in areas of high-level policies, see chapter 7 of this book.

lead to the conclusion that when comparing the European and the Nordic options in the period before EC membership in 1972 – and perhaps even later – the latter carried greater weight in the Danish foreign policy hierarchy than might be indicated by a superficial look at the course of events.

In large measure, the relative position of the two options has to be explained by their very different functions with respect to the internal Danish formulation of foreign policy.

It was no doubt the general European developments – and in part also global developments – that in the immediate post-war years created an interest in closer political and economic cooperation among European states. The thrust came from outside and attention, also in Denmark, was directed primarily towards integration in a broader European framework. In this sense, the European option had a higher ranking than the Nordic. However, since this external determination was more pronounced in Denmark than in Continental Europe, the government was generally as much pre-occupied with warding off the effects of European integration as participating in it. As an ingredient in this defensive posture, the Nordic option had an important dual function: on the one hand, it was a *means* towards strengthening the national position confronted by European challenges not easily managed in isolation, and – to a certain extent – even towards avoiding a strong European commitment; on the other hand, it also represented a highly appreciated alternative *goal* for economic and political integration.[22] This last function has been more prominent in the general public than within the political elite – at least since 1950. Due to the character of the Danish political system, Nordic integration as an alternative goal has nevertheless had a marked influence on official policy.

On this background, the historical record points to three features of Danish policy which indicate the high priority given the Nordic option.

First, the continued relevancy of this option in both political discourse and with regard to actual policy steps taken. It is remarkable that at least the perception of a Nordic alternative was kept alive in spite of the disappointments encountered and in spite of the objective limitations inherent in Nordic integration plans. These observations also have a certain bearing on the period after 1972. With EC membership, the Nordic option was finally abandoned as part of official government strategy, but its political relevance continued nevertheless. It remained a dominant point of reference in the argumentation of the EC opposition, which until the mid 1980s represented a majority of public opinion. Undoubtedly, Danish hesitation towards the deepening of the EC integration process may in part be explained on this background (cf. chapter 7).

---

22 Cf. Villumsen (1991) in regard to the last function. According to Borring Olesen and Laursen (chapter 7) Nordic integration as an alternative has also to be explained in the domestic context ("Nordic cooperation appealed to Danish Social Democrats as a lever to achieve political ends", this volume, p. 227).

Secondly, the necessity and importance attached to fully investigating the realism and implications of a Nordic alternative to European schemes by the decision-makers. This does not imply that a Nordic solution was always regarded as the most preferable. It might represent an intermediate step towards a broader solution or an integral part of it. In some form, however, the Nordic perspective always had to be put on trial. This was the case especially for domestic reasons. The thorough attempt to create a Nordic economic union, in 1968-70, was probably a precondition for the government's success in obtaining a majority of 'yes' votes in the 1972 EC referendum.[23]

Third, Danish willingness to go further with respect to integration in depth when the framework was Nordic than when it was Continental (Branner 1992: 311-13). This tendency, characteristic of the pragmatic Danish approach to integration (see below), may already be observed in the Scandinavian federation plans put forward by Social Democrats at the end of the war. When in the 1950s Danish governments in general showed no inclinations toward participating in supranational constructions, Denmark worked for a strong institutional set-up whenever the Nordic countries were involved. Similarly, NORDEK was a far-reaching project, in which Danish negotiators had worked for endowing the common institutions with a high degree of independence.

The choice between 'little' and 'great' Europe

So much at this point for the European-Nordic axis in Danish foreign economic and integration policies. The other axis to be dealt with when analyzing the period up to 1972, the choice between 'little' and 'great' Europe, was more circumscribed in its duration as an object of more intense political attention, since its salience was linked to the evolution of European market plans in the 1950s, especially in the latter part of the decade. The options involved nevertheless reflect another long-standing and basic issue in post-war Danish foreign policy.[24]

When speaking of 'the construction of Europe' the implementation of a greater European solution already by the end of the 1940s was already a given high pri-

---

23 This point has subsequently been made in an article by the leader of the Danish negotiating team, Christensen (1993: 145).
24 The concept of 'great Europe' in Danish post-war history needs a short explanation. It is possible and probably also correct to argue – not least from the perspective of the post-Cold War period and when focussing on security policy (see below) – that ever since 1945 an all-European pillar existed in Danish foreign policy aside from the four, traditionally outlined (cf. note 16). This all-European pillar, however, functioned in the latter part of the 1940s as a kind of corollary to the global one and had not acquired any noticeable standing in respect to foreign economic and integration policies when the erection of the Iron Curtain in 1947-48 fundamentally changed external conditions. Thus, the geographic area referred to here by the term 'great Europe' is restricted to the western, non-communist part of Europe.

ority goal of Danish decision-makers. As the issue of Europe's future construction had not received much attention in political debate, however, this goal was only to a very limited degree associated with the question of options in foreign policy. Denmark joined the Marshall Plan/OEEC in 1948 and a year later the European Council without any explicitly elaborated conception of the kind of Europe to be preferred (see below). This situation changed when the continental sector integration schemes were launched from 1950. In the following years, until the end of the decade, the choice between 'little' and 'great' Europe acquired ever greater importance in the Danish foreign policy universe.

Throughout the period, the 'great' European solution remained primary, and Danish governments actively – but in vain – worked for its realisation. Three interrelated factors accounted for this policy.

Probably the most fundamental factor has to do with *economic* deliberations. The configuration of Danish trade relations implied that any division of Western Europe placing Britain and West Germany in separate market blocs would be highly disadvantageous to Danish interests. Throughout the 1950s, the overriding concern of Danish foreign economic policy was to avoid this eventuality and – when it nevertheless happened – to alleviate the negative consequences by obtaining separate arrangements and by supporting every move towards overcoming the split.

Basic, economic concerns were by no means unrivalled by others. Denmark's preference for a broad European solution must also be understood in the context of *general foreign policy* deliberations – as expressed in a memo worked out in the Foreign Ministry in the Autumn of 1950, when the creation of a 'little Europe' was in its formative stage:

> "Denmark's interests, both economic and political, have such close linkage to the Continent that a closer confederation of Germany, France, the Benelux countries and Italy can lead to Danish isolation, for which it can become difficult to find compensation in a confederation with the other Scandinavian countries and eventually Great Britain. As far as I can discern, Danish policy should take its point of departure in our full participation in every significant European cooperation, especially when Germany is participating. On the other hand, our links to Sweden, Norway and Great Britain are so intimate that we cannot enter into a European cooperation in which these countries do not participate. Consequently, we ought to seek to oppose any group formation in Western Europe."
>
> (Memo of 4 October, 1950 by Max Sørensen, legal advisor in the Foreign Ministry, quoted from Branner 1993: 38; my translation)

It appears from the note that the threatening division of Western Europe represented a most difficult dilemma for Denmark – not only in economic but also in political terms. Although being a Scandinavian country with close overseas ties to Great Britain, Denmark risked political isolation by remaining outside an emerging 'little Europe' on the Continent. The only way out of this dilemma was to work for unity in Western Europe. Danish reluctance to enter into more binding arrangements with the Continental group must in part be accounted for by the desire not to eliminate Denmark's possibilities to actively pursue this goal. However, a Danish strategy of non-commitment in regard to European integration also accorded with considerations of political affinity. No group of countries ranked higher in this respect than the Nordic countries and Great Britain, whereas uneasiness prevailed concerning the prospect of closer affiliation with the Continental countries, especially West Germany.

As it turned out, Denmark's economic interests did not run entirely counter to its political aims and foreign policy inclinations. When in Autumn 1952, Danish membership in the European Coal and Steel Community was placed on the agenda, inquiries in the Foreign Ministry showed that economic considerations were not sufficiently convincing to warrant membership. The option was subsequently turned down on political grounds: membership of the ECSC would represent too great a deviation from the general foreign policy orientation of Denmark (Sørensen 1992: 117; Branner 1995: 125). Tensions between economic and political considerations became more acute later in the decade but never developed to the point where, the government seriously contemplated abandoning its primary strategy of achieving a 'great' European solution.

Into this calculation also entered a third, though probably less compelling, factor, one which had to do with *ideological considerations*. As will be shown later, the Danish approach to the form which European integration should take, was characterized during this period by a high degree of pragmatism. The issue of surrendering sovereignty was at this stage not yet an important obstacle to Danish participation in the Continental integration process. Nevertheless, a cautious and rather disengaged attitude prevailed in this regard, further supporting the non-committing strategy and the goal of reconciling the two emerging blocs.

On the background just sketched, and considering subsequent Danish EC policy, it becomes interesting to determine the more exact status of the 'little European' option, which from early of the 1950s had become externally feasible. The internally conditioned preference for the 'great European' solution and political reluctance towards 'Alleingang' into 'little Europe' in the 1950s was counteracted by mounting disadvantages resulting from a possible weakening of economic ties to the continent, (especially West Germany) (Sørensen 1992: 109-11) and by actual developments which – by the end of the decade – had led to the failure of negotiations on a wider free trade area (WFTA) and to the consolidation of 'The Six' by the the creation and initial policy measures of the EEC. Under these circumstances, the 'little European' option gained domestic acceptance, although it never became an option which Danish governments actively worked for.[25]

Three features of Danish policy in the period from the start of the WFTA negotiations in Summer 1956 until the Danish decision three years later of entering

---

25 For analyses of the Danish market policy dilemmas at the end of the 1950s see Nielsson (1966), Laursen (1993), Nüchel Thomsen (1993) and Laursen and Borring Olesen (1994).

EFTA are relevant when trying to evaluate the degree to which the 'little European' option had become acceptable among leading decision-makers: (1) the Danish *'open door' policy*, (2) the prevailing *'market policy' approach*, and (3) 'Little Europe' as a *fall back position*. Viewed in combination, these characteristic features are indicative of the priorities in Danish European policy during the latter part of the 1950s.

Considering the serious dilemmas confronting Denmark in this period an 'open door' policy became almost a necessity. Governments had to take into account that, the 'great European solution', might fail; in this case, a mere continuation of Denmark's existing market position was considered untenable.[26] Therefore, alternatives had to be prepared or kept open. Apart from EEC membership, these alternatives primarily included partial membership in the EEC, i.e., participation in the agricultural market; and a Nordic customs union, which could be either broad or narrow in scope. In addition, the conclusion of bilateral agreements, primarily with Germany, and a free trade area covering non-members of the EEC, i.e. the fate of the EFTA solution, entered the calculations at various stages. While none were considered optimal, all alternatives became part of the Danish strategy.[27] Thus, full Danish EEC membership was only one among several alternatives to the most preferred option, and – as will be shown below – not the most important.

From early 1957 the membership option was placed on the political agenda. When (in January) more detailed information was received in Copenhagen on the agricultural provisions in the forthcoming Treaty of Rome, Danish farming interests were aroused. Agricultural organisations demanded Danish accession to the treaty; and in the influential farmers party 'Venstre' (the Liberals), a process was initiated which by the end of the year officially turned the party into an adherent of Danish membership. The existing consensus on foreign policy among the leading political parties was hereby broken. The situation also demanded new deliberations in the Foreign Ministry, which by the end of January 1957 proposed two possible courses of action for Denmark: either full membership ('option A') or membership of the agricultural part of the treaty ('option B') with the latter as having priority.

On this background, and from the negotiations which followed upon the implementation of 'option B', at least one conclusion stands out: the Danish approach to European integration in the 1950s – as also later on – was almost exclusively dominated by market policy considerations, and more specifically by the aim of securing Danish agricultural interests. This approach led Denmark to ask for partial membership in the EEC, which in the view of leading representatives of 'The Six' demonstrated a lack of understanding of the entire philosophy laid down in the Treaty of Rome and, on this account, not surprisingly was turned down.[28] There was – at least at this stage – no room for a Danish à la carte membership.

---

26 In hindsight, it may even be argued that this solution was unrealistic; for a discussion, see Bloemen (1996).
27 However, the later EFTA option was not considered worth striving for.
28 The conception among 'The Six' of Danish 'Europeanness' is treated in Branner (1997). See also section 3.2.

Furthermore, it is possible to conclude that the option of full membership had not been ruled out beforehand by Danish governments. The low status of the Foreign Ministry's 'option A' was underlined when foreign minister Jens Otto Krag, in February, briefed the main Danish business organisations. Nevertheless, available sources show that under certain conditions, the government would have applied for full Danish membership of the EEC.

One indication hereof is a statement made by Krag during a July 1957 parliamentary debate. Hard pressed by the spokesman of the Liberal Party, Per Federspiel, the foreign minister acknowledged that in case a satisfactory solution for Danish agriculture could not be achieved within the framework of the WFTA negotiations, the government might opt for an accession to the Treaty of Rome. This Danish position was further spelled out few months later during a conversation between Krag a and Reginald Maudling, the British leader of the WFTA talks. According to notes made by Krag, Maudling gave evidence of the belief that Denmark would join The Six, if current negotiations failed. In confirming this impression, Krag added that such an outcome would be deplored by the Danish government, but that economic necessity would force it (Thomsen 1993: 115).

Obviously the full membership option was seen by the Social Democratic Government as only a last fall back position. However, its political relevance remained high until the very end of the Danish decision-making process, i.e., until Parliament, in July 1959 and with great hesitancy, came out in favour of Danish membership of EFTA. Throughout 1959, Denmark had stressed the negative consequences of creating an alternative grouping and had used its continued open door policy as a means of obtaining concessions in EFTA negotiations. In the end, when Danish demands had largely been met, a majority in Parliament, including only the three governing parties, voted for EFTA membership.

In conclusion it should be stressed that during this crucial period of Danish European policy, the 'great' European option, which had a solid base in both economic as well as general foreign policy considerations, remained unrivalled as the government's priority option. Relatively early on, the Nordic solution was abandoned, membership of The Six existed only as an unwelcome fall back position, and EFTA membership was seen as a temporary and very unsatisfactory outcome of the entire process. When combining these priorities with the actively pursued Danish attempt at participation on an à la carte basis in the Continental integration process, it is possible to discern a pattern in Danish European policy from the 1950s up to the present.

Central elements in the subsequent Danish policy which belong to this pattern are first of all: the rapid decisions to join Britain in applying for EEC membership in 1961 and 1967; the NORDEK experiment at the end of the 1960s as a stepping stone towards subsequent entry into the EC; the emphasis by the decision-making elite on economic advantages and concrete results when arguing for Danish EC membership and supporting EC integration steps; the hesitant and half-hearted approach to union plans resulting in reservations about the treaty obligations; and, finally, the enthusiastic endorsement of EU enlargement plans in the 1990s. All elements may be traced back to the pattern identified as characteristic of Danish policy in the 1950s.[29] Instead of a detailed analysis of these subsequent developments, we shall in the following continue our search for more general propositions.

3.2. The identification of three general tendencies

In the preceding section, emphasis has been placed on tendencies rather than on concrete decisions. In this section, we shall move a little further up the ladder of abstraction. The purpose is to integrate the findings already made into a more general conception of what constitutes the characteristic features of the Danish approach to post-war options.

It seems appropriate to distinguish between three features. The two first, the policy of limited engagement and the policy of fragmentation, have already partly been introduced. The third one, the policy of pragmatism, specifically pertaining to the European aspect of Danish foreign and domestic policy, forms part of the traditional political culture in Denmark, explored in more detail in chapter 5.

3.2.1. The policy of limited engagement

In large measure, the presentations of Danish political behavior made up till now can be summarized under the heading of this sub-section, at least insofar as we are dealing with Danish policies towards NATO and the EU. Although membership of these two principle international organizations of post-war Danish foreign policy presented entirely new foreign policy options for Denmark, enabling the country to free itself from a long standing bilateral dependency on Germany, Denmark in both cases approached the membership question with considerable reserve.

In the case of NATO, this has been dealt with above: Danish preference for a Nordic solution has been emphasized. In the case of EEC/EC membership, such hesitancy is not so conspicuous when dealing with official government policy. When the issue first arose at the very inception of the EEC in 1957, Danish rejection of membership must be viewed primarily in the context of the complicated market situation at the time. However, no hesitancy was shown when possibilities existed for membership together with Britain, even where the other Nordic countries were left out. In 1961 and 1967, Danish applications were submitted just of hours after the British. Again in 1970, when prospects for enlargement seemed brighter than on previous occasions, no doubts existed in the Danish government –

---

29 Elements of continuity in the Danish approach to European integration had already been observed in Hansen (1969) when comparing Danish responses to the Briand proposal of European Union in 1930 with post-war policies (p. 16).

or among the vast majority of the members of the Danish Parliament – as to the politically desirable goal of seeking membership. And negotiations were brought to a satisfactory conclusion without great complications.

That 'hesitancy' nevertheless seems an appropriate characterisation of the Danish approach to the EC membership question is due to two additional, interrelated, circumstances. First, Danish governments, while requesting admission, constantly had to face wide-spread and outspoken opposition from a substantial part of the population. Already in the end of the 1950s when the issue was first politicized, the popular strength of the anti EEC movement was visible. In Spring 1963, leading politicians of the pro EEC parties doubted that a referendum would have been won if held on the basis of agreements reached at the just completed, unsuccessful enlargement negotiations (Branner 1997: 144). And although continued polls during the 1960s showed only negligible opposition to membership, the previous pattern reappeared in the early 1970s, when the issue again acquired top priority. Just six months prior to the October 1972 referendum, which endorsed Danish admission to the EC by 63% of the votes cast, polls had registered a slight majority of voters opposed to membership.

The second factor relates to Danish emphasis on the economic aspects of membership. No enthusiasm for 'the European idea' had ever motivated Danish politicians in their policies towards Europe. The overriding consideration had always been how best to safeguard Danish foreign economic interests. Since popular opposition was primarily directed against the political and cultural aspects of increased integration, and since governments believed they had convincing arguments in regard to economic advantages, their inclination towards stressing the economic aspects was reinforced whenever decisions required public campaigning. By the same logic, wider implications of membership were played down. As a result, already in the late 1950s and during negotiations in 1961-63 key decision-makers of The Six and members of the Commission were suspicious of Denmark's 'Europeanness', a suspicion which was hardly reduced in 1970-72. Although officially endorsing plans for further integration, the Danish willingness to actually follow up on these plans was evidently very small. Only on one point, however, did Denmark put forward an outright reservation: cooperation in the security field (a possibility opened up by the Davignon plan), would not occur with Danish participation.

After becoming part of the two organizations in several respects, Danish subsequent policies reflected the country's ambiguous attitude when entering. Denmark has often been labelled a foot-dragging member of both NATO and the EU. More soberly, we may speak of a policy of 'limited engagement'.

This policy has been most visible within the framework of NATO. Although by the beginning of the 1960s Denmark had become fully integrated into the military command structure of the alliance, governments in general kept up a reserved attitude towards membership obligations. Normally, three aspects of this low-profile Danish NATO policy have been stressed: the decision in 1953 not to allow foreign bases on Danish soil; the rejection of the stationing of nuclear weapons in Denmark during peacetime; and defense expenditures which have by far fallen short of alliance requirements. Recent research has revealed that Danish reservations also were pronounced in a number of other respects (Villaume 1994). One study, has even characterised Danish behavior in the alliance as 'semi-neutrality' (Holbraad 1986).

The Danish limited engagement policy has also characterised Danish EU policy in certain respects. Up to 1990, it involved a consistent rejection of all Union plans, upholding the right of veto as stipulated in the Luxembourg compromise of 1966, continued emphasis on circumscribed economic aims of the community, and an unwillingness to alter power relations among the central institutions. To a certain degree, Danish EU behavior resembles the low-profiled NATO behavior just described. In spite of the reservations mentioned, however, and despite the fact that from the perspective of the late 1990s no member country rivals Denmark in reservations, the term 'limited engagement' does not fully reflect all the elements of Danish EU policy.

One modification pertains to the evolution of official policy, which – despite the new reservations embodied in the Edinburgh Agreement of 1992 – has been characterised by a tendency to move from a passive to a more active line, increasingly supporting steps entailing both widening and deepening of EU integration. This process undoubtedly has much to do with experiences of leading decision-makers at both the political and administrative levels, thus reflecting a predominantly intentional spill-over effect as defined in neo-functional integration theory. In terms of party attitudes the process is most manifest when studying the evolution of Social Democratic policies. By the middle of the 1970s organized internal opposition, which had included highly influential party members, had dissolved. By the end of the 1970s, the Social Democrats were in favour of stronger and more effective EC measures not only in the environmental and social fields but also in common economic and energy policies. A regular turn-about occurred when ratification of the SEA was completed in 1986. The party now came out in favour of abolishing the right of veto in new areas and ended up endorsing Union plans in 1990. By the end of the 1990s it had become increasingly evident that the party top aimed to overcome Danish reservations of 1992.[30]

A second modification relates to the fact that Denmark has probably been the most rule-abiding member of the community. Denmark continuously came out on top of the Commission's list of how national governments had implemented directives concerning the internal market. In the 1970s, Danish governments had prided themselves in honouring commitments contained in the Treaty of Rome to a greater extent than other member states. It became part of the goals of the Danish EC presidency in 1978 that the other members should live up to Danish standards (Rüdiger 1995: 175-76). In the day-to-day workings of the institutions, Denmark

---

30 Cf. the analysis in chapter 10 of this volume.

has generally played a constructive role, involving itself in the active pursuit of necessary compromises. These endeavours primarily reflect typical features of Danish political culture (cf. Knudsen 1992 and 1993), but they also demonstrate a desire to fulfill obligations ensuing from membership in a serious way, and, thus, reveal a less reserved attitude than the analysis of the concrete policy line is apt to indicate.

3.2.2. The policy of fragmentation

The configuration of Danish foreign policy in a number of separate arenas, referred to previously, was hardly to be interpreted as a result of a deliberate small state strategy on the part of Danish governments. To a large extent, this fragmentation was imposed upon Denmark from the outside, and not before the 1960s was it consciously defined as forming the basis of the country's foreign relations. However, the concrete manner by which Denmark has defined its participation in the various fora, the priorities attached to them, and the way they have been balanced against each other is primarily the product of a domestic political process. How deliberately a small state perception has been part of this process remains an open question, but the ensuing behavior, i.e. the policy of fragmentation – observable up to the present – it least fits well into a general small state strategy.

By 'fragmentation' of foreign policy (or 'functional compartmentalization') we refer to 'the attempt to spread the promotion of national interests over several fields, but in such a way that the promotion of a particular set of goals is concentrated in one arena, and – of course – the most congenial one' (Due-Nielsen and Petersen 1995: 38; cf. Schou 1990: 187). Fragmentation diminishes the problem of overload in the foreign relations of a small state, but the primary advantage has to do with the risk of entrapment which small states tend to encounter when participating in international organizations.[31] This risk will tend to increase if the pursuit of national interests in more than one foreign policy field, typically security and economics, is concentrated in one particular organisation, thereby providing larger states with more effective means for pressuring the smaller ones.

A Danish policy of fragmentation is observable from the very beginning of intensified multilateralism in the early post-war period. When Denmark accepted participation in the Marshall Plan for European recovery in 1947-48, it was repeatedly emphasised by leading politicians, especially among the Social Democrats who took over government responsibility in November 1947, that Danish adherence would have no consequences for the prevailing anti-bloc security policy. Still, in May 1948, the prime minister stated that Danish Marshall participation and OEEC membership should be regarded exclusively as means of promoting Danish economic interests without endangering Denmark's position outside the two

---

31 On the dilemma of small states in international organizations between entrapment and abandonment see chapter 3 and 4 of this volume.

emerging blocs (Borring Olesen, 1994a: 31-32). When developments a year later had brought an end to Danish neutrality, Danish governments embarked on a similar strategy of fragmentation with regard to NATO membership. There should be no doubt that this membership did not prevent Denmark from concentrating its value promoting policies in other fora, i.e. primarily in the global (UN) and the Nordic arenas.

However, the policy of fragmentation has until recently been practised most conspicuously in the domain of Danish EC/EU membership. The emphasis laid on the economic aspects of European integration may be interpreted as part of this policy. In this respect, it is significant that the term 'market policy' continued to be used synonymously with 'European policy' for a long period after the question of choosing between different market blocs was no longer on the political agenda (cf. chapter 2). As a member of the EC, Denmark kept the different aspects of cooperation strictly compartmentalized for several years, even to the point of maintaining two different ministries – one responsible for foreign economic policy (community matters) one for general foreign policy (to which belonged the EPS and other non-treaty matters). On the insistence of Denmark, foreign ministers could not meet in both capacities, which often meant that successive meetings of the same persons would be held in two different capitals.

In political terms, the most significant consequence of Danish EU fragmentation policy has been a consistently pronounced resistance towards equipping the EU with a security dimension. To what degree this resistance can and should be upheld under international conditions prevailing since the beginning of the 1990s, however, is a matter of controversy among politicans – and among researchers. In section 4.2 below we shall return to this topic.

3.2.3. The policy of pragmatism

A high degree of pragmatism is probably the most characteristic feature of Danish political culture (cf. chapter 5). Essential features of this pragmatism are the willingness to enter compromises, a desire for workable solutions instead of high-flying declarations, and a tendency among political parties to depart from ideological dogmatism. It is not difficult to detect such features in Danish EU policy. Pragmatism is reflected in the way Danish negotiators approach the day-to-day problems of the Community, in Denmark's ability to implement common decisions, in Denmark's insistence on concrete measures and dislike of long-range, mostly unrealistic aims.

The European policy of Denmark, as manifested in the greater part of the postwar period, may also be interpreted, however, as an exception to the pragmatism typical of Danish political life. The tenacity by which Denmark has for many years resisted all Union plans, her long upheld rejection of curtailing the right of veto, and her continued efforts to hold core elements of statehood (i.e. army, police, currency and citizenship) out of the integration process run counter to the image conveyed of Danish political pragmatism. An underlying current in the Danish policy thus appears to have been a rather dogmatic insistence on safeguarding national sovereignty.

In the following, an attempt will be made to demonstrate that – despite evidence to the contrary – Danish European policy on the question of sovereignty is also characterised by pragmatism rather than dogmatism.[32] As a point of departure for this discussion, we may relate to the traditional distinction made in the literature on the early history of European integration between states adhering to federalist, versus functionalist principles.

When employing this distinction, there can be no doubt that Denmark belonged to the functionalist camp. On closer inspection a clear-cut division into two camps, however, hardly corresponds to historical reality. Two sets of observations warrant a moderation of such a dualism.

The first moderation relates to the motives and concrete behavior of the so called *federalists*. Historical research, based on the recently released archives, shows that the Continental states, usually regarded as federalists, on the whole were diligently pre-occupied with safeguarding their own national interests when engaging in the integration process. Federalist goals were not, as public statements tended to show, at the centre of decision-maker's attention. They were subordinated to the pursuit of limited national aims or functioned as a guise for the pursuit of such aims. This holds true for the two great powers, France and West Germany, as well as for the small Benelux states.[33]

When studying the *functionalist* states more closely it becomes evident that it is rather misleading to speak of a homogenous group of states in terms of integration policy. It can be shown that the prevailing Danish attitude deviated from that of its partners in the functionalist 'camp'. Compared to British and Norwegian policies the Danish approach to European integration in its formative years was much more pragmatic.

All the 'functionalists' were pragmatic in the sense that they focused on the solving of concrete problems and did not pay much attention to long term goals of integration. But the pragmatism of Danish decision-makers was of a nature that they can not be regarded as functionalists in the normal sense of the term.[34] In concrete and circumscribed areas, supranational steps and strong institutions were accepted if it could be argued that they were practical means of solving political and economic problems. Furthermore it was accepted that, adapting such means would

---

32 This thesis is discussed in more detail in Branner (1992); see also Branner (1995).
33 The preeminence of national priorities in the early European policies of The Six has been stressed in Griffiths (1995).
34 The term 'functionalism' here refers to *political* conceptions of the time regarding means and goals in European integration, and not to its application when dealing with *theories* of integration.

eventually lead to a closely integrated Europe. Neither on part of the decision-makers nor on the part of the population is it possible to detect any noteworthy apprehension about the idea of a United States of Europe in the early phase of the integration process.[35]

In the 1960s, Danish foreign minister Per Hækkerup could publicly endorse this idea, explicitly arguing that a unification of Western Europe would be to the advantage of small states. In his book on Danish foreign policy Hækkerup wrote:

> "Under the given conditions, where two giants dominate world politics, the small and relatively small European countries have the possibility to make an effective impact, and thereby pursue their interests in the best possible way, only when they act as a unity. When such a unity can also serve as security against the internal disputes which for centuries have ripped Europe apart, one can only view with good will the idea of a politically united Europe."
>
> (Hækkerup 1965: 123)

The small state argument was further advanced when discussing the advantages and disadvantages of maintaining formal sovereignty:

> "The decisive question in this connection must be whether our possibilities to exert influence are increased by an obligatory cooperation with other states, with whom we share common interests and ideals. This question must ... undoubtedly be answered in the affirmative. By cooperating, we take upon ourselves obligations and formally restrict our freedom of action, but the actual freedom of action is expanded because the cooperation increases our possibilities to exert influence on the common policy on an equal footing with the states who participate in the cooperation. Especially significant is that participating in the cooperation gives us the possibility to promote our views before the greater powers have established – or perhaps even locked up – their policies."
>
> (Hækkerup 1965: 124)[36]

---

35 It is noteworthy that the foreign minister, when presenting the Statute of the European Council for ratification in Parliament in June 1949, explicitly referred to the long-term goal of creating a United States of Europe. In 1950 Gallup polls showed 60% in favour of a United States of Europe (Branner 1993: 59-60).

36 Hækkerup's belief in supranationality as a means to further the interests of small states is expressed even more strongly in a newspaper article which appeared while Denmark was still negotiating EEC membership: 'In regard to the form of cooperation, experiences from the economic field show that the interests of small countries are best protected when co-operation is arranged within strong organizations in which proposals are initiated by impartial supranational institutions working under the necessary democratic control' (*Berlingske Tidende*, 1 January, 1963). The same view was voiced in an interview with a Norwegian paper (*Aftenposten*, 19 October, 1962).

Despite such utterances and the undogmatic attitude of Danish decision-makers, Denmark remained closer to the functionalist than to the federalist camp. On the level of practical politics, this can be explained by Danish foreign economic interests and a greater foreign policy affiliation with the Nordic countries and Great Britain than with the Continental states.

On the question of the Danish position between functionalism and federalism three further observations are necessary. They all point to the danger of too much emphasis on Danish federalist inclinations.

First, since Denmark, until the early 1970s, did not actively participate in the supranational integration process, 'federalist' statements on the part of Danish decision-makers were not severely tested and should be seen as expressions of non-binding opinions rather than as a part of concrete policy steps. A similar interpretation pertains to opinion polls registering a majority in favour of a United States of Europe (cf. Nielsson 1966: 276). *Secondly,* until the 1970s, the issue of supranational integration lacked political salience – except for a few years around 1960. Only a handful of politicians attempted – mostly in vain – to engage the parliament, the government and the public in a debate on Europe's future and the possible role of Denmark in the process leading to a more united Europe.[37] And they were thus free to expound their views without risking political set-backs. *Thirdly,* a clear distinction between a short- and a long-run perspective was characteristic of the argumentation applied by the Danish exponents of an undogmatic approach to European integration (Branner 1992: 310-11). Although the goal of a United Europe implying the dissolution of the nation-state system was accepted, it was regarded as belonging to a distant future. In the meantime, the necessary political and economic conditions had to be ensured.

The fragility of the Danish federalist thinking was already demonstrated, during the first debate on Danish membership of the EEC at the end of the 1950s, and when membership was in sight in the early 1970s it had virtually receded. In any event it was no longer publicly expressed by leading politicians.[38] Pragmatism concerning the question of sovereignty, and the ultimate goal of integration had given way to the symbolics of stressing nation-state identity;[39] pragmatism was now but a means by which Denmark pursued its foreign economic interests. In large measure, this development may be accounted for by the greater involvement of the public in the decision-making process and by the exigencies of the yes/no alternative in a referendum campaign. While opponents of Danish membership were able to mobilise extensive support by arguing on the level of ideology, proponents chose to play down the ideological aspects by arguing that the implications of EC

---

37 A sample of early Danish views on European unity is collected in Laursen (1988).
38 The night before signing the treaty of admission in January 1972, Danish prime minister Jens Otto Krag, confessed to his top advisors that the Danish step was part of a development which in the long run would lead to a United States of Europe. See Christensen (1993: 147). Compared to similar, but earlier statements by leading Danish politicians (see above) Krag did not attribute any positive value to this development.
39 Cf. the terminology applied by Ulf Hedetoft in chapter 9 of this book.

membership for the continued existence of an independent Danish nation-state were minimal, if not entirely nonexistent. The issue of sovereignty – for a longer period – had lost its element of pragmatism in Danish political discourse.[40]

After Denmark became a member of the EC, the policy of Danish governments has tended to reflect a rather dogmatic approach to the deepening of integration. This dogmatism was evident during the ratification process of the SEA in 1985-86. While the parliamentary majority rejected the Act on account of the institutional innovations involved, and while the prime minister declared Union plans for 'stone-dead', solid support was given by both the political parties and the voters to the economic aim of creating an internal market without restrictions on free movement of goods, services, capital and people. However, although the great majority of the population since Danish membership continuously has preferred to see the EC develop along intergovernmental lines, pragmatism in regard to the surrendering of sovereignty never completely disappeared from official policy.

The strengthening of the supranational Commission as a means to enhance the position of small states was endorsed in the Danish response to the Tindemansplan for a European Union in the mid 1970s (Lehmann Sørensen 1978: 276); although involving a serious curtailment of national independence in regard to economic policies, the 1978 Franco-German plan to create a European Monetary System was conceived as highly advantageous to Danish interests and, thus, actively supported by the government. Despite opposition voiced against institutional changes produced by the SEA, the parliamentary majority had no difficulty accepting the key integrative element of introducing majority voting concerning single market directives. This kind of pragmatism, where the surrender of sovereignty was clearly subordinated to the pursuit of specific Danish interests, became even more manifest in the period after 1986, especially when analysing the policies of the 'vulnerable' parties,[41] hitherto sceptical or outright opposed to increased integration (i.e. the Social Democrats, the Social Liberal Party and the Socialist People's Party).

On this background, the situation which has evolved during the 1990s resembles previous patterns of behavior and policy. The institution of referenda has again highlighted the issue of surrendering sovereignty, forcing the political elite into a temporary withdrawal of its support for a deepening of European integration. In the context of Danish domestic politics, it is symptomatic of the pragmatic Danish political culture that it has been possible to arrive at an official platform with regard to Danish participation in the Union development comprising almost the entire political spectrum, i.e. 'The national compromise' of 1992 leading to the Edinburgh Agreement. However, it is also symptomatic that the initial Danish pragmatism about increased integration – despite official reservations – seems the most dominant feature characterising attitudes in the political elite at the turn of the century.

---

40 Cf. chapter 2, section 4.
41 Cf. the terminology applied by Jens Henrik Haahr in chapter 10.

4. Historical and Theoretical Perspectives

The final part of this chapter contains a number of conclusions to be drawn from the foregoing analysis. Its main purpose, however, is to place the findings in perspective, both historical and theoretical. Three kinds of perspectives will be dealt with.

The first one concerns a completion of the previously mentioned three-step analysis. The foregoing steps have created the basis for the formulation of more general propositions on how Europe and European solutions fit into the over-all foreign policy universe of Danish decision-makers, and how Danish European policy should be interpreted in the frame of Danish traditions, as analysed in chapter 6. The second perspective draws in developments in the 1990s, which in several respects has turned Danish foreign policy in new directions. An attempt shall be made to compare the degree of change which took place in the latter part of the 1940s and in the 1990s, and on this basis evaluate how the characteristic features of the Danish approach to the 'European option' fit into the new conditions of the 1990s. Finally, the third perspective is devoted to a theoretical discussion, elaborating on the small state approach and drawing on elements from theories of foreign policy change.

4.1. Denmark after 1945: low priority of the European option

The analysis undertaken here makes it possible to draw some interesting conclusions regarding the position of 'Europe' and the status of specific 'European options' in the formulation of post-war Danish foreign policy. Obviously, general conclusions are difficult to make, since neither 'Europe' nor 'European options' are precise terms and because Danish policy varied over time and had a variety of aspects. We shall nevertheless argue, on the basis of the previous sections, that 'Europe' – perceived as a political issue – in the period until 1990 did not occupy a position equalling its importance to Denmark in terms of history, geography and economy. Put differently, the over-all conclusion to be drawn is that European solutions did not carry the weight which an objective or 'realistic' analysis would warrant. Instead they were either discarded, avoided or given inferior status compared to other solutions. In the next sub-section, this conclusion will be modified but not refuted in light of developments in the 1990s.

In various ways, the data presented underpins the above conclusion. In the first place, we may return to the initial Danish inclinations after the end of World War II, when internal and external conditions for formulating foreign policy in Denmark completely changed, creating options which had hitherto been suppressed, non-existent or not regarded as worth pursuing.

The German defeat released Denmark from a one-sided and long-standing dependency on a neighbouring great power; the emergence of the Cold War made it possible for Denmark, for the first time in this century to enter into an alliance providing security against a potential threat; and among European states we see a new willingness to overcome age-old rivalries opening up for far-reaching integration projects. Altogether these external developments were indicative of the huge increase in foreign policy options which a small state like Denmark experienced after 1945. In addition, on the domestic scene a strong reaction gathered political weight during the years of occupation and right after liberation against the hitherto practiced policy of passive adaptation. Thus, in the first period after the war, no strong domestic, politically based, obstacles against a reformulation of basic foreign policy tenets were apparent; hence the government was able to make use of the new, externally conditioned opportunities.

What we have been able to substantiate in the preceding analysis is a striking discrepancy between some of these basic premises and the actual evolution of Danish foreign policy in the first post-war period. No doubt, Danish governments attempted to take advantage of the fundamentally altered and in most respects strongly improved conditions for foreign policy making. However there was no easily discernable correlation between the new conditions and the policy pursued, nor did Danish behavior amount to a simple adaptation to these conditions. Several of the key features in Danish policy of this period did not reflect the explosion in foreign policy options.

The global and the Nordic orientation, of course were, a reflection of the new foreign policy 'independence' of Denmark and the possibilities accruing from the altered conditions. In two respects, however, these orientations signalled an inclination to remain on a familiar track in regard to foreign policy.

In the *first* place, they both represented a minimalistic approach to foreign policy change under the conditions prevailing after 1945. As sub-options, and as shown in section 2.1., they had a high standing in the foreign policy hirarchy already before the war; and it was a sign of continuity rather than change when, after the German collapse, they were given highest priority. In terms of foreign policy tradition, they furthermore constituted the central elements in the internationalist part of the Danish tradition (see chapter 6). Seen in this light, their new prominence was not surprising. What was surprising was the strength and profundity of the Nordic engagement. No single reason can suffice as a full explanation, but the suppression of the internationalist strand of thought in the previous period may form part of it.

Second, the emphasis on the global and the Nordic dimension functioned as an inhibition towards a stronger engagement in other dimensions of foreign policy. Most convincingly, this effect has been demonstrated with regard to the Atlantic dimension. Yet the same effect was, less conspicuously, evident when analyzing the way Denmark approached the specific European questions. In the Danish perception, until the end of the 1950s an alternative image of both political and economic integration existed in the form of a Nordic vision. And although this image was transformed into reality to only a limited extent, it held Denmark from establishing closer ties to the European continent.

In continuation of these observations, it seems important to emphasize that 'internationalism', as the term has been defined in Chapter 6 of this book, in the perception of leading Danish decision-makers, had only a very restricted link to the Atlantic and European dimension of Danish foreign policy.[42] In general, these dimensions rather represented the other part of the tradition, e.g. 'determinism'. In the motives leading the Danish government to accept NATO membership in 1949, there were few traits of a new 'outward-looking' foreign policy orientation based on solidarity with like-minded countries. 'Internationalism', even in the traditional usage of the term, was not yet part of the mental universe of Danish decision-makers.[43] Reorientation in the security field amounted to a pre-occupation with avoiding the danger of Denmark being placed in a military vacuum and consequently, also a certain willingness to spend more on national defense. When, in 1954, Denmark acceded to German admission into NATO, this decision was again, in the internal context, rooted in purely national concerns. Finally, it belonged to the 'deterministic' thinking in security policy that Denmark, despite NATO membership, or even in part because of this membership, did not cut the string to the old-time non-provocative behavior vis-à-vis a threatening great power neighbour.

In other fields of immediate post-war foreign policy, the decisions did not have the same dramatic implications as in the security field. It is thus more difficult to investigate the importance and relevance of 'deterministic' thinking in Danish European policy. Nevertheless, it seems hard to avoid the conclusion that a parallel approach prevailed here.

The mere fact that Denmark approached European questions from a predominantly economic point of view is in itself indicative of deterministic thinking, implying an elimination of options contained in the new development characterising relations among West European states after 1945. In this sense, the policy of fragmentation functioned as a shield keeping Denmark away from close involvement in wider European questions.

Notwithstanding this fragmentation, when analyzing the motives, there was a certain overlap between the security and the European aspects of Danish foreign policy. Danish reluctance towards NATO membership and the subsequent low-profiled NATO policy not only stemmed from a preoccupation with narrowly defined national security concerns, but also from a desire to avoid a deterioration of East-West relations. Similar motives lay behind Danish European policy. Danish decision-makers – in spite of the economic approach – were not blind to the security implications of European integration. Insofar as integration was a means towards overcoming old antagonisms between European great powers, it was – albeit from

---

42 See section 3. Internationalism, its opposite ideological strand, determinism, and the interplay between them are seen in chapter 6 as the constituting elements in a dualistic Danish foreign policy tradition.

43 Cf. the analysis in Lidegaard (1996: 567-88), who argues that a 'national' rather than a 'cosmopolitan' conception dominated official foreign policy in the initial post-war period. For a similar but not identical view see Branner (1990).

the sidelines – greeted as an important positive factor. However, in an influential leftist opinion West European integration was also seen from early on as part of an undesirable process towards increased bloc-building and international tension. Thus again, the 'internationalist' part of the Danish tradition was not channelled into this new field of foreign policy opportunities represented by European integration – on the contrary.

The tendency towards 'determinism' rather than 'internationalism' in early Danish European policy has been reinforced by the emphasis on the defensive rather than offensive aspects of European integration. From the very beginning, Danish governments were pre-occupied with warding off the negative consequences of intensified cooperation. This process began when the OEEC initiated its policy of liquidating quotas without a parallel lowering of tariffs. In the 1950s and 1960s, the optimal market solution for Denmark did not materialise; instead, governments had constantly to choose among lesser evils, often attempting to obtain exemptions from plans, agreed upon by others, in order not to incur too heavy financial losses. Later on, as a member of the EC, Denmark has diverted much political energy into preventing more far-reaching integration projects being carried out; and Danish governments have been kept to this task by a population apprehensive of surrendering sovereignty.

No doubt, even the defensive Danish line is indicative of the salience of European issues in Danish foreign policy throughout the post-war period. However, Danish responses show remarkable similarities with those made in earlier periods when European issues also loomed large on Denmark. Instead of active involvement, Denmark has in many respects sought to escape external pressures. Quite in accordance with determinist thinking, options have been seen largely as threats and not as opportunities.

From the perspective of the entire period up to 1990, the initial Danish inclinations were reflected in the three general tendencies identified in section 3. Viewed separately as well as in combination, these tendencies, as the above discussion has shown, are testimony to the low priority of the European option. How does this assessment stand in light of the dramatic events in the years around 1990, with an entirely altered international situation? The next sub-section addresses this question.[44]

4.2. Denmark and Europe in the 1990s: A new beginning?

From a Danish point of view – as well as from the point of view of most other European states – the external changes occurring around 1990 were comparable in scope and intensity to the changes in the latter part of the 1940s and the beginning of the 1950s. In both periods, changes were of a two-fold nature. On the one hand

---

44 A more specific treatment of Danish options concerning European integration at the beginning of the new century is to be found in chapter 14.

we have during the last decade again been witness to a reorganisation of the entire international system after a 'war' lost by one of the leading great powers. Whereas the new system emerging in the 1940s took the shape of bipolarity, the international system since 1990 is characterised by unipolarity with the United States as the only superpower left. In both cases, however, small powers were confronted with an increased number of foreign policy options – due either to the establishment of new international organizations or to new roles assigned to them.

Remaining with the specific European environment external changes in the two periods have also been profound. Besides the repercussions of the systemic changes on the European level, a partially independent development has taken place on this level by, respectively, the commencement and intensification of Western European integration. No matter how far-reaching the drive, launched in the mid 1980s, towards increased economic and political unity among the EU member countries turns out to be, it seems no exaggeration to maintain that a qualitatively new step in speeding up the integration process has been taken by the transformation of the EC into the EU and the subsequent implementation of EMU plans.

In general, Danish reactions to the external changes brought about since the end of the 1980s have been very pronounced. In the view of most observers, a dramatic shift in the overall foreign policy line has occurred, with Denmark now pursuing a policy of what has officially been labelled 'active internationalism'.[45] When comparing the post-Cold War changes of Danish policy with the post-World War II changes, three interrelated features of 'active internationalism' are especially worth emphasizing.

First, Denmark in the past decade has continued to take own foreign policy initiatives. Although observable in many international fora, not least the UN and the OSCE, this feature has probably been most manifest with regard to the Baltic states. From early on, Denmark supported the liberation movements in these countries, subsequently took the lead concerning diplomatic recognition, and has since then been a primary spokesman on the issue of Baltic integration into Western institutions, i.e. NATO and the EU.

Denmark's Baltic policy also illustrates two other novel features of its foreign policy. The initiatives taken by Danish governments mentioned above are all at variance with a long held policy of not offending or provoking a neighbouring great power representing an actual or potential security threat to Denmark. Not least the fact that Denmark as the only European member of NATO actively confronted with outright opposition from Russia, has worked for Baltic membership is witness of this change of policy. Moreover Danish policies in other fields demon-

---

45 Changes in Danish policy towards a new activism are stressed in Holm (1997 and 1998), Due-Nielsen and Petersen (1995), and Heurlin (1994). See also chapter 5 and 6 of this book. To some analysts who interpret Danish behavior as a reflection of small state adaptation to a new American world order, the changes are less dramatic; i.e. Hansen (1996) and Villaume (1999). An overview of various conceptions is given in Branner (2000). On the term 'active internationalism', see Holm (1998).

strate a new willingness to stand up against great powers, e.g. Denmark's promulgation of a UN resolution in 1997 severely criticising the human rights situation in China.

In its bilateral relations with the Baltic states, Denmark has stressed the military aspects of cooperation. Considering Denmark's formerly low profile NATO policy, not to speak of the almost defenseless Danish neutrality stance prior to World War II, the new emphasis on military means by Danish governments in the 1990s indeed amounts to a true about-face. Further evidence of a 'militarisation'[46] of Danish foreign policy is the remarkably strong Danish presence in former Yugoslavia, where Denmark, when fighting was culminating in 1994, had the largest per capita number of military personnel stationed. An offspring of this engagement has been the Danish lead in efforts during recent years to establish a permanent UN Stand By force (SHIRBRIG), whose headquarters has been located close to Copenhagen.

When combining this rather sketchy presentation of developments in the 1990s with the foregoing analysis in this chapter, at least two kinds of conclusions may be drawn; one pertains to the degree of foreign policy change, the other to the position of the European option.

First, a comparison of changes in the latter part of the 1940s and in the last decade reveals that the relationship between domestic and external changes are not the same in the two periods. Upheavals on the world scene and in Europe, though of an equivalent magnitude, had a remarkably different impact on the over-all foreign policy line of Denmark in the two periods. Only in the second period did domestic changes match the external ones. This difference is even more remarkable when considering that – compared to the 1940s – no noticeable internal push outside decision-making circles existed in the 1990s demanding foreign policy change.

A *second* conclusion may be derived by once again examining the elements of Danish 'active internationalism'. While this policy, as shown above deviates in crucial respects from past behavior, it also contains ingredients which reflect continuity – not least in regard to the position of the 'European option'.

When viewing the geographic dimensions outlining the main content of Danish foreign policy, it is the continuity of priorities that remains remarkable. Danish active internationalism of the 1990s thus points to the continued weight placed on the global and the Nordic dimensions. In large measure, initiatives have been led into these two dimensions – with the Baltic states now replacing the other Scandinavian states in the regional context. In the perception of Danish governments and in their concrete actions, both dimensions have acquired a new and more central position in the field of security policy. At the same time, the continued importance of Danish NATO membership has been stressed, an official report stating that 'NATO

---

46 The term is used in Heurlin (1994). Here it is said that the 'new' Danish foreign policy is characterised by four tendencies: internationalisation, Europeanisation, militarisation and democratisation.

will remain the irreplaceable guarantee for the territorial integrity of Denmark' (Foreign Ministry 1993: XII). No doubt, the line followed by Denmark in the 1990s in its security policy reflects the new possibilities which external changes have created in the two traditional dimensions of Danish foreign policy activism. However, it is hard to avoid the conclusion that this line represents at the same time a deliberate attempt to steer clear of a European option in this field, highlighted by the continued Danish rejection of WEU membership and continuing Danish reservations over the Common Foreign and Security Policy of the EU.

However, it would be an exaggeration to postulate that the thrust for change and greater activism characterising Danish foreign policy in the 1990s have had no impact on the direction and content of Danish European policy. As a result of external developments, the European option has loomed larger. In at least three respects, this has manifested itself in Danish policy changes: both officially and among political parties, it is now recognized that Danish EU policy not only concerns Danish economic interests but involves political issues in a broader sense, hereby also opening up for the European level of European policy.[47] In large measure, the transformation of the former EC into the European Union is accepted, hereby outdating the old membership debate and replacing it with debate on more or less union; and finally, there is a willingness to accept and even to a certain degree advocate supranational solutions to common problems, primarily in the environmental and social field – and recently also in the field of taxation.

Danish activism is thus also visible on EU matters. Nevertheless, in summing up the position of the European option at the turn of the century, we should stress that a final decision concerning what previously has been called the integration option has not been reached. Instead one is tempted to state that the three general features characterising Danish European policy in the post-war period remain valid. The changes enumerated above amount to a *pragmatic* rapprochement to the integration scenario; the continued emphasis on fora other than the EU in matters of security and normative policy signifies a desire to maintain a high degree of *fragmentation* in foreign policy; and the great impact which public opinion due to the institution of referenda has on official policy entails that Danish European policy in the foreseeable future will continue to be characterised by a *limited engagement*.

As pointed out in chapter 6, Danish foreign policy has in the 1990s retained its dualistic character. A continuity is observable in the 'internationalist' and the 'determinist' parts of the tradition. External changes have not as yet fundamentally altered the established arenas of Danish internationalism, but have instead created unprecedented possibilities for this internationalism to flourish. Although signs of change are visible, Danish European policy has been slow to adapt to these external changes, thus demonstrating the continued relevance of the determinist element in the tradition.

---

47 Cf. the terminology presented in chapter 2, section 3.

4.3. Implications for analysing small state behavior and foreign policy change

This chapter has focussed on the small state aspect of Danish foreign policy; likewise, attention has been directed towards the degree of change which this policy has undergone. Still, theoretical ambitions have been rather limited. In part by combining the two approaches just mentioned, we shall in this last section indicate how the analysis may contribute to existing theory, especially concerning theories of foreign policy change.

We may start out with a few observations on the general theme of internal and external determination of foreign policy. Although generalisations regarding the behavior and conditions of small states in international relations have been hard to underpin, widespread consensus seems to exist at least on the rather trivial proposition that the foreign policy of small states tends to be more determined by external developments than is the case for larger states. In support of this proposition, the present study has shown how the scope of options in the Danish case has been greatly influenced by changes in the external environment; World War II and the immediate post-war period completely reversed Denmark's situation regarding the number of available foreign policy options.

Our study also indicates that the degree of foreign policy change, which an enlarged scope of options will trigger off, not to speak of the choice made among options, may for a small state also be largely domestically determined. In Danish post-war history, goals formulated as part of a foreign policy tradition have structured the priority given to various options, and have thus largely determined whether external changes would prompt equivalent foreign policy changes. The remarkable inertia in the years following 1945 compared to the swift reversal of main foreign policy postures after 1989 is illustrative of this point.

In continuation, it seems relevant to ask how it is possible to measure degrees of foreign policy change. To this end, a useful scheme has been set up by Charles Hermann (1990), who identifies four distinct levels of change: *adjustment change, program change, goal/problem change* and *international orientation change*.[48] The first level does not represent change in the proper sense, since it amounts only to minor alterations of a quantitative kind. 'What is done, how it is done, and the purposes for which it is done remain unchanged'. The next two categories relate to means and ends: a shift in methods to achieve a specified goal involves a lesser degree of change than is the case when the goal itself is being replaced by another goal, i.e. the purposes of the foreign policy of a country are reformulated. The highest level of change, international orientation change, is defined as 'the redirection of the actor's entire orientation towards world affairs'. This kind of change is

---

48 Hermann's entire scheme also includes a categorization of agents of change: 'leader driven', 'bureaucratic advocacy', 'domestic restructuring' and 'external shock' (Hermann 1990).

multidimensional: it involves the actor's approach to a host of other actors, to several issues and to all aspects of foreign policy.

The findings presented in this chapter suggest that the applicability of the categories set up by Hermann is highly dependent on the size of the state whose foreign policy is being analysed. Using concepts from adaptation theory, small and large states differ with respect to stress sensitivity and influence capability.[49] As the Danish case shows, this difference has implications for the degree of change, which the various categories signify.

A high degree of stress sensitivity means that external changes have great impact on the conditions relevant for formulating foreign policy. Thus for states with high stress sensitivity, i.e. small states like Denmark, pursuing the same goal may imply rather dramatic changes in methods. Viewed from the outside, a foreign policy change may amount to goal changes or even international orientation change, while a closer study of motives and priorities rather indicates a mere change of means, i.e. program change. In the terminology of Charles Hermann, the change in Danish foreign policy in the years after 1945, highlighted by the abandonment of a long established policy of neutrality in favour of an alliance membership, could easily be categorized as international orientation change. According to a number of interpretations made in recent years (see chapter 6, section 2.1.) this change, however, was more a reflection of Danish adaptation to external changes than formulation of new foreign policy goals.

On the influence side as well, foreign policy changes should be evaluated differently with respect to small and large states. The greater influence which large states are able to exert implies that they are in a better position than small states to draw up their own independent foreign policy goals. As a consequence, goal changes tend to be more frequent among large states, a tendency enforced by their involvement in a greater number of international issues. In contrast, small states do not so easily reach the level of goal changes, and when this level is reached, it tends to represent a greater degree of change than is the case for large states. The continuity in Danish foreign policy goals across periods of international upheavals, demonstrated here and in chapter 6 may be considered an illustration of this point.

This leads us to an observation on the importance of the time dimension in analyses of foreign policy change. For the historian, of course, this dimension is inherent in the discipline itself – and including it when evaluating policy changes is therefore self-evident. From a theoretical point of view, the problem is that the historian rarely attempts to categorize or give a more explicit formulation of the elements of change he/she is studying. On the other hand, in an analytical scheme like Hermann's the time dimension is left out. In the analysis of the Danish case, the drawbacks of this omission stand out.

Changes at one point of time necessarily have to be understood and evaluated on the basis of later changes. This holds true for the short period between 1945 and

---

49 For a discussion of these terms see chapter 3.

1949, but seems especially evident when examining the entire span of time since the end of World War II – or even further back. Without a comparison of the immediate post-war period with the period since the end of the Cold War, one tends to exaggerate the elements of change involved in the latter period. What we are witnessing today, as already indicated, may demonstrate the implementation of policy goals, formulated in earlier periods, and which were more or less subdued during the Cold War. In other words, the placing of a policy change on a specific level is meaningless – also from a theoretical point of view – unless one considers the dimension of time.

One final note relates to the normative aspects of theories of change and stability in foreign policy. It seems to be a tendency among scholars in this field to view changes from either a negative or a positive perspective, reflecting the prevailing evaluation of historical developments at the time of study. When Kjell Goldmann, around 1980, embarked on his study of foreign policy stability, he was explicitly motivated by a concern for the continuity of detente policy on the part of the two superpowers. Similarly, Charles Hermann (1990) regarded ongoing international changes as positive and desired theoretical efforts to be supportive of this development. Without discarding these normative motivations, I would like to stress two pitfalls which the study of Danish foreign and European policy reveals.

Considering the foregoing discussion, it seems evident that before being able to arrive at normative conclusions regarding the degree of change, one should to take the temporal dimension into account. Danish difficulties in adapting to a new world after World War II and the tendency to remain stuck in traditional priorities and concerns – even after becoming a member of NATO and the EC – have often been negatively evaluated. However, it is highly probable that this inertia has been a prerequisite for Denmark's ability to launch a more active foreign policy in the 1990s (cf. Branner 1990: 90). A relatively low degree of change in one period may lay the ground work for a greater degree of change in a later period.

The second point relates to the differences between small and large states. Evaluations of the kind mentioned above view change and stability in foreign policy exclusively in an *international* context. Whatever normative yardsticks one applies, this perspective, of course, is highly important. Yet it would, be a mistake to leave out the *national* perspective – also for the sake of a well functioning international system. The defense or even the strengthening of national values is a legitimate concern in the foreign policies of both kinds of states. Smaller states, however, normally have fewer possibilities than larger ones to impose such values on others. Since external changes are often brought about as a result of competing great power ambitions, inertia on the part of small states may be a means towards the maintenance of national values. This observation is especially pertinent with regard to European integration. In any case, it goes a long way towards explaining some of the characteristic features of Danish European policy.

Literature

Amstrup, Niels (1978): "Grønland i det amerikansk-danske forhold 1945-1948" in Niels Amstrup and Ib Faurby (eds.), *Studier i dansk udenrigspolitik,* Århus: Forlaget Politica.

Bloemen, Erik (1995): "A Problem to Every Solution. The Six and the Free Trade Area", in T. Borring Olesen (ed.), pp. 182-196.

Branner, Hans (1972): *Småstat mellem stormagter.* Copenhagen: Munksgaard.

Branner, Hans (1987): *9. april 1940 – et politisk lærestykke?*, Copenhagen: DJØF Publishing.

Branner, Hans (1990): ""Vi vil fred her til lands …". En udenrigspolitisk linie 1940-1949-1989?", *Vandkunsten* 90/3, pp. 47-90.

Branner, Hans (1992): "Danish European Policy since 1945: The Question of Sovereignty" in *M. Kelstrup (ed.).*

Branner, Hans (1993): "På vagt eller på spring? Danmark og europæisk integration 1948-1953" in *B. Nüchel Thomsen (ed.)*, pp. 29-64.

Branner, Hans (1995): "Denmark and the European Coal and Steel Community, 1950-1953" in *Thorsten Borring Olesen (ed.)*, pp. 115-128.

Branner, Hans (1997): "Small state on the sidelines: Denmark and the question of European political integration", in George Wilkes (ed.), *Britain's Failure to Enter the European Community 1961-63*, London: Frank Cass, pp. 144-163.

Branner, Hans (2000): "Traditioner og optioner i dansk udenrigspolitik" in S. v. Dosenrode (ed.), *Dansk udenrigspolitik. Muligheder og udfordringer ved det 21.århundredes begyndelse*, Copenhagen: Rådet for Europæisk Politik.

Christensen, Jens (1993): "Danmark, Norden og EF 1963-1972" in *B. Nüchel Thomsen (ed.).* -

Due-Nielsen, Carsten and Nikolaj Petersen (eds.) (1995): *Adaptation and Activism: The Foreign Policy of Denmark 1967-1993*, Copenhagen: DJØF Publishing.

Foreign Ministry (1993): *Principper og perspektiver i dansk udenrigspolitik*, Copenhagen: Udenrigsministeriet.

Griffiths, Richard (1995): "The National and International Ramifications of Post-war Europe" in *Thorsten Borring Olesen (ed.)*, pp. 24-39.

Goldmann, Kjell (1988): *Change and Stability in Foreign Policy*, New York: Harvester.

Haagerup, Niels Jørgen (1956): *De Forenede Nationer og Danmarks sikkerhed*, Aarhus: Aarhus University Press.

Hansen, Birthe (1996): "Dansk Baltikumpolitik 1989-1995" in Svend Aage Christensen and Ole Wæver (eds.): *Dansk Udenrigspolitisk Årbog 1995*, Copenhagen: DUPI.

Hansen, Peter (1969): "Denmark and European Integration", *Cooperation and Conflict*, 1969/1, pp. 13-46.

Hermann, Charles F. (1990): "Changing Course: When Governments Choose to Redirect Foreign Policy", *International Studies Quarterly*, 54,2.

Heurlin, Bertel (1994): "Nye prioriteringer i dansk udenrigspolitik", pp. 30-50 in *Dansk Udenrigspolitisk Årbog 1993*, Copenhagen: DUPI.

Heurlin, Bertel (1995): "Denmark: Security Policy and Foreign Policy – a New Activism" in B. Heurlin (ed.), *Security Problems in the New Europe*, Copenhagen: Copenhagen Political Studies Press, pp. 96-117.

Holbraad, Carsten (1986): "Denmark: Half-hearted Partner" in Nils Ørvik (ed.), *Semi-alignment and Western Security*, London: Croom Helm, pp. 15-60.
Holm, Hans-Henrik (1997): "Denmark's Active Internationalism: Advocating International Norms with Domestic Constraints" in Bertel Heurlin and Hans Mouritzen (eds.), *Danish Foreign Policy Yearbook 1997*, Copenhagen: DUPI, pp. 52-80.
Holm, Hans-Henrik (1998): "And Now What – Denmark? Danish Foreign Policy Turns Activist" in Georg Sørensen and Hans-Henrik Holm (eds.), *And Now What? International Politics After the Cold War*, Aarhus: Politica, pp. 18-41.
Hækkerup, Per (1963): "Europa vil samles", *Berlingske Tidende*, January 1.
Hækkerup, Per (1965): *Danmarks udenrigspolitik*, Copenhagen: Fremad.
Kelstrup, Morten (ed.) (1992): *European Integration and Denmark's Participation*, Copenhagen: Copenhagen Political Studies Press.
Knudsen, Tim (1992): "A Portrait of Danish State-Culture: Why Denmark Needs Two National Anthems" in *Kelstrup (ed.)*.
Knudsen, Tim (1993): "Det går nok – et essay om dansk statskultur og eurokratiet", *Politica*, 1993/3, pp. 269-87.
Laursen, Finn (1988): "The Discussion on European Union in Denmark" in Lipkens and Loth (eds.), *Documents on the History of European Integration*, Berlin: Walter de Gruyter & CO, pp. 566-527.
Laursen, Johnny (1993): "Mellem fællesmarkedet og frihandelszonen. Dansk markedspolitik 1956-1958" in *B. Nüchel Thomsen (ed.)*.
Laursen, Johnny and Thorsten Borring Olesen (1994): "Det europæiske markedsskisma", in Tom Swienty (red.): *Danmark i Europa 1945-93*, Copenhagen: Munksgaard, pp. 93-160.
Lidegaard, Bo (1996): *I kongens navn. Henrik Kauffmann i dansk diplomati 1919-58*, Copenhagen: Samleren.
Milward, Alan S. and Vibeke Sørensen (eds.) (1993): *The Frontier of National Sovereignty*, London and New York: Routledge.
Mouritzen, Hans (1988). *Finlandization: Towards a Theory of Adaptive Politics*, Aldershot: Avebury.
Møller, John Christmas (1945): *Det tyske problem*, Copenhagen: Nyt Nordisk Forlag Arnold Busck.
Nielsson, Gunnar P. (1966): *Denmark and European Integration. A Small Country at the Crossroads*, unpubl. Ph.D diss., University of California, Los Angeles (microfilm at Royal Library, Copenhagen).
Olesen, Thorsten Borring (1993): *The Lesser Evil. The Danish Social Democratic Party and the Decision to Join the Atlantic Pact, 1948-1949*, Working Paper, Aarhus: Institute of History, Aarhus University.
Olesen, Thorsten Borring (1994a): "Jagten på et sikkerhedspolitisk ståsted. Socialdemokratiet og holdningerne til sikkerhedspolitikken 1945-1948" in B. Nüchel Thomsen (ed.), *Temaer og brændpunkter i dansk politik*, Odense: Odense University Press, pp. 15-54.
Olesen, Thorsten Borring (1994b): "Brødrefolk, men ikke våbenbrødre – diskussionerne om et skandinavisk forsvarsforbund 1948/49", *Den jyske Historiker*, no. 69-70, pp. 151-178.
Olesen, Thorsten Borring (ed.) (1995): *Interdependence Versus Integration. Denmark, Scandinavia and Western Europe 1945-1960*, Odense: Odense University Press.
Pedersen, Ole Karup (1970): *Udenrigsminister P. Munchs opfattelse af Danmarks stilling i international politik*. Copenhagen: G.E.C. Gad.

Petersen, Nikolaj (1978): "Optionsproblematikken i dansk sikkerhedspolitik 1948-49" in Niels Amstrup and Ib Faurby (eds.), *Studier i dansk udenrigspolitik*, Aarhus: Forlaget Politica, pp. 199-236.

Petersen, Nikolaj (1979a): "Danish and Norwegian Alliance Policies: A Comparative Analysis", *Cooperation and Conflict,* vol. XIV, pp. 193-210.

Petersen, Nikolaj (1979b): "International Power and Foreign Policy Behavior: The Formulation of Danish Security Policy in the 1870-1914 Period" in Kjell Goldmann and Gunnar Sjöstedt (eds.), *Power, Capabilities, Interdependence*. Beverly Hills: Sage, pp. 235-69.

Petersen, Nikolaj (1990): "Denmark's Foreign Relations in the 1990s", *The Annals, AAPSS*, no. 512, pp. 88-100.

Petersen, Nikolaj (1991): "Atlantpagtbeslutningen" in Carsten Due-Nielsen, Johan Peter Noack and Nikolaj Petersen (eds.), *Danmark, Norden og NATO 1948-1962*, Copenhagen: DJØF Publishing.

Rosati, Jerel A., et al. (1994): *Foreign Policy Restructuring: How Governments Respond to Global Change*, University of South Carolina Press.

Rüdiger, Mogens (1995): "Denmark and the European Community 1967-1985" in *Due-Nielsen and Petersen (eds.)*, pp. 163-188.

Scavenius, Erik (1948): *Forhandlingspolitikken under besættelsen*. Copenhagen: Steen Hasselbalchs Forlag.

Schou, Tove Lise (1990): "Danmark i den økonomiske og politiske integration i Europa", in M. Kelstrup (ed.): *Nyere tendenser i politologien,* bd. III, Copenhagen: Forlaget Politiske Studier.

Seymour, Susan (1982): *Anglo-Danish Relations and Germany 1933-1945*. Odense: Odense University Press.

Sjøqvist, Viggo (1962): *Peter Vedel. Udenrigsministeriets direktør.* Vol. II, Aarhus: Aarhus University Press.

Sjøqvist, Viggo (1973): *Erik Scavenius. En biografi.* Vol. I, Copenhagen: Gyldendal.

Sørensen, Carsten Lehmann (1978): *Danmark og EF i 1970erne*. Copenhagen: Borgen.

Sørensen, Vibeke (1992): "How to Become a Member of a Club without Joining. Danish Policy with respect to European Sector Integration Schemes, 1950-1957", *Scandinavian Journal of History,* vol. 16, pp. 105-25.

Sørensen, Vibeke (1993): "Between interdependence and integration: Denmark's shifting strategies" in *Milward and Sørensen (eds.)*, pp 88-116.

Sørensen, Vibeke (1995): "Nordic Cooperation – A Social Democratic Alternative to Europe?" in *Thorsten Borring Olesen (ed.)*.

Thomsen, Birgit Nüchel (ed.) (1993): *The Odd Man Out? Danmark og den Europæiske ntegration 1948-1992*, Odense: Odense University Press.

Villaume, Poul (1994): *Alliereret med forbehold. Danmark, NATO og den kolde krig*, Copenhagen: Forlaget Eirene.

Villaume, Poul (1999): "Denmark and NATO through 50 Years" in Bertel Heurlin and Hans Mouritzen (eds.), *Danish Foreign Policy Yearbook 1999*, Copenhagen: DUPI.

Villumsen, Holger (1991): *Det danske Socialdemokratis Europapolitik 1945-1949*, Odense: Odense University Press.

Woyke, Wichard (1985): *Erfolg durch Integration*. Bochum: Studienverlag Dr. N. Brockmayer.

CHAPTER 12

Danish EU-Policy Making

Søren Z. von Dosenrode

1. Introduction

An often heard argument in favour of Danish membership in the European Union is that "it gives influence". Through membership, Denmark can participate in European policy processes and can thereby influence it. The European Union (EU) is a huge and complex system that profoundly influences the political systems of the member states, as well as some states outside it. Large and important areas of Danish society are now governed directly by EU directives and regulations, or they are less directly influenced by the norms and ideology of the EU. This article attempts to analyse the question of who decides the official Danish EU-policies.[1] Principle focus will be on the national policy formulation process: Which actors decide what in which settings? We will concentrate on the interplay among the major networks, where the key actors are four central groups of national actors in the Danish policy-making process: Parliament, the government, the civil service and the interest organisations. The main argument of this paper is that an important part of legislation directly influencing Danish citizens is not made by parliamentarians, but by networks dominated by civil servants and interest organisations.

This article will begin examining the EU decision-making system, following the phases of the policy cycle. This will provide an impression of the framework in which the Danish EU decision-making process takes place. We will then turn to the Danish EU decision-making system, looking first at the formal national EU decision-making, and then proceeding to an analysis of the networks where different sectors and actors interact in the shaping of Danish EU-policy.

The *analysis of the EU and of EU policy-making* has often taken its point of departure in the notion of the EU as an arena of traditional foreign policy making, in the theories of integration (stressing structures and processes), or within the field of (public international) law (viewing the EU as a new entity *sui generis*). The policy analysis approach has concentrated on liberal democratic systems (Schumann, 1993). However, there is no obvious reason why one should not try to use the insights of the policy analysis approach when analysing the EU, as has recently been done by for example Bulmer (1994) and Peterson (1995). A policy analytical approach has thus been chosen as a framework for this article. Within the comprehen-

---

1 This article deals mainly with the day to day EC policies in the "first pillar" of the EU treaty. This pillar has a different quality than the two other pillars.

sive insights of this approach, this article draws especially upon the concepts of "the policy cycle" and of "policy network analysis".

The phases of the policy cycle may vary a bit in number (e.g. May & Wildavsky 1978 or Sabatier and Jenkin-Schmith, 1993). In this essay we use Héritier's concept of a five-phase cycle, the phases being: 1) problem definition, 2) agenda-setting, 3) policy-formulation, 4) implementation, and 5) policy-reformulation or policy-termination.[2]

The policy cycle is a conceptual and a heuristic tool; in the "real world" the policy process often moves in a less linear and less orderly fashion. Using the policy cycle does however prevent us from overlooking important phases in the entire policy process.

When analysing situations of interaction between actors, the policy network approach seems well-suited as a supplement to the policy cycle.[3] An additional argument for focusing on policy networks is that they affect the policy outcome. In this essay, Héritier's definition will be used, as it opens up the possibility for both formal and informal interactions, seeing them as a whole (see Héritier 1993: 432):

> "Policy networks are here defined as predominantly informal (but also formal) interaction between actors, mostly organisations or individuals (as members of organisations) with differing or mutually dependent interests."[4]

The term "policy network"[5] is used in its genetic way, covering a variety of network types ranging from policy communities at one end of the continuum to issue-networks at the other (Rhodes & Marsh 1992: 182).

The policy network approach has the advantage, that it is useful for the analysis of open and closed policy networks (Pappi, 1993: 87), and for the analysis of interactions between different types of actors, over longer periods of time and across hierarchies. It is also useful for grasping the relations of actors outside the formal setting. Compared to the legalistic tradition, for example, the network approach urges us from the start to look for other actors and procedures than those mentioned in laws and procedures. According to Parsons (1995), "The strength of the network approach is that it provides a metaphor for this complexity which "fits" the technological and sociological changes of modern society" (p. 185)

---

2 Héritiers (ed.) (1993). May and Wildavsky discuss the advantages of using the policy cycles as a methodological tool (1978: 10). The criticism raised against the policy analysis in general, and the policy cycle in particular, is discussed by Héritier (1993), as well as in Parsons (1995).
3 For a discussion of the network approach as method and concerning definitions, see Rhodes & Marsh (1992), Pappi (1993), and Parsons (1995).
4 My translation from the German. The original German text (Héritier, 1993: 432): "... Politiknetzwerke werden hier [...] definiert als überwiegend informelle (aber auch formelle) Interaktion zwischen Akteuren, meist Organisationen oder Einzelpersonen (als Mitglieder von Organisationen) mit unterschiedlichen, aber wechselseitig abhängigen Interessen."
5 In the following text, the terms "policy network" and "network" are used synonymously.

Frans van Warden (1992) has developed a scheme for the analysis of networks. Van Waarden suggests concentrating on three main dimensions, and it is these which will also be used in this article: 1) the actors involved, 2) the main function of the network, and 3) the power relations.

2. EU Policy-Making[6]

There are several differences between a "normal", liberal democratic state and the EU.[7]

One of the most striking features of the EU, seen with both political and historical eyes, is the rapid development into something looking very much like a new state. The Pörtschach decision of October 1998 taken by the European Council to meet when necessary (in 1998 it met 4 times, 1999 it met 6 times), has tremendously strengthened the influence of the member-states, in a way not conforming to official EU-ideology. The European Council will now have time not only to lay down the overall strategy of the Union but to follow up on initiatives, and delve into individual cases as well. In other words, it looks very much like a (coalition)-government. This decision will have major consequences; the frequent meetings of the European Council, and the power that follows, will take its toll on the Commission, in spite of its new dynamic President Prodi. The Commission will change into a strong, central administration. In the same manner, the General Affairs Council will lose some of its power as "supreme council of ministers". In the member-states, the consequence will be a strengthening of the prime minister's power, as he, and not the foreign minister, is member of the European Council.

With something that resembles a government (European Council), a central administration (Commission), a parliament (EP), a court (European Court of Justice), a national bank (ECB), a currency (Euro), an embryo defence (the decision taken in October 1999 to go on with the plans of creating an EU-defence force of 30.-100,000 man), and the ongoing work of the reflection group on a EU-constitution including basic rights, *all* the traditional attributes of a state are present.

Still, if one disapproves of the above analysis, a most striking feature of the EU is the handing over of national sovereignty from the member-states to a supranational organisation that enacts binding legislation for the member-states. Below the supranational level there is a national level consisting of 15 states, all of liberal democratic character. Below the state-level there is an increasingly important subnational level of regions. These structures create a hyper-complex decision-making process. The power of the individual member-state executive has been constrained

---

6 This section is based on results of interviews with "EU policy-makers" made by the author between 1989-1996, on memoranda from the Danish Civil Service, and on the Swedish Government's survey on the first experiences of the EU membership (SOU 1996). This combination of data ensures a broad scope as well as a survey period of 7 years.
7 For a detailed analysis of the EU as a policy-making system, as well as of the EU policy circle, see von Dosenrode (1997).

by the increasing integration process, especially by the increased use of qualified majority voting in the Council of Ministers. Even as a *collegium*, the state executives have lost influence, as Marks, Hooghe and Blank argue (1996: 353f.). Thus, we are dealing with a very complex policy making system.

In the EU, as well as in a liberal democratic state, the first step of the policy making process is the *problem definition*. In this first phase, the game in the EU is per definition both open and "muddy". The EU decision-making process can be most effectively influenced in this phase and in the agenda-setting phase which follows. This is why the member-states seek to get involved in these phases, insofar as they want to shape the substance of the later phases.

The Commission, being responsible for the problem-definition, is clearly the most important actor in this phase. The Commission's responsibility derives from its "monopoly of proposals". If an issue looks interesting, the Commission will begin by sounding out their closer partners, mainly interest organisations, in order to obtain an initial impression. This is a fairly closed process. The opinions of organisations or "experts" may be solicited, but no one has a "right" to be heard at this important stage; the "partner organizations" of the Commission are not chosen according to national representation or other objective criteria. In day-to-day policy, only the Commission and the "chosen few" are decisive actors. Sometimes the organisations that have been consulted report back to their national administration, but it is not necessarily so. For these reasons, it frequently happens that the member states do not know that the Commission is preparing an initiative. This makes it hard for them to influence this phase.

It is not unusual for more than one of the Commission's General Directorates (GD) to be working on similar cases at the same time. Apart from the apparent loss of resources, it makes it hard for the national civil servants to identify the Commission"s standpoint. Subsequently, the national preparation of a strategy of influencing the process is impeded.

In spite of its unclear character, the phase of problem definition is obviously of great importance. However, acknowledging that there is a political problem is not the same as *setting it on the political agenda*, i.e., deciding that one must try to solve it. It takes political power to put a new issue on the agenda.

If the first "soundings" are positive, a functionary will draft a proposal. The draft proposal will be submitted to one of the many committees of the Commission, in which interest organisations, national-experts etc. are represented. Here the Commission obtains initial feedback on the national positions. The Commission will often consult the national attachés too. Thus, the national administrations can find out about an initiative relatively early. Nevertheless, the game is still being played among EU-functionaries and representatives of interest organisations, other national experts and eventually national civil servants. It is not yet the politicians" game.

As for the content of the agenda, Héritier has pointed out that the majority of issues on the agenda are old issues or routine-questions, and that only a small part are actually new questions (1993: 87). That this statement is also true for the EU appears in the Commission"s own "Recherche sur l"exercice du droit d"initiative de la Commission en 1991" (cited in Nedergaard 1994: 151f). Only 16% of the initiatives taken by the Commission in 1991 were new (6% having come from the Commission itself, 8% initiated by the Council and 2% being demands from either the EP or the European Court of Justice). The remaining 84% were the result of obligations arising from the treaty, from already agreed upon programs, from actions taken by the member-states, etc. Thus, it is clear that putting new issues on the EU policy agenda can be much harder than taking up issues falling within long established EU competencies.

The role of the Commission remains extremely important in this phase. It is the Commission who decides if, when, and in what form an issue will officially be placed on the agenda of the Council as a proposal. When an issue has been placed on the Commissions internal agenda, it must pass through the Commission bureaucracy. This procedure, the same for all kinds of proposals, is described by Spence (1994: 104).

The relatively small size of the Commission's administrative apparatus makes it very dependent on external advice and information throughout the entire agenda setting phase. Moreover, it is easier to legitimise an issue being placed on the agenda if the Commission can show a broad approval for a proposal. Such a proposal also stands a better chance of remaining on the agenda. Thus, the Commission will continue consulting expert committees of mixed background, e.g. national civil servants, academics and interest groups. The Commission is also known to be very open to lobbying from interest organisations. Most groups experience little difficulty in gaining access to Commission officials (Dosenrode & Sidenius 1999: 14ff.).

At this stage an interest organisation can bring an issue onto the agenda or prevent this; it is one of the most important stages in the EU decision-making process (cf. Andersen & Eliassen, 1993: 30). However, it is the privilege of the Commission to decide whom to consult. Neither national parliaments nor "the people" as such are actors in this phase. Moreover, it should be kept in mind that the Commission rarely accepts proposals not in line with EU ideology.

Despite the openness of the Commission to lobbyists and despite the Commission's right to initiate measures, etc., Mazey & Richardson claim that it is still the member states and their representatives who generally set the agenda (1994: 176). The argument is sound, if one distinguishes between political and technical issues. Concerning the technical issues, which are by far more numerous, it is the Commission that dominates (see below). The collegium of Commissionaires have the right to pass initiatives on to their respective administrations and to alter proposals from the General Directorates. In some cases, the national governments are able to influence the agenda-setting through "their" Commissionaire, or through the Commissionaire's cabinet. There are no reason to believe that this practice will change with the Prodi Commission. However, the success of national attempts to influence the policy process are very much dependent on the personality of the Commissionaire and on his or her standing in the Commission.

When an official proposal is finally drafted, we leave the realm of the Commission and enter the phase of *policy formulation*. However, this does not mean, that the Commission functionaries have no more work or influence; they will follow 'their' proposal all the way through the process, including the Council of Ministers.

More traditional analysis of the EU decision-making process have concentrated upon the policy-formulation phase. It is from this phase onwards, that the ministers – and national parliaments – enter the scene. In the later part of this phase we see the summits and nightlong negotiations so well-known from media coverage, however, these events, one dare say "happenings", constitute only a small part of the daily routine.[8]

It is under the auspices of the Council that negotiations now take place in the COREPER (1&2) and its working-groups. For the "A-points" on the agenda of the Council (non-controversial; settled by the civil-servants), most of the activity lies in the firm hands of the civil servants and, depending on the modus, of the EP. For the more controversial points on the agenda (B-points), one can divide the phase into a preparatory part run by the civil servants, and a second part led by the ministers. The national civil servants, often experts in their fields, are extremely important. It is they who decide whether a proposal is "controversial" or not (i.e., whether it is an A- or a B-point); and it is they, with their knowledge of national EU policy-making, who prevent possible political or controversial topics from turning into "B-points". They know that if they sell out a bit of their "national policy" one day, they may often win it back the next day when another topic is being negotiated.[9]

In this phase, we have different actors: the initiative now rests with the Council and the national civil servants, especially the "lonely experts" in the working groups, who are the main targets of lobbying activities. According to the procedure laid down in the treaties, however, the Commission and the EP can play important parts, too. Compared to the previous phases, this phase is much more closed to external influences.

Seen from the Commissions point of view the *implementation phase* is the weakest link in the chain.[10] In a national setting government and Parliament can be fairly sure of the implementation of their decisions. They have means of controlling and enforcing implementation. This is not the case for the Commission. Hence, implementation can easily turn out to be the phase where the conflicting

---

8 With the Amsterdam Treaty, there is one main procedure for making EU legislation (co-decision) plus several variations. For a description of these procedures, see the newest edition of Nugent.

9 For an analysis of the kinds of negotiations within the Council, see Schumann (1993: 414).

10 The Danish Foreign Office publishes an annual survey showing which countries have been (or are about to be) brought before the Court in Luxembourg. The sheer number is of course only the tip of the iceberg; but it gives a rough impression of which countries are "good" and which are "bad". Denmark notoriously belongs to the "Musterknaben".

points, that were so carefully wrapped up in a typical EU package, now reveal themselves. The European Commission relies heavily on the member states for implementing and monitoring directives and regulations (From & Stava 1993).

Although one could expect the *policy-reformulation phase* to be more or less the same as the policy-formulation, this is not necessarily the case. In the period after implementation (and before reformulation), the advantages and disadvantages of the regulation or directive are visible. This could be expected to be *the* opportunity to correct faults. However, this is not necessarily so. Due to the Commission's very rigid understanding of rules the national civil servants find that correction of regulations seldomly take place (interview, November 1995).[11] The experience of the civil servants must be seen in the light of the Commission's struggle for competence.

Reformulation of policy brings with it the permanent problem of finding a new compromise for the 15 member states. Bureaucratic resistance to changing an already implemented procedure must also be overcome. These obstacles work against radical changes. Thus, one can consider the reformulation of EU policy to be a rather futile exercise. The still new president of the Commission, Prodi, has promised changes; time will tell if he succeeds, but it is not an easy task to change decade-old habits.

3. The Actors and their Interplay in the Formulation of Danish EU Policies

Let us now focus on Denmark as one of the 16 decision making centres in the EU policy-making process. How is the Danish stand made? Which actors are involved in the domestic decision-making process? First, we will describe the formal, institutionalised EU coordination and -decision-making procedure. We will then examine the networks involved.

3.1. A Survey of the Formal Danish EU Decision-Making System

The formal part of the Danish EU coordination and decision-making procedure revolves around coordination and consultation committees on various levels, with different actors. At the lowest level one finds the EC Special Committees (EF-Specialudvalgene).[12] In 1999, there were 32 such committees. Their task is to coordinate

---

11 Professor John Toy, University of Sussex, stressed the same point, stating on Danish Radio (P1, 27 February 1996), that the rigidity of the EU system prevented changes, although it was acknowledged that the procedures were unsatisfactory.
12 Both the EC Special Committee and the EC Committee are called "EC" and not "EU", because their field of action concerns mainly the old EC-treaty.

the viewpoints of the involved ministries concerning a single issue or policy, e.g. agriculture or the internal market. The work of this level was thought to be of a specific and technical nature, but it includes strong political elements, as well. The next level is the EC Committee (EF-Udvalget), a senior officials" coordination committee, which according to Thygesen has three tasks: a) to solve the (rare) conflicts in the Special Committees according to the general rules of Danish EU policy, b) to filter out political from administrative issues, and c) to guide the former to the government (1986: 58). In addition, the EC Committee monitors the development of the EU in general. The coordination function of the EC Committee should be emphasized: With 32 special committees, it is one of the EC Committee's most important tasks to secure that the recommendations of these committees are not contradictory. The highest administrative level in the Danish EU decision-making system is the Government, especially its Foreign Political Committee (Regeringens Udenrigspolitiske Udvalg). Its main task is to decide the Danish stand on issues that are negotiated in the EU (in all three pillars). Before the government can participate in the meetings of the Council in Brussels, it must obtain the approval of the Folketing, or rather, it has to ensure, that there is not a majority against its stand. This is ensured by the European Committee (Europa udvalget). Compared to the traditional administrative tradition, the Danish EU coordination process can be characterised as strongly centralised, but it is at the same time flexible, and many questions are solved informally (cf. Dosenrode, 1993b).

3.2. The Interplay Relations

In this part we will look at the two important networks in Danish EU policy formulation, the administrative – corporative network, and the parliamentary network.

3.2.1. The Administrative – Corporative Network

This conglomerate-network consists of 34 semi-autonomous sub-networks; the networks of the 32 special committees, the coordination-network, and the ministerial network.[13] The main task of the conglomerate-network is to prepare the administrative aspects of Danish EU decision-making process. It must ensure that Denmark has a coherent and if possible, well-argued stand to defend in the Council of Ministers.

---

13 The term "conglomerate-network" implies a situation, with a group of interlinked networks, all of which they participate and shape the group's output. As the conglomerate-network contains 32 special-committee-networks, they will, in spite of their large differences, be treated in a general fashion.

The Special Committee Networks

The *function* of the special committees has always been to coordinate the view points of the involved ministries and to make a recommendation for what the Danish position should be: Already in 1972, it was stated, that the ministries were responsible for knowing the opinion of the important interest organisations. Thus, the purpose of the network involves a) establishing contact between the civil service and the IOs, b) exchanging information, c) coordination of actions in relation to the Commission, d) general cooperation in policy formulation, implementation and the subsequent legitimation.

When an issue has been through the European Committee of the Parliament and has been negotiated and decided in Brussels, a directive will normally be the result. The directive must be implemented, and here the IOs also get involved. The IOs are traditionally involved in preparing the implementation of Danish laws, and the same is now the case with EU laws. The civil servants, together with the IOs, supply the detailed regulations of the directive.

There are basically two kinds of special committee networks, distinguished from each other by their *actors*: Those made up only of civil servants, and mixed committees containing civil servants and representatives of IOs. Pedersen & Pedersen found that it was mainly industrial and branch organisations which have close contacts to the civil service, and that labour market organisations were involved only to a lesser degree (1995: 19). The ministers of the involved ministries and the EC Committee belong to the category of peripheral actors. They do not participate directly in the meetings of the committee, but they have a formal veto-power as well as direct and close contact to the core-actors.[14]

Each special committee should be regarded as an interdependent network, with a high degree of autonomy. *Structurally* it includes a core-network, consisting of the main actors entered around the relevant special committee, and a broader network including other important actors: Ministers, the EC Committee and the Ministry of Foreign Affairs. In spite of a certain horizontal, or egalitarian, character of the networks the key actor is the chairman and his ministry. Normally it is the chairman (his ministry) who formulates the proposed Danish position and who coaches it through the process.

The networks are tied together by both formal and informal links on several levels. A recent survey concerning EU matters indicates that 55% of the Civil Service have either daily or monthly contacts with IOs (Pedersen & Pedersen 1995: 19). Thus, we can speak of a general high density of relations. Pedersen & Pedersen's analysis of corporatism in Denmark demonstrates the increasing importance of routine informal contacts, taking different forms, between the Civil Service and the IO. They also point out that there has been an increase in contacts since the Single European Act was put into effect (1995: 17-20). However, the

---

14 Both to the IO representatives and to the civil servants.

findings of Pedersen & Pedersen indirectly point towards a potential problem within the civil service: if 55% of the ministries have close contacts, this implies that the remaining 45% do not have these close contacts. This situation could lead to tensions and conflicts between the "European" and the "National" ministries.

All actors within a core-network have their own potential for action and exerting power (e.g. Pappi 1993: 87); otherwise they would not be members of the core of the network. The power of the IOs derives from several sources. First, they represent knowledge. Second, their acceptance and cooperation give the decision an appearance of legitimacy, when it is to be implemented. The IOs represent political power in the Danish political system and in the EU, where they are often involved in problem-definition and in the agenda-setting of the Commission. A third source of power is that the support of the IOs improves the chances that no major changes in the proposal of the special committees network will be made when it passes through the parliamentary network. Fourth, the support of important IOs supports a ministry in the inter-ministerial struggles over resources and prestige. The general impression, however, is that the Civil Service has been able to increase its influence at the cost of the IOs.

The tradition of consensus decision gives the recommendations of the special committee considerable weight towards peripheral actors as well as towards the Parliament, but this tradition also has its exceptions, and there is a tendency towards majority decisions taken by the core-members.

The Coordination Network

This network is centred around the EC Committee (EF-Udvalget). Its main *function* is to coordinate the recommendations coming from the network of special committees, i.e., to ensure that there is a single Danish position. This function is important due to the fragmented character of the network, with its 32 sub-networks. The *actors* are civil servants. There is a group of permanent members representing the ministries with many EU activities; other ministries participate on an ad hoc basis.

As mentioned, the Civil Service is not monolithic. There are immanent conflicts, for example, between the Ministry of Finance and the Ministry of Foreign Affairs, between the ministries of Trade and of Environmental Protection, and between the Prime Minister's Office and the Ministry of Foreign Affairs.[15] The EU problematic is no exception, and, as mentioned, the IOs are important means in these "struggles" within the network.

---

15 Interviews reveal that the prestige of the Foreign Office has not been restored after the blow of the Danish "No" to Maastricht. The sector ministries do not take the Foreign Office seriously any more. The Prime Minister's Office has therefore assumed increased responsibility for the Danish EU policy process.

The Ministerial Network

The ministerial network is the last sub-network of the conglomerate-network. Its main *functions* are, first, the political and administrative preparation for "selling" the proposal to the Foreign Political Committee of the Government, the parliamentary EU-network, and subsequently in Brussels (the minister as "salesman"). The minister is the official bridge between the parliamentarian and the administrative – corporative network. Second, the minister has a role as political legitimiser; neither the IOs nor the Civil Service are entitled to suggest new bills; this being the prerogative of the government (or of members of parliament). Third, the minister and the Government's Foreign Political Committee serve as troubleshooters. In the rare cases where conflicting interests are not resolved within the special committee network (or in the EC Committee), it is the involved ministers or the Government who must make the final decision. Fourth, the relevant minister or the Government may lay down guidelines for Denmark's over-all EU policy. Fifth, the minister in question may serve as an important communicator. Only the minister can call a minister from a foreign country; no Danish permanent secretary, no matter how senior, can pick up the phone and call the German Chancellor or the British Prime Minister. Former Danish Prime Minister Poul Schlüter could and did, and one can assume that the current prime minister, Poul Nyrup Rasmussen does the same. These functions give the minister and the government an important role in the Danish EU decision-making process.

The *actors of the ministerial network* are the ministers representing the Government and the Civil Service, including the senior civil servants, from heads of section and up. Thus, the network is small and the boundaries quite clear. The Civil Service can only act as an instrument of the minister's power. On the other hand, the minister is very dependent on the expertise of the civil-service.

3.2.2. The Parliamentary Network

The *overall framework* for the parliamentary network is, of course, the Parliament. As in most other countries, foreign policy in Denmark is considered a governmental prerogative (Danish Constitution § 19). The Parliament, however, is getting increasingly involved in the conduct of foreign policy. Hence, we witness a mixture of the legislative and the executive functions. According to the Constitution, the Parliament elects a Foreign Political Council (Udenrigspolitisk Nævn). The Government must inform the Foreign Political Council of activities and discuss with it any future decisions of major importance.[16] As foreign policy, in contrast to national policy, is seldom made in the form of laws (which have to be prepared and

---

16 Bjøl quotes Bruun's definition of major foreign-politiy decisions as those having major domestic consequences (1982: 135).

passed by the Parliament), this paragraph ensures that Parliament is kept informed. The Parliament has created 3 standing committees for foreign political issues (European Committee, Foreign Policy Committee and Defence Committee). When laws on these issues have to be passed, they will be prepared by one of these committees.

The instruments for influencing the Government's foreign policy have been laid down in the Constitution and in the Rules of Procedure of the Parliament. There are two basic means of exerting influence. Either the MPs can propose a law on a foreign-policy topic (Constitution § 41), or they can ask a parliamentary question, which may lead to a parliamentary resolution, which is binding of the Government (Constitution § 53 and Parliamentary Rules of Procedure § 20 and § 21).

The Parliament also sends delegations to various international organisations (NATO, OSCE, WEU, etc.), and there are annual debates on foreign policy and on the EU. The Parliament's internationalisation has increased since World War II. Debates on Danish EC membership in the 1960s and early 1970s can be seen having prepared Parliament for the activity of the 1980s. During the 1980s the Parliament debated foreign policy issues several times, speaking against the stand of the Government. As a result, the Government had to follow the parliamentary majority, against its own stand.[17] Due to the security policy debates and the broad public interest in EU affairs, the Parliament has become more accustomed to thinking internationally.

The parliamentarians are of the opinion that their work is becoming increasingly internationalized, but that their influence on this issue is declining. To alter this situation, a working group on foreign-policy questions was set up in 1995. The group was to make suggestions on how to increase the influence of the Parliament on foreign policy. The result was a report with concrete suggestions for improving coordination, better information and fewer committees treating foreign polity issues (Redegørelse og indstilling fra Arbejdsgruppen vedr. Udenrigspolitiske Spørgsmål, 18. Oktober 1995). These proposals were accepted and implemented.

The European Committee is the most successful of the Folketing's "foreign political committees". It is the centre of the parliamentary EU network. Its *functions* are (1) to inform the Parliament on developments in the EU in general and on Danish stands in particular, (2) to provide the Parliament the possibility to influence Danish EU policy in order to legitimize it, and (3) to act as the last means of coordination. Unintentionally, the meetings of the Committee also serve as (4) a rehearsal for the Minister before his "performance" in Brussels. Thus the Committee's task is to control and influence Danish EU policy in the name of the electorate.

The 17 members of the Committee meet on Fridays, and the issues on its agenda are those about which the Council of Ministers are going to negotiate the following week. The minister or ministers, who are going to negotiate in Brussels review all

---

17 See e.g. the "footnote policy" of the 1980s and the debate on the 1986 Single European Act.

the points on the agenda. The minister can choose to give the committee either an orientation (if the government does not expect a decision to be made at the meeting of the Council) – or if the government expects the Council to make a decision a concrete negotiation proposal.[18] The members of the Committee may pose questions and make suggestions to all points on the agenda. The minister has to be certain that there is no majority against his proposal. When he has secured this, he has got his "mandate". The "mandate" has three aspects: (1) agreement on the subject matter, (2) agreement on which allies to search, and (3) "the elastic", i.e. the freedom of action for the negotiator (interview with Steen Gade, November 1995).

The committee is the point of intersection of the parliamentary and administrative corporative network. The actors who constitute the hard core of the network consist of the 17 members of Parliament and their alternates. They are represented according to their party strength in Parliament. The members are often senior in their party, e.g. former ministers or EU spokesmen and have often been members of Parliament for several years. Thus, they have a large knowledge. The ministers are members of the network in a broad sense. They are necessary actors; they are the link in communication between the parliamentary and the administrative – corporative network. In the narrow sense, however, they are not "full" members: They do not have the competence to authorise negotiations, as the members of the committee de facto have. The ministers may bring civil servants along to the meetings of the European Committee, but these cannot substitute for the ministers.

Among the actors, one obvious group is lacking: the Danish MEPs. The European Committee has tried to maintain contact with them for several years, but it was first realised that the MEPs could be of use after Denmark had lost an important case regarding food additives. The usefulness of the MEPs stems from the new powers of the EP on environmental, health and consumer protection issues. In May 1994, the Folketing decided that the Government had to inform the Danish MEPs on the Danish policy. In spite of the lost cases, and in spite of the relevance as an extra channel of influence, the MEPs are not involved as often as they could be. Speaking on Danish radio (20 January 1996) the Foreign Minister stated that the Government had a duty to inform the MEPs only "if possible", and that questions of environment, health and consumers rights were complicated, taking time to prepare thoroughly, etc. The Government was in fact saying that it was not interested in this possibility of influence.[19]

---

18 The oftheard complaint, that the Committee is notified too late is only partly true. It is true, that it normally first gets notified when an issue has been on the agenda of the special committee. However, a proposal is often discussed several times in the Council and thus returns to the special committee, too.

19 This view is surprising, as the EP and the MEPs could be useful in a number of ways: (1) for influencing the decision making within the EPs competencies (a growing area), (2) as an alternative means of drawing the Commission's attention to an issue, through the MEPs right to ask public questions to the Commission, and (3) as an information network, to hear "what's up" in Brussels.

Despite the negative governmental attitude towards the MEP, the European Committee repeated that a close working relation between itself and the MEPs was desirable (1999 report). Basically, however, no change has happened. What happens is; 1) that the foreign minister invites the Danish MEPs for a lunch meeting once a year, "to tell us what we already know" as one Danish MEP phrased it; 2) the head of the Danish Permanent Representation to the EU has introduced a regular series of meetings with Danish MEPs for mutual information. This initiative, which began 1998, seems to work well. Its purpose, of course, is to make Danish MEPs aware of the Danish Government's attitude to certain policies, and to make them bring these points of view into the debate in the EP.

There are two kinds of power relations in this network: the party political one (which is not discussed here), and the relation between the administrative-corporative network and the parliamentary network.

The "Danish-model", understood as a potentially effective parliamentary control of the government's stand prior to the negotiations in Brussels, rests on two interconnected factors: 1) the tradition of constructive cooperation between government and opposition and 2) minority governments, i.e. a situation where the Parliament can bring down the government, if they do not execute parliamentary wishes. In Western Europe, only Norway, Sweden and to a degree Spain have the same tradition of minority governments. The parliamentary culture, especially the tradition of "constructive opposition" is equally rare outside Scandinavia. Thus, one may speak of a Danish model, but the potential for "exporting" it seems rather limited. Until now, only Sweden has tried to adopt it.

The power of the committee is increased by 1) the high political standing on knowledge of the members, and 2) the time pressure, insofar as a Danish stand, a "mandate", must be formulated by the end of the meeting. In practice, the committee seldom gives the minister a "mandate" that does not correspond to his own position. More often there are minor changes: as the conglomerate network is aware of the opinions the minister is going to encounter, the minister tends not to present something he knows is unacceptable to the majority.

The structural framework of the Committee thus gives it a central position with potentially strong powers (e.g., the right to give a mandate and the potential to bring down the Government). In spite of being informed at a fairly early stage, there are severe restrictions on the actual powers of the Committee, First, there are only 17 members to look at all the proposals, and they are members of different parties, which prevents close cooperation and specialisation. The workload is huge, especially for the representatives of minor parties. Second, the committee may be informed early, but they are excluded from the important stage of problem definition and normally from the agenda setting-phase as well. Thus, their possibilities are limited to changing details in a proposal, or to turning it down; it is hard, if not impossible, to substantially change the proposals. Third, the power of the European Committee is further weakened by the influence of the administrative-corporative network: the support of the IOs and the recommendations of the

Options and Decision-Making 395

Civil Service can make it difficult to oppose the government's stand. Fourth, the parties, to which the committee-members belong, are often related to IOs, thus limiting the freedom of action of the MPs. The memo sent to the Committee by the Government includes a survey of the opinions of the IOs. If the IOs are positive, the members of the Parliament will seldomly turn down the proposal. Finally the Parliament tends to be more positive towards the EU than the majority of the population, who are very sceptical. This scepticism in the population tended to paralyse the Committee and the Parliament especially from the Danish "No" to the Maastricht-treaty in 1992 untill 1998-99.[20] This last factor is perhaps the most important. Not being allowed to think in a visionary fashion, the Committee used most of its time to examine and criticize minor details. This left the initiative to the administrative-corporative network. This situation is only beginning to change now, in 2000.

In spite of the obvious dangers of simplifying matters, one can answer the question of "who decides" in the process of formulation of Danish EU policy in this way: by and large it is the administrative-corporative network, i.e. civil servants in cooperation with the interest organisations which decides. They decide on daily EU-affairs. The European Committee could potentially influence the Danish stand concerning major policy decisions such as those related to Intergovernmental Conferences. However, due to the only slowly declining paralysis of the Parliament, the Danish contribution to important EU-conferences has been meagre, and it probably will continue to be so in the nearest future. The government coalition would either break down or the parties would be punished by the electorate if they played active roles.

3.2.3. Strategies of the European Committee

In their interactions with the administrative-corporative network the strategies of the MPs as members of the Committee have been incremental. One could speak of an ongoing process, beginning with the law on accession to the EEC. This law stipulated 1) that the Parliament had to be informed on an annual basis on developments in the EC, and 2) that the Government had to inform a parliamentary committee on EC legislation which would be passed by the Council of Ministers (§ 6). Thus, the starting-point was the right to be informed, nothing more. After just one month of membership, the majority in the Danish Parliament imposed upon the minority government the task of checking that there was no majority in the Danish Parliament against the Government's stand on an initiative to be voted on in the Council of Ministers (Folketingstidende 1972/73 Sp. 3355). The aim of the com-

---

20 The major party political actor, the Social Democrats (the Prime Minister's party), are internally divided on the EU issue. The same is true for the Social Liberals (the Foreign Minister's party). The division is not so much within the parliamentary groups, as it is within the party organisations and among the members.

mittee was to democratize the Danish part of the EU decision-making process. There has been a process leading to the right to give mandates, to be informed earlier, to be informed better etc.[21]

However, the Committee has still been criticised for a lack of efficiency by some of its members.[22] Often it boils down to manpower: 17 persons cannot keep track of all the proposals coming in. The Memorandum from 1994 (Beretning om regeringens orientering af Folketinget om EU-sager, 20. maj 1995) created the possibility to utilize the other standing committees of the Parliament for hearings. This possibility is now being used. How well it works differs very much from committee to committee and from minister to minister.[23] It would seem natural to take steps to acknowledge the fact that the EU is penetrating all or most of the legislative work. One could then delegate the tasks of the European Committee to the other standing committees of the Parliament and allow the European Committee to take care of coordination and general institutional questions. Implementing a solution with the European Committee as a coordinating "super committee" would on the one hand institutionalize a hierarchy in the Parliament, something which the other parliamentary committees would not accept without a struggle, and on the other hand the European Committee would have to get used to not prying into all details in all cases, as well as learning to trust the competence of the sector committees.

Another existing, unused possibility to coordinate, monitor and influence the decision-making process is the already described closer contact to the Danish MEPs, a possibility used in other EU member states such as Germany. In Denmark, these contacts are only being build up now, and are conducted by the Ministry of Foreign Affairs, not the Parliament.

Two innovations of the European Committee in its 1996 agreement with the Government could potentially strengthen the Committee's influence. The first concerns the implementation of EU directives. Of the 127 directives transferred into Danish law in the period 1994-95, only 27 were transferred by law, i.e. through the Parliament. The others were transferred administratively, i.e. without the Parliament knowing in which form the often very broadly formulated directive was

---

21 For a concrete and impressive display of this strategy, see the memoranda of the Market Committee/European Committee 1972-1999.
22 In the new regulation on cooperation between Government and Parliament, several of these shortcomings in the Danish part of the EU decision-making system have been identified and addressed (cf. Beretning afgivet af Europaudvalget om Folketingets behandling af EU-sager 27. september 1996).
23 Some ministers when called for consultations have been neglecting the EU questions in other Committees than the European Committee. They argue that they would answer these questions the following Friday in the European Committee. Other Committees have layed down procedures, that ensure that EU-related questions are scrutinized by the experts, e.g. in the Environmental Committee or in the Committee on Trade and Industry.

transferred and then implemented (Steen Gade, interview November 1995). Since 1997, the ministry responsible for the implementation has to inform the European Committee on the implementation.

The second innovation of the European Committee concerns the directives adopted by the EU-Commission and other "administrative" rules enacted in Brussels, without direct involvement of the Council of Ministers. The European Committee is now going to be informed about these cases. They will be led on to it by the administrative-corporative network. The urgency of this need can be illustrated with the remarks of Danish civil servant, who noted that "as soon as I have agreed to the new regulation, it is law in Denmark" (interview 1995).

The 1999 report of the European Committee introduced "open meetings", in an effort to provide more transparency to the decision-making process and to give the Danish MEPs an opportunity to participate in meetings of the committee. The results, so far, are meagre; the MEPs do not turn up, and the interest of the press is low. Explanations could be, that one cannot make any decisions, and the whole setup looks like a possibility for the politicians to promote themselves and not much more.

The main problem is that the Parliament seems to have constructed a strong and efficient means of control over the Danish part of the EU decision-making process but remains very reluctant to use it. The Parliament is only slowly overcoming its paralysis, and it is drowning itself in detailed questions in the European Committee. As a result the initiative drifts to other, more dynamic actors. Civil servants – backed up by the interest organisations – feel obliged to act on behalf of the elite; the elite to which they also belong.

4. Conclusion: Efficiency and Democracy in the Danish EU Decision-Making Procedure

The objective of this article was to analyse how Danish EU policy is made and who is involved. As the EU has developed into something looking more and more like a new state, it seems reasonable to conclude our discussion by examining related questions of efficiency and democracy.

Danish civil servants, ministers and MPs share the opinion that Denmark's interests are being well looked after in the European decision-making process. Denmark "gets more than it gives". This indicates a reasonable efficiency, and is related to the phase in which the administrative-corporative network is involved, i.e. the later ones. The conglomerate-network, or some of its actors, may often be involved in only the third, decision-making phase, having been excluded from the two previous and essential phases. As mentioned, it is not a question of having the "right" to be involved. Thus, "efficiency" basically implies the ability to change and adapt the already formulated proposal to Danish interests, but not to decide on its substantive content, nor whether to decide if it should be on the agenda at all.

This is essentially a *reactive* efficiency, fully in accordance with the ideas of the founding fathers of today's Union.[24]

How to reach efficiency in promoting the Danish stand could be the subject of another article (See Dosenrode, 1993b: 294-340). Apart from the always stressed emphasis on having a well-coordinated and well-argued case, a typical Danish characteristic is the strategy of being a "unitary actor" in the EU. Looking at the structure of Denmark's industry, trade etc., as well as the size and resources of the IOs, we obtain a picture of a typical small state with small units. Probably as a consequence of these limited resources, Danish trade unions, employers", industrial, manufacturers" and agricultural organizations see the necessity of uniting forces in order to promote their opinions in Brussels. Using the Danish EU co-ordination system (the conglomerate network), i.e. pooling the resources, seems to offer large advantages to all the involved actors, thus maintaining the system. The IOs obtain a lobbyist, the minister, who participates at key meetings.

It is how these comparatively smaller changes and adaptations in the later phases of the decision-making process will appear, that are the de facto substance of the Danish EU policy. And it is these positions that are formulated by the administrative-corporative network, and normally accepted by the European Committee of the Parliament.

The question of democracy has been somewhat circumvented in this article. However, as a few relevant questions have risen during this analysis, let us briefly discuss them.[25] If one wants to examine the democratic aspect of Danish EU policy-making, one must look at the EU-level as well as the Danish level.

By employing the model of the "policy-cycle", our attention was drawn to the first phases of the policy process. Let me now draw attention to a couple of democratic problems at the European level under the two headings "transparency" and "accountability".

It is the Commission that has the institutionalised right to initiate policies within the Union, a right which normally lies with an elected parliament, that is legitimized through elections. The Commission's legitimation lays in its pursuit of an ideology, that of European integration, as defined by the treaties. All member states have accepted this role of the Commission as "defender of the faith", when accepting the aquis communautaire by becoming members. One could argue that it is

---

24 This analysis has emphasised the Danish view, and has often posed the question of, how Denmark presents its stand, how Denmark gains influence, etc. In this context it is useful to remember, that the Founding Fathers of the EU explicitly wished to exclude the member states from interfering with the decision-making process, as they expected that the member states would pursue strictly national interests, rather than the common good of the EU. They thus created not only a Council of Ministers, but also a High Authority (later Commission). When one is talking about "pursuing Danish interests" one is proceeding against the spirit and the idea of the Union, which was and remains that of promoting the interests of the whole of the Union. But one is fully in accordance with the Pörtchsach-spirit.
25 The democracy question is not the main topic of this essay. It has been treated elsewhere (e.g. Kelstrup, 1995).

necessary for the Commission to be kept free of attempts by the member states to exert national influence in the first phases, so that it can fulfill its role. Seen from a Danish point of view, from a "transparency" point of view, it is a problem that the first phases of the policy cycle are closed, and that the meetings in Commission's working groups are not fully documented from the very first soundings and onwards. This makes it impossible to see whether the Commission has adopted a sound argument, or whether a proposal has been based on false premises. Equally problematic is the lack of rules concerning whom to invite to participate in working groups and unofficial hearings. If it is not possible to find ways to hear a representative part of the involved interests, then at the very least it should be possible to add a list to the proposal sent to the Council of Ministers. This list should mention all the actors who have been involved, together with a brief statement of their contribution. These traditional Danish (and now Swedish) stands are inspired by the small state experience, i.e., that where there are no rules, power relations decide. Rules on who is to be invited and on "openness" in the administration of the EU institutions, would further help consolidate the rule of law.

Whether it is an EU civil servant or a civil servant within Danish Central Administration proposing a law is all the same, one could argue. However, there is an important difference; a Danish civil servant works on behalf of his minister, who is responsible to the Parliament; there is accountability. In theory, the civil servant can be controlled and held responsible. Such control is only very rudimentary in the case of the civil servants of the Commission.

Compared to the Danish understanding of democracy, the first very important part of the EU decision-making process is not democratic – if one understands "democratic", as having something to do with public legitimation through elections, possibility of controlling how a decision was made, the possibility of participation, and the possibility to hold a decision-maker responsible for his decisions.[26] And this is a problem, because so much of the Danish policy process is mainly in the hands of organisations having only a limited democratic legitimation themselves.

The importance of "transparency" and "accountability" have become especially prominent following the qualitative jump towards increased statehood that appeared with Maastricht and Amsterdam. As long as the cooperation is fairly limited and of a somewhat technical character, openness and transparency may mean less. However, when the project is to build a "real" union and when there is neither a sense of community among the involved peoples nor a strong trust in the "motor of the integration", i.e. the Commission, it becomes vital to the whole project that the two concepts be taken seriously. Lord Acton once exclaimed that "power corrupts, absolute power corrupts absolutely". To prevent the suspicion of abuse of power, transparency and accountability are essential for the European project.

In the analysis of decision-making at the national level, we highlighted a number of aspects, that limit the influence of "Denmark" and the Parliament. Due to the design of the EU policy-making system, Denmark as well as the other member

---

26 See Kelstrup (1995).

states are involved at a later stage in the EU policy process, thus giving the Danish EU policy formulation a reactive aspect. This is in itself "ideologically correct", as the EU was designed to limit the member states" pursuit of national interests at a supranational level. The problem here is the shadowy character in which especially the actions in the first phases of the policy process occur.

In general, "all" the involved Danish actors felt, that "we" did well in the negotiations in the Council of Ministers, i.e. in the later phases of the decision-making procedure. However, we also saw, that "we" consist basically of the actors of the administrative-corporative network. In spite of its formal powers, the Danish Parliament is on its way to becoming disconnected from the decision-making procedure due to a mix of paralysing fear of making unpopular decisions and a tremendous workload within in the European Committee. In other words, the efficiency is created without the Parliament.

Another feature which makes Denmark special is the high level of information on the EU among the population. The EU has regularly been a topic in public discussions, due to the referenda following each of the large decisions on European integration (membership itself, the SEA, Maastricht, Amsterdam and EMU), as well as the debates ahead of EP-elections. Thus, in the EU-context Danish membership and its foundations are democratically legitimated to a great degree. Seen from this perspective, the Parliament's carefulness in EU-matters reflects the doubts and concerns of the population, and its impotence could thus be legitimized. The consequence, however, remains the same: a very reactive policy towards EU issues, both on a day-to-day basis and concerning input for the great historic decisions.

The Danish model, understood as strong parliamentary control, with the Parliament being informed of the Government's stand on current EU affairs before the sessions of the Council of Ministers, as well as the Government's need to have its proposed stand accepted by Parliament before entering the negotiations (mandate), is on the one hand based on a parliamentary culture of "constructive opposition", implying cooperation and normally an attempt to reach as broad a consensus as possible, and on the other hand a tradition of minority governments, leaving the governments in a vulnerable situation if they do not follow the wishes of the parliamentary majority. Thus, the potentially strong instrument of parliamentary control associated with the "Danish model" seems to be of limited use in other states.

This essay ends on a slightly pessimistic note concerning the democracy aspect of the EU policy-making process. Although the EU increasingly looks like a state, it is not yet democratic; and an unanswered question is if it at all is possible to make it so. The output from the EU system does not live up to the democratic standards of legitimation. This output then goes through the national Danish EU decision-making system, where the influence has been drifting away from the parliamentary network and its democratic legitimacy, to the administrative-corporative network, where there is no such legitimacy. The legitimate fear is, that "efficiency", understood by the conglomerate network having only limited legitimation, is starting to overtake "democracy".

Literature

Andersen, Svein S. and Kjell A. Eliassen (eds.) (1993): *Making Policy in Europe,* London: Sage.

Bjøl, Erling (1982): "De udenrigspolitiske beslutningsprocesser" in *Dansk Udenrigspolitisk Årbog 1981,* Copenhagen: Samfundsvidenskabeligt Forlag.

Bulmer, Simon J. (1994): "The Governance of the European Union: A New Institutionalist Approach", *International Public Policy,* vol. 13, nr. 4.

Caporaso, James A. (1996): "The European Union and Forms of State: Westphalian, Regulatory or Post-Modern?", *Journal of Common Market Studies,* vol. 34, no. 1.

Christensen, Jørgen Grønnegård (1994): *Centraladministrationen: organisation og politisk placering,* Copenhagen: DJØFs Forlag.

Christensen, Jørgen Grønnegård & Peter Mink Christiansen (1992): *Forvaltning og omgivelser,* Herning: Systime.

Commission of the European Communities (1991): *The Regions in the 1990s,* Brussels & Luxembourg: The European Commission.

Dosenrode, Søren Z. von (1993a): *Westeuropäische Kleinstaaten in der EU und EPZ,* Chur & Zürich: Verlag Rüegger.

Dosenrode, Søren Z. von (1993b): "Den optimale minimalløsning – Danmarks administrative tilpasning til EF", *Nordisk Administrativt Tidsskrift,* no. 4.

Dosenrode, Søren Z. von (1995): "Going NUTS: amter, delstater og kantoner i Europa", *Nordisk Administrativt Tidsskrift,* no. 2.

Dosenrode, Søren Z. von (1997): "Networks in Danish EU-Policy-Making", *European Studies,* no. 20, Aalborg University.

Dosenrode, Søren Z. von & Niels Chr. Sidenius, (1999): Lobbyisme i EU – Udfordringer for Danmark, Rådet for Europæisk Politik, Forlaget Systime.

Edwards, Geoffrey & David Spence, (eds.) (1994): *The European Commission,* Harlow: Longman Current Affairs.

From, Johan, and Per Stava (1993): "Implementation of Community Law: The Last Stronghold of National Control" in Andersen and Eliassen (eds.) (1993), pp. 55-67.

Heidar, Kurt & Einar Berntzen (1995): *Vesteuropeisk Politikk,* Oslo: Universitetsforlaget.

Héritier, Adrienne (ed.) (1993): "Policy-Analyse – Kritik und Neuorientierung", *Politische Vierteljahresschrift,* Sonderheft no. 24, Westdeutscher Verlag.

Hill, Michare (ed.) (1993): *The Policy Process – A Reader,* New York: Harvester & Wheatsheaf.

Haagerup, Niels Jørgen & Christian Thune (ed.) (1986): "Folketinget og udenrigspolitikken", *DUPI-hæfte* no. 1, Copenhagen: DJØF Publishing.

Kelstrup, Morten (1995): "Om det danske demokrati og den europæiske integration" in Madsen, Nielsen og Sjöblom (ed.) (1995), pp. 365-403.

Lynn, Jonathan & Jay, Antony (1989): *The Complete "Yes Minister",* London: BBC Books.

Madsen, Morten & Hans Jørgen Nielsen & Gunnar Sjöblom (ed.) (1995): *Demokratiets mangfoldighed – Tendenser i dansk politik,* Copenhagen: Forlaget Politiske Studier.

Markedsudvalgets beretninger & betænkninger.

Marks, Garry; Lisbeth Hooghe and Kermit Blank (1996): "European Integration from the 1980s" in *Journal of Common Market Studies,* vol. 34, no. 3, September, 1996, pp 341-78.

May, Judith V. & Aaron B. Wildavsky (eds.) (1978): "The Policy Cycle", *Sage Yearbook in Politics and Public Policy,* vol. 5, Beverly Hills & London: SAGE.

Mazey, Sonia and Jeremy Richardsen (1994): "The Commission and the Lobby", in Edwards and Spence (ed.) (1994), pp. 178-212.

Nedergaard, Peter (1994): *Organiseringen af Den europæiske Union,* Copenhagen: Handelshøjskolens Forlag.

Nugent, Neill (1994): *The Government and Politics of the European Union*, 3rd edition, London: The Macmillan Press Ltd.

Pappi, Franz Urban (1993): "Policy-Netze: Erscheinungsform moderner Politiksteuerung oder methodischer Ansatz?", in Héritier (ed.) (1993), pp. 84-96.

Parsons, Wayn (1995): *Public Policy*, Aldershot: Edward Elgar.

Pedersen, Ove K. & Dorthe Pedersen (1995): "The Europeanization of National Coporatism. When the State and Organizations in Denmark went to Europe together." *COS-rapport nr. 4/1995*, Copenhagen: Copenhagen Business School.

Peterson, John (1995): "Decision-making in the European Union: towards a framework of analysis", in *Journal of European Public Policy*, vol. 2, no. 1.

Rasmussen, Hjalte (1994): *EU-ret og EU-institutionerne i kontekst*, Copenhagen: Karnov Forlag.

Redegørelse og indstilling fra Arbejdsgruppen vedr. Udenrigspolitiske Spørgsmål, 18. oktober 1995.

Rhodes, R.A.W. & David Marsh (1992): "New directions in the study of policy networks", in *European Journal of Political Research*, vol. 21, no. 1-2.

Sabatier, Poul A. and Hank Jenkin-Schmith (eds.) (1993): *Policy Change and Learning – An Advacacy of Coalition Approach*, Boulder: Westview Press.

Schumann, Wolfgang (1993): "Die EG als neuer Anwendungsbereich für die Policy-Analyse: Möglichkeiten und Perspektiven der konzeptionellen Weiterentwicklung", in Héritier (ed.) (1993), pp. 394-431.

Spence, David (1994): "Staff and personal policy in the Commission" in *Edwards and Spence (ed.)*, pp. 68-102.

SOU (Statens offentliga utredninger), Utrikesdepartementet, nr. 6, Stockholm 1996.

van Waarden, Frans (1992): "Dimensions and types of policy networks", *European Journal of Political Research*, vol. 21, no. 1-2.

Tygesen, K.E. (1986): "Den danske EF-beslutningsproces" in Niels Jørgen Haagerup and Christian Thune (eds.). *Folketinget og Udenrigspolitikken*, Copenhagen: DJØF Publishing, pp. 55-68.

Wallace, Hellen, Willian Wallace & Carol Webb (ed.) (1987): *Policy Making in the European Community*, 2nd edition, Chichester: John Wiley & Sons.

Westlake, Martin (ed.) (1995): *The Council of the European Union*, London: Cartermill Publishing.

Abbreviations

CAP	Common Agricultural Policy
COREPER	Committee des representantes permanente
ECB	European Central Bank
EP	European Parliament
EU	European Union
GD	General Directorate of the Commission
IO	Interest Organisation
MEP	Member of the European Parliament
MP	Member of (the Danish) Parliament (Folketing)
SEA	Single European Act
TEC	Treaty on the European Community
TEU	Treaty on the European Union

CHAPTER 13

Integration from Below: Local Government in Denmark in the Process of Europeanization

Kurt Klaudi Klausen

International politics has focussed its attention primarily on international organizations and interstate relations, mainly from a policy point of view. This article argues that local governments also play a role in processes of internationalization and integration, and that we may learn more about this role by studying both political and administrative changes at the local level.

This article focuses on the meaning of internationalization at local level, particularly the impact of the EU. It describes how Danish local authorities have reacted to the challenges presented by increased Europeanization, and gives local authorities a new role in the processes of internationalization.

In contrast to the influence local governments can have on domestic policy areas, they play no role in Danish EU-policy. Local governments are not engaged in the formulation of Danish foreign policy. Internationalization and Europeanization have different meanings at the local level – it is not international politics. Internationalization at the local level primarily means interregional and cross-border economic, cultural and social integration. Second, internationalization has to do with political integration, that local authorities are represented in international organizations which formulate policies at the international level.

Nevertheless, local governments have come to play an increasingly important role as new legitimate actors on the international scene, and in the long run this may determine the overall European integration process. While the impact of local governments and of their umbrella organizations on Danish EU-policy thus remains indirect, their actual performance nevertheless constitutes a challenge to the old order insofar as they are pushing forward the integration processes from below.

Internationalization – a silent revolution

Throughout Europe, local governments have started to adapt themselves to the impact of an increasingly internationalized world and of the EU as a new European power centre (Goldsmith and Klausen 1997). This situation is also occurring in the Nordic countries (Gidlund and Jernick 2000; Baldersheim and Ståhlberg 1999) including the non-EU-member Norway (From and Stava 1995). The reaction patterns differ from country to country but there are also several common features.[1]

In any case, the reactions by local authorities to the increasing internationalization of their affairs represent a silent revolution. It is silent because it appears sporadically, diffuses and penetrates incrementally and, because it does not attract much political debate and public attention, it is not on the agenda in local election campaigns and there is no public debate on the pro's and con's of this process of internationalization. Still it is a revolution, because it potentially challenges the old order in which local authorities primarily took care of local matters and did not engage in regional development and international activities. It is a revolution in so far as it changes a number of roles and relationships which we used to take for granted. Local is no more just local in its orientation and context it is internationalized just as the other way around where international politics have become domestic.

Internationalization is nothing new to Danish local government. For centuries, large towns such as Copenhagen, Aarhus and Aalborg, have had experiences with internationalization through trade, as have almost all cities with harbors. This situation is seen in the other Nordic countries as well. Similarly, border regions have had a long tradition for disputes and conflicts which within the last decades have turned into cooperation. And since World War II almost every major city in Denmark and in the other Nordic countries has had twinning-arrangements with cities in other countries.

All these international activities, however, seem insignificant within the overall scope of the tasks performed by local governments. They do not occupy much time or many resources and have had no significant influence on Danish foreign policy. This situation is about to change, however, because of the ever more intense integration in the EU brought about and stimulated by a number of EU laws and regulations on an increasing number of policy areas and by EU funding opportunities (Bennet 1993; Bongers 1992; Jørgensen 1999). In this process, local governments become new players in the regional integration of Europe (Bullman 1994). One way of looking at this is to focus attention to new systems of "multi-level governance" (Hogue 1996). Whereas the concept of governance (Rhodes 1997) covers some of the topics discussed here at local and regional level, the concept of multi-level governance, however, is aimed at another level and at other actors than those who are in focus here. Most crucial, however, seems to be the way in which key actors are perceiving their situation and initiating new internationally oriented initiatives, often as a general inclination in some local governments to look abroad for new challenges and partners for cooperation. Some of these developments are qualitatively new. We are seeing the development of international relations and activities that pose a potential challenge to the old order.

---

1 This article is based on research on the internationalization of local government in Denmark and twelve other European countries. Surveys and case studies were carried out from 1990 and are reported in Klausen and Jensen (1993), Goldsmith and Klausen (1997) and Klausen (1998).

Europeanization – impact at local level

Looking at the findings from the survey and case studies of internationalization in Danish counties and municipalities (amter and kommuner) we find a number of striking features (see also Klausen and Jensen 1993; Klausen 1996; Klausen 1998):

1. twinning-arrangements have changed form and focus;
2. new institutions have appeared;
3. new organizations are established;
4. new collaborative/cooperative initiatives and strategic plans have developed;
5. the EU is a driving force;
6. but in the findings of proactive scenarios local actors and networks are more important than funding opportunities.

The international activities taking place at this level may be labelled Europeanization, since most of the efforts are European in their orientation and since the EU can in many ways be seen as a driving force. The research clearly shows that from the mid 1980s a qualitatively new situation has arisen due to the laws and regulations deriving from the establishing of EU's internal market. Prior to the internal market, most of the international activities of Danish local governments were within the framework of traditional twinning-arrangements; afterwards an increasing number of policy-fields and activities have been internationalized.

From the 1950s to the 1970s, *twinning-arrangements* tended to be established with cities in the other Nordic countries, and the aim of the contacts was social and cultural exchange. Throughout the 1980s and 1990s, twinnings have been made with sister-cities all over the world, though predominantly with other cities within the European Union. Recently cities in the former Eastern Block have been included, and especially cities in the Baltic area. Twinning with Central and East European cities has been stimulated by EU programmes, which encourage cross-border cooperation and East-West development initiatives.

The municipality of Odense may serve as an example (Odense Kommune 1994). The development of twinning arrangements – apart from a few exceptions – becomes clear when looking at the time when Odense's arrangements were established: in 1946 with Norrköping and Östersund (Sweden); in 1947 with Trondheim (Norway) and Tampere (Finland); in 1948 with St. Albans (England); in 1963 with Kópavagur (Iceland); in 1975 with Petach-Tikva (Israel); in 1980 with Upernavik (Greenland) and Groningen (The Netherlands); in 1984 with (Iri)Iksan City (South Korea); in 1986 with Columbus (USA); in 1988 with Klaksvik (the Faroe Islands) and Shaoxing (China); in 1989 with Funabashi (Japan); in 1990 with Izmir (Turkey); in 1992 with Brno (The Czech Republic); in 1992 with Katowice (Poland); in 1992 with Kaunas (Lithuania); in 1993 with Schwerin (Germany). In their deliberations over their policy of internationalization, Odense's city council has established four main objectives and two priority geographical areas (Poulsen 1996). The four objectives are:

1. Internationalization should work as a "door-opener" to local industry, export of public procurement systems and tourism, thereby constituting a key element in the policy for local economic development,
2. internationalization should strengthen mutual relationships between people at the social and cultural level;
3. internationalization should strengthen cooperation between the public and private sectors;
4. internationalization should strengthen the position of Odense in an international network.

The two priority geographical areas are the former Eastern Europe and the EU member states.

The expansion of the twinning-arrangements throughout the world, has also brought about a change in substance. They still focus on social and cultural exchange and cooperation. To this end they help to increase mutual understanding (and peacekeeping), an understanding which also produces symbolic support, and can therefore enhance the legitimacy of those local authorities involved. This is particularly true for smaller municipalities. Apart from this interest in cultural and social contact, however, large municipalities and counties are increasingly focusing their twinning activities on issues and programs which stimulate trade and industry. Whenever a delegation is sent out to sister cities, individuals from private enterprise participate alongside representatives from public sector organizations, interest organizations and politicians. As mentioned, this effort has been stimulated by the EU, as well as by policies and special grants from national authorities.

Since the latter half of the 1980s and throughout the 1990s, *new institutions* have developed in the administration of the municipalities and counties to sort and redistribute information and to coordinate initiatives internally as well as externally. Reeducation programs on the EU and international issues have been introduced, internationalization is on the agenda at staff meetings and among heads of department, and international issues, notably EU laws and regulations, are routinely incorporated into daily practices (Klausen and Jensen 1993; Jensen 1995). In this way, internationalization and EU-affairs become a natural part of everyday life in local administration, though, of course, more conspicuously so in some departments than in others.

At the same time, *new organizations* have been established to cope with these matters, both within local government administration, locally in cooperation with private interest groups and internationally. The organizational changes typically take the form of an "international office" with responsibility for keeping up to date on information and to service other parts of the local system, including external interest groups (private enterprise, other interest groups etc.). This office may be situated at the town hall and be strictly public or it may be located elsewhere and established as a cooperative unit comprising representatives from private enterprise and other interest groups. In the latter case – which is very common alongside with EU-info centers – the office typically functions as a local and/or regional development agency in which internationalization and international issues are but one aspect of a larger portfolio of tasks. We also find a number of new organizational set-ups established as combined public-private organizations operated in order to generate projects and service private and public organizations on a fee-for-service basis (Bertelsen 1996; Udby 1996). In addition, a number of cities, municipalities and counties have established their own offices abroad. Most often they are located in Brussels, but some local authorities have also opened offices in the Eastern European cities along the Baltic Sea.

Similarly, the respective umbrella organizations of the counties and the municipalities (Amtsrådsforeningen and Kommunernes Landsforening) have engaged themselves in international activities both with regard to servicing their members in Denmark and by creating lobbying institutions in Brussels. It is worth noting that while these offices serve political purposes (both as service institutions for their home organizations and to the Danish members of the committee of the regions) the offices established by the counties and the municipalities function as attachés for local trade and industry and as sources of information for their political constituencies that is, they have no political function and mandate.

An interesting development is the *new collaborative/cooperative initiatives* established by institutions, organizations and networks among partners who hitherto had not cooperated, initiatives which to a large extent have resulted from internationalization and integration in the EU. These take the form of cooperation among municipalities and between them and local enterprise (Udby 1996), between municipalities and the counties (Bertelsen 1996; Vedel 1996) and between cities and regions throughout Europe (Kristiansen 1996; Svendsen 1996).

These endeavors often form parts of strategic plans aimed at local and regional development, as is the case for large towns such as Aalborg (Christensen 1996), Aarhus (Udby 1996), Odense (Poulsen 1996) and the Danish capital Copenhagen (Svendsen 1996). In these plans international initiatives are seen as but a part of a larger, strategic plan. Internationalization is now taken seriously, and has profound consequences on the way in which new institutions, organizations, cooperative initiatives and programs are established and implemented.

Many of these undertakings are stimulated by EU-funding, and may thus be seen as a logical consequence of a very deliberate regional and structural policy of the EU, with the creation of structural funds having the special goals/priority objectives and common programs such as INTERREG, Leader a.o. Our research shows that local authorities build up their international activities around these funding opportunities when regions have become eligible to seek funding in Brussels, as is clearly the case for the northern part of Jutland (Christensen 1996) and the island of Bornholm (Kristiansen 1996). Hence, we may conclude that the *EU is a driving force* in the Europeanization of local government.

It is also easy to point out the motives behind this, both on behalf of the EU (and the Commission in particular) and of local governments. Looking at EU policies, it is evident that the EU is seeking to stimulate economic and political integration in general, and that regional integration is a part of this endeavour, both insofar as weak regions must be stimulated in order not to counter processes of integration and/or stand outside the dynamic processes of integration, and insofar as good relations to regional authorities are important in order to ensure that EU policies are implemented. Moreover, the local and regional levels are of importance to the EU because new EU policies may be generated at these levels and "jump over" national governments at times when they may not be to agreeable as seen from the Commission. To this end, we find the structural funds, the common programs, the idea of partnerships and of subsidiarity, the vision of a "Europe of Regions" and a "Europe of Cities". The Committee of the Regions may be seen as a vehicle for strengthening this subnational and regional integration politically.

The local authorities, for their part, are motivated in their endeavors by a wish for influence and representation at the new power-center from economic and industrial motives and by a wish to strengthen their local autonomy vis-à-vis the state. In some instances they may even have their own political interest in "jumping over" the state. The interest in being represented at the new power-center is achieved through representation in international organizations (this of course, is done only by a few people) and via the offices of the umbrella organizations of the counties and the municipalities. The economic and industrial interests are carried through by the new cooperation and organizations at local level and by the offices abroad. The quest for local autonomy vis-à-vis the state shows e.g. in the negotiations about the responsibility for structural funds, and in the activities aimed at new regional and cross-border cooperation. The interest in jumping over the state level, however, may be less pronounced for Danish local governments because their interests tend to be represented by the umbrella organizations of the counties and the municipalities. However, such motives may be strong in Germany, France and Great Britain (Goldsmith and Klausen 1997).

The fact that the EU may be seen as a driving force and that there are motives which create a mutual interest between local authorities and the EU cannot account for all the initiatives we find at local level. Some areas which do not have good funding opportunities are very active, while others which have such opportunities do not seem to manage them professionally. We find these patterns throughout Europe (Goldsmith and Klausen 1997). Internationalization takes a number of forms and varies throughout the country, but the patterns – apart from distinctive Northern and Southern European features – are strinkingly similar among/between the countries. They range *from a "counteractive scenario" to scenarios or strategies which may be termed "passive", "reactive", or "proactive".*

Local governments taking the proactive scenario are leading the way in taking new initiatives towards Europeanization – they undertake all the above-mentioned initiatives organizationally as well as politically. Those local governments belonging to the reactive type are followers who tend to imitate these actions of the proactive local governments without adding anything new. Local governments who are in the passive mode await what is going to be the outcome of such endeavors and continue to deliberate as to whether they should join the others. Finally, those belonging to the counteractive type actively try to obstruct Europeanization initiatives. Our findings show that most local governments have remained in the passive mode, that a growing number of them are undertaking a more reactive scenario, and that only a few can be characterized in terms of proactive scenario.

The scenarios of the proactive, reactive, passive, counteractive strategies of local governments are not distributed in accordance with whether or not the areas are eligible for funding, whether or not they are rural or urban, etc. Other factors must be decisive. According to Goldsmith and Klausen (1997), these other factors are associated with central *actors, networks and learning processes*, so that the key issue revolves around how these actors perceive the opportunities and threats of their situation and how they manage to persuade other local actors to undertake new initiatives. Initiatives often stem from central actors and networks of actors within the administrative system who meet, communicate and exchange ideas and experiences.

It is most important to note that the features of the proactive and passive scenario are not exclusively tied up to and dependent upon EU-funding opportunities, since these funds are very likely to cease and/or be reallocated in the next funding period, and most certainly when the new Member States enter the EU. Hence EU-funding opportunities can not be taken for granted.

Perspectives on the role of local governments – integration from below

Until the late 1980s, local governments played no role in the processes of internationalization and integration in the EU, in what has here been called Europeanization. This has changed.

The aforementioned social and cultural activities of the twinning-arrangements clearly play a role in the social integration of Europe. It is not a major role but is nevertheless an important part, and should not be underestimated in comparison with other aspects of local government activities in the field of internationalization. Social and cultural exchange have the capacity to enhance mutual understanding and respect, to make an emotional impact on individuals and groups (Jepsen 1996). Nevertheless, twinning arrangements do not constitute a new role for local government.

A new role appears, however, as municipalities and counties pursue economic integration at local and regional levels. They develop strategic plans in which internationalization becomes an integral part, and they act in order to promote local and regional economic development (as has been made possible by laws 383 and 384 –

a very recent development). Typically, this is done both within the framework of twinning cooperation and within programs supported by the EU to stimulate cross-border regional integration. It is in this respect that the new organizations and institutions, both at home and abroad, are of importance. The local authorities' new role as actors in the field of economic development changes previous relationships between the public and the private sector as well as between local governments and the state. Local governments become a more important partner for private enterprise and are able to act more independently of the state.

The latter is also the case when we turn to the new role of local government in the processes of political integration. We may talk of the internationalization of problems and decision making (Thaarup et al. 1996) and many problems, as well as decisions of importance for local government, have been internationalized. This forces local politicians to take on new roles, and these are played out in a number of arenas. Twinning-arrangements are also political actions both symbolically and in actual practice. They play a (minor) role in the peacemaking and particularly peacekeeping processes, and they are certainly intended to stimulate interregional development. Other international arenas and political fora in which local government representatives make policy include the Committee of the Regions, Eurocities, the Union of Capitals, the Union of Baltic Cities and the North Sea Commission.

Local governments of the proactive and reactive scenarios are pushing forward European integration politically, economically and socially. The actors at this level include those individuals and groups who take the initiatives at local level, typically the city manager, the mayor, internationally oriented people within public institutions (school teachers, etc.), private enterprise (local tycoons, CEOs) and voluntary associations (social, cultural and political interest organizations). These actors perform their activities through the new internationally oriented institutions and organizations. Even if this process is stimulated by the deliberate policies of the EU, we may conclude that the endeavors of local governments constitute an integration from below.

The new roles of local government are not played by all local politicians of course. Only some of them are active in this field. We also find that in many cases actors outside the political system are pushing for these new developments, i.e., local interest organizations, the private sector and the administrative system. It could be argued that when the administrative system is pushing things it is not in accordance with the ways in which democracy is supposed to work. Some observers would probably argue that in general, internationalization at the local level constitutes a partial depoliticization at local level (both because of the processes and of the change of focus). In this sense, internationalization, like many other complex features of today's political reality, potentially strengthens the administrative while weakening the political side of local government.

What we find striking, however, is that whenever local politicians, who hold power and are central actors at local level, are engaged in this and make it their policy, we usually find the proactive scenarios. In these cases local politicians engage themselves and produce the needed visions, strategies and plans in order to keep internationalization processes on track and render political legitimacy to these processes. All too often, however, this is not the case. The internationally oriented activities appear at random and are mostly the result of initiatives taken by the administrative system. To further promote internationalization at the local level political will and leadership are needed which can produce these internationally oriented visions, strategies and plans (Gjelstrup, Olsen and Klausen 1996).

Internationalization and Europeanization constitute challenges to local governments. These challenges not only confront local government but also point to potential conflicts and changes at other levels. This can be seen, for example, in the disputes about administration and political decision-making with regard to the structural funds of the EU. Here we find the umbrella organizations of the municipalities and the counties negotiating with the relevant national Danish ministries over the allocation of administrative responsibility and discretionary decision (Klausen 1998). In these matters, the local authorities have a common interest. This can also be seen in their conduct of affairs in their Brussels offices, whereas we find them disagreeing on many other subjects.

In this way, the internationalization process reveals a number of conflicts to be embedded in existing structures and relationships: the relationship between central and local governments; the relationship between the umbrella organization of the counties and the municipalities; the relationship between municipalities and counties; the relationship among competing counties and municipalities; the relationship between politicians and bureaucrats; the relationship between the public and private sector.

Local governments are gradually becoming new legitimate actors on the international scene. Just as international affairs are no longer a matter to be dealt with exclusively by the Foreign Ministry but also a part of everyday life in other parts of national government, the Danish government is no longer alone in these endeavors. There is no unitary actor but many actors on the international scene. Up to now, Danish local governments have not been influential with regard to the EU policy of the Danish state, but this possibility is not to be excluded in the future. Local governments are pushing forward processes of integration from below, and in many ways they have already become a driving force behind further integration. This will probably turn out to be so much more important at times when such processes may have come to a halt at other levels, e.g., in intergovernmental negotiations. Such a vision shows the potential of the silent revolution which is Europeanization.

Literature

Baldersheim, Harald and Krister Ståhlberg (1999): *Nordic Region-Building in a European Perspective*, Aldershot: Ashgate.

Bennet, Robert J. (ed.) (1993): *Local Government in the New Europe*, London: Belhaven Press.

Bertelsen, Ole (1996): "Erhvervsrettet internationalisering, Ringkjøbing Amt" in Kurt Klaudi Klausen (ed.). *Erfaringer med Internationalisering i Amter og Kommuner*, Odense: Odense Universitetsforlag, pp. 79-93.

Bongers, Paul (1992): *Local Government in the Single European Market*, Colchester: Longman.

Bullman, Udo (hrsg.) (1994): *Die Politik der dritten Ebene. Regionen im Europa der Union*, Baden-Baden: Nomos Verlagsanstalt.

Christensen, Henning (1996): "Et EU-målområde, Nordjyllands Amt" in Kurt Klaudi Klausen (ed.). *Erfaringer med Internationalisering i Amter og Kommuner*, Odense: Odense Universitetsforlag, pp. 25-43.

From, Johan og Per Stava (eds.) (1995): *EØS og lokalforvaltningen: gjensidig påvirkning? Utfordringer, muligheter og innflytelse for kommunesektoren*, Oslo: Kommuneforlaget.

Gidlund, Janerik and Magnus Jerneck (eds.) (2000): *Internationalization of Subnational Governance*, Lund: Publica.

Gjelstrup, Gunnar, Henrik Olsen and Kurt Klaudi Klausen (1996): *Perspektiver på internationalisering i amter og kommuner*, København: Projekt Offentlige Sektor.

Goldsmith, Michael and Kurt Klaudi Klausen (eds.) (1997): *European Integration and Local Government*, London: Edward Elgar.

Hooghe, Lisbeth (1996): *Cohesion Policy and European Integration. Building Multi-Level Governance*, New York: Oxford University Press.

Jensen, Lars Thore (1995): *Internationalisering i de danske amter*, Odense: Institut for Erhvervsret og Politologi, Odense Universitet.

Jepsen, Lauge (1996): "Den lille kommune, Bredebro Kommune" in Kurt Klaudi Klausen (ed.): *Erfaringer med Internationalisering i Amter og Kommuner*, Odense: Odense Universitetsforlag, pp. 109-115.

Jørgensen, Birthe Holst (1999): Building European Cross-border Co-operation Structures, Copenhagen: Ph.D. Thesis, Institute of Political Science, University of Copenhagen.

Klausen, Kurt Klaudi (ed.) (1996): *Erfaringer med Internationalisering i Amter og Kommuner*, Odense: Odense Universitetsforlag.

Klausen, Kurt Klaudi (1998): "Explaining Local Government EU Activities as Business Promotion", *Current Politics and Economics of Europe*, Volume 8, number 3, pp. 297-320.

Klausen, Kurt Klaudi (2000): "Conflict and Harmony in the Internationalization of Danish Local Government" in Gidlund and Jernick (eds.): *Internationalization of Subnational Governance*, Lund: Publica.

Klausen, Kurt Klaudi og Lars Thore Jensen (1993): *Primærkommunerne og EF*, Politologiske Skrifter fra Institut for Erhvervsret og Politologi, no, 1/1993. Odense Universitet.

Kristiansen, Orla (1996): "Danmark, Baltikum, Europa, Bornholms Amt" in Kurt Klaudi Klausen (ed.): *Erfaringer med Internationalisering i Amter og Kommuner*, Odense: Odense Universitetsforlag, pp. 175-191.

Odense Kommune (1994): *Årsberetning 1994*, Odense.

Poulsen, Henrik (1996): "Internationaliseringens mange strenge, Odense Kommune" in Kurt Klaudi Klausen (ed.): *Erfaringer med Internationalisering i Amter og Kommuner*, Odense: Odense Universitetsforlag, pp. 117-133.

Rhodes, Richard A.W. (1997): *Understanding Governance. Policy Networks, Governance, Reflexivity and accountability*, Buckingham: Open University Press.

Svendsen, Klaus Robert (1996): "Hovedstaden, Københavns Kommune" in Kurt Klaudi Klausen (ed.): *Erfaringer med Internationalisering i Amter og Kommuner*, Odense: Odense Universitetsforlag, pp. 151-173.

Thaarup, Bent m.fl. (1996): *Internationalisering i det offentlige*, København: Projekt Offentlig Sektor Vilkår og Fremtid.

Udby, Jørgen (1996): "Systemeksport og nye samarbejdsmønstre, Holstebro Kommune" in Kurt Klaudi Klausen (ed.): *Erfaringer med Internationalisering i Amter og Kommuner*, Odense: Odense Universitetsforlag, pp. 59-77.

Vedel, Hans Minor (1996): "Institutionalisering of professionalisering, Århus Kommune" in Kurt Klaudi Klausen (ed.): *Erfaringer med Internationalisering i Amter og Kommuner*, Odense: Odense Universitetsforlag, pp. 45-57.

CHAPTER 14

Danish Integration Policies: Dilemmas and Options

Morten Kelstrup

1. Introduction

It is amazing to see how the project of European integration which started few years after the Second World War, has developed into the present European Union. During the last 50 years the project has – with "ups and downs" – changed the economic and political organisation of Europe. Today, around the turn of the century, the European Union is a major part of the political structure of Europe and a major actor in the international political system. In the present phase of European history all states in Europe are challenged by the changes in Europe's political organisation made by the project of European integration. They are not only challenged to formulate their policies towards – or within – the European Union, they are also challenged in their domestic structures by the political system of the European Union.

The changes of the EC/EU have taken place continuously, yet the changes have been greater in some phases than others. The European Community had a stagnating phase in the 1970s and the beginning of the 1980s. But an important change was initiated in the EC in the middle of the 1980s resulting in a new dynamism which led to the Single European Act. Another important change occurred – as a continuation and further acceleration of the integration processes from the 1980s – after the end of the Cold War with the reforms in Maastricht in 1991which led to the formation of the European Union in 1993. Maybe "Maastricht and its aftermath" should be seen as the most important "constitutional moment in the history of the European Union".[1]

Yet, since the agreement in Maastricht on the Treaty on the European Union we have seen further steps in the European integration: the initiation of the process of further enlargement of the EU, the Schengen Agreement on free movements within the EU, the Amsterdam Treaty, Agenda 2000, further steps towards the creation of an "area of freedom, security and justice", the realisation of the Economic and Monetary Union (the EMU) and the initiation of its third phase in the beginning of 1999. In addition, the conflicts in the former Yugoslavia in the 1990s, which culmi-

---

1 Joseph Weiler identifies "Maastricht and its aftermath" as a the most important "constitutional moment in the history of the European Union", Weiler (1999 : 4).

nated with NATO's intervention in Kosova, have given new impetus to changes in the European security structure, to a strengthening of the common foreign and security policy, and to further involvement of the EU in European security. Other initiatives could also be mentioned, as for instance the work on a charter on fundamental rights for the people living in the Union as well as other topics included on the agenda of the intergovernmental conference of the year 2000.

It is difficult to describe the situation of the EU at the turn of the century on the basis of all these changes and initiatives. The number of issues and perspectives is great, and it is not easy to paint a larger picture of the present and future EU. Many developments point to a situation in which the EU is in a new, very decisive phase, at the edge of taking further steps towards more intense economic and political integration. Yet, as so often, the situation is also filled with challenges and uncertainties. The EU is, partly as a result of its earlier action and partly because of new developments, confronted with new problems, not least the problems of combining its coming enlargement with up to 12 or 15 states with reforms of EU's institutional structure. With the very comprehensive – and some will say overloaded – agenda, some foresee a coming crisis for the EU. Others predict that the EU, once more challenged with crises, will react to these by taking new important steps towards further integration.

Challenged with this development, it becomes a major task for the European states to find the strategies and policies they want to pursue in regard to the future process of European integration. As it has been discussed extensively in other parts of this book, a state's foreign policy – and also its integration policy – depends on its internal and external environment. The policies depend on history and traditions, and on domestic institutions and actors. The policies also depend on the international setting and the character of the integration system. As discussed, in particular in chapter 4, integration policies in regard to a supranational and transnational system are different from policies towards an intergovernmental integration system. Thus, the growing integration in the EU is also a challenge to states to redefine their integration policies. And it is also a challenge to the *ways* in which the integration policies are defined. Partly, the complexity of the EU and the very many kinds of involvement which a member state has in the EU, make it difficult for the states to act as unitary actors. This problem – and the danger of diffusion of the integration policy – in some ways sharpens the needs for having explicit policies.

The purpose of this chapter is to discuss the problems of integration policies with special regard to Denmark's dilemmas and options in her relation to the European Union at the turn of the century. A major purpose is to attempt to identify what we might call *"strategic options"* for Denmark in regard to the present and future European integration. By *options* we mean courses of action available to a given actor at a certain time. Options, for instance for a government in its foreign policy or integration policy, are primarily defined from the outside – as courses of action available in the international system – but also from the inside, depending on internal acceptability.[2] By strategic options we mean more general policy alternatives which an actor has in regard to its position within and attitude towards a specific political system. In this connection we talk of strategic options in regard to European integration, i.e. the general policy choices in regard to the state's position and attitude towards EU's present and future political system.

It is difficult to identify the strategic or long term options for Denmark in relation to the EU for many reasons. One reason is that strategic analysis is a difficult kind of analysis. Being directed towards the future, it has to deal with uncertain perspectives. Another reason is that since the Danish policy towards the EC/EU has been rather non-committed, fragmented and pragmatic, in major aspects it also tends to be rather unarticulated. [3] In addition, there are many dilemmas in regard to Denmark's integration policy. A consequence is that we have very little to build upon in making this kind of analysis.

The aim of the chapter is not to reach any specific, normative view on one recommendable strategy for Denmark, nor – directly – to take part in the political debate in Denmark on her policy towards European integration. But, since the aim is to contribute to the identification of major policy choices, the analysis does – unavoidably – have a certain involvement in the political debate on this issue. In particular, the chapter indirectly takes the stand that it is important to have political analyses that are able to identify relevant dilemmas and to differentiate between different political options. Yet, the emphasis is on major perspectives and better conceptualisation, not on specific recommendations.

2. On the analysis of Denmark's integration policies

2.1. On Denmark as a semi-integrated actor

The following discussion is based on two premises: Firstly, that the EU has developed beyond being an intergovernmental system and has become a relatively integrated political system comprising different modes of decision-making, including supranational decision-making. And, secondly, that Denmark can be seen as a semi-integrated actor within the EU. By *a semi-integrated actor* we understand an actor which is part of a greater social or political system. It is an actor which has some independence, but which also depends on the greater and more encompassing system and has a specific position and, possibly, specific roles in relation to the greater system. The more encompassing system has a certain structure within which the semi-integrated actor is positioned, and the greater system might itself be an actor. Thus, semi-integrated actors might also be understood as actors within actors.

An analysis of Denmark as a semi-integrated actor within the EU implies on the

---

2 See also Branner's discussion of options in chapter 11.
3 See also Branner's analysis in chapter 11.

Options and Decision-Making 417

one hand that we analyse the character of the EU, and also, since strategies and policies will be future directed, that we develop an understanding of the future prospects of the EU. On the other hand an analysis of Denmark's position as a semi-integrated actor should also include an analysis of the internal basis for Danish decision-making as it can be seen in the present phase of history, also the internal constraints on Danish decision-makers. Before commenting on this, I will, though, recapitulate some of the major perspectives for this kind of analysis.

As discussed earlier in this book, integration policy is, as foreign policy, formed on the basis of history and tradition. Policy formulations are always embedded within established discourses and institutions. Thus, the policy formulations of a state is also bound by traditions, former policies, earlier formulations and – more or less – established discourses. At the same time, external conditions are important. When external conditions are changing fast, there will most likely be a tension between the challenges from the changed international environment and the hitherto formulated and somewhat institutionalised discourses and policies. In addition, the formulation of new policies have to take account of the necessity of public support, and the generation of public support for new policies will normally require some continuity from earlier policies and discourses. Thus, sometimes it is likely to be very difficult for collective actors to break away from traditions or views which in some other way have been institutionalised.[4]

2.2. *On the relationship between state sovereignty and the status of semi-integrated actors*

Some might ask the questions: Can states also be sovereign when they are semi-integrated actors? What is the relationship between sovereignty and the status as semi-integrated actors? Obviously, these are questions which could lead to an extensive discussion of the concept of sovereignty and its status in regard to the present changes in Europe. It will be too much to go into this discussion here. My general view is that it is possible to keep the formal understanding of states as sovereign and at the same time talk of states as semi-integrated actors.

Clearly, the understanding of Denmark as a sovereign state is an institutionalised understanding deeply embedded in the Danish tradition which cannot easily be changed. When processes of change appear and practices develop which somehow are at odds with the formal view, a discrepancy might appear, a tension between the formal view on sovereignty and the accepted practices. In my view, this is what is happening, and it is implied in the understanding of Denmark as a semi-integrated actor. On the one hand we can accept the traditional point of view of

---

4   This also implies that it is an important question how fast adaptation to new circumstances can take place. But equally it is interesting to analyse what happens when such adaptation is not taking place, or – vice versa – when it is taking place too fast.

international law, that Denmark is fundamentally a sovereign state.[5] Denmark has – on the basis of its constitution – entered the European Communities (and European Union), and the Danish authorities have, in accordance with the Danish constitution (...) delegated some of their authority to the bodies of the European Union.[6] Thus, although it has chosen to delegate authority to the EU, Denmark is still a sovereign state. And Denmark is – as other states – in a constitutional position to withdraw this delegation, not without responsibility in accordance with international law, but without any fundamental constitutional disruption. On the other hand through the participation in the EU, new and special kinds of dependency are established. Denmark as a state takes part in the EU's decision-making system, and Danish citizens and other legal subjects are bound by decisions taken by the Community. Further, Denmark is influenced by the effects of the decisions taken in Bruxelles. And since the EU has developed into a political system which comprises about all political sectors, Denmark must be considered as deeply integrated in the EU. Said differently, Denmark is at one and the same time a formally sovereign state and a semi-integrated actor.

2.3. Different kinds of integration policies for Denmark in relation to the EU

When a state gets more involved in a process of integration, its policy of integration becomes more differentiated. We might, as explained in more detail in chapter 4, see integration policy as part of the state's foreign policy in the very early phase of integration, but from a certain level of integration the policy towards the integration system becomes more differentiated. If we use the theory of adaptation we might distinguish between the following five different types of integration strategies or policies:[7] 1) "relative isolation", 2) "reluctant political integration", 3) "balancing and optimizing integration", 4) "dominant political integration" and 5) "alternative political integration". Within this categorisation, we will expect Denmark to follow a "balancing" strategy. This view might be used as base for further

---

5 One should be aware of the importance of formal national sovereignty as a "fall back position": If things, in the impressive attempt to restructure European politics, goes very wrong, it is a possibility to insist on the formal sovereignty and use it for taking delegated authority back. Thus, the formal position might also have a certain "insurance-function" in relation to "worst case" developments, a function which most likely will remain latent and never be used. In addition, it gives the well known benefits of being recognized in international organizations etc.
6 Since the basic authority in Denmark rests in the constitutionally sovereign people, it is also – in principle – possible for the Danish institutions to withdraw formally from the integration process. Thus, there is nothing against – at a formal level – that Denmark withdraws its delegated authority.
7 See also Petersen's contribution to this volume, Kelstrup (1993), and Petersen (1995).

elaboration of more specific strategies, partly strategies relating to the integration system and partly strategies relating to the domestic scene.[8]

Yet, when the integration has developed so far that the actor in question is a semi-integrated actor within the new political system, the policy of the actor "proliferates" into different aspects or dimensions of integration policies. As described in chapter 4, these aspects, which can be seen as a further differentiation of the categories above, can be described as: 1) policy towards participating or not, 2) policies in regard to position within the integration system, 3) policies in regard to institutional changes in the integration system, 4) policies in regard to the internal output or policy of the integration system, and 5) policies in regard to the external output or policy of the integration system. Within each of these dimension we can make further distinctions. For instance, in relation to a state's "position" within the integration system, we might distinguish between participation without reservations and with reservations, and we might distinguish further between different kinds of "conditionality" of participation. In regard to institutional change, we might differentiate between policies that support further supranationality and policies that do not. Yet, a further specification could relate to the already established institutions within EU's political system, for instance policies that support further power to the European Council vs. policies that support the European Parliament or the European Commission. In relation to the policies towards internal and external output, we might distinguish between policy in different fields or sectors. For instance the policy within the security field might be distinguished from other, possibly more "pragmatic" or "economic fields".[9] In the following discussion I shall briefly attempt to use these categories in a discussion of Denmark's present and future integration policy. Yet, first, I shall comment on a few historical perspectives.

3. Denmark's policies towards European integration

3.1. Historical reflections on Denmark's integration policy

Which integration strategies have Denmark followed through the course of history? We have given a brief description of the Danish policy towards Europe in the introduction to this book. In addition, the other chapters in the book have each characterised and analysed different aspects of the Danish policies. I shall not attempt to summarise the analyses in the preceding chapters. In general, it is not easy to characterise the Danish policies.[10] I shall, however, point to some important aspects which shall form a basis for the following discussion of Denmark's dilemmas and options in the present situation in the beginning of the year 2000.

---

8 See Petersen's contribution to this volume.
9 Thus, the categories that Nikolaj Petersen employs in his chapter in this volume can be seen as a specification within such an overall framework.
10 Cfr. though other contributions to this volume and DUPI (2000).

It has been shown that Denmark has very deep traditions, and that the Danish foreign policy traditions are rooted in fundamental traits based in the history of the Danish people and the Danish state. An important interpretation is that although Denmark has a small state tradition, this is not Denmark's only tradition. Rather, we have a duality consisting of the small state tradition and a tradition which builds upon the earlier and stronger multicultural Danish state (see Uffe Østergaard's chapters). Somewhat in parallel to this analysis, it has been argued that Denmark does not only have a "deterministic" small state foreign policy tradition supplemented by a compensatory "internationalism", but has a more independent internationalistic and activistic tradition (see Branner's chapter 6). Some of the traits from these two traditions can be found in present days politics. Said differently, parts of the present Danish politics can be interpreted as a revival of parts of the Danish tradition, and for instance the Danish "active internationalism" from 1990 can be seen as based on deep historical roots.

In other chapters it has been shown that Denmark has given relatively low priority to its European policy in the first decades after 1945. Denmark gave a high priority to the 'great' European option, which had a solid base in both economic as well as general foreign policy considerations. As Hans Branner writes in chapter 11, reminiscences of this can be found in later Danish policies "including the rapid decisions to join Britain in applying for EEC membership in 1961 and 1967; the NORDEK experiment at the end of the 1960s as a stepping stone towards subsequent entry into the EC; the emphasis by the decision-making elite on economic advantages and concrete results when arguing for Danish EC membership and supporting EC integration steps; the hesitant and half-hearted approach to Union plans resulting in reservations about to treaty obligations; and, finally, the enthusiastic endorsement of EU enlargement plans in the 1990s. All elements may be traced back to the pattern identified as characteristic of Danish policy in the 1950s."

As Nikolaj Petersen points out, Denmark joined the European Community in 1973 on a highly selective identification with EC goals. The primary motivation was economic, and politicians advocating membership focused almost entirely on the economic benefits of joining in the referendum campaign prior to membership. Denmark's identification with EC/EU's goals has in general been low in the areas of foreign and security policy and especially in constitutional-institutional policy. Thus, Denmark's priority has been that security and defense should be dealt with within NATO. And in relation to EC/EU's institutional aspect, the Danish policy has in general been reserved towards supranational and federalist elements, having preference for an intergovernmental structure.

In general, Denmark's policy towards the EC/EU has been described as characterised by "limited engagement", "fragmentation" and "pragmatism" (Branner, chapter 11). One might argue that there was a change towards greater commitment to the European project in the late 1980s, after the referendum in 1986, in particular caused by the change of attitude within the Social Democratic Party (SDP). As Jens Henrik Haahr argues, the single market plans in the 1980s constituted in the view of the SDP (and also of the Social Liberal Party and also parts of the Socialist

People's Party (SPP)) an important societal change which gave new international conditions. It led the SDP, the SPP and the Social Liberal Party to support the introduction of majority voting in the EC in new areas. And from 1988 to 1991 there was a high level of agreement in Danish policy towards the EC, i.a. an agreement which formed an important part of the background for the acceptance by the majority of the political parties of the Maastricht Treaty. Yet, one might also argue that the "No" at the referendum on the Maastricht Treaty in 1992 changed this more active EC/EU policy. In stead, the predominant Danish policy became the one codified in the so-called "national compromise". The compromise included an "active part" which stipulated a basis for an active Danish integration policy based on high priority to i.a. democracy, openness, subsidiarity ("nærhed"), environmental concerns and employment. And it included the four "reservations" mentioned in the introduction, that Denmark should avoid far reaching Danish participation in four areas of EU policy: the single currency, defence cooperation, the common citizenship, and supranational cooperation in justice and home affairs. One might say that the "national compromise" and its confirmation in the Edinburgh Agreement and in the subsequent referendum on "Maastricht and Edinburgh" in 1993 changed Denmark from being a reserved or reluctant member of the EU to a "member with reservations".[11]

It is no exaggeration that since 1993 the four Danish reservations have played an important and maybe even dominating role in the debate on Danish policies towards the EU. Yet, seen in hindsight it is clear that there has been – and still is – very different interpretations of the Danish reservations.[12] One might talk of two rather different strategies in regard to the way in which the reservations should be interpreted. One interpretation is that the reservations give Denmark a "time out" which can give the Danes the possibility of seeing how the development will be within the different problem areas and thus give them possibilities of cancelling the reservations later, possibly one by one, depending on the circumstances. This interpretation has clearly been supported by the Liberals and the Conservatives, and at least also partly by the Social Democratic and Social Liberal government. The other interpretation, supported by the Socialist People's Party and the "no-movements", sees the reservations as permanent conditions for Denmark's participation in the EU, not as something temporary which should easily be changed but rather as a basis for Denmark's more general policy within the EU.

It can be discussed how Denmark's integration policy since 1993 as "a member with reservations" shall be characterised. One interpretation is that Denmark after 1993 returned to the policy of limited engagement, fragmentation and pragmatism. Major elements of this interpretation seem plausible. Thus, the reservations can be seen as a sign per se of limited engagement. Denmark's reservation in regard to defence can be seen as a policy line of fragmentation (wanting defence issues treated in NATO). The construction of the "compromise" can in itself be seen as a very

---

11 See also DUPI, (2000 : 225 ff.).
12 See DUPI, (2000 : 261).

pragmatic approach. One might argue however, that there have also been new and more active elements in the Danish EU policy after 1993. The policy of the Danish government can be seen as a policy which at the one hand accepted the four reservations, but on the other hand went nearly as far as it could in an active participation within the communities. The active Danish policy in the negotiations of the Amsterdam Treaty is an indication of this. Also Denmark's acceptance of the Schengen Agreement is such a sign. In the debate about the Amsterdam Treaty it was recognised by the Government as well as by the political parties that the Danish EU policy is, primarily, political and not only a question of Danish economic interests. Thus, in this respect part of the Danish "fragmentation" has been abandoned.

One might also argue that in the interpretation of the Danish reservations, the Government has shown a considerable "pragmatism". This pragmatism has in some ways run somewhat contrary to the policy line of limited engagement. Although there has been some uncertainty as to which of the two "reservation-strategies" the Government has followed, most interpreters will probably claim that the government has chosen – at least in its external policy – to regard the reservations as only temporary. Internally, the government has in general adhered to a consensus-oriented policy line (compare also Hedetoft's chapter in this volume). The Government has been giving many guarantees that the Danish reservations will be respected and only changed after a referendum, but it has also attempted within such an overall commitment to get as much possibility for active engagement in the EU as possible. Lately, i.e. in the spring 2000, there has been a certain move which challenges the consensus-oriented policy. The Government decided to hold a referendum in regard to the reservation on Danish participation in the Euro-cooperation in September 2000 with the clear indication that the government want Denmark to participate fully in the Euro-cooperation. One might see this as a clear indication that the Government follows the policy of regarding the reservations as temporary, and maybe the decision on the new referendum can also be seen as an indication that the Government now attempts to follow a more active and integrationist policy and to get public support for this.

3.2. Some general features of the Danish integration policy

Let us on the basis of the reflections above try to summarise the Danish integration policy, using the dimension presented above.[13]

1) One aspect of Denmark's integration policy towards the EC/EU relates to Denmark *participating or not participating* in the EU. One might say that this question became a major issue in the 1960s, articulated around the question whether Denmark should apply for membership, as Denmark did in 1961, 1967 and

---

13 Cf. also the discussion of different levels of European policy in chapter 2, also fig. 1, p. 50.

again in 1970. The question of membership was the major issue in the Danish referendum in 1972, and the result of the referendum decided formally this question. The solution was found, once and for all, some might say, others might say that the question was not decided in any definitive way by this first referendum. The rather strong "People's Movement against the EC" kept the issue alive. The debate on the referendum in 1986 was in many ways also about Denmark's general position as a member or a non-member of the EU. In the later referenda, the membership issue has not been as dominant, and most interpreters will say that from the late 1980s there is a rather general acceptance that the membership issue has been decided. Yet, the issue is not quite dead. The People's Movement against the EU still exist, and it is still represented in the European Parliament. The membership issue is still articulated in the referenda, and it is heard as a complaint from some that the referenda in Denmark on EU issues tend to politicise the membership issue. This having been said, the Danish policy seems to be relatively consolidated on a membership course.

2) Another aspect of Denmark's integration policy relates to Denmark's *position* in the integration system, here the EU. We are dealing with a question which arises for Denmark as a member of the EU as it does for other members. The state in question might attempt to be in the centre of the integration process, but it might also place itself with some reservations, keeping outside part of the common policies. Obviously, if the integration system develops with differentiated speed, possibly within a framework of flexibility, the question of a state's position in the system becomes crucial. Thus, the prediction is that this dimension is a very important aspect of the integration policies of all semi-integrated actors in the EU.

Denmark's policy has, as described, been that of a "reserved member" which was transformed into the position of "a member with reservations". Yet, it should be noted that within this position there are very many sub-positions, and that Denmark in the period 1988-91, and again in the late 1990s, has followed a more active and influence-oriented policy.

3) Integration policies might also be characterised in regard to the existing institutional system and *the changes* which the state might want in this institutional system. As the institutional system of the EU has evolved, it becomes important not only to have a policy in regard to the general character of the system as such (for instance in regard to the question whether – and to which degree – the system should be supranational). It also becomes important to have policies in regard to other issues, for instance to the character of constitutionality in the EU or to the allocation of competences between the community institutions and the member states. In addition, it is relevant to have policies towards different aspects of the institutional system. For instance, with the importance of the European Court of Justice which has evolved as an important, integrationist actor, it is also required to have a policy towards the position and practices of the Court.[14] In parallel, it is important

---

14 Interestingly enough, this policy is not only a policy of the state in question, but relates also to the practices of the individual national courts in a state and the attitude which it take towards the EU's legal system.

to have policies in regard to the powers of the European Parliament and with respect to the rules of decision making, for instance the rules for Qualified Majority Voting in the Council, the (lack of!) rules for the system of Commitology etc. Since institutional questions will be extremely important in the future EU, not least in combination with enlargement, this dimension of a state's integration policy seems to have growing importance.

Denmark's policy in institutional matters has, as described above and in other chapters, been very intergovernmentalist and institutionally conservative. One might add that Denmark's policy has been pragmatic in the sense that Denmark has accepted to adapt to the gradual changes of the institutional system. Some of the Danish reservations can be seen as an attempt to formulate barriers to this adaptation – or at least to institutionalise a certain inertia in the adaptation process. Maybe, in some ways Denmark has in this followed its own tradition as a small state, accepting – although it has not been very articulated – that Denmark in institutional matters act within a power structure in which Denmark has only limited influence. Interesting enough, Denmark accepted a more active, institutional policy with the national compromise (working for more democracy, more openness, and subsidiarity). As an institutional policy this has been very selective and not followed by much success. One might – by analysing Denmark's position in regard to the different intergovernmental conferences – find more specific indications of Denmark's integration policy in regard to the institutional dimension, but it is remarkable that the concrete dimensions of this aspect hardly play any role in the public debate in Denmark. The domestic discourses seem to be so dominated by the question whether "we get more or less union", that it makes articulation of more differentiated institutional policies impossible.

4) We might also characterise integration policies in regard to the *internal policy output* which the state in question wants of the integration system, i.e. its policies in relation to the participating societies. Within this we might distinguish in many ways between different kinds of policies. We might for instance differentiate between economic, ecological, socio-cultural, legal, political, military and possibly other aspects of integration policies. We might also distinguish between market orientated, regulative and distributive policies. In general, with the growing importance of EU-legislation (comprising 60-80 % of the total legislation of the member states, depending on the way of calculating this), obviously the interest in the kind of internal policy output is growing. As some has remarked, we do not only in relation to the EU have the difficult problem of understanding the "nature of the beast", we also have the problem of understanding the "colour of the beast" (Johansen 1998). The EU is – by becoming a politically important system – also becoming a political battlefield between advocates of different political orientations and different political and/or social and economic interests. For instance, one of the effects is that the interest in "lobbying" the EU-system has increased. Paradoxically, it might be appropriate also for governmental bodies to act as lobbyists in Bruxelles (as this,

for instance, is done by local governments, see Kurt Klaudi Klausen's contribution to this volume).

Denmark's integration policy has gradually acquired an important dimension related to the policy output of the EU system. Although being a reluctant EU-member, Denmark rather soon engaged in the formulation of an active EU policy in the ecological field. Part of the "national compromise" in 1992 pointed, as mentioned, to an active engagement in this area and in relation to employment. And the partially "renewed activism" in relation to the EU in the 1990s has been related to Danish engagement in selected policy fields. In general, though, the thinking in Denmark in relation to policy formulation through the EU seems underdeveloped and mainly restricted to insights found in the Danish central administration and in parts of the lobbying system.

5) Finally, integration policies can be characterized with regard to the external policy of the new integration system, here the EU. As the EU becomes stronger as an international actor, not only in the economic but also in the security field, the importance of having a policy towards the EU's various external roles and possibilities is growing. Thus, we see an increased importance also of this dimension of the states' integration policies, and also a need for differentiating policies within this policy field.

Denmark's integration policy in regard to the EU as an international actor has been marked by a certain ambivalence. Economically, it was by joining the EC accepted that the EC/EU has the competences in trade policy. Regarding foreign policy, Denmark has been supportive of the EPC-cooperation which lead to the Common Foreign and Security Policy (CFSP), and Danmark has been rather active within this cooperation. Yet, Denmark has placed one of its important reservations in regard to future defence cooperation within the EU. One of the effects of this is that Denmark must stay outside EU's engagement in peace keeping operations. Some will regard this as an "unintended consequence" of the Danish policy since the major aim of the reservation was to avoid the emergence of a proper EU defence capacity.

The general picture of the different dimensions of Denmark's integration policy is that in many dimensions there is a need of a much more articulated and differentiated policy. If and when Denmark's policy is characterised by "limited engagement", "fragmentation" and "pragmatism", this stands somehow in contrast to the need for formulation of basic policy goals and the need for differentiated policy formulations. A main argument in the following part of this article will be that Denmark's rather general integration policy is being challenged even more by the present and coming development of the EU.

4. On the EU's development in the late 1990s and in the beginning of the 21st century

4.1. On the EU and globalization

In the following I shall very briefly discuss some of the major aspects of the EU's development in order to identify the perspective for future integration policies of states in regard to the EU. It is important that the relations between states and the EU are not discussed in isolation as a zero-sum game, but are taken to include other aspects of the international development which also challenge the nation states. Formulated in very general terms, the nation states are presently involved in an increasing globalization. By globalization we might understand the formation of social systems across state boundaries. In particular, we are experiencing a growing economic globalization, the internationalization of the economy or the further development of global capitalism, as we might call it. This globalization is not new, it has been going on for at least two centuries. But it has acquired new dimension, not least related to the internationalisation of capital markets.

It is important that there are two very different perspectives on the EU and globalization. In one perspective the EU furthers globalization. The establishment of the "four freedoms" furthers the markets and competitiveness on the markets. The common European currency, the Euro, is also furthering this liberalisation. On the other hand, the EU has a function in regard to regulation of globalization. By insisting on concerns with social aspects of labour, environment protection, health, employment, regional development etc. the EU is able to regulate aspects which might otherwise be neglected. I shall return to this aspect of the EU later.

4.2. EU's latest developments and prospects for further change in the EU

It has already been indicated that the European Union seems to be in a new, very decisive phase, at the edge of taking further steps towards more intense economic and political integration. As mentioned in the introduction to this chapter, the EU has undergone important changes in several important areas in the latest years, and the EU is in a process of transformation, challenged with a very heavy agenda. In the following I shall briefly point to some of the possible and/or likely developments of the EU.

The EMU:

A very important step in the European integration was the agreement in the Maastricht treaty on the formation of the Economic and Monetary Union. Subsequently, the realisation in the beginning of 1999 of the third phase of the EMU, the so-called "Euro-cooperation" with the establishment of a common currency and a common set of institutions, represents an important step towards closer integration in Europe. It was in many ways a surprise that 11 of the EU-countries managed to start the Euro-cooperation. It was not least due to the political choice for European integration made by the German chancellor Helmut Kohl, and to the French-German cooperation around the process of German unification. There is no room here for discussions of the perspectives of the Euro-cooperation, but probably it can easily be accepted that the most likely development is that the Euro will lead to a much closer economic cooperation between the "Euroland" members. Analyses might differ concerning the prospects for the Euro-cooperation. Some see the most likely perspective as a relatively harmonious cooperation between the participating states, a cooperation which will lead to further cooperation and harmonisation. Others focus more on the many possible problems within the EMU, not least problems caused by unequal economic development within the EU or "asymmetrical chocks". The perspective could easily be that these problems will lead to a further politicisation within the EU and – on that basis – even further pressure for increased political cooperation (see also Kelstrup, 2000). Without going into details of the debate on these perspectives here, it shall be concluded that the prospect is that the Euro-cooperation will lead to further, important steps in the European integration.

The security development of the EU:

The crisis in the former Yugoslavia and NATO's intervention in Kosova in 1999 did in many ways challenge EU's role in relation to European security. The crisis in Kosova exposed the European dependence on the US, and European reactions to the intervention have i.a. been to engage in further action within the security sphere. There has already been appointed a spokesman for the Common Foreign and Security Policy, and it was in December 1999 at the meeting of the European Council in Helsinki agreed that the EU should in 2003 have a military force of 50-60.000 soldiers which can be used in crisis management. Without going into details on these plans and the organisational structure of the decision, the general conclusion must be that the EU is taking important steps in regard to this dimension. The most likely development is that this aspect of the EU will be strengthened even further.

Cooperation in legal and home affairs: The creation of an "area of freedom, security and justice":

Since the Maastricht Treaty there has been intensified cooperation in legal and home affairs. In 1998 in the Amsterdam Treaty it was specified as a goal to create an "area of freedom, security and justice", and the Schengen Agreement was included in the Amsterdam Treaty. The initiatives have been followed with a plan of action and several declarations from the European Council. The policy field has developed into one of the most important for EU's future cooperation.[15]

The enlargement of the EU:

As it is well known, the EU is preparing for its next enlargement. At present 13 states, mainly from Central- and Eastern Europe, have applied for membership, and it is likely that even more states will line up in the queue of applicants. Negotiations are going on at the present with the applicant countries. Without going into any evaluation of the difficulties and prospects, enlargement can be understood as a very important perspective for the EU's future. The perspectives linked to enlargement are extremely important, for Europe as such and for the EU. The positive perspective for Europe is that enlargement makes it possible, through the EU, to stabilise a peaceful, prosperous and united Europe. There are, however, many possible negative visions, for instance that the enlargement process will be postponed, frustrating the applicant countries which will turn their attention away from the EU. Or that the enlargement will create internal problems in the EU, making internal cooperation in the EU much more difficult. Without going into these perspectives, enlargement can be taken as a very important perspective for the EU.

Institutional change of the EU:

Already now the EU is going to undertake institutional change at the intergovernmental conference of the year 2000. Partly, this is due to unsolved institutional problems from the Amsterdam negotiations. The major perspective was that the EU should undertake institutional changes in order to be prepared for the admittance of new members, yet the negotiations on these changes were unsuccessful.

The most likely perspective for the future is that there will be much more fundamental institutional changes on EU's agenda. In a somewhat crude interpretation one might claim that there is a dilemma for the EU in regard to a future enlargement. On the one hand the EU seems so committed to enlargement that it seems necessary to take these steps. On the other hand some of the leading participating members see a danger in having an EU with about 25 members, a situation which could easily lead to a loosening not only of the decision-making procedures in the EU, but also of the integration itself. This concern has led several leading politicians in the EU to articulate thoughts on the need to establish a "small federation" within the EU. This has most recently been articulated by the German foreign minister, Joschka Fischer, in his capacity, notably, as leader of the Green Party and not as foreign minister (Fischer, 2000). One of the central differences between the recent suggestions for such a "small federation within the Union" is whether it is "the original six", the "Euro-11" or some other special collection of "core-states" that should take part in the small federation. (Wernicke, 2000).

---

15 See an elaborate description in DUPI, (2000 : 145ff.).

Obviously, some of the most radical suggestions for institutional change shall be interpreted as "balloons" testing new ideas. But the radical thoughts on EU's future institutional structure should be a clear indication that the question will be on EU's future agenda, and that it is necessary to have an integration policy which also take this into account. The most likely development seems to be that the process of institutional reform will continue at new intergovernmental conferences beyond the present one.

General reflections:

The purpose of this brief enumeration has been to point out that the EU does have a heavy agenda. Other areas for major changes could be mentioned, for instance the steps taken towards a Charter of Fundamental Rights. The most likely development is that rather great changes are to take place, and that there will be a pressure for more integration. This – obviously – presents a challenge to all the European states for formulating their policies towards the future European integration. We should add that it is not only states that have the problem of finding strategies in relation to the process of European integration, it is also a task for parliaments, parties, interest groups, media and individual citizens – and maybe also courts and individual governmental agencies.

In order to foresee coming developments of the EU it might be useful to speculate in negative scenarios. This should be done, not in order to be negative or produce alarming results, but in order to predict the kind of problems that might arise. For instance, one might argue that it is likely that the development in regard to the EMU or in regard to the enlargement will create severe problems either for individual states or maybe for certain regions. If such problems arise, the first reaction will probably be to articulate the problems in the domestic system and in the political system of the EU. In the first round, this will lead to a politicisation within the EU. This, in itself, will imply that the demands for problem management through the EU-system will increase, a process which might lead to further integration. If, on the other hand, the EU shows to be inefficient in solving the problems, a very likely development will be that local politicians will blame the EU. This process might initiate a "negative spiral" of delegitimation which will make it harder for the EU to gain sufficient legitimacy. Such actions could provoke "rupture" with the EU.

Negative scenarios might include thoughts which we in relation to processes of globalization know about different forms of "reaction". Changes brought on too fast which create problems too severe for certain groups or regions might provoke different kinds of "reaction forces". In the extreme, we could get "the 1000 Haider's Europe". Such a development will be very severe and lead to serious problems in Europe's political structure. The action initiated in 1999 against Austria is only a vague indication of the kind of conflicts that could arise. However, the most reasonable overall expectation is that the EU will react to such tendencies. These reactions will, one should expect, lead to further politicisation within the EU and to further integration of EU's political political system.

5. The internal dependencies of the Danish government in relation to the EU-policy

The approach applied here takes for granted that a state's integration policy is very dependent on domestic factors, including history, traditions, domestic institutions and actors. I shall not attempt to analyse these domestic factors anew. In general, the internal setting for the Danish Government has not been changed in any dramatic way in recent years. The polls still indicate that the Danes are very divided in their attitude towards the EU and that rather many, maybe a majority, are sceptical towards giving away authority or sovereignty to the EU. As analysed by Hedetoft and Haahr in this volume, there are important dilemmas in regard to the domestic basis for the Governments integration policy. The vote in 1998 in favour of the Amsterdam Treaty showed with 55.1% in favour, a rather positive attitude to the governments policy. Yet, in regard to the referendum on the Euro-cooperation the polls show that attitudes are divided and still so uncertain that an outcome in either direction seems possible.

6. On dilemmas and options in the Danish integration policy

Now, how can we on the basis of the analysis above identify dilemmas and options in the Danish integration policy. The major interpretation in the following section is that there are several rather severe dilemmas in Denmark's integration policy. These dilemmas are, it is argued, becoming even greater in the present phase of EU's development because of the likelihood that EU's integration is increasing. If the picture presented above of EU's present situation is true, we can expect that the EU with its heavy agenda is taking important steps towards further integration. The political and economic integration is already so developed that Denmark is to be considered as a semi-integrated actor. And the realisation of the Euro-cooperation and the likelihood of enlargement and further institutional reform will create even further pressure for clearer integration policies. This is also true if the EU, as it is expected in this analysis, will become more politicised.

6.1. Dilemmas

When there is a high tension between two courses of action, two policies, there might be a "dilemma". A *dilemma* is a situation in which there is a basic choice between two courses of action both including specific distribution of advantages and costs. Dilemmas might for instance arise in a situation in which a semi-integrated actor is confronted with a new, important step in the integration process. The actor might either have to accept this new step – with the costs that this might imply – or reject this step, with the cost that such a choice might imply. Another dilemma could arise in a situation in which a government is bound by the domestic and the external scene at the same time. The situation might be that by following the demands from the external scene the government will have severe disadvantages on the domestic scene, or vice versa. I shall briefly describe four different dilemmas which exist in relation to a semi-integrated actor's integration policy.

It should be added though, that it is a special question whether there are ways out of dilemmas. Often the strategy in relation to a dilemma is to not choose one or the other alternative, but "reinterpret" the situation and thus add to the possible courses of action. Thus, dilemmas might not only be more or less severe, but also more or less fixed. In addition, we might distinguish between "real dilemmas" and perceived dilemmas. Some real dilemmas are not perceived, and vice versa.[16]

The integration dilemma

The integration dilemma is the dilemma which an actor, possibly a state, experiences when it is confronted with a new important step towards further integration. The situation might be that the actor has to chose between *either* participating in the more intensified integration (with the possible risk of being "entrapped", being forced to accept decisions which it would otherwise reject) *or* on the other hand rejecting the new integration step (with the risk of being "abandoned", left outside the integration process or losing influence within this). The integration dilemma has been discussed elsewhere, in particular in Nikolaj Petersen's contribution to this volume, and shall not be elaborated here.[17]

A major contention in regard to the integration dilemma is that it might increase as the degree of integration increases. The cost of breaking loose might become greater, while the possibility for others to force the integration process further, might also become greater. This implies that the intensified integration of the EU might intensify the integration dilemma for the states that do not find it in their interest to go "all the way" in the integration process. On the other hand, if it is accepted within the integration system that there should be a certain "flexibility" in regard to each state's participation, this might loosen the integration dilemma.

The democracy dilemma

The democracy dilemma is related to the understanding that – if democracy only exists in combination with statehood – there are only two democratic strategies for European integration, a strategy for democracy in the member states and a strategy for democracy in an EU-state. On the assumed premise, democracy is *either* to be developed in the present nation states. The negative consequence is that important decisions at the European level are left as uncontrolled by democratic political structures. *Or* democracy is to be formed at the European level as "the nation state

---

16 The problem is also that we can only identify "real dilemmas" as observers, i.e. with the uncertainties which this implies.
17 Kelstrup (1993: 154) and chapter 3 and 4 in this volume.

written large", for instance with the formal establishment of state-like democratic institutions at the European level with the negative consequence that it might undermine democracy in the existing states. The democracy dilemma cannot be elaborated in this context.[18] But it is important to recognize the dilemma and to reflect on the premise, the close link between our understanding of democracy and statehood. My contention is that we need to develop our understanding of how democracy can be strengthened beyond the nation state without undermining the gains which have been reached for democratic values and institutions at the state level. In order to do so, it is of special importance to develop our thinking about democratic legitimacy. On this basis it is possible to formulate strategies for democratizing the EU, also without the a priory implication that the EU should become a (federal) state.

The inside/outside-dilemma

The inside/outside dilemma is that a government might have to choose *either* to act dominated by concerns in regard to its external environment, with the possible cost of not being sufficiently attentative to domestic concerns, *or* to act dominated by internal concerns, with the possible cost of not being sufficiently attentative to external concerns. The tension between a politicised external scene and an equally politicised domestic scene will create demands on the government from both directions, and a government might well find that it has no "room of action", or maybe even that it has a "negative room of action": that it is impossible to find solutions without severe costs. There are different strategies in such a situation. One strategy is a) to give priority to the internal scene and, for instance, to find the best domestic agreement (for instance a "national compromise" or another consensus-based solution) and then to present this externally with the risk that it might cause severe external problems. Another strategy is b) to choose a policy in accordance with the governments analysis of the external situation and to pursue this policy with less regard to the internal conflicts that this might cause (for instance with the acceptance of a "divided nation" as a consequence). A third strategy could be c) to attempt to play the optimal roles internally and externally at the same time *with* possible inconsistencies. An effect of this policy of "hidden inconsistencies" would easily develop into an active "policy of diffusion", possibly leading to loss of trust and support either at the domestic or the external scene – or both.

The old/new discourse dilemma

The old/new discourse dilemma is that an actor, typically a government, might have to choose between *either* a new discourse which might be necessary in order to formulate policies and strategies that are relevant in regard to a new, complex external constellation (with the possible cost that this new discourse is not under-

---

18 For a discussion of this and the question of democratic legitimacy, see Kelstrup (2000).

stood sufficiently and therefore not generating support), *or* the formulation of policies in old and established discourses which can mobilise traditional support (but might have the cost that the policies that gain support are inadequate in regard to the actual problems). This dilemma seems relevant in very many established institutional settings, certainly not only in politics. But it is also relevant in regard to integration policy, in particular in periods in which new kinds of political organisations emerge and in periods of swift change. The dilemma is mentioned here, because a major problem in relation to international integration seems to be that such phenomena are poorly understood.

The strategies related to this dilemma have a certain parallel to the strategies in the inside/outside dilemma. Typically in this dilemma, the actor will choose discourses which are well known to the domestic public and are known as effective in generating internal support. This might sometimes give a "room of manoeuvre" in areas which are excluded from the chosen discourse. For instance, such a mechanism might explain why major actors choose to articulate an economic discourse – for instance in the Danish referenda – even when it is obvious for all well informed persons that major problems are political. Obviously, education and general insight in new conditions presents a possibility of getting out of the dilemma mentioned here. Yet, in periods with many changes one might fear that policies have to be formulated within old discourses in spite of their inadequacy.

The conflict/diffusion dilemma

The conflict/diffusion dilemma is that an actor *either* might formulate a specific policy as a unitary actor with the advantage of having specific goals and objectives and having the ability to pursue this in practice, but with the disadvantage that the goals might provoke disagreement, political conflict and possibly lead to lack of support. *Or* the actor might avoid such policy formulation, leave policy questions in diffusion and lack of clarity with the "advantage" that opposition to the "hidden" policies might be very difficult, but with the cost that the actual policy might loose direction and that support might also be lost by the diffuse strategy.

This problem is highly relevant in regard to integration policy. As described in chapter 4, there are tendencies of diffusion in later stages of integration processes. In many ways the Danish decision-making process in regard to the Danish EU-policy is organised with the aim of making Denmark an unitary actor in regard to the EU.[19] Yet, there are tendencies which undermine this ambition.[20] In some ways it is exactly the tendencies toward diffusion which make it of particular relevance to work for explicit policy formulations.

All these dilemmas seem relevant in relation to a semi-integrated actor's formu-

---

19 See also Dosenrode's analysis of the Danish EU decision-making in chapter 12.
20 Among these are the involvement of local government in the EU-system, see Klausen's analysis in chapter 13.

lation of its integration policy and also for the formulation of Denmark's integration policy[21]. Yet, as mentioned, some of the problems might be circumvented.

6.2. Options

What are then the Danish options in relation to the EU in the present phase of European integration? In attempting to answer this question we might first use the differentiation between different dimension of integration policies mentioned above in order to identify relevant options and then discuss which of these options we should regard as major choices and thus as strategic options.

1) Should Denmark participate in the future EU or not? Obviously, this is a major strategic choice. The basic understanding of the political parties of most of the Danish population seems to be that this choice has been taken.[22]

2) Which position should Denmark take or attempt to take in the future European political structure? Obviously, this cannot be answered in any exact way with all the uncertainties about Europe's future. The major options can in a rather inexact way be regarded as attempts to place Denmark either in the "core" of EU's present and future political system, in its periphery or maybe in between the two possibilities. The terminology is somewhat vague and inexact, since it is rather unclear what we mean by "core". If we imagine that the ideas about "a federation within the Union" are materialised, obviously being in the "core" will imply that you become part of this "narrow" federation. This is a rather demanding solution that probably would imply that Denmark, essentially, gave up its statehood. On the other hand in another institutional construction of the EU there might be the possibility of participation as a "full member without reservations". But there might also be the possibility of a position as a "member with reservations", i.e. with participation in major part of the community but with important exemptions, possibly the same as now, possibly with other exemptions.

3) What should the policies be in regard to future institutional changes in the EU? Relevant questions in this regard are related to the Danish attitude towards further supranationality in the EU, towards an expanded scope of the EU, towards further

---

21 We might also speak of a state/nation dilemma (Wæver 1995). I have chosen not to include this in order not to complicate the analysis too much. It is difficult to apply this dilemma to integration because integration penetrates both state *and* nation.
22 It might be relevant, though, to keep it as a "reserve" position that Denmark – if things in the EU goes very wrong – might have the formal option to withdraw the formal authority which has been delegated to the EU, cf. also the brief discussion above on the relationship between semi-integrated actors and sovereignty. A parallel can also be drawn to the debate about whether Denmark after, eventually, accepting the Euro-cooperation can or cannot withdraw later. It seems to be a formal possibility, but in practice it is impossible.

"democratic elements" in the EU, etc. Clearly, the Danish debate on these issues must be informed on goals and ideas pursued of other European actors and with inclusion of analyses of Europe's "possible institutional futures".

4) What should the policies be in regard to EU's internal output, EU's substantial policies? Relevant questions in this regard has to do with policy formulation at the EU level. Does Denmark, for instance, work for the establishment of elements of a welfare state at the EU level? If we take for granted that the nation states are confronted with globalization, is it then the most viable policy to attempt to secure social and environmental concerns through action at the EU-level, or is it better to choose a national strategy? Which kinds of policies do we want at the EU-level in the intersection between market and competition concerns and ecological concerns? How are we positioned in relation to the priority between monetary policies vs. employment policies, etc.? The scope for this kind of policy definition is rather large. And as integration increases, these political choices grow in saliency.

5) What should be the policies in regard to EU's external output, EU's function as an external actor in the trade field, in the security field and possibly in regard to other areas in which the EU can influence the building of international regimes? A major question is related to the priorities in EU's influence on international regimes, for instance whether social and ecological concerns are given priority to environmental concerns. Behind this lies the very important question of the role of the EU in regard to economic globalization. As mentioned, EU's present function in this regard seems to be ambiguous, and one might see the EU as a political space for different strategies in this regard. Another major question is related to EU's military dimension, and – maybe treated as a separate question – EU's possible function within peace keeping.

6.3. Strategic options in regard to the EU

A major strategic option in regard to the EU has to do with the degree of engagement in the integration process and the willingness to go far into the integration process. Denmark might choose to become what we can call an *A-member* of the EU, being a full participant in all relevant fora. This would clearly be a change away from the present position as *a member with reservations* and a change in the traditional the policy of *limited engagement*. The alternative to becoming an A-member would be a continuation of some kind of reservation and limited engagement, what we might describe as the strategy of becoming a *B-member*.[23]

A problem with the strategy of becoming an A-member might be that the EU may develop a political structure which allows some states to form a "federation within the Union", i.e. to let some states become what we might call A+-members:

---

23 See also DUPI, (2000).

Members that might want to go so far in the integration process that they, essentially, give up their own statehood. Confronted with this, an A-member might also have to mobilise reservations. Another problem with a strategy of becoming an A-member is related to the domestic scene. Is it possible to get sufficient support for such a policy? Are the costs related to this strategy that domestic societies become "divided nations" and maybe also for some political parties that they become divided?

A problem with the strategy of becoming a B-member might be that such a status diminishes the possibilities of political influence in the EU. It is somewhat uncertain whether this is true or not. In particular, it is very relevant whether the future EU is created in a way which allows for states to have specific reservations and thus B-member status, or whether this is regarded as an anormality. An additional problem is related to the specification of the reservations of a B-member status. One could argue that there is a danger in "fixing" reservations as it has been the case – at least partially – for the four Danish reservations taken in 1992. One could imagine other kinds of B-status, and maybe one could also define positions as having B+ or B- status.

Another strategic option seems to be the choice of strategy in a situation in which the nation states – and the welfare states – are challenged by globalization. It might be formulated as a major choice whether a strategy for securing social and environmental concerns is followed primarily as *a national strategy* or as *an EU-strategy*. Since the discussion of the pro's and con's of these two strategies is too demanding in this context, I shall limit myself to this indication of a strategic choice.

It is also possible to place the focus of the strategic choice at the domestic level. Thus, it can be seen as a major choice whether a policy of *maximising national consensus* is chosen as compared to a policy of domestic politicisation and *acceptance of majority dominance*. The negative effect of optimising national consensus might be that this might be done in categories that are inadequate or in a long term perspective problematic in relation to the EU (compare the old/new discourse-dilemma). The drawbacks of the acceptance of a majority dominance are rather obvious, i.e. the emergence of domestic cleavages. A further danger is, evidently, that in the extreme case the majority might change, giving a severe disruption in the integration policy.

Obviously, there might be some links between the different strategic options. For instance, it is rather certain that a policy of becoming an A+ member of the EU will cause severe internal cleavages in the Danish electorate, and this might also be a consequence of an A-member strategy. On the other hand it might be expected that a B or B + strategy could be defined in a way which gave a rather high, if not necessarily optimal, national consensus.

These indications of strategic options for Denmark in relation to the EU are rather vague and in many ways highly inadequate. They are, however presented, as an attempt to structure a policy field which normally is left unstructured. In many ways the dilemmas mentioned above have such a severe influence on the formulation of integration policies that they tend not only to hamper strong policy formulations but also to inhibit differentiated analyses of policy formulations.

7. Conclusions

The purpose of this article has been to discuss Denmark's integration policy towards the EU and the dilemmas and options which Denmark experiences in the present phase of history. The main view has been that Denmark has already become a semi-integrated actor in relation to the European Union, that the EU is undergoing a new transformation, and that this is going to challenge Denmark even further.

The view is also that integration policies from a certain stage of integration proliferates. Thus, there are many aspects of the integration policies, and similarly there are many tasks and dimensions in the development of the integration policies. The analysis has in particular been undertaken in regard to five major questions, but even within these there are many other sub-questions.

The article has drawn upon the historical analyses undertaken in other chapters of this book. Historically, Denmark's policy towards Europe after 1945 was first dominated by a realist inspired small-state conception. Yet, as Branner and Østergaard have shown, the Danish traditions are more comprehensive, and the view of small state "determinism" which dominated in some phases (and corresponds to a realist inspired, small-state conceptualisation) has to be supplemented with the understanding that Denmark also has a rather independent tradition of active internationalism. In the first decades after 1945 Denmark's policy towards Europe had a rather low priority. The policy towards the EU can be characterised, as Branner explains, by limited engagement, a policy of fragmentation and a policy of pragmatism. This picture might be somewhat modified for the later part of the 1990s, but it still holds true in its main features also for this period.

On this background the article has presented the understanding that the European integration has taken important steps forward in the recent years, and that the EU is on the edge of taking new steps towards further integration. This is regarded as a challenge to Denmark, but also to Denmark's traditional EU policy. A major contention of the article is that the EU's integration confronts Denmark with several difficult dilemmas. Thus, there has been pointed to five different dilemmas: 1) The integration dilemma, 2) the democracy dilemma, 3) the inside/outside dilemma, 4) the dilemma between old and new discourses, and 5) the conflict/diffusion dilemma. Major problems arise from these dilemmas and their interplay.

The article concludes by considering Danish options in regard to the EU and discussing which of these we should regard as strategic options. Major options in regard to Denmark's position in the EU's political system are between Denmark as "a member without reservations", and Denmark as "a member with reservations". It is shown that there are problems to both of these options. If Denmark takes reservation, another debate follows on the *kind* of reservations Denmark might take, the assumption being that the reservations need not by necessity be the four reservations which were fixed in the "national compromise" of 1992.

The contention has been that if Denmark goes for a full participation, what one might call an A-membership of the EU, problems will arise at least in two areas. One problem is that the integration in the EU might very well continue, possibly with a concentration on some member countries which might want to go even further in their wish for political integration. Thus, "a federation within the Union" as a reaction to the EU's enlargement is not totally excluded, maybe even likely. Such a development will create a new dilemma for Denmark, a dilemma between being an A-member and what we might call an A+ member. The central question in relation to an A-member strategy is: where is the limit to integration? How is a balanced and stable structure found in which the Danish position might also be stabilised?

The other problem related to the A-member option is that it seems to be followed at the cost of internal cleavages in Denmark on the EU-issue. Already now the political cleavage on the EU-issue is one of the deepest political cleavages in the Danish population. It is not difficult to predict that this situation would become more severe, if an A-member strategy is chosen. Not to speak of the difficulties that an A+ member strategy might cause. Said differently, the internal costs in the form of an undermining of the high degree of consensus in Danish politics could be very great. One might add that certain parties might be hit rather seriously by such a development, not least, probably, the Social Democrats.

The contention is also, though, that the choice of a strategy of "reluctant participation" or "member with reservations", i.e. what we have called a B-strategy, might have important difficulties and costs. A major difficulty is to define the areas in which Denmark should not participate fully. A major cost could be that having reservations might diminish the Danish influence in the EU. Whether this is true or not is, however, somewhat uncertain.

Finally, it has been suggested that other strategic options might be related to the choice of strategies towards globalization, in particular whether one chooses a national or a European strategy for securing social and environmental concerns in the confrontation with economic globalization. It lies beyond the scope of this article and this book, though, to explore this further.

Literature

Beetham, David and Christopher Lord (1998b): *Legitimacy and the European Union.* London and New York: Longman.

DUPI (2000): *Udviklingen i EU siden 1992 på de områder der er omfattet af de danske forbehold,* København: DUPI

Fischer, Joschka (2000): "Vom Staatenverbund zur Föderation – Gedanken über die Finalität der europäischen Integration", http://www.gruene-ger.de/themen/bund/fischer.htm

Gustavsson, Sverker (1998): "Defending the demodratic deficit" in Albert Weale and Michael Nentwich (eds. 1998), *Political Theory and the European Union. Legitimacy, constitutional choice and citizenship.* London: Routledge, pp. 63-79.

Hix, Simon (1999): *The Political System of the European Union,* London: Macmillan

Johansen, Helle (1998): "Exploring the Colour of the Beast: Hegemony and Political Projects in the European Union" in Anders Wivel (ed.) (1998), *Explaining European Integration,* Copenhagen Political Studies Press, pp. 297-320.

Kelstrup, Morten (1991): "Danmarks deltagelse i det internationale samarbejde – fra pragmatisk funktionalisme til aktiv internationalisme?" (Denmark's participation in international cooperation – from pragmatic functionalism to active internationalism?). In Henning Gottlieb et al. (eds.), 1991, *Fred og Konflikt.* SNU, Copenhagen, pp. 289-311.

Kelstrup, Morten (1994): "Dansk EU-politik: Politikfastsættelse i et dilemma mellem diffusitet og fastlåsning" in Bertel Heurlin (ed.), *Danmark og den Europæiske Union,* Forlaget Politiske Studier, pp. 20-53

Kelstrup, Morten (1998): "Om det danske demokrati og den europæiske integration" in Morten Kelstrup and Peter Vesterdorf (1998), *Demokrati og EU?,* Rådet for Europæisk Politik, Århus: Systime, pp. 9-43.

Kelstrup, Morten (2000): "Legitimacy, Democracy and the European Union: Perspectives in the normative discussion of EU's future political structure", Copenhagen: Institute of Political Science: CORE working paper 2000/1.

Larsen, Henrik (1999): "British and Danish Policies towards Europe in the 1990s: A Discource Approach", *European Journal of International relations,* 5(4).

Nielsen, Carsten Due, and Nikolaj Petersen (eds.) (1995): *Adaptation and Activism. The Foreign Policy of Denmark 1967-1993.* Copenhagen: Danish Institute of Foreign Affairs, DJØF Publishing.

Pedersen, Thomas (1996): "Denmark and the European Union" in Miles, Lee (ed.), *The European Union and the Nordic Countries,* London and New York: Routledge, pp. 81-100.

Petersen, Nikolaj (1995): "Denmark and the European Community 1985-1993" in Carsten Due-Nielsen & Nikolaj Petersen (eds.). *Adaptation and Activism. The Foreign Policy of Denmark 1967-1993,* Copenhagen: Danish Institute of Foreign Affairs & DJØF Publishing, pp. 189-224.

Rasmussen, Hjalte (1993): *Towards a Normative Theory of Interpretation of Community Law,* Copenhagen: CORE-publication, Copenhagen Political Studies Press.

Weiler, J.H.H. (1999): *The Constitution of Europe. "Do the new clothes have an emperor?",* Cambridge: Cambridge University Press.

Wernicke, Christian (2000): "Brüssel steht vor dem Infarkt", *Die Zeit,* no. 20/2000.

Wæver, Ole (1995): "Danish Dilemmas: Foreign Policy Choices for the 21st Century" in Carsten Due-Nielsen and Nikolaj Petersen (eds.): *Adaptation and Activism: The Foreign Policy of Denmark 1967-1993.* Copenhagen: DUPI/DJØF Publishing, pp. 321-363

Økonomiministeriet og Finansministeriet (2000): *Danmark og Euroen.* København.

The Contributors

Hans Branner
Lecturer in the Danish High School and external Lecturer at the Institute of Political Science, University of Copenhagen, teaching in the fields of foreign policy and modern history. Former Senior Researcher at CORE and other projects. He has published books and articles on historical and theoretical aspects of Danish foreign policy in the 20th century, i.a. on "Danish European Policy Since 1945: The Question of Sovereignty" (1992), and has written several textbooks on international relations and Denmark's foreign policy.

Søren Z. von Dosenrode
Jean Monnet Professor and Associate Professor in International Relations at the Centre for International Studies, University of Aalborg, and Ph.D. in international relations. He is author of: *Westeuropäische Kleinstaaten in der EG und EPZ* (1993) editor of several books on European integration and has written many articles on the topic. Presently he is doing research on the Danish EU decision-making process.

Jens Henrik Haahr
Associate Professor in International Relations at the Danish School of Journalism and Ph.D. in political science. He has worked for various European Community Institutions. He is author of: *Looking to Europe. The EC policies of the British Labour Party and the Danish Social Democrats* (1993) and of several articles on European integration.

Ulf Hedetoft
Professor and Dr.Phil. in European Studies at the Centre for International Studies, University of Aalborg. Author of *Signs of Nations. Studies in the Political Semotics of Self and Other in Contemporary European Nationalism* (1995). He has written and edited many publications on nationalism, national images and political culture.

Morten Kelstrup
Senior Research Fellow at Copenhagen Peace Research Institute (on leave from a position as Jean Monnet Professor at the Institute of Political Science, University of Copenhagen). He is director of Copenhagen Research Project on European Integration (CORE). He has edited and contributed to several anthologies, i.a. *European Integration and Denmark's Participation* (1992) and is author of many articles on European integration, European Security and democracy.

Kurt Klaudi Klausen
Professor in Public Organization Theory, Department of Political Science and Public Management, University of Southern Denmark, Odense University. He is

co-editor of *European Integration and Local Government* (1997) and author of many books and articles, in particular on local government and public administration.

Karl Christian Lammers
Associate Professor in Modern History at the Institute of History, University of Copenhagen. He is author of books and articles on German politics, German fascism, the history of the Federal Republic and of the GDR, and on Danish-German relations in the post-war period, i.a. *Nationale Minderheiten im friedlichen Zusammenleben* (1993).

Johnny N. Laursen
Associate Professor in Modern History at the Institute of History, University of Århus. Ph.D. in History. He has in particular written on German history, Danish integration policy in the 1950's and 1960's and Nordic cooperation, i.a. *"Det nordiske samarbejde som særvej? Kontinuitet og brud, 1945-73"* (1998).

Thorsten Borring Olesen
Jean Monnet Professor and Associate Professor in modern European history at the Institute of History, University of Århus. He has publicised books and articles, i.a. on Italian fascism, contemporary Danish history, the security policy of the Danish Social Democratic Party and Nordic cooperation. He is editor of: *Interdependence vs. Integration: Denmark, Scandinavia and Western Europe 1945-1960* (1995).

Nikolaj Petersen
Professor in International Relations at the Institute of Political Science, University of Aarhus. He is author of several books and articles on strategic studies, European integration, European politics, Nordic foreign policy and foreign policy theory. He is co-author of a number of publications from the Danish Institute of Foreign Affairs. Presently he is working on a research project on the history of Danish foreign policy.

Uffe Østergaard
Jean Monnet Professor at the Center of European Cultural Studies, University of Aarhus. Director of the Danish Center for Holocaust and Genocide Studies. He is author of several books and articles on Danish history, national identity, Nordic identity and European identities, i.a. *Europa: identitet og identitetspolitik* (1998).